The Piozzi Letters

John Salusbury Piozzi Salusbury. Portrait by John Jackson. (Hyde Collection, Four Oaks Farm. Reproduced by permission.)

The Piozzi Letters

Correspondence of
Hester Lynch Piozzi, 1784–1821
(formerly Mrs. Thrale)

Volume 5
1811–1816

EDITED BY
Edward A. Bloom
AND
Lillian D. Bloom

ASSOCIATE EDITOR
O M Brack, Jr.

INTRODUCTION BY
Gay W. Brack

DELAWARE

NEWARK: University of Delaware Press
LONDON: Associated University Presses

Associated University Presses
440 Forsgate Drive
Cranbury, NJ 08512

Associated University Presses
16 Barter Street
London WC1A 2AH, England

Associated University Presses
P.O. Box 338, Port Credit
Mississauga, Ontario
Canada L5G 4L8

PR
3619
I.P5
Z48
1989
V.5

The paper used in this publication meets the requirements of the American National Standard for Permanence of Paper for Printed Library Materials Z39.48-1984.

Library of Congress Cataloging-in-Publication Data

Piozzi, Hester Lynch, 1741–1821.
    The Piozzi letters.

    Includes bibliographical references and index.
    1. Piozzi, Hester Lynch, 1741–1821—Correspondence.
    2. Authors, English—18th century—Correspondence.
    3. London (England)—Intellectual life—18th century.
    I. Bloom, Edward Alan, 1914–1994.   II. Bloom, Lillian D.
    III. Title.
    PR3619.P5Z48   1988   828'.609   [B]   87-40231
    ISBN 0-87413-394-7 (v. 5 : alk. paper)

Contents

Illustrations

Acknowledgments

"Those relations are . . . commonly of most value in which the writer tells his own story. He that recounts the life of another, commonly dwells most on conspicuous events, lessens the familiarity of his tale to increase its dignity, shews his favourite at a distance decorated and magnified like the ancient actors in their tragick dress, and endeavours to hide the man that he may produce the hero. . . . The writer of his own life has at least the first qualification of an historian, the knowledge of the truth. . . . [H]e that speaks of himself has no motive to falshood or partiality except self-love, by which all have been so often betrayed, that all are on the watch against its artifices. . . . [H]e that sits down calmly and voluntarily to review his life for the admonition of posterity, or to amuse himself, and leaves this account unpublished, may be commonly presumed to tell truth, since falshood cannot appease his own mind, and fame will not be heard beneath the tomb." Samuel Johnson's observations on the importance of autobigraphy in *Idler* 84 have served as guiding principles for the introduction to this volume. Mrs. Piozzi, now in her seventies, is less concerned about the great public events of her time, "conspicuous events" such as the Battle of Waterloo, except as they impinge on her increasingly narrowing personal world. For this reason the introduction, unlike those to previous volumes, spends less time providing the larger social and political context for reading the letters. Instead, Mrs. Piozzi is allowed to reflect on her personal concerns, to tell her own story, and to defend herself in her own inimitable way.

Readers will also note that in this volume many identifications are provided in the index so that it may be used more readily as a means of cross-reference.

Our greatest debt is to J. Kent Clark and Carol B. Pearson (Clark). The sharing of their experiences in seeing volume four through the press, and alerting us to possible difficulties, made our work much easier. Since we agreed to take on this project and began serious work on it in spring 1996, they have answered our queries and aided our research with unfailing patience. For this and for the warmth of their friendship we are most grateful.

Viscountess Eccles has generously provided us with photographs of the portrait of John Salusbury Piozzi Salusbury and the watercolor of Brynbella in her collection at Four Oaks Farm. Her wide knowledge of the Thrales/Piozzis has saved us from error on numerous occasions.

Most of the work on the volume was carried out on a summer fellowship at the Huntington Library. Roy Ritchie provided the fellowship, an office, and more personal encouragement to allow us to complete the project. Thomas V. Lange assisted us in solving several vexing problems. Cathy Cherbosque gave us useful suggestions about illustrations. Virginia Renner and the staff of Reader Services helped make our stay a pleasant and profitable one. Finally, special thanks to Martin Ridge for suggesting that we should complete the project, and for supporting in various ways this and numerous other projects over the years.

Other libraries have kindly assisted us in our research. We are grateful to C. J. Hunt, Dorothy Clayton, and Peter McNiven of The John Rylands University Library and to Marilyn Wurzburger, Special Collections, Arizona State University Library.

The following friends and colleagues solved or attempted to solve some of the last minute queries: Leslie Chilton, J. C. D. Clark, Taylor Corse, Robert DeMaria Jr., Scott Evans, David Foster, Nancy Gutierrez, Thomas Kaminski, Gwin J. Kolb, Mark Lussier, Curtis Perry, Gene Valentine, and Paul Zall.

Introduction

Mrs. Piozzi's correspondence for the years 1811–1816 depicts a woman whose horizons are rapidly becoming limited by infirmity and financial difficulties. An almost constant concern in her letters after 1812 is the increasing drain on her financial resources of Streatham Park, once the center of social life for Samuel Johnson and other literary luminaries. Her correspondence also records the full fervor and precipitous decline of her relationship with John Salusbury Piozzi Salusbury, her late husband's nephew and her adopted son, a decline framed by Mrs. Piozzi's quixotic gesture in deeding her beloved Welsh estate Brynbella to the young man so that he could leave Oxford and marry. And, as always in her correspondence after 1784, Mrs. Piozzi complains of the treatment accorded her by her daughters.

Yet, while the pressures of her financial affairs and the deterioration of her relationship with the only child who had not yet turned against her weighed heavily on her mind, Mrs. Piozzi was still able to develop new and interesting friendships, to follow news of war and peace, and to arrange for her retirement to Bath. Still, Gabriel Piozzi's long and terrible illness and his horrific death seemed to have robbed her of her lifelong curiosity and delight in the world. Instead, her letters reflect a growing sense of pessimism and alarm; she often compared the world of her youth with "this *Marble* Age; so *hard,* so *cold* and so *polished.*" Instances of public and private corruption abounded, she asserted: "surely surely one need not be like the old Man in Horace, to see plainly that Things grow worse and worse with the Rapidity of a Wheel pushed down hill increasing in Speed at every Rotation."[1] The past became increasingly desirable: "'Tis a strange Time—and strange Things are done in it. Nothing is as it *used to be.*"[2]

Perhaps the worst aspect of "this *Marble* Age" was its callousness: "Poor Miss Richards's Death—struck suddenly at 22 Years old with the Palsy; *did* however seem to affect ½ a Dozen Friends who depended on her for their Musical Amusement—for ½ a Dozen hours at least:—and *They* . . . were very good natured— because *Feelings* which I can remember quite the Rage, are now wholly *out* among those with whom I converse here."[3] Political standards had also degenerated from the days when she herself had hit the hustings for Henry Thrale: "Your Candidates are all preparing for the general Engagement no doubt: Mr. Waithman is expected to succeed for the *first City in the World.* He was bred a *direct Atheist.* A famous Fellow . . . known by the Name of Wicked Will, used to patronize, and teach him when a little Boy to stand on a Table, sing obscene Songs, and Spout Blasphemous Speeches; So he ends in an Orator, and a Democrate, and a *Fellow of Fire,* as his Friends call him."[4]

The fearful times called forth behavior both unseemly and unsafe: "Such Thunder and Lightning seldom occurs in our Island as I was out in that famous Thursday Night, when beautiful Greenwich suffered so:——but Fears are out of Fashion, and Ladies brave Dangers they would have shrunk from, when I was Young."[5] The world was surely tending toward some cataclysmic event: "Mercy on us! What Times my Darling comes of Age in!" she exclaimed to Salusbury, "The Plot is Thickening towards the 5th Act; and whilst others see *Sun-bright Prospects,* I am apt to believe that the Mist we live in, magnifies them. . . . I see and hear nothing *but* Dangers."[6]

Even the elements shared in Mrs. Piozzi's sense of a world in rapid and final decline: "The Weather is Cold beyond all Thought, beyond all Precedent I believe," she told her daughter Queeney. Reporting Queeney's response, she told Leonard Chappelow that, "Lady Keith says such a Snow was scarce ever seen in the Southern Parts of Devonshire."[7] Her anxiety even trickled into her increasingly rare literary discussions. Comparing Mme D'Arblay's latest book with the productions of Byron and Southey, she noted: "A Work descriptive of *Manners,* a Pen that is skilled to shoot Folly as it flies, will produce pleasing Contrast to these odd Performances—which hiding their heads in a Mist of Unintelligible Sublimity, make us *believe* they touch the Skies. . . . There is however Truth enough in what Burke says of Obscurity being a *Source* of the Sublime—Our Fancy has been sadly *let down* since Truth *illuminated* our Political Prospects. A new Fog arising would perhaps be better than the Certainties which are likely to follow soon."[8]

Mrs. Piozzi's pessimism coalesced into a general feeling that an unspecified doom was fast coming upon the country. References to "the last" began to appear in her correspondence: "I leave this Place on Friday 27: of May . . . and then home to dinner the *last* of this Month—Can the word be repeated without Seriousness? *ought* it? when such Changes of Place and Vicissitudes of Company, Connections &c. force the mind upon reflecting that *The Last* Hour is at hand to us all. . . . The *Enormous Occurrences,* the strange Circumstances that surround us all, contribute to hide lesser Objects from one's View. . . . We are all of one Mind and stare with Wonder at Events of which the Cause is scarcely visible." While first causes were shrouded in mist, immediate causes for this malaise were all too visible. Moral decline was seeping into every crevice, public or private: "The immediate one we must look for in Buonaparte's Madness. . . . With regard to *our own* Nobility and People of Fashion getting into these horrid Scrapes of Swindling and forging and Stock jobbing and the Lord knows what. . . . we need no longer say with Captain Macheath

I wonder we h'ant better company
upon Tyburn Tree!"[9]

Mrs. Piozzi, who had always exhibited keen interest in the behavior of her fellows, found little to applaud when the peace for which she had longed was negotiated, for peace brought out an orgy of self-indulgence: "I saw a Lady's Petticoat which cost 60 Guineas only Silver Gauze and She confessed it was to wear *one* Night only, no more." "Mean while the Appearance of Wealth displayed, is beyond my Comprehension. People think nothing of Paying 20£ for a Ticket to White's Ball; and 50 Guineas for a Dress—which they consider as impossible ever to put on again."[10]

Most intolerable was the "Wickedness" of the times. When Bonaparte escaped from Elba and England was once more engaged in hostilities, Mrs. Piozzi conflated his bid to regain power with England's increase in violence: "Oh my dearest Lady Williams! What Times are we living in! . . . The Events come forward as Scripture says they will do, like Pangs of Parturition; every Pain sharper than the last;—and now while the other Powers are *Threatening*, Buonaparte is *acting:* If Haste is not made, The Attempt to dethrone him will be vain. . . . It is a fearful Thing . . . to see how Wickedness does spread itself—— Forgery and Murder are Crimes which never used to be heard of, 200 Miles from Hyde Park Corner."[11]

Perhaps most unaccountable and therefore most wicked, was the political atmosphere surrounding Bonaparte's capture: "the wisest Men are bewildered by the strange Circumstances which surround us. One hears forty different Opinions in a Day;—and the next Day 40 other Opinions. What I like *least* is the Democratic Spirit of our own Folks—high and low.——The Walls exhibit inflammatory Words in every Street of London and of Bath;—and wash them out tonight as you please—The same Words or Worse, appear again Tomorrow."[12] Perhaps the strongest indicator of the country's imminent downfall was this loathsome graffiti; it demonstrated the people's collective madness in their support for England's most demonized enemy: "Well, the wonders that I have to relate are, that this Man, this Buonaparte, whom to dethrone such torrents of blood were willingly spilt; whom to depose, such treasures of money had been willingly spent, no sooner surrenders himself than we make an idol of him, crowd round for a glance of his eye, and huzza him as if he were our defender. . . . Had not Government prudently prevented his touching shore, hundreds, nay thousands, would have drawn him up and down in triumph. . . . as I went over Westminster Bridge last week, I saw we were building a new mad-house twice as big as old Bethlehem Hospital; and sure no building could be so wanted for Englishmen."[13]

The cessation of hostilities brought new discontents to civilian England and new alarm to Mrs. Piozzi: "These are Times when every body's best Wits are wanted—and I understand that much Pains are taken to excite Commotions in the Very heart of the Metropolis. *My* old Residence the Borough of Southwark is certainly run raving Mad, by what the Papers exhibit of their outrageous Resolutions; and *Britons to Arms* are printed on Hand-bills, and thrust under Doors whose Owners would be quiet if they could."[14] The hard times threatened the moral and economic fabric of the country: "The Times are indeed very bad— I told you long ago that bad Times were coming—tho' I knew not the Form they would appear in: That which is presented to us is formidable enough; for tho' the Corn in some of these Counties is got in, much remains out to perplex the Farmer and rob Gentlemen of their Rents.——Few of them even pretend to pay Taylors, Shoemakers, &c. So they shut their Shops, and increase the List of Bankrupts."[15]

The unrest in the countryside quickly spread to London. "I think no Emphasis Strong enough now," Mrs. Piozzi warned Salusbury, "to express the general Uneasiness, or particular Absurdity of the Londoners. Had Government not been provided with Guards for the Bank, Property would scarce have had a Name in England. . . . They attempted to take Arms from the Tower too: but there Government was beforehand with them, else half the Lives in London would have been lost by now."[16] Actually, all of England would soon be lost, Mrs. Piozzi feared, sure that her warnings were like Cassandra's: "While Salusbury reposes in the noiseless Tranquillity of Brynbella—and while you sit reading old History at Bodylwyddan," she chided John Williams, "and believing as Dr. Johnson did, that when *Consternation* was described by the Writers in pompous Terms,—nobody was *consternated:*—I have to assure you that War in the *Streets* of London and *Famine* in the Fields; are very serious, not to say dreadful Things. . . . The Rioters shewing a Disposition to Seize the Bank,—frighted our Moneyed Men—who wisely reflecting that half a Loaf is better than no Bread, will I doubt not quietly submit to see their 5 Per Cents become 4;—rather than witness a sudden Destruction of *all* Property by *Le Peuple Souverain.*"[17]

But when, worried for her safety, Salusbury offered her a refuge from the violence late in 1816, she declined, declaring with a trace of her old zest that, while it was frightful to live so close to scenes of turmoil, it would be more frightful to live insulated from them. Besides, she equivocated, "The blundering Rebellion is completely stifled—smothered like a Man bit by a Mad Dog in Ireland, between Two Featherbeds. . . . All is quiet: The foolish Creatures fancied they should have support from every Country Town; but Common Sense carried the Day, and saved the Nation from such Distresses as poor France experienced, and cannot yet recover from. . . . you see I learn something useful by living in the *World*—which my long Habits make necessary to my Existence;—it would be Shortened by playing the Recluse and not knowing what past *even close to me.*"[18]

"SHARPER THAN A SERPENT'S TOOTH":
The widow and her children

John Salusbury Piozzi Salusbury

By 1811 Mrs. Piozzi had moved Salusbury into a central position in her life, as she tried to fill the void left by her daughters' defection and the far larger void left by Gabriel Piozzi's death. He was to become a son who would compensate for her daughters' faithlessness and a companion who would compensate for her husband's loss.

When Gabriel Piozzi's brother offered his infant son Giovanni Salusbury to the Piozzis in 1794, Mrs. Piozzi clearly perceived that the little boy might become an effective weapon in her ongoing warfare with her daughters. In a *Thraliana* entry she juxtaposed a flareup of hostilities with her daughter Cecy Mostyn and Cecy's husband with the child's arrival: "Mr. Mostyn has written me an insulting Letter saying where's my *fine Breeding &c* & accusing me of interfering in his *private Affairs.* . . . He knows Piozzi & I are both ill, & Cecy sets him on to pinch us to Madness. A pretty Nest of Wasps they are to be sure. *I will get out on't tho'* before 'tis long. . . . I have sent for one little Boy from among my husband's Nephews, he was christened *John Salusbury:* he shall be Naturalized, & we will see if He will be more grateful, & rational, & comfortable than Miss Thrales have been to the Mother they have at length *driven to Desperation.*"[19]

Salusbury's advent seems to have had the hoped-for effect on Mrs. Piozzi's daughters: "the taking on of Piozzi's nephew astonished the four Thrale sisters. They felt embarrassment, as well as anxiety about their inheritance."[20]

In those early days, there was little to interest Mrs. Piozzi in the life of the little Italian boy, who she mentioned only in an offhanded way in her journal, calling him "Mr Piozzi's Baby" and the "little Italian Boy,"[21] and of whom she recorded little in her lengthy letters. But she was vitally interested in what the child could *become;* engineering his success and commanding his gratitude would, in large measure, compensate for her daughters' ingratitude and their refusal to be guided by her in any areas of their lives. She hinted her intentions to her friend Leonard Chappelow, declaring that, "Could I *but* live to see this John Salusbury a fine Fellow, and accounted one of the first Scholars at Eton; I really should think it a prodigious Happiness——and Yet a Lad is not fairly *launched* into the World till he quits the University——leaving Christ Church with *Eclat* for the Bustle of active Life."[22] Mrs. Piozzi was to find herself disappointed in this part of her carefully constructed plan for Salusbury's future. Never a happy scholar, Salusbury was underprepared and could not enter Eton. Mrs. Piozzi, who always refused to accept failure, immediately wrote to him that, "Much Vice and Folly will certainly be escaped by your not going to Eton."[23]

During Piozzi's terrible last illness in 1809, Mrs. Piozzi indulged herself in long letters to sixteen-year-old Salusbury, filled with vivid and horrifying details of his uncle's unremitting agony. Salusbury became increasingly important to her, both as a sort of human journal to whom she could pour out all her grief and fear, and as a source of whatever small comfort she could derive from his responses.

Several months after Piozzi's death in 1809, Mrs. Piozzi finalized Salusbury's denization, thus accomplishing the first part of her outline for his life.[24] This act was a preliminary, Mrs. Piozzi made clear to Salusbury, for the relationship they were now to assume. Each was to be central to the other's life: "So here I am— hoping if I *am* to live, that my Life may be useful to *You* . . . On *You* my thread of Temporal Existence is now suspended . . . and upon Your Feeling that it *is* so; upon Your Persuasion that we are linked together by Interest & Duty—I depend."[25] For her he was to take on the roles "both of *Protector* and *Protegé* united."[26] Such allegiance would be recompense for her kindness and generosity: Her "dearest Boy" had already cost her "so much Money and Care in these Dozen Years of his British Life."[27] Thus began what was to become a lifelong pattern of guilt-inducing statements masked with terms of affection.

Once she had established the centrality of Salusbury's role in her life, Mrs. Piozzi entered into the reciprocal role with gusto. She had always expressed pleasure in Salusbury's correspondence, albeit mingled with mild irritation at his problems with grammar and syntax. She now insisted that the sixteen-year-old's letters were vital to her very being. An 1810 letter indicates the paradigm shift. On 19 February Mrs. Piozzi sent Salusbury a writing desk, in the drawer of which she had placed her miniature. Three days later, not having yet received his thanks, Mrs. Piozzi issued a melodramatic demand that he write immediately: "I sit expecting my Dear Child's Letter from Newbury, and . . . I hear the Post Man knocking at every Door except poor No. 6. . . . Good Heavens! but here's the Post gone by—and no Letter from Newbury—Why surely my Dear Salusbury's hand could never have been stopt by any Accident from letting me know his Box was safe arrived. . . . *Dear* now for Mercy's Sake, write directly; and say you are alive. . . . Oh tell Pemberton and Mr. Shephard what an Agony I am in; and make *them* write if anything ails *you* which God forbid. . . . Oh Salusbury! have you no Pity? Write only two words—*Alive* and *Well.*"[28]

Mrs. Piozzi also attempted to align Salusbury against her daughters, often telling him that her "Enemies,""the Ladies" were jealous of him and were determined to find ways to hurt him, both socially and financially. His "old Aunt" would protect him, however, and ensure that, if he conformed to her wishes, her "own Family" would be *"forced* to confess that her favours" to him "have been all well deserved."[29]

Thus, by 1811, Mrs. Piozzi had already spent eighteen months in attempting to inculcate in Salusbury the notions that he owed her tremendous gratitude and loyalty and that part of his demonstration of loyalty was his unquestioning support for her in her unceasing strife with her daughters.

Much of Mrs. Piozzi's 1811 correspondence with Salusbury was devoted to fashioning his identity and her own as it related to his. The worldly, witty, independent Mrs. Piozzi had become "poor Aunt," with Salusbury cast as her "Support": "How well is my kind and Considerate *Friend,*——my best-loved Salusbury—acquainted with the Constitution of his poor Aunt! whose *thin-worne* Mind though shining still perhaps, in conversation or Correspondence; is no longer buoyant as it used to be: but begins to want support from his more youthful and elastic Powers." In an excess of the emotion with which she had lately invested her relationship with Salusbury, she wrote, as though to a lover: "so sweet, so wise, so lovely is your Letter, that if I am too restless for expectation of good Sleep tonight, I will put it under my Pillow as I used to do those from Your Uncle. Ah Salusbury! how have You and Yours withdrawn my whole heart from its old Channel!——never well cut indeed for my Affections to flow in; but where they *did* flow uniformly and tranquilly, however inclined to Dulness and Stagnation."[30]

With others, Mrs. Piozzi adopted the same extravagant tone when she spoke of Salusbury: "If I *am* to live on . . . I might lay up Sixpence o'Year for the Child of my age, and as the Mahometans call an adopted Boy—The Son of my *Soul.*"[31] It was clearly important that her friends sympathize with her intention to leave much of her estate away from her daughters; they would do so only if convinced that he was highly deserving. She continued to fashion an eminently deserving Salusbury in letters to her friends. Writing to Lady Williams from Cheltenham, where she had taken Salusbury for Christmas, she asserted that, "such Civilities were surely never lavished upon perfect Strangers—as were bestowed on Salusbury and Myself upon our first Arrival." Refusing to succumb to the blandishments of Cheltenham, however, the virtuous Salusbury "left me for Enborne last Monday; notwithstanding a Thousand Temptations . . . but *Steady* should be his Motto; and none of their Seducements could perswade him to change His day."[32] Indeed, her new friends were singularly impressed, not only by his steadiness of purpose, but by the "Prudence and Propriety of his Conduct."[33] Often resorting to hyperbole, Mrs. Piozzi applauded Salusbury's diligence and reminded him that his attention to duty was to result in further success: "Let Oxford, as Bath and Cheltenham have done—bear witness to my Darling's Triumph over Temptation; and to the Power of restraining Grace over his pure and honourable Mind."[34]

Linked to his virtue and prudence was Salusbury's filial regard for his Aunt: "I could not come thro' Llangollen, the Snows were higher than the Carriage in a less dangerous Road—but I had an able-bodied and active-Souled Youth to take Care of me, who makes Friends wherever he goes." Although prudent, Salusbury was no prude: "my young Spark rounded his Christmas Holydays with a gay Ball, and returned (more willingly than any other Boy on Earth would have done,) to his Studies at Enborne."[35]

Always during this period there were the reminders, subtle and not so subtle, of the enormous debt of gratitude Salusbury owed her: "my Heart confides in the good Sense and good Principles of Dear Salusbury," she wrote to her nephew on 17 March 1811. "I tell you that 'tis upon *no common* Boy, Hundred Pound Feasts have been bestowed——whilst even a new Gown is grudged to *herself* by his Affectionate Parent."[36] Included in her reminders were subtle admonitions about the behavior that would guarantee her continued approbation: "Counting the hours till we meet, does me most good, and the Certainty of your deserving more than I can do, and even all that I can wish." "Be you good, and wise, and well, and happy; and let the Visions of your future exemplary Conduct raised Night and Day by my Fancy and Fondness,—Fly out at the Gate of Truth not Fiction." "Mean while we have *ourselves* to think about—meaning Dear Salusbury and me:—Poor Aunt! whose Happiness now hangs but by *one* Thread; Your Conduct in Life. . . . Whilst we use our Wits rightly, We shall weave a Strong Bond for ourselves of Amity, Affection, and Esteem—a triple Cord which cannot be broken—between my Darling Salusbury and his *confiding* Parent."[37]

Looming large for both Salusbury and his "*confiding* Parent" was his twenty-first birthday in September 1814. If she lived until that date, Salusbury would become her residuary legatee. Mrs. Piozzi continually recurred to this momentous date in her letters. Although there is no evidence that her fears were justified, she seemed to live in terror of Salusbury's succumbing to depravity before he achieved his majority: "My truly beloved *Nepos* as he calls himself, is the *Ne plus ultra* of all good Boys. But Boyhood is done with now, and Manhood is begun——or to speak strictly *Adolescence.* Let us get thro' this fiery Tryal of Youth, and congratulate ourselves on the Year of Emancipation.——The Angel of God . . . still watches over *early Virtue,* and will preserve its Votaries from the Destruction destined for them."[38]

While they waited together for the all-important event, Mrs. Piozzi—against the advice of friends—set about achieving another goal: seeing Salusbury matriculate at Christ Church, Oxford. Earlier she had been warned of the iniquity prevalent in the college: "Good old Tall Townsend," she'd told sixteen-year-old Salusbury in 1809, "says 'Oh now for Pity do not put that fine-pure hearted Boy to Christ Church; it is the wickedest College in Oxford—any other College, Oh *any* Place but Christ Church.' . . . I am confident Sir—(was my Answer,) that Salusbury will be thrown into dreadful Temptations at Christ Church;—but when he and I saw the Porcelain Manufacture together at Coalbrook Dale, we saw that when they had turned the Plate, and shaped it elegantly—and painted a beautiful Figure of *Virtue* or *Religion* on it——The Man was at last obliged to put it in a *Furnace* and *burn it in* before the Plate was fitted for use.——Aye (replied Townsend) in a *Furnace,* but Christ Church when my Son was there, might be considered as a *Crucible* that would melt down Gold itself."[39]

But in this regard Mrs. Piozzi was obdurate. She had decided when Salusbury was very young that Christ Church was the entrée into the world of affairs for young gentlemen and to Christ Church Salusbury would go—even at the risk of annihilating that moral character of which she was so tender. In 1812 she accomplished her design, even though his tutor Charles Shephard had tried to stop her, feeling that, as with Eton, Salusbury was underprepared. In May, Salusbury received a defiantly triumphant letter from his aunt that must have terrified him; early on he had exhibited a distaste for any kind of scholarly activity, which became more pronounced as he grew older: "My dearest Friend! my best-loved Salusbury will perhaps scarcely wonder that I am critiseized by my watchful Acquaintance for the *Too-kind* Deed I have so fearlessly committed in sending my Darling Gentleman Commoner to Christ Church: Mr. Shephard of Enborne is most openly severe upon me, and I confess myself as *Ill-prepared* for his Severities, as he says You were *ill-prepared* for Oxford. What Schreech Owls!"[40]

Mrs. Piozzi strained to develop a parallel between the risk she was taking in sending Salusbury to Oxford and the risk she took when she married his uncle: "Let you and I live so as to shew them how wrong they were! and what true cause we have to scorn their schreeching. Did not your dear Uncle's Conduct justify my partial Confidence towards Him in the Eyes of all Mankind? and did he not *force* them to retract their ill founded Opinions?—Yes, Yes; so will *his* and *my own* incomparable Salusbury. I feel that all will end just as I wish, and of course I despise their Malice. . . . with God's Grace and my Care; your *Dangers* will not be so *great,* nor Your *Fortune so small* as they pretend to fear, and to lament. We shall do very well in 'Spite of false Friends and professed Enemies. . . . how very malicious People must be to endeavour at destroying My few Pleasures *now*—at 71 Years old!—and such an Innocent, praise-worthy Pleasure as rejoycing over my Darling Child's respectable Situation in early Life. . . . I *will* rejoyce that Dear Piozzi's Nephew and my own adopted Son——is as I always intended he *should* be, if a Good Boy——one of the Gentlemen Commoners of Christ Church."[41]

Even though she believed that it was imperative that Salusbury attend Oxford, Mrs. Piozzi was often vexed by his behavior there. For example, although she provided him with a most generous allowance—five hundred pounds per annum—Salusbury quickly managed to overspend it and to have bills sent to her. One such instance occurred in October 1811, almost immediately after he matriculated: "After fretting and frighting myself into a nervous Fever, I have this Day the Happiness to hear *of* my Inestimable Pug from *Stroud* with a 40£ Claim enclosed. Hamlet likewise has written to say Your Silver Plate went from London on the 19th but he has had no Letter from you acknowledging its Receipt; so *his* Intelligence which arrived Yesterday, increased my Terrors, lest some harm had happened." Added to this anxiety was Mrs. Piozzi's vexation that he was enjoying himself too much to be a good correspondent: "It now appears however that you were alive on the 22d: and do write to me *now* for Shame, if not for Love. Indeed I see neither Common Sense nor Knowlege of the World in persisting to think it a heavy Tax on Life to spend 3 Minutes in writing every Week 3 Words—*safe, well,* and *happy.* . . . the *last* of them implies the Conservation of your Virtue."[42]

Indeed, conserving Salusbury's virtue had become a major issue with Mrs. Piozzi, whose letters were liberally sprinkled with moral admonitions. Clearly, her initial defiant stance had given way to her fears: "Nothing in *My* Power, no nor in *Buonaparte's* Power, could make *you* happy with a Spotted Conscience."[43] Apprehensive that he would fall into bad company, thus fulfilling her friends' predictions, Mrs. Piozzi continually admonished Salusbury: "Dearest,—*Dearest* Boy! keep out of these worthless People's Company as much—as You can." In order to bring the lesson home, Mrs. Piozzi would enumerate his recent sins of omission and commission: "The Word *Boy* puts me in mind of poor Uncle: if he saw this Letter, and heard of the Wine Bill, and the Plate Bill—and *my* Complaints that you never write——and *Your* Humour of forbearing hitherto to accept any Profession; I think he *would* say '*Charming Boy!* I am very glad; He is spoiled *enough* now.'" But Mrs. Piozzi had long ago learned that, for a woman, anger seldom gained her point. Whenever she indulged in the luxury of railing at Salusbury for a real or imagined iniquity, she concluded by wheedling. She depended too heavily on Salusbury for comfort and affection to risk alienating him: "I cannot calm my Spirits even by reading Prayers;—have Pity on my Nerves, and write before I am too ill to beg of you: and don't feel *angry* but *Sorry* that I can neither eat nor sleep for want of a Letter."[44]

Such was the pattern of Mrs. Piozzi's correspondence with Salusbury until his marriage in 1814. When she did not hear from him frequently she wrote anguished letters, demanding sympathy, gratitude, and affection: "My dearest Child If you are Ill what *shall* I do? what *can* I do for my Darling? . . . If you are well, Your Heart is made of Stone; but No, I'm certain there has been some Accident."[45] Guilt-inducing statements permeated her letters: "It was high Time to write Dearest Salusbury—a too anxious Heart was just beginning to poyson all my Pleasures." And over all floated thinly veiled threats that he, like her daughters, could be disinherited. Constantly dangling the carrot of Brynbella, she warned: "you must pray for my Life, and deserve the Advantage of it by prudent Conduct."[46]

In subtle comparisons of Salusbury's careless behavior toward her and her daughters' long-term neglect, she emphasized that faithless offspring always fared badly: "Meanwhile I am just come from hearing Gods Curses denounced on Fornicators, Drunkards—and Those who Curse Father or Mother——*Lady Keith* ran through Bath Three Days ago, and did me the honour to take Breakfast. . . . Your *fair* Friend and Confident, and my professed Enemy—The dainty Widow of Segroid; has written *her* Enquiries in a fond familiar Style. . . . If I write more You will not read it I suppose, You are so *immersed in Business——Dear* Fellow!"[47]

Salusbury quickly found himself in a dilemma. Severe when he failed to write, Mrs. Piozzi found cause for anxiety even when he wrote dutifully and often: "My foreboding Soul felt *something* when the Postman knocked his smart Rap; and I was glad (God forgive me) that Mr. Lane was sick, instead of my Darling being seized with these Illnesses, which carry People off so Suddenly. . . . tho' I see Company enough, yet I feel miserably deserted at home somehow."[48] Perhaps worse than her lamentations were the veiled threats, which he learned to expect even in letters that stated that she had just received one of his: "My precious Creature had more need think of his poor Aunt's *Health* than her Anger. . . . It is however a foolish Thing to encrease my natural Tendency to Agitation, by *your Silence;*—a very foolish Thing indeed: and one Day or other you will repent it."[49] When Salusbury remonstrated with her at the extravagance of her concern, she responded: "Reproaches never do any Good Dearest Salusbury, and tho' I am as jealous of your *Affection,* as you purpose being of your Wife's *Love:* I seldom burst out till Fears for your Safety fling me quite off my Guard."[50]

Mrs. Piozzi's primary care, however, was not for the safety of Salusbury's health, but for his virtue; she was terrified that he could not withstand the blandishments of "this *Marble* Age. . . . The Atrocities which roll off other People's Minds Impress mine very forcibly indeed;—and when I look on the deserving Lad of my heart . . . Tears of Apprehension for his Virtue's Safety, stand in my long-experienced Eyes."[51] Salusbury was not only overspending his liberal allowance, but was balking at making a career choice. And he was ensconced at Christ Church, the college about whose moral decay she had been warned. If he fell from grace, her enemies, the "Ladies," would triumph. She must ensure that Salusbury remain a worthy candidate for his share of her estate.

At this early date, Mrs. Piozzi had not declared, at least publicly, an intention to leave her entire estate to her "darling Boy," recognizing that to do so would create an "Appearance of Impropriety and Disrespect to my first husband's Representatives."[52] Still, as long as he continued virtuous she intended to be generous to Salusbury, even if he refused to engage in a profession—although, still striving to bend him to her will, she contrived to make life without a profession sound a paltry thing indeed: if "you can perswade Some good Girl to marry you this Time *Three Years*—I will *give* you all I *can* leave You, and you may go abroad together and *save* Money, if you will not stay at Home and get Money—which would be a likelier Plan for Happiness, and Law the proper Profession. Whatever befalls—except *your* Ill behaviour—or Choice of what I call a Mop-squeezer, or flanting Miss from a Gaming House like——I shall be ever far more *Yours* than my own."[53]

In May 1812, after one year at Christ Church, Salusbury announced that he wanted to leave Oxford at the end of the school year. The announcement must have produced a series of conflicting emotions: acute embarrassment because she had risked alienating those who had argued against enrolling Salusbury in Christ Church and had proudly boasted that her "darling Boy" was a "Gentleman Commoner;" enormous relief that when he left Oxford he would be free of the corrupting influence of Christ Church; and, most importantly, keen gratification. He was leaving in order to return to Brynbella—and to her: "You are the best of all wise Boys, and the wisest of all good ones, in wishing to leave Oxford, and come home with poor Aunt—to take Care of her."[54] Salusbury, who had no such intention, spent most of the following year visiting friends and making merry with the full purse that "poor Aunt" provided.

During this period, Mrs. Piozzi enjoyed a remission of the pessimism that had dogged her since Piozzi's death: "My 71st Birth Day was like my *Life* stormy and rainy Morning and Afternoon; but clearing up fine *late in the Evening;*—and the *Night* very tranquil and brilliant."[55] Her wonderful sense of fun reasserted itself: "What were you doing at Nantwich?" she asked Salusbury. "Were there Races in that Country? It used to be ill calculated for such Amusement. Here they come, here they come, here they come; There they go, There they go, There they go: is the Sport of a Horse Course——It comes In, It comes in, It comes in; It goes out, It goes out, It goes out; is *my* Sport looking at the Tide."[56]

Mrs. Piozzi had little time to enjoy the relief afforded by Salusbury's removal from Oxford, however; the "Ladies," afraid that he was going to succeed to their mother's Welsh estates, were agitating for reversionary proprietorship of the properties. Incensed and anxious, Mrs. Piozzi rushed to London to confer with her legal advisors. Finding her property rights secure, a still-angry Mrs. Piozzi decided to take a decisive step; on 19 April 1813, she made a new will, giving "*every* Thing I *possess*, and every Thing I *claim:* or am, or shall be intitled to" to Salusbury. He was to take possession of Brynbella on 9 September 1814, the day he came of age, in order to escape the legacy tax.[57]

Having settled the estate on Salusbury, Mrs. Piozzi turned her attention to finding him the right wife. He was going to be the squire of Brynbella and, therefore, a desirable match: "The Estate is *mine*, and if mine *Yours*,—bestowing it as I wish on a Young Woman of Honour and Credit to us both. . . . And the Lady of your Choice will not be *very ill off*. . . . Do not undervalue Your own Importance——Such Person, Mind, and Fortune—tho none of them Gigantic, have good *Symmetrical Pretensions.*"[58] A short two months later, Salusbury announced his choice: Harriet Maria Pemberton. He had known Harriet, the sister of his best friend, for five years, although Mrs. Piozzi was not aware that he had long since fallen in love with her. She seems to have received the news with equanimity rather than enthusiasm, telling Dr. Whalley in an uncharacteristically subdued letter that her "fortune" as regarded Salusbury "will not be a fortune to rejoice or to lament over." If he "would not thrust himself forward in the career of ambition" but had elected instead the "sober path of private life in hope of domestic happiness, what can I do but pray for his success, and promote it as far as I am able?"

Harriet's family was, at least, a respectable one: "The family he connects with are, in all appearance, much respected by their neighbours; very honourable, and very ancient; proud Salopians! *plus noble que riche*; but individually well bred and agreeable."[59] Always resilient, however, Mrs. Piozzi soon recovered from whatever mild disappointment she felt about the match, wisely deciding to form a friendship with Harriet, thus ensuring that her all-important relationship with Salusbury would continue. Harriet, equally wise, sent charming letters, liberally laced with sympathy for Salusbury's "poor Aunt's" aches, pains, and solitary state.

Having secured Salusbury's financial future, Mrs. Piozzi spent much of fall and winter 1813 engaged in legal procedures that led to Salusbury's formal adoption. His name was "properly Gazetted" so that he could become a legal member of the Salusbury line of succession. This was another direct hit at the "Ladies": "The Gazette has given him Permission and Authority—nay *Command* to assume my Arms Name &c. *now*," she told Harriet, "and Mrs. Mostyn *must* change her Style when She directs to him again."[60] Attempting to enlist Harriet's support in her internecine strife with her daughters, she implied that the Ladies would, if possible, harm Salusbury in some way: "My Name and Arms are his *own* now, and in no one's Power to wash off his Carriage when he keeps one; a Trick which Malice *might* have plaid to give *me*—more than *him*—Mortification——but he *is* my Son at last—in true Earnest; my Son by Adoption, inserted into the Pedigree of my Descent, and registered in the Herald's College—so there's an End of such Designs if there were any."[61]

In spite of her determination to make Salusbury her legal son and heir, Mrs. Piozzi must often have felt frustrated and disappointed by his inability—and disinclination—to think and behave like a true child of Hester Lynch Piozzi. A poor scholar, he took no interest in intellectual, cultural, or political matters. She was not even able to pique his interest in the political events shaping the country. Complaining to her young friend John Williams (who possessed all the qualities of intellect and ambition that Salusbury lacked), Mrs. Piozzi compared her adopted son with herself at the same age: "Shall we praise or blame Dear Salusbury's utter want of all Curiosity concerning any one Thing but the pretty Girl he is attached to? *That* Disposition appears to me among the odd Things one stumbles over—but I really have Individually much Reason to rejoyce that he has taken Shelter (tho' in a Shed,) from the Storms that seem gathering round in every Direction. *I* should at his Age have felt inclined to go out and look at the Lightning,—by which Means I should have got blinded;—and he, *will keep his Eyes.*"[62]

But Mrs. Piozzi could not complain too loudly or too publicly about Salusbury. She had, after all, *chosen* him as her son and heir, and could never admit that she might have been mistaken. Therefore, as she had done when her attempts to secure Eton and Oxford careers for him had failed, she began to make revisionist excuses for Salusbury. His refusal to follow a profession quickly became a further proof of a virtue almost heroic: "from [Salusbury] I do confess to expect, all that his high Sense of Religion and Honour will prompt him to; They have kept him *poor* in Comparison with the Rich and Gay, but in his *State* of *Competence* he may be *prosperous;* and to deserve Success, is better than to enjoy it," she told Harriet.[63] To a contemporary of Salusbury's with ambitious career plans, Mrs. Piozzi defended her adopted son: "The same conduct no more suits two different Men, than the same coat does. . . . There are so many Cross Roads in our Journey thro' Life, and they are so dirty and so dangerous—one is contented to see a young Man make Choice of a clean and a straight one; however unadorned by Flowers, and however undiversified . . . by Elegant Turns, and sometimes *too serpentine* Windings."[64]

Mrs. Piozzi did not intend, however, that Salusbury's aversion for settling on a profession should indemnify him from all responsibility. When he at length returned to Brynbella, she left him in charge while she went to inspect Streatham repairs. Mrs. Piozzi's apparent aim was to make Salusbury grow into the squireship he desired. Unfortunately, Salusbury had no training for the position and quickly ran into difficulties. When he applied to Mrs. Piozzi for ready cash, however, she, who had always kept his purse filled, refused him, apparently favoring the sink-or-swim approach. If he wanted the role of squire he would have to earn it: "Ah my Dearest Salusbury! can you make me believe that a Fellow bent on his own Business, and residing closely like yourself on his own little Income . . . will ever feel real Distress."[65] This was the start of money squabbles that were to last until her death.

In November 1814 Salusbury and Harriet were married. Mrs. Piozzi attended but did not seem to feel much joy on the occasion, telling Dr. Whalley only that the families "went to Church on the *seventh* of this Month, and the happy Younglings jumped into their Carriage and away to *their own Brynbella,* leaving me a while to comfort Mrs. Pemberton at Condover Park Salop for Loss of her Harriet Maria."[66]

Tension between Mrs. Piozzi and Salusbury began to grow. Her steward, Alexander Leak, was furious with Salusbury for sending Brynbella tax bills to her. Leak had long believed that Mrs. Piozzi's affection for Salusbury was misguided: "His want of Gratitude make it less excusable, this is the return you meet with from Him for whom You have made Yourself, and so many others Miserable."[67] Even more distressing than the tax bills were the rumors that Salusbury, failing to discharge his financial obligations for Brynbella, was, instead, making unnecessary changes to the house. Most painful for Mrs. Piozzi must have been the news that Salusbury had converted the library to a maid's room. And he was felling the trees that she and Piozzi had planted to improve the estate.[68] A rueful Mrs. Piozzi exclaimed, "Oh Dear! I am ready sometimes to wish a little of the Money I spent there, was in my Pocket now."[69]

Even worse than Salusbury's depredations was his silence. Throughout his minority, Mrs. Piozzi had been able to pressure Salusbury to maintain a dutiful correspondence. Now, with her estate his own, the flow of correspondence became sluggish. Bitterly, she compared Salusbury with her daughters: "I have no Letters from him but upon *Business,* and none from the Ladies at all——It is not who is *deserving* of my favour that I think about; All five are *deserving* young People, with regard to their *Conduct in Life*——and as to Affection towards *me.* All are *alike* Affectionate!!!"[70]

Money was an ongoing source of friction. While Mrs. Piozzi was trying to recover from the heavy expenses incurred during Streatham Park repairs, Salusbury, aware that most of her income was encumbered, was still pressuring her to assist him with Brynbella debts. Mrs. Piozzi, however, was determined that, since he had preferred marriage and a small income to a profession and "taking care of poor Aunt," he would have to live with the consequences. He was no longer her chief care and concern: "Present me most kindly to your . . . fair Consort. . . . But do not believe me *now*—as of old Time—restless about dear Salusbury, and apprehensive for his Safety and Happiness," she told her nephew on 21 February 1815. "I can only pray for a long Continuance of his Comfort, and Delight in the Road he chalked out for himself." Still vexed by his refusal to follow a profession that could have provided financial security, Mrs. Piozzi began to subtly twit him on his lack of ambition: "Sir Nathaniel Wrax<all> had nothing at starting into Life except Talents and Education: but in India they were serviceable to him, and he married to Advantage as I remember; and he has been a Writer for Government and they seldom fail rewarding their Friends by Place or Title or something."[71]

Salusbury's excited announcement in March 1815 that Harriet was pregnant intensified Mrs. Piozzi's bitterness: "My dearest Salusbury may assure himself I keep up my Health and Spirits as well as I can. . . . My Hot Houses and Green Houses are to pay *Treble* Tax; other People who are so taxed, can tear their Hothouses and Greenhouses away; but I am bound by Law to keep mine up— so much for *my* Causes of Felicity. I am glad yours—as you deem them such— are increasing."[72] So piqued was Mrs. Piozzi by Salusbury's euphoria that she uncharacteristically wrote Lady Williams, from whom she ordinarily hid her frustrations with Salusbury: "I suppose the fair Lady of Brynbella will be taken double and treble Care of; being such a *Petted* Darling both of Mother and Husband."[73]

The birth of Salusbury's first child, Hester Maria, caused a temporary cessation of Mrs. Piozzi's growing animosity, but the respite was short-lived. Responding to an emotional letter from Salusbury, detailing the newborn's illness, Mrs. Piozzi, who had survived many such crises, accorded him little sympathy: "My dearest Salusbury is now learning by cruel Experience what every Book on every Shelf could have told him long ago: that Life is full of Cares, and that all our Pleasures however short lived—and however imperfect, are purchased and paid for by bitter and severe Pains. What You are Suffering, is Suffered . . .

by *every*body. It is not I believe One Person in 40000 who rears all their Offspring; and those which are brought up, cost their Parents much health, much Peace, much Time and much Money. I have myself lost Eight at various Ages:—some within the Month, some within the Year; one at Three Years old, a *Son;* and one Son at 11. From those that remain, I have as You know four Grandchildren—— and their turning out Well must compensate."[74]

Increasingly, Mrs. Piozzi complained openly to her friends about Salusbury's neglect. Omitting mention of her cold response to the frightened father, she told Sir James that, "That little Thoughtless Thing Salusbury—has kept me all this while in hot Water about his Baby——wrote the *pathetic* Letter you saw:—— and then, never (in answer to all my Enquiries) sent Word whether the Child lived or died."[75] Lamenting the straitened circumstances caused by her Strea- tham debts, Mrs. Piozzi asserted that Salusbury had grown as callous toward her poverty as her daughters: "People see me live as I do, and think I mean a long Continuance in the same Course of Wretchedness——but I am the more Tired of it, as I see so little Pleasure given to those who should render my Situation more Comfortable by at least affected Assiduity——but neither real Daughters nor adopted Son have ever dropt a hint as if I was living beneath myself."[76] Her children's behavior was bound to shorten her life, she hinted: "*My* Life *cannot* now be a long one; The Ladies and Mr. Salusbury are all very ill humored."[77] "Is Mrs. Salusbury again in the Family Way?" she asked Lady Williams. "Her Husband's Letters seem embarrassed somehow; and appear somewhat *very like very Ill-humoured.*"[78]

Nevertheless, Mrs. Piozzi professed herself surprised and disturbed when Salusbury remonstrated with her about the tone of her correspondence, noting in her "Pocket Book" entry for 20 February 1816 that she had "received a *strange* Letter from Salusbury, as if he had a Mind to quarrel with me!!! Is he going out of his Mind?"[79] Responding to Salusbury, she asserted that, "I am so little accustomed Dearest Salusbury, to be called roughly to Account for my Expres- sions, and find so few People ill pleased with my Correspondence, that I am at a Loss to answer your Accusation. . . . My Temper however may possibly be soured by Time and various Vexations——tho' I now do remember something of a Similar Disposition to quarrel on your Part, last May 1815—when I under- went a heavy Censure for some Omission of Ceremony. We will if you please beware of the Third Time."[80]

Peace was restored—if only temporarily—when Salusbury finally achieved a measure of distinction, becoming "Sheriff of the County of Flint,"[81] a largely honorary position. Delighted, Mrs. Piozzi saluted him from her lodging at Speen Hill: "From this once favourite Spot of Dear Uncle's, when pretty Salusbury came bounding over Hill and Dale to enjoy our Company who ran to embrace him;——do I address The High Sheriff of Flintshire and 'Squire of Bryn- bella. . . . Ah Dearest Salusbury! when out of this Window my Eye catches the Scenes we once saw together . . . how many Recollections croud my Mind!"[82]

But celebrating this honor could not restore the intimacy that had existed— at least in Mrs. Piozzi's mind—before Salusbury's marriage. When at last her Streatham artifacts were auctioned, Leak suggested that no catalogue should be sent to Salusbury. He had long asserted that the financial problems that led to the forced sale were due to her too generous support of her adopted son's whims. Mrs. Piozzi demurred, rather from prudence than from affection: "Making Enemies—especially of young People—is however always imprudent, and tho' I am inclined to be wholly of your Mind about Mr. Salusbury;——[the auctioneer] *ought* to send him the Catalogues. . . . Not a *Priced* one tho'; for I don't want him to see every 20£ I possess, or dispose of: Those days of Confidence are wholly over between *us*."[83]

The halcyon days of affectionate parent and dutiful son would never be recovered.

Mrs. Piozzi's Daughters

The days of affectionate parent and dutiful children had long ago ended for Mrs. Piozzi and her surviving daughters, Hester Maria (Samuel Johnson's "Queeney"), Susanna, Sophia, and Cecilia. They had been shocked, embarrassed, and outraged when, in 1782, their mother not only fell in love with but insisted on marrying her daughters' music master. After eighteen months of violent antagonism, the marriage took place.[84] The estrangement between mother and daughters was irretrievable, although they occasionally exchanged coldly correct letters. Little of their enmity appears in these letters, but Mrs. Piozzi regularly rehearsed her daughters' sins of omission and commission in her correspondence with others.

Perhaps as galling to her daughters as the marriage was her adoption of "Mr. Piozzi's nephew,"[85] who, coming to England in 1798, was immediately perceived as a threat to their inheritance. And, as both her correspondence and her *Thraliana* entries for the period make clear, the perception was accurate. Perhaps to assure that Salusbury would never become alienated through their baleful influence, Mrs. Piozzi began early on to fashion him as innocent victim of those wily predators, the "Ladies."[86] His only recourse, she made clear, was to cling to her protection. And, indeed, in 1811 the Ladies declared that Mrs. Piozzi's Welsh estate, Bachygraig, intended for Salusbury, was rightfully theirs. She had no more right to dispose of Bachygraig to a personally chosen heir than she had to dispose of Streatham Park, in which she held only a life-interest, they asserted. Mrs. Piozzi was agitated and indignant. While the Ladies' father had disdained her ancestral home in Wales, Piozzi had revered it, lavishing money as well as loving care on its restoration and improvement. Angrily, Mrs. Piozzi disputed her daughters' claim: "Did they imagine Dear Piozzi would have lived 25 Years in a Dream, spending Thousands after Thousands on other People's Property!—and Lord Keith—a Man of Business—can he Think—that my Estate was not settled on my Second husband and my Children by *him*?" she fumed to John Oldfield, her attorney. "All this came into my Head since you left me scarce recovered, my Amazement at these Doubts and Disbeliefs of my Power over an Estate which has undergone a good many Pulls, but which is I hope—and the Disposal of it——firmly fixed by the great Disposer of all human Possessions."[87]

Mrs. Piozzi considered the Ladies the bane of her existence, even calling Cecilia "my professed Enemy."[88] Yet Cecilia was the only daughter who seems to have attempted to maintain a relationship with her mother. There is evidence that Cecy, even though she sided with her sisters in matters of financial interest, was still an affectionate daughter, visiting at Brynbella and urging Mrs. Piozzi to return the visits: "The wretched backwardness of the Season and the deadly dullness of the dear Vale, one feels doubly when quite alone, but of that I'll say nothing, that you may not retard your return; in your next Letter I hope to hear some mention of it. . . . you will find me just where you left me; unless impatient for your return, Black Nancy and I set out to meet you."[89] Cecy seemed to have the farming skills that Salusbury was never able to attain, often requesting fowl or other barnyard animals from Mrs. Piozzi: "Mrs. Mostyn begs me to send her some live Guinea Fowl, and mentions her Increase of Poultry with great Pleasure: She seems well and gay."[90]

With such open good will, perhaps Mrs. Piozzi and her youngest daughter could eventually have grown closer—until rising conflict over Streatham Park, pitting mother against daughters, put an end to any notion of détente.

Streatham and Its Woes

The Streatham Park estate was fairly extensive, consisting of eighty-eight acres, eighteen freehold and 70 copyhold. According to the plan drawn up by Clement Mead, Mrs. Piozzi's surveyor, the house "faced Tooting Bec Common, due north, standing about 90 yards back from Tooting Bec Road. . . . It was approached by a sweeping drive about 100 yards long from the lodge gates. . . . Behind the [house] are the stables, coachhouses, greenhouses, outbuildings and melon ground. To the west, extending to Green Lane (now Thrale Road), are seen the walled kitchen gardens and *graperies.*" The grounds also featured a gravel path and a two-mile-long paling, added by Mrs. Piozzi, both of which encircled the park.[91] Henry Thrale's will had only provided Mrs. Piozzi with a life-interest in the property. At her death it would revert to her daughters. During her life she was required to maintain the property whether or not she lived there. Any repairs needed after her death to bring it to its original state could be charged to her residuary legatee.

In 1798, having decided to make their home at Brynbella, Gabriel and Hester Piozzi attempted to deed Streatham Park to her daughters. Upon the daughters' refusal, they resolved to let the property and were able to find a succession of suitable tenants.[92] During 1810, however, Mrs. Piozzi began to experience considerable difficulties with her current Streatham tenant and by 1811 had come to consider long-distance management of the property a burden and trips to London to oversee the estate's management unpleasant, writing to Lady Williams and her sister-in-law that she preferred to stay away from the "Plagues" of Streatham.[93] Mrs. Piozzi's life-interest was becoming more of a burden than a benefit and, upon the advice of her old friend Dr. Whalley, she began to contemplate selling it to her daughters: "It appears to me a good Project, Lands sell high at present, and if the Garden should not prove an Incumbrance—That

Place might fetch a Sum the Interest of which would encrease my Income."[94] Such an increase was important to Mrs. Piozzi; she had determined to leave the bulk of her estate to Salusbury and wanted to make it as valuable as possible: "If I *am* to live on——as People fancy, and as I sometimes *hope* for Three Years and ½: I might lay up Sixpence o'Year for the Child of my age, and as the Mahometans call an adopted Boy—the Son of my *Soul.*"[95]

Mrs. Piozzi's friend and lawyer, Charles Shephard, believed it was fairly certain that, if her daughters proved recalcitrant, another purchaser for her life-interest could quickly be found, an opinion that Mrs. Piozzi received with the mixed feelings she was always to display toward this property: "Charles Shephard gives hopes of Streatham Park being set to Sale, and *good* hopes of a good Purchaser," she wrote optimistically to Salusbury, adding however, "*Hopes!* of seeing The Vault where lies my Mother close to the Husband whom She chose for *me* Sold. . . . Yet 'tis the Thing I now most wish to see Effectuated and do earnestly pray that the Affair may be finished with the Ladies in *dumb Show.*"[96]

The "Ladies," however, demonstrated little interest in purchasing a property that would revert to them upon their mother's death. Angry, Mrs. Piozzi wrote letters critical of their behavior, both to Salusbury and to sympathetic friends. Reprising her remark that she would like to deal with the "Ladies" in "*dumb Show,*" Mrs. Piozzi described her plan of action in more detail to her friend Leonard Chappelow: "I am going to London . . . just to see what the Ladies mean to do about old Streatham Park——Doctor Whalley gave me a hint as if Selling it would be eligible, but the fair Principals——my amiable Reversionaries are Silent; and I have done being amused with *Dumb-Show* Transactions: a *Pantomime* of such Importance would only leave *me* the Character of *Mother Goose.*" She was not selfishly concerned for herself, Mrs. Piozzi implied; her daughters would benefit as much from this sale as she would: "my heart applauds the Project as likely to profit all Parties." However, she asserted, her daughters' advisors were more concerned with agitating her than with proffering advice on how to effect a reasonable and just outcome: "Davies wrote me such Letters about the Place as gave me very serious Concern," she told Chappelow. "But he is so tenderly attached to pretty Mrs. Mostyn and her Triumvirate as you call them, that I must forgive his hurrying my Spirits—The sooner I depart, The greater *their Advantage.*"[97]

Once set in motion, latent animosities stirred by the Streatham Park negotiations rapidly escalated. It was reported to Mrs. Piozzi that, not content with refusing to purchase her life-interest, her daughters had decided that she had no right to sell any item in the house, asserting that their father meant them to have the contents in their entirety. A furious Mrs. Piozzi relayed the report to Salusbury, whom she assiduously cultivated as her ally against the "Ladies": "I have heard by a Side-Wind that our Ladies mean to contest My Power over the Plate, Furniture, &c. their Father left——which they aver was only for My Life.——A fine Affair! Why 30 Years ago, in Sight of all the Executors I made Mr. Perkins a Present of the Furniture belonging to the Borough-house . . . Why did they not object to such a Measure?——The Plate I *sold*——except a Bread Basket and Candlesticks I gave Miss Thrale last Year and the Year before:

If they were not left to my Disposal Why were they accepted? . . . I have charged [my lawyer] to make strict Examination that no dormant Claims may come out against my *Residuary Legatee*. . . . They shan't hurt *Thee*."[98]

Mrs. Piozzi, not content to let her emissaries and lawyers handle the matter, personally contacted her relations to try to settle the vexed issue, but was frustrated in her attempt at a resolution: "Lord Keith and Mrs. Hoare were both very bitter to me about these Matters, and I wish from my heart The Place was sold, and that I were to take my last Leave of it." Mrs. Piozzi was particularly distressed that her daughters were apparently contending that even the furniture and paintings purchased for Streatham by her second husband should revert to them: "My poor Piozzi laid out 2000£ on The Furniture of that Place about the Year 1790, and hung up some very valuable Pictures. . . . I thought myself very goodnatured indeed in leaving them (as I have done) with her Father's Furniture—Portraits &c. to Lady Keith. An Idea has however been started, I know not by which of the Ladies, as if the Household Goods of both Southwark and Streatham Dwelling Houses was not bequeathed to me by Mr. Thrale *except for Life*," she reported to Dr. Whalley.[99]

Much of Mrs. Piozzi's anxiety over the disposition of Streatham and its contents was occasioned by the fear that her daughters' animosity would take the form of revenge on Salusbury, her residuary legatee, after her death: "We will see *all Through* when I get to London," she assured the much concerned Dr. Whalley, "So That poor dear Salusbury may have no Incumbrances or dormant Claims fall upon him after my Death who have so little that I *can* give him without an Appearance of Impropriety and Disrespect to my first husband's Representatives."[100] Her immediate fears were allayed, however, when Alexander Leak, her steward at Brynbella and a steady and supportive friend until his death, found an Abstract of Henry Thrale's will in which her sole possession of household effects was made clear. Elated, yet still angry at what she believed was her daughters' deliberate harassment, Mrs. Piozzi told Salusbury that, "All that Stuff about selling Streatham Park was a permitted *Dupery* after all, and I as usual the Dupe.——They know it cannot be sold it seems." To emphasize the separation between her "first husband's representatives" and the "child of my soul" she added, "and I shall tell Charles Shephard so today when I go to Windle's with my Will *rewritten;* 'designating you by the Name of John Salusbury Piozzi, commonly called and known by the Name of John Piozzi Salusbury . . . now my own dear and adopted Child.'"[101] All constructive negotiation appeared at an end.

The cycle of retaliation slowly intensified. On 12 March 1812 an anxious Mrs. Piozzi advised Leak that her daughters were seeking a new way to injure her: "Doctor Whalley called today; says Streatham Park *must be repaired*, or worse will befall me: he advises to begin directly." She was despondent: "I suppose They must begin again; and make it smart again; and I shall have as kind Returns as before——no Hope of putting Money in the Funds: Dr. Whalley thinks the Ladies are offended."[102] She learned what form retaliation for that real or perceived offense would take when Salusbury reported that Cecy Mostyn had threatened that she and her sisters would sue their mother's heir for Streatham repairs. Knowing her daughters well, she warned, "Mrs. Mostyn's Threats were the Threats of the whole Family, and I feel much alarmed,"[103] later adding, "If I do not repair the Place before my Death, or your coming of Age—They would certainly fall on my Executors for Dilapidation."[104] That Dr. Whalley had assessed the situation correctly was borne out by Mrs. Piozzi's summary of the conflict to her friend and Brynbella physician W. M. Thackeray: "My nerves have had a new Shock in the Anger of my beautiful Daughters for a Fault committed (if a Fault) most unintentionally on my Part. But having heard that they threw out Menaces of making my Successor amenable for Dilapidations at Streatham Park—I resolved to repair [it]. . . . So I sent Mead—my old Surveyor who you know built Brynbella, & bid him set to Work." But this attempt to pacify her daughters was understood by them as simple arrogance: "but the Ladies were enraged, said *their Property* was ruining by my Agents; & the Letters were dreadful; and I am at my Wits end; while the Men complain that my Daughters *insult them*; and *they* storm at the Men for injuring their Place."[105] But, Mrs. Piozzi bitterly insisted, the injury, if any, was to *her*, not to her daughters. The repair of Streatham, she asserted, would be a "dreadful Drawback on my Comforts for the remainder of my Life; but I hope my Daughters will live long and happily to reap the Benefit: and it is certainly *better* . . . that *their* Pleasure should be consulted rather than that of their Affectionate Mother."[106]

Her daughters and their husbands viewed Mrs. Piozzi's behavior as equally subversive. Lord Keith urged his wife to act against the tree-cutting at Streatham: "I do not believe your Mother has any Right to cut Trees at that Rate . . . Mr. Shephard is a Vagabound and finds it his interest to Inflame a Mind too apt to be so against her Children and she by a Momentary approbation from a flattering cur is soothed from the Reflection of her improper Conduct, which I daresay Ranckles her now and then, if Vanity would permit her to Confess it— The Act is the Most uncivil I ever heard of."[107] Mrs. Piozzi's behavior, Lord Keith asserted, was both retaliatory and a ruse to make herself appear to be the victim of her daughters' cruel machinations. Mrs. Piozzi, he insisted, had determined "to excite an opposition on your parts . . . and thereby furnish pretexts for her Complaints of unfeeling undutiful and the like." He also expressed his sympathy for "the times at Streatham and for all you have suffered first and last," and contrasted his wife's nature with her mother's: "you have a heart capable—it were well others had the like, even at the expense of some Learning."[108]

Mrs. Piozzi meanwhile was busy campaigning for her own sympathetic responses. While she had written peevishly to Salusbury that "Charles Shephard says Mrs. Hoare writes him *Spitefull* Letters about Streatham Park;—says *She* will send a *Surveyor* to see what Trees he cuts, that *we* may not *ruin The Place* that belongs to *Them*,"[109] her pathetic letter on the same subject to her Streatham contractor, Clement Mead, provided an inventory couched as a loving mother's poetic history of these trees: "I write to say that it would break my heart to offend the Ladies—when I am going to all this Expence merely to please them. You have not surely cut down any of our old favourite Ornamental Timber near the house——My Lime Tree for example, near the Glass Door of the Library; the Theophrastus with its Green and Silver Leaves in Driving to the Place:—or

Miss Thrale's Oak close to the little Pond by the Summerhouse, which was planted when Lady Keith was born; or The Scarlet-flowring Maple going to the Summerhouse; or Mr. Thrale's Walnut Tree at the Summerhouse Door almost. No, nor the Sycamore in the middle of the Octagon Court, or the monstrous Poplar, which monstrous as it is I put with my own hands into the Ground very near the Stable. Write, and set my Nerves at rest."[110]

Mr. Mead, however, apparently was not given to the sympathetic responses for which Mrs. Piozzi longed, for when she wrote to him on 16 May she forsook her role as loving mother, opting instead for the role of injured—and offended— party: "My dear Mr. Mead can scarcely think how his Letter, and one from Mrs. Hoare received the same Moment——shocked me: ——I little thought I was offending the Ladies by spending Such Sums of Money on a Place which will be *theirs the sooner*, for the Concern it gives me to hear them consider that as an Injury, which I meant as a Benefit. For God's Sake cut no more of their Trees, I wish these had all been left standing——and the House left to fall——if they like that better——but It was told me they wished it repaired;——and with what other Timber could I have repaired it?"[111]

Fortunately for Mrs. Piozzi's *amour propre*, her old friend Dr. Whalley could be counted on for the sympathy that Mead failed to extend. Seeking his assistance in recruiting a new steward for Brynbella so that Leak could supervise Streatham repairs, she quavered, "My dear Doctor Whalley will wonder to see I can write one Line steadily, by the Time he comes to the End of this Letter, but I will finish my Request—before I begin Grievances." Mrs. Piozzi continued perfectly "steadily" and sensibly about her business necessities, making a practical assessment of the requirements of the Brynbella stewardship. Turning to her Streatham "Grievances," however, she assumed the tone of a hapless victim of forces she did not quite understand and against which she was completely helpless: "Oh Heavens! how shall I ever bear the Sight of Streatham Park? or how will its Reversionary Proprietors bear the Sight of poor H: L: P? I fear I have now Sinned against them without *hope* of reinstatement to favour. Mrs. Mostyn having menaced little Salusbury pretty sharply last Summer, what they would do to *him* if I was to die; and how they would pinch him for dilapidations of their Seat in Surrey; Charles Shephard counselled me to repair and reside in it next Spring——to shew them it was habitable. I therefore recommended Mead, a Surveyor whom I have long known; and he selected such Trees as were overshadowing, and ruining the house, and has *cut them down*. Down came the Ladies though, in high Wrath; and terrified the Man, and wrote most Insulting Letters to Shephard——*cruel* and *bitter* ones to poor me. . . . I am afraid to face any of them while they are so angry."[112]

Dr. Whalley provided all the sympathy that Mrs. Piozzi could want: "I am sorry that ripe age, or reflection, have not, *yet*, impressed your Daughters with a due sense of their filial duties. It makes one fear that the *Stone* in their Hearts will never be removed. It is a stumbling Block to their respectability; but let it not prove one, any longer, to your peace. Your adopted Son, I trust, and verily believe, will recompence you, for all the wrong you have suffered from your *legitimate* Daughters. I am glad that you have, at last, determined to put Streatham in thorough repair < > doing it, you will know the *worst*, will save yourself from bickering and Heart burning, and dear Salusbury from eventual insult and expence. You will live long enough, I doubt not, to fetch up, more *much more*, than the cost of these Repairs, and then a Fig! for the fine Ladies, your fashionable daughters."[113] Thus fortified, Mrs. Piozzi resigned herself to the inevitable, but continued to fret about the inordinate expense of the Streatham repairs, cautioning Mead, "do not drive me to unnecessary Expences to please any Ladies living by the Mortification and Ruin of . . . H: L: Piozzi."[114]

In the midst of Mrs. Piozzi's fears for Streatham, she was struck by a competing emotion: the joy of acquisition. While she was reluctant to pay for renovation of the structure itself, she delighted in ordering new wallpaper, upholstery fabric, furniture, and pictures to adorn the inside: "You must write to Southey, and bid him send Patterns of Papers. That in the Eating Parlour however, *must* be a darkish Slate-Colour; because nothing else will suit the Pictures, and suit the Furniture *too*. . . . A White Satten Ground with rich White Flowers on it,— rather Small than large Pattern, will be best for the Drawing Room certainly."[115] Mrs. Piozzi's planning and purchasing continued until, she reported to Salusbury, "the Place is a Paradise; and every thing except *Necessaries*—Pots, Spits Beds and so forth; in elegant Order."[116] At this point, the renovation had cost Mrs. Piozzi almost £2000.

Streatham's current value and its liabilities continued to weigh heavily on Mrs. Piozzi's mind; she recognized that she could not implement her original plan of living in the house when the repairs were completed. In consultation with Leak, she decided that she must bring in another tenant to offset the financial burden of renovation and maintenance. Settling on a "fine, Elegant, Showy" Mr. Anderdon as a prospective tenant, Mrs. Piozzi, clearly amused, described a meeting with him at which her daughter Susanna was present. His behavior indicated that he felt himself "as high and mighty as the highest," and his tone indicated that he felt that he would be "doing [the] House no Small Honour to *Think of it:*——A House (said he) bosomed in Trees, The Sun never Shining on it." Standing beside a daughter who had protested vigorously against all timber cutting, Mrs. Piozzi "could hardly look grave at *that* Objection——He will he says, Set the Scythes to work; for he loves Landschape Gardening. . . . Miss Thrale looked but little pleased. . . . our Ladies are *so* earnest to have every Thing as it was in *their* Time."[117]

As they were often to do in the coming years, negotiations with the prospective tenant fell through. Mrs. Piozzi resolved to make Streatham pay its own way until a long-term tenant could be secured and began issuing instructions for crop production with the experience born of years spent handling farm affairs for a sick husband on a landed estate. Proceeds from produce and crop sales, she directed Mead, were to finance the remainder of the Streatham renovation. Mead's efforts to defray expenses, however, proved unsuccessful, and at the end of the summer an agitated Mrs. Piozzi poured out the anguish caused by this financial drain: "Dear Mr. Mead's Letters are enough to make one Wild. Why must the hot houses tumble down after all this Ocean of Money spent on the Place? and why must Potatoes sell for nothing at Streatham, when they bear a good Price every where else?" Adding to her sense of injury was Mead's request that Leak return immediately to Streatham: "How can You think of my sending Leak to London *now* just before Harvest and Planting Season?——Must I be ruined in Wales and Surrey both? and both at the Same Time?"[118]

Bad news about the dismal state of Streatham repairs flowed in, while repair costs spiraled. Mrs. Piozzi, panic-stricken, told Mead that Thomas Windle, one of her attorneys, had seen Streatham, "where he says the Rain is now raining *in* after 1250£ has been paid, and the new Cielings damaged!! Oh dreadful! and Mr. Mead calling for Money——when the Front of the House is discoloured even before *all the Ladies* have Seen it. . . . For God's Sake do not fright me out of my Senses, as well as out of my Money; but recollect that it is Inhuman to force me on Spending so for an Estate I have only my Life in. . . . send me word how *little* Money—not how *much* is absolutely necessary to make the Place *profitable*. . . . Oh Mr. Mead! I little thought to have heard that Rain could enter such *costly* Roofs as *mine* and spoil my new Cielings and Beds, even *before* they are *used*.—Oh *poor* H: L: Piozzi!!"[119]

Apparently it was finally borne in on Mrs. Piozzi that no amount of anguished pleading would render Mead sympathetic, for a later letter to him begins coolly and dispassionately. She was clearly emotionally exhausted: "Mrs. Piozzi earnestly wishes to hear that Mr. Mead has finished with Streatham Park. . . . When Mr. Mead's Account is made out . . . It will be the happiest Day She has seen many Years—when She reads his Name at the bottom of a Receipt in full of all Demands. . . . which God speed, for I am weary to Death on't."[120]

Further increasing her bitterness was her daughters' habit of visiting her at Streatham to gauge the state of repairs, visits that meant empty conversation, empty compliments, and further strain on Mrs. Piozzi's almost-empty purse: "The Ladies were here Yesterday, Mrs. Mostyn and Mrs. Hoare," she reported to Salusbury on 6 June 1814. "I shewed them a Tree that was tearing the House down faster than I can build it up——Oh cried Sophia, The Place would be *frightful* without that Tree—I shewed them a *dead* one, and begged Permission to cut *that*, which they graciously afforded. . . . Oh! I was cross and spiteful enough, and the Visit has given Me the head Ach and a bad Night's Sleep. The continual Laugh and *Te he* of fine Ladies, possesses a Power of depressing my Spirits beyond all telling."[121]

Finally, the house was habitable, and, after considerable negotiation, a suitable tenant was found. Mrs. Piozzi was once again able to indulge in the luxury of complaining about the occupant at Streatham: "Count Lieven is my tenant, and pays me liberally, but so he should; for his dependants smoke their tobacco in my nice new beds, and play a thousand tricks that keep my steward, who I have left there, in perpetual agony."[122]

Once the disposition of Streatham seemed settled, Mrs. Piozzi, as she had long intended, retired to Bath, where, unlike earlier stays, she had to secure inexpensive lodgings. According to the figures provided by Leak, the total cost of Streatham repair, interior design, and furnishings came to a ruinous £6500, of which debt Mrs. Piozzi had already managed to discharge £4000. The dreary burden of the final £2500 however, which had to be discharged without recourse to the resources of Brynbella, now in Salusbury's hands, permeated every aspect of Mrs. Piozzi's life: "poor old dowager as I am, the remainder ke[eps] me marvellous low in pocket, and drives me into a nut-shell here at Bath, where I used to live gay and grand in Pultney Street," she complained to Reverend Robert Gray on 27 November 1814.[123] Yet Mrs. Piozzi was still able to summon up optimism, realizing that, with the income from the Streatham crops and the irritating but profitable tenant, the debt would finally be paid and that in "Three or four Years, *I will yet be as sleek as a Mole.*"[124]

As irritating as she claimed to find the presence of Count Lieven at Streatham, therefore, his absence was to be far more distressing. In March 1815, as she was beginning to feel the relief that came with less straitened circumstances, she discovered that, once again, her situation had become desperate: "comes a Letter from cruel Count Lieven the Russian Ambassador," she cried to Lady Williams, "to say that such is the Pressure of these dreadful Times, he shall never be able to Enjoy my beautiful Place again; and as he does not like (of Course) to pay for what he has not, begs to be *off* &c."[125] Nor was her anguish due simply to the loss of an eligible tenant. Leak's figures had not included her obligations to her attorney and she had not been able to find out the extent of her total indebtedness. Her anxiety on this account impelled her to make a valiant declaration and a grim resolution: "Mr. Windle will not tell me what I owe him, and fighting in the Dark is to me dreadful," she declared to Leak. "Let us know the worst of every Disaster, because Fear—which is emplanted in us as a Preservative—ceases when it can preserve us no longer; and Courage comes of its own Accord——when Escape is out of the Question."[126] To Lady Williams she avowed: "Truth is, I can make no Purse at all: but by resolutely living in a mean habitation and keeping no Servants &c. I shall escape Arrests, and pay all the [Streatham Park] Debts . . . by the Time Two Years are out."[127]

Yet even while she determined on last-resort measures, Mrs. Piozzi clung to the small hope that the Count could be made to pay his lease debt. Realizing that legal means would yield little return, she resolved on charm to effect what coercion could not: "I am going to write the Count a long French Letter in answer to his *very polite* but *very afflicting* Communication,"[128] she told Leak on 16 March 1815, elaborating on her strategy to Salusbury: "every Friend to whom I have shewn [the Count's] Letter, *feels* that I have no Chance of obtaining my Money by any *serious Demand* of it. He is *a privileged Man.* I have written him a Sort of gay Supplication——filled with Compliments and Predictions of Success against Buonaparte, but still *pressing my Suit* that he will *pay his Fortune-telling Sybil* the whole Years Rent. . . . and now and then a Thought crosses my Mind that it is *possible* he may be a *Man of Honour.*"[129] A few days later, Mrs. Piozzi provided the Leaks with a translation of her altogether delightful letter:

Count Lieven's Letter while its Politeness does me honour, goes near to break my Heart.——I let my House to your Excellency only because tyrannic Circumstances surrounding me, took from me all possibility of Inhabiting it myself. And now to lose my Pains at last, after Expences so enormous! and lose my Tenant too who did me so much Honour.—Dreadful Moments! I hoped that these Political Storms which tear up the strong Oaks would at least have spared the feeble and worne-out Willow, which bends before the Wind. Ah My Lord! your Excellency has already paid Two Quarters—you will think me worthy Your Care——You will pay the other two.—And I might say if I had not too much Discretion:

That if my poor Three hundred Pounds were necessary to tame the Fury of These terrible Foes——they should be yielded up at once——but without *Them* The World will soon obey *your* Command; and the Muses will be bound for *me—this once*. Fortune has no Oracles against Victorious Russia: but you must give Life to your Sibyl that you may hear her Predictions in Your Favour.[130]

On 18 March Mrs. Piozzi recorded in her "Pocket Book" that she had received Count Lieven's "Quarterage £150." And the Count had established the "showy" Mr. Anderdon as "sub-tenant" in his place.

Even though the count had finally paid her a portion of his lease obligation, however, the vexed question of the appropriate disposition of Streatham remained. In a series of letters that reflected her increasing ambivalence toward Salusbury, she first solicited his recommendation on the matter and then rejected it. Responding sarcastically to Salusbury's advice to lease Streatham to a new tenant, Mrs. Piozzi expressed her "appreciation" for his counsel: "I thank you for your Letter Dearest Salusbury and have the Pleasure to say that Your Opinion is everybody's Opinion——*I must let Streatham Park*." Ultimately, however, the situation was too critical for derision, as, she made clear, Salusbury would realize if he cared enough to give careful consideration to the matter: "They who give me the Advice do not know as You must necessarily know— the Evils which possibly,—nay probably—may result. Leak will leave me; I shall have no Person on the Spot to guard those Pales from being plucked up and burned, which have cost me such Thousands putting down."[131]

Although Mrs. Piozzi peevishly insisted that "everybody" had advised her to "let" Streatham again, such was not actually the case. Her old friend Dr. Myddelton had recurred to an earlier plan, first submitted to her by Dr. Whalley as early as 1811: "having well weighed all the Circumstances of your Situation, I am perswaded that the best Mode you can adopt, is to offer your Life-Interest in the House, Premises, and Park with all the Pictures estimated at 5000£ and the Furniture 3000£——to your Daughters for 6000£." Admitting that such a proposal would probably be rejected, he noted that each daughter in turn should be allowed an opportunity to refuse the offer, noting that the individual offers undoubtedly would also be refused. This would free Mrs. Piozzi to strike a good bargain on the open market. "Rely upon it, you will *thus*, dispose of the whole to advantage."[132] Apparently considering that the plan had merit, Mrs. Piozzi demanded Salusbury's opinion: "You will doubtless take Advice from your Friends: and will communicate to me what is Your own Opinion after having consulted them."[133]

Having solicited his advice for what she clearly considered an eligible course of action, Mrs. Piozzi blasted Salusbury when he seconded Dr. Myddelton's proposal, intimating that he did so only to ensure that his prospects would not suffer. Streatham, long a source of frustration and worry, whose maintenance made retirement to Bath in dignity and comfort an impossibility, was instantly transformed into a source of pleasure, of precious and bittersweet memory: "*I will not give* the Place; and I *cannot* bear to sell . . . poor dear old Streatham Park—The Residence of my Youth, The Pride of my Age," she indignantly responded to Salusbury. To part with her "Husband's Gift,——His Childrens old Streatham Park," Mrs. Piozzi rather surprisingly asserted, would preclude her "living or dying in Peace." Striking out at what she conceived to be his real concern she added, "You are welcome to *all I have*——except my Honour and Conscience; The Loss of *them* would deservedly shorten my Life. . . . you must be as contented as you *can,* with my out-living my Debts, and leaving you the Personalty as it stood when you saw and admired it."[134]

As if to confirm her determination, Mrs. Piozzi followed this letter with a note to Ann Leak: "I have written Mr. Salusbury Word that I *will* not give away the Place—which I see frights *him*,——and that I *cannot* sell the Place, which would I'm sure—kill *me.* The Tenor of my Letter is such,—*He will Think no more on't.*" The episode seemed also to have temporarily diminished Mrs. Piozzi's frustration with the straitened circumstances into which her Streatham difficulties had plunged her: "With Regard to my living close I am respected for it by People of Sense and People of Birth: and . . . 'Those who want least, are most like the Gods who want nothing.' By the Time I *do* want Delicacies, I shall be able to afford them honestly."[135]

By the following month, however, her philosophic resolve had dissipated and the theatrical language in which she described Streatham to her young friend Sir James Fellowes, about to see the property for the first time, bore no resemblance to that in which she rhapsodized about the estate to Salusbury. Nor did her complaints about the terrific drain on her purse bear any resemblance to her stoic acceptance of "living close": "when you see Streatham Park That Gilded Millstone which weighs me completely down; and when You have spoken to my Steward Leak—no Distress of mine will Surprize You. *Such a Place* to keep in Repair!!"[136]

Although she had castigated Salusbury for suggesting that she sell her life interest in Streatham, Mrs. Piozzi, violent declaration to the contrary, was still considering this option and had, in fact, approached Lady Keith with a proposal, receiving through her solicitor a request for more particulars. The Keiths, she responded, could have "Pictures and Bronzes and *everything* to be sure, The House and its *Contents.*"[137] While waiting for news from the Keiths, Mrs. Piozzi described her Streatham negotiations to Lady Williams—in highly revisionist terms. Interestingly, for Welsh consumption, she changed her interpretation of Salusbury's role to that of affectionate and supportive son; contrasted with Salusbury's warmth was her daughters' cold vindictiveness: "I suppose my real Possessions at Streatham Park must all be sold to my Daughters if I am so urged and forced to part with them.—Dear Salusbury and Doctor Myddelton—who saw that Place when he was in Town, do nothing but press me to get rid of it— and a Neighbour in the Village of Streatham wrote to me Two Months ago or more, to say that if I would offer it to Lord Keith *he* would purchase for 6000£. . . . since they were all so warm in the Cause—*I did offer it*—and received nothing for my Offer but Silent Neglect." Now that it appeared that the Keiths might not accept her offer, Mrs. Piozzi, who only a few weeks before had fiercely upbraided Salusbury for seconding someone else's idea that she sell Streatham, panicked at the notion that the place would be left on her hands: "the House and Estate are Taxed so high with Tythes &c. . . . that it will be a Millstone round my Neck to ruin me: and [Leak], and everybody is wishing me well rid on't. So if they will purchase—*let them.*"[138]

Mrs. Piozzi's suspense over the possible Streatham sale lasted until early July 1815 when, as she told Harriet's brother, she heard that "every Expectation of Purchasers at Streatham Park is completely over." That her daughters had cruelly conspired to raise and then dash her hopes she had no doubt: "they have had their Hoax—and I am where I was."[139]

Regardless of her anger at the ladies, however, it was important that civil relations be maintained. So once more she developed a revisionist account of her attempt to sell her Streatham life-interest; this time the beneficiary was her daughter Cecy. In the newest version of the Streatham story, Mrs. Piozzi had been a most unwilling actor in the sale attempt, not agreeing to it until she had been bullied beyond her ability to withstand the pressure; Dr. Myddelton was metamorphosed from disinterested and sincere friend to a scoundrel whose objective had been (why, was not made clear) simply to foment trouble: "You are right enough in laughing at me for troubling Doctor Myddelton about my pecuniary Affairs; but Solemnly do I protest to you that not contented with volunteering his unsought Services—he all but *forced* them on me, and *what could I do?* He and a Neighbour of mine at Streatham—Mr. Dalgliesh, never let me rest all Winter till sometime in May they persecuted and perswaded me to offer Lord Keith my *long* Life and *large* Possessions for 6000 Pounds or Guineas. Then came Letters from Solicitors . . . and an infinite deal of Disturbance—till last Week came a Release from some of the Lawyers employed—saying Lord Keith knew nothing of the Place or its Value, and Mrs. Piozzi might do what She pleased with it.—So much for Facts; and I hope as mine Hostess Quickly says, *here be Truths.*"

It was not enough that Cecy accept the story of Mrs. Piozzi's persecution and betrayal as truth, however. Because Cecy questioned the severity of Mrs. Piozzi's financial problems, she also had to be made to understand that her once financially independent mother was now destitute because of the expenses incurred to rescue and protect her daughters' inheritance: "*Your* Arithmetic alone can make my Income 3000£ and *Your* Imagination alone, turn my wretched Habitation into a good House. . . . And Whatever Surplus of Riches you can find me; must buy these Annuities and Mansions that you tell me of—till then I feel happy in not being Threatened (*as I have been*) with Arrests. . . . I have spent 6500£ on the *House* and Paling; 500£ more on recovering the Garden, Park &c. from Destruction. . . . I hope once more *Here be Truths.*"[140]

While her neighbor Mr. Dalgliesh was a scoundrel in the version of events that Mrs. Piozzi retailed to her daughter, he managed to maintain his benevolent image in her other discourse. Writing to Leak two days after she had reviled Dalgliesh for beleaguering her into the ill-fated attempt to sell Streatham, she chirruped that, "That dear Mr. Dalgliesh behaves to me like a Brother. I have repaid his kindness with *Confidence* . . . and have assured him of my own good Spirits and Resolution to bear what God sends; and free myself as *soon*, but as *quietly* as I can."[141] With Mr. Dalgliesh himself, she continued to discuss the prospect of ridding herself of Streatham—with no sign of coercion: "I do long to see and converse with you about that Purchase-Business, which my Thoughts have hardly dismissed from a Notion of Possibility; I will have a clearing up of The Mist it is enveloped in: for this odd Uncertainty is a wretched Existence."[142]

While she cast the hapless Dalgliesh as villain in her apologia to her daughters, it was her daughters themselves that she cast in that role as she wrote bitterly to her friends about the abortive Streatham sale. Reiterating her contention that her daughters had perpetrated a cruel "hoax," Mrs. Piozzi told Lady Williams that, "My own Family pretending an Inclination to buy my Life in old Streatham Park, and take the Furniture, Books, Pictures &c. giving me 6000£ at once——made me believe I should pay all I owed. . . . But after increasing my Lawyers bill . . . here am I left worse than I was before."[143] As though she had never protested to Cecy that she was forced to put Streatham on the market, she sought support from Sir James Fellowes for continued attempts to sell her life-interest, attempts that she must make as a result of her daughters' duplicity: "I must make the most of my House now they have left it on my Hands, must I not? *may* I not? and like my Countrymen at Waterloo—Sell my *Life* as dear as I can." In her next attempt to wriggle off the Streatham life-interest hook, Mrs. Piozzi's personal combat was to be with Count Lieven's subtenant, John Anderdon, to whom she again offered her life interest, but of whom she expected little: "The Battle with Anderdon will be fought tomorrow.—I make sure of losing the *Field*; My Generals are unskilful."[144] Mrs. Piozzi's gloomy prediction proved too true: "[You] will wish to hear how all ends . . . in mere Smoke at least for the Present," she told Sir James.[145] Once again, Mr. Anderdon declined to purchase.

The failure of this second endeavor at a private sale at last determined Mrs. Piozzi to attempt a public one: "All my scruples and delicacies are . . . at an end," she told Dr. Whalley, "and if you hear . . . that H. L. P.'s house is advertised for public sale, believe it; for I will get all I can now."[146] Still she vacillated about the form the sale should take—should she sell lock, stock, and fire screens, or attempt to divest herself only of the house and grounds? Leak continually prodded her to make up her mind; it is a measure of their friendship that she responded to his intent rather than to his language: "As you say it is high Time to determine; and my Determination . . . ['tis] to Sell the Contents of poor old Streatham Park." Her foremost concern, however, was to ensure that her course of action would not cause financial harm to Salusbury nor fire once again the Ladies' indignation: "unless I can so dispose of the Shell and the Grounds as to bear me quite harmless—and my Residuary Legatee harmless also—from all Dilapidations and Demands:—[I will] *give* it by a Deed of Gift to my four Daughters. Do you think they will accept it?" she asked her steward. "I am dubious."[147]

Finally, Mrs. Piozzi came to a firm decision—everything must go; Leak drew up the advertisement, which appeared in February 1816:

Streatham Park/ Late Residence of Mrs. Piozzi/ Mr. Squibb (in conjunction with Messrs. Matthews and Taylor, of Fenchurch-street) has the honour of announcing to the Nobility and Gentry, that in the course of next month will be offered to their notice, by Public Auction, the valuable Contents of the above distinguished Residence; comprising the rare and curious Library of upwards of 2000 Volumes, principally selected by the celebrated Dr. Johnson. A Collection of choice Pictures, the productions of the most eminent Masters of the Italian, Flemish, and English schools, a few excellent engravings, an assemblage of rare old China, a few valuable antique Bronzes, &c. &c.—— Also the elegant Household Furniture, the greater part of which is recently new. At the same time will be Let by Auction, the elegant Mansion, with suitable offices, large productive gardens, and about 70 acres of valuable meadow land."[148]

Instead of relief that she was soon to be disburdened of Streatham, however, Mrs. Piozzi reacted with indignation when she saw the advertisement. Her business sense told her that Leak had acted precipitously, and she wrote to his wife: "My good Dear Leak, Tell your too hasty Husband from me, that I have seen the Advertisement at length—and confess my Amazement—What! expose a Summer Residence to Sale while Frost and Snow is on the Ground! . . . The very *Sight* of the Grounds in Winter must check and chill every Wish for the Place. . . . Stop the further Advertisements Dear Leak for Pity. . . . [it] has put me quite out of Breath by its Hastiness."[149] Leak, upon whose own business acumen Mrs. Piozzi usually relied, responded with, perhaps, justifiable irritation: "I have . . . stoped the advertisement of the Sale about which, I am sorry to find, You think I have acted Hastily. . . . The Time I had proposed for the Sale was not at all too early. The People were beginning to be very anxious about it . . . many have been to enquire about the Books and Pictures, and seem to think them very valueable."[150]

Leak's vexation was not directed alone at Mrs. Piozzi's alarm at his timing of the Streatham sale. Far more injurious was her determination that Sir James, about to marry, should spend his honeymoon at Streatham, and, perhaps, enjoy the house so much that he would purchase it. Leak found himself unable to convince Mrs. Piozzi that such a visit would exacerbate her financial problems; there would be extra taxes to pay and services to provide. But there was a subtext to Mrs. Piozzi's whimsical decision: she wanted Sir James to see and experience the munificence with which she had lived before the death of her husband: "I should like that he should know what Expence I lived at, when *last* an Inhabitant of Streatham Park: and what was our Establishment," she told Ann Leak. "Make Leak speak freely to Sir James about *every* Thing."[151] Complicating the issue still further were the fantasies in which Mrs. Piozzi saw Sir James as the new owner of Streatham—and herself as frequent and delightfully welcome guest. Life would finally regain a measure of that warmth that she had known there with Piozzi. When Sir James visited and then sang the praises of the estate, Mrs. Piozzi responded with a pathos, clearly not manufactured, that expressed her yearning to go home again: "Oh I do think you are taking a fancy to Streatham Park; and that there is a little Cordial Drop of Comfort at the bottom of my *Old China Cup* left yet." So real was her fantasy of Sir James as owner and host of Streatham that she even began to paint its pictures for him: "Whenever I come to Streatham Park (and never will I see it more unless I see *You* sitting there at Bottom of your own Table;) The Room where my Mother's Portrait hangs—*must* be *yours.* The Dressing Room will be for your use you know, and Lady Fellowes will keep Possession of Her own Apartment. . . . Bessy is pulling the Pen out of my hand to make me be dressed. . . . Be quiet Bessy; Who knows but you and I may have an Airing of a Hundred Miles to take together one of these Days?"[152]

Gamely, Leak struggled to save her from her own folly: "Sir James has not the least Idea of continuing here more than a few Weeks, which will I fear be very injurious to the Sale, it will be too late and People will be Ill Humoured, with being so long kept in expectation."[153] Mrs. Piozzi responded with an appeal to Leak's sympathy that yet rang true: "my Hope is to pass one happy Week with him and his Lady there, before I see old Streatham Park no more. That hope has Sweetened my Existence. . . . I have had Misery enough with Streatham Park—and my Heart is set on *one Week's* Comfort in it."[154] She won.

With Sir James ensconced at Streatham, Mrs. Piozzi immediately put her plan of a happy week's entertainment there in action, cloaking her acceptance of an invitation long hinted at as necessitated by her business concerns: "I really do mean to avail myself of Lady Fellowes's extraordinary Good Nature and come to You, just for one little happy Week. I *must* come to Town you know, about rewriting my Will &c.—against I *have something to leave.*"[155]

To Salusbury she indicated that the reason for her visit was to conclude, if possible, her Streatham affairs: "Sir James and Lady Fellowes . . . have invited the Mistress of the Mansion to visit *Them* and settle Matters somehow—by public Sale or private Contract." Even though she realized that the "public Sale" of Streatham was almost certainly inevitable, she still clung to the hope that her daughters would at last agree to a "private Contract": "If he offers me his Carriage to go about in, I shall wait on my Daughters, and obtain their final Determination,—Their Pardon if possible."[156] Mrs. Piozzi was quickly disabused of the notion that she could obtain either. Three days later she related the details of Sophia's calm indifference to her mother and her determined rejection of her mother's proposals: "[Mrs. Hoare] behaved neither with Kindness nor Cruelty, but complete Indifference—till the Business I came upon was mentioned—— and *that* She negatived according to the Parliamentary Phrase,——without *a Division.* . . . Well then said I lightly, 'Speak in Time or 'tis going, going *Gone,*' imitating an Auctioneer. You have not lost Your Spirits was her Observation—— No, 'tis enough to lose my Money and my Peace of Mind I think."[157]

Compounding the bitterness of Sophia's indifference was the sting of her query about Mrs. Piozzi's recent tenants: "How did Your Russians behave?" Mrs. Piozzi later recorded an emotional response that she may or may not have given to Sophia, a response that held her daughters responsible for the ills that had befallen the estate—and its owner for life: "They smoked Tobacco in Bed, and put the Place in perpetual Danger of Fire——to Them succeeded Mess:

Anderdon and Co. whose *little* Children rubbed their Bread and Butter into my best Carpets, ruined my nice new Mattrasses . . . while the bigger Boys wrote on My new painted Walls, and cut the Wainscot with Pen Knives. Oh!—continued poor H:L:P.—my Heart is Sick of the Place and the Tenants and the Torments and the Tormentors; *You refuse* all Connection with it, and mine shall end next Week. . . . Catalogues shall be made out, and a Public Sale proclaimed. So ended our Conversation."[158] And so ended her relationship with her daughters. Shortly before her encounter with Sophia, Cecy, without even notifying her mother of her intent, left the country: "*My* Life *cannot* now be a long one; The Ladies and Mr. Salusbury are all very ill humoured, and Mrs. Mostyn has let Segroid for Three Years, and will go abroad—I dare say without ever saying Adieu Mamma! . . . I shall never see Cecy again."[159] Cecy did not return to England during her mother's lifetime.

Having finally accepted the fact that her daughters would never yield to her entreaties that they lift the burden of Streatham from her, Mrs. Piozzi gave final approval for the sale, which began in May. While the house and property were entailed on her daughters, she could sell the life-interest she held in both. Once the sale started, Mrs. Piozzi entered into the transaction with spirit, elated that she would once again have adequate funds, and curious about who was providing them. Of primary interest was the disposal of the Reynolds portraits of her old friends: "Johnson sold magnificently; I expected more for Garrick, and more for Reynolds."[160] Most importantly, Mrs. Piozzi was finally rid of her "gilded millstone": "So the Place goes to a Mr. Elliott . . . *let it go!!* Tis enough to make *any* one go mad: I shall have *Money* however, and no further Debts or Trouble with the Place, and that is a great Matter. . . . he will perhaps take some of the Furniture, and *perhaps* too, the Place will not be degraded by his Residence."[161]

Mrs. Piozzi realized enough profit to allow her to salvage at least one precious possession from the "general Wreck." She described her reasons to Sir James Fellowes, succinctly reducing the long-past trauma surrounding her decision to marry Piozzi to a few sentences: "Mr. Watson Taylor wrote after me to beg [the Murphy portrait] . . . but I am no longer poor, and when I was—There ought surely to be some Difference made between Fidelity—and Unkindness. When Burneys were treacherous and Baretti boisterous against poor inoffending H:L:P. dear Murphy was faithful found among the faithless, faithful only he.

> He, like His Muse, no mean retreating made,
> But follow'd faithful to the silent Shade.

Equally Attached to both my Husbands—he lived with us till he could in a manner live no longer; and his Portrait is now on the Canal with that of Mr. Thrale coming to Bath——my Mother whom both them adored—keeping them Company."[162]

The Streatham ordeal was finally over. Gone forever were any hopes for a renewed relationship with her daughters or for the recovery of her intimacy with Salusbury. But she did have something of value to look forward to; she could now become what she had long wanted to be: "an old Bath cat."

The Joys of Bath

Many years earlier, Mrs. Piozzi, newly arrived in Bath, asserted that, "I always did love it better than London, and so I do still."[163] Since Piozzi's death it had been her intention to retire to this city, where she enjoyed fond acquaintances, good talk, and enough cultural stimulation to satisfy her intellectual cravings. And she, who prized loyalty highly, felt allegiance to the Bath residents who supported her during her Streatham distresses. It was here that she made the friends who were to become most important to her emotional and mental well-being after Salusbury's marriage. And it was here that she denied a renewal of friendship to those who, like Frances Burney D'Arblay, had supported her daughters in opposing her marriage to Gabriel Piozzi. Mrs. Piozzi never forgave disloyalty.

When Mme D'Arblay returned to England and France in 1812, her family, aware of her distress over her rift with Mrs. Piozzi, tried to reconcile the two. Between 1 September 1812 and 17 May 1813, Marianne Francis, Mme D'Arblay's niece, wrote at least thirteen letters to Mrs. Piozzi in which she announced the arrival of her aunt, mentioned her name, or pleaded her cause. Finally, after Mme D'Arblay had major surgery in France, Francis pleaded that her aunt "was so desirous of something kind and conciliatory, and is, perhaps, poor thing, in a most dangerous state, I think if you can bring yourself to send anything like a kind message, it would be a most christian act in you, and give great happiness to her."[164] On 12 May 1813, the day before she left Streatham for a visit to Bath, Mrs. Piozzi called on Mme D'Arblay, but she was not at home. The next day Mrs. Piozzi described the episode to Salusbury, implying that her new Bath friendships promised more than did renewal of intimacy with a woman she would always distrust: "When Connections are once broken, 'tis a foolish Thing to splice and mend; They never can (at least with *me*) unite again as before. Life is not long enough for *Darning* torne *Friendships;* and they are always a Proof however neatly done, that the Substance is *worne out.* A new Dress can better be *depended* on."[165] Lest Queeney should join in urging her to resume her acquaintance with Mme D'Arblay, Mrs. Piozzi obliquely reminded her of her former friend's treachery; accompanying Mrs. Piozzi to Bath in 1784, ostensibly to support her when she sent Gabriel Piozzi away, she had betrayed her position of trust, supplying Queeney with details of Mrs. Piozzi's unaltered love for Piozzi. From that time on "Little Burney" became the "Aimable traitresse."[166] "They tell me Madame D'Arblaye is writing: busy in *Some* useful Way no doubt. Do you recollect when we were forming (for Sport) a female Administration, and She enquired what Provision should be made for *her?* Oh says Doctor Johnson; We will send *Little Burney out for a Spy.*"[167] Mrs. Piozzi spoke from bitter experience when she reiterated, "*New* Acquaintance are best; They *can* have no *old Malice.*"[168]

Mrs. Piozzi was more fortunate in the "New Acquaintance" she made in Bath: "The Bath People are those who I depend on for my *Social* Comforts in future, not the London ones," she told Salusbury.[169] "*You* who are blest with the Companion of Your Choice may live delighted and see no one else: but I, poor

Solitary Cast-off, could not breathe without Light and Noise and Acquaintance:—Droppers-*In* as I call them, and justly:—for they do drop-*in* by ones and twos and Threes all Morning."[170] When the bulk of her income was encumbered for Streatham expenses, Mrs. Piozzi's Bath acquaintances seemed to double their attention to her "Social Comforts," providing entertainments she could not herself afford, and continuing their visits to her "nutshell" of a house: "You scarce can think how kind these dear Bath People are. If I were to win the Golden Prize in this Lottery—I would never spend my Winters out of Bath."[171] Never was she made to feel an object of charity: "Bath is very amiable indeed, and very kind. The *only* Place I should imagine where dressing like a Pauper, and living like a Hermit—my Self-Love is never offended by Negligence or disrespect."[172] Her friends' devotion earned her deep gratitude. Speculating on the increase in income she would enjoy after she discharged her Streatham obligations, she declared that she would spend her clear 2100£ "among Friends I have made for myself—when they *must* of necessity have been disinterested in their Kindness;——because it has not be[en] in my Power to give a Glass of Wine, or even a Dish of Tea to anyone for the Time I have spent away from Wales and Surrey."[173]

Foremost of these acquaintances was Sir James Fellowes, a wealthy young physician whom she met in January 1815. Over the next few years, his marriage notwithstanding, Sir James was her most trusted intimate, replacing Salusbury in her affections and confidence. With Sir James she was by turns playful, witty, self-pitying, and admonitory—very like the Hester Lynch Piozzi that the young Salusbury had known: "Why Dear Sir James Fellowes! Peter the Cruel was surely *Your* Ancestor instead of *mine*. After the Thousand Kindnesses You and your charming Family—Hombres y Hembras had heaped on your ever obliged H:L:P;—to run out of the Town so, and never call to say Farewell. Ah! never mind; I shall pursue you with Letters."[174] And pursue him she did, with letters which must have touched and flattered him: "How kind You are and how partial! And what an unspeakable Loss shall I have when you enter on a London Life and London Practice—Dr. Holland who writes about the Ionian Islands is going to London to *practise* and exchange the *Cyclades* for the *sick Ladies*: He has been a Lyon here for Three whole Days. I caught the *Queue du Lion* and passed one Evening in his Company.——But a whole Menagerie would make me no Compensation for Exchange of Sentiment in Friendly Converse——Oh do make haste to Bath and let me lament my Fate to You personally."[175] From her responses to Sir James it is clear that he returned her affection: "My dear Sir James Fellowes, not contented with heaping kindnesses on his poor little Friend; *Thanks* her for her good Opinion; and *Thanks* her for the Tenderness of her Expressions——when Alas! 'tis only honest Truth that tears the first from my Heart; and relaxed Sensibility makes the other flow spontaneously from my Pen. 'But so few People will give *one* Leave to love them' would Doctor Collier say continually. They are always (added he) doing some what to hinder me from feeling or expressing my Regard. Now nobody can take a more opposite Course from this than Sir James Fellowes, who certainly now stands a fair Chance of being suffocated with Kind Words Wishes &c. Bear 'em as you may therefore."[176]

While Bath's inhabitants were the chief charm of the city, the place itself provided a balm for a mind and body exhausted by contending with her family: "I shall retire to Bath and wash away the Remains of Worldly Care—at the Pump."[177] Investing the Pump with near magical properties, she claimed that, "These hot Springs too are so comfortable, they wash away Sorrow and Care."[178] Little disturbed the town's tranquillity: "We have no Occurrences to relate: Bath goes on as it used to do: now a Coffin pushing you off the Pavement, and now a Base Viol Case."[179] Responding to news of political unrest surrounding London's elections, she described Bath: "Bath is quiet, and will remain so: a Town dedicated either to Sickness or Amusement will not be disturbed by Political Transactions; and our Folks are only thinking on the Election of a Master of the Ceremonies."[180] To Lady Williams, who pressed her to take a cottage near Brynbella when her finances were settled, she playfully described a possible alternative: "I might be tempted (with a freed Income) to take a comfortable House *here* and end my Days—an old *Bath Cat*—Snappish at the Card Table, sullen at the Conversation Parties——and passionate With the Maids at home——following them up and down Stairs with a Cambrick Handkerchief in hope of finding Dust on the Mahogany Bannisters."[181] Under continued prodding, Mrs. Piozzi made clear her commitment to Bath: "Bath is the best Place for Single Women that can be found; and the Friendship I have experienced here, leads me to choose it as a *last*—perhaps a *lasting* Residence. The Water is become quite necessary to my Health, and the Society will grow still more agreeable to me, when I have a less inconvenient Dwelling. . . . Ah Dear Lady Williams! I should feel as strange in Denbighshire *now* as Dear Sir John—in *Bath*."[182]

Mrs. Piozzi would have one more trauma with which to deal, however. Her beloved steward, Leak, arriving in Bath immediately after concluding the balance of her Streatham affairs, fell "very Ill in Danger."[183] His condition rapidly deteriorated: "Leak not safe at all; a raging Rheumatic Fever expected. Doctor Gibbes called. Terror returned, the Man will sure enough die in the House." Two days later, the forty-one-year-old Leak lay "A Corpse in the House of poor H: L: P."[184]

Finally, however, comfortable income reestablished, the resilient Mrs. Piozzi prepared to put her plan for a real home in Bath into action, closing a sad episode of her life and opening a new door: "My affairs here being all settled, Streatham Park disposed of, and my poor steward, Leak, being dead, I have got a pretty neat house and decent establishment for a widowed lady, and shall exist a true Bath Cat for the short remainder of my life, hearing from Salusbury of his increasing family, and learning from the libraries in this town all the popular topics—Turks, Jews, and Ex-Emperor Buonaparte, remembering still that now my debts are all paid, and my income set free, which was so long sequestered to pay repairs of a house I was not rich enough to inhabit, and could not persuade my daughters to take from me—

'Malice domestic, foreign levy,—nothing
Can touch me further;'

as Macbeth says of Duncan when he is dead. Things will at worst last *my* time I suppose."[185] Mrs. Piozzi spoke prophetically. She was to indulge in minor trips and to spend one unhappy fall and winter away from her beloved Bath, but she was, indeed, to be a "Bath Cat" for the rest of her life.

Notes

1. HLP to TSW, 20 December 1811.
2. HLP to Q, 29 February 1812.
3. HLP to Q, 28 March 1812.
4. HLP to JSPS, 27 September 1812.
5. HLP to Q, 15 May 1813.
6. HLP to JSPS, 23 December 1813.
7. HLP to Q, 17 January 1814; HLP to LC, 18 January 1814.
8. HLP to Clement Francis, 9 March 1814.
9. HLP to JW, 7 May 1814.
10. HLP to HMP, 15 June 1814; HLP to Ly W, 18 June 1814.
11. HLP to Ly W, 29 March 1815.
12. HLP to Ly W, 30 April 1815.
13. HLP to TSW, 13 August 1815.
14. HLP to Ly W, 5 November 1816.
15. HLP to JSPS, 9–10 November 1816.
16. HLP to JSPS, 6 December 1816.
17. HLP to JW, 25 December 1816.
18. HLP to JSPS, 17 December 1816.
19. *Thraliana* 2:984.
20. Hyde, p. 266.
21. *Thraliana* 2:992–93. There are only eleven mentions of Salusbury in *Thraliana* between 1798 and 1809, the year the journal ended.
22. HLP to LC, 22 May 1799.
23. HLP to JSPS, 26 September 1808.
24. Hyde, pp. 283–84.
25. *Thraliana* 2:1094, n.3.
26. HLP to JSPS, 7 June 1809.
27. HLP to JSPS, 7 June 1809.
28. HLP to JSPS, 22 February 1810.
29. HLP to JSPS, 2 March 1810.
30. HLP to JSPS, 9 March 1811.
31. HLP to TSW, 20 February 1811.
32. HLP to Ly W, 28 February 1811.
33. HLP to MW, 6 March 1811.
34. HLP to JSPS, 10 March 1811.
35. HLP to LC, 16 March 1811.
36. HLP to JSPS, 17 March 1811.
37. HLP to JSPS, 30 [March 1811]; 4 April 1811; 16–17 April 1811.
38. HLP to JSPS, 27 April 1811.
39. HLP to JSPS, 22 February 1810.
40. HLP to JSPS, 18–19 May 1811.
41. HLP to JSPS, 18–19 May 1811.
42. HLP to JSPS, 27 October 1811.
43. HLP to JSPS, 27 October 1811.
44. HLP to JSPS, 27 October 1811.
45. HLP to JSPS, [December 1811].
46. HLP to JSPS, 12 February 1812.
47. HLP to JSPS, 12 February 1812.
48. HLP to JSPS, 29 February 1812.
49. HLP to JSPS, 15 May 1812.
50. HLP to JSPS, 28 April 1812.
51. HLP to TSW, 20 December 1811.

52. HLP to TSW, 28 March 1811.
53. HLP to JSPS, 28 April 1812.
54. HLP to JSPS, 18[–19] May 1812.
55. HLP to Ly W, 28 January 1812.
56. HLP to JSPS, 27 September 1812.
57. Ry. Ch. 1258; HLP to JSPS, 19 April 1813, n.5; to HMP, 4 February 1814.
58. HLP to JSPS, 24[–26] April 1813.
59. HLP to TSW, 3 August 1813.
60. HLP to HMP, 15 December 1813.
61. HLP to HMP, 23 December 1813.
62. HLP to JW, 13 July 1814.
63. HLP to HMP, 23 December 1813.
64. HLP to JW, 1 June 1814.
65. HLP to JSPS, 23 June 1814.
66. HLP to TSW, 19 November 1814.
67. AL to HLP, 22 December 1814.
68. Ann Leak to HLP, 19 March 1815 (Ry. 609.7).
69. HLP to AL, 16 March 1815.
70. HLP to Ann Leak, 19 April 1815.
71. HLP to JSPS, 21 February 1815.
72. HLP to JSPS, 9 March 1815.
73. HLP to Ly W, 30 April 1815.
74. HLP to JSPS, 20 September 1815.
75. HLP to JF, 16 January 1816.
76. HLP to JF, 26–27 [January 1816].
77. HLP to Ann Leak, 25 February 1816.
78. HLP to Ly W, 26 February 1816.
79. Entry for 20 February 1816; HLP to JSPS, 21 February 1816, n. 1.
80. HLP to JSPS, 21 February 1816.
81. *GM* 86, pt. 1 (1816): 273.
82. HLP to JSPS, 27 March 1816.
83. HLP to AL, 19 May 1816.
84. Queeney was twenty when HLT married Gabriel Piozzi, Susanna was fourteen, Sophia thirteen, and Cecilia only seven. A fifth daughter, Henrietta Sophia (Harriet), died at age five in 1783, while the battle over the proposed marriage was raging.
85. Giovanni Salusbury Piozzi, eventually John Salusbury Piozzi Salusbury. Mrs. Piozzi always called him Salusbury.
86. Mrs. Piozzi's sardonic term for her daughters.
87. HLP to John Oldfield, 1 July 1811.
88. HLP to JSPS, 12 February 1812.
89. CMM to HLP, 26 April 1812.
90. HLP to AL, 4 May 1812.
91. HLP to Clement Mead, 6 November 1812, n. 2. The estate no longer exists.
92. *Thraliana* 2:985.
93. HLP to Ly W and MW, [16 February 1811].
94. The purchaser of a life interest enjoyed all the profit from rents and crops on an estate. In return the purchaser was liable for all taxes and tithes, as well as for all repairs. The agreement ended with the death of the seller.
95. HLP to TSW, 20 February 1811.
96. HLP to JSPS, 9 March 1811.
97. HLP to LC, 16 March 1811.
98. HLP to JSPS, 17 March 1811.
99. HLP to TSW, 28 March 1811.
100. HLP to TSW, 28 March 1811.
101. HLP to JSPS, 27 April 1811.
102. HLP to AL, 12 March 1812.
103. HLP to JSPS, 15 March 1812.
104. HLP to JSPS, 28 April 1812.
105. Clifford, p. 431.
106. HLP to AL, 19 March 1812.
107. Clifford, pp. 431–32 n. 2.

108. Clifford, pp. 431–32 n. 2.
109. HLP to JSPS, 15 May 1812.
110. HLP to Clement Mead, 16 May 1812.
111. HLP to Clement Mead, 20 May 1812.
112. HLP to TSW, 25 May 1812.
113. TSW to HLP, 16 June 1812.
114. HLP to Clement Mead, 13 August 1812.
115. HLP to Clement Mead, 6 November 1812.
116. HLP to JSPS, 24[–26] April 1813.
117. HLP to AL, 10 May 1813.
118. HLP to Clement Mead, 6 August 1813.
119. HLP to Clement Mead, 16 August 1813.
120. HLP to Clement Mead, 23 March 1814.
121. HLP to JSPS, 6[–7] June 1814.
122. HLP to Reverend Robert Gray, 27 November 1814.
123. HLP to Reverend Robert Gray, 27 November 1814.
124. HLP to HMP, 15 June 1814.
125. HLP to Ly W, 21 March 1815.
126. HLP to AL, 16 March 1815.
127. HLP to Ly W, 21 March 1815.
128. HLP to AL, 16 March 1815.
129. HLP to JSPS, 24 March 1815.
130. HLP to Ann and AL, 26 March 1815.
131. HLP to JSPS, 2 April 1815.
132. Reverend Robert Myddelton to HLP, quoted in HLP to JSPS, 12 April 1815.
133. HLP to JSPS, 12 April 1815.
134. HLP to JSPS, 19 April 1815.
135. HLP to Ann Leak, 19 April 1815.
136. HLP to JF, 9 May 1815.
137. HLP to Ann Leak, 27 May 1815.
138. HLP to Ly W, 15 June 1815.
139. HLP to Edward William Smythe Owen, 9 July 1815.
140. HLP to CM, 12 July 1815.
141. HLP to AL, 14 July 1815.
142. HLP to Robert Dalgliesh, 23 July 1815.
143. HLP to Ly W, 16 July 1815.
144. HLP to JF, 31 July 1815.
145. HLP to JF, 7 August 1815.
146. HLP to TSW, 13 August 1815.
147. HLP to AL, 22 October 1815.
148. The *Morning Chronicle*, 12 February 1816, quoted in HLP to AL, 13 February 1816, n.3.
149. HLP to Ann Leak, 15 February 1816.
150. AL to HLP, 22 February 1816, quoted in HLP to Ann Leak, 15 February 1816, n.1.
151. HLP to Ann Leak, 15 February 1816.
152. HLP to JF, 21 February 1816.
153. AL to HLP, 26 February 1816, quoted in HLP to AL, 1 March 1816, n.1.
154. HLP to AL, 1 March 1816.
155. HLP to JF, 9 March 1816.
156. HLP to JSPS, 27 March 1816.
157. HLP to JSPS, 30 March 1816.
158. HLP to JSPS, 30 March 1816.
159. HLP to Ann Leak, 25 February 1816.
160. HLP to AL, 12 May 1816. The Johnson sold for £378, the Garrick for £183.15, and the Reynolds self-portrait for £128.2.
161. HLP to AL, 12 May 1816. Robert Elliott was a rope, hemp, and flax merchant in Wapping.
162. HLP to JF, 30 May 1816.
163. HLP to Jacob Weston, 18 December 1798.
164. *Journals and Letters*, 7:118–23.
165. HLP to JSPS, [13-]14 May 1813.
166. *Journals and Letters*, 7:119, n. 11.
167. HLP to Q, 15 May 1813.

Short Titles for Major Manuscript Repositories

Barrett

The Barrett Collection of Burney Papers, British Library, London, 43 vols., Egerton [Eg.] 3690–3708

Berg

The Henry W. and Albert A. Berg Collection, New York Public Library, New York City

Bodleian

Bodleian Library, Oxford University

Bowood Collection

The Bowood Collection of Thrale-Piozzi letters in the possession of the marquis of Lansdowne, Bowood House, near Calne, Wilts.

Brit. Mus. Add. MSS

British Museum [now British Library] Additional Manuscripts

C.R.O.

County Record Office[s], England, Wales, and Ireland

Harvard University Library

Houghton Library at Harvard University

Historical Society of Pennsylvania

Historical Society of Pennsylvania, Philadelphia

Huntington Library

Henry E. Huntington Library, San Marino, California

Hyde Collection

The Donald and Mary Hyde Collection at Four Oaks Farm, Somerville, New Jersey; and at the Houghton Library, Harvard University

N.L.W.

National Library of Wales, Aberystwyth

N.P.G.	The National Portrait Gallery, Trafalgar Square, London
Osborn Collection	James Marshall and Marie-Louise Osborn Collection at the Beinecke Rare Book and Manuscript Library, Yale University
Peyraud Collection	The Paula F. Peyraud Collection of Piozzi letters and marginalia, Chappaqua, New York
Pforzheimer Library	The Carl H. Pforzheimer Library, New York City
The Pierpont Morgan Library	The Pierpont Morgan Library, New York City
Princeton University Library	Firestone Library at Princeton University
P.R.O.	Public Record Office, Chancery Lane, London
Ry.	The John Rylands University Library of Manchester, England
Victoria and Albert	Victoria and Albert Museum Library, London
Yale University Library	The Beinecke Rare Book and Manuscript Collection at Yale University

Locations of miscellaneous collections of Piozzi manuscripts not listed above are identified at the foot of each relevant letter under *"Text."*

Short Titles for Hester Lynch Piozzi's Manuscripts and Books

"Account Books"

"[Gabriel Piozzi's] Accounts, 1784–1792," Drummond's Bank, Charing Cross, London

Anecdotes

Anecdotes of the Late Samuel Johnson, LL.D., During the Last Twenty Years of His Life. London: Printed for T. Cadell, 1786.

"Appeal"

"Mrs. Piozzi's Appeal against the *Critical Reviewers*," *Gentleman's Magazine* 71, pt. 2 (July 1801): 602–3.

British Synonymy

British Synonymy: or, An Attempt at Regulating the Choice of Words in Familiar Conversation. 2 vols. London: Printed for G. G. and J. Robinson, 1794.

"Children's Book"

For "The Children's Book or rather Family Book" from 17 September 1766 to the end of 1778 (Hyde Collection), see Hyde, Mary. *The Thrales of Streatham Park.* Cambridge and London: Harvard University Press, 1977.

"Commonplace Book"

"The New Commonplace Book." Random entries made by HLP after the completion of *Thraliana*, the first entry written at Brynbella in 1809 and the last in 1820 at Penzance (Hyde Collection).

Florence Miscellany

Florence Miscellany. Florence: Printed for G. Cam, Printer to His Royal Highness. With Permission, 1785. Hester Lynch Piozzi contributed the preface and nine poems.

French Journals	*The French Journals of Mrs. Thrale and Doctor Johnson.* Edited by Moses Tyson and Henry Guppy. Manchester: Manchester University Press, 1932. Hester Lynch Thrale's *French Journal* (1775) includes pp. 69–166; Hester Lynch Piozzi's *French Journey* (1784), pp. 191–213; Samuel Johnson's *French Journal* (1775), pp. 169–88.
"Harvard Piozziana"	"Poems and Little Characters, Anecdotes &c. Introductory to the Poems." 5 MS vols., 1810–14, for John Salusbury Piozzi Salusbury. Harvard University Library, MS Eng. 1280.
"Italian and German Journals"	"Italian and German Journals, from 5 September 1784 to March 1787," 2 MS notebooks (Ry. 618).
"Journey Book"	"Journey through the North of England and Part of Scotland, Wales, &c." 1789 (Ry. 623).
Letters	*Letters to and from the Late Samuel Johnson, LL.D.* 2 vols. London: Printed for A. Strahan and T. Cadell, 1788.
"Lyford Redivivus"	"Lyford Redivivus or A Grandame's Garrulity." [Signed by] "An Old Woman" [1809–15] (Hyde Collection).
"Memoirs"	Autobiographical Essays: For Sir James Fellowes, December 1815. Thirty-six MS pages bound into Johnson's *Letters.* Princeton University Library. For William Augustus Conway, May 1819. Eleven MS pages bound into *Observations.* Hyde Collection. See also Mrs. Piozzi to the Proprietors of the *Monthly Mirror,* 17 June 1798, Huntington Library, MSS 20831, and vol. 2, *The Piozzi Letters.*
"Memorial"	"Memorial of H. L. Piozzi against John Cator Esq." [autumn 1792]. John Rylands Library, MS. Ry. 611, and Appendix, vol. 2, *The Piozzi Letters.*

Merritt

Piozzi Marginalia. Edited by Percival Merritt. Cambridge: Harvard University Press, 1925.

"Minced Meat for Pyes"

"Minced Meat for Pyes" (1796–1820), a collection of extracts, jottings, quotations, verses, &c. Harvard University Library, MS Eng. 231F.

Observations

Observations and Reflections made in the course of a Journey through France, Italy, and Germany. 2 vols. London: Printed for A. Strahan and T. Cadell, 1789.

Old England

Old England to her Daughters. Address to the Females of Great Britain. [Signed by] "Poor Old England," penny broadside. London: Printed by J. Brettell for R. Faulder, ca. June 1803.

Retrospection

Retrospection: or A Review of the Most Striking and Important Events, Characters, Situations, and their Consequences, which the last Eighteen Hundred Years have Presented to the View of Mankind. 2 vols. London: Printed for John Stockdale, 1801.

"Thrale Estate Book"

"Accounts of the Estate of Henry Thrale, also Guardian Accounts with the four Thrale Daughters." MS in Hyde Collection.

Thraliana

Thraliana: The Diary of Mrs. Hester Lynch Thrale (later Mrs. Piozzi), 1776–1809. Edited by Katharine C. Balderston. 2d ed. 2 vols. Oxford: Clarendon Press, 1951. The original MS, 6 vols., is at the Huntington Library, San Marino, California.

Three Warnings

The Three Warnings. Kidderminster: Printed by John Gower, 1792. This work appeared originally in Anna Williams, *Miscellanies in Prose and Verse* (1766).

Three Warnings to John Bull

Three Warnings to John Bull before He Dies. By an Old Acquaintance of the Public. London: R. Faulder, 1798.

"Verses 1"	"Collection of Hester Lynch Piozzi's MSS Poetry." 140 leaves, of which 60, i.e., 120 pages, contain HLP's original poetry (Hyde Collection).
"Verses 2"	"Collection of Hester Lynch Piozzi's MSS Poetry." 34 pages of Hester Lynch Piozzi's verse plus 19 blank pages (Hyde Collection).
Welsh Tour	*Mrs. Thrale's Unpublished Journal of her Tour in Wales with Dr. Johnson, July–September, 1774.* In A. M. Broadley's *Doctor Johnson and Mrs. Thrale,* pp. 155–219. London and New York: John Lane, 1910.

Short Titles for Secondary Sources

We have used standard encyclopedias, school and university rosters, biographical dictionaries, law lists, peerages, armorials, baronetages, knightages, medical and clerical rosters, town and city directories, almanacs, and so forth. Along with these we have consulted annual army and navy lists; *Boyle's Court Guide: Royal Kalendar;* the Reverend William Betham, *The Baronetage of England,* 5 vols. (1801–5); the numerous editions of Burke's *Peerage and Baronetage* as well as Burke's *Landed Gentry;* Burke's *Royal Families of the World,* 2 vols. (1977); Burke's *Irish Family Records* (1976); George Edward Cokayne, *The Complete Peerage,* revised by Vicary Gibbs, et al., 13 vols. (1910–59); *The Complete Baronetage,* 6 vols. (1900–1909); W. A. Shaw, *The Knights of England,* 2 vols. (1906); Howard M. Colvin, *A Biographical Dictionary of British Architects, 1660–1840* (1954; 1978); Joseph Haydn and Horace Ockerby, *The Book of Dignities,* 3d ed. (1894); Gerrit P. Judd IV, *Members of Parliament, 1734–1832* (1955); and Sir Lewis Namier and John Brooke, *The House of Commons, 1754–1790,* 3 vols. (1964).

These works will be cited only when specifically appropriate.

AR	*The Annual Register, or a View of the History, Politics, and Literature. 1758–.* (See Mrs. Piozzi to Mrs. Pennington, 4 August 1794, n. 10.)
Baronetage	Cokayne, George Edward, ed. *Complete Baronetage.* 6 vols. Exeter: W. Pollard, 1900–1909.
Bayle	*The Dictionary Historical and Critical of Mr. Peter Bayle.* 2d ed. 5 vols. London: Printed for J. J. and P. Knapton [etc.], 1734–38.
Boaden	Boaden, James. *Memoirs of Mrs. Siddons, Interspersed with Anecdotes of Authors and Actors.* 2 vols. London: Henry Colburn, 1827.
Boswell's Johnson	*Boswell's Life of Johnson.* Edited by George Birkbeck Hill and L. F. Powell. 6 vols. Oxford: Clarendon Press, 1934–64.

Broadley
Broadley, A. M. *Doctor Johnson and Mrs. Thrale.* London and New York: John Lane, 1910.

Brooke
Brooke, John. *King George III.* New York: McGraw-Hill, 1972.

Campbell
Campbell, Thomas. *Life of Mrs. Siddons.* 2 vols. London: Effingham Wilson, 1834.

Chandler
Chandler, David G. *The Campaigns of Napoleon.* London: Weidenfeld and Nicolson, 1966.

Clifford
Clifford, James L. *Hester Lynch Piozzi (Mrs. Thrale).* 2d ed. Reprinted with corrections and additions. Oxford: Clarendon Press, 1968, 1987 (with a new introduction by Margaret Anne Doody).

Corr. George IV
The Correspondence of George, Prince of Wales, 1770–1812. Edited by A. Aspinall. 8 vols. New York: Oxford University Press, 1963–71.

Décembre-Alonnier
[Joseph] Décembre-[Edmond] Alonnier. *Dictionnaire de la Révolution française, 1789–1799.* 2 vols. Paris [1866–68].

Diary and Letters
Diary and Letters of Madame d'Arblay. Edited by Charlotte Barrett. 7 vols. [1842–46.] London: H. Colburn, 1854.

Dodsley
A Collection of Poems in Six Volumes by Several Hands. [Edited by Robert Dodsley.] London: Printed by J. Hughs, for J. Dodsley, in Pall-Mall, 1765.

Doody
Doody, Margaret Anne. *Frances Burney. The Life in the Works.* New Brunswick, New Jersey: Rutgers University Press, 1988.

Early Journals
The Early Journals and Letters of Fanny Burney, vol. 1 (1768–73). Edited by Lars E. Troide. Oxford and Montreal: Oxford University Press; McGill-Queens University Press, 1988–

English Poets
Johnson, Samuel. *Lives of the English Poets.* Edited by George Birkbeck Hill. 3 vols. Oxford: Clarendon Press, 1905.

Farington   *The Diary of Joseph Farington.* Vols. 1–6 edited by Kenneth Garlick and Angus D. Macintyre. Vols. 7–16 edited by Kathryn Cave. New Haven and London: Published for the Paul Mellon Centre for Studies in British Art, Yale University Press, 1978–84.

Genest   Genest, John. *Some Account of the English Stage, from the Restoration in 1660 to 1830.* 10 vols. Bath: Printed by H. E. Carrington and sold by Thomas Rodd, Great Newport Street, London, 1832.

GM   *The Gentleman's Magazine.* Edited by Sylvanus Urban. London, 1731–1907.

Hawkins   Hawkins, Sir John. *The Life of Samuel Johnson, LL.D.* 2d ed. Revised and corrected. London: J. Buckland, et al., 1787.

Hayward   Hayward, A., ed. *Autobiography, Letters and Literary Remains of Mrs. Piozzi (Thrale).* 2d ed. 2 vols. London: Longman, Green, Longman, Roberts, 1861.

Hazen   Hazen, Charles Downer. *The French Revolution.* 2 vols. New York: Henry Holt, 1932.

Hemlow   Hemlow, Joyce. *The History of Fanny Burney.* Oxford: Clarendon Press, 1958.

Highfill   Highfill, Philip H., Jr., Kalman A. Burnim, and Edward A. Langhans. *A Biographical Dictionary of Actors, Actresses, Musicians, Dancers, Managers & Other Stage Personnel in London, 1660–1800.* Carbondale and Edwardsville: Southern Illinois University Press, 1973–93.

Hodson   Hodson, V. C. P. *List of the Officers of the Bengal Army 1758–1834.* 4 pts. London: Constable; Phillimore, 1927–47.

Howell   *Epistolae Ho-Elianae, The Familiar Letters of James Howell.* Edited by Joseph Jacobs. 2 vols. [1645–55.] London: David Nutt, 1892.

Hyde   Hyde, Mary. *The Thrales of Streatham Park.*

Cambridge and London: Harvard University Press, 1977.

Hyde-Redford   The Hyde Edition of *The Letters of Samuel Johnson*, vols. 1–5. Edited by Bruce Redford. Princeton, N.J.: Princeton University Press, 1992–94.

Idler   *The Idler and the Adventurer.* Edited by W. J. Bate, John M. Bullitt, and L. F. Powell. Vol. 2 of *The Yale Edition of the Works of Samuel Johnson.* New Haven and London, 1963.

Jerningham   *The Jerningham Letters (1780–1843).* Edited by Egerton Castle. 2 vols. London: Richard Bentley and Son, 1896.

Jesse   Jesse, J. Heneage. *Memoirs of the Life and Reign of King George the Third.* 2d ed. 3 vols. London: Tinsley Brothers, 1867.

Johns. Misc.   *Johnsonian Miscellanies.* Edited by George Birkbeck Hill. 2 vols. Oxford: Clarendon Press, 1897.

Johns. Shakespeare   *Johnson on Shakespeare.* Edited by Arthur Sherbo. Vols. 7–8 of *The Yale Edition of the Works of Samuel Johnson.* New Haven and London, 1968.

Journals and Letters   *The Journals and Letters of Fanny Burney (Madame d'Arblay).* Edited by Joyce Hemlow et al. 12 vols. Oxford: Clarendon Press, 1972–84. Especially vol. 7, edited by Edward A. Bloom and Lillian D. Bloom (1978); vol. 8, edited by Peter Hughes et al. (1980): vols. 9–10, edited by Warren Derry (1982).

Knapp   Knapp, Oswald G., ed. *The Intimate Letters of Hester Piozzi and Penelope Pennington 1788–1821.* London, Toronto, and New York: John Lane; Bell and Cockburn, 1914.

Lefebvre   Lefebvre, Georges. *The French Revolution.* Vol. 1, *From its Origins to 1793,* translated by Elizabeth Moss Evanson. Vol. 2, *From 1793 to 1799,* translated by John Hall Stewart and James Friguglietti. London: Routledge and Kegan Paul; New York: Columbia University Press, 1962–64.

Lloyd	Lloyd, J[acob] Y. *The History of the Princes, the Lords Marcher, and the Ancient Nobility of Powys Fadog, and the Ancient Lords of Arwystli, Cedewen, and Meirionydd.* 6 vols. London: T. Richards [Whiting], 1881–87.
London Stage	*The London Stage 1660–1800.* Edited by William Van Lennep, Emmett L. Avery, Arthur H. Scouten, et al. 5 vols. in 11 and index. Carbondale: Southern Illinois University Press, 1960–79.
McCarthy	McCarthy, William. *Hester Thrale Piozzi: Portrait of a Literary Woman.* Chapel Hill: University of North Carolina Press, 1985.
Mangin	[Mangin, Edward.] *Piozziana; or, Recollections of the Late Mrs. Piozzi, with Remarks.* London: Edward Moxon, 1833.
Manvell	Manvell, Roger. *Sarah Siddons: Portrait of an Actress.* London: Heinemann, 1970.
Marshall	Marshall, John. *Royal Naval Biography.* . . . 4 vols. London: Longman, Hurst, Rees, Orme, and Browne, 1823–35.
Nichols	Nichols, John. *Illustrations of the Literary History of the Eighteenth Century.* 8 vols. [7 and 8 by John Bowyers Nichols.] London: Nichols, Son, and Bentley, 1817–58.
O'Bryne	O'Byrne, Richard William. *A Naval Biographical Dictionary.* 2 vols. London: J. Murray, 1849.
Oxford Proverbs	*The Oxford Dictionary of English Proverbs.* 3d ed. Revised by F. P. Wilson [1970]. Oxford: Clarendon Press, 1982.
Parliamentary History	*The Parliamentary History of England from the earliest Period to the Year 1803, from which last-mentioned Epoch it is continued downwards in the work entitled "Hansard's Parliamentary Debates."* 36 vols. London: Printed by T. C. Hansard [etc.], 1806–20.
Pastor	Pastor, Baron Ludwig Friedrich August von. *The History of the Popes, from the Close of the Middle Ages.*

40 vols. London: J. Hodges et al., 1891–1953.

Peerage   Cokayne, George Edward. *The Complete Peerage of England, Scotland, Ireland, Great Britain and the United Kingdom.* 2d ed., rev. and enl. Edited by Vicary Gibbs et al. 13 vols. London: St. Catherine Press, 1910–59.

Poems   *Poems.* Edited by E. L. McAdam, Jr., with George Milne. Vol. 6 of *The Yale Edition of the Works of Samuel Johnson.* New Haven and London, 1964.

Prayers   *Diaries, Prayers, and Annals.* Edited by E. L. McAdam, Jr., with Donald and Mary Hyde. Vol. 1 of *The Yale Edition of the Works of Samuel Johnson.* New Haven and London, 1958.

Queeney Letters   *The Queeney Letters.* Edited by the marquis of Lansdowne. London: Cassell; New York: Farrar and Rinehart, 1934.

Rambler   *The Rambler.* Edited by W. J. Bate and Albrecht B. Strauss. Vols. 3–5 of *The Yale Edition of the Works of Samuel Johnson.* New Haven and London, 1969.

Rasselas   *Rasselas and Other Tales.* Edited by Gwin J. Kolb. Vol. 16 of *The Yale Edition of the Works of Samuel Johnson.* New Haven and London, 1990.

Redford   Redford, Bruce. *The Converse of the Pen.* Chicago and London: University of Chicago Press, 1986.

Repertorium   Winter, Otto Friedrich. *Repertorium der diplomatischen Vertreter aller Länder seit dem Westfälischen Frieden (1648).* Vol. 3, 1764–1815. Graz-Köln: Verlag Hermann Böhlaus, 1965.

Rothenberg   Rothenberg, Gunter E. *Napoleon's Great Adversaries: The Archduke Charles and the Austrian Army, 1792–1814.* Bloomington: Indiana University Press, 1982.

Sale Catalogue   *1. Streatham Park, Surrey. A Catalogue of the . . . Household Furniture . . . a Collection of Valuable Paintings . . . also the Extensive and Well-Selected Library . . . the genuine Property of Mrs. Piozzi . . . will be sold by Auction, by Mr. Squibb, on the Premises, on Wednesday the 8th of May, 1816, and Four following Days (Sunday excepted). 2. Collectanea Johnsoniana. Catalogue of the Library, Pictures, Prints, Coins, Plate, China, and other Valuable Curiosities, the Property of Mrs. Hester Lynch Piozzi, Deceased, to be sold by Auction, at the Emporium Rooms, Exchange Street, Manchester, by Mr. Broster, on Wednesday, [September 1823] the 17th instant, and [six] following days, Saturday and Sunday excepted. Chester.*

Seward, *Anecdotes*

Seward, William. *Anecdotes of Some Distinguished Persons, Chiefly of the Present and Two Preceding Centuries.* 4 vols. and supplement. 2d ed. London: T. Cadell, Jr., and W. Davies, 1795–96.

Seward Letters

Letters of Anna Seward: Written between the Years 1784 and 1807. 6 vols. Edinburgh: Archibald Constable and Co.; London: Longman, Hurst, Rees, Orme, and Brown, William Miller, and John Murray, 1811.

Shakespeare

The Riverside Shakespeare. Boston: Houghton Mifflin, 1974.

Siddons Letters

Burnim, Kalman A. "The Letters of Sarah and William Siddons to Hester Lynch Piozzi in the John Rylands Library." *Bulletin of the John Rylands Library* 52 (1969–70): 46–95.

Spectator

The Spectator. 8 vols. London: Printed by H. Hughs for Payne, Rivington et al., 1789. This is Hester Lynch Piozzi's copy, bought in 1794, with her marginalia (Peyraud Collection).

Stanhope

Stanhope, Philip Henry, fifth earl. *Life of the Right Honourable William Pitt.* 4 vols. 3d ed. [1867]. New York: AMS Press, 1970.

Tilley

Tilley, Morris Palmer. *A Dictionary of the Proverbs in England in the Sixteenth and Seventeenth Centuries.* Ann Arbor: University of Michigan Press, 1950.

Walpole Correspondence

The Yale Edition of Horace Walpole's Correspondence. Edited by W. S. Lewis et al. 48 vols. in 49. New Haven, 1937–83.

Warton   Warton, Thomas. *The History of English Poetry, from the Close of the Eleventh to the Commencement of the Eighteenth Century.* 4 vols. London: J. Dodsley et al., 1774–81.

Watson   Watson, J. Steven. *The Reign of George III, 1760–1815.* Oxford: Clarendon Press, 1960.

Welsh Journey   Johnson, Samuel. *A Journey into North Wales, in the Year 1774.* In *Boswell's Johnson* 5:427–61.

Wheatley   Wheatley, Henry B. *London Past and Present.* 3 vols. London: John Murray; New York: Scribner and Welford, 1891.

Wickham   Wickham, The Reverend Hill, ed. *Journals and Correspondence of Thomas [Sedgwick] Whalley, D.D.* 2 vols. London: Richard Bentley, 1863.

Names and Abbreviations of Major Figures in the Piozzi Correspondence

AL	Alexander Leak (1776–1816)
CB	Charles Burney (1726–1814)
CMT ⎤ CMM ⎦	Cecilia Margaretta Thrale (1777–1857); in 1795 Mrs. Mostyn
DL	The Reverend Daniel Lysons (1762–1834)
EM	The Reverend Edward Mangin (1772–1852)
FB ⎤ FBA ⎦	Frances "Fanny" Burney (1752–1840); in 1793 Mme d'Arblay
GP	Gabriel Piozzi (1740–1809)
HLS ⎤ HLT ⎬ HLP ⎦	Hester Lynch Salusbury (1741–1821); in 1763 Mrs. Thrale; in 1784 Mrs. Piozzi
HMP ⎤ HMS ⎦	Harriet Maria Pemberton (1794–1831); in 1814 Mrs. Salusbury; in 1817 Lady Salusbury
HT	Henry Thrale (1728 or 1729–81)
JB	James Boswell (1740–95)
JF	James Fellowes (1771–1857); in 1809 Sir James, knight
JMM	John Meredith Mostyn (1775–1807)
JSPS	John Salusbury Piozzi Salusbury (1793–1858); in 1817 Sir John, knight
JW	John Williams (1794–1859); in 1830 Sir John, second baronet; in 1842 Sir John Hay-Williams
LC	The Reverend Leonard Chappelow (1744–1820)
Ly W	Margaret Williams (1768–1835) of Bodelwyddan; in 1798 Lady Williams
MF	Marianne Francis (1790–1832)
MW	Margaret Williams (1759–1823) of Bath
PSW ⎤ PSP ⎦	Penelope Sophia Weston (1752–1827); in 1792 Mrs. Pennington
Q	Hester Maria "Queeney" Thrale (1764–1857); in 1808 Lady Keith
RD	The Reverend Reynold Davies (1752–1820)
RG	The Reverend Robert Gray (1762–1834)

SAT	Susanna Arabella Thrale (1770–1858)
SJ	Samuel Johnson (1709–84)
SL	Samuel Lysons (1763–1819)
SS	Sarah Siddons (1755–1831)
ST ⎫ SH ⎭	Sophia Thrale (1771–1824); in 1807 Mrs. Hoare
TSW	The Reverend Thomas Sedgwick Whalley (1746–1828)
WAC	William Augustus Conway (1789–1828)

Genealogical Abbreviations

cr.	created
fl.	flourished
M.I.	monumental inscription

Editorial Principles

Manuscript Sources

All letters are arranged chronologically. Mrs. Piozzi's correspondence creates few textual problems since she prided herself on her penmanship and wrote with a strong hand. We have transcribed literally, changing only what we believe would detract from clarity. We have retained original spellings, capitalization, and punctuation. Certain accidentals—the omission of a period or a closing parenthesis—are silently emended. Superior letters are lowered. Her intermittent use of an elision to form a past tense—a usage that she came to see as outmoded—is normalized: e.g., "defer'd" becomes "deferred." Most abbreviations—except in a few instances or in addresses and postmarks—are expanded.

Mrs. Piozzi's paragraphing can puzzle. Occasionally she follows normal practice by dropping a line and then indenting. At other times to indicate a new paragraph she merely extends a space on the same line. Sense usually dictates where a visibly uncertain paragraph begins. Dashes, similarly, are hard to decipher since her lines for that mark can be of any length or even appear as a seemingly extended ellipsis. Dashes, consequently, are transcribed as "—" or, when elongated to suggest emotional response, as "——".

The writer's address is shown at the upper right of the letter along with the date. The complimentary close and signature for each letter are presented in run-on fashion with slash marks to indicate line breaks or divisions. At the foot of each letter are provided, where available, repository, address of recipient, and postmark. Franked letters are marked as such.

Pertinent complementary correspondence usually appears in notes in order to explain obscurities, clarify cryptic remarks, or solve problems. In a few instances, however, when Mrs. Piozzi answers a letter—say, of Sarah Siddons, Leonard Chappelow, Joseph Cooper Walker, or Daniel Lysons—point-for-point, we incorporate in the body of the text the letter that initiated or continued the correspondence.

Generally, square brackets "[ ]" signal such defects in the holographs as blots, tears, seals, and oversights. In addition, when a date of composition is conjectural, it is enclosed in square brackets and annotated. Angle brackets "< >" indicate places where a printed date, as in a postmark, a word, or a phrase is blurred. When warranted by the context, emendations are made within the appropriate square or angle brackets.

Printed Sources

Texts are reprinted literally although erroneous datings and obvious misprints are corrected with explanations when necessary, and certain typographical eccentricities, such as the arbitrary and inconsistent use of small capitals in words and phrases, are not reproduced.

We have consistently used the names of Welsh counties as HLP would have known them. Since 1974, however, following reorganization under the Local Government Act (1972), the new county of Clwyd, e.g., was created from Flintshire, most of Denbighshire, and the Edeyrnion district of Merioneth. Similarly, the new county of Gwynedd was formed out of Anglesey, Carnarvonshire (or Caernarfonshire), the rest of Merioneth, and the Conwy valley in Denbighshire.

The Piozzi Letters

Letters, 1811–1816

TO LADY WILLIAMS AND MARGARET WILLIAMS

[Cheltenham]
[16 February 1811]

My dear Lady Williams

will I hope begin now to wish for a Letter from Cheltenham: so here is one dated Saturday 16: This Place really appears to me to have been well chosen this Year when a London Jaunt would have been poysoned by the Plagues concerning Streatham Park.

I have dispatched Leak thither—*Chargé d'Affaires*—to speak with Agents, Assignees &c., and learn Mr. Charles Shephard's real best Advice; while I remain here to amuse myself with Seeing my Dear Salusbury so well amused.

His Sport however ends next Monday sennight, and he returns to Enborne for a Couple of Months, after having so well deserved all the Pleasure I can give him, that I have consented to make out a nice Dance and Supper on Thursday 21 that We may in some Measure return the numerous Civilities and showy Entertainments to which We are Invited every Evening.

The Society here is really very pleasant; and the People are Not fastidious but willing to make their Pleasure out of each other.

Every one is rejoycing in the good News, and praising the Prince Regent; whose amiable Forbearance makes Stock *rise*, and the Faces of disloyal Democrates to *fall*.[1]

We have had a contested Election,[2] but 'tis over; and all seem pleased that Guise sits Member, while both Parties join to applaud Mr. Dutton's Conduct, and graceful Exit.[3]

Mrs. Dutton was the hon: Miss Legge who your Ladyship remembers at Vronew.[4] Her Mother (who married Lord Stawell) was Daughter to my oldest Friend *Esther* Hanmer of Escoyde, first Wife of Asheton Curzon—who has had two Since her, and is expected to lead another Lady to Church very soon.—[5]

He is like Katherine de Berayne.[6] Now kind Lady Williams You must write to *me*, and tell how the dear Children come on, and how this Weather agrees with Sir John's Grounds: and how the Mine prospers, and how Wheat rises, and how you are not afraid of the Phantom our Folks here have conjured up concerning Lucien Buonaparte's making himself a Favourite in Wales[7]——and selling our 13 Counties to his Brother who is to step over from Ireland and take ready Possession. But I conclude this Letter and begin one—upon the same Sheet to Miss Williams——who shall have the Disposal of all my Compliments and who knows how Sincerely I love and respect my Dear Lady Williams and her Darlings to Whom I am ever True and faithful while/ H: L: Piozzi

My dear Miss Williams

It is an old Italian Saying: "That *Mountains* never *meet,*—but *People* can scarcely be *parted.*"[8] In this Village, Centre almost of England: I have met Ladies from *Raasay*, that Island of the Hebrides,[9] which Doctor Johnson so celebrates in his Scotch Tour;[10] and Women from *Rome* whom I remember——(or their Families,) when I was passing *My* happy Days upon the Continent.

This is odd enough—is not it? and pretty enough.

Here is too much Card-playing——and such Suppers, as nobody thinks of giving at *Bath;* or any but very Showy People, in *London.* House Rent comfortably *low.* The Dust Basket I inhabited last Spring—No. 60 Welbeck Street cost me 16 or 17 Guineas o'Week: We have a Clean habitation here for 3 and Room enough for Salusbury and me. This is prodigious advantage, and Dinners are expected from *no one.* The Richardsons are here, and Lady Frances Beresford—Lady Charlotte Gould, Lady Grant, Lady Lushington and a long *Et cetera.*[11] The Old Countess Buckinghamshire fixed at the Loo Table,[12] and Miss Cornwallis just gone to Town.[13]

Droppers-*In* all Morning, and Conversation Parties every Night. A lovely Mrs. Bagwell whose Countenance, (not Figure,)[14] resembles our beautiful Lady Callender,[15] is most admired of any one; but Salusbury says pretty Mrs. Richardson's *Welsh Eyes* have most Expression.[16] She was a Miss Philips of South Wales you know. Farewell! and among your present Felicities forget not an Old Friend, and faithful Servant./ H: L: Piozzi.

Remember me to all you love, and don't let me be fretting for Letters when I have lost my Companion.

Text Ry. 3 (1807–1811). *Address* Lady Williams/ Bodylwyddan/ St. Asaph/ Flintshire/ North Wales. *Postmark* CHELTENHAM 17 FE 17 <101>.

1. The Prince of Wales resented the restrictions written into the regency bill by the Perceval ministry: restrictions on creating new peers, on granting pensions, on handling the king's property or being responsible for the king's person. He urged his brothers to protest the constraints and chose his advisors from the Opposition. Determined to bring down the Perceval government, he wanted to substitute another, probably led by Lords Grenville and Grey. But toward the end of January, when the king's health was said to be improved, the Prince of Wales seemed to favor the continuation of Perceval and his ministers. By 4 February he told Perceval that his government was secure and that Grenville and Grey had been dismissed. Political tensions relaxed as the Prince took the oaths as regent and planned his first levee on 20 February.

2. HLP refers to the Gloucester county election. The two contenders were Berkeley William Guise (1775–1834), second baronet (1794), and John Dutton (1779–1862), second baron Sherborne (1820).

The *Courier* (30 January) announced the results of the first day's poll: "Sir W. B. Guise . . . 263/ the Hon. Mr. Dutton . . . 147." Guise's majority continued to mount until Dutton, "the Peers' nominee . . . declined on the 10th day" the continuation of the poll (*The Times,* 9 February).

3. The election was important for, as *The Times* of 9 February pointed out:

"if a trio of noble families is to appoint county members, as has been attempted in this case, the whole principle of representation is vitiated in its very elements, and we had better be without a House of Commons altogether. We have heard enough of rotten boroughs, but this was an attempt to sink Gloucestershire into a rotten county. . . . We hope and trust that Sir William Guise will demean himself in a manner becoming the high confidence which has been reposed in him; and that his conduct in Parliament will be as honourable as the triumph of the county in his behalf has been glorious."

4. On 11 August 1803 John Dutton married Mary Bilson-Legge (d. 1864), daughter of Henry Stawell (1757–1820), sixth baron Stawel (1760) of Somerton and Mary, née Curzon (see HLP to Margaret Owen [12 February 1799], n. 5).

5. Assheton Curzon (1729/30–1820), cr. baron Curzon of Penn, Bucks. (1794), viscount Curzon (1802). In 1756 he married Esther Hanmer (d. 1764); in 1766 Dorothy Grosvenor (d. 1774); in 1777 Anna Margaretta (Trecothick), née Meredith (d. 1804).

6. For Katheryn of Berain's three husbands, see HLP to PSP [ca. 26 July 1800], n. 12.

7. For Lucien Bonaparte at this time, see HLP to Ly W, 28 February 1811.

8. Cf. John Ray, *English Proverbs*, who traces the proverb to the Greek and French; *Oxford Proverbs*; etc.

9. John Macleod, ninth laird of Raasay (ca. 1710–1786) and Jane, daughter of Macqueen of Rigg (d. 1780), had thirteen children, ten of whom were daughters: Flora, Margaret, Janet, Catherine, Isabella, Julia, Jane, Anne, Mary, and Christiana.

The women, who married other Macleods, were Catherine, who married her first cousin John of Eyre, a lieutenant in the Royal Navy, and had no issue; Julia, who married Olans of Bharkasaig, and had four daughters; and Jane, who married her cousin John of Colbecks, had three sons (died young) and five daughters.

See Alexander Mackenzie, *History of the Macleods with Genealogies of the Principal Families of the Name* (Inverness: A. and W. Mackenzie, 1889), 375–89.

10. *A Journey to the Western Islands of Scotland* (London: W. Strahan and T. Cadell, 1775).

11. Frances Arabella Leeson (d. 1840), daughter of the first earl of Milltown, had married in 1791 Marcus Beresford (1764–1797), a grandson of the first earl of Tyrone.

Lady Charlotte Browne (d. 1852), daughter of Valentine, earl of Kenmare, married 13 May 1802 George Goold (1779–1870), second baronet (1818).

In 1788 Mary Forbes (1769–1852) married Alexander Grant (1760–1820), fourth baronet (S., 1796).

Fanny Maria (d. 1862), daughter of Matthew Lewis, under-secretary of war, married Henry Lushington (1775–1863), second baronet (1807).

12. The dowager countess of Buckinghamshire, Albinia, née Bertie (1738–1816), had in 1757 married George Hobart (1731–1804), third earl of Buckinghamshire (1793).

13. Elizabeth Cornwallis (1774–1813) was the daughter of James (1742/3–1824), bishop of Lichfield and Coventry, dean of Durham, fourth earl Cornwallis (1823).

14. Either Mary, née Hare (d. 1812), the wife of John Bagwell (ca. 1751–1816) of Marlfield, Clonmel, M.P. for county Tipperary (1801–6); or their pregnant daughter-in-law, Margaret Croker (d. 1873), originally of Ballynaguard, county Limerick, who had in 1808 married Richard Bagwell (ca. 1778–1825), M.P. for Cashel (1799), dean of Clogher (1805–25).

15. Margaret (Kearney), née Romer (d. 1815), had married Sir John Callendar, or Callender, in 1786. See HLP to JSPS, 19 February 1810, n. 2.

16. Samuel Richardson (1739–1824) of Hensol Castle, Pendoylan, Glamorgan (and of Newent, Glos.) was a grand juror at Great Sessions, sheriff of Glamorgan (1798), a founder of a bank in Cardiff in the 1790s, and an agricultural reformer. See the "Diaries of John Bird," in the South Glamorgan Reference Library, MS.2.716.

Prior to settling at Hensol Castle, which Richardson purchased in 1789, he married Harriet Philips. They had one surviving son, Henry, born 17 July 1791, and therefore a contemporary of JSPS. See the "Pendoylan Baptism Register"; "Lease and Release of Hensol Castle," 12 and 13 December 1815, C.R.O. Glamorgan.

TO THE REVEREND THOMAS SEDGWICK WHALLEY

Cheltenham
20: February 1811.

I begin by thanking my very dear Doctor Whalley for his kind—*kind* Letter, and Important Communication. It appears to me a good Project, Lands sell high at present, and if the Garden should not prove an Incumbrance—That Place might fetch a Sum the Interest of which would encrease my Income; and——If I *am* to live on——as People fancy, and as I sometimes *hope* for Three Years and 1/2: I might lay up Sixpence o'Year for the Child of my age, and as the Mahometans call an adopted Boy—The Son of my *Soul*: in Contradistinction to the Heirs of their Body begotten &c. My Agent and Counsellor Charles Shephard must be consulted as to *Securing* me the Life Interest of A Capital so obtained by my Permission to sell: and when His Advice is added to *your* Advice; I will not Suffer old Prejudices to stand in the Way of my Daughter's Advantage and My own.[1] Such a Scheme too, looks like Confidence in the Funds; which is consolatory in these Days of Doubt and Terror: I will come to Town before You leave it if possible—Tho' the People here are most un*de*servedly, and un*re*servedly kind, and we are fondled and Fêted as if we came to confer a Benefit; instead of rubbing away Rust, and chasing away Care. I thought it a good Place for Salusbury to finish his Christmas Holydays in——better than *always* shooting &c. and not so senseless a Mode of Amusement as running from Theatre to Theatre, from Spectacle to Spectacle in London; where no Ideas are obtained; no polished Manners are observed in so short a Moment as we had to command: for he leaves me next Monday Morning and in this little Fortnight I could scarce have entered him into any elegant Society——So much for my own Vindication in choosing *these Boards* to make our *petit Debût* upon.

Is the Prince of Wales seriously ill?[2] And are Lord and Lady Derby going to separate?[3] The one would be a heavy Calamity—The other—a melancholy Proof *indeed* of the Vanity of human Wishes. I rejoyce that our charming Siddons is well and gay; I saw Miss Cornwallis here: She seems in better Health now, and is laying her fine Heart out on a beautiful Baby Niece[4]——So I trust is Miss Thrale,—cy devant *Susan:* and Lady Keith says the Child has been ill——Oh Dear! I hope no harm will come to it——meaning Lady Keith's valuable Infant.

I *did* hear something of your having protected a wretched ill-used Lady, but know not the Particulars: I knew it was *not* my dear Lady Kirkwall. Her Husband is canvassing the *Borough of Denbigh*——*I think he* wants somebody to take Care of *him*.[5]

My lovely Friend Marianne Francis has been almost blind this Year,[6] and My *old* Friend Sir William Weller Pepys has gone and sate with her, for comfortable Chat.[7] You should have done so *too*; it would have been a nice Place, and such Conversation would have cured her of caring whether She ever got her Eyes again.

Adieu Dear Sir, and pray add to the Delights of Cheltenham, that of finding settled here Two of the ten Beautiful Daughters of Raasay—so often mentioned by Johnson in his Tour and Letters—They married other Macleods, and the Beauty of *their* Girls shews that they have no Tendency to Degeneration. Add another Thing to our Delights; that we pay Three Guineas o'Week for a better and much a *cleaner* Habitation than the Dust Basket I inhabited last May and June in Welbeck Street, for which 17 Guineas walked Weekly out of the Pockets of/ my kind Friend Doctor Whalley's/ ever grateful as Obliged Servant/ H: L: Piozzi.

Salusbury begs you will honour *his* Respects with Acceptance.

Text Berg Collection +. *Address* Rev: Doctor Whalley/ No. 45./ Baker's Street/
London. *Postmark* CHELTENHAM 21 FE 21 1811; A <   >.

1. At the suggestion of TSW, HLP hoped that her daughters would buy out her life interest in
Streatham Park and so relieve her of the care and cost of an estate that she rarely used. Much of
the spring of 1811 was given over to futile negotiation.
2. On 6 February the Regency Oath was administered to the Prince of Wales and in the days that
followed he was well and busy. On 18 February the *Morning Chronicle* claimed that he was ill and,
despite a repudiation by the *Courier*, e.g., on 19 February, there was public concern.
The *Morning Chronicle* had alleged:
The "Prince Regent has been confined to his room by a lameness, occasioned by a wound which
he received sometime ago by a horse treading on his toe. Mr. Home discovered on Friday that one
of the small bones was dislocated. On Saturday he was blooded. And from the inconvenience of
standing for a length of time, his intended Levee is adjourned till to-morrow se'nnight—before
which time the Surgeons expect him to be perfectly re-established."
3. The untrue rumors that Lord and Lady Derby were to separate after fourteen years of marriage
were typical of the gossip that circulated in resorts like Bath and Cheltenham.
4. Jemima Isabella (d. 1836), the child of James Mann Cornwallis (1778–1852), fifth earl (1824),
and Maria Isabella, née Dickens (d. 1823).
5. Lord Kirkwall was to sit for Denbigh Borough from 1812 to 1818.
6. On 15 February 1811, MF wrote:
"Since I had the happiness of writing to you last, my dearest Mrs. Piozzi, I have been as blind
as Samson—as lame as Mephibosheth—and I wish I could add as patient as Job. I began to look
about seriously for my *third* warning . . . but the *deafness* happily never came; and the rheumatism,
blindness and all are gone off. . . . If I can continue to recollect such a queer name as Sir William
Pepys's, I *ought;* for he has been very good, coming to see and amuse me during my misfortunes
. . . and always talked of *you* and made me laugh with Stories you told *him* 20 years ago" (Ry. 583.70).
Actually, MF began to experience optical difficulties early in January. According to Clement Francis
on 8 January (Ry. 584.168): "The other day at Richmond, She felt a small pain in her Eye, it increased
next day, and on coming to Town became so seriously painful, that She could bear no light, and
Was consequently obliged to sit in total darkness. . . . [Mr. Phipps, the oculist] put her in terrible
Torture lancing her Eye, putting sharp stuff into it &c. . . . Much Ulceration on the Eye lid. But She
is doing Well as the Norfolk Folk say and hopes soon to answer your letter."
7. For Sir William Weller Pepys, see HLP to SL, 26 February 1785, n. 9.

TO LADY WILLIAMS

Cheltenham
28: February 1811.

My dear Lady Williams
will do herself no harm by taking fat Dolly in lieu of pretty Mary. She is
perfectly honest, sober, and chearful about her Business—and as good a House
Maid as the next House Maid I think. They all like to eat as much, and do as
little as they can.—My purpose is to get *English* ones *this* Time, and see what
they will do.
Your Ladyship's Story of Lucien's Insolence is admirable, and I dare say perfectly true.[1] The poysoning Business too; how dreadful![2] Colonel Wardle has
flourished away finely:[3] nothing can quiet these naturally restless Spirits.
Our Ball and Supper was much liked, and will I fear be in the public Papers,
but I could do no less: for such Civilities were surely never lavished upon perfect

Strangers—as were bestowed on Salusbury and Myself upon our first Arrival. He left me for Enborne last Monday; notwithstanding a Thousand Temptations, particularly Lady Lushington's delightful Evening—but *Steady* should be his Motto; and none of their Seducements could perswade him to change His day. I wish Mr. Williams of Bodylwyddan his Friend and Namesake had been of our pleasant Party. I shall enquire for Mrs. Kingscote, and leave her a Card.[4]

Leak has been in London, and has seen Dear Mr. Charles Shephard, and seen Streatham Park—and brought me better hopes——We may possibly come to some Accommodation: I wait here to know how I can please the Ladies without Injuring myself—and am told, that a common Friend to all of us, has struck out a Way.[5] When I know more I will tell your Ladyship and Sir John, to whom I am so much obliged.

Leak set off for Wales yesterday, and poor Glover cries, faints and screams by Turns, so that We can hardly hold her.—but Doctor Jenner promises to do her good.[6]

Provisions are monstrously high here—Butter 2s. the Pound. Coals very dear, Poultry excellent and reasonable: and the Weather very mild as can be.

Lord Kirkwall's Advertisements are Strange Things Dear Madam! are they not? Will he really canvass Denbigh?—and carry it? We have had so much Electioneering Nonsense about these Counties and Boroughs; one dreads the very name on it.

Adieu! and present me kindly to all the Darlings: to their Papa, Their Uncle, Aunt and all who remember Their own/ H: L: P.

Text Ry. 3 (1807–1811). *Address* Lady Williams/ Bodylwyddan/ St. Asaph/ Flintshire/ N. Wales. *Postmark* CHELTENHAM 1 MA 1 1811 101.

1. The name of Lucien Bonaparte had occupied the attention of the British since the autumn of 1810. On 3 October the *Courier* reported "that Lucien Bonaparte is under British protection. He was not taken prisoner." Two days later the *Chester Chronicle* explained "that being required by his *Imperial* brother to repudiate his wife and bastardize his children, in order to take . . . a new wife, *a la Napoleon*, preparatory to his being appointed to *the Government of Rome*," he escaped "on board of an American vessel, with what valuables he had at hand, and effected a retreat to Sardinia, where he has placed himself under the protection of the English Government, who, for his greater security, have directed him and his family to proceed to Malta, till the pleasure of Government is known."

Never expecting to become a prisoner of war, he was just that. Therein lies his "insolence" or annoyance. According to the *Courier*, 4 January: "In consideration of Lucien Bonaparte's family, which consists chiefly of females, a good deal of pains has been taken in providing him with a comfortable residence [in Ludlow]: in other respects, he is treated as a prisoner of war, and is subject to whatever restraints Government thinks proper to impose."

2. The "Poysoning Business" grew out of reports similar to the following: "About eight months since, Napoleon sent an invitation for the appearance of Lucien's two eldest daughters, and his son Charles, at his Court. Charlotte only, who is 17 years of age, was permitted to avail herself of this imperial favour. She remained there about two months. Her return was rather precipitate; and for some reason or other . . . demonstrations of implacable resentment have been ever since so unequivocally manifested by Napoleon, that his brother was at length induced to make preparations for his removal" (*Courier*, 4 January 1811).

3. For Gwyllym Lloyd Wardle, see HLP to Ly W, 1 May; to Q, 20 June; to LC, 13 December (all in 1809).

4. A sister of Louisa Pennant, Harriet Peyton (b. 1778) had married in October 1794 Thomas Kingscote (d. 1811) of Randalls, Surrey.

5. TSW.
6. Edward Jenner (1749–1823), who received his M.D. from St. Andrews in 1793, discovered the smallpox vaccine in 1796.

TO MARGARET WILLIAMS

Cheltenham Wednesday
March 6: 1811

My Dear Miss Williams.—

Your Letter was a very kind one, and I owe You many Thanks for it: The good Advice shall not be lost assure yourself, if I live to make *new Disposition.*

Salusbury is a fortunate Fellow in finding and in making Friends: 'Tis astonishing how he has pleased the People of this Place; who—every one of them meet me (now he is gone back)—with some Instance of the Prudence and Propriety of his Conduct whilst among us.

Mrs. and Miss Macleods, and Lady Grant are indeed a charming Family; much attached as You say to The Bamford Heskeths,[1] and quite the first People here—Tho' we have Quality Folks enough too—but nothing of higher *Extraction* than the Lairds of Raasay I believe.

You will have heard how soon poor dear old Hamilton followed his hapless Daughter.[2] Lady Aldborough finds it a famous Windfall for *her:*[3] tho' the Accident of injuring an Artery in letting Blood, has deferred her present Pleasures and Enjoyment. Mrs. Pennant's Sister is not yet here,[4] and many of our Winterbirds will take flight soon, making room for a gayer Set—Tho' we have been very gay *too.*—Balls, Suppers, Feasts, Breakfasts have succeeded one another ever since I have been at Cheltenham, and are scarce over now.

My own Anxiety concerning Streatham Park is not quite removed, but Charles Shephard writes me Encouraging Letters; and If I can but live four or five Years—All may yet be well, for my Dear Boy and for myself; but he is *fated* I think to pass his *early* Years in wishing a long Continuance of my *late* ones. Next Month will take me to London for 3 or 4 Weeks—no more. Dear charming Lady Kirkwall is so pressing with her Invitation I shall certainly accept of it, while he is fixing at Oxford:—and then come home to repose my Empty Purse, and cool my Head after our Christmas Gambols.

Lady Derby is never seen Separate from her Lord They tell me; and yet there are Reports of Disagreement—which nobody seems to understand.—We are likewise made to believe Sir Watkin Williams is dying,[5] and Lord Kirkwall actually incites to canvass the Borough of Denbigh. Can such Things be? The Sale of Lleweney Effects are advertised I see. Surely I shall get some of my old Ancestor's Armour—Sir John the Strong's Spurs at least——or his Sword to hang up at poor Bachygraig.[6]

I am writing now to put Lake in Mind to bid for them.

Adieu Dear Miss Williams! Present me most affectionately to all Friends at Bodylwyddan as I am ever/ Theirs and Yours most faithfully/ H: L: Piozzi.

Text Ry. 8 (1808–1812). *Address* Miss Williams/ Bodylwyddan/ St. Asaph/ Flintshire/ North Wales. *Postmark* CHELTENHAM 6 MA 6 1811 101.

1. Robert Bamford-Hesketh (d. 1815) of Bamford Hall and Upton, had married in 1787 Frances, née Lloyd (d. 1797), heiress of Gwyrch Castle, Denbighshire. Their children were Lloyd (1788–1861), Robert (d. 1815), John (d. 1870), Frances (d. ca. 1860), and Ellen (d. 1864).
2. The Reverend Frederick Hamilton died in Bath in February 1811, aged ninety-three. His daughter was Jane Holman, who had died in June 1810.
3. For Elizabeth, Lady Aldborough, see HLP to PSP, 4 October 1798, n. 2.
4. For Harriet Kingscote, see HLP to Ly W, 28 February 1811, n. 4.
5. For Sir Watkin Williams-Wynn, see HLP to LC, 17 June 1798, n. 11.
6. Sir John Salusbury (d. 1612). His sword was one of the "rareties" at Llewenny. See *Thraliana*, 2:975, n. 2.
According to Salusbury genealogical legend, Sir John the Strong "had two Thumbs on each Hand, was eminent for performing singular Feats, and he married Lady Ursula Stanley [illegitimate daughter of Henry, fourth earl of Derby], & had by her a son whose Name was Henry & was the first Baronet of the Family" (*Thraliana*, 1:275).

TO JOHN SALUSBURY PIOZZI SALUSBURY

Cheltenham
9: March 1811.

How well is my kind and Considerate *Friend*,——my best-loved Salusbury— acquainted with the Constitution of his poor Aunt! whose *thin-worne* Mind though shining still perhaps, in conversation or Correspondence; is no longer buoyant as it used to be: but begins to want support from his more youthful and elastic Powers. With such Support however, it would be graceless to feel Depression of Spirits; and I will learn—as the Apostle teaches,——to be content.[1]

Poor Lady Meredith's sudden Seizure at the Card Table however, gives a temporary Shock to everyones Nerves here;[2] Young Barrett[3] had just paid her 200£ She won of him, and down She dropt in an Apoplectic Fit——Prelude to many more no doubt:—her State of Insensibility lasted an hour—Doctor Jenner is in London giving Evidence in the Berkeley Cause[4]—all the other Physicians of the Place have been called in, tho' Mrs. Bagwell[5] who has never left her Bed since our Ball,—employs one of them perpetually. Her Husband is returned from Ireland and attends her with great Assiduity. What Young Women these are to be so taken with dangerous Illness! Would It not force one upon Reflexion? Would it not make one feel that Feasts and Frolics are no good Preparatives for the only unchangeable Condition of Mankind! I am not pleased either with Lake's Delay to write, nor quite free of Apprehensions that something has happened wrong at dear *dear* Brynbella. But so sweet, so wise, so lovely is your Letter, that if I am too restless for expectation of good Sleep tonight, I will put it under my Pillow as I used to do those from Your Uncle.

Ah Salusbury! how have You and Yours withdrawn my whole heart from its old Channel!——never well cut indeed for my Affections to flow in; but where

they *did* flow uniformly and tranquilly, however inclined to Dulness and Stagna-
tion—Charles Shephard gives hopes of Streatham Park being set to Sale, and
good hopes of a good Purchaser.—*Hopes*! of seeing The Vault where lies my
Mother close to the Husband whom She chose for *me* Sold to a Jew, or Stock
Broker perhaps. Yet 'tis the Thing I now most wish to see Effectuated and do
earnestly pray that the Affair may be finished with the Ladies in *dumb Show*.
They write civil Letters about any thing else, and never name the Place of their
Youth; from whence They seemed weaned as well as myself. But *I* have my own
natural and paternal Acres to recur to, and I have a Boy, a dear adopted Son,
to accept and improve them. And after taking my *last Leave* of my *first* Settlement
in this World, home I will go, and wait for *his Arrival*. This is a mere Effusion
of my Heart—mind;—written between Your Letter's coming *In*, and the Post
going *out*—So I will take My Darling Child's Advice, and brush up my Looks,
and dine at Mrs. Doyne's.[6] The Countess of Buckinghamshire gives a Breakfast
Fête next Tuesday and came and wrote *herself*—not Miss Dere—to invite me.

Now then Farewell! best and Dearest of all Creatures to Your Affectionate H:
L: Piozzi.

I keep hanging after the Richardsons[7] and Northeys,[8] because You loved *them*,
and I doat on that Mr. Reed of the Crescent[9] because he says *You love me*. Selfish
enough and simple enough, but so it is.

Now tell whether I shall come to Newbury in April or to Oxford in Early
May? I will do as You would have me, and as you find best for your own Pleasure
and Advantage.

Robert calls me to give the Letter, tis almost 4 o'Clock.

Text Ry. 585.91. *Address* John Piozzi Salusbury Esq./ at The Rev: T. Shephard's/
Enborne/ near Newbury/ Berks. *Postmark* CHELTENHAM 9 MA 9 1811 101 (In
JSPS's hand "Received March 12th 1811. Answered Do 14th Do").

1. 1 Timothy 6:8; Hebrews 13:5.
2. HLP refers to the first wife of Joshua Colles Meredyth (1771–1850), of Pelletstown; sheriff of
county Dublin, 1793; knighted (as the first son of a baronet) on 16 May 1793, being then captain in
the 89th Foot.
    On October 14: "In Dublin, aged 64, [died] Sir Barry Colles Meredyth, bart. father of Sir Joshua
M. . . . on whom his title and estates have devolved." See *GM* 83, pt. 2 (1813): 506.
    Sir Joshua had married in 1795 Maria, née Coyne Nugent, who was to die, aged thirty-five, on
15 October 1813, the day after her husband succeeded as eighth baronet.
3. Eaton Stannard Barrett (1786–1820) was a native of Cork who received his B.A. from Trinity
College in 1805. Although he entered the Middle Temple, London, he was apparently never called
to the bar. A writer of satires, he was best known for *All the Talents, a Satirical Poem in Three Dialogues*,
written under the pseudonym of Polypus in ridicule of the Grenville ministry.
4. Frederick Augustus Berkeley (1745–1810), fifth earl of Berkeley (1755) married Mary, née Cole
(d. 1844), daughter of a "Publican and Butcher." According to her oath in 1811 before the Lords'
committee for privileges, the marriage was first celebrated 30 March 1785, and subsequently, without
question, in May 1796. Lord Berkeley settled Berkeley Castle and his other estates on their first son,
William Fitz Hardinge Berkeley (d. 1857), who from 1796 onwards was styled Viscount Dursley.
    With the earl's death in 1810, William could not succeed to his father's honors on the grounds of
illegitimacy, the marriage of 1785 not having been verified. This decision was to be made on 1 July
1811 by the Lords without dissent. The honors then passed to William's younger brother, Thomas

Moreton Fitz Hardinge (later FitzHardinge) Berkeley (1796–1882), who was the fifth but first legitimate son of his parents.

5. See HLP to Ly W and MW, [16 February 1811], n. 14.

6. Annette Constantia (Uniacke), née Beresford (d. 1836) had taken as her second husband on 2 July 1805 Robert Doyne (1782–1850), of Wells, county Wexford.

7. See HLP to Ly W and MW [16 February], n. 16.

8. The Reverend Edward Northey (1754–1828), canon of Windsor, later of Box, Wilts. and Woodcote, Epsom, Surrey, had married 3 March 1794 Charlotte, née Taylor (d. 1837). Their elder son, Edward Richard (1795–1878), was a friend of JSPS.

9. The houses in the Crescent (today the Royal Crescent) were built between 1805 and 1810 and were intended mainly as lodgings for seasonal visitors. We cannot, therefore, identify Mr. Reed with any certainty, his name not being listed in any of the Cheltenham rate books.

TO ALEXANDER LEAK

Sunday
10: March 1811.

If Leak knew the Uneasiness caused by his Silence he surely would have written before now. Ten Days have elapsed since he left Cheltenham, and no Accounts from dear Brynbella either *before* or *Since*——altho' no one can know better than he does, that however Streatham Park may occupy the Mind of its once happy Mistress during its *present unsettled State*, all her Care and Affections have reverted to her native and natural home: an anxious Love of which will make her most solicitous for its Safety and Welfare while She remains able to write/ Herself/ H: L: Piozzi.

If any harm has happened to Leak himself—(which God forbid,) He would surely have sent Word by some Means.

Text Hyde Collection. *Address* Mr. Alexander Leak/ Brynbella/ near/ Denbigh/ North Wales. *Postmark* CHELTENHAM 11 MA 11 1811.

TO JOHN SALUSBURY PIOZZI SALUSBURY

Sunday Night
10: March 1811.

Incomparable Salusbury! The sweet Promise given in Your Letter dated Wensday the 6th of March—of clearing out that well-regulated Mind of yours, so as to receive future Impressions; deserves *Pages after Pages* of approving Tenderness from Me, whose Prayers are perpetually directed to request for You, as happy a Future in this transitory Life, as can consist with permanent Felicity in the next. Nor am I—like Eastern Bonzees, or Carthusian Monks disposed to think that Heaven is to be purchased only by sublunary Sorrow. A good Man scarcely *can* be very sorrowful;—his Chearfulness is increased by Consciousness of good Intention

What nothing Earthly gives or can destroy,
The Soul's calm Sunshine and the heart-felt Joy;

is Virtue's Prize: as your Friend Pope says.[1]—Long! long may you enjoy it! Let Oxford, as Bath and Cheltenham have done—bear witness to my Darling's Triumph over Temptation; and to the Power of restraining Grace over his pure and honourable Mind: *my* Sun will set delightfully indeed, and leave my Soul no Sentiment but Gratitude in her last Stage of temporal Existence.

Meanwhile I am foolish enough to wish the Year 1814 was nearer.

I shall want *you*, more than You *Me* by that Time. Lake's Letter is arrived—dictated by a half sullen, half querulous Spirit. And Robert——is either out till one o'Clock in the Morning, or sitting in my Servant's hall surrounded by a rascally Set of Waiters from the Rooms, and other Worthies of a like Description——I cannot part with him as you know—and as he knows—come what may; till we arrive in London. I cannot trust myself to a Sick Maid and an Ignorant Infant,——we should not get ten Miles out of the Town. Well! never mind: my Two Months are up the first Monday in April, and I am in *no Danger*——keeping so very little Money in the house, and plenty of Friends round. Let us talk of a Young Fellow in higher Life but I suppose of no more Thoughtful Temper than poor Robert, and like him led away by Vicious Company: *Charles Henry* by Name, and Hero of the Novel I promised our Friend Pemberton.[2] He was brought up as you both are, and have been; at a private School; and was a favourite with his Master[3]——Lord Moira his Uncle I think—at least his Protector.[4] From the University he dropt into the gay Scenes of London, and Lady Aldborough—Sister to poor Jane Holman—fastened on his Heart. They led a fashionable Life for Some time, till her fair Daughter's Charms rivaled her own—and for an hour he prefered Lady Emily.[5] The Crime was known, the Noise was loud; Lord Moira withdrew his Protection, and the young Man fled, but fled with undiminished Gaiety to Dublin, where he had Hosts of Friends. There, by mere Chance he met in Merion Square his old Preceptor Mr.—Such a one; and accosting him familiarly with My dear Sir—I'm glad to see *you* here——to which no Reply was given—Why don't you know Charles Henry? he exclaimed; No Sir, indeed I do not was the Answer; from my Charles Henry I had formed far other Expectations——Good Morrow.—The Blow however well deserved came suddenly, and struck deep. The Youth went home was seized with something of a Shivering Fit, and calling up the Person that he lodged with, bid her enquire his old Preceptor out, and give him a little Note which he was holding in his hand.——The Purport of it was "I am struck with Death; my Heart is broken, but let me feel your Hand in mine once more—While yet my own is capable of the Impression." The Tutor flew to his Dear Boy's Relief, and found him overwhelmed with Guilt and Shame: administered the kindest Consolations—gave him the Sacrament, witnessed his Will by which he left the little All he had—3000£—in Stock only, to the poor worthless Girl he thought he had seduced:—and wrote a Letter Henry dictated—endeavouring to awaken Lady Aldborough's Mind to a Sense of her Dangerous Courses.——She spurned his Counsel and hated only his Preference of Lady Emily:—but now, that Her ill Health follows so fast upon her Lover's Death——dear Mrs. Orr[6] (who told me these particulars) begins to feel some hope of *her* Conversion—Mrs. Orr is Niece to poor old Hamilton's Lady[7]—Cousin to these Girls—as I call them—The Countess and Jane Holman. And now is not this a Melancholy Story?—a Sunday Night Sermon? I leave off here and go to Bed, if anything occurs (in my Dreams) The Morning shall relate it. God bless you Dearest—and fail not still to fear God and love/ Your own Aunt/ H: L: P.

Lady Meredith is recovering—as Mr. Thrale recovered; to relapse again as Mr. Thrale relapsed; with every Appetite sharpened by Disease; and consciousness of Danger lulled fast asleep.

Morning is come, The 11th Morning of this Month Monday—and all my bills to pay—I have sent the Cook off——our present Cook; She belongs it seems to a House of Ill Fame across the Street, whither my Mutton goes by Pieces at a Time. My Throat however is uncut still; and I lay no more Meat upon my own Account than if it was cut already. We shall do better now without any one in her Place——The new Servant intended for Brynbella I have a complete Character of:—This was but a Temporary Business, and one can't wonder. Whilst you are well and wise and good: No Care (except how to be thankful enough) shall come near the Heart of your/ H: L: Piozzi.

Give best Regards to Pem: I expect a kind Invitation from You both.

Mrs. Pennant of Downing is come; I am thinking how her Son's Play or Puppet Show would look[8]——by my Salusbury's Ball and Supper.

Text Ry. 585.92. *Address* John Piozzi Salusbury Esq./ at The Rev: T: Shephard's/ Enborne/ near Newbury/ Berkshire. *Postmark* CHELTENHAM 11 MA 11 1811 101 (In JSPS's hand "Received March 13th 1811. Answered Do 14th Do").

1. *Essay on Man*, 4.167–70.

2. The hero of the novel is not Charles Henry but the title character of *Charles Henly; or the Fugitive Restored*, 2 vols., by Sarah Green, published in 1790.

3. The anecdote of Charles Henry seems to have circulated among Irish friends at Cheltenham. Because she was relatively unfamiliar with the names and persons, she made identification subordinate to a moral lesson for JSPS.

4. Francis Rawdon-Hastings, second earl Moira, had associations with the surname of Henry. His half sister, Catherine (d. 1780), had married in 1764 Joseph Henry of Straffan, county Kildare. Along with three daughters, they had two sons: John Joseph and Arthur (ms. 385, Genealogical Office, Dublin Castle; now at the National Library of Ireland). In short, had there been a *Charles* Henry, Lord Moira would have been his uncle.
For Lord Moira, see HLP to Henry Barry, 19 October 1789, n. 4; and to PSP, 19 September 1793, n. 11.

5. For Emily, the youngest daughter of Lord and Lady Aldborough, see HLP to PSP, 4 October 1798, n. 2.

6. Probably Elizabeth Orr, née Daniel (d. 1835), originally of Belfast, county Antrim. See the "Prerogative Wills Index," P.R.O., Ireland.

7. For Rachel Hamilton, who died in 1805, see HLP to Ann Greatheed, 2 April [1788][b], n. 4.

8. The son of David (1764–1841) and Louisa (née Peyton) Pennant, residents of Downing in Bodfari, the younger David (1796–1835) was three years the junior of JSPS. He attended Harrow (1807–13) and matriculated at Christ Church, Oxford, 27 January 1814. See also HLP to Thomas Pennant, 2 June 1795, n. 3.

TO THE REVEREND LEONARD CHAPPELOW

Cheltenham
Saturday 16: March 1811.

My dear Mr. Chappelow's Letter shall not lie an hour unanswered, nor my ever true and kind and partial Friend Mr. Este's good Natured Remark on my Conduct,—unacknowledged.[1] I was glad by Lord Torington's Franked Cover, to find at least *one* Contemporary above Ground:[2]——You are our *Junior* you know.[3] Pluto will not touch poor Mrs. Hamilton I hope——She had Punishments enough *here*—had She not?—so had Jane Holman whose Deathbed I witnessed; and Doctor Whalley's demi-divine Behaviour to her.—Wretched Lady!![4]

I could not come thro' Llangollen,[5] the Snows were higher than the Carriage in a less dangerous Road—but I had an able-bodied and active-Souled Youth to take Care of me, who makes Friends wherever he goes; The People here were so *very kind* on our Arrival, I felt bound to make them some Compensation—— So my young Spark rounded his Christmas Holydays with a gay Ball, and returned (more willingly than any other Boy on Earth would have done,) to his Studies at Enborne.

I am going to London *in* a fortnight and *for* a Fortnight——just to see what the Ladies mean to do about old Streatham Park——Doctor Whalley gave me a hint as if Selling it would be eligible, but the fair Principals——my amiable Reversionaries are Silent; and I have done being amused with *Dumb-Show* Transactions: a *Pantomime* of such Importance would only leave *me* the Character of *Mother Goose:* though my heart applauds the Project as likely to profit all Parties——but then we must talk it over. Abbe Davies wrote me such Letters about the Place as gave me very serious Concern; and afterwards told a Man I sent to enquire,——*That it was all a Joke*. But he is so tenderly attached to pretty Mrs. Mostyn and her Triumvirate as you call them,[6] that I must forgive his hurrying my Spirits—The sooner I depart, The greater *their Advantage:* Not so my dear, Affectionate Salusbury, a valuable Child to me, and very justly beloved by your old Friend and his old Aunt/ H: L: Piozzi.

He is at Enborne now with Mr. Shephard—brushing up for College. Lord Torington is right not to take L'Eau Medicinale,[7] and you are right to take it—— new-arrived Gout it may drive away[8]——but such a Lease as it has taken long ago of poor Lord T's Tenement——how will it dislodge? Had Piozzi known of it 20 Years back, I should not yet have used *my Widow Seal*——but never mind;—Sequor.

Text Ry. 561.144. *Address* Rev. Mr. Chappelow < > *Postmark* < >
1811.

1. HLP responds to LC's whimsical letter, dated from Ham Common, 14 March, which began: "Are you dead or alive?—alive and aLive Like, says Mr. Este:—and she is giving, in conformity with her hospitable and amiable generosity—fine suppers &c. &c.—at Cheltenham. And her Fine boy Salisbury is doing the honours of her entertainments.—And she is in perfect health and spirits.—And when does she come to London? That she alone can tell you" (Ry. 563.92).
2. For John Byng, fifth viscount Torrington, see HLP to Q, 22 March 1810, n. 21.
3. LC was born in 1744, HLP in 1741.
4. LC had written that "during my Confinement in the winter . . . I prepared papers for my executors—and I have reserved yours every one—would you believe it—its number 212—We must all by and by *depart*—I see poor Mr. Hamilton is gone to Elysium to see his wife—if *Pluto has not got hold of her*—and his singing Daughter."
5. HLP comes as close as she ever would in disputing the word of the Ladies of Llangollen who, according to LC, "put me in a passion. They will have it you are in London—What said I—and i Little I not know it. No—no I shall hear of her when she comes.—"
6. LC had written: "3 days ago—I met Mrs. Mostyn—with one of her Little Triumvirate—she Looked extremely well, in good spirits."
7. Eau Medicinale was "the celebrated medicine which in gouty complaints produces extraordinary effects." Although its ingredients were unknown, "it has no mineral in it. & its quality is of a vegetable nature. . . . at present, as no medicine will suit all constitutions, objections have been made to it on acct. of unfavourable effects having been produced in some instances" (Farington, 11:3873).
8. According to LC's letter: "Thank God I am now recovered, but I have been coughing all winter—and nursing a gouty hand—but I was determined, not to be in many days agony.—Mine was the first fit—but tolerably severe.—I treated my maiden fit—with as much care and gentleness— as the virgin had reason to expect—I took the Eau Medicinale 3 successive nights—and on the 3 night—I most effectually succeeded in conquering, the warm virgin who so violently had taken me by the right hand.—in short 20 drops taken for 3 nights—sickened my companion, and I rejoice that I am at least for a time divorced.—I wish I could at least for a time persuade my good old present Landlord Lord Torrington to try the experiment, which has given such universal relief to 1000ds.—He is too obstinately determined against it—and flys into a passion, when we mention it to him."

TO JOHN SALUSBURY PIOZZI SALUSBURY

Cheltenham Sunday
17: March 1811.

My dearest Child's last kind Letter I took from the Post Office myself this Morning as I came from Church——The last but *one* lived in my Pocket till this came; It says how welcome *mine* are; and that my Admonitions are not lost. Oh! I am well perswaded—that altho' I *have* preached to cold Ears crammed full with Cotton——The dying Swan will ever have to say non canimus Surdis.[1] When the black, deep, dividing Gulph is passed by your poor Aunt, you will consider these Pages as her Shadows; and prize them accordingly—not for their Wit, because the Head that has nothing better than Wit in it, is scarce worth a Stroke from a French Guillotine: but for the Heart which dictates every Line; and which I hope will not beat above Three Strokes more, if Ever by Your Conduct—or my Calamity, (in losing my Reason,) Dear Salusbury ceases to be Master of it. The

Servant and the Mare are *Your own,* and if you have no better Luck than I have had, there is a Chance of Plague enough with both. Mr. Reed of the Crescent thinks there is a Club of Infernals here, and I think if there is such a Thing—— Robert belongs to it——but Let'n bite'n (as the Booby Lad said of the Tyger;) a' can't hurt *we.* I wish that nothing vexed me more than Robert! but I have heard by a Side-Wind that our Ladies mean to contest My Power over the Plate, Furniture, &c. their Father left——which they aver was only for My Life.——A fine Affair! Why 30 Years ago, in Sight of all the Executors I made Mr. Perkins a Present of the Furniture belonging to the Borough-house[2]—You saw it there; Why did they not object to such a Measure?——The Plate I *sold*——except a Bread Basket and Candlesticks I gave Miss Thrale last Year and the Year before: If they were not left to my Disposal Why were they accepted?——But the News comes not from Charles Shephard, and may be false: I have written to him about it, and charged him to make strict Examination that no dormant Claims may come out against my *Residuary Legatee:* but that all may be cleared and settled whilst I have the Power of reimbursing myself in my own hands.——For such I *have,* Therefore You may say Let'n bite'n.—They shan't hurt *Thee.*

All Argus's Eyes[3] however are barely sufficient to keep one from being tricked out of one's Money, one's kindness and one's good Opinion. A Friend here said She would recommend a Young Gentleman of Christ Church to your particular Regard—

> I thanked her on my bended Knee
> And drank a Quart of Milk and Tea[4]

as Prior said but when I dived into the Character of this approved Intimate—— I found from a Man who knew him in early Youth, that at 12 or 13 Years old he had most *dishonourable* nay truly *dishonest* Propensities——and that there was even Question of a Silver Spoon!!

How far the Current of such innate Meanness can be worked clear from 12 Years old to 20 I cannot tell;——but tho' I liked his Conversation well enough, My Heart turned away from all Thought of my *Child's* Acquaintance with him.

Early Vices contaminate a Character for ever, Early Virtues sanctify one; The Literature obtained before 18—is that best remembered in our Progress to 80: And The Man who drinks heavy Loads of Strong Beer during the Dinner— finds them count heavy on his Head towards Midnight; he can't keep Pace with a Companion who never begins till the Cloth is taken away; besides that if you rub the Early Bloom off a beautiful Plumb,—it will gain no more Maturity tho' it still hangs upon the Tree. A French Writer would say Suivez vous autres la Chaine de tout cela.

I have no Objection to have *you* remembered, You *are* remembered by every body here; all are asking when I got a Letter, and I enclose one from Mr. Chappelow which will amuse You.[5] The Mr. Este he mentions, gave me your curious little Sedan Virgil 20 Years ago;[6] and has been ever my true and disinterested, and sincere and useful Friend—'Spite of our constant Difference of Opinion concerning Politics &c. &c.[7] He will now love Salusbury because he is My

Boy. What a Sweet-blooded Creature it is!! Should it ever fall in your way to do his Progeny any Service—forget not what I said of him.——Now don't you fancy me lowspirited——I shall do well enough, and walk up the Mount at Marlborough I hope, as I did for the first Time in 1751—but as poor Chappelow says—We must depart.—*My* Journey will be deferred I dare say till I have settled this Streatham Park Business——God Almighty has been so good to You in bringing it out now when no harm can Come of it; but is not our Friend Edward Pemberton indignant against the Ladies?

I am glad there are but Two Weeks now before I see you once more in your present State, and give you a true School boy's Kiss.——Pray Sir, (as you are so soon to be a Gentleman at large) how did your Honour's Servant go down to Brynbella? My Darling had no Money to pay his Expences I fear: and Plimmer Arrian will become a Serious Consideration to us soon.[8] But my Heart confides in the good Sense and good Principles of Dear Salusbury. I tell you that 'tis upon *no common* Boy, Hundred Pound Feasts have been bestowed——whilst even a new Gown is grudged to *herself* by his Affectionate Parent——and/ anxious Friend/ H: L: Piozzi.

Oh Pray recollect to ask if Vashti is the real name of any woman, or given her for a Joke.[9]

Mrs. Pennant is come hither to consult Dr. Jenner about her Sister's sick Husband: She says Lord K. will carry his Election. West and Biddulph who married the two Miss Myddeltons have quarreled, and the first gives his Interest to Lord K—— to spite the other.[10]

Charles Shephard is out of Town, so gives no Answer to my anxious Letter:——I hope 'tis only a false Alarm after all.

Text Ry. 585.94. *Address* J. P. Salusbury Esq.

1. See Virgil, *Eclogues*, 10.8.
2. For John Perkins and HLT's gift to him in June 1781, see John Field to HLP, 28 December 1791, n. 2.
3. A monster in Greek mythology who (depending on the source) had a third eye in the back of his neck, or four eyes—two before and two behind—or as many as one hundred eyes. Panoptes never closed all of his eyes.
4. See *Alma*, 3.222–23:

> The youngster, who at nine and three
> Drinks with his sisters milk and tea.

5. LC's letter of 14 March (Ry. 563.92) with its "How does—Young Salisbury?—with me, as well as with every one who knows him—he is a great favourite."
6. Publii Virgilii Maronis, . . . *Opera indubitata omnia, ad doctiss. R. P. Jacobi Pontani castigationes accuratissime excusa*. (Sedani, ex typogr. et typ. novissimis Jannoni, 1625).
7. HLP distrusted Charles Este as much for "&c. &c." as for his "radical" politics. See HLP to Sophia Byron, 1 September [1789]; and to Charles Este, 26 June 1793.
Despite her differences with Este—and even anger—she never dismissed him, as had one of her favorite conservative newspapers, the *True Briton* on 1 January 1796: "Mr. Este.—Some conversation happening to take place relative to this extraordinary character, a Gentleman observed, 'the name of that man never should be mentioned but upon the *first of April.*'"
8. HLP apparently is being playful with two dialect words related to "plim" (swell out, increase

in bulk) and "ary" or "harry" (the act of robbing or plundering). That is, are HLP and JSPS to increase their financial resources by pillaging or other illegal means? HLP uses the term later in HLP to JSPS, 9 March 1815.

9. Vashti was the queen of Ahasuerus (Xerxes I), king of Persia. She was repudiated by him and succeeded by Esther. See the Book of Esther, esp. chaps. 1 and 2.

10. For the marriage of Maria Myddelton to Frederick West, see HLP to LC, 8 or 9 June 1798, n. 7. For the marriage of her sister Charlotte to Robert Biddulph, see HLP to Ly W, 9 February 1810, n. 1.

For the Myddeltons of Chirk Castle, see HLP to LC, 17 June 1798, n. 3.

TO LADY KEITH

25: March 1811.

My dear Lady Keith is too kind in troubling herself a Moment about my Petition, *for* whom I have little Care, and *with* whom I have no Correspondence.[1] The Duke of Gloucester has my heartiest Wishes.—It is so pretty in him to try, and it is so offensive to resist and repel every Effort of the Royal Family to please and conciliate Mankind.[2]

Baby must keep her little Bowels open, and her Gums will open too.

You ask me who is Doctor Charles Burney? I reply That he is a Man so celebrated for Greek Literature that he is considered as a Bishop expectant.[3] That he is The *Son* of old Doctor Burney, The Brother for whose Relief when he was *not* a Bishop expectant Madame D'Arblaye wrote her Novel called Evelina, and Sold it for Ten or Twenty Pounds.[4] That he is The Man who about Seven and Twenty Years ago presided over a Magazine in which all Libels on H: L: Piozzi were received which other Repositories of the same Sort had rejected as over scurrilous; That he is The Man who about seven years ago at Bath sent me a most flattering Letter, and requested the *honour* of my Acquaintance.[5] That he is The Man—I shewed your fine Abraxas to—on *that Occasion;* and he knew no more about the Matter than my Chambermaid. That he is the Man I went last Spring to hear preach at St. George's Bloomsbury, with his Niece Miss Marianne Francis; but we were disappointed, and heard only his Imitator who told us of the polite Athenians, The Vain-Glorious Romans, and I know not who beside. That he is the Man who *keeps* the great Grammar School at Greenwich[6] where the Boys learn Eschylus, Sophocles &c. and come away Saying that he *keeps* the famous Sabrina educated by Mr. Day—for his *Housekeeper.* Cætera desunt. Did you expect such an Answer? I trow *not.*

Poor Duc D'Albuquerque and the Culprit, had *Themselves* too strongly in their own Hearts and Minds.[7]—They lose their Senses and their Lives thro' Egotism— I have kept both by caring so very little about myself——but by the same Trick I have caught Cold—a rare Thing for me to do—but even a favourable March brings Tendency towards Ill Health, so does October: one never passes either without a rough Salute: Lord Keith must make haste to be well.

You used to love Literary History, I confess *myself fond* of it to excess; and this new Edition of Pope's Works by Bowles will of course ruin me;[8] A Gentleman here has lent it for my Reading, and so keenly *vient l'Appetit en mangeant,* that I feel I must buy, and carry it home to Wales. The Story in it of Dr. Waterland's Agony at being mistaken for Warburton kept me in a loud Laugh even when alone.[9]

I am in Love with Cecy's Doctor Jenner here: and wish to get him the *original* Edition of dear Hogarth's Anaylsis of Beauty with the Plates—*Quarto.* Could you direct me where to apply for such a Treasure? I would not give my own away—*unless to save the Nation.* If you have Friends among the Book-fanciers, they could direct one;[10] you know of Course that Paul Whitehead wrote it for Hogarth under his Direction——Hogarth pretended not to Literature, or Abilities for Composition.[11]

I shall be in Town for Two or Three Weeks in April at Lady Kirkwall's Manchester Street; but shall have no Time for any Thing but shake hands, and God Bless; as my Furlough like my Paper will only serve to say that I am ever Affectionately Yours/ and your Sisters' H: L: P.

The People here are giving Balls and Suppers and Fêtes and Dejeuners—all Day and all night, and every Day and every Night——and yet persist in perswading Themselves That *none was like* ours—so I'm glad.—

How stands You Peeresses towards the Berkeley Cause? *We* all wish for the eldest son here in Gloucestershire.——Jack Gillon's Will is thrown into Chancery I hear; but never mind![12] I suppose I am Sure of my Shakespeare. Possession we are always told, counts for nine Points in the Law.[13]

Oh! I forgot: tho' Sunday still reminds me of a Monument over our Pew, where lies Anna Caroletta Maria Wife to Sir Francis Hartwell Bart. Daughter to John *Elphinstone* Esq. aged 45.[14]

> Adeste! Juvenes! Lugete;
> Fuit enim pulchra, Pia;
> Seb ob Pietatem pulchrior.

Pretty enough! Does Lord Keith acknowledge his Cousin? And is there any more to be Said of her?

We have some Relations here at Prestbury—Sir William Fowler's Grandchildren—who married My Mother's Aunt.[15] The same degree of Kindred as Dear Lucy Mackay who lives in Baker Street[16]—and the rakish Marquis of Headfort.——They are poor, proud, and pretty.[17]

Adieu—Your Ladyship's *tripsey* Mother will be knocking at your Door (I think so at least) next Saturday Sennight: and if You are not at home I shall ask for Baby.

Write to me once more tho'.

Text Bowood Collection. *Address* R: H: Baroness Keith.

1. HLP had written three relatively short notes to Q in February and March prior to the twenty-fifth: on 21 February to ask about the baby, who had been ill; on 28 February to relate anecdotes on death; on 11 March to present the request of John Gillon's old servant for a position. Unable to

use the woman herself, Q had apparently involved the charitable and compassionate duke of Gloucester in finding her a place.

2. For William Frederick, second duke of Gloucester, see HLP to PSP, 5 November 1803, n. 5.

3. The road to ecclesiastical preferment was made possible for Charles Burney Jr. through the intervention of Martin Davy (1763–1839), M.D., D.D., and master of Caius College, Cambridge. Davy put Burney's name forward as a candidate for the degree of M.A., in 1808. He was also to receive the degree of D.D. from the archbishop of Canterbury in 1812.

For Burney's livings in 1810 and 1811, see HLP to Sophia Byron, 8 June 1788, n. 6. According to Marianne Francis to HLP on 28 May 1811, "he will have had at 45, more than 2000 a year Preferment, after having been but 2 years in the Church" (*Journals and Letters*, 7:27, n. 10).

4. *Evelina* was sold in 1778 to the bookseller Thomas Lowndes for twenty guineas, with her brother acting as "agent" in the transaction.

That Charles Burney Jr. could have used some "Relief" in that year is true, since he had been expelled from Cambridge in the autumn of 1777 for stealing books from the Caius College library. There is, however, no indication that FB shared, or ever intended to share, her meager profits with him.

5. See HLP to Charles Burney Jr., 24 January 1807, n. 3.

6. About 1811 Charles Burney Jr. was to turn over the mastership of the profitable Greenwich school to his son, Charles Parr (1785–1864). As a result of the transfer, the older man took up residence in his rectory at Deptford, bringing with him his wife, Sarah "Rosette," née Rose (1759–1821), and Sabrina Bicknell (see HLP to JSPS, 27 July 1810, n. 7).

7. On 18 February 1811, "at half-past eleven at night, in Portman-place, Edgeware-road, in his 37th year" died José Maria de la Cueva, "the Duke of Albuquerque, Ambassador Extraordinary from Spain, Grandee of the First Class, General of the Spanish Army, &c. &c." Angered by "some insinuations and neglect of the Junta of Cadiz, [he] had been almost incessantly employed, for some time past, in drawing up a vindication of his conduct, which he had just printed in 4to." On 15 February "he was seized with a most alarming paroxysm of mental derangement," which grew steadily worse until he died.

On 2 March he was given virtually a state funeral in deference to his active role in the armies of the Patriots, to his skillful march by which Cadiz was preserved, and to his overall opposition to Bonaparte.

See *GM* 81, pt. 1 (1811): 197–98, 290–92.

8. *The Works of Alexander Pope, Esq. in Verse and Prose. Containing the Principal Notes of Drs. Warburton and Warton: Illustrations, and Critical and Explanatory Remarks, by Johnson, Wakefield, A. Chalmers, F.S.A. and others.* . . . By the Rev. William Lisle Bowles, 10 vols. (1806). Lot 223 in the first day of the sale of the books from Brynbella (17 September 1823). See *Sale Catalogue* (2).

9. See Bowles's edition of Pope, 9:38ln.–82n.: "In his last journey from Cambridge to London, being attended by Dr. Plumtree, and Dr. Cheselden the surgeon, he lodged the second night at Hodsden; where being observed to have been costive on the road, he was advised to have a clyster, to which he consented. The Apothecary was presently sent for, to whom Dr. Plumtree gave his orders below stairs, while Dr. Waterland continued above; upon which the Apothecary could not forbear expressing his great sense of the honour which he received, in being called to the assistance of so celebrated a person, whose writings he was well acquainted with. The company signified some surprise to find a country Apothecary so learned; but he assured them, that he was no stranger to the merit and character of the Doctor, but had lately read his ingenious Book with much pleasure, *The Divine Legation of Moses.*" When someone reported the apothecary's error, Waterland, enraged, accused him of being "ignorant in his profession, and unfit to administer any thing to him . . . and notwithstanding Dr. Plumtree's endeavours to moderate his displeasure, by representing the expediency of the operation . . . he would hear nothing in his favour, but ordered him to be discharged, and postponed the benefit of the clyster till he reached the next stage."

The confusion centered on William Warburton (1698–1779), bishop of Gloucester (1759), author of *The Divine Legation of Moses* (1737/38), and the theologican Daniel Waterland (1683–1740), a polemicist against the deists.

10. Published by subscription: *The Analysis of Beauty,* written with a view of fixing the fluctuating ideas of taste, with two plates (London: Printed by J. Reeves for the Author and sold by him at his house in Leicester-Fields, 1753).

Copies of this edition were difficult to obtain by those who had not subscribed. See the edition of this work prepared by Joseph Burke (Oxford: Clarendon Press, 1955), xxiv–xxv. HLP's copy with manuscript notes was lot 296 in the second day of the sale of the books from Brynbella (18 September 1823). See *Sale Catalogue* (2).

11. HLP quotes an old rumor. Paul Whitehead (1710–44) was a friend of Hogarth, but there is

no evidence that he participated in the composition of the book. His name emerged from "the allegation that Hogarth . . . had it written for him by collaborators. Several prints show Hogarth in the company of a group of satellites, who perform the dual office of composing his text and puffing it in the reviews" (p. xxvi). According to Burke, "It is clear that Hogarth did not take easily to literary composition. . . . The artist has evidently worked on his manuscripts by fits and starts, and in widely differing moods. . . . the general impression left by the drafts is one of intermittent accretion and painful replanning" (p. xxxi).

12. John Gillon's will was first signed on 18 July 1809, then signed with a codicil on 13 December 1809. It was proved 20 January 1810.

The will was entered in chancery early in 1811 and there it remained until the final Decree and Order was issued on 26 July 1816 (P.R.O., Chancery Index, C/33/1759–61).

The case was debated in chancery before the master of the rolls. The plaintiffs were the chief beneficiaries of the will, who were in essence suing the executors, particularly A. W. Robarts, for holding on to much of the money and failing to honor the bequests outlined in the will. The case ended with the master of chancery's decision to replace the original executors (those who were still alive) and to appoint others in their place.

13. Gillon left "to my respectable friend Mrs. Piozzi my edition of Shakespeare bound in real morocco by Reed" (P.R.O., Prob. 11/1507/32).

14. Francis John Hartwell (1757–1831), cr. baronet (1805) after being knighted in 1802, was an admiral, colonel of Deptford and Woolwich Volunteers, director of the Greenwich Hospital. He married first on 12 February 1781 Anne Charlotte Maria, née Elphinstone (d. 6 June 1809). He married second on 27 January 1812 Louisa, née Aldridge (d. 1843).

15. HLP refers to William Fowler (d. ca. 1717), cr. baronet (1704), who had married Mary, née Cotton (fl. 1660–1681), the sister-in-law of Philadelphia Lynch Cotton, HLP's grandmother.

Their grandchildren, originally four, were the offspring of Sir Richard Fowler (1681–1731), second baronet, and his wife Sarah, née Sloane (fl. 1685–1740).

16. For Lucy Mackay, née Jones, see HLP to PSW, 28 July [1791], n. 2.

17. Thomas Taylour (1757–1829), second earl of Bective, viscount Headfort, and baron Headfort in the peerage of Ireland (1795); cr. marquess of Headfort (1800). He had married on 4 December 1778 Mary, née Quin (1758–1842), who bore him four children.

TO THE REVEREND THOMAS SEDGWICK WHALLEY

Cheltenham Thursday Night
28: March 1811.

Though as my Dear Doctor Whalley says—I have not yet been invaded by the Torpor of old Age—non sum qualis eram[1] in any respect:—My Mind is worne as *thin* as an old Sixpence—and shines—if it does shine just as the old Sixpence does, from mere *beating out*. These Events, or rather *Transactions*, and I *hate* a Transaction; help to hammer it all away.[2]

We shall meet on Fryday next—and that consoles me: Shephard says the Assignees will not give up the Lease, so we are all at a Stand about old Streatham Park—The Trees in Front of which are I find disputed,[3] Tho' I feel sure Mr. Thrale bought them for a small Sum of Palmer the late Duke of Bedford's Steward—when the Duke was a Baby.[4] My being sure is however no Proof, and Papers were things I was never talked to about—in those Days.

Lord Keith and Mrs. Hoare were both very bitter to me about these Matters, and I wish from my heart The Place was sold, and that I were to take my last Leave of it—This Journey to London.[5] My poor Piozzi laid out 2000£ on The Furniture of that Place about the Year 1790, and hung up some very valuable

Pictures there—especially the Heads of Torquato Tasso—and Doctor Beccarelli by Titian and Murillo.[6] The fine Chimney Piece by Locatelli too, which caused a long Lawsuit in old Days between Mr. Locke then of Norbury Park, and the Artist: was purchased by us, and set up in Room of the Wooden one We found there——&c.[7] I thought myself very goodnatured indeed in leaving them (as I have done) with her Father's Furniture—Portraits &c. to Lady Keith.[8] An Idea has however been started, I know not by which of the Ladies, as if the House-hold Goods of both Southwark and Streatham Dwelling Houses was not be-queathed to me by Mr. Thrale *except for Life* and Charles Shephard is now making out a Copy of his Will to ascertain this Matter, because that will make a Differ-ence indeed.

We will see *all Through* when I get to London,—So That poor dear Salusbury may have no Incumbrances or dormant Claims fall upon him after my Death who have so little that I *can* give him without an Appearance of Impropriety and Disrespect to my first husband's Representatives. He is indeed an Affection-ate good Child; of an open Temper, and generous Heart, visible in a Counte-nance that makes him Friends wherever he sets his Foot.[9]

Mr. Hopkins Northey who brings You this Letter in Consequence of his polite Solicitation for *Commands* to Town, has been very kind to Salusbury[10]—so has every body, and *our Ball* was much liked.

The News from Spain is indeed truly glorious News. Why our People fight——as they *used* to do.—Cressy, Poietiers, *Minden*, Maida[11]——and now Barrose.[12] When will the French leave off saying that Englishmen can be success-ful only at Sea? I hope Lord Wellington will follow up General Graham's Lesson to their Conviction of the Contrary.[13] I expect to find London illuminated for Massena's Defeat, on my Arrival; and Dear Doctor Whalley's House brightest, as its Master's true Loyalty is purest and clearest.

Lady Kirkwall's Invitations are so tenderly pressing, and her pretty Self so partial to me and to my Friends—no Wonder you love one another.[14]

Lord Kirkwall and She will I dare say agree to pass their Old Age together after cheating one another of their Youth.[15]

> When Love and Genial Years are flown
> And all the Life of Life is gone[16]

but we have all been very silly now for Six Thousand Years, and Hannah More herself will not mend us. What a Mind *there* is! Solid and Sterling—not light Paper Currency of mere Nominal Value during the People's Fancy to give and receive it as such——While *You* however, and Sir William Pepys, and a very few more partial Friends contribute Your Help to hold up the falling Fund;—Despair shall not come near Your still Obliged and grateful/ H: L: Piozzi.

Text Berg Collection +.

1. Horace, *Odes*, 4.1.3.
2. HLP responds to TSW's letter of 27 March 1811 (Ry. 564.19), in which he summarizes his efforts to have Streatham Park purchased by the "Daughters." "But I have not been so ready to

answer your friendly, and pleasant Letter as I ought, in all reason to have been. The torpors of Age (which you are peculiarly *gifted* never to feel) and the fritterings away of time in this hurry, scurry metropolis, must plead my excuse. However, I had nothing to communicate respecting dear old *ill* used *Streatham*, or I would have roused myself to write. I spoke to Lord Keith, on the subject, doing your wishes, respecting your Daughters, all honor. His Lordship informed me that your confidential Lawyer, and *theirs* had met on the subject and that he hoped every thing would be settled to your mutual satisfaction. Lawyers, added his Lordship, can best manage these matters. And so they *can*, replied *I*. Here the topic ended, as it would not only have been useless, but indelicate and officious in me to have interfered further."

3. Abraham Atkins' creditors had seized the Streatham Park lease and would not surrender it. Indeed, they went further to claim certain trees (valuable for timber) as their rightful property.

4. For Francis Russell, fifth duke of Bedford, see HLP to LC, 27 December 1795, n. 7. For Robert Palmer, see HLP to Q, 4 June 1785, n. 7.

5. HLP's daughters, dissatisfied with the maintenance of Streatham Park, never seriously intended to buy out their mother's life interest in the estate. See HLP to JSPS, 27 April 1811.

6. During the third day of the sale (i.e., 10 May 1816) of the contents of Streatham Park, Titian's portrait of Tasso (lot 69) and Murillo's of Beccarelli (lot 70) were sold to the merchant John Kymer of Wood Lodge, Streatham. The Titian sold for £37.16 and the other for eight guineas. See *Sale Catalogue* (1).

7. HLP refers to Giovanni Battista Locatelli (1735–1805). He was born in Verona but lived in London from 1778 to 1790. A sculptor and woodworker, he is best known for his works of "Faith" and "Hope" in the Cathedral of Verona and the statue of Pietro d'Albano in Padua.

We have discovered no evidence that Locatelli's complaint against William Locke ever reached a resolution in a law court. Despite the protracted legal wrangling, Locatelli either retained or recovered possession of the chimney piece, which the Piozzis purchased for £100 in 1790. Three payments to the artist are listed in their bank account at Drummond's, Charing Cross.

8. If HLP left HT's furniture and paintings to Q, then she did so in her 1809 will, which is missing. But in her will, signed and witnessed on 19 April 1813 (Ry. Ch. 1258), she left "*every* Thing I *possess*, and every Thing I *claim*: or am, or shall be ever intitled to. Whether in Possession, Reversion, Remainder or Expectancy: wheresoever it may be found in England, Wales, or Italy at the Time of my Decease. And all my Estate and Interest there *In Trust* and *in Trust only* for the aforesaid *John Salusbury Piozzi* commonly called and known by the Name of *John Piozzi Salusbury* until he shall attain the Age of Twenty one Years [9 Sept. 1814]—*And Then* to the Use of the Aforesaid *John Salusbury Piozzi* . . . his Heirs, Executors, Administrators and Assigns for ever, according to the Nature and Quality of the said Estates and Property respectively. And in Case the said *John Salusbury Piozzi* . . . should die before he attains the Age of Twenty one Years . . . *Then* I give and devise the same *in like Manner* to my Eldest Grandson *John Salusbury Mostyn* . . . hereby revoking all and every other Will or Wills."

9. HLP responds to TSW's praise of "darling Salusbury, whom you cannot love too well, and *for whom*—in *my opinion*—you cannot do too much. He is the delight of your Eyes and will be the Staff and solace of your age. There is a marked Character in him that wins affection and inspires confidence. May God preserve his Life, and Health, and then I am convinced, he will never cause you shame, or anxiety."

10. William Richard Hopkins Northey (1753–1826), of Oving House, Bucks., and Suffolk Lawn, Cheltenham, J.P., a captain in the army, and aide-de-camp to the duke of Richmond when lord-lieutenant of Ireland.

11. Crècy in northern France is the site for the great victory of the English under Edward III over the French commanded by King Philip of Valois (26 August 1346). The English were outnumbered three to one in this early campaign of the Hundred Years War.

The battle of Poitiers, the second of the three great English victories in the same war, was fought between the forces of King John of France and Edward, the "Black Prince," on 19 September 1356.

The battle of Minden, in the Prussian province of Westphalia, was fought 1 August 1759 between the Anglo-Allied army under the command of Duke Ferdinand of Brunswick and the French under Marshal Contades. In this battle, important in the Seven Years War, British infantry supported by Hanoverian troops decisively defeated the French cavalry.

In 1806, at Maida in Calabria, British troops under Sir John Stuart defeated the French, commanded by Reynier.

12. *The Times*, 26 March, reprinted a letter from General Graham, first published in the *London Gazette Extraordinary* (25 March). He began his letter by announcing the battle he fought on 5 March: "My divisions being halted on the eastern slope of the Barrosa height, was marched about 12

o'clock through the wood towards the Bermesa. . . . On the march I received notice that the enemy had appeared in force on the plain, and was advancing towards the heights of Barrosa. . . .

"But before we could get ourselves quite disentangled from the wood, the troops on the Barrosa hill were seen returning from it, while the enemy's left wing was rapidly ascending. At the same time his right wing stood on the plain, on the edge of the wood, within cannon-shot. A retreat in the face of such an enemy, already within reach of the easy communication by the sea-beach, must have involved the whole allied army in all the danger of being attacked during the unavoidable confusion of the different corps arriving on the narrow ridge of Bermesa nearly at the same time."

The infantry being "hastily got together, the guns advanced to a more favourable position, and kept up a most destructive fire. . . .

"In less than an hour and a half from the commencement of the action, the enemy was in full retreat."

13. *The Times*, 26 March, devoted its lead article to the victory of Barrosa, pointing to the losses on both sides and comparing this victory to that of Maida. "They are both among the proudest illustrations of the superiority of British discipline and courage. Without speculating upon the ultimate consequences of General Graham's victory, the immediate advantages resulting from it cannot be said to be too dearly purchased. The Isle of Leon and the mainland . . . has been opened, and the enemy so completely humbled, that they never attempted to come out of Chiclana, and share this pious office with our troops [i.e., the burying of the dead]."

Thomas Graham (1748–1843), K.B. (1812), cr. baron Lynedoch (1814), in 1810 succeeded General Sir John Coape Sherbrooke (1764–1830) in Portugal and was sent to Cadiz with the rank of lieutenant general, to assume command of the British defense against the French. In February 1811, en route from the Isla with an expeditionary force, he attacked the French blockading army. The result was the victory of Barrosa on 5 March.

For the latest news concerning Wellington, See HLP to JSPS, 16 April 1811.

14. Lady Kirkwall, separated from her husband, was living at 38 Manchester Street, Manchester Square.

15. HLP's wishful thinking agrees with TSW's, who wrote: ". . . Lord Kirkwall is in Town, and has called on me. But I had rather he would call, and hurriedly, on his charming, virtuous, and deserted wife. I hope, yet, [to see] them living happily together."

16. See HLT to SJ, 15 July 1783, in *Letters*, 2:267; *Thraliana*, 2:825.

TO JOHN SALUSBURY PIOZZI SALUSBURY

[March 1811]
Saturday 30: Your Letter
this Minute arrived

I am too happy to see my Darling's hand,—to complain of the shortness of his Letter. Nay I did not deserve a longer, for I was very sick and very cross when I broke off last—and felt that if it were not for You I should cry nunc dimittis with true Sincerity. My Inside is better now, and my heart hopes for a Happy Meeting.——Hope shows her Front-face tho' to Young Folks alone; To me She begins to put on that peculiarly Picturesque Appearance Sir Joshua has given her in the Window of New College Oxford—pale and flying away somehow.[1]

Shall we ever visit it together? Oh Yes! the first Week of next May.

Leak wrote me word that he had the honour of a Letter from Mr. Salusbury, the first he ever had; and seemed quite proud of It. Oh he knows now who he is to look *up* to; and will behave accordingly. Mean while he has acted wisely in another Matter: because—finding Charles Shephard so silent, I sent to bid

Leak look among old Papers for some Evidence of Streatham Park and South-wark *Plate,* Furniture &c. belonging to Me absolutely as the Lawyers term it——Well! The sharp Fellow found a complete Abstract of my first husband's Will—and ran with it to Oldfield;[2] and I got *his* Letter, Oldfield's last night, to say *all is safe.* Charles Shephard had written, and said he *hoped* all was safe, but that the Will should be copied (an expensive Operation,) and Counsel's Opinion should be taken.—Another heavy Expence;—but all of it well bestowed.

We shall know the best and worst; and my present Peace and your future Fortune shall not be disturbed any more with these Conjectures. They made me mortal *sick*—That they *did*; but I held Glover fast, that She should not send for Dr. Jenner; and give the Ladies hopes before their Time——so every body saw me abroad next Day, and nobody knows anything ailed me. Counting the hours till we meet, does me most good, and the Certainty of your deserving more than I can do, and even all that I can wish. May we but see these Three Years and a half thro'—*Together.*

Poor pretty Lady Gardner whom You and Pemberton must remember at Bath, is dead;—Lord Carington's Daughter.[3] And a Miss Stewart, who danced at our Ball, drowned herself last Week at Rodborough[4]—her Mother Lady Stewart a Widow, is gone out of her Mind upon it.[5]

If you get good Pens, and I get such as these, our Hand Writing will be exactly alike.

Young Wraxall behaved in such a Manner here, that his Parents cried out both in a Breath "how Happy Mrs. Piozzi is in her Boy!! Ay, Ay, better adopt a Child than have one of our own You see."[6]

They told me this Themselves,——and I told *Them* how much more Comfort I enjoyed in the *Son of my Soul,* than anyone could do in the *Heirs of their Body begotten*—to use a Law Term.

So farewell Dear and only Dear Salusbury, and bring little Agnes to visit your true and tenderly/ Attached/ H: L: P.

This Letter is folded wrong, and written wrong, except the kind Expressions—*They* are all *right.* But I have no Pens left, and scarce any thing else—all packing up for *Monday*; and no Time to write the Stuff over again, because it must go to Post directly, or you will see me before my Letter.

Dispose of my Compliments as they ought to be disposed of, and let us love one another as well in September 1814 as/ We do on the 30th of March/ 1811./ Tis all that's wished on Earth by H: L: P.

Text Ry. 585.97. *Address* John Piozzi Salusbury Esq./ at The Rev: T: Shephard's/ Enborne/ near Newbury/ Berks. *Postmark* CHELTENHAM 30 MA 30 1811 <101> (In JSPS's hand "April 2nd 1811. Do 3rd Do").

1. HLP refers to the Reynolds' window, inserted in 1785, in the Ante-Chapel in New College. It is the only window ever designed by Sir Joshua.

The subject of the upper window is that of the Nativity. The lower range of lights contains seven panels of the virtues. Hope, the third panel from the right end, is depicted in profile and as if to take flight. What HLP, therefore, implies is that only the young are sufficiently naive to expect a sight of Hope's "Front-face."

2. For John Oldfield, an attorney at Bettws Abergelle, see HLP to JSPS, 5 March 1809, n. 1.

3. For Lord and Lady Carrington, see HLP to JSPS, 13 December 1809, n. 5. Their third daughter Charlotte Elizabeth (d. 27 March 1811) had married in 1809 Alan Hyde [Gardner] (1770–1815), second baron Gardner (1809).

4. There is no entry for Miss Stewart's burial in the Rodborough parish register (PMF 272/1) or in that for Stroud (P320 IN 1/8), the largest neighboring town. The bishop's transcripts for Cheltenham reveal nothing, nor do the coroner's inquest records for 1811 (C.R.O., Gloucestershire).

5. The unidentified Miss Stewart may be the daughter of John Stewart (ca. 1740–1797), fifth baronet of Castlemilk (1781), who ca. 1770 had married his cousin Anne, née Stewart (d. 1821). Or she may be Elizabeth, the daughter of Simeon Stuart (d. 1779) of Hartley Mauduit, Hants., third baronet (1761), who had married a Miss Hooke.

6. Charles Edward Wraxall (1792–1849) was the second son of Nathaniel William Wraxall, cr. baronet (1813), and Jane, née Lascelles (d. 1839).

TO MARGARET WILLIAMS

Cheltenham
31: March 1811.

My Dear Miss Williams

will find this Letter a dull one; but Cheltenham grows a dull place between the Seasons, and my Intention is to quit it now very soon indeed.

The Clause in Mr. Thrale's Will concerning his bequest to me of the Furniture, Plate &c. is known to no one *in Wales* I should think, so well as by Mr. Oldfield; and it would be bad indeed should the Report have sprung from him; I have no Fears.

My Visit to London will probably be a long-Leave-taking of poor Old Streatham Park, but at my Age every Year must be a Leave-taking of Friends, Pleasures and Companions.

We have taken an agreeable Leave of the Winter, which was I think never succeeded by so beautiful a Spring. There used to be a Speech about The Peck of March Dust being worth a King's Ransom;[1] and as Land gets to be worth more, and Kings to be valued at less than ever—We will suppose that such a Proverb may come true at last.

Buonaparte's Son fills the News Papers, and delights the French who are here;[2] The News from Spain is less welcome to them, but I fancy the Game is very near up in that Peninsula: unless by some Crane-neck Turn such as the Tyrant's Affairs have often taken, they would put themselves on a new footing.

Mrs. Pennant has been here a pretty while; but the Physicians seem to have small hopes that her Tender Cares will be Successful. She looks extremely well, her Husband and Son are expected.[3]

I hope charming Lady Williams and her little Flock are well. It seems long since I heard from dear Bodylwyddan but this Letter must be Answered to me at The Viscountess Kirkwall's No. 38. Manchester Street. I hear my Lord is likely to be a Lucky Candidate for our Borough of Denbigh.

Poor Lake writes us Word he has had Money taken from his Drawers at Brynbella—'Tis a Sad thing to think People are not honest even at such a Distance from the Capital—but this Paper Currency is too easy Carriage.

Adieu dear Miss Williams; present me with all Affection and Respect to the Family which have been ever so kind and obliging, to theirs and Your own/ Faithful Servant/ H: L: Piozzi.

When comes home your Young 'Squire? *Your* amiable Nephew? I shall see *mine* at Oxford before I see Home again.

Text Ry. 8 (1808–1812). *Address* Miss Williams/ Bodylwyddan/ near St. Asaph/ Flintshire/ N. Wales. *Postmark* CHELTENHAM 1 AP 1 <   > 101.

1. See HLP to PSP, 10 March 1799, n. 1.
2. For François-Joseph-Charles, see HLP to Q, 22 March 1810, n. 2.
3. Louisa Pennant helped to care for her brother-in-law, Thomas Kingscote, who died in April.

TO JOHN SALUSBURY PIOZZI SALUSBURY

Salthill Thursday Night
4: [April 1811].

My dearest Salusbury shall not be without a Direction to me in London—come what may. Let me soon see a kind Scrap at The Viscountess Kirkwall's No. 38 Manchester Street.

What I have learned here at Salthill is That nothing ails The Queen but an Increase of the old Lameness She has always suffer'd—a Bone Spavin it would be called if Agnes had it; Mine in my Arm's a Blood Spavin——But as you do not want to Sell poor Aunt;—no matter for her Blemishes. What I have done here is writing to the Dean of Christ Church, You should have made me do it at Newbury—but this was the Way Mr. Shephard directed me—and when he or his *Butler* answer, I will let you know. It was certainly right to say that tho' I was with Lady Kirkwall You were not.

So turn over and read The true Copy.

Mrs. Piozzi presents her most respectful Compliments, and as the Dean did her the honour some Time ago to say that he would be so obliging as to write and tell when her Nephew Mr. Salusbury was to be at Oxford—begs Permission just to mention her own Change of Place: lest a Letter going into Wales might be too long returning back to her who is for The Present at The Viscountess Kirkwall's No. 38 Manchester Street London.

Mr. Salusbury however is not with Them—He is at the Reverend Mr. Shephards Enborne Berks.

Mrs. Piozzi begs Leave to present her best Compliments to Mrs. Hall.

Well! I suppose this is a Model of Propriety to my old Friend Anna Maria

Byng's Husband. I wonder if her Brother Edmund will find me out in London or whether he has forgotten us completely.

Tis past 10 o'Clock and Glover is sick and *Hill* and wants to Sleep—so I must go to Bed who do not wish it—but no matter—

Be you good, and wise, and well, and happy; and let the Visions of your future exemplary Conduct raised Night and Day by my Fancy and Fondness,— Fly out at the Gate of Truth not Fiction.

See Virgil's ending of the sixth Book.[1]—So God bless my Dearest and Adieu— remembering/ That I must be Yours/ While/ H: L: Piozzi.

Give Pemberton a kind Shake of the hand for me, and tell me in your next that Mr. Shephard is better.

The Nose has I hope done bleeding.

Robert put up the odd Volume of Shakespear belonging to Botham's among my Books,[2] and made me rob the People and play Pelican Fanny.[3]

Text Ry. 585.98. *Address* John Piozzi Salusbury Esq./ at The/ Rev: T: Shephard's/ Enborne/ near Newbury/ Berks. *Postmark* MAIDENHEAD <22> (In JSPS's hand "Received April 6th 1811. Answered Do 8th Do").

1. The sixth book of the *Aeneid* (lines 886–901) ends with Anchises exciting his son with a love of fame and with Aeneas fleeing the realm of Tartarus through the ivory gate, speeding to the ships and revisiting his comrades. "Then straight along the shore [he] sails for Caieta's haven."
2. Peter Botham (fl. 1775–1814), a merchant at 8, Old Jewry, whose residence, as listed in *Boyle's Court Guide* (1807), is 4, Grosvenor Gate, Park Lane.
3. HLP likens herself to one of the natural wonders still being exhibited in London's museums and menageries—e.g., the Great Room over Exeter Change. "This inhabitant of the Wilderness, History gives an extraordinary Account, for its Paternal Affection and Care of its young" (DL, *Collecteana*, 2:33–34). Specifically HLP draws upon the unfounded legend that the pelican feeds and revivifies its young with the blood from its breast.

TO JOHN SALUSBURY PIOZZI SALUSBURY

Tuesday
16–17: April 1811.

The Letter of my truly Dear one was delightful to me——It gave me such renewed hope in your Virtue and Good sense, when I perceive you felt on your return from the Altar how true his Words are—who says "Pure Religion before God and the Father is this—to help the fatherless and Widows in their Affliction, and *keep Yourself unspotted from the World.*"[1] Go on then happily; hold the strait Path; your Eyes fixed forward——remembering—

> True 'tis a narrow Road that leads to Bliss,
> But right before, There is no Precipice;
> Fear makes Men look aside, and so their Footing miss.
>
> Dryden.[2]

These Lines written by no Modern Poet, beat all that Walter Scott, or the new Poem can boast—Oh what a Poem that is!! The Curse of Kehama is its Name, and a famous Dish of Moon shine will its Readers find it.[3] Lady Kirkwall and I sate up one Night and finished it——

> If finish may be call'd which End has none,
> Distinguishable in early Line or late;
> For Each seem'd either—

like the Portrait of Death in Milton's Paradise Lost.[4]

Sweet Lady Kirkwall! She was pleased with your Letter, but you should write to her Separately, and ask for her Babies; and offer them your future Services. She is so kind, it is quite inconceivable, and much more beautiful since You saw her last. Her Prudence and Piety are actually charming——and if you had seen the Men's Looks at Lady Lansdowne's Assembly last Night,[5] following her pretty retiring Eyes; You would have loved and pitied her.

Mean while we have *ourselves* to think about—meaning Dear Salusbury and me:—Poor Aunt! whose Happiness now hangs but by *one* Thread; Your Conduct in Life. The Young Hammersleys when I signed a formal Order to their House for answering Your Call on them for 125£ every Quarter —seemed as if wondering at the Liberality of the Allowance. And after praising me for my exactness, Said that one grand Source of this World's Sorrow was the strange Negligence most people treated their Money Concerns with—which a Sixpenny Account Book would relieve them from. For Mercy's Sake my Love do not ever suffer, or make me suffer by such silly Neglect: know what you have, and what you Spend, and what is left——It is no difficult Matter——but in this case like as in one more serious; *Fear* makes Men look aside and so their footing miss.[6] Italians say wisely There are but Three Things to care about: our Soul, our Body and our Purse.—English People add Knowledge but as an Adjunct rather than a Principal: because without some Knowledge We shall have no Virtue——and indeed Our Lord's condemnation of the unprofitable Servant, his curse upon the barren Fig tree, and his severity towards the Man who hid his Talent in a Napkin;—prove the necessity of keeping our Wits keen by the polish of Book Learning.[7] It is hard enough to get thro' the World creditably and with a clear Conscience, altho' one obtains all the Assistance that past Times' long Experience can bestow:——but how we should arrive happily or even *safely* into Port, without Pilot, Rudder or Compass—I guess not.

Literary Employment is good for Health likewise. A Man gets heavy, fat, and Lethargic who suffers his Intellect to sleep and rust; filling the Body with gross humours, which Exertion of the Spirits in Study—clears and refines—nor can those expect full Power over their *Minds* any more than over their *Horses*, if Care is not taken to force our Ideas on Subjection, making them come and go at our Command. Tom Lloyd is dying now of that Disease—He never recovered his Son Holland's death;[8] The Man's Image has haunted him, till at length it hunts him fairly out of temporal Existence. Langton and Northey live on—in their

Quarrel;[9] The Town only laughing at the Expence and Trouble they take to call one another Rogue and Rascal.

Lord Cochrane committed some slight Act of Tyranny at Malta, and was cited by their Courts of Law which he despised; and they confined him for Contumacy of course—so he 'scaped out o' the Window, and came home with Intention of appealing to our Admiralty Court—*They* —bid Him perform Quarantine, because of coming from Malta:—but he 'scaped away again; and seems possessed with a Spirit of running away from every thing but the King's Enemies; he is an eminently brave and gallant Officer.[10] The Retreat of the French before Lord Wellington has been horrible: burning and massacring the poor Inhabitants as they ran forward——leaving whole Villages in Flames.[11] No Scenes can equal, no Disgust can surpass the Sight of a Country which has been a Theatre of War. God keep Great Britain from *tels Horreurs*——all Words but those of *Attack* and *Defence* are banished at such Moments: all Tender Feelings blunted by Revenge.

Meanwhile you perceive my Property is safe (in the Defence of a merciful Providence) from the Attacks of my Enemies.—But I may go next and ask the Attorney General[12] if Bachŷgraig is my own—for it seems the Ladies call it Their Place quite familiarly——and a female Friend said to me two Days ago—She wondered I did not purchase it. Purchase my own Father's house! replied I—purchase Bachygraig!!——Of Whom? Oh Dear! well! I did not know Mr. Thrale had left it You *unconditionally*.[13]

Mr. *Thrale* leave it!!! What Nonsense: I think the People have taken leave of their Senses.

Pray for the Continuance of yours and of my own, Dearest Child of my Cares, dearest Friend of my Heart—as you are. Whilst we use our Wits rightly, We shall weave a Strong Bond for ourselves of Amity, Affection, and Esteem—a triple Cord which cannot be broken[14]—between my Darling Salusbury and his *confiding*/ Parent/ H: L: Piozzi.

We dine at Mrs. Hoare's today.
I wish Pem would write——and I wish to know if your Nose bleeds.
Wednesday 17: April 1811.

Text Ry. 585.102. *Address* John Piozzi Salusbury Esq./ at The/ Rev: Thomas Shephard's/ Enborne near Newbury/ Berkshire. *Postmark* AP 17 1811 (In JSPS's hand "Received April 18th 1811. Answered Do 20th Do").

1. See HLP to JSPS, 6 December 1810.
2. *The Conquest of Granada*, Pt. 1, 4.2.459–61. See also *British Synonymy*, 2:75.
3. *The Curse of Kehama*, a long poem by Robert Southey about Hindu mythology, appeared in 1810. Of it and other modern poetry, HLP writes in "Minced Meat for Pyes": "These new writers Southey and Walter Scott who as Dr. Young expresses it, have Souls, that *Wander wild thro' Things impossible* are not difficult Authors to Imitate—I should like well enough to try, but that

> My Hairs are Gray, my Limbs are Old,
> My Heart is dead, my Veins are cold."

4. HLP's playful adaptation of *Paradise Lost*, 2.666–70.

5. Henry Petty, afterwards Petty-Fitzmaurice (1780–1863), third marquess of Lansdowne (1809) had married on 30 March 1808 Louisa Emma Fox-Strangways (1785–1851), fifth daughter of the second earl of Ilchester.

6. Proverbial, as in Tilley, F 138; M 230. Cf. Shakespeare, *Richard III*, 2.2.130.

7. For the "unprofitable servant" who "hid his talent," see Matthew 25:24–30 (see HLP to JSPS, 9 September 1807); for the parable of the fig tree, see Mark 11:13–14; for the "Man who hid his Talent in a Napkin," see Luke 19:20–26.

8. For Holland Lloyd and his father Thomas, see HLP to PSP, 22 October 1798, n. 7; to Charlotte Lewis, 20 September [17]89, n. 7.

9. Probably George Langton (1772–1819). For Northey, see HLP to TSW, 28 March 1811, n. 10.

10. For Lord Cochrane, see HLP to Ly W, 1 May 1809, n. 4.

HLP refers to his legal battles with the Maltese admiralty court, which he accused of chicanery, and his subsequent imprisonment by it in 1811. Urged to escape by a senior naval officer, then stationed at Malta, he was given files with which to cut through the bars. By means of a makeshift ladder, he reached the ground. "In a few minutes he was in a boat, and, catching the English packet, was soon on his way to Sicily. Thence, after retrieving his precious table of charges [the source of contention], he travelled to England."

As Lord Cochrane concluded the narrative in his autobiography: "nothing could exceed the chagrin of the Admiralty officials [in Malta] at having lost, not only their table of charges, but their prisoner also. No one had the slightest suspicion that I had gone to sea, and that in a man-of-war's boat. Yet nothing could better show the iniquitous character of the Maltese Admiralty Court than the fact that my escape was planned in conjunction with several naval officers present in harbour, who lent me a boat and crew for the purpose; the whole matter being previously known to half the naval officers present with the squadron, and, after my escape, to not a few of the seamen, all of whom must have been highly amused at the diligent search made for me the next day throughout Valetta, but still more at the *reward offered for those who aided me in escaping.* Yet not a word transpired as to the direction I had taken."

See Henry Taprell Dorling, *Men o' War* (London: P. Allan, 1929), 131–32; Cochrane's *The Autobiography of a Seaman* (London: Richard Bentley and Son, 1890), 311–20.

11. A *London Gazette Extraordinary*, 7 April (printed in the *Courier*, 8 April 1811), published Lord Wellington's dispatches on the fighting between 5 and 11 March in Pombal, Redinha, Cazal Novo, and Foz d'Aronce.

"I am concerned to be obliged to add to this account, that [the conduct of Masséna's troops] throughout this retreat has been marked by a barbarity seldom equalled, and never surpassed. . . . they have since burnt every town and village through which they have passed. The convent of Alcobaca was burnt by order from the French head-quarters. The Bishop's palace, and the whole town of Leyria, in which General Drouet had had his head-quarters, shared the same fate."

12. Knighted in February 1805, Vicary Gibbes (1751–1820) had a long legal career, serving, e.g., as solicitor general and attorney general to the Prince of Wales, as chief justice for Chester, and as solicitor general in Pitt's last administration. HLP refers to Sir Vicary as attorney general (7 April 1807 to May 1812).

13. The quarrel over the ownership of Bachygraig continued until 1813. See HLP to JSPS, 19 April 1813.

14. Ecclesiastes 4:12.

TO JOHN SALUSBURY PIOZZI SALUSBURY

London
27: April 1811.

My truly beloved *Nepos* as he calls himself, is the *Ne plus ultra* of all good Boys. But Boyhood is done with now, and Manhood is begun——or to speak strictly *Adolescence.* Let us get thro' this fiery Tryal of Youth, and congratulate ourselves on the Year of Emancipation.——The Angel of God who preserved the three

Young Israelitish Captives from the Heat of Nebucadnezzar's Furnace, still watches over *early Virtue,* and will preserve its Votaries from the Destruction destined for them; and turn (as in their Case) even bitter Enemies into admiring Friends——read their Story—in the best and most eloquent of all Books:—after Scripture Language, none but that of Milton can be borne; and he says in a Spiritual Character.——

> Mortals that would follow me,
> Love Virtue;—She alone is free:
> She can teach you how to climb
> Higher than the Sphery Chime;
> Or if Virtue feeble were,
> Heav'n it self would stoop to *her.*[1]

When Comus invites you to his Court—Think upon Milton's Lady and her Brothers—when Infidel Arguments assault your Piety, and The Fool not only says in his Heart,—but with his *Voice*—"There is no God."[2]——Remember the Three Children as they are called, whose Song is in all our Prayer Books;[3] and their Story in the 3d: Chapter of Daniel. The Persian History says they were all of them under 20 Years of Age.[4]

Dear precious Salusbury Adieu: I shall be at Oxford on the 2d: or 3d: of May. —The Expences here—(tho' I am ruining sweet Lady Kirkwall) are very heávy; and the Death of an old Superannuated Sister of Mr. Thrale's forces me back into new deep Mourning, after I had bought all my Clothes.[5] But what would the Ladies *say* was I not to respect their Family?

All that Stuff about selling Streatham Park was a permitted *Dupery* after all, and I as usual the Dupe.——They know it cannot be sold it seems——and I shall tell Charles Shephard so today when I go to Windle's with my Will *rewritten;* "designating you by the Name of John Salusbury Piozzi, commonly called and known by the Name of John Piozzi Salusbury the Nephew of my late husband Gabriel Piozzi and now my own dear and adopted Child."[6]——And this Trouble I have taken chiefly to make your Mind easy, as I saw some one had put it in your Head that the other way *might* (tho' it could not) have been caviled at.

I shall do this Deed no more now till the Year 1814[7]—and then we will enjoy *our own* Brynbella if God grants us Life, and preserves your steady Spirit in the Way to his Salvation: and we will have no oppressive Rod over us gathering their Tythe on *our* Estate you shall see. Till then I must save something to pay for Changes and Renewals. Leak has behaved beautifully after all, and sold my Timber for more than he expected——and I have struck Cecilia Siddons from among the Legatees—and Streatham Parish, where I have only a Blister on my Back stuck fast for as long as I shall live—Vexatious!!

I am quite afraid of shewing you my frightful Richard—more hideous than even the last Richard—but no matter; handsome Robert is I fear a horrible Creature, deserving to be dismissed out of the Lists of humanity.

My Cough is bad, but who can wonder? with foul Air, close Rooms, number-less Vermin, and *no milk.* I shall perhaps leave it at Salthill. I have left 500£ at

Hammersley's and George says he has explained all clearly to you and hopes you will be regular in your Accounts like Your daily more and/ more Affectionate/ H: L: Piozzi.

We never open Door or Window here till 10 o'Clock.

You really must write to Lady Kirkwall herself about the China Ware for Breakfast Arrangements. I hope it came safe to Christ Church.

Text Ry. 585.105. *Address* John Piozzi Salusbury Esq./ Christ Church/ Oxford *Postmark* < > (In JSPS's hand "Received April 28th 1811. Answered Do 30th Do").

1. The Spirit concludes *A Mask* ("Comus") with lines 1018–23, those quoted by HLP.
2. Psalms 14:1.
3. The Song of the Three Children, verses 29–68, which appears in the apocryphal addition to Daniel, was incorporated into the Book of Common Prayer (sec. 17) as a part of Matins.
In the prayer book, the song of praise begins "O all ye works of the Lord, speak good of the Lord: praise him and set him up for ever." It concludes with "As it was in the beginning, &c."
4. By the Persian History, HLP meant Xenophon's *Cyropaedia* from which she learned that boys remained such "until they are sixteen or seventeen years of age, and after this they are promoted from the class of boys and enrolled among the young men" (1.2.8). Associating Daniel's young friends Shadrach, Meshach, and Abednego with this chronology, HLP used them as prototypes of unassailable piety for the eighteen-year-old JSPS. She refers to the story again in HLP to JSPS, 20 February 1812.
5. Frances, née Thrale (1726–1811) was the widow of Samuel Plumbe. For the latter, see HLP to Q, 21 December [1796], n. 15.
6. HLP delayed signing the will until 19 April 1813. Written in her own hand, it was notarized and witnessed by Joseph Ward of 44 Bedford Square.
7. There is an HLP will, signed 19 April 1814 and witnessed in North Wales, that duplicates that of 1813. A copy of the later will is now at the Pierpont Morgan Library.

TO JOHN SALUSBURY PIOZZI SALUSBURY

Brynbella—Greener and
lovelier than ever
18–19: May 1811.

My dearest Friend! my best-loved Salusbury will perhaps scarcely wonder that I am criticized by my watchful Acquaintance for the *Too-kind* Deed I have so fearlessly committed in sending my Darling Gentleman Commoner to Christ Church:[1] Mr. Shephard of Enborne is most openly severe upon me, and I confess myself as *Ill-prepared* for his Severities, as he says You were *ill prepared* for Oxford. What Schreech Owls!—Let you and I live so as to shew them how wrong they were! and what true cause we have to scorn their schreeching. Did not your dear Uncle's Conduct justify my partial Confidence towards Him in the Eyes of all Mankind? and did he not *force* them to retract their ill founded Opinions?— Yes, Yes; so will *his* and *my own* incomparable Salusbury. I feel that all will end just as I wish, and of course I despise their Malice.

> For Piozzi's Sake, welcome all Torments past;
> And for your *own* Sake, welcome ev'n the last.

Write to me meanwhile, and recollect that at our truly beautiful Brynbella lives her who loves you best; write to me, letting Your Pen run as Your Tongue would do, were we together: and remembering that with God's Grace and my Care; your *Dangers* will not be so *great*, nor Your *Fortune so small* as they pretend to fear, and to lament. We shall do very well in 'Spite of false Friends and professed Enemies: Do not be perswaded that my Fondness for you is *capricious*;—it is founded on *Your Merit*; and no one but *Yourself* can lessen or Injure it. Be you but *resolute* to fear God, and attend his *Table*, where we best obtain Strength for opposing Temptation.[2] Whitsunday begins the next Month; and your Term will be ended, and you may go to Church where You *will* I trust; and mingle in a Croud of those who know you not. *I* always *seek* such Opportunities; I hate to be watched at my Devotions for my own Part,—and in a Croud—one is always most alone——and free to exercise One's own Thoughts.——Doctor Gillies says that *Whit*Sunday is so called, not from *White* as I am *sure* it is; but from Eight— 8,—*huit* in French:[3] meaning the 8th Sunday after Easter. The best Explanation is in Nelson's Feasts and Fasts——I hope you have that Book, and I wish you would read it—There is much true Piety in that too much neglected Volume, and much Sound Learning.[4]

My Health is greatly mended since the fine Weather; Leak goes to Liverpool soon,—half upon Business half Pleasure: when he returns, we will be very busy; and you shall see Grand Resultàt as the French phrase it. Dear! precious Salusbury! be chearful and make *me* so; whose Happiness depends on Your *deservings*:——and whose *Hopes* of your exemplary Conduct are so *high*——a *Fall* would surely kill me.

Let us in the Interim never repent of anything but our Sins—It was none in me to send you to Christ Church; A Man must be Somewhere——if he is a *Man*; and as to my making a *Baby* of the Person meant for my Comforter, my Counsellor, and my Friend—I see no Sense in *That*, nor no Virtue.

You may rationally enough retard the Progress of *your* eldest Son at the same Age;—but my Point is to ripen and bring forward the Mind on which my own means to repose in the *near Close of Life*; and when you read this Letter 20 Years hence, You will say *I was right*.

The World in which you must live, and I must die, is not new to you *now*—— London, Bath, and Cheltenham have all spread their Snares, and as little Bowen expressed himself—*made a dead Set at you.*[5] Two Years more—for we have shortened the Term—will finish this fiery Tryal of Oxford: and as you Will be then close upon 20 Years old——You shall (if all has gone to my Approbation) find yourself unruined, notwithstanding the Croakers; and with a *Gentleman's* Income, whether or no A *Gentleman Commoner's*. So much for Indignation, Tho' I am still nettled, and stung and smarting No wonder.

My Opus Magnum goes on very slowly, but does not stand quite still:[6] The Weeks come round too quick however, and find too little done. One recollects too seldom that *Sloth* is one of Scalken's seven Vices: Indeed the Devil is more *concealed* in that Picture than in any of them. Did I tell you that our William the 3d: of England held the Candle while his Countryman painted that sleeping Figure—till the hot Wax ran down and burned his Fingers? it is a Fact not quite generally known.[7]

This Letter will not go now till Monday—Ay, Monday 19 May: I write it over Night after reading Prayers to my English Servants——When does your Post come in? what hour I mean? because in such great Cities Letters doubtless arrive every day——one will be brought me from Christ Church in the Morning——how very malicious People must be to endeavour at destroying My few Pleasures *now*—at 71 Years old!—and such an Innocent, praise-worthy Pleasure as rejoycing over my Darling Child's respectable Situation in early Life. Such as so Many Youths are wishing for——but I will not be disturbed by their Tales of Wonder or of *Plunder*: I *will* rejoyce that Dear Piozzi's Nephew and my own adopted Son——is as I always intended he *should* be, if a Good Boy——one of the Gentlemen Commoners of Christ Church.

So Good Night Sweet Angel, and enjoy the comfortable Sleep procured by a good Conscience——The consciousness of being *her* sole Delight who is/ with hourly-increasing Love/ Your ever/ Affectionate/ H: L: P.

The Country never, no *never* was so pleasant; and Seven Weeks more will bring you home to *your own* Brynbella—which will be greatly improved by the Addition of Mrs. Parry's Land,[8] and turning the Road away to Tŷ Bach—when I can do it——and we hope to begin this Summer——God send it may be so, that the Expence may fall on *me* while my Income can bear it;—and not upon my Titmouse.

I have heard *of* Lady Kirkwall at last—not *from* her; but Marianne Francis and She have struck up an Intimacy[9]—Pray did Clem: come to Oxford as *he said*? My Locket went very Safe, I'm sorry you lost Yours: Is the Talisman in being?——< Mercy >! how it does Thunder and Lighten!

Write to me soon: I feel frighted lest You should have caught Cold, walking thro' the Wet in these unmeaning Processions.

Text Ry. 585.108. *Address* John Piozzi Salusbury Esq./ Christ Church/ Oxford. *Postmark* DENBIGH 224.

1. HLP acknowledges JSPS's admission certificate to Oxford, issued 8 May 1811 (Ry. Ch. 1257): "Quo die comparuit coram me Joannes Piozzi Salisbury . . . et subscripsit Articulis Fidei, et Religionis; et juramentum suscepit de agnoscendâ supremâ Regiæ Majestatis potestate; et de observandis Statutis, Privilegiis, et Consuetudinibus hujus Universitatis./ J. Cole Vice Can."

2. See Ecclesiastes 12:13; Psalms 37:39; 1 Corinthians 10:21.

3. For John Gillies see HLP to Sophia Byron, 11 August [1788], n. 10.

4. See *Mr. Nelson's Companion for the Festivals and Fasts of the Church of England, Made More useful, and instructive, by reducing each solemnity into a practical Discourse. To which is prefix'd some account of Mr. Nelson's life and writings, with a true copy of his last will and testament*. By William Kirke, M. A. (London: A. Bettesworth and E. Curll, 1715).

In the above work (chap. 22), Robert Nelson (1656–1715) defines and explains Whitsunday, which is so called "partly from the glorious Light of Heaven, which was this Day sent down upon the Earth from the Father of Lights; but principally, because . . . those who were baptized, put on White Garments, as Types of that Spiritual Purity they received in Baptism, and which they were obliged to preserve in the future Course of their Lives" (p. 141).

5. The Bath apothecary, William Bowen.

6. That is, "Harvard Piozziana."

7. Gotfried (Godfried) Cornelisz Schalcken (1643–1706) was a Dutch genre painter. Active among artists at the Hague and Dordrecht, he went to England in 1692 and probably remained until 1697.

HLP makes an obscure association between her own dilatory composition and a figure of Sloth, although we have no evidence that Schalcken painted the Seven Vices.

The "Fact not quite generally known" about the painting of William III had been recorded by Walpole on Vertue's authority. Schalcken, who was partial to illumination by candlelight, "gave his majesty the candle to hold, till the tallow ran down upon his fingers." The picture in question (one of several by Schalcken depicting the King) is no longer known.

See *Anecdotes of Painting in England; with some Accounts of the principal Artists; and incidental Notes on the other Arts; Collected by the late Mr. George Vertue; and now digested and published from his original MSS. By Mr. Horace Walpole*, 3 vols. (Strawberry Hill, 1762–63), 3 [1763]: 131; Christopher White, *The Dutch Pictures in the Collection of Her Majesty the Queen* (Cambridge: University Press, 1982), 116–18 and plates.

8. She was the widow of Edward Parry (d. 1806) of Tan y Bryn. See "Land Tax Assessments," C.R.O., Clwyd.

9. On 27 May 1811 (Ry. 583.76), MF had written: "there is *one* thing for which I believe I never thanked you . . . and that is, for introducing me to Lady Kirkwall. . . . dear Lady K has been so sweet and kind since you left London that I am grown really to love her from my heart—She has done us the honour to come here several times—and I think there is a nobility of *mind* about her— a generosity of Soul, and a *delicacy* of character, which together with that sweet winning way of hers, are very uncommon, and to me, quite irresistible—and She has been so *wickedly* used—suffers so cruelly about her Babies—the tears stand in her fine eyes whenever she mentions their names— that it's hard to say whether most pity or indignation are excited at the recollection."

TO JOHN SALUSBURY PIOZZI SALUSBURY

Brynbella Wensday Night
13: June 1811.

If my Dearest Angel knew what Happiness this Last Letter has given his poor Aunt——*he* would sleep the better——as *She* will be *sure* to do this Night. I had been Thinking and fretting lest this *adorable Dean* (whom I love *now*,) should have disapproved your Flash;——and here comes a Letter to say he was not only *Civil, but Kind*. Oh keep his Favour carefully, my best Salusbury; and enjoy the Fruits in *this* World, of that exemplary Conduct, which will *ensure* Your Felicity in the next. Young Fitzhugh's Report will pass instantly to *our Ladies* with whom his Mama is intimate—and so is Mrs. Siddons——and I shall be the happiest of human Creatures.[1]

The World is such a Field of Battle, some Generalship is always required: but the grand Safe Guard is the *Old Red Cross* which was shewn to Constantine you know, when he went out to fight Tyrant Maxentius——with the Words under *In hoc Signo vinces*. It is the same Standard from which *Satan* The *Adversary* has ever hastened to fly——*literally* and *figuratively:*[2] and Lord Wellington has driven Massena before him by its protecting Virtue—The Colours of England are Constantine's old Red Cross on a blue Ground.

So far Knowledge—now comes Ignorance. I have not the slightest Guess what my Darling can mean about——*Taking up my Collections*——what Collections hast thou to take up Dear Child? no Collections of Money I much fear, so I enclose a Dandy's Egg, meaning a *Ten Pound Note*: and do let me know *instantly* that it comes *safe to hand*.

I am sorry about Agnes—*very* sorry: but the Horses and Bulls *will* break their Legs I think; do not let the new Gig break *yours*.

George Hammersley will come here in July he says, I shall be glad *you* are here to make him welcome. Mr. Maughan walked round with me this Morning—and promises seriously to put me out of my Pain concerning the Allotments against Planting Season. We are to know our Fate in August.

This has indeed been a happy Day——Your Account of the Dean's good nature does delight me: pray make my Respects to him, and Compliments to his Lady, and take a polite Leave of him before you come home Thro' *Llangollen* to your/ *anxiously*, and *tenderly* attached/ H: L: P.

The 29th of June ought to be our Tythe-Setting Day—and we *ought* to be cutting Hay—but the Weather is *so* cold. Do not tell any one that I send you Money so. I want People to say how *prudent* Mr. Salusbury is—and always leaves something in the Banker's hand &c. So God bless My only Love, and protect from evil his beautiful Body and Mind. Mrs. Thelwall Salusbury was Overturned in her Coach close to old Offley Place—The Glass broke, cut the carotid artery in her Neck, and She died in ten Minutes.[3] The Captain who lives at Denbigh, is gone to comfort them:[4]—but what Accidents there are in the World!! when I think on them my Heart trembles for its Titmouse.

You say nothing of your little Fête. Læta non luxuriosa I suppose—plena non tumida——Quintilian's Receipt for a good Style.[5]

Adieu! I am in *famous Spirits*.

You never mention my Riddle and that is very cruel; I thought it such a funny one.

Look in the *inside* and tell if it comes safe *tell directly* and call it the *Dandy* lest your Letter should be seen.

Text Ry. 585.114. *Address* John Piozzi Salusbury Esq./ Christ Church/ Oxford. *Postmark* DENBIGH 224.

1. HLP refers to William Anthony Fitzhugh (1794–1881), who matriculated at Christ Church, Oxford, on the same day as JSPS. He was to become rector of Street, Sussex, in 1821 and of Belshford, county Lincoln in 1826.
For his parents, William and Charlotte Fitzhugh, see HLP to PSP, 22 May 1802, n. 5.
2. For Constantine and his standard, see HLP to DL [16 October 1796], n. 6.
3. She was Elizabeth, née Offley. Her husband, Thelwall (d. 1814), was the fifth son of Robert and Gwendolen Salusbury of Cotton Hall, Denbigh. Having received his LL.B. from Cambridge in 1791, he became rector of Llanfair-Kilgeddin, Monmouthshire, in 1801, and rector of Llanwern in 1803.
Mr. and Mrs. Thelwall Salusbury sat in the coach with three others. "Mrs. T. Salusbury sat in the middle. The night was dark. . . . the Driver was sober, & accustomed to the road. The Chaise was overturned in a narrow lane. . . . Mr. T. Salusbury being very heavy in His person could not be got out of the Chaise with[ou]t some difficulty. When Mrs. T. Salusbury was taken out she was dead. No other of the party was hurt except a scratch on the arm of one of the Children" (Farington, 11:3915). In fact, Mrs. Thelwall Salusbury's head went through the window, the broken glass cutting one of the arteries of her neck, "& she died before She could be got out of the carriage" (ibid., 1:3912).

4. The "Captain" was Sir Robert Salusbury.
5. Quintilian says, "læta, non luxuriosa . . . grandia, non tumida" (*De Institutio Oratoria*, 12.10.80).

TO JOHN SALUSBURY PIOZZI SALUSBURY

Brynbella Thursday
27: June 1811.

My best of all Boys has sent me a very kind Notice of the when, where and how I am to expect him: Your short Letters do indeed always contrive to make me amends even for long Silences;—but this was not short—nor the Silence long. You are a Dear fellow That is the Truth; and now I go repeating to myself all Day, that the Day after Tomorrow I *shall* repeat to Myself—how on That Day sennight Saturday 6 July Home comes My Salusbury——Even *frowning* Betty *Smiles* at the Thoughts of it:—and my Anxiety about the Tythe-setting remains suspended whilst I read your comfortable Account of your Servant.—I am fitting him up a tidy Room.

Don't you remember how we all rejoiced when these Tythes were set for 300£?—This last Year they *have* brought me in 375£ and now tho' the Common is not enclosed, nor the Allotments fixed on, (which will add much to their Value,)—Oldfield has set them for 423£ minus only one Shilling——Is not this an *Improving* Property?——Ah Dearest Salusbury! and shall anybody *touch* it but *You*? Not if you keep your Virtue, and I keep my Wits, which God preserve for your Sake.

Rees of Bachygraig[1] and Leak for H: L: Piozzi go Partners in the Tythe of Bachygraig.

I have embroidered a bright Butterfly (worthy your old Schoolfellow Dale,)[2] upon my *Hand*; for I had no Tambour or any other Frame: and mean it for an Ornament of your Rooms at College. I feel quite glad that every thing will be safe that is left there, and gladder than I can express, that you are leaving them for a While. The Dear Bodylwyddan's Happiness has I much fear, seen its best Days.[3] Doctor Johnson always said—*out* of his Book, as well as *in* it; That the worst thing he knew of human Life was—"That altho' The Vice of *one* Individual can often make many Miserable, The Virtue of one Individual can Seldom make many happy."[4] Well! *your* Virtue will at least make *Two* People happy, Yourself and your Affectionate Aunt/ H: L: P.

Pray invite Pemberton to Brynbella,—he knows his Apartment and his Welcome. Those who really love *You* my Heart embraces *cordially.*——Those who do *not* must necessarily feel a Coldness in their Reception at *my* House, which will be yours; when you shall say to Them "*Terra quam calcas, mea est.*" The next Post carries Stroud his Money for your Wine[5]—so *that* is paid, and may be enjoyed. 'Tis only good Men like yourself that can have any Enjoyment of this World, or well-founded hope in the next. Mrs. Myddelton was here Yesterday—

She says She loves Mr. Salusbury because it appears to *her*—*That he loves me.* Truly Dear Madam was the Reply, "My Heart quite depends upon his Affection for its Support—It was *my* Turn at the Beginning of *his* Life—at the Close of *my* Life——it will be *his.*"

Mr. Oldfield carries this to the Post, and I hope you will have it before you leave Oxford, and come on Your Way the Wrexham Road rejoycing: Every body tells me, and I gather it besides from Your Letters—that the Post delivers Letters out on Sunday at Oxford: You will perhaps find another at Longnore, but I could not delay the News of the Tythes:

I told you it would be 500£ by the Time you come of Age, and sure enough so it will. Oh that the Tythes in Caernarvonshire would keep pace with them![6] But that is hopeless—and indeed scarcely would it be fair—because this costs Money in Renewals, and that does not.

They are making a noise and a casting up all round me and I can only [tell you] I *am* but not half enough how much I am Yours/ H: L: P.

I expect another Letter for *some* Place, *any* Place to say you are safe and coming.

Text Ry. 585.117. *Address* John Piozzi Salusbury Esq./ Christ Church/ Oxford. *Postmark* St. Asaph 218.

1. In her "Pocket Book" (Ry. 616), 24 August 1810, HLP wrote: "Tenant People came to talk about Bachygraig—I seemed to like the People and they—Me. Hope I made tolerable Advances."
On 29 November 1810 an indenture was signed between HLP and "John Rees of Moor side in the parish of Hope in the County of Flint, Farmer, and Samuel Rees the Elder of Moor side." According to the indenture, they were to rent "All that Capital Messuage or Tenements with the Appurtenances situate lying and being in the Parish of Dymerchion . . . known by the Name of Bachegraig now or late in the Occupation of Widow Gittens . . . (Save and Except that part of the woodland now inclosed and to be inclosed and all Timber and other Trees Wood and Underwood of what Growth or Species soever now standing." For this the Reeces would pay an annual rental of £321 for a term of twenty-one years. See Ry. Ch. 1017.
The indenture was signed by HLP (with AL her witness) and by John and Samuel Reece (with John Oldfield their witness). The spelling of Reece is taken from the appropriate signatures.
2. James Charles (1791–post 1820) was the son of James Dale of Glanville's Wooton, near Sherborne, Dorset. The young Dale, who had prepared at Wimborne and Enborne, matriculated at Sidney College, Cambridge (1811), receiving his B.A. in 1815 and his M.A. in 1818.
3. HLP refers to Sir John Williams's brother, Fleetwood, his insolvency, and his marital infidelity.
4. The sentiment appears in a speech by the Princess Nekayah in *Rasselas,* chap. 26.
5. Richard Stroud, Virginia Coffee House, Cornhill, London.
6. HLP refers to her property in the parishes of Llangwadl and Tydweiliog, near Pwllheli in Carnarvonshire.

TO JOHN OLDFIELD

Sent Monday Morning
1: July *1811.*

My dear Mr. Oldfield
as well as myself felt so agitated by our Fryday Morning's Conversation that

I dare say he forgot poor Salusbury's Letter: but no matter; I wrote to him at Mr. Pemberton's Longnor near Shrewsbury where he Spends a Day.

I wonder if Mr. T. Lloyd's Son or his Female Servant could tell whose Authority that good Man considered as so *Undoubted*: They must know what Friends were in his Confidence.[1]

Did they imagine Dear Piozzi would have lived 25 Years in a Dream, spending Thousands after Thousands on other People's Property!—and Lord Keith—a Man of Business—can he Think—that my Estate was not settled on my Second husband and my Children by *him*? I was Younger then, by two or Three Years than Lady Keith was when She married. Mr. Ray, my Executor drew the Will we cannot find,[2] because he and Old Macnamara of Streatham thought *that* would bind the Business firmer,—and that very Mr. Ray is Trustee to Lady Keith and Mrs. Mostyn both, and says that *both* the Husbands behaved ill to *him* who I know to be a Man high in Fortune, and of Consummate honour. And he was very well with Lady Keith in 1810—I dined at her house and met him; but he has since had a Difference with *My Lord*.

I will write and ask him for the Counterpart——that is—if he *has* the Counterpart of my Will giving all to Piozzi; because Old Macnamara being a Roman Catholic had a sharp Eye to Disqualifications,—and advised me to make a Will in his favour after we returned from abroad.

All this came into my Head since you left me scarce recovered, my Amazement at these Doubts and Disbeliefs of my Power over an Estate which has undergone a good many Pulls, but which is I hope—and the Disposal of it—— firmly fixed by the great Disposer of all human Possessions in the hand of Dear Mr. Oldfield's ever Obliged and faithful/ H: L: Piozzi.

Do pray come to us next Week, pray do: call it Business or Pleasure, but a Visit from You, would do me *so much good for my Health*.

Text Ry. 533.27; copy of a letter to Mr. Oldfield.

1. This letter to her solicitor is concerned with HLP's quarrel with her daughters over the ownership of Bachygraig and her right to bequeath it to a personally chosen heir.
2. HLP's will was signed 4 September 1793. It was witnessed by John Jones of Mortimer Street, Robert Ray of Lincoln's Inn, and Leonard Chappelow of Hill Street.
This will (Princeton University Library) reaffirms her marriage contract of 19 July 1784 (Ry. Ch. 1239) in which she shares all her wealth and estates with GP. In the 1793 will he is named her sole heir and her property becomes his, "his Heirs and Assigns."

DR. JOHN PERKINS, JR., TO HESTER LYNCH PIOZZI

Coventry. High Street
22 September 1811.

Dear Madam

It is not without unusual sensations of deference and respect that I take up my pen to address you, from whom a variety of occurrences has separated me since my childhood; and were it not for that felicity of memory for which I have heard you, Madam, repeatedly praised, I should with reason, fear that so inconsiderable a being as myself must long since have escaped your recollection.[1]

A romantic stream of events, Madam, has hurried me through various scenes, various stations in life, and various climes, since I left the calm retreats, which your villa at Streatham afforded the studious, to proceed to Dr. Parr's for my education:[2] I was then about to dip my feet, for the first time in the ocean of human life.

After two years, past with that venerable and learned man, I contracted marriage with an amiable and well educated young person, whose fortune however had been reduced by unforeseen and irremediable misfortunes to nothing. This served as a source of dissention between myself and family, and occasioned a breach which neither time, nor the hardships I have experienced during nine years captivity in France has as yet been able to close.

I am now returned from the Continent, to establish myself as a Physician in my native Country. (I ought to have already mentioned that I have made Medicine my profession for these seventeen years.) By the persuasion of a friend, I have fixed upon Warwickshire as my place of residence, where I am environed by the friends of my youth, and have every reason to expect ultimate success. These latter circumstances which are the more interesting and agreable to me, because during a long series of years I have been unused to the smiles of Fortune would however have infinitely more charms for me, If I were permitted to enjoy the distinguished honour of your friendship, and were not allowed to flatter myself with the hope that you had not entirely forgotten him, whom your goodness formerly induced you to hold over the baptismal fount.—I should, Madam, be yet more happy if I were allowed to visit you in your enchanting retreat, and to assure you personally with how much sincerity of esteem/ I remain/ Your obedient and dutiful servant/ John Perkins M: D:

Text Ry. 556.159. *Address* Mrs. Piozzi/ Vale of Clwyd/ Denbighshire. *Postmark* COVENTRY 23 SE 23 1811.

1. This letter should be read in conjunction with the letter of 1 October 1811 from his father.
2. See HLP to Robert Ray, 20 January 1798, n. 3.

JOHN PERKINS TO HESTER LYNCH PIOZZI

Brighton
1 October 1811

My dear Madam

Accept in first instance my very best thanks for your kind letter of the 28 Ult., to the enquiries it contains, I shall give you a short narrative by way of answer as best enabling you to form your own Judgment and direct your Conduct.[1]

My son John was brought up as you may remember with every care and expence that a kind Parent could bestow to qualify him in holding hereafter with the rank of a Gentleman, the situation in life which I enjoy. He was introduced into the business and soon afterwards formed the connection which has separated him from his family—it was not want of fortune alone *in his Wife* that brought upon him my displeasure, but want of *character*, with Education and the brightest prospects before him he married a common abandoned Profligate, to say nothing more my dear Madam, an Inmate and companion of Lady Worstleys[2] and a Partner in her profligacy, all this known to him at the time—a Father of a Family could not overlook this. However I did not abandon him. As he could not continue in my business I sent him to College with a liberal allowance to qualify as a Physician, set him up in London at a considerable expence, from whence he fled to the continent in debt. It was at that period My Wife saved the Child you saw at Bath from the wrack.

After several years of Imprisonment and folly on the continent he returned last Winter with his Family to England, with a load of debt from which I relieved him.

He had however in all his Misfortunes or Imprudences improved his Knowledge and certainly possesses Talents which might make him a useful and ornamental Member of Society.

I therefore stepped in once more to save him from ruin and by the exertions of my Friends have settled him at Coventry, where if he will remain Steady, quiet, honest, and Industrious he *must* do well—This is the History.[3]

There is much more which had better be passed over. If you should write to him my dear Madam you may render him some service, in Exerting those strong abilities you possess, to perswade him to remain quiet where he is, to persevere in the hopes of Success, to Endeavour to retrieve his Character and to make some amends for the many years that passed away in banishment, in disgrace, without profit or good and to remember he has *with him* a Wife and three Children who have hither to depended upon his Father for their daily bread—You may thus serve your Godson and oblige an old Friend who still retains his esteem and due sense of your Many Excellent qualities which allways was and ever will be admired by/ Your Obliged and Most Obedient Humble Servant/ John Perkins.

Text Ry. 556.160. *Address* Mrs. Piozzi/ Brynbella/ near Denbigh/ N. Wales. *Postmark* OC 2 811.

1. Dr. John Perkins Jr., now thirty-seven, was HLP's godson, whom ca. 1790 she sent to study with Samuel Parr at Hatton, Warwickshire, as a private pupil. See *Thraliana*, 2:849, n. 4. About 1793, he dropped out of school, out of his father's business, which he sampled, and made an unfortunate marriage (at least, according to the elder Perkins). He then went to Edinburgh to study medicine and received his M.D. in 1797. Unable to maintain his London practice, he fell into debt, fleeing to France with his wife and three of his children, but leaving his eldest daughter with her grandparents. See HLP to Q, 17 January 1806 and n. 26. In France he was imprisoned, allowed to return to England only in 1810, where he set up a new practice, this time in Coventry. Eager to renew his friendship with HLP, the younger Perkins wrote to her on 22 September. Before replying, she sought his history from his parent. This letter is John Perkins's answer to her request.

2. Seymour Dorothy Fleming had in 1775 married Richard Worsley (b. 1751), seventh baronet (1768) of Appuldurcombe, who died intestate and without male issue on 8 August 1805 of "an apoplexy." As a consequence, a jointure of £70,000 reverted to his widow, whose marriage portion was £80,000. See *AR*, "Chronicle," 47 (1805): 492.

3. The tension between son and father never abated. In his will, the elder Perkins divided his property among his wife Amelia and their four sons: Henry (1776–1855), Frederick (1780–1860), Alfred Thrale (1781–1828), and Charles (1785–1851). To his eldest son "for which I have provided otherwise five hundred pounds for mourning." The will had been signed 7 May 1812 and proved 5 December 1812. See P.R.O., Prob. 11/1539/552.

TO DR. JOHN PERKINS, JR.

9: October 1811.

Dear Sir

On receiving your Letter I wrote to your good Father, whose Severities you seem very causelessly to complain of. The Education he bestowed on You was not rendered useless by Parsimony, The Money you have received at his hands would have made many a Man rich, and many a Man happy; who possessed not the Tenth Part of your Abilities—With regard to your Marriage, The World and he have been completely of the Same Mind; and I saw one of your Children under his Protection at Bath about seven Years ago:—Mr. Perkins tells me you have three at Coventry.

For *their* Sakes dear Sir be careful of what's left, whether Fortune or Character: 19 Parts out of 20 surely suffice the lightest Head or Heart to fling away—— and Conduct is perhaps more necessary in *Your* Profession than in any other. A Physician's Reputation depends on a Thousand Things beside Talents and Learning: Those that Employ him can seldom judge of his Excellence, Those who reject—pretend not to know in what he is deficient—but Regularity of Behaviour will give Dignity to Gentleness of Manners—and keep out the dangerous Enemy *Contempt* which is to a Character what Surgeons call the *Ignis frigidus* the Sphacelated Part—that soon destroys all Life in the Constitution.

To be respected with your Powers of Mind Sir, requires little more than to be quiet: keep still in your Place nor let People *suppose* you have Leisure to make Visits fourscore Miles from the Spot fixed on as your Residence.

A Medical Friend once told me he owed much of his Prosperity to *keeping home*.[1] People always knew where to find me, was his Expression—and in a Country Town where he like you once chose to reside, it is really of great Importance.

But I will obtrude on you no longer—*This* Letter you drew upon yourself by claiming as Godmother/Yours and Your Family's/ very sincere Friend and Servant/ H: L: Piozzi.

Text Ry. 533.28; a draft.

1. Dr. W. M. Thackeray, who lived in Chester.

TO JOHN PERKINS

9: October 1811.

My dear Mr. Perkins
   may command my Pen worne out as it is if the Precepts it conveys can be of any Use. I annex the Copy of my Letter to your Son, and hope he will at length be tired of ranging the World and stay quietly at home. It is a Melancholy Consideration to think how little Benefit is brought to Body, Soul, or Purse by Superior Talents, and to *me* who have always made my Pride and Pleasure out of Literary Acquirements it is particularly afflicting but we can't help These Things—When the Dice are once Thrown We must play them the best we can; I hope Mrs. Perkins continues well and her little Amelia,[1] and that *She* will remain under Your Protection, till She obtains that of a good Husband. So God bless you my good Sir, and see on the other side how I have schooled our young Doctor, but he really drew the Lesson on himself.
   I am ever his Wellwisher, and *Your/* most faithful Servant/ H: L: Piozzi—

Text Ry. 533.29.

1. See HLP to Q, 17 January 1806, n. 26.

TO JOHN SALUSBURY PIOZZI SALUSBURY

Sunday Night
27: October 1811.

Oh dearest Salusbury!
   How I should like to give You *Toko,* as you are used to call a Stroke with a little Stick. After fretting and frighting myself into a nervous Fever, I have this Day the Happiness to hear *of* my Inestimable Pug from *Stroud* with a 40£ Claim enclosed. Hamlet likewise has written to say Your Silver Plate went from London on the 19th but he has had no Letter from you acknowledging its Receipt;[1] so *his* Intelligence which arrived Yesterday, increased my Terrors, lest some harm

had happened. It now appears however that you were alive on the 22d: and do write to me *now* for Shame, if not for Love. Indeed I see neither Common Sense nor Knowlege of the World in persisting to think it a heavy Tax on Life to spend 3 Minutes in writing every Week 3 Words—*safe, well,* and *happy.* Those Words are all I want—as I well know the *last* of them implies the Conservation of your Virtue.——Nothing in *My* Power, no nor in *Buonaparte's* Power, could make *you* happy with a Spotted Conscience.—

What a hideous Story is this of the Clown and the Nobleman![2] Methinks Lady Ann Crofton had more Need to run Mad about such an Accident than poor Bradbury[3]——The whole however is suppressed, and not a News Paper named it after the first and second Day.

Dearest,—*Dearest* Boy! keep out of these worthless People's Company as much—as You can.——The Word *Boy* puts me in mind of poor Uncle: if he saw this Letter, and heard of the Wine Bill, and the Plate Bill—and *my* Complaints that you never write——and *Your* Humour of forbearing hitherto to accept any Profession; I think he *would* say "Charming *Boy*! I am very glad; He is spoiled *enough* now."

Farewell! Laughing or Crying I am ever Yours,/ and *only* yours Whilst/ H: L: Piozzi.

The Horse does not recover as he should do: The Swelling falls down to his Knees—and he feels something which prevents his Lying down in the Stable— but Owen says he will *come up for sure,* because he eats and drinks, and is well *at his Heart.*

I cannot calm my Spirits even by reading Prayers;—have Pity on my Nerves, and write before I am too ill to beg of you: and don't feel *angry* but *Sorry* that I can neither eat nor sleep for want of a Letter.

Is *it* come to the Dean's Ears? I fancied so by what your *only* Letter from Christ Church said of his kind Reception.

Text Ry. 585.122.

1. Thomas Hamlet (fl. 1770-1820) was a jeweler and silversmith at 1 Prince's Street, Soho.

2. HLP refers to Lady Crofton's son, Hamilton. Previous to his sailing to India, where he was to serve as an aide-de-camp to a general, he took rooms at the Crown Inn, Portsmouth. There he met Mr. Bradbury, a famous clown, who owned a "valuable snuff-box . . . in the shape of a large hunting watch." Shortly after displaying it to Crofton and two other gentlemen, Bradbury missed his box. When questioned about it, Crofton denied having seen it and stated that his room at the inn had been robbed. In the course of an investigation at the inn, it was learned that two other rooms had been burglarized.

Crofton, who was suspected, appeared unconcerned. Only when an attempt to search his person was made, did he confess to the robbery. Thereupon he "caught up a pen-knife and was detected in the act of cutting his throat, with as much force as is used with an unsharpened knife." He was prevented from doing himself harm and charges against him were pressed. See *AR,* "Chronicle," 53 (1811): 134–37. See HLP to TSW, 20 December 1811.

3. Anne Crofton, née Croker (d. 1817), was elevated to the peerage of Ireland (an honor intended for her husband Sir Edward, who had died in 1797) by the title of Baroness Crofton, of Mote, county Roscommon.

TO THE REVEREND ROBERT GRAY

Brynbella
13th November 1811.

Of Fray Gerundio I never heard except from Baretti, who was always talking about him; and as veracity was never among Baretti's merits, it may very possibly be more nearly connected with the translator than I was aware of.[1] Preaching is however a favourite topic of ridicule among Spanish wits. There is a comedy, exceedingly laughable, by Calderon della Barca, called the 'Devil turned Preacher,' which I used to read thirty years ago;[2] but I have no books in that language here, so it fades away too fast from my mind. Old Macklin used to say, there was a geography in humour:[3] I am convinced there is one in oratory. That preaching which would impress a London congregation would roll over our folks here and leave no trace: as the tail of the serpent comes nearer the mouth meanwhile, extremes meet in *everything*; and there is a rage for pulpit instruction that I did never observe in my younger days, but which marked the early periods of church history, and marks these late ones. There is likewise a visible disposition to inordinate vices not dreamed of forty years ago, but bearing strong resemblance to what one reads of in the first and second centuries. Knowledge increases too in a wonderful manner, but the science ends in a wonder after all. Witness the aeronauts, the galvanists, the vaccinators, and a long etcetera of philosophers who turn the flame downwards, and burning our diamonds to death, find them to be *charcoal*. Never was poor Nature so put to the *rack*, and never of course was she made to tell so many *lies*. The thing Fourcroy says which best pleases *me* is, that of all our human anatomy, the brain holds out longest from decay.[4] *Ainsi soit-il.*

Text Hayward, 2:268–69.

1. José Francisco de Isla (1703–1781), a translator and Jesuit preacher, made the name of Fray Gerundio apply to one who spoke on religious or ecclesiastical matters with affected erudition and bombastic cleverness. See Father Isla's *Historia del Famoso predicadore Fray Gerundio de Campazas* (1758).
  Baretti is said to have planned a translation of the *Historia* into English. While he never saw this work through, he did write a preface for it, which was apparently published in his lifetime.
2. HLP wrote about this play, which "beats them all for humorous oddity," in *Retrospection*, 2:444. According to Bruce W. Wardropper, HLP's attribution is dubious. The Devil plays a declared role in at least four Calderón plays: *El mágico prodigioso*; *El Josef de las mujeres*; *Las cadenas de Demonio*; and *El diablo predicador, y mayor contrario amigo*. Wardropper speculates that the last is the play in question. See B. B. Ashcom, *A Descriptive Catalogue of the Spanish Comedias Sueltas in the Wayne State University Library and Private Library of Professor B. B. Ashcom* (Detroit: Wayne State University Libraries, 1965), 27.
3. For the actor Charles Macklin, see HLP to SL, 31 December 1785, n. 5.
4. Antoine-François de Fourcroy (1755–1809), comte de Fourcroy, *Leçons Élémentaires d'Histoire Naturelle, et de Chimie*, 2 vols. (Paris, 1782), 2:707–8. See also his *L'Art de connoitre et d'employer Les Médicamens dans les Maladies qui attaquent Le Corps Humain*, 2 vols. (Paris, 1785), 1:368–71.
  HLP was intrigued by Fourcroy's assumption and noted it in "Harvard Piozziana," vol. 4.

TO JOHN SALUSBURY PIOZZI SALUSBURY

[December 1811][1]

My dearest Child

If you are Ill what *shall* I do? what *can* I do for my Darling? Oh send and tell me.—If you are well, Your Heart is made of Stone; but No, I'm certain there has been some Accident.

This is the 16th Day since Your last Date; It never, *never* was so before, I have looked back and counted.

A Letter from Shephard by mere Chance convincing me you were in Being on the 6th or 7th of this Month, has served as the sole Comfort of/ poor/ H: L: P.

Turn over and accept my Thanks, Prayers, and Blessings for this timely Renewal of a wretched Existence which but too surely does depend on your *Life*, *Character*, and *Behaviour* as the Hawkers express it, who will soon be crying Mr. Crofton's up and down the Street.[1]

> But here the Letter comes at last,
> Like Dinner after too long Fast.
> When the made-Dish—its Sauce grown Thick,
> Makes one half happy, and half Sick.
> Ah Salusbury! had *You* hung one *Hour*
>   On those sharp Hooks of Expectation,
> That my poor Heart in pieces tore;
>   How you'd have stormed with Indignation!
> But you acknowledge 'twas not right,
> And promise not to kill me quite.
>
> Before that Day arrives, pray read
> Miss Seward's Book, You *must indeed*.
> At least *Two Letters*, where She praises
> The Piozzis in such polished Phrases.
> But for that Cordial to my Pride,
> I really think I must have died.[2]
>
> From *You* no kind Return e'er came,
> For Chronicle or Epigram:
> And what much Stranger will be found,
> No Notice of Your Twenty Pound.
> Will you have more? Oh hang the Pelf:
> Only keep *Well* and *Good Yourself*.
>   Volume 1st Page 254 and Page 335.

The Books are in every Shop Window, step in and read those Passages—don't buy them: because I suppose—I *must*.

You are a dear Creature after all, for telling me *what ailed you*, and *how much*——I was so afraid you had broken a Blood Vessel: but now I will *try* to eat and sleep once more, if it so pleases God. Let me never again be above a Week without some Scrap to convince me you are *alive*——or what am I caring for?

These high roaring Winds, rushing Rains, and utter Solitude (since I broke my Carriage) would make Buonaparte *Melancholy*, but they have another Effect on *Me* which I *like less still*.

At present I will say my Prayers and haste to Bed——The Scolding does *me good*:

You remember we agreed to change Characters—You the cross old Uncle, and I the good Child: but in my *spelling book* I learn that the Word Scold has never an *h* in it.

Adieu, There is a little of the *Old Stuff* yet left you see, in Your own *half-exhausted*, but still tenderly and anxiously/ attached H: L: P.

Pray does not Vacation begin next Monday Month? do write and tell me.

Text Ry. 585.118.

1. The reference to Crofton would indicate that the letter was written in December 1811.

2. For the six-volume edition of Anna Seward's *Letters*, see HLP to Q, 31 January 1810, nn. 16, 17. The letters to which HLP alludes praise her and GP equally. See particularly that to the Reverend Doctor Warner, 7 March 1786, in which Seward comments: "[HLP's] fine talents, and the ungrateful abuse of Dr Johnson, upon this marriage, after the years she had devoted to rendering his life happy, ought, and will interest every benevolent heart in her destiny. Such hearts will rejoice to see envy and malice disappointed by the devoted attachment of the highly obliged Piozzi, and his acknowledged virtues" (1:254–55).

TO THE REVEREND THOMAS SEDGWICK WHALLEY

Brynbella
20th December 1811.

My dear Doctor Whalley's *enchanting* Head was made to talk in a happy hour for me, who sit so much alone, and felt while I was reading it the Pleasures of Society——It was a sorry Trick tho' to shew my Letter, and I never called her (indeed I never *do* call her) *Mrs.* Hannah More——you know *Doctor Johnson* turned a stupid Fellow out of his Room once for calling Milton *Mister John*.[1]

Well never mind; I have made *her* laugh before now, &c. so I have dear Siddons—who still continues to make every body cry.

Mrs. Stafford's Situation is an Interesting one, and likely to attract Attention from the Great and Gay;[2] because there is a little private Pretension to Benevolence still left in this *Marble* Age; so *hard*, so *cold* and so *polished*.——Lighthearted as I *seem*, The Atrocities which roll off other People's Minds Impress mine very forcibly indeed;—and when I look on the deserving Lad of my heart as you sweetly call him, Tears of Apprehension for his Virtue's Safety, stand in my long-experienced Eyes.

Your Profession would have been a *Guard upon it* through Life's perilous Journey—more perilous by far than in *our Young Days* when Guilt was certainly Punishment in this World, but now its frequency will I fear take off all du<e> Abhorrence. The hideous Tale of Hamilton Crofton for Example, which as it appears ended in Nothing;—and now Mr. Walsh's Business:[3]—surely surely one need not be like the old Man in Horace, to see plainly that Things grow worse and worse with the Rapidity of a Wheel pushed down hill increasing in Speed at every Rotation:[4] but Whilst Britannia herself condescends to live by keeping a Brothel in Hindostan, who can wonder at her Subject's Wickedness on this Side the Water?——every Sentiment of *Honour* must be lost, as well as every Remains of *Virtue*.[5]

Lady Kirkwall had the Satisfaction her Dutyful Heart panted after; She *did* cross the Wintery Seas safe, and find her Father alive:[6] Poor Poor Lady Kirkwall! I hope She will call on me coming back, She has with her *my* Friend and hers, that pretty Miss Francis, whose Execution of difficult Passages in Music is only equalled by her Skill in Scholastic Learning.—I tell her always She is like a Quack Doctor, delighting in Matters of Difficulty: that of making Lady K—— happy is not the easiest among them, whilst her Babies are detained from her Sight;[7] The Counsels of a Parent denied her in future and her Husband canvassing a Part of the King's Dominions where he has not *now* a Foot of Land— having sold Lleweney before he thought about Denbigh.

So now I will release you; and trust to the charming Friends you are with, to keep Lassitude and Torpor far away——They fly from the Name of Mrs. Lutwyche.[8] The worthy and amiable Master of the Mansion will make his house ever agreeable to his Guests—and le Chevalier de Malte will tell you that en la Cuisine tout se trouve.[9]

If tis a Plague to write, (which never appeared to me from any of the truly delightful Letters I have received from kind Dr. Whalley,) stay till you come to Monstrous London, *then* do me the honour of a long Account *how* monstrous grown.

I saw the Hindoo Superstition of *Globe*, *Wing* and *Serpent*, implying *Dominion*, *Conservation*, and *Destruction* coming into use as an Upholsterer's Ornament when I was last there, but finding nobody understood me when the Remark was made——it was not worth while to repeat it: Claudius Buchanan's book however Set me o'thinking on it again. How very awful are these Times Dear Sir! Public and private Occurrences bearing Such a Red, and Menacing Aspect— yet Knowledge increasing all the while; and Virtue herself—dead as She is,— Galvanized into momentary Exertions. People *are shocked* even on the 20th December 1811 at the Murders in Shadwell.[10]

Once more Adieu, and continue for 20 Years more that Partiality for her and her Memory, which has for 30 at least been the Vaunt and Consolation of/ Your Obliged and Faithful Servant/ H: L: Piozzi.

Text Hyde Collection. *Address* Rev: Thos. Sedgwick Whalley/ at Lutwyche's Esqr/ Marlbro' Buildings/ Bath. *Postmark* DENBIGH 224.

1. See *Boswell's Johnson*, 4:325 and n. 3.

2. Mary Stafford lived at the lodging and boardinghouse she owned at 30 Gay Street, Bath, from about April 1811 until the end of December 1817. See "Walcot's Poor Rate Books," Guildhall, Bath.

3. Benjamin Walsh, M.P. for Wootton Bassett, absconded with a large sum of money stolen from the solicitor general, Sir Thomas Plumer.

According to *The Times*, 11 December 1811: "The sum originally placed in the hands of the broker was £21,000 for the purchase of Exchequer Bills. About £5,500 only of that sum were expended in that way on Thursday morning last. In the evening, the broker [Walsh] waited upon his principal, to state that the order could only be executed in part; and that he had paid the remainder of the cash to the amount of £15,500 into Gosling's and Co. the Knight's Banker; to prove which, he produced a receipt from the house for that sum, which entirely satisfied Sir T.P. It was perfectly true, that about five o'clock on the Thursday, the broker paid into the house of Gosling and *Co*. his check on Curtis and Co. on account of Sir T.P. to the amount in question; but it was at too late an hour to clear the draft in the usual way; and no suspicion being attached to the transaction, the matter stood over until next evening; when it was found that there were no effects at the broker's bankers. Sir T. was immediately apprised of the circumstance, and on the same evening drove down to Hackney, to require an explanation; when he learned from the broker's wife, that her husband had gone to Ireland. It was not until then that Sir T. was convinced he was duped of his money, and took the means to recover it. The several ports were telegraphed on Saturday morning on the business, but at that period the fugitive had two days' start."

For further on the "Walsh Business," see HLP to Q, [29] February 1812.

4. HLP is combining from two Horatian poems the metaphoric wheel and image of the beleaguered, unhappy old man. The metaphor of the wheel is derived from *Odes*, 3.10.10 (lines 9–12) and the portrait of the old man from *Ars Poetica* (lines 169–74). HLP had used the portrait of *senex* in a letter to TSW, 23 April 1801, n. 3.

5. HLP alludes to the revelations made in Claudius Buchanan's new book, *Christian Researches in Asia* (Cambridge: J. Deighton; London: Cadell and Davies, 1811).

In "Harvard Piozziana," vol. 4, she wrote: "I know not however what London—or what England can do to wipe out the stain thrown on her by this new Book of Claudius Buchanan [on Hindostan] . . . where Britannia does curiously keep an actual and positive *Brothel* consisting of 400 Dancing Girls besides Boys for their Idol's [the Jaggernaut] avowed Pleasure: and cooly receives the Profits of *their Abomination* as an article of Commerce."

Several years later she wrote in the "Commonplace Book": "Jaggernaut in East India devours chiefly Boys and Females—*Human* Creatures, why do not these Missionaries for Shame go to Orissa and put a final End to *that* Abomination? 'Tis a Joke to pretend Zeal for God's Worship, and suffer *our own* Subjects in Ireland and India to continue in gross Idolatry——because Avarice would cry out in both Countries if Conversion indeed came forward. . . . the rich Indians pay our People for Permission of Crimes which in England would be punished with Death——*if* openly perpetrated."

6. Baron de Blaquiere was to die on 27 August 1812, at Bray, county Wicklow. HLP believed Lady Kirkwall to be too attached to her father. When reading Steele's *Spectator* 449 about the twenty-three-year old Fidelia, who could not be drawn "from the Side of her good old Father," HLP wrote in the margin, "She is like Lady Kirkwall" (6:307; 1789 ed.).

7. Lady Kirkwall had two sons: Thomas John Hamilton, aged eight, and William Edward, now six. By the spring of 1811, Lord Kirkwall gained custody of them. See Lady Kirkwall to HLP, 15 August 1811 (Ry. 580.26), and particularly 12 September (Ry. 580.28):

"Tell me my dearest beloved Friend if You know that my dear Infants are in Wales, or with Lord Kirkwall, or where?—how strange must this request appear to you—how would the relation shock your heart were I to tell you how first detained from me by stratagems and under pretences as unworthy as they are malicious. They are even prevented writing to inform me of their health and preservation!—My heart is choaked up—with the contending emotions of a Mother I suppose who loves too sincerely for her own happiness. God forgive those who cause me this wanton and unnecessary vexation."

8. For William and Mary Lutwyche, see HLP to MW [ca. April 1808], n. 2.

9. The Chevalier de Malte was Pierre-Marie-Louis Boisgelin de Kerdu (1758–1816), royalist, soldier, and travel writer. See particularly his *Ancient and Modern Malta . . . also, the History of the Knights of St. John of Jerusalem*, 3 vols. (London, 1804). During the Revolution, he emigrated to England, remaining there until the Bourbon restoration in 1814.

10. A family named Marr were found brutally murdered by thieves, their heads battered by a heavy mallet. Dead were the shopkeeper Marr, his wife, their infant child, and the shopboy. The incident occurred on 7 December 1811. See *AR*, "Chronicle," 53 (1811): 157 ff.; *The Times*, 9 December 1811.

On 19 December, just two streets away from the lace and pelisse warehouse owned by Mr. Marr at "29 Ratcliffe-highway," there were "More Murders," still "another scene of sanguinary atrocity." The victims were Mr. Williamson, owner of the King's Arms public house in Old Gravel Lane, Mrs. Williamson, and her maid, Bridget Harrington; all had their throats cut, their bodies battered and mutilated. See *The Times*, 21 December 1811.

TO THOMAS CADELL AND WILLIAM DAVIES

Brynbella
8: January 1812.

Mrs. Piozzi presents her best Compliments and Wishes of a happy New Year to Mess. Cadell and Davies:[1]

They know perfectly that She never printed any thing but the Anecdotes of Dr. Johnson——The Observations made during the delightful Years She past in Italy;—The Synonymes,—British Synonymy it was called:—and the Retrospection:[2] which She heartily wishes had been published from their House.[3] She leaves her Portrait and her Fame to *their* Mercy, who will have much more Care for them than She has; and who have been always very obliging.——One further favour would be however particularly welcome to her: It is, that The Portrait should be sent to her Nephew John Piozzi Salusbury Esq. Christ Church Oxford; where he is A Gentleman Commoner—and—strange to say—feels desirous of having an Old Woman's Picture in his Rooms.[4]——I did write to Mr. Jackson, and begged *him* to send it, but by some Mistake the Letter was returned me from the Post Office.

I shall like to have the *Print* here at Brynbella——The House my *late* Husband built. Bachygraig is the Name of my old Family Seat in Denbighshire, first Inhabited by Katherine Tudor de Berayne[5]—Cousin and Ward of Queen Elizabeth;[6] and with her consent married to Sir John Salusbury my Immediate Ancestor— Then Possessor of Lleweney Hall[7]—which my Uncle sold to Lord Kirkwall's Father—who has lately disposed of it to a Purchaser.[8]

Text Charles D. LaFollette Collection, Corning, New York. *Address* Mess: Cadell and Davies/ Booksellers/ London. *Postmark* ST ASAPH 10 JA 10 1812.

1. HLP throughout this letter alludes to a little-known publication of Cadell and Davies. Comprising only six pages, it is called *Portraits of Gower, Piozzi, Wilmot, Rose, Beaumont & Scott*. The work is dated 1811.
2. HLP neglects to include the *Letters* (brought out by Cadell) among her publications.
3. *Retrospection* was brought out by John Stockdale, who—HLP believed—rushed her through the printing process, allowed proof errors to stand, and refused to print an index.
4. For HLP's portrait by John Jackson, printed by Cadell and Davies (n. 1 above), see HLP to JSPS, 19 February 1810. The portrait is reproduced as the frontispiece to volume four of this edition.
5. For Katheryn of Berain, see HLP to PSP [ca.26 July 1800], n. 12. For her association with Bachygraig, see HLP to SL, 4 November 1785, n. 1.
6. Katheryn of Berain was the daughter of Tudur ap Robert Vychan and his wife Jane, whose father, Sir Roland Velville (d. 1527), was a natural son of Henry VII. Katheryn and Queen Elizabeth (whose father was the legitimate son of Henry VII) were therefore cousins. Moreover, according to Welsh tradition, Katheryn was said to be a ward of the queen.

7. For HLP's ancestor, Katheryn's first husband, see HLP to PSP [ca. 26 July 1800], n. 12.

8. For the sale of Llewenny to Thomas Fitzmaurice by Sir Robert Cotton, see HLP to PSW, 6 October 1792, n. 2; for its sale by Kirkwall to the Reverend Edward Hughes of Kinmel, see HLP to MW, 18 February 1809, n. 3.

TO LADY WILLIAMS

Tuesday
28: January 1812

I snatch up some old *Gilt* Paper to tell my dear Lady Williams that I have always a true sense and feeling of her Kindness. Salusbury set off this Morning; I follow on Thursday the Day after Tomorrow. My 71st Birth Day was like my *Life* stormy and rainy Morning and Afternoon; but clearing up fine *late in the Evening;*—and the *Night* very tranquil and brilliant——So may it be/ with your Dear Ladyship's/ ever obliged and faithful/ H: L: Piozzi.

I will take Care of my Little Commission, and am glad Mr. Williams did not expose himself to such rough Weather.[1] Give to Sir John and him My very best Regards.

Text Ry. 4 (1812–1818).

1. The eighteen-year-old JW, who went off to Rugby for his last term prior to his admission at Cambridge on 13 June 1812.

TO JOHN SALUSBURY PIOZZI SALUSBURY

No. 16 Pultney Street Bath
Ash Wednesday 12: February 1812.

It was high Time to write Dearest Salusbury—a too anxious Heart was just beginning to poyson all my Pleasures of which every one is offering Me choice. The People at the Pump still whisper one another—That's Mrs. Piozzi;—and Invitations never came more frequent, even in my best Days. All goes well but the Money-Stuff; and I was never so *forced* upon Prudence in *that* Way before.

Well! If Oldfield and Maughan have Seized 515£ instead of 489£ We have got the whole Bryn,—Lime kiln included; and our Acquisition stops only at the Cottage *beyond*:—beside good Allotments near Gwern ŷ coombe, and Some Arable, at which I rejoyce; because that will mend our Tythes, and increase the Value of our adjacent Farms. The Fencing and Planting of what is appointed Wood Land, will cost us 500£ more.——So you must pray for my Life, and deserve the Advantage of it by prudent Conduct. Meanwhile I am just come from hearing Gods Curses denounced on Fornicators, Drunkards—and Those who Curse Father or Mother——*Lady Keith* ran through Bath Three Days ago, and did me the honour to take Breakfast; She is the only Person I have seen who did not ask for *You*.

Your *fair* Friend and Confident, and my professed Enemy—The dainty Widow of Segroid; has written *her* Enquiries in a fond familiar Style——desiring *best Remembrances to Old Sarum*.[1]

If I write more You will not read it I suppose, You are so *immersed in Business*——*Dear* Fellow! but do let me add to your Occupations, that of looking out a Lap Dog for poor Lady Clerke, who buried Ladi last Week with all the honours of War;[2] Mr. Townshend wishes her a new Favourite,[3] because She is *so* sad, and *so* sick——his Kindness towards *you* quite affects my Heart and Spirits. Edmund Byng is my frequent Visitor—he hopes the Dean and you love each other.[4] Had *I* been Dean, I should have looked on any Man who Travelled on the Day appointed for a general Fast,—with some Degree of Coolness.[5]

Adieu Dearest Salusbury! beg your Friend's Pardon for me, and tell him I don't make Court to him for want of Beaux, because I have Plenty here at my Command; but because I wish him to continue his Partiality for/ Your Affectionate Aunt and *his*/ Faithful Servant/ H: L: P.

The young Roscius is coming here to act *four* Times for *five* Hundred Pounds;[6] I will try to see him play Hamlet.——I wish he would give *me* A Benefit:—he wants 500£ no more than I do; what can he mean by such a Performance? Every body is enraged at the Attempt.

Text Ry. 585.132. *Address* John Piozzi Salusbury Esq./ Christ Church/ Oxford. *Postmark* BATH FE 12 1812.

1. CMM's pun on Salisbury/Salusbury. Old Sarum, an ancient British settlement near Salisbury, served once as the residence for the kings of Wessex.

2. Byzantia Cartwright (d. 1815) had married in 1792 the Reverend William Henry Clerke (d. 1818), eighth baronet (1778).

3. For the geologist Joseph Townsend, see HLP to JSPS, 22 February 1810, n. 1.

4. For Edmund Byng, whose brother-in-law was Charles Henry Hall, dean of Christ Church, Oxford, see HLP to JSPS, 22 February 1810.

5. The *London Gazette* of 14 January contained "a proclamation for the observance of a General Fast" on 5 February in England and Ireland, and on 6 February in Scotland. See *GM* 82, pt. 1 (1812): 84.

6. See the *Bath Chronicle*, 20 February:

"Saturday [15 February], after a retirement of four years, partly spent at College, and partly in rural seclusion at his estate in Shropshire, Mr. Betty, the celebrated Young Roscius . . . again appeared on the Bath stage, in the character of the Earl of Essex. . . . It was an arduous trial; criticism, which had been formerly disarmed by the consideration of his tender years, was now alive to scan his errors with all the rigour of impartial justice, and freely censure in the man those faults which had been left unnoticed in the boy. The event, however, has afforded a full confirmation of his superior Talents: his performance as Essex, though by no means faultless, was replete with all the fire and energy of true genius." This judgment of Betty's performance was also voiced by the *Bath Journal*, 17 February.

For William Henry West Betty, see HLP to LC, 17 November 1803, n. 2.

MASTER BETTY
THE YOUNG ROSCIUS.

born at Shrewsbury, September 13th 1791.

Engraved by W. Leney after a Drawing taken from life by S. Ramsey.

William Henry West Betty. Engraved by W. Leney after a drawing taken from life by S. Ramsey. (Reproduced by permission of the Henry E. Huntington Library and Art Gallery, San Marino, California.)

TO LADY KEITH

No. 16 Pultney Street Bath
18: February 1812

I was just going to complain of my Dearest Lady Keith when I was made to feel
I had nothing to do but thank her. You should not so *Soon* have hazarded those
good Looks and clear Voice in a thick Atmosphere—but *Holydays* some how,
are never long enough—Pray make haste and be well, and love Claudius Buchanan, for he is a first-Rate Creature. The Idolatry is nothing less than *new*,
and by no means a strange one——What shocks *me* is our People taking Money
for permitting Crimes in India, which they would punish in England—and
looking on such Abominations with Coolness, thinking and saying—Ay! Why
some People worship Jaggernaut we see,[1] and some worship Jesus Christ;—
Every one to his Taste,—but *let us secure the Money.* Can Ruin be warded off
from a Nation of such Principles? by any Set of Men or Ministers——*I trow not.*
    We hear only the Echoes of les On-dits—and they sound fearfully to my
Ears,—but Echo multiplies sometimes, and so we don't believe when she Speaks
Truth and *Singleness.* The best is that Baby keeps well and sprightly, She will
have much to see—perhaps to do—Tho' to be *Pars maxima* is scarcely *per se*
desireable, it is greatly to be wished for those we best love, that nothing should
be too high or too hard for them, if called upon.
    The Pantheon must have been greatly altered to make it interesting—as a
Theatre:[2] I remember it fitted up for such a vast while ago, and a paltrier Thing
could not have been made in Pasteboard: as a Winter Ranelagh The Appearance
was grand and imposing.[3]
    We have got the Roscius here—a fat Aledrinking Country Squire, but he acts
Hamlet on Thursday, and I will venture my Neck for the Sport of seeing how
500£ for four nights can compensate the Probability of Disgrace, and the certainty of stepping on these boards with every united Prejudice against him.[4]
Are you a Man? says Lady Macbeth—Ay a bold one too replies her Husband[5]——'Tis like betting on a Game at Whist with the four Honours against
one the first Deal. Will he come thro'?
    Well Well! Joanna Baillie has the truest Notion of how Passions agitate the
human Mind of any Author since old Shakespear's Time. Her making the brav-
est General possible even *die of Fear*—is to *me* delightful,[6] who used to make
you laugh by saying how Marechal Turenne or the Duke of Marlborough would
have been a Jest to the Glazier's Boys for their *Cowardice,* if they had been set
to clean a London Window of some Second Floor poized on a tottering Board.[7]
    What is this Nonsense of Miss Owenson? and how is She Lady Morgan?[8]—
Is it all a Joke? or as the People used to say 40 Years ago—Is it all a Hum?[9]—I
remember their saying Hannah More was my Lady Somebody, and she went to
Bed with a Fever for Grief and Rage:[10] I fancy this little Tit will bear the Report
less impatiently.
    Cecy Mostyn persists there is Contagion in the Air this Spring: Twelve People
were prayed for one Day in Denbigh Church and The Bell tolls *here* incessantly:

but no Death ever affected so large a Number of People with unfeigned Tender Sensations as that of dear charming Dimond:—who left this Life with not a Debt or a Duty unpaid—having passed it in a Situation never accounted *particularly* amical to Religion or Virtue, he went thro' without ever having been seen drunk or heard swear by either Family or Acquaintance: leaving his Character unsullied by *any Vice* and enjoying Health, high Spirits, and active Manners to Three Days before he died——"There goes handsome Dimond! blythe as a Bird," was the Exclamation of a Friend the Evening before he was seized.[11]— And the clergyman who had administered the Sacrament to him in the Abby two Sundays before——could scarcely sob out the Burial Service.[12] Oh may I die the Death of the Righteous![13]—nothing could equal its Tranquillity and Happiness.

Meanwhile favour me from Time to Time with Hints of what may be expected in *this* World, where whilst I *do* remain, I shall be ever Affectionately Yours/ H: L: P.

Text Bowood Collection.

1. Claudius Buchanan had been writing about the Hindu superstition of Juggernaut as early as 1805 in his *Memoir of the Expediency of an Ecclesiastical Establishment for British India*. His most explicit description, however, occurs in *Christian Researches in Asia* (Cambridge: T. Deighton; London: Cadell and Davies, 1811):
"The throne of the idol [Juggernaut] was placed on a stupendous car or tower about sixty feet in height, resting on wheels which indented the ground deeply, as they turned slowly under the ponderous machine. Attached to it were six cables, of the size and length of a ship's cable, by which the people drew it along. Upon the tower were the priests and satellites of the idol, surrounding his throne. . . .
"After the tower had proceeded some way, a pilgrim announced that he was ready to offer himself as sacrifice to the idol. He laid himself down in the road before the tower as it was moving along, lying on his face, with his arms stretched forward. . . . and he was crushed to death by the wheels of the tower. A shout of joy was raised to the God. He is said to *smile* when the libation of the blood is made" (pp. 25–27).
2. A theater and public promenade, the Pantheon on the south side of Oxford Street, was designed by James Wyatt, R.A., and opened in 1772. When the Opera House burned down in 1789, the Pantheon—no longer fashionable—gave the operatic company a home in 1791. But the Pantheon was itself destroyed by fire in January 1792. A second, less-successful Pantheon arose. This was razed in 1812, and a third, equally unsuccessful Pantheon opened in the following year.
3. For Ranelagh, see HLP to PSW, 10 July 1789, n. 1.
4. Betty played Hamlet on 20 February (*Bath Journal*, 17 February). Of it and his other performances, the *Journal* on 24 February 1812 pointed to "his improved talents, and the most flattering and unquestionable proofs of the high estimation in which they are held by the public."
5. *Macbeth*, 3.4.57–58.
6. HLP refers to Osterloo, an imperial general, in Joanna Baillie's tragedy called *The Dream*. It appears in *A Series of Plays in which it is attempted to delineate the stronger Passions of the Mind*, vol. 3 (London: Longman, Hurst, Rees, Orme, and Brown, 1812).
7. Henri de la Tour d'Auvergne, vicomte de Turenne (1611–75) one of the greatest of French commanders, was killed in the third of the wars between the English and the Dutch (1672–78).
John Churchill (1650–1722), the most famous British general of his time, became duke of Marlborough on 14 December 1702. His name is associated with the victories of Blenheim, Ramillies, Oudenard, and Malplaquet during the War of the Spanish Succession.
8. Sydney Owenson [Lady Morgan] (ca. 1783–1859), originally of Dublin, was so successful as a novelist that in 1811 she was invited to become a permanent member of the marquess of Abercorn's household. There she met her patron's physician, Sir Thomas Charles Morgan (1783–1843), becoming his second wife in January 1812.
9. A colloquialism for *cheat* or *bamboozle*.

10. During the Blagdon controversy, Hannah More was said to have married the Reverend George Crossman, rector of Blagdon, Somerset. See HLP to LC, 17 September 1801, n. 4.

11. William Wyatt Dimond suffered a cerebral hemorrhage on Christmas Eve, 1811, and died on 2 January 1812 in Norfolk Crescent, Bath. He was buried close to the tomb of actor James Quin in the Abbey Church, where but two Sundays before—in apparent good health—he had received the sacrament with the Corporation of the city.

For Dimond, see HLP to SL, 15 November [1788], n. 2.

12. "On the Sunday following [Dimond's] demise, an enlightened and truly worthy Divine (the Rev. Dr. Tomkyns), in an eloquent and impressive sermon, most feelingly alluded to the melancholy event, and pointed out the character of Mr. Dimond as an example to society of public worth and domestic virtue." See *GM* 82, pt. 1 (1812): 90.

13. Numbers 23:10.

TO JOHN SALUSBURY PIOZZI SALUSBURY

Bath Tuesday
20: February 1812.

My Dearest Salusbury

I write at Sir Walter James's Request to beg the favour of you to go and visit his Son at Trinity College.——It seemed to me that Mr. James ought to have left his Card first—as *Semi Noble,* but it seems a Christ Church Man is not to receive Visits from Gentlemen of other Colleges, unless he *leads the Way.*[1]

Here are many showy Fellows here—with their Necks stiffened, and their Heads on one Side: whether by Fashionable *Cravats* or fashionable *Complaints* I know not; but my Heart recoils at the Sight of them. The Women too are pretty—and *odious*: giving their Partners a Pocket-handkerchief to hold for them which has wiped *their* Face, and blown *their* Nose all down the Dance:—a Mode of managing usual upon the Continent; but I never saw it in England till now.

God preserve us from such Examples either of Elegance or Morality.

Tell Dear Pemberton he must read the Countess and Gertrude;[2] It is a very useful, and to me a very entertaining Work: tho' I do not hold—with the Authour—that unless a Man is made wretched by the Severity of his Guardians or Parents from Seven Years old to Seventeen——and hardly dealt with by the World afterwards from 17 to 27—he can never be good for any thing here or hereafter!! Mercy on us! what would in that Case become of *You* or of your Friend.[3]

Indulgence however like *too wide* Stays has its Temptations and its Inconvenience: nor can any but an *excellent* Horse *indeed*, be trusted with a light hand and a Snaffle.

I feel more and more glad every Day that your Time of Tryal approaches to an End; He who guided the three Children in Scripture from the fiery Furnace can alone bring you thro' *unburnt*——*They* were not even *singed; they* prayed incessantly for Protection, *They* did not rely on themselves.[4]

May my incessant Petitions be heard for *his* Safety, who is still too fondly beloved/ by his affectionate/ H: L: P.

Text Ry. 585.133.

1. The second son of Sir Walter James, John (d. 1818) had matriculated at Trinity College, Oxford, on 20 September 1811. Not taking a degree, he was to serve for a short time as minister plenipotentiary to the Netherlands and to marry Emily Jane Stewart (d. 1865), daughter of the first marquess of Londonderry. See *GM* 88, pt. 1 (1818):647.
2. Laetitia-Matilda Hawkins, *The Countess and Gertrude; or, Modes of Discipline,* 4 vols. (London: F. C. and J. Rivington, 1811).
3. In the preface to *The Countess and Gertrude* (1: xiii–xiv), where pleasure is scorned and adversity made the rule of life, "The motive to our undertaking originated in the vexation produced by being compelled to see . . . very few children made happy by the indulgences lavished on them by their parents, very few parents reaping the expected fruits of indulgence, and very few young persons who, on quitting the paternal home, can face the realities of life without injury to their temper, ship-wreck of conscience, or a lamentable demonstration that fortitude and submission are not amongst the *accomplishments* they have acquired."
For the maxim of "severity and indulgence," see HLP to RG, 7 January 1801, n. 1; to Q [21 June] 1801, n. 6; to Ly W, 16 July 1815, n. 2.
4. For the story of Hananiah (Shadrach), Mishael (Meshach), and Azariah (Abednego), see Daniel 3:19–28. She had used the story earlier in HLP to JSPS, 27 April 1811.

TO JOHN SALUSBURY PIOZZI SALUSBURY

Saturday Night
29: February 1812.

God preserve my dearest Salusbury! and preserve him for the Girl that will make him *most* happy—*I* should not think that could be Louisa Wynne.[1]

My foreboding Soul felt *something* when the Postman knocked his smart Rap; and I was glad (God forgive me) that Mr. Lane was sick,[2] instead of my Darling being seized with these Illnesses, which carry People off so Suddenly.

The Regent had just Superseded Sir Charles Cotton, and given the Command of *his* Channel Fleet to my Lord Keith; when the Baronet dropt down dead in an Apoplexy; and never heard the Event.[3] This was happy—so far as relates to *our* World: how he was prepared for that he entered on so unexpectedly:—God and his Conscience know.

Charles Shephard will be here on Thursday, and I am glad; because he'll bring the Banker's Book and tell about Streatham——besides tho' I see Company enough, yet I feel miserably deserted at home somehow. A new Frightful Footman and a Baby Boy—Leak is gone home to meet Maughan &c.:[4] and I boyl a *Rabbet in a Coffeepot* to Save Money, which glides too quick away; and every Guinea of which goes to my heart that is not spent *on* you or *for* you—Pug as you are!! Heaven send you Safe from that _____ Place: Mr. T: Shephard may fill the Blank up.

My House is Nine Pounds o'Week;[5] The Drawing Room good, the Dining Parlour not amiss;—Two Bed Chambers on the Ground-Floor for Pem and You— one much too *large,* the other much too *Small.* You and he must Compliment about them—who has the best: I will make the worst as good as I can—but shall not put it to rights till I know you are coming. Oh how I do count the

Days! Shall you not come *together*? And Was not Dear Pem shocked at the Story of Crewe's Aunt Mrs. Bulkeley—dying of her Son's Ill Conduct—Wretched Lady![6]

You really must go and see Mr. James; *That* Family is under a Cloud of heavy Apprehensions, but do not mention it: Some Claimant has started up, new come from India, that says Sir Walter has usurped the Fortune which of good Right belongs to *him* alone.[7] A fine World is My Sweet Salusbury venturing upon; borne on the Bladder of *Hope*,[8] and of *Tomorrow*. But Love, Duty, and Friendship are three good strong Cards, if we can but twist them cleverly together, and Cement them with the best Gilding we can get.

Marianne Thelwall has lost a famous Match I hear;[9] the young Man's Father said she drest too gay, and had too little Turn for Œconomy—So She has preferred fine Ribbons to a good Establishment, and must abide the Consequences.—Fools! as Charles Shephard says—Egregious Fools!

Farewell! tomorrow is Sacrament Sunday, and I must call my Thoughts away— even from *You*—Tonight. My Father, and his two Brothers, and *their* Father all died Suddenly, when such Accidents were far less frequent.[10]—How ought *I* then to keep my great Account clear! Remember in Your Prayers sometimes Your own poor H: L: P.

The Hot Bath waits—Adieu my Dearest Creature!

Text Ry. 586.136. *Address* John Piozzi Salusbury Esq./ Christ Church/ Oxford. *Postmark* BATH <   >.

1. Louisa Wynne was the daughter of Jane, née Wynne (d. 1811) of Voelas, Denbighshire, who in 1778 had married Charles Finch (d. 1819), son of the third earl of Aylesford. Like two of her brothers, Louisa may have assumed the name of Wynne or, while retaining the surname of Finch, was known to the local gentry by her mother's maiden name.
She was to marry in 1822 Count San Martino d'Aglio, Sardinian minister to London, and to die in the same year.
2. Having studied at Eton, Henry Thomas Lane (1793–1834) matriculated at Christ Church, Oxford, on 31 October 1811. He left without a degree, dying at Middleton House in Sussex.
3. Charles Cotton (b. 1753), fifth baronet (1795) of Madingley Hall, Cambridge. A distinguished naval officer, he was made admiral in 1808 and commander in chief of the Mediterranean Fleet in 1810. Shortly before his sudden death on 24 February 1812 at Stoke, near Plymouth, he was appointed commander of the Channel Fleet.
Officially, Lord Keith's promotion to replace Sir Charles was not announced until March. See *GM* 82, pt. 1 (1812): 287.
4. Despite his misgivings, Leak was able to negotiate successfully for the enclosure of common land desired by HLP. On 9 March 1812 (Ry. 609.2) he wrote to her:
"I have this Day Received Your Letter, Inclosing a Draft on Mess. Hammersley for 57£—and am very sorry to observe the reluctance with which you part with it. I think I need not say the Money is not going to be expended for My advantage; nor is it to be expended on projects of My advising, I sincerely wish the Inclosure had not been persisted in, and you know such was My advice at the Time. Your affairs might then have been more concentrated, and Your Expenditure much reduced, and Yourself more Happy because able to put more Money in the funds, for My Own part I had no wish to engage in all this intricate business."
5. HLP was again renting a house at 16 Pulteney Street, Bath.
6. The son of Richard Crewe (d. 1814), a major general in the army, Willoughby (1792–1850) matriculated at Christ Church, Oxford, on 1 February 1810. In 1819 he received a B.C.L. from St. Alban Hall. By 1836 he was rector of Mucklestone, Staffs., following the death (19 February 1836) of the Reverend Offley Crewe.

His aunt was Jane *Eleanor* Bulkeley, née Ord, a Bath resident, who had come from Ludlow, Salop. She was the widow of Richard, who left her saddled with debts—those owed him and those he owed.

If Mrs. Bulkeley was made "wretched" by her son's behavior, she did not acknowledge this fact in her will. She left the bulk of her not-very-large estate to her two sons—the elder Richard, and Samuel. Her will had been signed 27 April 1806 and was proved at London on 2 April 1812. See P.R.O., Prob. 11/1532/154.

7. The scare over a "Claimant" proved to be without foundation. Sir Walter James's will in 1829 indicated that the estate devolved upon his grandson, Walter James (1816–ca. 1857), when he should reach the age of twenty-one. Walter is described by his grandfather as "the son of my dear and deceased son John James." For the will, proved 21 November 1829, see P.R.O., Prob. 11/1762/648.

8. For "Buoyant on bladders filled with hope," see Matthew Green, *The Spleen*, line 51.

9. HLP's relative, the Reverend Edward Thelwall (d. 1814), had two daughters. The elder was Marianne (d. 1865), who on 25 March 1824 married Thomas Bulkeley Owen (1790–1867) of Tedsmore Hall, Salop.

See HLP to the Reverend Robert Myddelton, 28 March 1805, n. 5.

10. HLP's father John, on returning from Offley on 18 December 1762 "dropped down dead—of an Apoplexy" (*Thraliana*, 1:304). His two brothers were Henry (1710–ca. 1758) and Sir Thomas. Their father was Thomas, who died in 1714. All these men, according to *Thraliana*, "died in less than four Hours from their Seizure" (1:524).

TO LADY KEITH

Saturday
[29] February 1812[1]

I congratulate myself and You and all the Nation Dearest Lady Keith on the Appointment of such a Commander for the Channel Fleet; and above all I congratulate Sir Charles Cotton on his happy Removal and Escape from being superseded—he was a Cadet of the House of Maddingley.

Oh! don't you recollect tall Mr. Langton's eldest Son *little George*? who had a Taste for Fortification his Papa said,—at 5 Years old—and when they retired to live in Kent, You made dear Dr. Johnson laugh by observing that with such help *Rochester would be impregnable.* Well! Little George is a Tall Man himself, and has a Son 17 Years old by a Relation of Sir Walter James:[2] They met at my House Yesterday and amused me no little. Poor Mr. Langton's Account of his good Father, bursting with Greek[3] and with Religion as he said, and leaving him the Estate——diminished 4000£ o'Year!!—and then exclaims the Man—Johnson could say—Sit anima mea cum Langtono![4] A fine Fellow to take Chance of Heaven with! that has ruined me and my Seven Children.—And are not you a *Worse*? replies the Baronet, who now in the 1st: Year of your own *Widowerhood* quarrel with your eldest Boy about a Girl who he would marry, but you tear her from him by Threats of leaving Langton Hall away——and marry her *Yourself* tho' but Sixteen Years old. A curious Scene was it not?[5]

Veniamo ad altro.

Resistless Roscius has overcome all his Difficulties, and Silenced if not softened the Tongue of Prejudice——he has acted Six Nights and filled the Streets with Crouds turned from our Playhouse Door.

You always loved him and will like to hear with what unbounded Rapture they applauded. I saw Him Twice; approved his Hamlet, and admired his Alexander.[6]—None of his Precursors had the Dignity he displayed in the Scenes with Rosencrantz and Guildenstern, the haughty Scorn he shewed of their close Treachery; or the half crazy Triumph in the Scene where Players act before the King and Queen——he seemed so eager to detect, and to express his Detection, neither he nor his Audience could half sit it out. All this without the help of *Features*—or a *Form* distinguished from the commonest of Men; but

> before such Merit all Objections fly,
> Pritchard looks slim, and Garrick six feet high.[7]

I who remember Barry's sweet Tones,[8] and fine Symmetric Figure, expected to be little pleased with the young Hero in Lee's ranting Tragedy——but he did look so like a son of Jove when he reproved Lysimachus's Freedom; and so filled up one's Notion of Comus when he said

> Gay as the Persian God ourself will stand
> With a crown'd Goblet in our lifted hand &c. &c.[9]

that I felt nothing but Delight from my Evening's Amusement, and remember his Voice *only* as articulate.

'Tis a strange Time—and strange Things are done in it. Nothing is as it *used to be.* We have an Earls Daughter here whose Son by her first Husband will be a Duke—walking in Milsom Street Arm in arm with *un autre Femme publique.* We have another Woman of high Quality by *Marriage,* living quite openly with an untitled *Cher Ami*—by whom She has a Son, who I am told must be Marquis of _____ in due Time; because her own Lord cannot and dare not speak upon the Subject. "These be Miracles—or you make them so," says a Character in Ben Jonson's Comedies:[10] I hate being a Miracle-maker, Yet are these Things out of the common Course——Robbers too! Why at Bath a Robber was no more expected than a Rattle Snake, and Three Nights ago Evill's Shop was broke open, and some Trinkets of small Value taken thro' the cut Shutter.[11]

I'll say no more.—You never told me what was the General Opinion about Miss Seward's Letters, or whether they amused You[12]——my Young Taste was attracted to Lady Lansdown's fine *China Ware* beyond all her other Possessions—Those Two Bottles were famous Things indeed.—I suppose Mr. Benjamin Walsh when his Certificate is signed, and he begins the World anew; will dazzle us all with *his* Finery;[13] and I hope Hamilton Crofton in a *high Collar* will lead up the Ball with some of the Ladies I have mentioned.

Whilst I am saying God bless you and Your Baby, comes Intelligence that Roscius braves the Hornet's Nest called London;[14] and yields to the Seducements of some Managers there—I am really very Sorry.

Text Bowood Collection.

1. Saturday was 29 February.
2. Bennet Langton had married 24 May 1770 Mary, née Lloyd (1743–1820), the widow of John

Leslie (ca. 1698–1767), tenth earl of Rothes (1722). They had six daughters and three sons. Their eldest son was George (1772–1819), who had married Elizabeth, née Mainwaring (d. 1811). Of George Langton's three sons, HLP alludes to John Stephen (b. 1794).

3. For Bennet Langton, friend of SJ and professor of ancient literature at the Royal Academy, see HLP to LC, 30 September 1796, n. 5.

4. *Boswell's Johnson*, 4:280, 530–31.

5. If this remark refers to George Langton, who was in the first year of his "*Widowerhood*," then HLP quotes rumor: he never remarried.

6. Betty had performed Hamlet on 20 February and Alexander in Nathaniel Lee's *Alexander the Great* on 27 February.

7. The second line should read, "Pritchard's genteel, and Garrick six feet high." See Charles Churchill, *The Rosciad*, lines 851–52.

8. For Spranger Barry, see HLP to PSP, 22 May 1802, n. 9.

9. See Nathaniel Lee, *The Rival Queens*, 3.435–36 (the concluding speech).

10. Lovewit in *The Alchemist*, 5.1.39.

11. See the *Bath Journal*, 24 February:
"A most daring attempt at robbery was made on Tuesday night last, on the premises of Mr. [W.] Evill, silversmith . . . in the Market-place. The villains succeeded in boring a hole in the rail of the shutter, the pannels being lined with iron, and cutting a pane of glass, but were fortunately disappointed in obtaining their expected booty, the valuable property having been removed the preceding evening."

12. For HLP's persistent interest in Anna Seward's *Letters*, see her letters to Q, 31 January 1810, nn. 16, 17; to JSPS [December 1811].

See, e.g., the overall favorable review in *GM*, which published lengthy extracts from the *Letters*: 81, pt. 2 (1811):154–56, 241–46, 350–53, 446–49, 635–38; 82, pt. 2 (1812):345–46.

GM concluded that Miss Seward's *Letters* "will long be read with avidity . . . as they are almost all addressed to persons either eminent themselves as authors, or as excellent judges of literature; and as they contain numerous explanatory passages relating to persons whose lives are only partially known to the publick; and, finally, as they give us the unreserved opinion of one well qualified to criticise the different publications of a considerable period of times" (82, pt. 2:345).

HLP's interest in the Seward *Letters* stemmed from her attractive portrait that emerged in the correspondence. See, e.g., the letter to TSW, 6 October 1787, and another on the same day to William Hayley (1:335–40).

13. See the *Courier*, 27 February:
"The following has been printed by order of the House of Commons:
"The Lord Chief Baron to Mr. Secretary Ryder,/ Feb. 15, 1812.
" . . . But doubts having occurred to Mr. Justice Le Blanc and myself . . . the case was reserved for the Judges to consider whether the facts proved amounted to the crime of larceny. The argument of Counsel concluded last night; and the case was considered by ten Judges present . . . who were of opinion that the facts did not, in estimation of law, amount to felony. The prisoner having been convicted of that offence, I am humbly to recommend him as a proper object of his Majesty's pardon."

14. Planning to play in Bath only from 15 to 29 February, Betty extended his engagement to include performances from 7 to 29 April. (He chose not to go to London.) His roles at the Theatre Royal, Bath, included the leads in Henry Jones's *The Earl of Essex*; John Brown's *Barbarossa*; *Hamlet* and *Macbeth*; John Home's *Douglas*; Thomson's *Tancred and Sigismunda*; John Hughes's *Siege of Damascus*; Aaron Hill's *Zara*; Ambrose Philips' *The Distressed Mother*; Nathaniel Lee's *The Rival Queens*; and Sheridan's *Pizarro*.

TO JOHN SALUSBURY PIOZZI SALUSBURY

Wednesday
4: March 1812.

I shall ruin my Dearest in Postage if I do not enclose him a Dandy—but you must keep the Oxford Debts as low as ever you can, we are so hard run this

Year—Maughan has had his 515£ without my borrowing Money however. So if *They* are not quite out of Bounds, *We shall do.*

Here are pretty Girls enough to crack any Man's Crown, who care about them——A Miss Myddelton the handsomest, and I think least agreeable among them:[1] but *very* handsome Indeed.—Let dear Pemberton take care of his Heart, or lose it to *my* Liking——Saucy Enough! but you shall See my Choice for him. Lord Berwick has raveled his *Stocking* into a fine <Louse-Ladder>;[2] and I doubt not but the Lady will mount *up* it, and be proud;—such Ladies always are.

Have you heard of Alexander Winch's fine Exploit?[3] lost for 14 Days—a Compleat Disappearance! He left his Parents Pretending to go to Cambridge—but turned aside from the *right* Path——Quere whether he ever was in it?——and got into a Drunken Quarrel about Sir Charles Oakley's Daughters[4]—and into a Duel—and went to his Parents' Bedside, and stood there all Streaming with Blood in the Dead of a dark Night. The Father sent off for Colonel Glover, an old Brother Officer to *advise with*—and begged him bring his eldest Daughter to console Mrs. Winch whose Life is still despaired of.[5]

What a Punishment for every possible Offence against Heaven! Must it be to the *Mother* of *Alexander* Winch. Have you heard of the *Toasts drank in* Hell, at Satan's last Party? I think one of them should have been this young Parricide. Oh frightful! Here comes a Letter from Leak saying that he is building our Wall upon the Bryn but cannot go on without Money. He has given 8£ for a Drill in London[6]—and wants 100£—from Hammersley's:—his Account of Streatham Park is *rueful.*[7] Fine Times for your poor H: L: P.

Mr. Byng is among our gayest Fellows,—Tomorrow I expect Charles Shephard and shall be glad at heart to see him and talk over the Money-Stuff.

Tinker is well and merry—Martha madder than ever, and Jack Savage *dead*—— Such is the News from Wales: of more Importance to You and I than the Regent's Reconciliation with His Princess—tho that's a good Thing if it be true.[8]

Write to me the Instant this Bit of Paper comes safe—These are not Moments to lose any thing. Keep your own Health, and tell me how Mr. Lane does. God bless my Darling and Adieu says his H: L: P.—Oh tell what Day I may expect You.

Text Ry. 586.137. *Address* John Piozzi Salusbury Esq./ Christ Church/ Oxford. *Postmark* BATH < > 1812.

1. Probably Caroline May (1796–1850), the eldest daughter of the Reverend Robert Myddelton of Gwaynynog. She was to marry the Reverend William Carr Fenton (d. 1855), of Grinton Lodge, York.

2. Thomas Noel Hill (1770–1832), second baron Berwick (1789) had married Sophia Dubochet (1794–1875) on 8 February 1812.

3. Alexander John Wynch was born ca. 1792 in India. The son of Colonel Alexander Wynch (d. 1812), onetime of the East India Company's service, and Elizabeth, née Read, he was admitted to St. John's, Cambridge, in 1810, matriculated at Michaelmas in 1811, but left without a degree.

The elder Wynch, who had large estates in the East Indies and England, directed no lasting anger against their only child. Indeed, he divided his property between his son and his wife, Elizabeth.

For the will of Alexander Wynch, signed at Bath on 30 November 1812 and proved at London on 4 March 1813, see P.R.O., Prob. 11/1543/169.

4. For Sir Charles Oakeley, see HLP to PSP, 9 March 1800, n. 9.

He had fourteen children, of whom five daughters survived: Henrietta (d. 1868); Georgina, already married (1804) to R. Kynaston; Louisa, married (1806) to George Reid; Amelia (d. 1878), married in February 1812 to Chappel Woodhouse (d. 1815); and Helena (d. 1859).

5. The eldest daughter of Colonel John Glover was Anna (d. post–1825).

6. AL, in his letter of 9 March (Ry. 609.2), pointed out that "It was not a Drill but a Chaff cutter which you paid for last Year and which I think you have seen at Work in the Stable."

7. Unoccupied since Abraham Atkins became bankrupt in 1810, Streatham Park had grown dilapidated. Its condition was to be the focus of a new quarrel between HLP and her daughters.

8. More Bath rumor. *The Times*, the *Courier*, and the *Morning Chronicle*, e.g., are silent on the possibility of a reconciliation and, indeed, there never was one. In 1812, in their descriptions of the Regent's various courts, levees, and dinners, the newspapers did not mention either the name of Princess Caroline or her presence at these festivities.

TO ALEXANDER LEAK

Bath Thursday
12th: March 1812.

I enclose you Forty Three Pounds—making the whole *one Hundred*——and must follow Lord K's Example for a while of being indebted to my own Servants.

Not the Fruits of the Enclosure however, but of Frolics to Bath and London, which I *do* grudge from my Heart; and not the Expences either of Farm or Common.

Doctor Whalley called today; says Streatham Park *must be repaired,* or worse will befall me: he advises to begin directly, and Mr. Southey who repaired it for Mr. Piozzi, putting up Marble Chimney Pieces where Mr. Thrale left Wooden ones &c.—is here;[1] and Mead who built Brynbella is his Friend; so I suppose They must begin again; and make it smart again; and I shall have as kind Returns as before——no Hope of putting Money in the Funds: Dr. Whalley thinks the Ladies are offended.[2]

Mr. Jones of Bryntirion was offended because his Recommendation to the Curacy was not accepted,——so he made me wait for my Money *out of Spite.*[3] Everybody is easily offended——and find it no difficulty to Spite The unresisting/H: L: Piozzi.

Mr. Shephard comes tomorrow—I shall be glad to see him: I wonder how we offended Cloughs and Wynnes,[4] and I wonder likewise how letting the Farm would mend anything especially when Corn bears so good a Price—it may surely pay for Drill and Chaff cutter.[5]

I hope Your Health mends with this change of Weather, and That the Money will come Safe, and you will write Word.—

Text Hyde Collection. *Address* Mr. Alexander Leak/ Brynbella/ near Denbigh/ N: Wales.

1. James Southey (fl. 1757–1820) was an auctioneer and appraiser, located in Tooley Street, London.

For Clement Mead, see HLP to PSP, 22 May [1793], n. 8.

2. HLP summarizes the nature of the quarrel with her daughters in a letter to W. M. Thackeray, dated 30 May 1812.

"My Nerves have had a new Shock in the Anger of my beautiful Daughters for a Fault committed (if a Fault) most unintentionally on my Part. but having heard that they threw out Menaces of making my Successor amenable for Dilapidations at Streatham Park—I resolved to repair, & partly resolved to inhabit it when repaired,—instead of paying House Rent every Spring—while that Place was tumbling down. By all means said my wise Counsellor Mr. Charles Shephard, By all means said my wise Steward Leak; & both agreed there was plenty of Timber on the Premises, which really wanted cutting. So I sent Mead—my old Surveyor who you know built Brynbella, & bid him set to Work, & I called Charles Shephard—*Ranger* but the Ladies were enraged, said *their Property* was ruining by my Agents; & the Letters were dreadful; and I am at my Wits end; while the Men complain that my Daughters *insult them*; and *they* storm at the Men for injuring their Place" (Clifford, p. 431).

3. Thomas Jones (1754–1824), of Brynterion, high sheriff of Carnarvonshire (1818), rented land owned by HLP in that county.

4. HLP responds to the following in AL's letter of 9 March (Ry. 609.2): " . . . it is but a few Hours since the Cloughs and Wynnes of Denbigh were Galloping their Horses and Hounds, on a Hunting party through Your Shrubberys, over the little Bridge on the rivulet, and round the House. Indeed [I] had some difficulty in keeping them out of the Garden. But it is to no purpose to Complain, nobody here will redress our grievances, the Verdict here is always against us."

5. In his letter, AL had recommended the following in part to silence HLP's money complaints: " . . . You had better lett Your Farm and then none of these expences will occur, and keep nothing but your House and Gardens as Mrs. Mostyn do." Nonetheless, AL offered some good news regarding the sale of the crops.

"I have Thirty Hobbets of Barley going to Hollywell to Morrow, for which I am to have Thirty Guineas brought back, and then I shall begin on the Wheat. I believe it will sell well."

TO JOHN SALUSBURY PIOZZI SALUSBURY

Sunday Morning
15: March 1812.

My dear Salusbury

I hope you are coming *indeed* and coming *very soon*. Doctor Whalley wishes to see you Sadly, and he leaves this Place on Thursday next——he is much your Friend and takes a deep Interest in this horrid Streatham Business—Mrs. Mostyn's Threats were the Threats of the whole Family, and I feel much alarmed.[1]

Mean while my Dinner Party is put back to Saturday 21st and it will break My Heart if you prefer staying at Enborne.——

Make My Compliments there, and believe me ever too/tenderly and anxiously Yours/ H: L: P.

I do not feel well today, but my Executor is at hand,[2] and My Heir not far off.

Text Ry. 585.140.

1. CMM's letter is missing, but HLP summarized its threats in a letter to TSW, 25 May 1812: "Mrs. Mostyn having menaced little Salusbury pretty sharply last summer, what they would do to him if I was to die, and how they would pinch him for dilapidations of their seat in Surrey . . ." (Wickham, 2:353).

2. Sir Walter James. See her will dated 19 April 1813 (Ry. Ch. 1258). Her other executor—not at hand—was Sir John Williams.

TO ALEXANDER LEAK

Bath
Thursday 19: March 1812.

Nothing in Leake's Letter—not even the Ten Acorns, Surprized me so much as his Account of the Spring being too forward; while the Frosts here cut every thing to pieces, and Stop all Progress of Vegetation. We have now Three feet Snow upon the Ground, and the Cold is less insupportable.

Dr. Whalley and Mr. Shephard and Mr. Salusbury afford me good *Pleasant,* and good *literary* Talk;—but I think none of them wish me to *disregard my Money*: and all feel alarmed about Streatham, and urge me to speedy repair:——It will be a dreadful Drawback on my Comforts for the remainder of my Life;[1] but I hope my Daughters will live long and happily to reap the Benefit: and it is certainly *better* as will be every one's Opinion, that *their* Pleasure should be consulted rather than that of their/ Affectionate Mother/ and your true Friend/ H: L: P.

If you go to Surrey after Harvest, You may find or make the Place habitable for me in some ensuing Month perhaps; at present there is neither Pot nor Spit it seems; and The Ladies *say* The Rain is pouring *in*, which Mr. Shephard *denies*; who examined the Roof the Day before he came *hither*.

Bread rises, and Stocks fall every Day, and Coals the most necessary of all Articles are terribly dear indeed.

Text Hyde Collection. *Address* Mr. Alexander Leak/ Brynbella/ Denbigh/ N. Wales. *Postmark* BATH 19 MR 1812.

1. By 1815 HLP was to spend £6,500 on the rehabilitation of Streatham Park.

TO LADY KEITH

[Bath, 16 Pulteney Street]
28: March 1812.

My dear Lady Keith's Letter coming *unsealed*—by which I mean never sealed at all—Mrs. Hoare's Note dropped out probably, for no such ever reached Bath; at least not No. 16 Pultney Street. I take however good Note of Georgiana's good Health, and feel glad you mean to preserve it by speedy Removal out of a Town so pernicious to Babies. My Horror of Hooping Cough is such that I actually left Church one Day from hearing the fatal Sound too near me. Lord Keith must get well, and catch These French Ships himself, I dare say they'll wait for him.

Having two Oxonians with me and a Cambridge Man;—[1] They are called Mrs. Piozzi's agreeable Beaux;—(except by the Pump-Woman who says "There go the fine young Fellows who *live* with *Mrs. Piozzi*)*—You will not wonder that I send you a Latin Charade:—Tis written backwards like Witches' Prayers, The Tout Ensemble *first*; otherwise excellent in my Mind. It was the Cambridge Man made the Answer *sur le Champ*.

> Est Totum Flumen; caput aufer, splendet in Armis;
> Caudam deme, volat, viscera tolle-dolet.

> Vulturnus flumen; Turnus splendescit in Armis;
> Avolat en Vultur; vexat quoque corpora Vulnus.

But all our Amusements are not Classical: We have public Balls till 11 at Night, and private ones till 7 in the Morning, beside which Roscius returns on Monday Sennight, and our Theatre will be once more crouded. When I look to its beautiful Cieling and see the Works of Chevalier Casali which I recollect to have won Prizes on the *first* Exhibition of the Arts in my *Maiden Days*; and which Dear charming Dimond purchased from Fonthill, it glads my very Heart: but when I recollect again that at Fonthill Yet remains the likest possible Portrait of my Uncle Cotton King—and the more valuable Lady's last Stake painted expressly as a Present *to me* by my venerated Friend Hogarth[2]—Then does a little Tragic Feeling cross my Mind; and draw it from the very Elegant Perfection of our little Playhouse here, which is really a Model;—and so favourable to the Performers!—just the right Size and Shape.

But here comes your Second Letter, with Dear Sophia's obliging Note: The Mistake was to *me* only beneficial, and I am half ashamed to pepper and pelt you with Nonsense at a Time when Things of such Serious Import are passing thro' your fair hands.

The Changes of Weather are dreadful, very good for *tying up Bath Knockers* which otherwise never would rest. A good natured Mr. Harrison at my next Door would not tye up his, though he felt himself so *very near* his End—for fear of disappointing his *Wife and Daughter's Party: I may* (said he) live till tomorrow you know; and you will hate to put the People off——so he had a Hundred and Seventy Folks in his House till Two O'Clock of the next Morning—and by Noon he was a Corpse:—and the Ladies said truly *How good natured he was.*[3]

Poor Miss Richards's Death—struck suddenly at 22 Years old with the Palsy;[4] *did* however seem to affect ½ a Dozen Friends who depended on her for their Musical Amusement—for ½ a Dozen hours at least:—and *They* too were very good natured—because *Feelings* which I can remember quite the Rage, are now wholly *out* among those with whom I converse here.

But Adieu! Here is too much Folly, and *too much Fool* as your Oriental said of the Lord's Lady: poor Lord! Poor Lord! you remember. Farewell, and give the enclosed Note as a Proof I received one from Mrs. Hoare for which accept the sincere Thanks of yours and hers Affectionately/ H: L: P.

Compliments to Lord Keith with Cordial Wishes for his recovery.

Text Bowood Collection.

1. The Oxonians were Pem (see HLP to JSPS, 20 August 1808, n. 1) and JSPS; the man from Cambridge was the attorney Charles Mitchell Smith Shephard (see HLP to MW, 5 July [1807], n. 2).
2. For the material in this paragraph, see HLP to Q, 22 March 1810 and n. 14.
3. Clement Harrison, aged sixty-seven, of Bathwick Parish, was buried on 15 March. See "Burial Register," St. Mary's Church, C.R.O., Somerset.
Harrison, a man of considerable substance, owned property in Middlesex and Lincoln counties, as well as in Bath, where he had a house on Great Pulteney Street. His wife, Elizabeth, née Naylor, upon his death became the guardian of their three children: Robert James, a student at Oriel College, Oxford; Elizabeth Frances; and Harriet. His will was signed 27 December 1811 and proved at London on 4 April. See P.R.O., Prob. 11/1532/171.
4. Louisa Richards died unexpectedly during a concert tour away from Bath. Her burial was unrecorded until 10 June 1812. See "Bath Abbey Burials," C.R.O., Somerset.

TO JOHN SALUSBURY PIOZZI SALUSBURY

No. 16: Pulteney Street, Bath
18: April 1812.

My dearest Dear

And how kind it was in you to write directly So! I really feel quite *obliged* by it. Pem: told the Girls whom we met by Troops at Mrs. Horneck's,[1] Your merry Nonsense about their *wet Pocket Handkerchiefs*, which would as I said to Mrs. Lutwyche become by that means proper Inhabitants *pour leurs Ridicules.* But I think young Roscius has more Power over their Fears by *his* Passion—tho' acknowledged to be fictitious; than you obtain with Yours (no less affected) tho' pretending to be genuine.

Dear Pemberton! we parted but this Morning—and he did look *So* grave! I felt myself quite flattered. God send him Safe to you; These vile Mail Coaches have my true Aversion, but he had the prudent Fear of five Guineas before his Eyes. Every one is wiser than Salusbury and his Silly Aunt. *Our* Paper Money flies like the Paper Kites in Spring. Will that Season ever arrive this Year?— nothing springs in this Warm Valley; how must it be at Brynbella! I sent you Leake's Account of how many Trees he had planted. And so the Dean was very kind after all[2]—I expected he would be so; graceful Confession of a Fault always conciliates the Mind of old Men towards Young one,—It acknowledges *their* Superiority. How different is the Confession of real *Sin* to him who alone can forgive it; and whose Eyes are too pure to suffer Guilt in his Presence!

Oh keep as far as may be *your* dear Soul unpolluted, and pray sincerely for Celestial Grace, which only *can* preserve it——No one can guess how *Soon* his Accounts may be called for.

Fleres si scires unum tua Tempora Mensam,
Nunc rides, dum sit forsitan una Dies.

If you *thought* You should live but a Month, how you'd cry!
Yet you laugh, tho' you *know* You tomorrow may die.[3]

You are very good natured in wishing me to amuse myself; and so I *will* go out and chat with the Folks, while they like to chat with me. General and Mrs. Leighton have asked me to Dinner on Wednesday next[4]—and I do believe there is a Party somewhere that Evening, which I might go to; but for my vile Trick of losing the Invitation Cards, now I have lost my young Friends that used now and then to separate and class them for me.

You will do very well at College without your *Companions* and *Acquaintance* now you have with you an old and favourite Friend.[5] Oh how different are those two Characters!—The light Wines of Italy so delicious on the Spot in a Warm Summer, but *quite* incapable of Carriage to England;—are the true Emblems of agreeable Society; while the pure East India Madeira that has crossed the Line and Tropics two or three Times—not ill resembles a real and true Friend.

Well! here am I returning to my Desk after the noisy Siege of Damascus,[6]— where however I sate very comfortably with pretty Lady Wilmot[7] and her two Old Beaux—Lord Northesk[8] and Sir Richard Bedingfield,[9] who took Care and put me safe in my Sedan—for I ran to the Theatre with my *Servitorello,* my *petit Laquais* following. Roscius surpassed himself; and I saw Miss Fellowes making her Hands sore with Clapping.[10]

Eudocia was a poor dull Innocent,[11] but the Play was applauded whole, and some Passages were catched at by the Audience, and adapted (I think) to *The Times.*

Lady Collier has tempted me to *her* Box on Tuesday—[12] Betty acts Tancred,[13] and then I will have done with such Nonsense. It is however Scarce 9 o'clock, so late Hours are not connected with my Dissipation; and I kept my Word to Pem: and dined upon Veal Broth and Rice only: Your Company seduced me, and I have been living too well of late.—Shall I go to Mrs. Lutwyche's tomorrow Evening? The Colliers pretend to desire it. Farewell and remember how you are/ beloved by your true and tender/ Parent, Your own/ H: L: P.

Let me have a Letter once o'Week, and then I shall not *dun* you.

Text Ry. 586.141. *Address* John Piozzi Salusbury Esq./ Christ Church/ Oxford. *Postmark* BATH AP 19 1812.

1. Frances Gould (b. 1752) had married on 3 May 1791 Charles Horneck (d. 1804), a general of the 62nd Regiment. On 5 October 1812 she became TSW's third wife in what was to be an unhappy marriage; the couple separated. She was to die 16 September 1832 at her lodgings in the Belvidere, Bath. See the *Bath Chronicle,* 20 September 1832.

2. JSPS confessed that he had traveled on 5 February, a day appointed for a general fast. See HLP to JSPS, 12 February 1812.

3. HLP assumed that both the Latin and English verses were by LC. See the "Commonplace Book" under *Chappelow.* But Hayward implies that the Latin couplet was a commonplace, a friend

of his having read it "on a beam, dated 1626, of an old timbered post-house between Sheffield and Lichfield" (2:385).

4. Baldwin Leighton (1747–1828), sixth baronet (1819), of Loton Park, Salop. He served in the army and was wounded in the American War; he was on active duty as a brigadier general in Portugal (1798) and in the West Indies (1801). By 1803 he was a major general, by 1809 a lieutenant general, and a full general by 1819. He became governor of the garrison of Carrickfergus, Ireland, in 1817.

He had first married in May 1780 Anna, née Pigott (1746–1800), of Edgmond in Salop; and second in November 1802 Louisa Margaretta Anne, née Stanley (d. 1842), of Alderley Park, Cheshire (*GM* n.s. 17 [1842]:227).

5. Edward Pemberton, at the age of eighteen, had matriculated at Christ Church, Oxford, on 29 January 1812.

6. Betty played the role of Phocyas in John Hughes's *The Siege of Damascus.*

7. For Mary Anne, Lady Wilmot, see HLP to Ly W, 9 February 1810, n. 7.

8. William Carnegie (1758–1831), a Scot, seventh earl of Northesk (1792). He entered the navy in 1771 and rose steadily. By 1808 he was vice admiral of the blue and two years later vice admiral of the red. In 1814 he became an admiral, subsequently rear admiral of the United Kingdom (1821–31), and commander in chief at Plymouth (1827–30).

On 9 December 1788 in Paris, he had married Mary, née Ricketts (1757–1835), niece of John Jervis, earl of St. Vincent.

9. Sir Richard Bedingfield (1767–1829), fifth baronet (1795), had married Charlotte Georgiana, née Jerningham.

10. Ann Fellowes (1765–1844) was the elder daughter of William Fellowes (1737–1827), M.D., and Mary, née Butler (1738–1819). As the sister of JF, she was to figure in HLP's correspondence from 1815 onward.

11. The leading female character in *The Siege of Damascus.*

12. HLP refers to the second wife and widow of George Collier (1738–95), of West Hill, Surrey, who was knighted in 1775. Rising in the ranks of the Royal Navy, he was made a vice admiral in 1794. She was Elizabeth, née Fryer (1760–1831). Their marriage had taken place on 19 July 1781. See *GM* 101, pt. 2 (1831): 651.

See HLP to JSPS, 14 May 1813, and n. 5.

13. Betty performed as Tancred twice while in Bath: on 25 February and 21 April.

TO ALEXANDER LEAK

Sunday
26: April 1812.

I feel sorry indeed that Leak's Fatigues agree so much worse with *him* than Privation does with his poor Friend and Mistress. I have almost lived *literally* on a Crust since the Dear Boys left me, and Glover will bear witness I have not even bought a Saffron Cake for my own eating. Chickens will be as costly at Brynbella as here by Your Account——pray do your own Way about them, and do not let me be ruined by *Pecking* to Death.

The Dogs are Salusbury's only Amusement when in the Country; *Their* Barley must be charged to *his* Account.

I hope You will be amused at Chester to see Dr. Thackeray; and tell him that I never passed six Months with so few Complaints for Six Years at least; and the Physicians here all wonder to see me so well. It has been a horrible Season for health.

The Affair at Badajoz affects every body, and blights all happiness like the East Wind.[1] You will see Sir Walter James's Loss of his eldest Son in the Gazette:

His other Son is come home *Ill* from *Oxford* and will go into a Consumption[2]——
but if this new Claimant succeeds in getting the Estate, Girls will be as good as
Boys to him;[3]——his Heart is breaking in the Mean While however.

My Young Ladies have none of them written for a very long Time indeed[4]——
when Streatham Repairs are begun, they will be kinder. Mrs. Wynne of Llewessog is at Bath——and civil.[5]

I am glad the Dear Animals at Brynbella are well, If Venus's Calf is a Bull, we
must call him Cupid of Course. Mr. Rees was very good natured to come and
assist Magpye. Newton paid only 160£ but has explained *why*: it will be 200£ in
November when I shall want it as bad: he kept back the Property Tax for both
half Years at once.[6]

The Wax Candles are the very Things that have inflamed Leedham's Bill;[7]
Barrett's was only six Guineas and a half.[8] Our Coals are not wasted: Wine and
Porter in Bottles went off merrily while Shephard and Pemberton Staid,—of the
Small Beer I know nothing.

250£ has however served me from the 2nd of February to the 2nd of May,
notwithstanding Gifts and Expences: as much more will pay my Weareables,
and Hired Things (I hope) and Taylor's Bill, and keep me alive till the 2d: June,—
when 140£ must discharge the House Rent——and then my Estimate will be
completed——only the Journey home——640£. All this if Dear Salusbury and
his Friend keep away from me the Whitsun Week,——for if they return, it will
not be Sufficient—according to my Estimate of Debts here.

supposing them

To the	Taylor	£ 25	:	0	:	0
Mrs.	Glover	13	:	0	:	0
Mr.	Leedham	40	:	0	:	0
Mr.	George	6	:	10	:	0[9]
	Sloper	5	:	10	:	0[10]
	Slack	10	:	0	:	0[11]
	Lucas	8	:	10	:	0[12]
	Evill	8	:	10	:	0
	Arnold	6	:	0	:	0[13]
		£ 123	:	0	:	0.

If Mr. Harrison keeps true to his Time however, all will go well:[14] and Money
left to discharge *Debts of Honour* as I call those of Oxford—The Rioters will do
as much Mischief as The Scarcity,[15] I am very sorry about it indeed, and am
with every good Wish/ Your true Friend/ H: L: P.——

Chickens are 5s. o'piece, Asparagus 12s o'Hundred: You may be sure I eat
none of either.

General Donkin says it was a glorious Sight—The Storming of Badajoz;—and
that old John Duke of Marlbro' would have rejoyced to see the Courage of our

Officers and Men. 51 of the first Rank were knocked down from the Scaling Ladders—and died cheering their Soldiers. *His* Son is alive;[16] Mrs. Glover likewise is in Transports—*her* Boys are unhurt among murdered Thousands.[17]

Text Hyde Collection. *Address* Mr. Alexander Leak/ Brynbella/ near Denbigh/ N. Wales. *Postmark* BATH AP 26 1812 109.

1. Wellington's capture of Badajoz on 6–7 April was costly to the Allies. They lost some thirty-three hundred men during the assault and another fourteen hundred during the preparatory action. Six generals had been wounded and four colonels killed. The Allied troops took vengeance on the Spanish population and for three days the town was sacked. From a military point of view, the victory at Badajoz prepared the way for the Allied invasion of Spain and the success at Salamanca. See *GM* 82, pt. 1 (1812): 378, 573–75.

2. Francis James, a captain in the 81st regiment, fell at Badajoz. The other son was John, home from Oxford because of illness.

3. Sir Walter had four daughters: Jane married in 1803 John Trower, of Berkeley Square; Mary Anne (d. 1845) married on 9 May 1808 Lieutenant Colonel John Byng (1772–1860), later baron Strafford of Harmondsworth (1835) and earl of Strafford (1847); Frances in 1823 married Horatio Davies; and Charlotte Elizabeth (ca. 1792–1820) married in 1817 Captain Franz Friedrich von Lerber (1782–1837), a member of the Sovereign Council of Berne and by 1820 a major general in the Swiss artillery.

4. The quarrel between HLP and Q, at least, was to climax in the middle of May, after which there was no exchange of letters for a year. Yet Q must have written before the end of April since HLP on 1 May 1812 wrote a response. Moreover, CMM wrote a friendly letter to HLP, dated 26 April (Ry. 572.29). This is reproduced as the next letter in the edition in order to offer some indication of mother-daughter feelings.

5. For Anna Maria (Mostyn) Wynn, see HLP to LC, 30 March 1795, n. 1.

6. See HLP to John Gillon, 18 November 1799, n. 2.

7. Stephen Leedham, "Grocer, Tea-Dealer, and Cheese-Monger," located at 21 Green Street, Bath, from ca. 1805 to 1812. In the latter year, his shop is listed as being located at 1 New Bond Street Buildings.

8. HLP refers to Barrett and Beaumont, wax chandlers, at 4 Haymarket, London.

9. Thomas George, "Hatter, Hosier, and Men's Mercer," 6 North Parade, Bath. He practiced his trade at that address from ca. 1806 to 1824.

10. Either Isaac Sloper at 6 Wade's Passage, Bath, or John Sloper, at 8 Wade's Passage. The former appeared in the Bath directories from 1809 to 1824, the latter from 1809 to 1829.

11. S. and W. Slack, merchants, from ca. 1805 to 1812 at 5 Bath Street and 40 Milsom Street, Bath.

12. Either Christopher Lucas (fl. 1805–19), linendraper, at 11 Union Street; or Lucas and Reilly (fl. 1805–19), wine and spirit merchants, York House, Bath.

13. George Arnold owned the White Lyon Inn and Tavern (along with its stables) at Market Place, Bath, from ca. 1800 to ca. 1819. See the Bath directories for that period.

14. George Harrison (d. 1818), a timber merchant of Chester, had apparently contracted to buy some timber from HLP's land near Brynbella and Bachygraig.

15. HLP refers to the Luddite riots, which were beginning in Huddersfield, Dudley, and Nottingham. See *GM* 82, pt. 1 (1812):285. HLP's concern with such disturbances was to grow even as the riots spread. See her letters to JSPS, 15 and 18[–19] May 1812.

16. Becoming a major general in 1811, Rufane Shaw Donkin (1773–1841) had been and was to be involved in military actions on the east coast of Spain from 1810 to 1813. See HLP to JSPS, 20 March 1810, n. 10.

17. Her elder son was Octavius Augustus, or John Octavius (1789–1855), a captain in the Royal Regiment of Foot; her other son was Frederick Augustus (d. 1865), an ensign in the Royal Regiment of Foot. See HLP to JSPS, 22 March 1808, n. 6.

CECILIA MEREDITH MOSTYN TO HESTER LYNCH PIOZZI

Segroyt
April 26th [1812][1]

Dear Mama

You may justly say I am the worst of Correspondents but have been so fully occupied with Harry's departure, that it has prevented my doing or thinking of any thing else, otherwise I should have thanked you for your entertaining Letter a Month ago.—He is now in Town and will go to Plymouth with his Aunt and Baby very soon I hope, but the illness of old Miss Elphinstone perhaps will prolong their stay in Town, as I understand she is very bad.[2]—I am anxious for the Boy to be at Plymouth and messing with the Midshipmen, he will see the kind of Life he is likely to lead and be a better judge how he likes it.—[3]

The wretched backwardness of the Season and the deadly dullness of the dear Vale, one feels doubly when quite alone, but of that I'll say nothing, that you may not retard your return; in your next Letter I hope to hear some mention of it—having let my House in Town for the remainder of the Season, you will find me just where you left me; unless impatient for your return, Black Nancy and I set out to meet you, she comes occasionally and laments your absence, I gave her some Ducks eggs last time to put under one of your Hens, but mine will not sit or do any thing they are desired from the cold east Winds they tell me, The Cottage family however is much encreased by more Pigeons and white Guinea fowl—pray do not give yourself trouble about the common Guinea fowl but if any of your Servants return by the Coach into Wales *they* could perhaps come by the same conveyance.—If Salusbury, your Nephew is with you pray remember me to him, and that the Bryn is I hear planting at all rates. Your account amused me exceedingly of your *triumphant* neighbour's news about Mrs. Wynne and *your* laconic reply—it was the more amusing to me, as the following day I believe, Mrs. Wynne wrote word to some of her friends here, that you had invited her to your Concert, so Mrs. Wynne triumphed also I suppose![4]

I am sorry your friend Miss Williams is so ill, by me newspaper I see that Sir John Callender is dead, it will be thought *a happy release,* by his widow no doubt:[5] Mr. Thellwall's spirits may be bad, but from what his Sons said when we last met, his health is as usual I fancy and if *it is* his natural character to be the unprincipled person he professes to be by words and actions—more's the Pity, I think. We have lost Dr. Cumming for a time, probably you will meet with him at Bath.[6]

Pray tell me if you have read Childe Harold's Pilgrimage[7] or I says—Says I, or any of the new Books I see advertized.

It is scandalous to make you pay for such Pages of Inanity but you know the impossibility of getting Franks here.

Believe me yours affectionately/ *CMM.*

Text Ry. 572.29. *Address* Mrs. Piozzi/ Great Pulteney Street/ Bath. *Postmark* DEN-BIGH 22<4>.

1. The date of this letter can be determined by HLP's reference to it in her letter to AL, 4 May 1812.
2. Lord Keith's unmarried sister, Mary "Mally" Elphinstone (1741–1825) was the eldest daughter of Charles (1711–81), tenth baron Elphinstone and Lady Clementina, née Fleming (ca. 1719–99).
3. CMM's second son, Harry, was now thirteen and a favorite of his uncle, Lord Keith. Through the latter's efforts, the boy was sent to the Royal Naval College at Portsmouth from 1813 to 1816. He was to have a successful career in the navy, attaining the rank of commander in 1830, when he resigned his commission to live at Segroid.
4. For Mary Williams-Wynn of Llandgedwin, Denbighshire, see HLP to the Ladies of Llangollen, 23 September 1801, n. 7.
5. Sir John died on 2 April. See *GM* 82, pt. 1 (1812): 489.
6. For Dr. George Brownlow Cumming, see HLP to Ly W, 9 February 1810, n. 11.
7. The first two cantos of Byron's poem appeared in 1812, the third in 1816, and the last in 1818.

TO JOHN SALUSBURY PIOZZI SALUSBURY

Bath—Tuesday
28: April 1812.

Reproaches never do any Good Dearest Salusbury, and tho' I am as jealous of your *Affection*, as you purpose being of your Wife's *Love:* I seldom burst out till Fears for your Safety fling me quite off my Guard.—Does not your late Experience show, that one has every Reason for Fear of the most Dreadful Accidents? It was odd enough however that the same Fancy of writing down a String of Facts should seize us both at the same Moment.—The Wise Acres give me no Concern;—Such is Your odd Situation,—(and Pemberton's too)—That the People in general would feel an illnatured feel of Triumph if you did wrong—even those that could receive no Benefit from your bad Conduct:——and if you go to London next Year, Seducements from those whom it *would* benefit, must be expected.

The Price of Corn in Denbigh and Flintshire is dreadful: and while our wretched Cottagers are starving—how shall I grudge the Dogs and Poultry Barley Meal at 35s. the Hobbet!—its proper Standard You know is no more than 15s.

My own Expences here too are greater than I like, tho' we talk of a Crust; and tho' I walked to Mrs. Lutwyche's and home again last Sunday Evening. There was Mr. Burrell there,[1] who I liked very well, and it happened curiously that Chevalier Boisgelin related—as a good and pious Thing—The Conduct of the Flagellants at Rome in the Holy Week: just as I gave you and Pem: and Charles Shephard the Account of what I saw and heard at Milan:—when the Church was darkened, the Groans heard, and the heavy-sounding Lash falling—just before *us*, and behind the Black Curtain which divided us from the seeming Executioners—a Suddenly-illuminated Crucifix in one Corner Streaming with *real Blood du vrai Sang* was his Expression—and a Black Fryar pointing to it in the most vehement Manner—accompanied with pathetic Words and Action.

Oh Heavens! and what Hearts must those People have, who can contemplate such Representations! exclaimed Burrell; Let us go home Mrs. Piozzi, and thank God that we are Protestants.

Mrs. Lutwyche looked displeased,—for the Fitzgeralds were there,[2] besides two or three Foreigners—all Papists of Course: but *I* loved the Young Man the better for his Sensibility, and have not forgotten *Your* Interjection of Oh what Have I escaped!

If Peace should be proclaimed—as some expect;—You may perhaps like to go and see what you have escaped,—or from what at least the early Currents of Life compelled you to part![3]

What a Change that would make, in Yours and my Situation! Whilst I write, comes in old Jacob Weston,[4] whom you remember I suppose at Streatham Park— sent as a Spy I fancy by old attached Friends of *his* not *yours;*—who are all sighing to see me once more established at Streatham Park. Charles Shephard does not however open his Trenches on that Ground, till the Hay Harvest gives him Money for *carrying on the Works*: and little do they dream—any of them;— that if I *do* go thither, it will be for Your Sake, not for theirs: Mrs. Mostyn's Threats were not Things to be neglected, and if I do not repair the Place before my Death, or your coming of Age—They would certainly fall on my Executors for Dilapidation.

The Time however rolls on; and if you can perswade Some good Girl to marry you this Time *Three Years*—I will *give* you all I *can* leave You, and you may go abroad together and *save* Money, if you will not stay at Home and get Money— which would be a likelier Plan for Happiness, and Law the proper Profession. Whatever befalls—except *your* Illbehaviour—or Choice of what I call a Mop-squeezer, or flanting[5] Miss from a Gaming House like——I shall be ever far more *Yours* than my own H: L: P.

Give my best Regards to Dear Pem: and beg him to write next—you should take the Fatigue by Turns. Lady Leven sends to ask *my Nephew's* Company—I tell her he is gone away long ago.[6] So God bless the most precious Possession I ever had to boast—my dear Inestimable! Adieu.

My last five Shillings takes me this Minute to Lady Wilmot's Box to see Roscius in Rolla.[7] Farewell.

Text Ry. 586.143. *Address* John Piozzi Salusbury Esq./ Christ Church/ Oxford. *Postmark* BATH < >.

1. Henry Burrell (1776–1814) was an Oxonian, who received his B.A. in 1797 and M.A. in 1800. He became a barrister-in-law at the Middle Temple and secretary to Lord Eldon.

2. At least three Fitzgerald families were regular visitors to Bath. See, e.g.,:
The politician James Fitzgerald (1742–1835) in 1782 had married Catherine, née Vesey (d. 1832). She was to be created Baroness Fitzgerald and Vesey on 31 July 1826.
Maurice Fitzgerald (1774–1849), hereditary knight of Kerry and Irish statesman had married on 5 November 1801 Maria, née Digges la Touche (d. 1827) of Marlay, Dublin.
Thomas George Fitzgerald (b. 1778) of Turlough Park, county Mayo, and of Maperton House, Somerset, who had married on 6 September 1806 Delia, née Field (fl. 1780–1817).

3. In April, Bonaparte, aware of an impending struggle with the Russians and fearful of another northern coalition, made peace overtures to Great Britain through an intermediary. With such a peace, he would—according to people like Castlereagh—be able "first, to alarm the Northern Pow-

ers; and secondly, to entrap the English Government, by subsequently explaining that by the present dynasty of Spain, he meant not only the family of Charles IV. but his brother Joseph." Only two letters were exchanged: one of offer and another of rejection. See *GM* 82, pt. 2 (1812):74–75.

4. For Jacob Weston, see HLP to PSW, 27 June [1790], n. 3.

If he came as a "Spy" for HLP's daughters, he was within a few years to offer her financial assistance. See HLP to Ann Leak, 7 [March] 1815.

5. Obsolete form of "flaunting."

6. Alexander Leslie, later Leslie-Melville (1749–1820), ninth earl of Leven (1802), styled Lord Balgonie (1754–1802), was comptroller of the customs in Scotland from 1786 until his death, and a Scottish peer from 1806 until 1807.

On 12 August 1784, at Clapham, Surrey, he had married Jane, née Thornton (1757–1818).

7. See *Pizarro*, by Sheridan.

TO ALEXANDER LEAK

Bath Monday
4: May 1812.

I lose no Time to assure you I have received the Bill, and shall lose none in sending it to Hammersley's.

A vexatious Circumstance has arisen about the Hertfordshire copyholds—which *we conveyed over* here in Bath Two Years ago; but all our Trouble and Expence was flung away: for I am forced to sell them in my *Life Time*, by an Enclosure Act; which gives me nothing but the *dry Value*—as I am no Householder in the County:——so the nine Acres will go for 250£.[1]

Mr. Piozzi refused 500£ for them before You ever saw *him* or/ Your unlucky Friend & c./ H: L: Piozzi.

Mrs. Mostyn begs me to send her some live Guinea Fowl, and mentions her Increase of Poultry with great Pleasure: She seems well and gay.—I'm sorry you lose the Races.

Text Hyde Collection. *Address* Mr. Alexander Leak/ Brynbella/ near Denbigh/ North Wales. *Postmark* BATH 4 MY 4 1812 109.

1. For HLP's Hertfordshire copyholds, see her letter to William Wilshire, 26 April [1791], n. 2.

TO JOHN SALUSBURY PIOZZI SALUSBURY

Bath Fryday
15: May 1812.

My precious Creature had more need think of his poor Aunt's *Health* than her Anger; the Late horrible Assassination set my Nerve-shaken Frame into a Flutter that I feared might seriously injure it;[1] but a *resolute* Mind will do much—

and I *resolved* not to give way to the Terror it occasioned: It is however a foolish Thing to encrease my natural Tendency to Agitation, by *your Silence*;—a very foolish Thing indeed: and one Day or other you will repent it.

The News of Chatsworth being burned down by Rioters is of the most dangerous and alarming kind,[2] and those who spread it here all yesterday (if it is not true) did a great Mischief among our Invalids, who most of them have houses which they leave for purpose of drinking these Waters, and who cannot be sure we shall have them to return to, if The Sovereign People are to give the Word in this Way, with their Sink, burn, and destroy.

I hope the Dean will permit your coming; I shall be happier when we are under one Roof:—and as to Dear Pemberton, I think if I owe him Your last kind Letter—I never can repay the Obligation—Let me however be Thankful you are not at Cambridge. Loyalty, Orthodoxy, and Honour will I believe make their last Stand at *Your* University; at least if Things are not still more changed than I am aware of.

Mr. Percival was a worthy Man, and fit enough to be called at a short Notice; he died in the Discharge of his Duty, and even the Mouths of his Enemies bear Testimony to his Merits—but The Individual Loss is not what I mourn—Tho' my Great Grandmother and his were Sisters[3]—'Tis the Spirit of the Times: 'Tis hearing how a London Mob cheered a Murderer;[4] 'Tis the Speech of a Taylor's 'Prentice here in Bath: "Ay Ay—is the Minister killed? what a fine Fellow was he that struck the Blow! I would make his Clothes for nothing."

These are the Things that make one *half* wish to drop into the strong hands of the *Wellesleys* who best could tread 'em down.[5] We will however hope that Mr. Bellingham will have no Occasion for a Taylor.

See what a *Liverpool Bankrupt* is capable of![6]

Meanwhile old Hammersley the Banker is come here to die; and his Son George—sent for to be with him:[7] I felt it both my Duty and Interest to shew him every possible Attention, and took him to Lady Wilmots Party, where we *tried* to be happy, but could scarcely make it out for Fear and Anxiety: *my* Face was chearfullest, because I had a Letter in my Bosom just received from Oxford by Cross Post, before we set out on our Walk to Harley Place. I make my own Leave-taking Party on Wednesday the 20th——and hope and trust my Dear-one will be here to grace it.

Your Brother's Letter to *me* tells of Distress in Trade,[8] of Your Godfather's— Count Fenaroli's Treachery to the Family he pretended such Regard for; and says Your Papa is laid up hard and fast with the Gout[9]——exactly like his Brother I suppose.

They curse Commerce and *S*peculation, and *P*eculation and omne quod exit in *ation* I believe.

Charles Shephard says Mrs. Hoare writes him *Spitefull* Letters about Streatham Park;—says *She* will send a *Surveyor* to see what Trees he cuts, that *we* may not *ruin The Place* that belongs to *Them* &c. &c.[10]

Ask Pemberton if he does not recollect saying Those Girls were Salusbury's best Friends: but Pem: has more Sense than belongs to 19 Years of Age.

Be good Boys, and good Angels to each other——stopping each other, when either of you feel impelled by coarse *Appetite,*—(I will not honour such Feelings with the Name of *Passion*)——to slide down the black stream into the dirty Pond——*Oh pull each other back.*

God bless you then Dear Soul! and don't forget me.

I attend the Lectures of a Man who teaches Memory[11]——Is it necessary for me to *learn* to *remember* how sincerely and with what Affectionate Anxiety/ I remain *Yours*/ while/ H: L: Piozzi?

Write to say when I may expect you both.——

Text Ry. 585.145. *Address* John Piozzi Salusbury Esq./ Christ Church/ Oxford. *Postmark* BATH < > 15 < > 109.

1. On 12 May, HLP wrote into "Minced Meat for Pyes,"—"Mr. Percival assassinated puts every Thing else out of our Heads *here*," i.e., Bath.

Spencer Perceval (1762–1812), who had been first lord of the treasury and chancellor of the duchy of Lancaster since 1809, was assassinated by John Bellingham as he entered the lobby of the House of Commons on 11 May 1812.

2. The present Chatsworth House dates from ca. 1688 and is the seat of the dukes of Devonshire near Bakewell, north central Derbyshire.

The destruction of Chatsworth House was unfounded rumor prompted by the many riots throughout England on account of the high cost of provisions. So common were these riots that *The Times* coined a department for them under the rubric "Disturbances in the Country." See that newspaper for 17 and 23 April. When *The Times* on 12 May devoted its leading column to the "murder" of Mr. Perceval, it ran alongside it the following:

"The rioters have lately, in some parts, entered houses by night, in parties of 20 or 30, for the purpose of procuring arms. Two more attempts at assassination [at Leeds and Huddersfield] have been made, though happily without success. It is said that just before these riots broke out, several persons, known to be United Irishmen, arrived in the manufacturing districts from Ireland, for the purpose of binding the rioters together by oaths."

3. For HLP's great grandmother, see HLP to Q, 23 July 1805, n. 8.

Spencer Perceval's great-grandmother was Catharine, née Dering, who had married in 1680 John Perceval (d. 1686), third baronet [I.]. She was buried 5 February 1690/91 as "the Lady Katharine Persivall" at Chelsea.

4. Pointing to the following events, many people felt that Perceval's assassination portended an English revolution.

Shortly after Perceval's death, a mob gathered in Parliament Square and tried to rescue Bellingham from his guards. Not until midnight and with the help of a troop of horse guards was Bellingham removed to Newgate. The slogan "Rescue Bellingham or die" was pasted on walls, and in London taverns crowds were screaming, "more of these damned scoundrels must go the same way, and then poor people may live." In Nottingham and Leicester, bells were rung, bonfires lit, and mobs shouted their joy. See Denis Gray, *Spencer Perceval, The Evangelical Prime Minister, 1762–1812* (Manchester: Manchester University Press, 1963), 455–60.

5. HLP alludes to the strong-minded and conservative brothers of Arthur Wellesley, duke of Wellington.

Richard Colley Wellesley (1760–1842), second earl of Mornington (1781) and marquess Wellesley (1799) in Ireland. As governor-general of India, he triumphed over Tippoo and destroyed the empire of Mysore. From 1809 to 1812 he was foreign secretary in Perceval's cabinet.

William Wellesley-Pole (1763–1845), third earl of Mornington (1842) and baron Maryborough in the United Kingdom (1821). At this time he was chief secretary and chancellor of the Irish exchequer. In 1814 he was to become master of the mint.

Henry Wellesley, cr. Baron Cowley (1828), British ambassador to Spain (1811–22) and other embassies. See HLP to Q, 19 March 1809, n. 16.

6. Perceval's assassin was John Bellingham (b. ca. 1771), a native of St. Neot's in Huntingdon. As a young man he worked for a Liverpool firm at Archangel in Russia. There he became insolvent and was imprisoned for five years. He held the British government responsible. Upon his release and return to England, he tried to get compensation from the government. After two years of futile

effort, he felt he had to murder the prime minister. This he did by holding his pistol against Perceval's chest and firing. He then sat down on a bench to wait.

7. Thomas Hammersley was in fact to die on 22 October 1812, aged sixty-five, at Auberries, near Sudbury (the seat of his brother-in-law, Charles Greenwood). See *GM* 82, pt. 2 (1812): 496–97.

8. Either Giovanni Maria or Pietro.

9. For Giambattista Piozzi, see HLP to Sophia Byron, 1 September 1788, n. 5; for Luigi Fenaroli, or Fenarole, see HLP to Jacob Weston, 18 December 1798, n. 2.

10. While SH's letter is missing, those of Lord Keith are extant. He was furious about the cutting of trees at Streatham Park, and wrote four letters to Q on the subject. See, e.g., the one dated 15 May 1812:

"I do not believe your Mother has any Right to cut Trees at that Rate. . . . Mr. Shepherd is a Vagabound and finds it his interest to Inflame a Mind too apt to be so against her Children and she by a Momentary approbation from a flattering cur is soothed from the Reflection of her improper Conduct, which I daresay Ranckles her now and then, if Vanity would permit her to Confess it— The Act is the Most uncivil I ever heard of." (Bowood Collection). See also Clifford, pp. 431–32.

11. HLP alludes to a Johann Kaspar Spurzheim (1776–1832), German physician and one of the earliest advocates of phrenology, who annually gave a course of sixteen lectures "on the propensities, sentiments, and intellectual Faculties of the Mind"—i.e., "Craniology." See the *Bath Herald*, 24 December 1814. In her "Commonplace Book" HLP observed, in reference to Spurzheim, "What a Mountebank Business that Craniology is."

TO CLEMENT MEAD

Saturday
16: May 1812.

Mrs. Hoare having expressed much Anxiety concerning The Trees to be cut for Repairs at Old Streatham Park;

I write to say that it would break my heart to offend the Ladies—when I am going to all this Expence merely to please them. You have not surely cut down any of our old favourite Ornamental Timber near the house——My Lime Tree for example, near the Glass Door of the Library; The Theophrastus with its Green and Silver Leaves in Driving to the Place:—or Miss Thrale's Oak close to the little Pond by the Summerhouse, which was planted when Lady Keith was born; or The Scarlet-flowring Maple going to the Summerhouse; or Mr. Thrale's Walnut Tree at the Summerhouse Door almost.

No, nor the Sycamore in the middle of the Octagon Court, or the monstrous Poplar, which monstrous as it is I put with my own hands into the Ground very near the Stable.

Write, and set my Nerves at rest; and believe/ me much Yours/ Hester Lynch Piozzi.

Direct/ Mrs. Piozzi/ No. 16/ Bath.

I can't tell where or how to direct to Mr. Charles Shephard now he is *under Arms.*

Text Hyde Collection. *Address* Mr. Clement Mead/ Builder &c./ 34 Charlotte Street/ Fitzroy Square/ London.
Postmark BATH < >.

TO JOHN SALUSBURY PIOZZI SALUSBURY

begun on Monday Night
18 [-19]: May 1812.

My dearest Salusbury

You are the best of all wise Boys, and the wisest of all good ones, in wishing to leave Oxford, and come home with poor Aunt—to take Care of her.[1] I will not flatter either you or myself by saying I am as well as when we parted—How can I?—Depend upon it half of *the Dean's* Sickness is caused by Agitation of Mind for public Matters,——much more *mine*: whose Anxiety is increased by my Concern for *You*. Leak writes me Word that Risings are expected at Holywell—If that Bank should be destroyed, my 718£ is not worth seven Shillings——and such a Year as this! when both of us have spent double, ay treble the Money we ought to have done.[2]

My *seventeen* Weeks Bath are up on Monday 1st of June, but perhaps we might save something by meeting at Worcester, instead of your coming out of the way hither: Though I should delight to have your dear Company *directly*——The Moment the Dean is visible tell him you are coming away,—and *upon my Account*: Thomas Curr has deserved his Rheumatism more than he has deserved my Compassion;[3] 'tis hard his Master should suffer tho' for *his* Faults: but indeed I never saw Vice contented with *one* Victim, She insists upon Two or Three,— and often upon Two or Three Generations.

This is a Day of infinite Importance:——Should the Assassin be hanged quietly and unresistingly; All may yet go well. Should the Mob even *endeavour* at rescueing, or revenging him, Woe betide us![4]

Come home however, and mind your own Affairs; Come at least *nearer* home, that you may be sent for on any Emergence. Young as you are—(and in 3 Months you will be going for 20 Years old;) many have been called to act seriously and steadily:—and notwithstanding I have *indulged*——I never did *emasculate*—or breed you up in Effeminate Softness. My own *Courage* will outlive my own *health,* and if Things come to a rough Conclusion You shall not see me disgrace my Father's, or my Mother's Family.

They may make me Sick, they shall not make me Mean.

Will it amuse you to know that the pretty little Widow *Finette* Mrs. L. H. Moore, was married this Morning[5]——so was Mr. Elliott[6]—Brother to the Countess of Errol, who is scarce cold in her Coffin.[7]—Sir Walter James is at Cheltenham, whence General Le Fêvre went off quite openly—breaking his Word and Honour——like a true *Frenchman.*—[8]

My *Party* will now be *odious* to me, Salusbury's not here. And 'tis a Leave-taking Business too, and surrounded by melancholy Circumstances. Well! commend *me* to Miss Williams and old Boigelin. The first Thinks of her Grandpapa's Will, Debts &c.[9] The second—*only of His Manuscript* which never will be published.[10]

I think, that People will build and plant, and marry, and give in Marriage down to the very Day our Saviour comes to judge them—*see 24 Chapter Matthew*,

38 Verse: Mean while we *must* mind this World's Business while we Stay in it:[11] but we *must* remember too how short a Time that *is;* and that the next (thank God) will last for ever.[12] Be not seduced to *risque* it Dearest Dear! See what the Fools you meet with, risque it *for?* Tom Curr's Rheumatism!! A *Dog* is as wise, and more respectable.

God preserve You! but take care of your Dear Self Body and Soul, and render not vain the Prayers of/ your affectionate Aunt/ H: L: P.

Let me know what you determine about our Journey.——
Give my Love to Pemberton.—I am forced to send this by 9 o'Clock, so cannot tell how the great Affair went in London—because the Mail is not come in Tuesday Morning 19 May. And I want an Answer to this Letter.

Text Ry. 585.146. *Address* John Piozzi Salusbury Esq./ Christ Church/ Oxford. *Postmark* BATH < > 1812 <109>.

1. JSPS entered Christ Church as a student in October 1811. By the end of the university year, he wanted never to return, preferring to live at Brynbella (with a wife) and be the country squire.
2. When *The Times* on 12 May published the information, real or not, that the disturbances in the country over the high cost of provisions were now being fomented by the arrival of the United Irishmen, people like Leak and HLP worried about the safety of Holywell (with its attempts at manufacture and banking) and all of North Wales. In short, they expected the Irish to land at Holyhead, move through Flintshire to Chester, and thence to "the manufacturing districts" of northern England and the Midlands.
There is no record of serious disturbance at Holywell.
3. JSPS's servant at Christ Church.
4. Bellingham had been tried at the Old Bailey on Friday, 15 May 1812, found guilty, and hanged on the morning of 18 May. From the time of the assassination to the trial and execution, Bellingham asked no mercy, showed no sign of strain, and died quietly.
There was fear of an uprising to prevent the execution, as acknowledged by MF on 19 May (Ry. 583.97).
"Monday *has* past quietly over, notwithstanding my dearest Mrs. Piozzi's fears, and the sad assassin has been dispatched to *another* world, we won't say, a *better.* I lifted up my hands with horror, to hear a Gentleman this morning say 'he made a *fine* end;' because the Devil had so hardened his heart, and pride had thrown so much dirt in *one* eye, and revenge in the other, that he could not himself, poor wretched Monster . . . see the Magnitude of his crime. . . . Do you not rejoice that every vote, for the provision of poor Perceval's Family, was carried? His wife expecting to be shortly confined of her *twentieth* child!"
5. According to the *Bath Chronicle,* 21 May: "Thursday [14 May] was married at Queen-square chapel Major Waller to Mrs. Moore of Portland Place."
6. HLP is reacting to the announcement of the intended marriage of Freeman W. Eliott (b. 1781), originally of Antigua, to Margaret, the daughter of the Reverend George Strahan, vicar, St. Mary's, Islington, and prebendary of Rochester.
7. Alicia Eliott, born on 16 May 1775 in Antigua, became on 3 August 1796 the second wife of William Hay-Carr (1772–1819), seventeenth earl of Erroll (1798). She died in Norfolk Crescent, Bath, on 24 April 1812 and was buried on 1 May.
8. Charles Lefebvre-Desnouëttes, général de division (1808), captured in the Peninsular War, had been a prisoner in England since early 1809. By May 1812 he escaped to France, where he resumed his military career.
See the *Courier,* 11 May 1812:
"Another letter mentions the arrival in France of an *officer of distinction,* who had escaped from this country. There seems little doubt that this was Gen. Lefebvre, who, personating a German Count, took a post-chaise at Cheltenham, for London. Madame Lefebvre, attired in boy's clothes, passed for his son, and his Aide-de-Camp was valet-de-chambre." They went from London to Dover "where a smuggling boat being ready, he was conveyed to the coast of France. The Secretary of State

for the Home Department is said to have received a most insolent letter from him, in justification of his breach of parole."
9. MW's grandfather was John Williams (d. 1788) of Bodylwyddan, chief justice of Brecon, Glamorgan, and Radnor.
10. HLP predicted correctly. Boisgelin published nothing subsequent to 1810.
11. 1 Thessalonians 4:11.
12. Psalms 89:47.

TO CLEMENT MEAD

Bath
20: May 1812.

My dear Mr. Mead
can scarcely think how his Letter, and one from Mrs. Hoare received the same Moment——shocked me:——I little thought I was offending the Ladies by spending Such Sums of Money on a Place which will be *theirs the sooner*, for the Concern it gives me to hear them consider that as an Injury, which I meant as a Benefit.

For God's Sake cut no more of their Trees, I wish these had all been left standing——and the House left to fall——if they like that better——but It was told me they wished it repaired;——and with what other Timber could I have repaired it?

Pity it was not Sold last Year, and then we should all have enjoyed our Share of the Money, and they would have been Gainers. As it *is*—I insist only on *one* Thing, and upon *that* I insist Solemnly: namely—That you lay out no more on the Place, than the Profits of the Place produces; that if one Year's Rent will not serve——We may take *Two;* but still giving Credit till those Rents come in: for no Power on Earth shall make me lay out my ready Money where instead of *Thanks* I receive only *Reproaches.* That you may assure Yourself, so you know the Peril incurred by Expence upon Streatham Park——and I suppose You know likewise that a Thousand Pounds cannot be more foolishly spent *on my Part.*—

The Die however is cast; and I expect your Estimate/ remaining ever Sir/ Your True Friend and Servant/ H: L: Piozzi.

Pray why should I repair Hothouses or Boathouses built by Mr. Piozzi or Mr. Giles?

Sure 'tis sufficient if I leave all as it was left me by Mr. Thrale.

Text Hyde Collection. *Address* Mr: Clement Mead/ Surveyor &c./ Upper Charlotte Street/ Fitzroy Square/ London. *Postmark* BATH MY 20 1812 10<9>.

TO THE REVEREND THOMAS SEDGWICK WHALLEY

25: May 1812.

My dear Doctor Whalley will wonder to see I can write one Line steadily, by the Time he comes to the End of this Letter, but I will finish my Request— before I begin Grievances.

The kind Reception Mr. Almon[1] gave my Steward Leak, and the Offer he made him of an Intelligent Substitute, some Time that he came to Your house with My Compliments,—induces me to Enquire if the Person then mentioned, may be probably found by next Michaelmas, willing to come to Wales, and supply Leak's Place during the planting Season. I fancy he must be both active and able; as Leak complains of having too much Business, and too little Health to go thro' with it. No need to add how necessary how Indispensable is Honesty, and Skill in Agricultural Concerns. He must likewise have the Power of patient Endurance where the People he employs are sometimes stupid, and often perverse: They have wearied the last Man quite out: and if I should ever be impelled to make Streatham Park a comfortable Residence——perhaps Leak liking England better than Denbighshire might be more useful to me near London. But Oh Heavens! how shall I ever bear the Sight of Streatham Park? or how will its Reversionary Proprietors bear the Sight of poor H:L:P?

I fear I have now Sinned against them without *hope* of reinstatement to favour. Mrs. Mostyn having menaced little Salusbury pretty sharply last Summer, what they would do to *him* if I was to die; and how they would pinch him for dilapidations of their Seat in Surrey; Charles Shephard counselled me to repair and reside in it next Spring——to shew them it was habitable. I therefore recommended Mead, a Surveyor whom I have long known; and he selected such Trees as were overshadowing, and ruining the house, and has *cut them down*. Down came the Ladies though, in high Wrath; and terrified the Man, and wrote most Insulting Letters to Shephard——*cruel* and *bitter* ones to poor me, who will have little less than 1000£ to lay out, and Reproaches alone for my Reward.

Now tell me my Dear Sir—why These Afflictions, which are really no light ones at my Age; should not have produced Tears from those Eyes that cried over the Castle of Montval the other Night till I believe people thought me hysterical.[2]

It was very respectably acted, and well got up; and having never seen Siddons in the Character——I was content.[3]

I am discontented tho', and seriously discontented too, at the Thought of leaving this Place just as You come to it. I find all these enumerated Occurrences concur to make me who have Three good Houses, doat on a *dirty Lodging*—— but an Ass *does* prefer Thistles to Roseleaves you know;[4] and I can enjoy the Trees that grow in Sydney Gardens without caring about their Reversionary Proprietors.

Mrs. Lutwyche will tell you that I go to learn of a Memory Master who gives Lectures here——was not there one at Athens once? and did not Themistocles tell him he would rather learn the Art of Forgetfulness?[5]

Nothing new under the Sun.[6]

The Situation of Public Affairs seems to interest People chiefly from private Motives—wanting the Ministry which will patronize their Sons, Brothers &c.[7] I see no one sincerely vexed at the Thought of our Dissentions giving Pleasure to the Enemy——The Removal of Lucien Buonaparte is however a Sensible Thing let who will have advised it.[8]

Write to me Dear Sir, a long and kind Letter to Brynbella near Denbigh N. Wales, never forgetting that You have there a truly old Friend/ and gratefully Obliged Servant/ H: L: Piozzi.

What will Cecy Mostyn say? I am afraid to face any of them while they are so angry——but Charles Shephard is practising L'Art militaire among the Buckinghamshire Corps and will go on courageously.

Text Berg Collection +.

1. For Amans, TSW's confidential servant, see HLP to TSW, 11 May 1808, n. 2.

2. TSW's *Castle of Montval*, which began rehearsal by 11 May 1812, was produced at Bath's Theatre Royal on 19 and 28 May. See the *Bath Journal*, 11, 18, and 25 May 1812.

3. The *Castle of Montval* had opened initially on 23 April 1799. Whatever success it had in 1799 was owing to SS. See, e.g., the *True Briton*, 10 January 1799, which reported: "Mr. Whalley, the Author of the new Tragedy, coming forward to the Drury Lane Theatre, is one of the early friends of Mrs. Siddons, who strongly interests herself in the success of the Piece [and plays the Countess of Montval]. The zeal of friendship operating with a sense of public duty, will, therefore, doubtless urge her talents to their utmost force."

4. "An ass loaded with gold still eats thistles," etc. (*Oxford Proverbs*).

5. The story is told of Themistocles (ca. 524–ca. 459 B.C.), "easily the greatest man of Greece," that Simonides of Ceos (556–467) offered to teach him the newly invented "artem ei memoriae." Themistocles "replied that he would sooner learn to forget—no doubt this was because whatever he heard or saw remained fixed in his memory."
See Cicero, *Academica*, 2.2; *De Finibus*, 2.32.104; *De Oratore*, 2.299.

6. Ecclesiastes 1:9.

7. There was little satisfaction with the ministry, which made Nicholas Vansittart chancellor of the exchequer in place of Perceval. On 21 May James Archibald Stuart-Wortley-Mackenzie, an independent M.P. who had been a follower of Perceval and an admirer of George Canning, moved that an address be presented to the Prince Regent, begging him to act on behalf of an efficient administration. The House of Commons decided (in this revolt of the back-benchers) that the address should be presented not by the privy councillors but by Wortley and Lord Milton. On the presentation of the address to the Prince Regent on 22 May, the ministry resigned.
See *GM* 82, pt. 1 (1812): 483.

8. On 11 April 1811 the *Courier* announced that Lucien Bonaparte's family and entourage were "removing from the vicinity of Ludlow into Worcestershire," where he bought Thorngrove, near Worcester. If they were moved again—an event not particularly noticed in the newspapers of 1812— then the action was taken by the government to prevent the recurrence of an incident like General Lefebvre's escape. (Records show, however, that they continued to live at Thorngrove until 1814.)

THE REVEREND THOMAS SEDGWICK WHALLEY TO HESTER LYNCH PIOZZI

16 June 1812

. . . Mrs. Lutwyche informed you of my fair Prospect for the renewal of those domestic Comforts which I have, since I could observe, and reflect, valued above all others, and without which the Life, of Life, with *me,* is gone.—Your Lynx Eye, and quick perception, would enable you to distinguish Mrs. Horneck's Talents, and turn of Mind, on a cursory acquaintance; but they could not give you the full knowledge of her various and uncommon merits, that I have after a confidential friendship and Correspondence with her for more than 30: years.—I *know* she likes *you,* and I think I know you well enough to be confident that you like her; and when you know each other *au fond,* which I trust you will do, you will esteem and have a sincere affection for each other.—Next Winter, my Dear Mrs. Piozzi, I hope we shall see each other often, and without Form, and Fashion. And next May, I promise myself the delight of seeing you, and your Darling Salusbury at Mendip Lodge. Mr. and Mrs. Lutwyche (God permitting) I have engaged to meet you there; and sweet pretty Mary Mayhew,[1] and the Lad of your Heart, while we Elders commune gravely, may skip about. . . .

I am sorry that ripe age, or reflection, have not, *yet,* impressed your Daughters with a due sense of their filial duties. It makes one fear that the *Stone* in their Hearts will never be removed. It is a stumbling Block to their respectability; but let it not prove one, any longer, to your peace. Your adopted Son, I trust, and verily believe, will recompence you, for all the wrong you have suffered from your *legitimate* Daughters. I am glad that you have, at last, determined to put Streatham in thorough repair < > doing it, you will know the *worst,* will save yourself from bickering and Heart burning, and dear Salusbury from eventual insult and expence. You will live long enough, I doubt not, to fetch up, more *much more,* than the cost of these Repairs, and then a Fig! for the fine Ladies, your fashionable daughters. . . .

Text Ry. 564.22.

1. For Clementina Mary Mayhew, see HLP to Ly W, 30 January 1802, n. 7.

TO THE REVEREND THOMAS SEDGWICK WHALLEY

Brynbella
Monday 29: June 1812.

I direct to my Dear Doctor Whalley at Bath, tho' I do believe this anxious Evening sees him at London at the Theatre.[1] You who never forget old Friends will feel for our charming Siddons, tho' your heart is once more taking irrevocable Engagements: may they be happy as I wish, and as You deserve! It is Impossible to know Mrs. Horneck and not love her, equally impossible Not to see that She loves You; I am glad Things are to end so, and pray divide my cordial Congratulations between You. It will be a fine Holyday Time for Salusbury and me to spend May next at Mendip after my Sullen Penance with Workmen at old Streatham Park; but I am talking as if I expected the Longævity *you* have partly a Claim to, in right of your good Mother.

Are the much-tormented Ladies of Sir Walter James's Family out of their Pain yet? I pity the Females more than I do *him*, however his Company and Conversation delight me; Oh surely that agreeable young Christ Church Man will not go (as was apprehended) into a Consumption;—That would really be too dreadful.

We are in the midst of our Hay here, and make no Complaints of *our own* Crop; but sure enough the Produce of Mother Earth this Year will be but a Scanty one; whilst her Progeny increase with a Rapidity beyond my Comprehension.

The Dearness of Corn however is good for us farmers—up to a certain Degree; and this is my Tythe-setting Day, and we are all on Tip-toe——How exactly Does my excellent Friend describe my Character!

> I often think my buoyant Mind
> Is like a Bladder blown with Wind;
> Which flung upon the angry Tides
> Their utmost Fury still abides:
> From the high Wave unhurt can bound,
> Oft seeming lost, Often tost, but never drown'd.[2]

So if Brynbella prospers I will defy the *rough Estimate* of my Surrey Expences, which at any Rate had better fall on my full Purse, than on my poor Boy's comparatively empty one:——and I may be thankful their Menaces led me to enquiry, tho' the Sum I am threatened with is a tremendous one—not less than 1700£.

Dear Doctor Whalley let me have your good Wishes——and from Mrs. Lutwyche all She can spare: her *best* go to you I am confident. Commend me to the kind Friend—L'aimable Chevalier: he felt for me when he saw me severely fretted, I shall retain a grateful remembrance of *him*, whilst able to subscribe myself *Your* truly obliged/ and Faithful Friend, Servant/ &c. H: L: P.

My Health is not amiss, yet Mr. Chenevix's Shakespearian Exclamation does sometimes rise to my Lips.

> "Oh vain World!
> Thy hourly Use has shrunk me."[3]

I wish I knew where to buy the Castle of Montval—I want to read it to Salusbury.

Text Berg Collection + . *Address* Rev: Doctor T. S. Whalley at/ William Lutwyche's Esq./ Marlborough Buildings/ Bath. *Postmark* DENBIGH <224>.

1. SS "took her professional farewell of the stage on [29 June]. The play was 'Macbeth.' At an early hour a vast crowd assembled around the theatre of Covent Garden, and, when the doors were opened, the struggle for places became a service of danger. After the sleep-walking scene . . . the applause of the spectators became ungovernable: they stood on the benches, and demanded that the performance of the piece should not go further than the last scene in which she appeared. . . . The curtain was dropped for twenty minutes; after which it rose, and discovered Mrs. Siddons sitting at a table, dressed simply in white. She came forward amidst the most fervent acclamations, which for several minutes prevented her from speaking. When silence was obtained, she delivered, with modest dignity, but with much emotion, the [farewell] Address, written for the occasion by her nephew, Horace Twiss" (Campbell, 2:336–37). See also *The Times*, 30 June; Farington, 11:4151.

2. HLP's own verse, its central image indebted to Matthew Green's *The Spleen*. See "Harvard Piozziana," vol. 4.

3. The lines were spoken by Margaret, Duchess of Burgundy, in Richard Chenevix's *Henry the Seventh, An Historical Tragedy* (published 1812), 3.1.

For Richard Chenevix, see HLP to LC, 25 January 1803, n. 5.

THE REVEREND LEONARD CHAPPELOW TO HESTER LYNCH PIOZZI

London
July 7—1812
Tuesday.

Dear Madam—

Pray do write now and not then to Dear Sir Yours ever truely H. L. P.—

And what am I to say.—Why say that at last, we have a fine warm morning, 'tis 6 'Clock—and the Sun shines gloriously—but we have had dreadful frosty nights—the Mail coachmen declare that their fingers have been as cold as in January—and the kernels of the Wheat, filled with their dulcet vegetable cream, have been eventually so frozen that in some places they have perished and dropped from the ears—which are every [one] too short.—We must starve or depend upon the Americans.—I hope the Atlantic—will resume its old Title—we must call it the pacific Ocean—for to war with America would be dreadful indeed.[1]

I need not tell you, any thing about Mrs. Siddons and her Benefit, for you must have seen all in the newspapers.—Do you recollect any thing about Garrick and his farewell speech—when he quitted the stage?—It has been said that after he had finished his part, no more of the play was performed—and it was understood that the Last Act in Macbeth was not to be performed, after Lady M—walking in her sleep—and washing her hands, finished her part—but O. P.—made a dreadful disturbance and not one word of the <Farewell> could be heard.—

You saw in the Papers—the speech—'twas written by a young man, a Mr. Twiss,[2] son I suppose of the Man who married Mrs. Siddons's sister—4 lines were delightful—but so bad is my memory become that I cannot quote them—but the two words memory and moonlight will direct your Eye to them.—[3]

I have written 2 or 3 scrawls to the Recluses—The Dutchess of Richmond is with them this very day in her way to Ireland.[4]

Sarah Siddons as Lady Macbeth. Portrait by George Henry Harlow; engraved by Robert Cooper. (Reproduced by permission of the Henry E. Huntington Library and Art Gallery, San Marino, California.)

Have you in your neighbourhood any French prisoners?—The Llangollen Ladies are very Luck<y>—by the kind interference of Mr. W. Pole none are sent
to the Vale of Llangollen.[5]—What a wretch is this Philippon—I hope [he] will
be caught.—Had he capitulated at Badajos, the Lives of many English Officers,
and Men would have been saved—and by military Law we might have put the
whole Garrison to the Sword.[6]—We never had but one Officer who broke his
Parole in the Peninsula and Lord Wellington immediately sent him back again
to the Enemy.

What are we to do with the *Roman* Catholics[7]—for we are all Catholics.—It is
ridiculous to apply to Romanists the *general* Title, when that which is specific is
intended.—On Sunday Last—I was at White Hall Chapel 2 hours and ½. Your
New Bishop of Chester was consecrated by the A[rch] B[ishop] of C[anter-
bury].[8]—The Ceremony was long and very impressive.—A great number of
Ladies were there—and with the military I suppose there were near 1500 people there.—

The King is in a dreadful state.[9] Expresses were sent Last night for the Regent
&c. &c. &c.—and he is not better this morning.—Good God deliver us—we are
absolutely upon the Eve of Revolution and rebellion both in Church and
state.[10]—Your paper will tell you all—2 Bow street Heros have been for some
weeks mixed as Spys amongst the Rebels—taken their treasonable Oaths and
made many discoveries.—50 ringleaders are seized—and their Depots of Arms
and amunition discovered.[11]—Good Lord deliver us—says your sincere and very
faithful friend/ —L. C.

Text Ry. 563.100.

1. War had already broken out between the United States and Great Britain on 18 June 1812,
although the news had not yet reached England. When LC was writing this letter, he knew only
that "the American Senate had determined on war with this country by a majority of six. . . .
Whether [a declaration of war] received the final sanction of the American Government previous to
the arrival of the intelligence of the death of Mr. Perceval, and the revocation of the Orders in
Council, is not yet known." See *GM* 82, pt. 2 (1812):77.

2. SS's nephew, Horace Twiss (1787–1849) was in time to become a satirist and politician. Although always interested in the theater, he had been called to the bar on 28 June 1811. His verses
for SS's farewell performance in *Macbeth* on 29 June 1812 are quoted in Campbell, 2:338–39. See
HLP to LC, 10 July 1812.

3. The lines to which LC alludes are as follows:

> Yet, grateful Memory shall reflect their light
> O'er the dim shadows of the coming night,
> And lend to later life a softer tone,
> A moonlight tint,—a lustre of her own.

4. Charlotte Gordon (1768–1842), daughter of the fourth duke of Gordon, had married on 9
September 1789 Charles Lennox (1764–1819), fourth duke of Richmond and Lennox (1806). At this
time he was lord-lieutenant of Ireland (1807–13) and was later to be appointed governor-general of
Canada (1818–19).

5. The Ladies of Llangollen are reacting to the news of General Lefebvre's escape.
For William Wellesley-Pole, see HLP to JSPS, 15 May 1812, n. 5.

6. Armand Philippon (1761–1836) had begun his army career in 1778 as an enlisted man. With
the creation of a republican army, he switched his loyalties and service. Employed over succeeding

years in Italy, Switzerland, and Hanover, he served with the Grande Armée from 1805–7. Sent to Spain in 1808, he took part in the battle of Talavera and the siege of Cadiz. He became a baron and a général de brigade (1810). In March 1811, he was governor of Badajoz and withstood the first siege attempts of the British. Quickly (July 1811) he was promoted to général de division. He surrendered in 1812 only after being wounded and after the storming of Badajoz in April. Taken prisoner and brought to England, he was, however, able to escape and engage in the Russian and German campaigns.

7. There was a prolonged parliamentary debate from January to June on the "Catholic question": specifically, whether or not to remove "the civil disabilities" under which Catholics in Ireland "laboured." For the debate, which ended inconclusively, see *GM* 82, pt. 1 (1812): 166, 265, 282, 372, 467, 571, 658.

8. For George Henry Law, see HLP to JSPS, 19 February 1810 and n. 5.
Charles Manners-Sutton (1755–1828) had become archbishop of Canterbury in 1805.

9. "During the last fortnight of the month of June, his Majesty suffered a high degree of agitation; but was rather better on the 4th of July. . . . In the afternoon of that day, however, the paroxysm increased to a degree of violence." It continued "between 50 and 60 hours; and, on the 6th, he became a few minutes speechless." By 7 July the paroxysm had subsided and the king became tranquil again. See *GM* 82, pt. 2 (1812): 80.

10. The political rebellion had to do with the Luddites.
The Anglican Church, with its emphasis on rational piety, was being shaken by pietistic evangelism. By 1810, moreover, dissenters (particularly the Methodists) were able to adapt themselves more readily than the Anglicans to conditions in the new industrial cities. They built many small brick chapels and attracted craftsmen and artisans, small farmers and farm laborers, fishermen and miners.
LC feared the impact of the evangelical movement on the state church, evident, e.g., in the Anglican Clapham sect, and he feared the growing number of dissenters.

11. Report had it "that two Bow-street Officers had been in the neighbourhood of *Huddersfield* for nearly three weeks past, and that they had been *twisted in*, or, in other words, had taken the oath of the Luddites. By this means they had learned the proceedings and ways of those infatuated people, and had obtained the knowledge of the depôt where their arms were concealed. Warrants have been issued for the apprehension of 50 of the ringleaders, and a great number of them were taken into custody." See *GM* 82, pt. 2 (1812): 78.

TO THE REVEREND LEONARD CHAPPELOW

Brynbella
10: July 1812.

Dear Mr. Chappelow's

kind Scrap came safe, and gave me Pleasure; and very glad am I that my Letter to the Charming Siddons contributed towards giving you some.[1]

Horace Twiss's Verses are really very pretty ones, better perhaps than Whitehead's for Mrs. Pritchard; when She, in the same Character took Leave of the Stage in 1768.[2]

Mr. Garrick in Don Felix remained on the Boards till the Curtain dropt—*of Course*—it was in his Part to do so; and we were told that the Applause was unbounded.[3] Many of his Adorers received him in the Green room, or his own Dressing room (whichever was grandest) with Tears, Embraces &c. and some begged a Part of the Dress he acted in as a Keepsake—To Hannah More he presented the Shoe buckles I remember;[4] and She, the next Morning ran to Letitia Aickin, now Mrs. Barbauld with them in her hand to shew with what

Honours She had been distinguished.[5] That Lady viewed them, and pausing but a Moment cried out

> Thy Buckles dear Garrick thy Friends may now use,
> But no one hereafter shall stand in Thy Shoes.

With Regard to the Political World it is I believe crumbling about us apace; The great Performers have all left the Stage, and these miserable *Figurantes* finish the Ballet but lamely.[6]

The Moral World is in a new Way too. Lord and Lady Uxbridge, Lord and Lady Berwick have I believe no Objections made to them;[7] General Broughton has brought home Miss Poole, and all goes on *smoothly,* as *polished* Manners should do.[8] The natural World is cruelly disturbed in our West Indies; but that's another Hemisphere You know, and if it does rain Fire *there*—We care not.[9]

Our Corn affords a very scanty Prospect, my own is good enough, and Hay in Plenty: but there will be Distress, and Democratic Fancies, and Luddites in *every Riding.*[10]

John Bull resembles the Bull *Dog* in one Thing; for let that Animal be never so tame, take him with you in a Chaise,—and let that Chaise be in Danger of upsetting; Your Companion—well convinced *'tis all your Fault*—flies at your Throat:—as we do at the Government when Bread is at too high a Price.

But now we have no Government, our best Chance for Quiet is—we have no one to fly at: so for the Present I will think no more on't—My Tythes set ill I know, and sink in Value; and Stocks are dropt down to nothing: never Mind—— What did that Old Greek Fellow say when People asked him why he was not afraid? because I am *Old* replied he, and my Children are grown up—They may take Care of themselves.

So Adieu dear Mr. Chappelow; and beg Lady Bradford's Prayers for us all and for *me* because I am Your/ Faithful Friend and Servant/ H: L: P.——

Text Ry. 561.145. *Address* Rev: Leonard Chappelow/ No. 12 or 13/ Hill Street/ Berkeley Square/ London.

1. LC had written to HLP on 11 June 1812 (Ry. 563.98). In his letter he asked her to use her influence with SS to get him seven tickets for the actress's farewell on 29 June. SS procured the tickets for LC's party and on 18 June wrote to HLP:

"It is surely needless for me to assure you how truly gratifying it is to me to secure a letter from you, or how delightful it is to me to obey your wishes. Our friend Chappelow is, I hope, accommodated to his satisfaction, and as we both remember he never was any admirer of mine, he will probably see me take my leave without much of the regret which some few at least, I do believe, will feel upon that occasion. I am free to confess it will to me be awful and affecting. [To] know one is doing the most indifferent thing for *the last time* induces a more than common seriousness. . . . I feel as if my foot were now on the first round of the Ladder which reaches to another world. Give me your prayers, my good friend, to help me on my way thither, and believe me ever/ Your faithful and affectionate/ S. Siddons" (Broadley, 148–49).

2. Hannah Pritchard (1711–68) took leave of the stage on 24 April 1768 as Lady Macbeth. At that time, she spoke an epilogue written for her by Garrick. Another epilogue by George Keate (1729–97) was written for her farewell but never recited.

There is no evidence that the poet laureate William Whitehead (1715–85) wrote verses for Pritchard's farewell night.

3. For his farewell evening, 10 June 1776, David Garrick appeared as Don Felix in Susanna Centlivre's *The Wonder: A Woman Keeps a Secret*. The entertainment opened with a rhymed prologue written and spoken by Garrick in the form of an appeal for the Decayed Actors' Fund to which the profits of the evening were devoted.

"When the curtain fell on the play, the claps, it was said, sounded like muffled drums. A deep hush fell and the audience waited motionless and silent as Garrick came forward slowly and stood for a few moments unable to speak. Then in low, unrhetorical tones, he made a simple and moving speech." See Margaret Barton, *Garrick* (London: Faber and Faber, 1948), 264–65; Arthur Murphy, *The Life of David Garrick, Esq.*, 2 vols. (London: J. Wright, 1801), 2:135–36.

4. Hannah More probably met David Garrick and his wife in 1773 or 1774. She enjoyed their friendship, and their house became her second home. There she largely wrote her drama *Percy* in 1777. The actor gave it his enthusiastic care, saw to its production, wrote the prologue and epilogue for it, and helped her earn over £400 by it. For her part, Hannah More thought Garrick had purified the stage.

5. If Hannah More rushed to Anna Letitia Aikin (1743–1825) on 11 June, she saw the wife of the Reverend Rochement Barbauld (d. 1808). The marriage had taken place in 1774.

6. HLP lamented the demise of "The great Performers"—Pitt and Perceval—leaving ministers whose quarrels prevented efficient government action. When the Liverpool ministry resigned in late May in the face of the backbenchers' revolt, efforts were made by Marquess Wellesley and Lord Moira to form coalition governments. When they failed to form a ministry, the Prince Regent asked Liverpool to resume with his ministry as it had been constituted before the crisis began on 21 May. See *GM* 82, pt. 2 (1812): 68–69.

7. For Henry William Paget, fourth earl of Uxbridge (1812) and his wife, see HLP to Q, 19 March 1809, nn. 9, 15.

For Thomas Noel Hill, Lord Berwick, and his eighteen-year-old wife, see HLP to JSPS, 4 March 1812 and n. 2.

8. John Delves Broughton (1769–1847) of Doddington Hall, near Nantwich, Cheshire, was a major general (1808) in the army, although on the half-pay list since ca. 1799. On 5 June 1792 he had married Elizabeth, née Egerton (d. 1857), initially of Fulton Park, Cheshire. Broughton, a lieutenant general in 1813 and a general in 1830, became seventh baronet upon the death of his father on 23 July 1813.

Whoever Miss Poole was, she did nothing to upset the Broughton marriage.

For Broughton's will, see P.R.O., Prob. 11/2063/755, proved 2 October 1847.

9. *The Times*, 23 June 1812, devoted its lead column to the description of the volcanic destruction on St. Vincent. It quoted a letter from "Nevis, May 10":

"'On the 1st of this month, our whole island was much alarmed by various distant explosions, accompanied by a slight shock of an earthquake; the reports were, many of them, full as loud as those of heavy cannon; and a high surf was immediately observed, although there was no wind.'" These phenomena were explained by a volcanic eruption on St. Vincent.

"'The yellow fever has carried off many persons in the islands. We hear it has been fatal at Antigua, and at St. Kitt's, where many of the troops have died.'"

On 30 June, *The Times* devoted almost two columns to a detailed "Description of the Eruption of the Souffrier Mountain, on Thursday night, the 30th of April 1812, in the Island of St. Vincent."

10. The Luddites were the workmen of the industrial centers of England, who rioted in 1811–16. They systematically wrecked new machinery, to which they attributed unemployment and low wages. Local magistrates tried in vain to find them and prosecute. The government, therefore, made the war against the Luddites ferocious. To smash frames, to damage property, and to take Luddite oaths became capital offenses.

At this time, HLP refers to Luddite activities in the North and West Riding, Yorks.: specifically in Leeds (10 July), Huddersfield (11 July), Holmsforth (12 July), etc. See *GM* 82, pt. 2 (1812): 78.

TO CLEMENT MEAD

Brynbella
Thursday 13: August 1812.

I send You enclosed my good Mr. Mead a Draft on my Banker for 100£ and am glad Things are going on well, and in a Way to please the Ladies. They have surely every Reason to be pleased by what you tell me of your Proceedings, nay—*I almost think* you had better have asked for their Approbation to cut down that Row of large Poplars, which growing close by the Garden Wall, keeps the Sun from The Fruit; than go about to purchase Oak at the Rate you mention, when there are Oaks running to Decay all over the Park and Plantation——but you will cut no more till October, and by then You will have seen Mr. Shephard again; and seen the Ladies likewise: and I shall send up my own Steward to look how Things go, and when the Place will be fit to receive Me &c.——and In the Mean Time do not drive me to unnecessary Expences to please any Ladies living by the Mortification and Ruin of Your old Friend/ H: L: Piozzi.

Text Hyde Collection. *Address* Mr: Clement Mead Surveyor &c./ Charlotte Street/ Fitzroy Square/ London. *Postmark* DENBIGH < > 1812.

TO CLEMENT MEAD

Brynbella
2: September 1812.

My good Mr. Mead should have let me know that he received the Draught for 100£ quite safe. I sent it on the 14th of last Month *August:* and made it payable at Ten Days after Date.

Do pray write, and say you have had it; and tell me if you have heard from Mr. Shephard, and if you know how the Garden Things sell, and how Matters are going *on*. I feel many an *un*easy Feel about my Streatham Park Property, and am greatly afraid it will be a heavy Mill Stone[1] round the Neck of Your poor old Friend/ H: L: Piozzi.

Text Hyde Collection. *Address* Mr: Clement Mead Surveyor &c./ Charlotte Street/ Fitzroy Square/ London. *Postmark* DENBIGH 22<4>; 4 SE 4 1812.

1. See Matthew 18:6; Luke 17:2.

TO JOHN SALUSBURY PIOZZI SALUSBURY

Prestatyn Sunday
27: September 1812.

My Dearest Soul

I have got your last kind Letter dated Hardwicke—[1] and am glad You are happy: the Way to be happy is to be good; and Angels are happier than We, only because they are better.

Mr. Shephard's Letter may be charming, but to me 'tis useless; find out what we owe the Cur, and let him be paid *soon* or he will be paid *more*.[2]

My Thomas is delightful: cuts the Pudding I cannot eat into Shares; and gives it under the Windows to the savage Babies of this wild Place; who *Sing*, or rather *howl* to me in return. Never was so Wild or so Solitary a Place as Prestatyn: I shall have enjoyed all the high Equinoctial Tides, and will go home next Thursday—for tho' the Character of the Welsh is to love Solitude, to reflect on their own Descent, and despise Commerce, I begin to be tired of never, no *never* changing a Word with any human Creature but the Dipper.

I tried Miss Clarke,—but in vain:[3] So I asked her to lend me a *Book, any Book* said I, if it be but a Superannuated Novel. Oh Lord! was the unexpected Reply— "I never by any Chance am induced to read *any* Book except the Sporting Magazine and Racing Calendar."[4]—So I borrowed those; and to my much Amazement Saw Mrs. Piozzi's Name—*even there*.[5]

General Leake or Lake came to shew me how Tinker was recovered, and to complete his Cure by Sea Bathing: I hear by them, that our Barley and Oats are all *in*, and our wheat sown for next Year; in the beautiful Summer Fallow.—The Guinea o'Week Man, is to begin with October, so *your* Wishes are completing one by one; and when they are all completed, You will sigh for something *to wish*—like the Fellow in the Rambler when he has *buried* his Aunt.[6]

Buonaparte keeps his Spirit of Wishing warm, by a Desire of Dividing Russia;[7] and retaining the Sea Coast himself for purpose of annoying England: I wish only a Continuance of the Comfort your Good Behaviour gives me, and that I could avoid reflecting—so often as I do—on the Dangers of a London Winter and its Environs, to Your Heart, and my Purse.

Dear Pem: has written me a kind Letter—he has my true good Wishes. To the Ladies I send my best Compliments. What were you doing at Nantwich?[8] Did you go to see my Uncle's Seat at Combermere[9]—close by? or were there Races in that Country? It used to be ill calculated for such Amusement. Here they come, here they come, here they come; There they go, There they go, There they go: is the Sport of a Horse Course——It comes In, It comes in, It comes in; It goes out, It goes out, It goes out; is *my* Sport looking at the Tide.

What else does Life afford?——Yet am I desirous of enduring it for Two or Three Years, and if our Scheme of going NorthWards next Summer takes Place, I will bathe at Scarboro'.[10] The very best Place in our whole Island for the Purpose, where You may dance and I may dip in the Sea very pleasantly indeed, and among the best Company.

Your Candidates are all preparing for the general Engagement no doubt: Mr. Waithman is expected to succeed for the *first City in the World*. He was bred a *direct Atheist*. A famous Fellow in this Country known by the Name of Wicked Will, used to patronize, and teach him when a little Boy to stand on a Table, sing obscene Songs, and Spout Blasphemous Speeches; So he ends in an Orator, and a Democrate, and a *Fellow of Fire*, as his Friends call him——I think he will be a Fellow of Fire sure enough, but am Sorry he is half a Welshman.[11]

Charles Shipley has a Living given him in Oxfordshire and the Clergy are enraged.[12] The Bishop of Bangor called at Brynbella but I was here; so he saw nothing, and nobody.[13]

Farewell Dear and Inestimable Titmouse: I shall soon come over to your humour of hating Genius and Learning both, if the World goes on in this Way.

Mean While remember how you are beloved by Your Affectionate H: L: P.——

Text Ry. 586.148. *Address* John Piozzi Salusbury Esq./ White Lyon/ Shrewsbury/ To Care of Mrs. Tompkyns. *Postmark* < >.

1. A hamlet near Bishop's Castle in south Salop. JSPS was on his way to visit the Pembertons of Longnor.
2. The "Cur" was Thomas Curr, JSPS's servant.
3. Probably Charlotte (b. 1778), daughter of Joseph (1738–1807) and Sarah Clarke, née Rudsdell (d. 1786), of Northampton.
4. That is, *The Sporting Magazine or Monthly Calendar, of the Transactions of the Turf, the Chase, and every other Diversion interesting to the Man of Pleasure, Enterprize & Spirit*, 50 vols. (London, 1793–1817).
5. Only by inference is HLP mentioned in the *Sporting Magazine*'s anecdote: "When Dr. Johnson, on some occasion, was musing over a fire in a drawing room at Streatham, a young gentleman called to him suddenly, perhaps disrespectfully: 'Mr. Johnson, would you advise me to marry?' Johnson replied in an angry tone, 'I would advise no man to marry who is not likely to *propagate understanding*'" (37 [February 1811]: 301). The victim was HT's nephew Sir John Lade. See *Anecdotes*, p. 97; *Johns. Misc.*, 1:213, n. 2.
6. See *Rambler* 73 on the folly of wishing for future pleasures, especially those derived from material gain through inheritance.
7. On 16 July 1812 *The Times* announced the outbreak of war between France and Russia and the push of Napoleon's *Grande Armée* eastward on the road from Kovno via Vilna, Vitebsk, and Smolensk to Moscow. The same paper reported on 10 August that the latest advices from the Russian capital indicated, "Fresh levies to a large amount has been ordered, and corps of reserve were in motion from all parts of the empire towards the Dwina and the Dnieper. The total amount of troops which Russia had in the field is estimated in one of these letters at not less than 495,000 men."

The Russian forces were in fact deployed in two armies—hence HLP's reference to division. One force was commanded by Mikhail Barclay de Tolly, and the other—smaller in number—by Pyotor Ivanovich Bagraton. (Time was to show that they determined on a strategy of withdrawing on converging lines.)

On 22 September, *The Times* admitted that Napoleon was "still advancing into the Russian Empire, but without any particular triumph: he appears merely to have touched the Russian rear-guard in its retreat." Between 22 September and the date of this letter, newspaper accounts of the French in Russia did not alter appreciably although they were in fact in control of Moscow.
8. JSPS was attending the races at the Nantwich Meeting, Cheshire.
9. For Sir Lynch Salusbury Cotton, see HLP to Isabella Hamilton, 13 May 1805, n. 2.
10. For HLP's earlier visit to Scarborough, see HLP to PSW, 11 June [1789]; to LC, 12 July 1789.
11. Born in Wrexham, Robert Waithman (1764–1833) came to London before he was twenty. There he opened a linen draper's shop, earned considerable wealth, and retired in favor of his sons. An advocate of democratic principles, he was active in English politics. By 1794 he spoke out against the war with France and in 1796 was elected for the ward of Farringdon Without, becoming the ward's most dynamic orator.

In 1812 Waithman sought to represent the city of London but was defeated, although he polled

2,622 votes. He was not to be elected to Parliament until 1818, when for two years he unseated Sir William Curtis.

Waithman's Welsh ancestry was derived from his mother, Mary, née Roberts, who had married the senior Waithman (i.e., John, d. 1764), on 29 January 1761.

12. The son of the dean of St. Asaph, Charles Shipley (1784–1834) had matriculated at Brasenose College, Oxford, in 1802 and received his B.A. from All Souls' in 1806. He became rector of Finmere, Oxon., in 1812, and of Maypowder, Dorset, from 1814 until his death.

13. The grandson of a Huguenot who settled at Exeter, Henry William Majendie (1754–1830) was educated at Charterhouse and Christ's, Cambridge, where he received his D.D. in 1791. He had been ordained a deacon in 1774, a priest in 1783. From 1800 to 1809 he was bishop of Chester and from 1809 until his death bishop of Bangor.

TO CLEMENT MEAD

Brynbella
19: October 1812.

Dear Mr. Mead's last Letter—tho' a kind one, and acknowledging the Receipt of his 100£ half broke Mrs. Piozzi's heart to think of her having to pay the Duke of Bedford—38£ is it not? for the Sake of cutting those odious Trees which brought her Reproaches, She would have paid 38£ to escape.[1]

Her Steward Leak will She hopes bring her some less afflicting News from poor Streatham Park, which however She hopes by the favour of God to see once more in good Repair; and comfortably inhabited. Pray shew Leak the same Confidence that you would/ to your Old Friend/ H: L: Piozzi/ and tell him all that is done and is to do.

Text Hyde Collection. *Address* Mr. Clement Mead/ Surveyor/ Charlotte Street/ Fitzroy Square/ London.

1. HLP refers to John Russell (1766–1839), sixth duke of Bedford (1802), who was lord of the manor at Streatham.

The reason for HLP's indebtedness is explained in a letter to AL, 8 February 1813.

TO AMELIA PERKINS

Brynbella
6: November 1812.

Dear Madam

Your Son Alfred, having written to me So very kindly demands My best Acknowledgments, which I rather choose to direct to You, as I conclude he is gone to London upon Business, and that you will stay at Brighthelmstone— out of the way a while—or, let me See; You will be gone to Camberwell—Yes,

Yes, and to Camberwell I will send this Letter, expressive of my true Regards to your late excellent Husband and his Family.

May you Dear Madam receive from their Dutyful Attention all the Comfort which can in Such Cases be reciprocated—[1] and may We live to meet once more, and mingle our Tears for past Times and past Sorrows.

I hope to be at Streatham Park sometime next February till when and ever/ I remain/ Dear Mrs. Perkins's very faithful and sincere/ H: L: Piozzi.

Text Harvard University Library. *Address* Mrs. Perkins/ Camberwell/ Surrey. *Postmark* Holywell < > 1812.

1. This letter of condolence acknowledges that John Perkins, in his eighty-third year, had died on 31 October 1812 "at Brighton, in consequence of being rode against and struck down by a person on horseback during the races, on the Brighton Course, a few weeks since. . . ." See *GM* 82, pt. 2 (1812): 592.

TO CLEMENT MEAD

Brynbella
6: November 1812.

My good Mr. Mead

will find my Note altered by the Return of Leak;——You must write to Southey, and bid him send Patterns of Papers.[1] That in the Eating Parlour however, *must* be a darkish Slate-Colour; because nothing else will suit the Pictures, and suit the Furniture *too*——which being bright Red, requires a Slate Coloured Paper; *one* Shade darker than that we call *French Grey*.

I am glad the Outside shews so well to the Common;[2] and that on the 1st of January 1813, all will be in my own hand again Just 50 Years since the Place was first seen by/ Yours &c./H: L: Piozzi.

A White Satten Ground with rich White Flowers on it,—rather Small than large Pattern, will be best for the Drawing Room certainly——Give a kind Word from me to Southey; he is an old Acquaintance.

Text Hyde Collection. *Address* Mr. Clement Mead Surveyor &c./ Charlotte Street/ Fitzroy Square/ London. *Postmark* Holywell; 9 NO 9 1812.

1. For James Southey, see HLP to AL, 12 March 1812, n. 1.
2. Clement Mead's plan for Streatham Park, completed in 1816, is essentially that of 1822 made by J. and W. Newton, of Chancery Lane. The estate consisted of eighty-eight acres, eighteen freehold and seventy copyhold. The house "faced Tooting Bec Common, due north, standing about 90 yards back from Tooting Bec Road. . . . It was approached by a sweeping drive about 100 yards long from the lodge gates. . . . Behind the [house] are the stables, coachhouses, greenhouses, outbuildings and melon ground. To the west, extending to Green Lane (now Thrale Road), are seen the walled kitchen gardens and *graperies*. . . . The gravel path that went right round the Park" was part of Mead's plan as was the paling of about two miles extent that similarly encircled the park.

See H. W. Bromhead, *The Heritage of St. Leonard's Parish Church Stretham* (London: Hatchards, 1932), 39–43.

TO ALEXANDER LEAK

Wensday Night
13: January 1813.

I received Your Letter, and assure You that I sincerely wish Old Streatham Park had been under Leak's Care *long ago.*

In the mean Time Mr. Shephard writes me Word that he has paid Tythes, and Taxes and Coals, and Wages; and all Expences of the Place besides *above* 100£ to *the Surveyor.*——Just the *Set-offs* you said we might expect.

Mead writes to me most pressingly to be sure for *100£* and you say he should have *150£* but I will take his Word, and send him the Sum I have a Right from himself to think sufficient.

All Expectation from Shephard is vain; I see it is:—but I will not irritate or provoke him. Hammersley[1] has sent his 50£ to pay our Workmen here, and I am this Night come home from Bodylwyddan: whole Scores of Letters lying on the Table to be answered. One from Price in particular—dunning me for the 49£ of which I sent him 25£ by you, which he does not acknowledge.[2]

Pray tell me about Mr. and Mrs. Hoare, and if they are in good humour or no; I am as much afraid of them, as If I expected a Legacy: Miss Thrale writes very civilly. Mrs. Mostyn still in South Wales, but I fancy She is going to London. Dear Hammersley says I *must* not sell out, he is one of the few true Friends boasted by poor/ H: L: P.

Sir John and Lady Williams are no Enemies of yours—They both told me that if there ever was an honest and faithful Steward it was *You:* and I told them how much I must needs value a Character so seldom found by *anyone* much less so by their humble Servant.

Pray write soon again.

My dead Child—Salusbury—is not come home yet:—but he has *So few* Holydays!

Here comes a Tax Gatherer for 3£ odd Money—'tis well I had My five pound Notes.

Text Hyde Collection. *Address* Mr: Alexander Leak/ at Mrs. Piozzi's/ Streatham Park/ Surrey. *Postmark* 10 o'Clock; JA 16 1813.

1. For George Hammersley, see HLP to JSPS, 1 November 1810, n. 1.
2. For several years—at least since 1810—HLP had purchased foodstuff from Edward Price, who had taken over Badioli's Old Italian Warehouse, at 5 Haymarket, opposite the Opera House. See Ry. 598.66.

TO ALEXANDER LEAK

Thursday Night
21: January 1813.

Leak need not fear being forgotten at Brynbella, where every thing that *does* go right, goes right by his Direction. It is 1000 Pities you did not get sooner to Streatham Park, but *that* was nobody's Fault.

Our Work Folks have finished at Bachygraig and begun my Dear Master's favourite Work—pulling up the Hedge by the Ha! Ha!—The *Cut* as I call it;—— and laying all open to the Park. I *like* that Business because my poor Husband was always wishing to be about it——The Mountain Men are completely stopped by the Frost: I paid them 24£:0:0 last Saturday and our own Folks 21£:6:0—Kerby has sent his Account— 4£:14:0 and I would pay him by Draft but the Boobies I send for Stamps, bring me wrong ones always; he must wait till We have more Wit here.[1]

The Londoners are Sharper—witness Mr. _____, a *Dun*[2] certainly:—how much of the *other Thing*, We Welsh people may reasonably doubt.

Doctor Myddelton says A Man with a *good* Character is a Match for *Ten* that have bad ones, for I told him how you were situated; so you see our Neighbours that *are* Gentlemen, are certainly anything but Your Enemies.

Women *are treacherous* Creatures always, whether they look pretty pale and *interesting* as their own Phrase is; or blooming, *plump,* and drest in *constant Smiles:* I have ever warned the Men—especially the *very Young* and inexperienced from their Wiles[3]——Dear Salusbury has kept tolerably clear hitherto; I expect him home soon now from Lord Kenyon's,[4] and from the Wynnestay Ball in honour of our Queen's Birthday.[5]

Glover is bright again, and dining today at Mr. Rees's:[6] I wish She had a Good Husband and Children, and that I had an Annuity of 1000£ o'Year for her Life.[7] Thomas is got well. She is gone out to amuse herself, and has not even left me a Glass of Wine: No Matter, one always eats and drinks *too much,* instead of *too little.*

I wrote to Mrs. Hoare, and hope She will not—through *respectful Tenderness* towards *me*—suffer Southey to send down another Heap of Patterns to cost Heaven knows what for Carriage. *You* know (tho' it were uncivil to tell *her* so,) that I care not Sixpence about the Colours or the Patterns: but I *do* care to Spend The Money which must be spent, upon the house, rather than upon the high Road. If Mr. Hammersley comes to see the Place pray shew him every Civility; he is among those who behave best to *Me;*——and *he adores the Ladies.*

I have had no Letter from Mr. Shephard since that surly one I told you of— to which I replied by saying—"In short if you have any Money or if you are to receive any Money for which you do not make me out Debtor to You—Send it to Hammersley's: and if you *have not*——Why like the Man's Head in the Lyon's Mouth I may say—does he wag his Tail Gentlemen? Of Yes he wags his Tail:—— Why then

The Lord have Mercy upon me."

It is even so: for what Can I do in such a Case?—any more than the Fellow could?

Mr. Fell not having a Catalogue amazes me.[8] What can be become of the Catalogue he took under Mr. Gillion's Directions? Mr. Gillon used me very Ill about that Place you are living in, very ill *indeed:* but he's Dead, and left me his Shakespeare[9]——and He too adored the Ladies.

The Clergymen in Caernarvonshire are all at Daggers Drawing about my Curacies there; but Dr. Myddelton has written to Mr. Evans and I have written to Mr. Cotton assuring them that I will not be dragged into Contests between Persons I do not know if they walk into the Room.[10] Their Letters—desiring me (each of them) to *compel* the other by a Law Suit, came by the *same Post* with Mead's 9th January. I was finely off among them all to be sure.

Tell Mr. Mead I have received his Acknowledgement for the Money: and be careful of your health, and do not be Sick in *Earnest*—because that will be *no Jest* to/ H: L: Piozzi.

Owen can't take a Hare or I would send you one.

I wrote to Hammersley on Saturday 16th for 50£ again to pay the Work <men>, *but it is not come.*

Give my kind Services to Mr. Davies, and beg him to write; I will not mind his Jokes any more; tell him so.

I love Mr. <   > Davies.

Text Hyde Collection. *Address* Mr: Alexander Leak/ at Mrs. Piozzi's/ Streatham Park/ Surrey. *Postmark* 10 o'Clock JA 25 1813; 25 JA 25 1813.

1. Bowdery and Kerby, Jr., booksellers, stationers, binders, at 190 Oxford Street, near Portman Square. The firm billed HLP for the delivery of newspapers—the *Evening Mail* and the *Courier.* See Ry. 598.102.

2. An "importunate creditor" (Grose, *A Classical Dictionary of the Vulgar Tongue,* 1785).

3. HLP's adaptation of Proverbs 7:4-7.

4. A large landowner in North Wales and Salop, George Kenyon (1776–1855) became baron of Gredington in 1802. Educated at Christ Church, Oxford, he received his B.A. in 1797, M.A. in 1801, and D.C.L. in 1814. He was a successful barrister and bencher, elected a Tory M.P. (5 May 1802) and F.S.A. (17 November 1808). In 1803 he had married Margaret Emma, née Hanmer (1785–1815).

5. Wynnstay Hall (Denbighshire) belonged to the family of Williams-Wynn. At this time it was occupied by Sir Watkin Williams-Wynn. See HLP to LC, 17 June 1798, n. 11.

6. For the Reeces of Bachygraig, see HLP to JSPS, 27 June 1811, n. 1.

7. HLP achieved a partial success in her wishes: Glover married AL.

8. Nornaville and Fell, booksellers and stationers, of 29 New Bond Street, London, cataloged the library at Streatham Park in the spring of 1806.

9. For John Gillon's bequest, see HLP to Q, 25 March 1811, n. 13.

10. The struggle involved William Evans, curate of Llangwynnadl and Tudweiliog, and the Reverend James Henry Cotton. For the latter, see HLP to JSPS, 2 December 1809, n. 3.

TO CLEMENT MEAD

Brynbella
Saturday Night
23: January 1813.

My good Mr. Mead
may assure himself I shall not hurry Leak home, altho' I find being my own
Steward here—painful enough:——he knows he *must* come both to *cut* and *plant*
in Bachygraig Wood, and to get Trees into the Nursery here;
I received Your Acknowledgement for the Money. Tell him Mr. Salusbury is
come home, and has been told *every* thing, and feels towards him exactly as I
do——and is as well convinced of our Confidence being *at length* well placed;
as is/ Your faithful Friend/ &c./ H: L: Piozzi.

Desire Leak to write; and let him know that Mr. Roberts called for Property
Tax today, but I refused——not knowing what I owe till he comes home.[1]

Text Hyde Collection. *Address* Mr. Clement Mead/ Surveyor &c./ Upper Charlotte
Street/ Fitzroy Square/ London. *Postmark* DENBIGH 224; E 26 JA 26 1813.

1. For John Roberts, the tax assessor in Flintshire, see HLP to John Lloyd, 11 November 1809,
and n. 1.

TO ALEXANDER LEAK

Saturday Night
6: February 1813.

My good Leak must not be so miserable; You see *I* bear all with Fortitude, and
I have not drawn the Bankers so dry as I wrote you word. They have my Orders
and will soon have my Power of Attorney for taking out 1300£ and you may
have Money from *Them* for our Ash and Beech Trees, and do not let us Starve
the Cause——*buy them.*
What I meant by your *Promises* was the hope You inspired of my living to
replace the Money, and it will perhaps soon come back; The Garden will be
profitable.
Mr. Oldfield is here, and very angry at the People's plucking up the Trees—
as fast as we plant them—near Hugh Owen's.[1] He and Mr. Salusbury are considering what to do to prevent further Mischief—and I hope will succeed.
Our Oxen get very fat, I wish the Cows would Calve: Never was such Weather
seen certainly—quite a lovely Spring.
Purchase the Trees, and we will send the Bill to Hammersley's, and You shall
see all end well Yet.

My 1300£ will make 767£—and there is a little left yet in dear Pallmall,[2] enough to make up 1000£ but *do* drive on Mead and Southey, that we may get quit of them, and begin upon Gillow[3] and the Gardening, Fencing &c.

My Heart tells me every thing will prosper: If the Place brought Money when *No* Care was taken, it will bring *more* Money when it is likely to be looked over.

Have a good Heart, good Leak; and assure Yourself of the Esteem and Confidence—never yet repented by or of/ H: L: Piozzi.

Text Hyde Collection. *Address* Mr. Alexander Leak/ at Mrs. Piozzi's/ Streatham Park/ Surrey. *Postmark* DENBIGH 22< >; 4 o'Clock 9 FE 9 1813.

1. Probably Hugh Owens (fl. 1762–1815), a laborer of Tre'r Graig, near Brynbella.
2. At Hammersley's bank.
3. Robert and Richard Gillow, cabinetmakers and upholsterers, at 176 Oxford Road. The company began ca. 1780; by 1815 it was Gillow and Company. Under that name it continued until 1840.

TO CLEMENT MEAD

Brynbella
8: February 1813.

I am glad to hear Mrs. Hoare express herself as content with the House Dear Mr. Mead, but when She *is* content, why must we go on? What further Repairs do you wish for?, or why should you wish what the Ladies themselves do not want?

She says you are desirous of falling more Timber;——I wonder for *What*? Are You repairing the Offices, or Stables, or Coach house or something *quite necessary* for Use. *Pray* let me hear the Extent of our Operations, and *Pray* be satisfied when the Ladies are.

I long to see Leak, that I may learn what has been done, and what is yet to do: if he is set out before this reaches Streatham Park write by the Post to Yours ever/ H: L: Piozzi.

Text Hyde Collection. *Address* Mr. Clement Mead Surveyor &c./ Upper Charlotte Street/ Fitzroy Square/ London. *Postmark* DENBIGH 22< > 11 FE 11 1813.

TO ALEXANDER LEAK

Monday
8: February 1813.

I have this Moment received a Letter from Mrs. Hoare—appearing contented with the Repairs at Streatham Park,[1]—and wish Leak to tell me Why Mead presses to go on *repairing* when the Ladies *are content*? *They* hate the thoughts of cutting more Trees I see; and *I* hate the Thoughts of purchasing more Timber;—Mrs. Hoare says there are Things to cut in the Plantations; but that being Copyhold, it cannot be touched but by the Duke of Bedford's Permission, meaning a *paid for* Permission no doubt——I can not guess *for my own Part*, why more Repairs are wanted; but if Necessary—perhaps a slight fine to the Lord of the Manor would be Money well laid out—to hinder me from purchasing——or from stripping the Place naked——What *is* the fine?

Pray make me understand.

Mr. Salusbury is gone out to Dinner at Pontriffeth with Doctor Cumming who Slept there last Night,[2] and Mr. Mostyn Edwards who came to Brynbella, invited them both Together.[3]

While I write comes Thomas to tell that little Favourite has calved—a fine Heifer Calf——and both Mother and Daughter are doing quite well——It is a stormy Evening; and the Park two hours ago, covered with Sea Gulls from Prestatyn: I should have liked to have Seen those Waves with this high Tide and blowing Weather; They must have looked so very grand.

Doctor Cumming walked over our Mountain with Salusbury, and says he never saw Fences so beautiful——by what I gather from their Report the Job is almost done, if Mr. Davies would but do *his* Part, and I hope he will.[4] I wait but for Dear Hammersley to send his Power of Attorney, and then We will pay Mead what is necessary, and so on the others; and clear off with these Duns and Debtors.

I am hoarse with a Cold, otherwise very well Thank God, and I hope nothing wrong is doing while you are away; and I look sharp for next Saturday—— which I trust will bring you home safe and pay my Workmen both here and on *Kefn o'Dee.*[5]

There was a Threshing Machine going about from one Farmer's House to another a while ago—I went to see it, but Salusbury said it was a good Thing for nobody but poor Roger Jones;[6]——and very Expensive.—He will explain his own Meaning when You meet.

Our Thrushes sing as well as those in Surrey,—but we have no Nightingales: There were Plenty in the Plantations at Streatham Park—when Mr. Piozzi and I inhabited the Place. Sophia says——or her Letter implies at least, That the Grounds look very *bare*—The house very *neat* and the Books very Safe. Did you find my Grandfather's Portrait when a Boy in his Laced Cravat?[7] It should hang in the *Dressing Room:* his dear Daughter Hester Maria Salusbury—in the best Bed Chamber——her Name on the Back if I remember right; and I value that small whole Length by Zoffany,[8] beyond even the Heads painted by Sir Joshua— not only on my Mother's Account but on Account of the *Artist:*[9] and now Farewell my best good Leak, and don't be lowspirited; The Estimate was 1700£ and if it does cost 2000£——You know You say it will help to repay its own Expences Soon: but don't let us do *more* than is *wanted.*

Once more Farewell! and say what past between you and Mrs. Hoare: and assure yourself of the Most perfect Esteem and Confidence of/ H: L: P.

Text Hyde Collection. *Address* Mr. Alexander Leak/ At Mrs. Piozzi's/ Streatham Park/ Surrey. *Postmark* FE 11 1813.

1. Although a few letters passed between HLP and her three younger daughters in the second half of 1812 and early 1813, none seem to have been exchanged between HLP and Q from 1 May 1812 to 15 May 1813.
2. For Dr. George Brownlow Cumming, see HLP to Ly W, 9 February 1810, n. 11.
3. For Thomas Mostyn Edwards, see HLP to MW, 31 July 1806, n. 10. In 1813 Edwards lived in Pontriffeth. Two years later, he moved to Nannerch Cottage, and finally to Kilken Hall, Flintshire. For the identification of Edwards and other names associated with the Bachygraig and Brynbella estates, we are indebted to various parish records, maps, and lists in C.R.O., Clwyd. See also Thomas Mostyn Edwards's will, P.R.O., prob. 11/1798/219, proved 9 April 1832.
4. Hugh Davies (fl. 1736–1818) had rented Coed Robin, a farm on the Bachygraig estates, as early as 6 April 1756. It consisted of slightly more than thirty-nine acres and rented for approximately £30 annually. He or his son (similarly named) rented land on the nearby "Mountain" and is listed in "The Names of the Wellwishers of Sir John Salusbury Piozzi Salusbury of Brynbella, January 6, 1818."
   HLP, in the process of enclosing the "Mountain," wished Davies to move from that small portion of the land he occupied. Apparently, he did not "do *his* Part." See C.R.O., Clwyd, for the "Names" of Sir John's "Wellwishers"; also N.L.W., MS. 11103D and 11104C.
5. Kefn o'Dee is Cefn du, an upland heath area one mile east of Brynbella. HLP either rented Cefn du or owned it as part of the Brynbella estates. If the latter is true, then the land was sold before 1841 to Ann Elizabeth Allanson, who rented it to a John Evans. See the "Tithe Map, Flintshire," for 1841 (C.R.O., Clwyd).
6. The farmer Roger Jones owned or occupied a cottage and about one acre of land at Graig, fairly near Cefn du.
7. HLP's maternal grandfather was Thomas Cotton of Combermere (1672 or 1677–1715), second baronet (1712).
8. The Zoffany portrait of HLP's mother, painted ca. 1766, is now at Bowood House. See Mary Lightbown's catalog for the 1977 Zoffany exhibition at the National Portrait Gallery.
9. Johann Zauffely, generally called Zoffany (1733–1810), was born in Ratisbon but, after several years in Rome, came to England in 1758. A portraitist, he is perhaps best known for his paintings of actors in character. By 1769 he was admitted to the Royal Academy. Patronized by George III, for whom he painted a group of the Royal Family, he traveled widely on the Continent and as far as India. He died at Strand-on-the-Green, near Kew, and is buried in the Kew churchyard.

TO THE REVEREND THOMAS SEDGWICK WHALLEY

Brynbella
8: February 1813.

My dear Doctor Whalley

has been sick Miss Williams says,[1] and I am very sorry——but you are often Ill, and I thank God—never in Danger.——Elizabeth Cornwallis is *dead* The Papers tell me; and greatly shocked was I, at hearing the News——It was put *in* so oddly too; my Curiosity is raised, almost as much as my Concern; What did She die of?[2]

My Diet of Weak Mutton Broth and a Turnep, keeps me Yet in Hope of seeing lovely Mendip in May or June——but Fasting Welsh Women have a Strange Vis Vitæ in them, that is certain; because Mary Thomas mentioned by Mr. Pennant as a Medical Wonder in the Year 1770 died but a Week ago—at 90 Years of Age having been Bedridden 63 Revolutions of the Sun—or Earth!—very astonishing is it not, and quite possessed of her Intellectual Faculties——Hers was a *Contemplative* Life indeed, for She could not *read* any thing or *do* any thing but say her Prayers, and be fed once o'Day with a Bit of Bread weighing Two Penny Weights—and a Wine Glass of Water.[3] There is a Woman near Wrexham *now*, much in The same Way. Cecy Mostyn says You know, that as We have no Meat in Wales, we have always one of these Models of Temperance and Longævity before our Eyes; Pennant tells of *one* says She, Doctor Thackeray of another, and I am convinced *Mrs. Piozzi* will be *the Third.*—How comical!

Poor Lady Williams of Bodylwyddan will *not* be one: her Limbs are going to resemble Chevalier Boisgelin's,—to whom Dear Sir pray make my best Compliments and tell Mr. and Mrs. Lutwyche how happy I shall feel to see You all once again. Oh If I can but drive away all Thought of Streatham Park and its reversionary Proprietors, and take dear Salusbury a Drive round England this Summer——call upon *You*, and upon Doctor Gray who has been Seven Years inviting me, I may by *then* be glad to see the Place, and look how My Money has been spent at least. When you can write without its Fatiguing you, tell me *un petit peu* how the World goes, how Buonaparte gets his Conscripts in,[4] and when that Bubble will break, which has suffered so much Expansion, and exhibited such gawdy Colours. I thought the Russian Campaign must have been his last, but our Newspapers give an Idea of his Continuation in Power; and what Hope there is now of ever seeing him *really distressed* I cannot conjecture.[5] My Expectations ran too high, and have broken their own Necks.

Adieu my dear Doctor, and never forget the Friendship with which you have ever since the Year 1780 honoured Your/ poor Friend/ H: L: P.

Hannah More's Book has never reached us Yet.[6] Make my best Remembrances and Compliments to Mrs. Whalley. How is Sir Walter James's Health? and how is his Peace of Mind?

Text Berg Collection +. *Address* Rev: Doctor Thos. Sedgwick Whalley/ Queen Square/ Bath. *Postmark* DENBIGH <224>.

1. According to TWS's letter dated 13 February 1813 (Ry. 564.25):
"Miss Williams wrote you the truth. I have, indeed, been ill. . . . It has been severe, serious, and at one crisis, dangerous. . . . After being confined to my Bed or Bed chamber, more than five weeks, I crept down to dine in the back Drawing Room, ten days since, and have ventured out thrice, when the Sun shone, to take a little fresh Air in the Carriage. At my Age and with my debilitated Constitution, Recovery *must* prove slow, and cannot be perfect. I am still very low, weak, and emaciated; the *Shadow* of a *Shade*."
2. On 24 January 1813, "Miss [Elizabeth] Cornwallis, daughter of the Bishop of Lichfield," died. See *GM* 83, pt. 1 (1813): 187. According to TSW's letter: "She returned Home in high Spirits and apparently high health, from Church; and while stepping quickly towards the Fire *sunk* down and expired without a struggle or a groan."
3. According to the *North Wales Gazette*, 4 February 1813: Died "Last week, in the parish of Celynn, near Dolgelley, in the 89th year of her age, Mary Thomas, who had been bed-ridden during the long period of 65 years. . . . During the last ten years of her life, she took no other nourishment than a few spoonfuls of a weak liquid, and that but seldom. How life could have been preserved so long is a subject worthy the attention of the medical profession: for at the time of her dissolution, her body was completely exhausted, though her intellectual faculties continued unimpaired, till the last hour." See also Pennant, *A Tour in Wales*, 2:105–7.
4. HLP responds to reports in January of the further buildup of French troops: e.g., a "force of 350,000 men is ordered to be placed at the disposal of the Minister of War, in order to shew that

'there is no repose for Europe until England shall have been *forced* to conclude a peace.'" Moreover, Napoleon himself announced that 300,000 Frenchmen "will, in the course of February, be collected at Hamburgh, upon the Elbe, upon the Rhine, and upon the Oder, independent of 200,000" who are with the *Grande Armée*. The ensuing campaign," he adds, "will be opened with a French army, nearly twice as strong as in the last campaign." See *GM* 83, pt. 1 (1813): 79.

Introduced in 1799, conscription created fear and later opposition to Napoleonic power. As a French officer said, "Hitherto every call to the conscription has been looked upon as a call to death. . . . The conscription has been a double calamity to all the productive arts; while it has carried off from them useful hands, it has enhanced the wages of labour." See [Gotthilf] Theodor von Faber, *Sketches of the Internal State of France*, trans. M. Faber [*Notices sur l'intérieur de la France*] (London, J. Murray, etc., ca. 1811).

5. HLP was aware that the French army had evacuated Moscow and had begun its retreat in October 1812, and that by 18 December, Napoleon, having left his troops, had arrived at Paris. Despite such a defeat and the Malet conspiracy against him, he created by a senatus consultum, dated 5 February, an imperial regency. By letters-patent in the event of the emperor's absence from home and by prescriptive right in the event of his death, Marie Louise was made responsible for her son during his minority, granted the regency of the empire, and supported by a council of regency composed largely of the princes of the blood, etc.

6. *Practical Piety*, which had appeared in 1811, went through at least six editions during its first year.

TO JOHN SALUSBURY PIOZZI SALUSBURY

Coventry Sunday Night
11: April *1813*.

My dearest Dear

Was there ever such a Correspondent? Ah no—you reply—I would there were—at *Shrewsbury*. Well! since I *am* going to London, 'tis good to be within 95 Miles of it; and here I set up my Rest for *this* Night. The last was a *wretched* one at Wolsley Bridge,[1] where four Years ago I saw the first Swallows I remember; and now, tho' the Season is so much forwarder, not a Feather of any such Summer Bird has appeared yet.—My Money delayed me at Chester: Old Jackson had no Change,[2] and the Bank did not open till 10 o'Clock, so I could not pay the Bill, and *Charge* Chester! *Charge* is as good a Joke as ever; but the Honey there was so exquisite, I could not resist the Temptation of Sending you a Pot of it by the Denbigh Coach, and I do hope our Friend *Pem* will come and eat it with You: I sent him a tender Invitation.

The Hedges are not half as much out as in North Wales, and the Thrushes not in half the Song, that ours were—last Month.—No need to come to England either for neat *Stacks:* I have seen none that Hugh Owen would not be ashamed of.

Well! notwithstanding my very bad Headach, I went to Prayers in the beautiful Cathedral at Litchfield; and somehow I felt the Psalms—quite *appropriate*. The Chanting of the Litany was charming, and read by a fine Tenor Voice full and strong: a Dignatory of the Church I suppose—and I saw poor Dr. Johnson's Monument,[3] and David Garrick's;[4] and read Anna Seward's Inscription over her favourite Saville[5]——All old Acquaintance! all dead and gone!!

Quae Regio in Terris nostra non plena Laboris?[6]

Such will be my *Amusements* again at Streatham Park!![7]

The News Paper I find here, censures Mrs. Siddons's Reading, and says She pops her Head up and down to the Book ungracefully; using Eye Glasses &c. &c. The Public is hard to please, and I wonder She was tempted to try the Many-headed Beast again—at *her* Age.[8]

> And from the Dregs of Life hope to receive
> What the first sprightly Running scarce can give.[9]

Did you?—in order to continue Your *own* Life,—regard my Injunctions and take your Tamarind Whey for the *half* sore Throat you complained of?

I shall be like Lord Chatham's Flatterer The Duke of Some Place, who followed him out the House of Lords,—and holding up the head of his Sedan, cried:—— at least—Promise me *one* Thing; Promise me *one* Thing *dear noble* Friend!—do not forget to take Your Sack Posset going to Bed. Had you known the People as *I* did; You would have better relished the Ridicule of this Story.[10]

How did you pass *your* Sunday Evening? Mine is spent in hearing the laughers and Fleerers in the Street whinnying along to catch attention from Fools that walk by them: I never saw such Troops of Trollops in any Town but the Metropolis;—This Weather brings out all the *Stinging Flies* I suppose.

If you go to Bodylwyddan carry my best Compliments and if Oldfield comes, let me know what he says: and make him write to Robinson *himself* in *their own* Language, which will be better understood than *Mine* in Carey Street.[11]

I only tell the Man how wretched I am—and when he sees all Lincoln's Inn built and founded on the Wretchedness of Fools robbed by Knaves,—What can he care for *that*?

Adieu my best, my only Dear; and let me find a Letter from you at Hammerleys. If my strength will bear it, I shall run Threescore and odd Miles tomorrow, and send you Word I come alive to Dunstable; I know my Way thence to London on *Foot:* It was near my old Hertfordshire Residence till almost Your Age.[12]

Farewell and God preserve your Body, Soul, and Purse to the Wish and Prayer/ of your poor H: L: P.——

Text Ry. 586.155. *Address* John Piozzi Salusbury Esq./ Brynbella near Denbigh/ North Wales. *Postmark* COVENTRY 12 AP 12 1813.

1. A hamlet in Staffordshire.
2. The proprietor of Jackson's Hotel, whom HLP met in the spring of 1808. See HLP to JSPS, 11 June 1808, n. 1.
3. "In the dean's Consistory Court, adjoining the south Transept, is the bust of . . . Samuel Johnson, with this inscription. 'The friends of Samuel Johnson, LL.D./ A native of Lichfield,/ erected this monument,/ as a tribute of respect to the memory of/ a man of extensive learning,/ a distinguished moral writer, and a sincere/ Christian./ He died the 13th of December, 1784, aged 75 years.'" The sculptor was Richard Westmacott and the architect James Wyatt. See *A Short Account of the Lichfield Cathedral* (Lichfield: T. G. Lomax, 1823), 64.
4. Near SJ's M.I. and done by Wyatt and Westmacott is a bust of Garrick with the following inscription: "Eva Maria, relict of David Garrick, Esq./ caused this monument to be erected to the memory/ of her beloved husband,/ who died on the 20th of January, 1779, aged 63 years./ He had

not only the amiable qualities of private life/ but such astonishing dramatic talents,/ as too well verified the observation of his friend,/ 'His death eclipsed the gaiety of nations,/ and impoverished the public stock of harmless pleasure.' *Johnson*" (ibid., 65).

5. In the south transept of the Lichfield Cathedral is the M.I.: "Sacred to the memory/ of John Saville,/ 48 years Vicar Choral of this Cathedral./ Ob: Augusti 2ndo, 1803, Aetas: 67." This is followed by twenty lines of rhyming couplets which conclude, "Sleep then, pale mortal frame, in yon low shrine,/ 'Till angels wake thee with a note like thine'" (ibid., 89).

6. Virgil's *Aeneid*, 1.460.

7. In St. Leonard's Church, Streatham, HLP could read the inscriptions for HT and her mother, Hester Maria Salusbury. She could also visit the graves of seven of her children.

8. See the *Morning Chronicle*, 9 April. The review began by pointing out SS's "power of declamation—the energy of gesture, the electricity of expression." It continued, "but those were precisely the talents which she could but partially exert in the task of reading.—The constant reference to the book, and the incessant use of her eye-glasses damped the animation of the scene, and it was only when she came to a passage where she could trust to memory, that she assumed the commanding attitude of the Actress, and communicated the emotion which she so exquisitely felt.—We by no means say that her reading was tame or languid; for nothing could be more critically correct, but it is in the very essence of reading to abate from gesture and action."
SS was almost fifty-eight.

9. See Dryden, *Aureng-Zebe*, 4.1.41–42.

10. The anecdote grows out of the personality of William Pitt (1708–78), first earl of Chatham. His behavior and thinking exhibited pride and vanity so that he consulted only his own judgment. Haughty to his colleagues, he was servile before the king, and he demanded similar servility from those who expected his favor.

11. Edmund Robinson (d. ca. 1831), an attorney, of 1 Carey Street, Lincoln's Inn.

12. Offley Place.

TO JOHN SALUSBURY PIOZZI SALUSBURY

Easter Monday
19: April 1813.

My dearest's short Letter with Marianne's enclosed, shews that I have alarmed him; but from Mr. Robinson's Chambers what could come but Alarm?[1] He even appeared to enjoy the Agitation I was feeling, and seemed happy I was disposed to communicate it to You. How different was the Behaviour of his Clerk! who seemed restrained merely by dislike of betraying his Master from telling me when we were alone a Minute, that they were sending me to *seek* what they themselves *knew* could not be found.——You gave them the Slip *once* Madam said the Fellow, 30 Years ago; and you'll give it them *now*—if you are able to come from Dunstable this Morning to St. James's Street and then walk hither——and he winked at the Door of another Room where sate the great Mr. Robinson— and spoke all he said in a Smiling Whisper——which, when recollected kept me from bursting I believe with Terror and Indignation—especially at Robinson's rough Expression—of "I only say that Robson and Norris deserved a Horse Whipping[2]——and I wish I had the giving it Them: They have Jockied those charming Ladies out of their Estate"——Out of *mine* You mean Sir, I suppose; was the pointed Reply of your poor H:L:P.——I offered it the eldest Lady once, and She refused it. When a *Baby* said he:—of 19 Years old and a half I answered,—and I answered truly.—I told Mr. Ray the same Anecdote the next Day——*he* seemed shocked. Oldfield's Letter so wished and sighed for, came on Saturday last, *Easter Eve;* saying that the Letter Leak shewed him from Robinson was *conclusive,* and that I had no Business to have left Brynbella.—— Charming Oldfield! I am very glad &c.——His Letter says no Fine has been found at Ruthyn, and that it is *fair to presume* there will be *none* found any where else—but that he will continue to seek——*After the Circuit is over.* Fine Fellows! to put one's Peace, and one's Purse in the Power of!! Fine Fellows indeed! Oldfield's chief Care seems to be how Mr. Thrale's covenanting to levy this Fine, and forbearing to levy it, will affect his Representatives (meaning the Ladies) after my Death——What need *he* care about that I wonder! Ray and Robinson both assured me it could not affect *me* or my *Heir* in the least:——and why should Oldfield be zealous about the Ladies? I suppose he wrote it to shew how a Country Attorney could talk Law with the best of them, for he begged me to shew his Letter in Carey Street.

I shall talk to Ward about it,[3]——when we execute my *last Will.*[4] *He* never had a Fear or a Doubt——except of Their *Good Disposition* towards *Me.*

I have been to Streatham Park——Your Personalty there is really very considerable, better than I thought for; and Mead will take Inventories of all to the uttermost Trifle——Sir Walter James is a Man Miss Thrales cannot suspect; and he will be active and kind I do believe; and attentive to your Interest *here* as Sir John Williams will not fail to be in *Wales*——They are Your *true Friends,*[5] and so is dear Doctor Thackeray. If I come to any harm before we meet again—Shew your Executors this Letter, by which I *request* You to give Lady Keith the small whole Length Portrait of My Mother by Zoffanÿ,—and that of *her* Father, my Grandfather, painted in The Tower when he was a Child—Prisoner for his *Papa's* high Treason in opposing the Incroachments on Religion by James the 2d:—— old Sir Robert begged the Boy might be with him.[6] Likewise give her Mr. Thrale's Portrait by Sir Joshua Reynolds; and old Halsey's their Relation, with a Dog[7]—— and give Mrs. Mostyn the fine Baskerville Folio Bible with her Brothers and Sisters Births and Deaths written out in the first Blank Page,[8] and an old Chair worked by My *Great* Grandmother, with her Maiden Name Vere Herbert written on the Back[9]—If any of the Lasses wish for *my* earliest Writing Desk given me by that Lady's Daughter Philadelphia Lynch, my own Dear Grandmamma;— let them have it. Mrs. Mostyn likes any old odd Stuff of that sort, and I think you don't care about it. You should present her with the Chest at Brynbella too; 'tis marked *for* her, but I would not incumber my Will with Legacies.——Thraliana should be hers—or burned—but you may read it first, if t'will amuse You——only let it *never* be printed! oh never, never *never.* There is a Baby's Cabinet made by Dr. Johnson's Orders for Lady Keith when a Girl—You should *offer* it to her; and if refused, give it Mrs. Mostyn.

You were the wisest Fellow in the World to give Leak the Letter; and Oldfield had a heart of Stone, not to write you word how *near* to *quite safe* We were—he must have known Your Anxiety. Don't be lowspirited now though. They cannot take the *Power* from me of giving it to You—and No Creature but Yourself can take the Will and Intentions. Therefore be wretched no longer.

Mr. Ward's House No. 44 Bedford Square.

I have settled everything and Mr. Ward says all *is quite safe* tho' my Letters are but at *Barnet*[10] I Suppose. I was appointed so early at Wards. And now Dear Darling Adieu, and God bless you and love your poor Aunt/ H: L: P.

Mr. Ward's Ink is *so* dirty I was quite in an *Ag*[ony] lest my nicely written Will should be dirtied and he and his Clerks laughed at me.

Text Ry. 587.161. *Address* John Piozzi Salusbury Esq./ Brynbella/ near Denbigh/ North Wales. *Postmark* AP < >

1. Frightened by news sent to her by her Welsh attorney, John Oldfield, HLP left Brynbella on 9 April 1813, "and arrived [at London] in Three Days when Mr. Ray of Gower Street and Mr. Robinson of Carey Street shewed me a Deed made in 1775 in which Mr. Thrale covenants to levy a fine for settling my Welsh Possessions on our son, entailing the Same to Daughters in due Succession, should Mr. Thrale leave no male Issue——providing in the same Deed a Power of *Revocation* if Signed by him or by me during our *Joint Lives.*

"Now in that Year 1775 We went to France; and I fancy *forgot,* (I am sure *I* did) all about these Deeds and Settlements, which were witnessed by Mr. Thrale's Attorney Bateman Robson &c. &c. in proper Form and Order. In 1777 however, Mr. Thrale bought Pistill and Penucha; and by conveying them over to the same uses, might have recollected the Necessity of levying a Fine for the before-mentioned Estates; but no *Fine was levied,* for we sent and charged Oldfield to look; as you remember: and by no other Act could my Estate have been alienated from me Who had it in Fee Simple. One would think nevertheless that Mr. Thrale *apprehended* he had done something to injure me; for in 1780—The Month being October—and our Son dead Sometime back,—He made an addition by Interlineation to the Deed of 1775, giving *Me* a power of revoking the uses if I survived my Husband——and this Interlineation was reattested with all possible Care, by the selfsame Attorney Bateman Robson &c.——but I think there was no new Stamp to it.

"Well, after Mr. Thrale's Death which happened in 1781—My Uncle's Widow Lady Salusbury, between whom and myself a Lawsuit had long been pending, pressed me hard for Money; and I was obliged to Mortgage my Estate in Wales for 7500£——lent me by Mr. Cator.

"He . . . did not lend it me without knowing the Security was good, because upon the Draft of this Mortgage Deed, Mr. Ray and myself read Counsellor Waller's opinion . . . in which Opinion he treats the Reattested Deed of 1775 and 1780 as a Nullity . . . not because it was not duly Stamped a second Time——but because *no Fine had been levied*—which however Ray and Robinson unwilling to believe, forced me to make fresh Enquiry: thinking it scarce possible that Mr. Bateman Robson and Mr. Christopher Norris his Clerk and Successor could have been so *neglectful* as they deemed it; though my own honest Opinion is, that when Mr. Thrale had lost his only Son——These Estates grew of less Concern to him; and his last Wishes were to leave the whole of them at my Disposal.

"In the Year 1783 The Month April,—Cator knowing my Power over my own Fortune, came to my Bedside when I was in all Appearance a Dying Woman in Argylle Street,—and . . . insisted on my Settling all on my Daughter; but leaving me at my reiterated Request, a Power of Revocation.—— This Deed I signed, but this deed I *revoked* by my Marriage Settlement with your Dear Uncle, on whom I wished to bestow myself, and all I possessed. . . ." (This statement, dated 9 July 1813, appears at the conclusion of vol. 4 of "Harvard Piozziana.")

2. Bateman Robson (1719–91) and Charles Norris (d. 1789) were law partners with rooms at Lincoln's Inn, New Square. They had been affiliated since at least 1777 and both were certified to try cases before the Court of King's Bench.

For Robson, see P.R.O., Prob. 11/1210/479 (October 1791) and *GM* 61, pt. 2 (1791): 973; for Norris, P.R.O., Prob. 11/1187/35 (January 1790).

3. For Joseph Ward, see HLP to Jonathan Sterns, 30 October 1790, n. 3.

4. HLP's far from "*last Will*" was dated 19 April 1813, witnessed by Joseph Ward and W. Martin at 44 Bedford Square, London (Ry. Ch. 1258).

5. HLP in her 1813 will did "constitute and appoint Sir Walter James . . . now Resident at Bath, and Sir John Williams . . . of Bodylwyddan, Flintshire, my lawful Executors, and Trustees."

The will made clear that all was left to JSPS: "*every* Thing I *possess,* and every Thing I *claim:* or am, or shall be intitled to:" when he reached his majority on 9 September 1814. Should he die, however, before that date, "*Then* I give and devise the same *in like Manner* to my Eldest Grandson *John Salusbury* Mostyn . . . hereby revoking all and every other Will or Wills."

6. Thomas Cotton as a child was imprisoned in the Tower with his father Sir Robert Cotton (d. 1712), knighted at the Restoration and created baronet, 29 March 1677. Sir Robert had married Hester, née Salusbury (d. 1710), the sister of Sir John (d. 1684) of Llewenny.

7. Edmund Halsey (d. 1729), HT's great-uncle and successful brewer. For the rags-to-riches biography of Halsey, see *Thraliana*, 1:299–300; marginalia in HLP's copy of *Boswell's Johnson* (1816), 1:473–74.

8. The Holy Bible, containing the Old Testament and the New (Cambridge: Printed by John Baskerville, Printer to the University, 1763).

9. For Lady Vere Lynch, see HLP to DL, 9 July [1798], n. 5.

10. In Hertfordshire.

TO JOHN SALUSBURY PIOZZI SALUSBURY

Easter Tuesday
20: April 1813.

My dearest Dear

Oldfield says I had no need to leave Brynbella and how foolish it was; but I know how right and wise it was; and Ward says so too. We should always have had this black Cloud hanging over us; and they would have frighted you finely, soon as I was cold in Earth——Tho' I see clear They could not *materially* or *eventually* have *hurt* you. However now (as Ward says) they can make no *Battle at all;*——and He commends Your Delicacy for absenting yourself during my Temporary Struggle with *Them*, and final Settling for *You*. He is as *sure* no Fine has been levied as if he had Searched the Records *himself*.

Well now I must tell you I have seen Lady Coventry—kinder than the kindest, and asking for you. She has a pretty Daughter Lady Jane *17 Years* old would such an Article Suit you?[1] Lady Kirkwall kept me up till 12 last Night with her Tales of Woes and of Wonder.

Sophia Hoare was not *Cruel* but *very Cold:* I shook her out of her Ill Humour and made her follow—*That is* accompany Me to Siddons's,[2] and to Gillow's, where we chose Furniture.

This Moment Merrick Hoare calls on me; and says, and *acknowleges* that I have been *ill used:*—Oh Yes replied I, but like the Skinned Eels we read of in the Jest Book—*I am used to it.*[3]

No Time for another Word except Farewell and never forget what an active Friend You have/ found in Your Old Aunt/ H: L: Piozzi.

Text Ry. 587.162.

1. For Peggy Coventry, née Pitches, see HLP to PSP, 11 February 1794, n. 11. Her daughter was Jane Emily, born 3 July 1794. See "Christenings 1756–1812," St. Leonard's Church, Streatham, Greater London Record Office.

2. Seddon Sons and Shackleton, cabinetmakers and upholsterers, at 151 Aldersgate Street. The firm had been founded by George Seddon ca. 1775.

3. "A reverend gentleman, seeing an Irish fishwoman skinning some eels, said to her, 'How can

you be so cruel? don't you think you put them to a great deal of pain?'—'Why, your honour,' she replied, 'I might when I first began business; but I have dealt in them twenty years, and by this time they must be quite *used to it.'"* See James Pettit Andrews, *Anecdotes, &c. Antient and Modern* (1789 ed.), 122; *Thraliana,* 1:236; *Retrospection,* 2:460.

TO JOHN SALUSBURY PIOZZI SALUSBURY

Saturday Night
24 [-26]: April 1813.

Dearest Salusbury would say Well done Aunt! indeed; if he knew but how hard I work. Marking and cleaning the Streatham Portraits all Morning, then packing up Dear old Davies and the Band Boxes, to bring *him* to Mr. Embry's in Covent Garden to Dinner,[1]——*Them,* the Band Boxes, to Blake's Hôtel: where when I arrived my Apartments were gone—a new Family occupying 'em: and Bessy who had walked to London, was gone in Search of a New Lodging.[2] By the Time She returned however, a Family left Blake's Hotel, and I jumped into *their* Rooms on a Parlour Floor: but You see no Direction is Safe *but Hammersley's:* Davies was obliged to turn me off today, that his House might be cleaned out for Boys on Monday Morning next. What a Mercy that I can bear dashing about so: It was a mere Accident I got these Apartments; Where I have sate reading your darling Letters till the Bed &c. was got in Order—Dinner I always find enough of.

What a sweet Letter your *last* is! I fancy you have *seen* Oldfield or *heard* from him, you write in such Spirits——but I have had no Account of any Search he made since the Letter I told you about—where he says no Fine was found at Ruthyn; and that *it was fair to presume* none would be found at all: but that he would look diligently both at Flint and Caernarvon—After the Circuit was over——It made me wild to see him so cold about it; while we were standing on Sharp Pins.——But that Ward sayd—(like Mr. Moore,)[3] *He would pledge his Life, there was not an Atom of Danger*—adding that if it had not been done in *one* County—it would surely not be done in another: and on *his* Assurances, I have existed from Monday to this Hour—Saturday Night.——The Bills and Rogueries and Rascalities of Streatham Park going on all the While, and to an Extent beyond even *my* Fears, beyond even *Leak's*—I leave it to him to describe. Meanwhile the Place is a Paradise; and every thing except *Necessaries*—Pots, Spits Beds and so forth; in elegant Order. I forced Ray's Mother to see what I had spent upon it, making her confess it never was so beautiful for the 50 Years She has known it.[4] I do believe, (Dieu me pardonne) her Son and Robinson sent the Ladies, or the Ladies sent *Them,* to take Sir Samuel Romilly's Opinion whether they should not go to Law with me for cutting Timber to repair their House[5]— and you can hardly see to read in the Library now—*for Shade.* Mr. Ray has himself knocked down Trees truly ornamental, the Loss of which do in some Measure deform the Place; but Mrs. Hoare made no Objection to that in the least.—A Scotch Friend of Lord Keith's there, a Coal Merchant;[6] told *me* that his

Lordship meant to buy the Common in Front—The Manor in short; and some of us think he will propose to buy the whole, or to buy my Life out—or something—tho' Davies says *not*——*he* feels *sure* the Girls will not *suffer* him to do anything that can be an Accommodation to Your H:L:P.——The Manor is an Accommodation to *Themselves;* for if the Duke of Bedford lets the Common out on Building Leases—Their Place at my Death will lose more than half its Value. Dr. Myddelton has been Inexpressibly kind, and managed nicely for me about the Church *Rates, Pew* &c. Charles Shephard has been a ruinous Agent indeed.

Clement Francis shot me flying in Piccadilly, and protested he would spend Sunday Evening with me Will-or-Nill.[7] He certainly did deserve Company he drove his Gig all the way to Bath in *Quest of;*——This *is* Sunday Evening—— and whilst I expect *him* I write to *you.* Oh my Dear Salusbury! what a Preacher is Doctor Andrews;[8] and how *you* in particular would like him. I could not stand the Croud of a Noon Day Church, so went at 3 in the *After*noon among the *second best.* I received the Sacrament on Easter Day at seven in the Morning for the same Reason——Fear of being crushed or frighted to death. We were 600 Communicants even *then:* Four officiating Priests, and a double Consecration. What must it have been at 11 o'Clock Prayers?

Well! now concerning these Misses. If *no* Fine has been levied—The Estate is *mine,* and if mine *Yours,*—bestowing it as I wish on a Young Woman of Honour and Credit to us both. You may say of it as Touchstone says of Audrey,—a Poor Thing Sir, but *mine own.*[9]——And the Lady of your Choice will not be *very ill off*——She should therefore *Know her own Mind.* Do not undervalue Your own Importance——Such Person, Mind, and Fortune—tho none of them Gigantic, have good *Symmetrical Pretensions.* But the Clock strikes 8—and transports me to the Drawing Room at Brynbella; My Darling reading Prayers to his Family. Oh *hear* them merciful Lord! joins with him in Spirit, his own/ H: L: P.

Mrs. Hoare squeezed out an Invitation at last—I am to dine with her on Fryday and go to Siddons's Readings at Night—but Dr. Andrews reads better.[10] Monday *Morning* 26.

Text Ry. 587.166. *Address* John Piozzi Salusbury Esq./ Brynbella/ near Denbigh/ N: Wales. *Postmark* AP C 26 813.

1. For RD and his friend, the Reverend Edward Embry, see HLP to RD, 9 November 1799, n. 8.
2. HLP's first mention in these letters of Bessie Jones, a servant whose employment ceased only at HLP's death on 2 May 1821.
3. For John Moore, the apothecary and surgeon of Denbigh, see HLP to PSW, 15 September [1792], n. 3.
4. For Sarah Ray, see HLP to Q, 7 July 1787, n. 2.
5. HLP's joking allusion to one of England's most prominent lawyers, Sir Samuel Romilly (1757–1818).
6. Robert Dalgleish (d. ca. 1825), a resident of Streatham, rented land there from Crook, Ellison, and Bates from 1811 to 1820. He is listed in the London directories as R. Dalgleish, coal merchant, "Middle Scotland-yard Wharf," from 1799 to 1805; and from then to 1825 as Dalgleish and Taylor, "Great Scotland Yard Wharf." See Streatham "Land Tax Assessments," C.R.O., Surrey.
7. For Clement Francis, see HLP to JSPS, 14 [–15] April 1810, n. 3.
8. Gerrard Andrewes (1750–1825), D.D. (1807), rector of St. James, Piccadilly (1802–25), dean of

Canterbury (1809–25). The particular sermon to which HLP refers was first delivered "at St. Nicholas, Cole Abbey, Old Fish-street" on Sunday morning and repeated at St. James in the afternoon.

9. *As You Like It*, 5.4.57–58.

10. See *The Times*, 1 April 1813. "Under the patronage of her Royal Highness the Duchess of York. Mrs. Siddons has the honour of informing the Public, her Readings [at the Argyle Room] will commence on Thursday, April 8, and succeed in the following order:—" always on a Friday, 23, 30 April; 7, 14, 21 May. "The doors to be opened at half-past 7, and to begin at half-past 8, and to finish before eleven o'clock." According to the *Morning Post*, 9 April, her readings reached their high point when she went "through the Tragedy of *Hamlet* from the beginning of the Play to the end of the Closet scene."

TO LADY WILLIAMS

Blake's Hotel Jermyn Street
Tuesday 27: April *1813*.

While Snows are covering the Hills of Kent and Surrey and while Business surrounds *me* on every Side, my Heart turns to the View of Dear Bodylwyddan from the Windows of Brynbella. Let me hear how near to quite recovered is charming Lady Williams, and how amiable her sweet Girls look when playing on the Organ, singing to it &c.

The People here are Sickly; Such Violent and rapid Changes in the Weather affect every body, and Ladies wear Furs again, *now*; and Velvets, as if it was Christmas. Public Places are left to the Second and Third *Sets* as they are called, and private Routs, Balls, and Fêtes are the *vrai Ton*. Mrs. Siddons's Readings however are crouded; and what will make Your Ladyship laugh, crouded by Methodists and Quakers: who fancy they ought not to see a Drama represented, but find no harm in hearing one read.

I have not been yet to this new Amusement, but will try for admittance on Fryday, if such a favour may be obtained for *less* than four Guineas. My Streatham Affairs have been so ruinously managed, I certainly cannot give *more*.

London seems madder than ever *this* Year, People run—and well they may—to see a Man who walks on the Cieling instead of the Floor; his Head downwards: it must be a horrible Sight.[1] The Cossack too rides in the Park and shows himself to Thousands:[2]—but I dare not mingle in a Throng of any Sort, My Nerves won't Stand it.

Upon Easterday the Carriages at St. James's Church filled the whole Street: Our Waiters at the Hôtel counted 300 Coaches. I had myself received the Sacrament at *seven* in the *Morning* that I might escape the Crush at Noon Day:—— We were 600 Communicants even *then*. But the Populousness of this Town amazes those who have known it longest, myself among the rest.

A Procession to the Funeral of one of our East India Officers this Morning was very impressive——Six Cannon drawn before his Hearse——And such a prodigious Number of Soldiers—Musicians—Muffled Drums &c. I never saw such a Thing—or heard the Dead March in Saul played to such Perfection.[3] Mr. Gillow, my Upholsterer's Balcony in Oxford Street gave me a full View of the whole Transaction: and when I was *weary* of *counting* Carriages that followed the old General; I went in, and chose Furniture for Streatham Park House. Your Ladyship may *imagine* the Croud of Spectators, but I could not *describe* it.

Adieu! We give 15*d.* o'Pound here for Veal—common pieces; The loynes and Fillets are 18*d.* o'Pound. How we all live does amaze me. I eat a Chicken one Day and a Rabbet another, but can by no means afford to dwell in my own House: The Taxes, if I was caught sleeping there; would soon finish to devour me.—

Lady Kirkwall enquires for your Ladyship very Tenderly. She is full of Troubles, full of woes, and looks very Thin. I think I have no more to say except that Dear Dr. Myddelton is very well, and very friendly to my kind Lady Williams's/ ever Obliged and truly attached/ H: L: Piozzi.

Do not let Sir John nor his young ones forget me.

If you honour me with a Line Direct to Hammersleys—I can't be certain *where* I lodge but the Bankers are sure to know—and they live in Pallmall.

Text Ry. 4 (1812–1818). *Address* Lady Williams/ Bodylwyddan/ near St. Asaph/ Flintshire/ North Wales. *Postmark* AP 27 813.

1. See, e.g., the advertisement in the *Morning Post*, 3 April 1813: "Surrey Theatre. . . . The Sieur Sanches will Walk Against the Ceiling, and give his unparallelled Performances on the Slack Rope.—"

2. From *The Times*, 10 April 1813:

"Yesterday morning, the City was thrown into considerable bustle, by the arrival at the Post-office of two post-chaises from Harwich. In one of them were a Don Cossack, and a Russian officer. The former exhibited his pike, which extended several feet out of one of the post-chaise windows. This unusual sight soon attracted a crowd" everywhere the coach went.

According to the *Morning Post*, 15 April, "the name of the Cossack is Alexander Wittischensdt. He is in his fifty-fourth year, and had been allowed to retire from the service nearly fifteen years ago with a pension, the reward of his courage and good conduct. When he heard of the invasion of his country by the French, he quitted his retirement, and voluntarily enrolled himself and his two sons in defence of native independence. He was dressed in the plain Cossack costume, with a large pistol stuck on his left side, in a belt, a musket slung behind him, and a pike shod with sharp iron upwards of ten feet long." The Cossack had been sent by his government to arouse pro-Russian sentiment among the English.

3. HLP refers to the funeral of Major General Sir Barry Close who was forty-two years in the service of the East India Company.

On 26 April 1813 his remains "were interred with military honours in Marylebone church-yard. The following was the order of the procession from the house of the deceased in Gloucester-place to the place of interment:—/ Artillery with six Field-pieces,/ Firing party—two hundred men,/ Drums,/ Band,/ Two Porters,/ Lid of Feathers, The Horse of the Deceased,/ The Hearse,/ Two Coaches with Chief Mourners,/ Two Battalions of Infantry,/ Eight Mourning Coaches with Friends,/ A long train of private carriages."

For the officials and nobility presented, see *The Times*, 27 April; *Morning Post*, 29 April; *GM* 83, pt. 1 (1813): 497.

TO JOHN SALUSBURY PIOZZI SALUSBURY

Wensday Night
28: April *1813.*

My dear Soul

I write this by Leak—as I *said* I would: You must take 5£ from *Him* for my *promised* Donation; but go no further, and hold no Plates; and make no Promises Yourself.——Mr. Roberts[1] does not even pretend to Discretion, but to You and I it is absolutely necessary. Oldfield's very comfortable Assurance that no Fine has been levied,—secures our Peace of Mind, and Possession of our own Estate: The Covenant will certainly not affect the Heir of my Landed Property: a Property of which I am myself *seized in Fee:* nor did the *Enemy*[2] suggest any thing but a slight Dispute among the Ladies *themselves;*——and Mr. Ward thought even *That Fear*—nugatory. I will however make him give me his Opinion in *Writing;* Mr. Thrale I believe left no Residuary Legatee—who might have been perhaps in Some Measure answerable, but The Ladies are his Heirs; and have as Mr. Ward expressed it—no Remedy but to be quiet, because quarrelling would do them harm instead of *Good.* He has never been wrong yet, and my heart tells me his is right *now.* Let us have no more Alarms——Ray and Robinson half laughed when they said——Now what will Mr. Thrale's Daughters do to *each other* concerning the unexecuted Covenant?—Why interrupted I, what *can* they do?——Just nothing at all said Mr. Robinson:—Ray said Lady Keith would not like it.

I am come home from Streatham Park again tonight, and find 40 Letters to answer; Literary Stuff, Money Stuff, Visiting Stuff—and most Important of all (Leak says) a *Request* for Streatham Park to let it a rich Young Merchant newly married;[3] and save poor Mead,—my intended Ranger—from almost irresistible Temptations of burning Wood and charging Coal; paying one Price for Labour, and putting down another: every possible Opportunity of committing Petty Larcenies which no Skill of mine could *dis*cover or *re*cover. Mean while my Lord Stafford worries me for The Portraits——and *Three* he *will* have—as the Irish say anyhow—*five* I mean: Johnson, Baretti, Burney, Murphy and Goldsmith.[4] I am to tell you too that Mrs. Siddons has presented me an Admission Ticket for the Readings, and Wilson another for the European Musæum[5] and Doctor Gray will dine with me on Saturday, and see this curious *Memorandum* Book;[6] it is a true Manuscript sure enough, and the Proprietors will get 200£ by it.

I opened my last Bottle of the Wine brought from home—this Day, and have never touched Inn Wine with my Lips; So I lead a *Sober* Life in *one* Sense—a Mad one in another, for People find me out I can't guess how, and leave Cards—and croud about me, that I live in a Constant Whirl. This Night I write to Hammersley who recommends the

Tenant—*Anderdon.*
    Robinson.
    Oldfield.

Ward.
Mrs. Hoare.
Mrs. Siddons.

besides this long Prose to my only Dear Salusbury—The Sight of whom on the 1st of next June at Bath, will be the best Cordial to his harrassed, but/ ever true and tender Friend/ H: L: P.

I said nothing to Leak of the 20£ from Hammerleys Desk: You must take your five Pounds from *Leak.*

I shall have a terrible Loss of Leak—as a Counsellor, and Person to confide in; Thomas and Betty are very good indeed for Dash and Splash, and walk and run: and make no Difficulties nor Daintyfications.

They are very useful as can be, and very active.

Davies sends you kind Words—and Plummer would like to send Kisses[7]—— She longs to see Brynbella but Leak must send me Money, or what will become of poor Aunt?

Adieu! and God bless my Darling; prays everlastingly his H: L: P.

Mr. Anderdon wants the House for 3 Years *only.*

Text Ry. 587.168. *Address* John Piozzi Salusbury Esq./ Brynbella/ near Denbigh/ North Wales. [Hand-delivered.]

    1. John Roberts, the vicar of Tremeirchion. See HLP to PSP, 31 July 1803, n. 4.
    2. Edmund Robinson, the attorney. See HLP to JSPS, 11 April 1813, n. 11.
    3. A proposed tenant for Streatham Park at this time was John Proctor Anderdon (1761–1847), of Farley Hill, Berks., and Spring Gardens, London. He was a partner in the mercantile firm of Anderdon, Blois, and Company (2 Copthall Court, Throgmorton Street) between 1813 and 1818, and a member of the board of directors of the London Dock Company (see the *London Chronicle,* 7–9 July 1803).
    The second Mrs. Anderdon was Frances, née Casamajor (d. 1859), the first having died in 1811. Anderdon and his new wife did not rent Streatham Park in 1813; they did, however, sublease the estate from Count Lieven in 1815 for a short time. See also the *Bath Chronicle,* 17 January 1811; Farington 11:3923, 3927; P.R.O., Prob. 11/2049/90 (proved 3 February 1847), and IR/26/1760, ff. 118–19.
    4. For the art collector George Granville Leveson-Gower, marquess of Stafford, see HLP to MW, 28 May [1807], n.3.
    5. John Wilson (fl. 1755–1825), who described himself as "An American Loyalist from Charleston, South Carolina," founded in 1789 at 8 King Street, St. James Square, London, the European Museum for the Promotion of the Fine Arts and the Encouragement of British Artists, the "first picture market in Europe." See *New Descriptive Catalogue and Plan of the European Museum* (London: G. Smeeton, 1813), iii.
    6. "Harvard Piozziana."
    7. Mrs. Plummer, the housekeeper (and sometimes JSPS's "preceptress") at RD's school in Streatham.

TO JOHN SALUSBURY PIOZZI SALUSBURY

Saturday
1: May 1813.

Now I ought to write very *entertaining* Letters indeed; but I flatter myself my dearest Salusbury would rather they were *kind* ones; the kindest would scarcely express my Esteem and Affection.

I dined with the Hoares Yesterday——Lady Kirkwall when She heard I was going—*congratulated* me, and said "Ah Dear Creature! come home to the Bosom of your charming Family,—*That's* your *true Place* at last." Well! a Miss Webbe dined with us—a deserted Damsel of 30 Years old; very sensible and intelligent:[1] Robert once lived with her, but he played too much at Cricket She says; and neglected her old Father whom She took him to wait upon.

The next was going to hear Siddons read Macbeth:——Why She *acted* every Word of it—Witches and all: and having been ever *slow*, is now *tardy;* So we were kept till 12 o'Clock—no Music intervening, nor nothing to break the almost monotonous Uniformity: for tho' She does vary the Tone, She never changes the Key Note, by any Accident; in any Character. It was however a very great Performance, and tho' like Correggio when he saw Raphael's Pictures——*I* could have cried out Anch'*So*:[2] it was for the *Reading* alone; her Attitudes and Gestures, and Figure, are incomparable. The Crush and Squeeze however is so dreadful that as Macbeth says when he has committed the Murder——

> I'll go no more:
> I am afraid to think on what I've done,
> Look on't again I dare not——[3]

Much Distinction was paid to me both There and every where—I shall get sadly Spoiled: meanwhile I fear some thing bad for the *Mostyn Boys;*—Sophia says the youngest is taken from School, and is under Doctor Jenner's Care at Cheltenham because of his *Health*——Lady de Blaquiere said poor dear *Moussey* had had a great deal of Trouble about her youngest Son, and Lady Kirkwall gave unpleasant and unintelligible *Hints.*

Davies told me the eldest Boy called on *him,* and said Little *Tom,* meaning *Bertie* was to go to Sea with Lord Keith: and that he had wholly left Westminster——Davies replied *very likely;* and thought no more on't: but I feel sure all is not as it should be.[4]

Here are the most astonishing Specimens of Mona Marble to be seen in Piccadilly. One would think the whole Island of Anglesea was Marble—so beautiful is the Furniture it makes: and the Man who shews it—possesses an *Oak* Table of such surprizing Elegance and Beauty I remain amazed at it, and am quite sorry Leak did not see what British Timber was capable of.[5] Mr. Gillow has nothing to compare with it among his Foreign Woods. The Man in Piccadilly has got Bullock's Liverpool Musæum to shew at the Place, and a famous Exhibition it *is.*

I am in sad Case about this hateful Weather—The Ground is all a *Slop*; The Air like *Water Gruel*: nobody will go see Streatham Park till the Wind changes I suppose.

Worse and worse; while I was at this foolish Musæum;—Hammersley's People sent your Letter *here* they say:—I'm *sure* it was Yours—but nobody here has seen, or taken it *in*; I would not have lost my Letter for all their Stock of Curiosities: and This vile Accident will disturb my whole Comfort this Day. They should have let it lain quiet at the Bankers till I called or sent—but this vexatious *officiousness* has lost me my Letter completely;——and tomorrow is Sunday—I *can* have none tomorrow. How provokingly foolish.

Here comes the Dear Letter, and with it my Peace of Mind. Young Gray of Oriel College has presented me his Works:[6] every body civil—and I fancy nobody *kind* but our own Folks—Pennant and Myddelton—You shall be sure of The Merry Jests called Rejected Addresses[7]—Two Penny Post Bag &c. but the Table, with some other Trifles must go by Sea. It appears by your last that you *will* meet me at Bath: Do what suits You; Well assured that my *Reliance* is on Your *Discretion*; but my *Heart* will be most delighted in seeing, and *telling* you instead of *writing* it, how fond and how faithful is your Old Aunt/ H: L: P.

I will write again *Monday*.

This is miserable May Day I think:—Cold, rainy, wretched Weather, Sleet and Snow; and such a Heat in the Argylle Room last Night.[8] And such a Sharp Wind at the Door &c.!! I wonder how we survived it.

Text Ry. 587.171. *Address* John Piozzi Salusbury Esq./ Brynbella/ near Denbigh/ North Wales. *Postmark* MA <1813>.

1. HLP refers to a daughter of Elizabeth (d. 1803) and William Webb (d. 1806), of Streatham. The daughter was either Mary, born 15 October 1778, or Sarah, born 2 April 1780. See the relevant parish records, St. Leonard's Church, Streatham, in Greater London Record Office.

2. On 27 October 1777 SJ wrote to HLT: "You talk of writing as if you had all the writing to yourself, If our Correspondence were printed I am sure Posterity, for Posterity is always the authours favourite, would say that I am a good writer too. Anch'io sonô Pittore." According to Bruce Redford, this apocryphal remark, "I too am a painter," said to have been made by Correggio when looking at a work of Raphael, was attributed to him as early as the late seventeenth century (Hyde-Redford, 3:89).

3. *Macbeth*, 2.2.47–49.

4. CMM's youngest son was the twelve-year-old Thomas Arthur *Bertie*, who at the beginning of 1814 was to be permanently removed from Westminster and placed by Lord Keith in the hands of Captain Nash aboard the *Saturn*, a 74-gun man-of-war. See Hyde, 304.

5. HLP refers to the work of George Bullock (d. 1818), marble mason, sculptor, and modeler, who had a business in Liverpool from 1804 to 1814. The *Bath Herald* (8 April 1815) wrote of his "interesting discovery . . . [made] in Anglesea a few years since. He found in the centre of that island, and about seven miles from the Paris Mountain, some marble quarries, containing two beds of rocks, the one resembling in colour and effect the Oriental Porphyry, and the Verd Antique. [He] lately established in Oxford-street a public manufactory of Mona marble, the productions of which are scarcely equalled by the marbles of any age or country." See R. Gunnis, *Dictionary of British Sculptors 1660–1851* (London: Odhams Press, 1953), 68–69.

6. For Robert Gray, see HLP to JSPS, 15 December 1810, n. 4. His "Works" consisted of a twenty-seven page pamphlet, *Essays in Poetical Composition* (London: Printed for J. Hatchard, 1812).

7. The highly popular work of James Smith (1775–1839) was *Rejected Addresses: or The new Theatrum poetarum* (London: Printed for J. Miller, 1812).

8. HLP probably refers to the first [29 April] of two balls "at the Argyle Rooms, under the Patronage of the Countess of Cholmondeley, Countess Cowper, Viscountess Castlereagh, and Mrs. Boehm. . . . No ticket can be had at the Rooms, unless a voucher is produced from a Patroness." See the advertisement in *The Times*, 15 April.

TO JOHN SALUSBURY PIOZZI SALUSBURY

Tuesday Night
4 [–5] May 1813.

My Dearest Salusbury

Says—Pray write every Day; and then does not write every day *himself.* I have been wretched for want of a Letter since Morning, when Thomas came home from Hammersley's without one, and found Marianne Francis here to catch me the Instant I came out of my Bed Room; whence few Ladies would have stirred at all, had their Bowels been troublesome as mine. I took Her out however to the Somerset House Exhibition,[1] and likewise shewed her the Algebraical Boy, who told me when I said I had lived 72 Years and four Months, that——I had therefore passed 26400 Weeks, 633600 Days, 38016000 houis, and 2280960000 Minutes.—I am more shocked than amused at the Thought of having passed them no better. The Child is just 8 Years old—a Native of America.[2]

The Managers of the Institution for Sir Joshua's Pictures sent me their humble Thanks, and Permission to go see the Shew afore it opened, and place my fine Portraits where I pleased in the Room.—We went; and my Reception was most flattering, so I am paid in Vanity.[3] At some of these Places I met Windle and his Wife who were too civil by half;[4] and quite insisted on my giving them a Day &c. so sick as I was, I felt in no humour to refuse, because I thought the Visit would lead me to learn whether Shephard had paid *him* or not, and I fancy he has. Mr. Pennant of Downing likewise called on me today and Mrs. Merrick Hoare, to whom I affected gay Spirits and perfect health—her Husband's Picture is in the Exhibition.

There has been a strange Attack made on the Queen by a mad Miss Dickinson;[5] Tis said her Majesty's Terror was very great indeed:——The Town has left off talking of the Opera, and all the Discourse is of *This* frightful Story. Mead wants me to see the Pond drawn at Streatham Park—and Saturday to be the Day:—I want a Letter from You, and to write myself to Dr. Whalley.

8 at Night.

Marianne is gone home—Thomas waiting on her—The Weather warm but rainy, and my Bowels miserably affected, I guess not from what Cause: unless it was Rhubarb Tart, which I eat on Saturday with my *Six* Rev. Divines here at home.[6]

At The Dinners abroad I was most cautious; a Letter from you to morrow Morning will do me good——I feel fretted that your Oxford Correspondent is so likely to continue troublesome——You *do* take the only proper Method—by *disclaiming* all Friendship, and all Connection with such Trash: They can do *only*

Mischief. When She asks for a Character it will be best to say—I know nothing of her Merits——I know nothing of her but a Shameless persisting to follow up one who always wished—and always *did* keep clear of her; and ever assured her it was his fixed Resolution never to see or hear a Syllable concerning her. You see She keeps your Letters. The Truth is your own Words are full as good and proper, (better perhaps:) than any I can suggest; and your own dear Discretion must be your Guide. I am going to take some Thin Toast with fine Sugar and Ginger, and my own good Port Wine on it, for my Supper. I remember Leak and I stopping a Diarrhæa that poor Uncle was scourged with at Worcester once by that Remedy. You may be sure I dined today solely on Chicken Broth—— I will finish my Letter in the Morning and Say I am better, if Sleep should stop the Torment *to Night*. We shall see how it is by then. Meanwhile be *you* good wise and happy——and I can neither live nor die uncomfortably. God bless my precious Creature and Adieu!—Mr. Thompson the Coach maker will be here in the Morning, and say when my Carriage will be capable of taking me to Bath.[7] Once more, *Once* more, Good Night; and Angels guard my best-loved Boy, Farewell![8]

Well! I passed the Night—not happily—but without further Disturbance from my Bowels: and feel this Morning as if I had been under Will Hughes's Flail for a few Hours, so beaten, and so Sore: Lady Kirkwall's Notes and kind *Teizeries*— never let me rest. I shall be glad of some Bath Water to wash all the Nonsense away. I must pay my Devoirs to York Place today, as Mrs. Hoare called Me from my Chicken Broth to say her Sister was arrived Yester *Noon*. Oh come Thomas! and bring me the Letter from Hammersley's. Here it is; and I am tho' not *yet well*; Very happy, and very Thankful. You are quite right—getting rid of the Country Rust is a *very* dangerous Thing. God keep *Your* Virtue *well cased over*, with Rust, or any thing that will keep *it safe*. Leak and I always did and always shall differ on *that* Subject——he likes Mr. Salusbury to be a *fine Gentleman*, and I doat upon him for being a good Christian; because going to Court is a good Thing, but going to heaven is a better. Says H: L: P.

I shall certainly write every day, it is my truest Pleasure: and I shall now write to Dr. Whalley and Sir Walter James, They are both at Bath.

No News at all of those rich Anderdons.—

Text Ry. 587.174. *Address* John Piozzi Salusbury Esq./ at Brynbella/ near Denbigh/ North Wales. *Postmark* < >.

1. HLP refers to the forty-fifth exhibition of the Royal Academy, Somerset Place, which had opened 3 May. The exhibition was widely judged, most reviewers finding it unexceptional and failing to "display any pictures which justify that expectation." Earmarked for praise, however, were Turner's landscapes; the portraits of Lawrence, Beechey, and Owen; the painting by G. Dawe, "A Child rescued by its Mother from an Eagle's nest"; and one by J. Northcote, "Lion Hunting."
    See the *Morning Post*, 13 May; *Bell's Weekly Messenger*, 9 May; *The Times*, 22 June 1813.
2. The boy—seven or eight years old—was George Parker Bidder (1806–78), of Moretonhamstead, Devon. The advertisements of his talents, which were to continue for the next two years, indicated that "any question, however abstruse or complicated he answers with the utmost promptitude and correctness, though he does not at present know a figure. . . . The following questions, which have been recently proposed to him will afford some idea of his almost supernatural talent:

"Q.—In £100,735,641 how many farthings? Answered in one minute! 96,754,215,660 Farthings.— Q—If my horse stands me 9 ½d. per day, keeping, what will be the charge of 11 horses for the year? Ans. £158.18s. 6-½d.—How many Thirty-sevens in 4769? Answered in less than one minute! 128—Remainder 33."

See, e.g., the advertisements in the *Bath Herald* for 10, 17, 31 December 1814; *Bath Journal*, 19 December 1814.

After having been exhibited by his father, young George was educated at Edinburgh and became a distinguished engineer *(DNB)*.

3. According to a ms. description in the library of the Royal Academy, Piccadilly: "The British Institution, 1806–07. Established as a Rival to the RA at Boydell's Shakespeare Gallery in Pall Mall. Aimed 'to encourage and reward the talents of the artists of the United Kingdom.' Organized loan exhibitions of old masters for students to copy."

On 13 May the British Institution, largely through the effort of Sir George Beaumont, opened an exhibition of Sir Joshua Reynolds' portraits—"130 of his performances," which it borrowed "for the benefit of Students." See *GM* 83, pt. 1 (1813): 480. For HLP's loan, see her letter to Q, 15 May 1813.

4. For Thomas Windle, see HLP to JSPS, 6 May 1809, n. 2. On 1 October 1788 he married Jane Maxwell of Jamaica.

5. According to *The Times* (4 May 1813), an assistant mistress of the wardrobe, named Davenport, who had lived long under "the Royal protection," was emotionally affected by Princess Amelia's death. "She slept in the tower over the Queen's bed-room. About five o'clock [2 May] Her Majesty was awoke by a violent noice at her bed-room door, accompanied with a voice calling loudly for the Queen of England to redress her wrongs, and with the most distressing shrieks and screams imaginable. The Queen's bed-room has two doors: she used such violence as to break open the outer door but found herself unable to break the inner one." The shrieking woman, clad only in nightclothes, was overcome by a porter and seen by a doctor, "who ordered her a strait waistcoat; and she was sent off in a post-chaise, accompanied by two keepers, to a house at Hoxton for the reception of insane persons."

6. For a slight variation of the whimsy, see HLP to the Miss Thrales, 8 June 1807, n. 1.

7. Whatever work Lionel Thomson of 33 Mortimer Street did for HLP's coach, his bill came to £72.13 (Ry. 598.97–97+).

8. "Good night, sweet prince,/ And flights of angels sing thee to thy rest" (*Hamlet*, 5.2.359–60).

TO ALEXANDER LEAK

10: May 1813.

When Leak Said We could perhaps make 700£ o'Year out of Streatham Park by *living* there——we scarce permitted our hearts to hope *that possible;* out of which Taxes must have been paid, and Servants kept: how grateful ought I then to be, if Providence does really send me this fine, Elegant, Showy Mr. Anderdon! Mead will not Suffer me to stir from Town till he knows the Bargain is made.— He is, (rationally enough) afraid that the Ladies will make me suspicious of him. It would have set any one laughing to see Miss Thrale's Anxiety about the few Fish we found, and I carried *them* home a noble Dish of Carp, Eels &c. reserving the rest for my Friends.

The Desk Susan is afraid of having lost, I do verily believe went away with Doctor Johnson to His House when we parted, and I left London for Bath in the Year 1783; after Signing my Deed of Settlement, leaving a Power of Revocation. Poor Mr. Piozzi never saw the Desk in his Life, tho' She apprehended *he* used it for Musick; The Ladies certainly lost nothing by *him*.

Mr. Charles Shephard has never been spoken of among us, but they seem seriously displeased I did not prosecute the Family of Atkins:[1] What should I have gained by that? said I: *Revenge* was the Reply; *We* hoped you would have gone to Law with him.

Mead took a Checque from me today for 100£——and I shall now be forced to have new Chairs from Gillow, and a Carpet for the Drawing Room, beside Beds and Tables——and I fear the Globes must be made good.

Mr. Anderdon is as high and mighty as the highest, and thinks he is doing their House no Small Honour to *Think of it:*——A House (said he) bosomed in Trees, The Sun never Shining on it—I could hardly look grave at *that* Objection——He will he says, Set the Scythes to work; for he loves Landschape Gardening.

At his proposal of cutting the Windows down to the Ground, Miss Thrale looked but little pleased: Mr. Windle however calling here Yesterday, I asked *him;* and he says The Tenant must replace whatever he alters of *that* Sort—— and our Ladies are *so* earnest to have every Thing as it was in *their* Time——I was half mortified to think of My furnishing the Place so prettily, till This Man offered to take it——Lady Kirkwall too cries out—You will not surely let the Place without first offering it to *your own* lovely Girls! *Poor* Mrs. Hoare! why *mayn't She* have it? Will She take it? enquired I——Ah Surely She would, were *Dear Mamma* but to ask her.

I know not what Answer to make to such tender Speeches,——They quite confound *me.* My heart pants for home or for the first Step towards home, Salt Hill; and Salusbury to meet me at Bath. The Yellow Fog I breathe every Morning is not so Impenetrable as the Affectation that Surrounds me at Night—and when I am unwell, 'Tis too much to bear and live.——

There is meanwhile no Affectation in Susan Thrale's saying She would rather any one bought the Manor than her Brother in Law: for He like *them* She observed, would cover the Common with Houses; or with *any*thing to make his 4000£—into 40,000£. Lord Keith I understand laughs at the Ladies and at *me* about the matter——and resolves to take Care of his favourite Child and himself. No bad Lesson for/ H: L: P.

Mr. Hammersley must make the Bargain between Me and Anderdon after all: Mead says he spoke to *him* of an *Optional* Letting for 3 or 7 Years—but Hammersley seems so afraid of offending those charming Ladies——*I* should like the Idea of 3 or 7 Years very well——The Other Offer was a Mr. Harrison[2] who applied to Mead——Mrs. Anderdon claimed Acquaintance with Miss Thrale, and would have been civil, but Susanna would hardly return even her Curtsy——The Anderdons are gone into Hertfordshire and I can't sit here waiting their Return. I'll leave all to Hammersley.

Mr. Ward is to draw the Agreement and *convince* Hammersley that I *can* let it. I shall insist on their not Letting the Place (if tried) to any under Tenants who may ruin my Furniture.

Text Hyde Collection. *Address* Mr. Alexander Leak/ at Mrs. Piozzi's/ Brynbella/ near Denbigh/ North Wales. *Postmark* MA 10 813.

1. For the bankrupt Abraham Atkins, see HLP to JSPS, 13 November 1810, n. 2; also to Robert Ray, 20 April 1807, n. 1.
2. John Harrison (fl. 1789–1820), a surveyor at 324 Rotherhithe Street.

TO CLEMENT MEAD

Bath Thursday Night
13: May *1813*.

Dear Mr. Mead

will be glad to hear I am got safe to Bath—Pray direct there—*Post Office*, and let me know if that amiable Mr. Anderdon takes poor old Streatham Park or no: I hope he does; I hope he will not suffer me to be tempted by others, beyond what I can bear;[1] because I prefer him to every body, on his own Account as well as Mr. Hammersley's: and if I don't hear You have closed with him, I shall be grievously disappointed.

Whoever has the Place I will not separate the House from the Land——It shall go or stay *altogether*.

My Service to your Family and believe/ me Yours and Theirs truly/ H: L: Piozzi.

Text Hyde Collection. *Address* Mr. Clement Mead/ Surveyor &c./ Upper Charlotte Street/ Fitzroy Square/ London. *Postmark* BATH MY 14 1813; 15 MY 15 1813.

1. 1 Corinthians 10:13.

TO JOHN SALUSBURY PIOZZI SALUSBURY

Bath Fryday Morning
[13]–14: May 1813.

I do not like beginning a Letter with a Lie; yet certainly it is no Truth at all that I write this Fryday Morning. No; Dearest Salusbury, I write it Thursday Night, that it may *go* on Fryday Morning 9 o'Clock; and tell you—if at Shrewsbury— that I am at length within fourscore and twelve Miles of my *Inestimable*. It is not easy to say how happy that Thought makes me——I have been so exceedingly unwell of late, that the Servants as well as myself were (I believe) truly rejoyced to see me housed at Arnold's, under the Protection of his White Lyon.[1] *My* Joy was greater when we had fixed upon a pretty Lodging, No. 11 on the North Parade:——a cool and shady spot,—with all the Comforts round me of Town and Country united. Bath always shews well, come from what Place one will; and its near Environs are so much more beautiful than those of London,—'tis Incredible. Tho' I who have a house to dispose of on the Surrey Side of our great Metropolis, should say nothing against a Situation so admired. We have had Deluges of Wet here in the West; the Roads, and Carriages which *pass* the Roads, all look like December instead of May; and yet one Sees no Swallows, and except at Streatham Park I have heard no Cuckoo.

The Friends who called on me so diligently—as to distract me—in London; will be half offended at my leaving Town so abruptly: but I told nobody when I came, and why should my going away be announced?

Mrs. Opie and I never met, tho' We tried hard for it[2]——Mrs. D'Arblaye's Visits and caresses produced no Renewal of Acquaintance.[3] When Connections are once broken, 'tis a foolish Thing to splice and mend; They never can (at least with *me*) unite again as before. Life is not long enough for *Darning* torne *Friendships;* and they are always a Proof however neatly done, that the Substance is *worne out.* A new Dress can better be *depended* on.

Dearest dear Salusbury will take Care and keep *ours whole.*

I am sadly ashamed of my mad Countrymen's behaviour, which you describe so feelingly: Famous People for civilizing the So much tamer Hindoos!! and probably they subscribed nothing but their Noise and Folly: Was any Money given at last except by ourselves?—most likely not: and that which We gave, will perhaps never reach those it is designed for.

I am sick of it.

Direct to me Post Office Bath; Your Bed shall be slept in Tomorrow Night—— a very comfortable Apartment.

I have seen no Friends yet of course but the Hon. Miss Hay who I met in the Street.[4] If Lady Collier's Son comes home as She expects from India We shall have her *here* again,[5] but our *own* Stay is so short: just 25 Days I think from this Hour.

Well! The Time used to fly at Brynbella; and now it seems Three Months since I have seen *You* or *home:* We are always told that Variety shortens Life, and Uniformity lengthens it; but my Experience,—and our Separation says no to the general Rule.

Farewell! and fail not to continue That Affection and that Conduct which makes your Affection valuable for upon them depend the Life and Temporal Happiness of Your poor/ H: L: P.

8 Drops of Laudanum again tonight; and 80 Drops of Brandy: Bath Pump tomorrow Morning—instead of New Milk.

Text Ry. 587.184. *Address* John Piozzi Salusbury Esq./ White Lyon/ Shrewsbury. To be forwarded to him if in the Neighbourhood. *Postmark* BATH MY 14 <1813>.

1. George Arnold's White Lion Inn and Tavern, Bath. See HLP to AL, 26 April 1812, n. 13.
2. Amelia Opie, née Alderson (1769–1853), novelist.
3. Members of the Burney family, aware of FBA's pain over the rift between herself and HLP, had tried to reconcile the two women since the former's return to England in 1812. Between 1 September 1812 and 17 May 1813, MF wrote at least thirteen letters to HLP in which she announced the arrival of FBA, mentioned her name, or pleaded her cause.
HLP indicated only "cold" interest in FBA. In a letter dated 14 April, MF pointed out FBA's declining health and ended with a plea: as "she was so desirous of something kind and conciliatory,

and is, perhaps, poor thing, in a most dangerous state [she had a lump in her breast removed by surgery], I think if you can bring yourself to send anything like a kind message, it would be a most christian act in you, and give great happiness to her." This letter prompted HLP to call on her former *protégée* on 11 May. FBA, however, was not at home and HLP made no further efforts to renew the acquaintance at this time. See *Journals and Letters*, 7:118–123.

4. Margaret Hay (d. 1828) lived at 23 Gay Street, Bath. Related to the earls of Kinnoull, she was the daughter of Edward Hay (d. 1798), one-time minister plenipotentiary to the court of Lisbon (1757) and governor of Barbados (1772–73).

5. Of Lady Collier's four sons, HLP referred to Charles (1782–1818), who served as an officer in the Bengal Army or to Francis Augustus (d. 1849), who at this time was a captain in the Royal Navy in the West Indies.

TO LADY WILLIAMS

North Parade Bath
Fryday 14th May 1813.

If my dearest Lady Williams feels as much benefit from *any* Water, as I did to day from my old favourite Pump here at Bath, She will get well presently—and despise the little Chair. Between Morning Worries, and Evening Society, my Stomach and Bowels began to find themselves much disordered; and I ran hither for Refuge, taking no leave of the Gay and Great——The first Glass acted as an Immediate Cordial and I felt the Effects warming my very finger Ends—but it is not *everybody's* Medicine: my silly Servant Thomas swallowed a large Dose (for a Frolic) and could hardly find his way home thro' Giddiness and Fever. Do me the honour to present me kindly to Doctor Cumming;—he knows what to do, and you must be Obedient to Command. Salusbury is turned Hermit I believe, but he writes often; and I have quite pelted him with Letters——we shall have nothing to say when we meet——but how is dear Lady Williams?— on my Part;—on his, Oh she is a great deal better.

My heart trembles for Mrs. Hoare, whose increase of Flesh, and *disposition* towards swelled Legs precisely resembles that of the dear Lady I am now writing to—and between Your Ages there can be Scarce five Years I suppose.[1] Miss Thrale appears much more active and strong than her Sister, and is exceedingly like Mrs. Mostyn—of and from whom I hear nothing—unless that She was at Cheltenham a Month or Six Weeks ago.

The most curious Thing in London is a Boy Seven Years old only, born in America:[2] who gains Treasures of Money—merely by his strange Powers of counting it—How old are *You*? says the little fellow to me: 72 Years old and four Months was my Reply. Then—answered the Child you have lived so many Weeks, so many Days, so many Hours, and so many Minutes.——Father! continued he—Set down the Figures.—Set them down yourself my Dear, said I—— I *can't* Ma'am do *that,* for I have not learned to *write Yet.*—What an astonishing Creature! very ugly, and awkward, and has Six perfect Fingers on each hand. The Algebraists are all amazed at him; I wished for your Eldest Son to have been with me. Dear Soul! he called on me with Young Pennant at Blake's Hotel:[3]

but could not stay five Minutes—so did Mr. Fleetwood Williams;[4] *he* met Lady Kirkwall. She lives at 124 Mount Street Grosvenor Square, but complains of Heat and Dust; and meditates——as all People *say* they do——for two Months, a Retreat into the Country. Her Ladyship seems much engaged in Cares for her Brother who is abroad;[5] and Business Seems to amuse her.

I am *this Instant* got into my New Apartments and Meditate an early Visit to Miss Williams: arriving only last Night nobody has shewn themselves to me yet; I slept at the Inn of course: and carry this Letter to the Post Office in my Way to a Second Glass of the dear Pump.

Thunder, Lightning, and Torrents of Rain fell on the Metropolis one *Evening* at *11* o'Clock, when People were rising from Table to get ready for the Masqued Ball——I remember the Time when such Storms would have affrighted fine Ladies, but Cowardice is as much out of Fashion as Modesty.[6]

Present me most affectionately to the Dear Family; and Give my Grateful Respects to Sir John, believing me ever most faithfully *his* and your Ladyship's true Servant/ H: L: Piozzi.

Text Ry. 4 (1812–18). *Address* Lady Williams/ Bodylwyddan/ near St. Asaph/ Flintshire/ N: Wales.

1. Ly W was born in 1768, SH in 1771.
2. The advertisements for George Parker Bidder claim he was seven years old and a native of Devon. See HLP to JSPS 4[–5] May 1813, n. 2.
3. HLP was visited by John Williams II and by David, the only son of Louisa and David Pennant. See HLP to JSPS, 10 March 1811, n. 9.
4. For Ly W's brother-in-law Fleetwood, see HLP to JSPS, 15 December 1810, n. 10; HLP to JSPS, 27 June 1811, n. 3.
5. John de Blaquiere, second baron, was detained in France as a prisoner.
6. On 6 May the "Metropolis was visited by a severe thunder-storm. At eleven at night the vivid flashes of lightning produced considerable alarm; and were followed by peals of thunder, which resembled the explosion of a mine." See *GM* 83, pt. 1 (1813): 480; *The Times*, 10 May 1813.

TO LADY KEITH

No. 11: North Parade. Bath
Saturday 15: May *1813*.

It was a great Pleasure to receive Your kind Letter so soon after my arrival at this Place.—The Water did me a great deal of Good, and the Letter did me more. London hours and London Fog are certainly bad for Health, and you have been happy as well as *little Dear* in escaping them this Winter or Spring—for both are strangely blended.

Such Thunder and Lightning seldom occurs in our Island as I was out in that famous Thursday Night, when beautiful Greenwich suffered so:[1]——but Fears are out of Fashion, and Ladies brave Dangers they would have shrunk from, when I was Young.

Susette was with me at Streatham Park the last Time I saw it, and witnessed the Pictures all in full Beauty. Lord Stafford and his Subalterns never let me rest till I lent them Johnson and Burney, Baretti and Goldsmith, but they *do* look very well, so I am paid in Vanity.

Don't you remember a Portrait of this Duke of Bedford's Mother, in the Habit of our Queen's Bride Maid dressing a Statue of Hymen?[2] It has a very peculiar Appearance now from the Dress being obsolete—but I felt it interesting in a high degree.[3]—It is a marvellous Exhibition most certainly, and we may boast that Reynolds and his Tragic Muse can do what no other Artist or Actress dared have attempted.[4]—They can amuse hundreds—ay Thousands of fastidious Spectators, without any Assistance from others——Such *Self*-dependent Powers, do not I believe exist except in them alone. But after all Bath still looks beautiful, and I felt glad to see it once again.

Did I mention to dear Lady Keith a literary Curiosity that was shewn me in Town?—The Journal Doctor Johnson kept of our Tour in Wales? His Description of Hawkestone and Ilam render it valuable, tho' I suppose 100 Lines is all he gives them both:——If the Proprietor resolves to print it, he must exchange Peace for Pelf, and so I had the honour to tell him.[5] How well your Sisters look! Susanna asked me what was become of Doctor Johnson's old Desk? and I—not reflecting except on how many Things the Last Tenants took away; concluded they had taken that too: but my Notion is now,—hunting back my Memory— that I gave it him when we parted—along with a Carpet I had worked, and an old Silver Tea-Kettle and Lamp which had been my poor Mother's Virgin Establishment:—They all went to the Blackamoor,[6] with my Portrait by some of the Burneys.[7]

Apropòs They tell me Madame D'Arblaye is writing:[8] busy in *Some* useful Way no doubt. Do you recollect when we were forming (for Sport) a female Administration, and She enquired what Provision should be made for *her*? Oh says Doctor Johnson; We will send *Little Burney out for a Spy.*[9]

That Lord Keith is not immediately with you, I learn by the Direction of your Letter but my black Hand is always visible thro' the Cover; this cannot escape coming free.

Give my true Love to little one, and believe me ever most Affectionately Yours/ and hers H: L: P.

What a sad Accident at fine Lansdowne House![10] Old Streatham Park is [in] no Danger of *Wet* Rot, or *Dry* Rot *now,* for these future forty Years I believe; but Such Storms of Hail *must* break the Hothouse Glasses—new as well as old ones—I have seldom seen such a Tempest.

Text Bowood Collection. *Address* R: H: Baroness Keith.

1. In describing the thunderstorm of 6 May, *The Times* on 10 May reported that "part of the steeple of Greenwich Church was precipitated into the Church-yard. A public-house (the Mitre) was also injured. The weather-cock, with a large stone attached to it, perforated the earth several feet."

2. "This Duke" was John Russell, sixth duke of Bedford.

One of Princess Charlotte's bridesmaids on 8 September 1761 was Lady Elizabeth Keppel (1739–

Sarah Siddons as The Tragic Muse. Portrait by Sir Joshua Reynolds (1784). (Reproduced by permission of the Henry E. Huntington Library and Art Gallery, San Marino, California.)

68), daughter of the second earl of Albemarle. In 1764 she was to marry Francis Russell (1739–67), styled Marquess of Tavistock. The marriage ended tragically, he dying of a fall from a horse and she of tuberculosis. The sixth duke of Bedford was their second son.

3. The portrait of the duke of Bedford's mother, executed by Reynolds in 1761 for the wedding of King George III and Queen Charlotte, was hung in Woburn Abbey [no. 248] ca. 1766–67. Initially, however, it was exhibited at the Great Room in Spring Garden, Charing Cross, for the Society of Artists. It is a whole-length portrait of Lady Elizabeth Keppel "decorating a term of Hymen." See *British Museum Engraved British Portraits*, 4:247, item 1265.

4. Now at the Huntington Art Gallery in San Marino, California, the portrait of Sarah Siddons as *The Tragic Muse* was painted by Reynolds in 1784.

5. See SJ's *A Journey into North Wales, in the Year 1774*, in *Boswell's Johnson*, 5:433–34. HLP was able to see the manuscript through the efforts of the Reverend Robert Myddelton and the Reverend Henry Gostling White (1769–1846), who owned it in 1813. It was first printed in October 1816 by Richard Duppa in an unreliable edition. For the manuscript, see B.M. Add. MS. 12,070.

SJ saw Hawkestone and Ilam on 25 July 1774, describing it in six paragraphs contrasting the "turbulent pleasure" of the former with the "pastoral virtue" of the latter.

6. For Francis Barber, see HLP to SL, 6 December 1787, n. 6.

7. HLP's portrait by Edward Francesco Burney (1760–1848) is missing.

8. *The Wanderer* (1814) was to be FBA's fourth and last novel.

9. HLP's unusually snide paragraph is as much an attack on Q as on "Little Burney." The latter in 1784 passed on to Q secrets that detailed HLT's feelings for GP. From that time on "Little Burney" became the "Aimable traitresse." See *Journals and Letters*, 7:119, n. 11.

10. According to *The Times*, 13 May 1813: "A Paper of yesterday says, 'that a most alarming accident happened at Lansdowne-house, on Tuesday last [11 May], which had nearly proved fatal to a large party who were dining with the Marquis of Lansdowne, in Berkeley-square, by the centre roof of the house falling in, and some of the largest beams passing through into the dining room, from one of which Lord Gower, eldest son of the Marquis of Stafford, received a slight injury, but fortunately the rest of the company escaped unhurt. The disaster was occasioned by some of the principal timbers of the roof being eaten through by the *dry rot*.'"

TO CLEMENT MEAD

Bath Monday
17: May 1813.

Dear Mr. Mead

I am as sorry as there is any Need to be that Mr. Anderdon does not take the Place, but I am not *very* Sorry; I saw from the first he would *not* take it, and I told you so——but don't advertise it, I will not (during my Time) do the old House that Indignity.

Ask Mr. Wilson of the Europæan Musæum, King Street, St. James's, if he heard any more of a rich Mr. Parr he recommended me for a Tenant,[1] because I have no *Objection* to letting it, tho' I will have a high Price: and tho' I expect You to be a *faithful* Ranger, and see to the Selling of my Potatoes, the Profits of my Crop &c. The Hay must be in prodigious Quantity this Year I am convinced, and why *We* have no Gooseberries or Apricots to dispose of, for I see plenty about—You must *tell*.

Direct to me Post Office Bath, till Whitsun Week when we move to Mendip Lodge, Doctor Whalley's; and from thence home thro' Derbyshire &c. &c.

You will write *to Leak* when I am on my Journey——he knows the full Mind of/ H: L: Piozzi.

Hang up the *Horse* Prints, and the Prints from *Teniers* in the Hall where the Globes are: The Ladies can direct you where they used to Stand.

The Italian Prints from Roman Antiquities brought over by myself from *Rome,* hang in the Anti Chamber where the old China stands——The Print of my old Place in Wales goes to the Housekeepers Room[2]—it is a *Drawing* not a Print; and with it go the Map of Miss Susan Thrale's Working when a Baby: and Dr. Johnson's Print, and Mr. Halsey and his Dog. The Prints representing Corsica, and Turkish Tents, and Enchantments from Tasso, used to hang in the *other* Anti Room leading to our Eating Parlour.[3]

My old *Great* Grandfather—if he can be found, may go to the Housekeeper's Room——he spent one Year in The Tower of London, so he is used to be *misplaced.*—If you want further Directions Mrs. Hoare or Miss Thrale can give them.

Adieu! and God bless You, and Your amiable Family. Mrs. Mead can sort the Prints if She will take the Trouble.——[4]

Text Hyde Collection. *Address* Mr: Clement Mead Surveyor &c./ Upper Charlotte Street/ Fitzroy Square/London. *Postmark* BATH MY <17> 18<13>.

1. William Parr (fl. 1779–1817), a merchant whose business house was at 10 Norfolk Street, Strand.
2. HLP refers to a drawing of Bachygraig by SL.
3. On the third day of the sale of Streatham Park's contents, the following items were sold: lot 51—"six prints, after *Collins,* from Tasso's Jerusalem Delivered"; lot 52—"Les marchands des Chevaux et les Chasseurs, after *Wouvermans,* and six others from ditto"; lot 53—"L'Entretien and four others, after Teniers"; lot 54—"Vue de Skevrin, after *Ruysdall,* Vue de Santvliet, after *Vandrever,* two prints of Horses, and View in Corsica"; lot 55—"Seven Very Fine Prints Of The Interior Of The Vatican." See *Sale Catalogue* (1).
4. The second wife of Clement Mead was Emma *Eliza* Robson, one of the five daughters of the bookseller James Robson. See the letters of Mead to HLP from 1794 to 1796 (Ry. 607.14, 17, 36, 37). See also his will, signed on 10 June 1837, filed and proved 9 February 1839 (P.R.O., Prob. 11/1907/108).

TO THE REVEREND THOMAS SEDGWICK WHALLEY

No. 11 North Parade Bath
Monday 17: May 1813.

My Dear Sir

Is good Miss Williams quite correct when She tells me our kind Friends Doctor and Mrs. Whalley left Bath without having received any Letter from their so much obliged H:L:P.? I had the honour to write from Blake's London Wednesday the 5th of May——the 6th of May it was; promising half presumptuously to come to Mendip after the 6th of June. It is the 16th now; and I am happily enabled to *repeat* my Promise.[1] The amiable Lutwyches are wretched from *his* Rheumatism;—but I hope Danger is far away; and that We shall have a chearful meeting.[2]

London harrassed my Inside a little, but the Bath Pump is doing it a World of Good; and I *can* eat one small Bone of the Neck of Mutton *now.* Salusbury

and I have been separated for a long Time but I expect him this next Week——
Lord Lyttelton said you know as he walked round Ranelagh, that Pleasure and
Comfort always seemed to be in the next Box.[3] It has been so with me for these
Two or Three Months I think——May they long reside at Mendip Lodge, and
in Three Weeks be witnessed by Dear Doctor Whalley's Holyday Friends; who
mean to be with *him*, and his charming Lady Some Day in the Whitsun Week—
when these horrible Storms are all over.

Till then and ever/ believe me Your Faithful/ as Obliged Servant/ H: L: Piozzi.

Text Berg Collection +. *Address* Rev: Doctor Whalley/ Mendip Lodge/ near/ Bristol. *Postmark* BATH <M 18 > <109>.

1. As early as 13 February, TSW had promised himself "the delight of receiving you, and Dear
Mr. Salusbury, at Mendip Lodge, with open Arms and Heart, about the middle of Rose Month of
June" (Ry. 564. 25). See also TSW's invitation in his letters of 19 April and 19 May 1813 (Ry. 564.26, 27).
2. William Lutwyche's complaint was not rheumatism but gout, for whose alleviation he was to
spend June through September at Buxton.
3. For William Henry, Lord Lyttelton, see HLP to LC, 24 September 1808, n. 5.

TO MARIANNE FRANCIS

Bath Saturday
5: June 1813.

Think not Dear Marianne that I should employ Wit or Wisdom or Ingenuity if
I had them, in Defence of Public or Private *Entertainments.*—I do not think we
came hither to *entertain* ourselves or others; nor can suppose that the *best* of
them are considered as better than half permitted Follies—by those who judge
rightly—if any such there are.[1]

Meanwhile St. Paul you know quotes a Comedy of Menander,[2] who certainly
gave no better Lessons in Morality than poor Moreton;[3] and tho' the Clerks
ruined themselves and their Master at the Playhouse, it was probably the Fault
of *Auditresses* rather than Performers. Of the various Mortals I have known in
this "Worky-Day-World" my Heart and Experience tell me that few if any purer
Souls were ever dismissed their House of Clay than that of Dimond the Bath
Actor and Manager:——not a Debt unpaid, not a Duty unperformed: half the
Town followed him to the Grave with Tears, nor could the Clergyman who
administered the Sacrament to him in the Abbey Church only *one Sunday before;*
read the Burial Service over him without *Sobs.*[4] I who have often dined and
supped with him and his Wife always said, that no Man knew how to say Grace
but dear Dimond; and those who lived still more familiarly in the Family asserted the same of his Morning and Evening Prayers.

Garrick—tho' no spotless Character like *his*, was rather less a Rake than any
of the Wits who kept him Company: an Exemplary Husband certainly and a
beneficent Friend[5]——he was a better Thing still and <Several lines obliter-

ated.>——no Arrow sticks; so here is an honest Chronicle of People I never
thought of praising till you put me on't——and all without one Word of charming Siddons.

Well! now give my best Compliments and Wishes to your Aunt D'Arblaye——
whose Panegyric I have often made; and never recanted——Lady Keith's and
Miss Thrale's Letters are full of her whenever they write to me: and when her
new Book comes out, we shall hear the Echo of her Merited Praise I doubt not,
from London and from Paris. I know the People *say* these Murders fright them,
but much is said which one cannot believe.[6] What Dr. Johnson said once, I am
however daily *forced* to believe:[7] That He who committed a new Crime—or
committed any Crime in a new Way, so as to attract public Attention; was guilty
in a double Sense; for added he, some one else will do it before six Months are
out, perhaps *sooner*, and more People than one or Two; 'tis like the first Fellow
who <turns> his Back in a

<The> other <Men   die stood> firm but for him——how great therefore
is His Guilt? and how exemplary ought to be his Punishment? Was not the
Duke of Cumberland's Assassin he who led the Way to these Atrocities?[8] I think
so——Then followed the dreadful Death of Marrs, Williamsons,[9] Percival, and
the Farmer near Chester, who was murdered by His Wife Edith Morray and her
Sweetheart:[10] but none more unprovoked as it appears than this last——or that
which resembles it nearest—The killing Count and Countess D'Entraigues, as
they were stepping into their Coach.[11] The Idea of Joseph being condemned to
Wicklow Goal by Potiphar, an Egyptian Courtier, is ludicrous enough; but I am
perswaded many People go on thinking (when they *do* think) of what they
read——in precisely the same Way.[12] A Friend told me once that reading Pope's
Lines how some

> Man proceeded, and with round unthinking Face,
> He first the Snuff Box open'd, then the Case:[13]

why said the Reader that was wrong to be sure, because he should have opened
the Case first, to get at the Snuffbox.

Apropòs to Miss *Hett*, Her Grandfather by a Strange Disposition of his Wealth
has left her Forty Thousand Pounds *independant;*—lest She should be ill used—
he said.——A few Years will shew the Consequences of such Wrong-headedness
I doubt not.[14]

Farewell Dear Friend! direct to Dr. Whalley's Mendip Lodge near Bristol if
you write *soon*—if *late* to Brynbella;—Denbigh N. Wales. Accept our united Regards, and believe me ever Affectionately Yours/ H: L: Piozzi.

Text Berg Collection, m.b. *Address* Miss Marianne Francis/ at W. Wilberforce's
Esq./ Kinsington Gore/ Middlesex. *Postmark* 10 o'Clock JU 8<   >; BATH <   >.

1. HLP responds to MF's letter of 3 June (Ry. 583.114), in which she excoriated the theater as a
place of immorality.
2. In *Thraliana*, 2:1076, HLP wrote: "St Paul was much a reading Man we know; & scorns not
to quote Epimenides, Aratus and Menander."

Such information was part of a late Renaissance tradition enunciated, e.g., by Lancelot Andrewes. Thus, in "One of the Sermons upon the II. Commandment Preached in the Parish Church of St. Giles Cripplegate, Jan. 9 An. Dom. 1592": ". . . they find S. *Paul*, in matter of doctrine, alleaging *Aratus* a heathen Writer, in his Sermon at *Athens* [Acts 17:28]. And againe, in matter of life, alleadging *Menander*, a Writer of Comœdies, in his Epistle [1 Cor. 15:33]: and thirdly, in matter of report onely without any urgent necessity, alleaging Epimenides, or as some think Callimachus." See the Appendix to *Ninety-Six Sermons* (London: Richard Badger, 1629), 31.

3. The dramatist Thomas Morton (ca. 1764–1838) was recognized as a man of virtue and regular habits.

4. See HLP to Q, 18 February 1812.

5. HLP wrote of Garrick's moral stance in *Retrospection*, 2:394: "Even then, when custom had wiped off the blush from Nature's cheek, and vice was naturalized by the name of fashion, *even then he* swept away offensive passages from many plays, restored those which had good tendencies, gave no encouragement to vicious characters, and added to talents unseen before, and unexpected to be ever seen again, such beneficence of heart and integrity of character, as gave even the most strict moralists among us hope, that where the poison grew, there had we found the antidote."

6. Several murders had been committed in 1813, from January to the end of May. The most shocking had been the murder of Mr. and Mrs. Thomson Bonar at Chiselhurst on 30 May. When they were discovered the next day, Bonar was dead and his wife dying, both having been bludgeoned by their footman, Philip Nicholson. For him it was a spur-of-the-moment act for which "he can assign no motive . . . he had no enmity or ill-will of any kind against Mr. and Mrs. Bonar."

See *GM* 83, pt. 1 (1813):582–83 for an account of the Bonar murders; and pp. 80, 175, 382 for other instances of *"wilful murder."*

7. See particularly the last paragraph of *Rambler* 70 on the human instinct of imitativeness.

8. For the presumed attack on the duke of Cumberland, see HLP to TSW, 1 July 1810. Yet at the time of the attack, HLP questioned the guilt of the alleged attacker. In her 1810 "Pocket Book," she had written of her "Doubts concerning the Duke of Cumberland's Assassination" (15 June), and on 4 July her sympathy for "Poor Sellis."

9. See HLP to TSW, 20 December 1811, n. 10.

10. On 16 April 1812, *The Times* had reported the murder of George Murray, a farmer near Nantwich, his brains having been "dashed out, and his throat cut from ear to ear." The murder had been planned by the farmer's wife, aged forty, and a male servant, aged nineteen: "that in the night they fell upon [George Murray] with an axe, and beat him about the head, until they thought him dead, and struck out one of his eyes; they then left him, but he was yet living; they returned to their work of blood, and again retired, under the persuasion that he had breathed his last: they were still disappointed, and although the wife pressed the man to go and finish his master, he said he could not resume the task; and he refused, until she removed his scruples, by furnishing him with a razor: then the work was completed."

11. HLP refers to the murder of Louis-Emmanuel-Henri-*Alexandre* de Launay (1753–1812), comte d'Antraigues, a political adventurer, and his wife on 22 July 1812. Planning to visit Lord Canning, they were murdered by an Italian servant at Barnes Terrace, near London.

12. MF in her letter repeats a comic story told her by a woman who taught in a school for poor children near Dublin. "There is a place in County Wicklow for imprisonment; and the people call going to *jail*, going to Wicklow. The same Lady was asking where that good Joseph was sent by King Pharoah—'*sent to Wicklow* Maam' was the answer—meaning to *prison*. The *chronology* of Joseph in Wicklow Jail!" For the Joseph story, see Genesis 39:19–23.

13. See *The Rape of the Lock,* 4.125–26.

14. The rich Emily Frances Hett of Bloomsbury would die unmarried in 1839.

TO CLEMENT MEAD

Mendip Lodge
Langford near Bristol
14: June 1813.

Mrs. Piozzi sends Mr. Mead another Hundred Pounds; and when She looks over the Expence which Streatham Park has been to her——since this Year came *in*, which is not half *out* yet; She does really feel quite shocked.

Letting the Place will however do *no Good*; Mr. Mead must Set the Grass, and sell the Garden Produce to the best Advantage; and he must take the Money in Aid of Repairs, and Send her the Accounts to Brynbella remembering the Confidence She places in him, and resolving to do his best for the Interest of/ his true Friend/ H: L: Piozzi.

Text Karl I. Sifferman Collection.

TO ALEXANDER LEAK

Mendip Wednesday
23: June 1813.

I just write to say We certainly do mean to set out tomorrow, and feel impatient now to arrive at home: tho' it would be Silly to forbear seeing all the Beauties that present themselves in our way thither, and I do half expect being detained a Day by pretty Mrs. Wells of Piercefield.[1]

Hereford Cathedral too is worth looking at; we will—if possible contrive to be there on Sunday: There was a sharp Frost last Night, and so there was on the Night of the 16th of June, but *this* was worse still, and less to be expected on one of the longest Days throughout the Year——Mr. and Mrs. Lutwyche are gone fowards to Buxton, the very Journey I meant to take had my Purse proved stronger: they intend us a short visit at Brynbella if he is well enough[2]——which I hardly dare hope, but his Friends fancy Buxton is to cure him of all Complaints.

My Notion is, *we* may reach Shrewsbury on Tuesday; and if not detained in that Neighbourhood, come home directly: but still there are the Ladies at Llangollen who will not Suffer us to pass peaceably without calling on them.

I have at last heard from Mrs. Mostyn bidding me direct to *her* Post Office Weymouth.

Her Handwriting was very welcome to Your/ true Friend/ H: L: P.

Text Hyde Collection. *Address* Mr. Alexander Leak/ Brynbella/ near Denbigh/ North Wales.

1. For Harriet Wells, née Este, see HLP to LC, 1 May 1802, n. 2.
2. The Lutwyches never made the visit to Brynbella, returning to Bath immediately upon quitting Buxton. See Mary Lutwyche to HLP, 19 July 1813 (Ry. 556.140).

TO ALEXANDER LEAK

Chepstow
25: June at Night 1813.

After seeing Mendip and Piercefield and the fine Prospects from Wind Cliff Hill——We are beginning to turn our Heads towards Brynbella, and hope to sleep tomorrow Night at Hereford and go to Cathedral Service there—next Day. Fryday or Saturday—at *farthest* for that Reason, will take us to dear Home. I shall have spent exactly 3 Months in Rambling, and expect to see Hay Making in full Perfection. The Grass is cutting here all round us, and the People are hoping their Hay Harvest will compensate a Want of Apples seldom experienced. Mead says mine are not spoiled—They will be very valuable; and if those Potatoes we saw at Streatham Park prosper, That Place will run alone soon; and I shall have a better Balance than *Seven* Pounds next Year perhaps after all.

Cold Meat will be best if we come sooner or later than I mention; for one knows not how one may be detained on the Road, and we must see Tintern Abbey &c. The Weather is better for Travelling than for any other Purpose; a bright Sun and cool Air makes it charming, and our Passage across the Channel was very delightful indeed.

Doctor Whalley and his Lady are neither of them well, but Mr. Amans looks in good Health.

Mr. Salusbury is pretty well and so is his Affectionate/ Aunt and Your/ good Friend/ H: L: P.

Text Hyde Collection. *Address* Mr: Alexander Leak/ Brynbella/ near Denbigh/ North Wales. *Postmark* CH<EPSTOW>.

TO THE REVEREND THOMAS SEDGWICK WHALLEY

Brynbella
July 7th 1813.

My dear Doctor Whalley
——Said I must not write on the Road, and the Road lasted till Yesterday. We are but just come home, and feel Impatient to acknowledge the Happiness and Kindness we met with at beautiful Mendip—a Beauty celebrated sufficiently to justify her if Capricious, yet uniformly amiable and obliging. Have you and Mrs.

Whalley mended in Your Health? and have You heard how poor Mr. Lutwyche goes on? no longer *poor* Mr. Lutwiche I hope, but walking to Derby as he threatened; and directing his Course to Brynbella. Ours ran through Chepstow to Piercefield and Wind Cliffe, and Tintern Abbey and Monmouth; The Approach to which Town along the Common high Road has never been admired half enough, or I have never read the Notes of Admiration it deserves.

Through Hereford we drove to Ludlow Castle, and had the Fortune of a fine Day for every fine Sight on our Journey—particularly Tintern Abbey where the Gleams of Sunshine illuminating the Gloom caused by a Growth of Ivy somewhat too little checkt, felt really very striking. I never had seen so fine a Piece of Gothic before in any Country, and have not yet done wondering why such Places impress the Imagination with Ideas of *Antiquity* far more than can the Colisseum at Nice or Verona: tho' when they were erected, Monmouthshire was inhabited by Wolves I trust; not embellished with elegant and expensive Architecture. Well, through Hereford we ran forward to Ludlow, and saw the Place where grew the Wood, celebrated by Milton as the Habitation of *Comus* which Mrs. Whalley and I saw represented in the most *appropriate* Manner possible—only the Costume was somewhat *cold* for the Latitude of Ludlow——at least its *Appearance.*[1]

Shropshire Hospitality delayed us next, and we passed one Week with our agreeable Friends at Longnor, where among other Chat we learned that Lady Eleanor Butler had fractured her Arm, and dislocated her Shoulder—a Visit at Llangollen in our Way home, confirmed the Account; but She is well and merry, and was not Confined to her Bed an hour it seems:—So strong is her Constitution.

But I am too long talking of anybody but Lord Wellington; his useful Efforts will be felt far. The Ice is *Starred* as Skaiters call it, by Fall of the French in Spain: but the *Tread* will be rendered dangerous to Napoleon in the North.[2] And though his Subjects may be contented for a while to see their Country made a Barrack, because it was so lately a Slaughterhouse; we may be Sure they can't like it long—and Peace will be much accelerated by this Battle of Vittoria.[3]

Dear Mrs. Whalley has many Correspondents who will tell her the Particulars of the Regent's Fête;[4]—my Female Friends inform me that the newest occurrence there was the Miscarriage of Lady Caroline Wood, who was taken suddenly ill in the Ball Room, and conveyed to her House *in Blankets.*[5]

Che Mondo Mais! as the Italians express it.

Whilst I continue to make one of the Croud, I will continue to rejoyce in the flattering Distinction of a Friendship so valuable as yours has always been to Dear Sir Yours most faithfully/ H: L: Piozzi.

Dear Salusbury sends a Thousand Compliments.

If Mrs. Whalley should hear of a Place for *my Bessey* at Bath among Friends there, I think I could recommend her as a Valuable Servant—particularly where there are Sick People or Children.

Text Berg Collection +. *Address* Rev: Doctor Whalley/ Mendip Lodge/ Langford/ near/ Bristol. *Postmark* <DENBIGH 224>.

1. *A Mask* ("Comus") was first presented [1634] at Ludlow Castle to celebrate the earl of Bridgewater's election as lord president of Wales. HLP remembers particularly "this drear wood,/ The nodding horror of whose shady brows/ Threats the forlorn and wandering passenger" (lines 37–39).
2. After his defeat in Russia in 1812, Napoleon "in the North" faced an enlarged Sixth Coalition as Prussia joined Russia in March. The allied monarchs—Alexander and Friedrich Wilhelm—made their headquarters in Dresden and put their joint field army under Count Wittgenstein and Blücher.
    While HLP would have recognized the victories of Napoleon at Lützen and Bautzen in May, she knew from newspaper accounts that the exhausted French could not pursue the allied army. Moreover, there were newspaper predictions of the further strengthening of the Sixth Coalition with the addition of Austria, Sweden, and several German states.
3. HLP's interpretation of the allied victory at Vittoria (Vitoria) is virtually a summary of the newspaper accounts of the battle. Like them, she sees the battle fought on 21 June 1813 as Wellington's triumph, with France open to allied armies and forced to sue for peace. See the *Morning Post* and the *Morning Chronicle* for 5 May, particularly the former, which likened the victory at Vittoria to those "of Cressy, of Agincourt, of Blenheim."
4. On 30 June the Prince Regent "gave a ball and supper to a numerous and splendid party." Invitations had been sent to almost a thousand people; fresh flowers were brought from Kew, Kensington Palace, and Hampton Court, to decorate Carlton House. Eighteen tents were set up on the lawn, where supper was to be served. (Because of the heavy downpour of rain, few dared to use either the tents or the promenade that led to them.) The ball was a success, the queen and the princesses staying until after five in the morning and many of the guests until after six. See *The Times* for 1 and 2 July 1813.
5. HLP refers to Lady Caroline Stewart (d. 1865), daughter of the marquess of Londonderry, who on 23 December 1801 had married Thomas Wood (d. 1860), forty years M.P. for Brecknockshire.

TO THE REVEREND THOMAS SEDGWICK WHALLEY

Brynbella
Tuesday, 3: August 1813.

My dear Dr. Whalley seems, as far as I can judge, to have told my future fortune very exactly. It will not be a fortune to rejoice or to lament over; and, since this child would not thrust himself forward in the career of ambition, or list under the hard taskmaster Avarice, but prefer the sober path of private life in hope of domestic happiness, what can I do but pray for his success, and promote it as far as I am able?[1]

The family he connects with are, in all appearance, much respected by their neighbours; very honourable, and very ancient; proud Salopians! *plus noble que riche*; but individually well bred and agreeable.[2] He is with them at Parkgate now, on a sea-bathing frolic, and will bring them here on this day sevennight. I shall receive them kindly, and persuade them to wait patiently, if possible, till an early period in the year 1815.[3]

How many things may happen before that time, indeed, frights me, more than it will fright them. The mind's eye, like that of the body, flattens with age, and drives near objects to a distant perspective, hoping to obtain a clearer view. Youth sees distinctly through purer medium, and must be often deceived, before it can believe deceits exist at all. We must do as well as we can.

My old friend Sir Lucas Pepys is married again;[4] he says three years of complete misery was enough for him, and he will once more try to be happy. I were a monster not to pursue his course, whichever road he takes, with fervent good wishes; and dear Siddons ought to join with me.[5] Give her my best and kindest remembrances.[6] She will not help us to care about Austria's defection,[7] which I dread daily to hear of, but she will be sorry the plague is at Malta, because Gibraltar is so near that island, and we have such constant connection now with every part of Spain.[8]

Mrs. Mostyn is not come home yet. Hannah More does me much honour; she named me to Miss Marianne Francis, who caught her at Mr. Wilberforce's, and enjoyed an hour's tête-à-tête with her.[9] We have been parching with drought here, whilst your beautiful valley was drenched with rain; but

> Brynbella to Mendip sends grateful and greeting,
> And grieves that such mountains are hinder'd from meeting.

Mrs. Lutwyche has written, but her letter is more kind than cheerful: her good husband's best days are, I see, completely past. Whilst yet he lives he will enjoy a little *jeu de mots,* and, if you see him before me, do tell him how one of our new-fangled poets said to a friend of mine, that he had really made up a tolerable fortune, and would now marry and settle in the country, where, added he, 'I have already taken one step in my new character, by becoming a magistrate.' 'A magistrate!' re-echoes the merry man, 'a magistrate! why then do, dear sir, put your money in the Stocks, and send your poems to the House of Correction.'

This moment brings me accounts of poor Dr. Randolph's death, the Bishop of London.[11] Now let us see if Fisher stands well with his young princess, whose recommendation—if she enforces it the way we were talking of—must, I should think, be very powerful.[12] He was a charming creature when we knew him abroad, and called him the King's Fisher.[13] Our Bishop Cleaver[14] was the man appointed to show Oxford to Louis XVIII. of France: he commends the King's scholarship and good breeding extremely; but how odd it was, that when they opened a Virgil in the Bodleian, the first line presenting itself should be, "Quæ regio in terris, nostri non plena laboris.' 'Ah! monseigneur,' cried Louis Dixhuit, 'fermons vite, j'ai eu assez de ça.' 'Why, my lord,' said I, 'were you seeking the Sortes Virgilianæ on purpose?' 'No,' replied he, 'nor ever thought of it.'[15] Once more, adieu! dear sir, and continue your partial kindness,/ So valued by your/ H: L: Piozzi.

Adieu! dear Dr. Whalley, and present me most kindly to your fair and amiable lady, and make sweet Siddons recollect the happy hours we have spent together. Lady Keith is well, and has her youngest sister with her.

Text Wickham, 2:365–67.

1. HLP had learned of JSPS's intended marriage to Harriet Maria Pemberton (1794–1831) early in July.

2. For the Pembertons of Longnor, see HLP to JSPS, 20 August 1808, n. 1.

3. JSPS was to marry on 7 November 1814, two months after his twenty-first birthday.

4. Sir Lucas Pepys married secondly, on 29 June 1813, Deborah, née Askew (1764–1848).

5. Sir Lucas was once SS's physician; see HLP to TSW, 3 June 1790, n. 5.

6. According to TSW's letter, dated 22 July (Ry. 564.28): "Dear solemn, sublime Siddons is to grace my Mountain Eyrie the 1st of next Month. I wish you could have met her here. You alone possess the Talent of making Melpomene laugh, as if she were transformed into her Sister Thalia."

7. Anticipating Austria's joining the Sixth Coalition, England instead found her indecisive during the month of July—or at least English newspapers found her too eager to resume negotiations with Napoleon. On 14 July the *Courier* reported that "a short dispatch from Buonaparte announces the arrival of the Austrian Minister, Count Metternich, at Dresden, and his having several conferences with Maret."

On 28 July the same newspaper wrote that "Austria is rumoured to have insisted on a prolongation of the Armistice [with France] to afford another opportunity for removing the difficulties in the way of negociation."

8. *The Times* on 27 July 1813 announced that "In consequence of the yellow fever being prevalent at Malta, and being supposed to be at Carthagena and other places in the Mediterranean, it is said to be the intention of Government to order all vessels to perform quarantine which may arrive from that quarter, until it is known that the contagious disorder has disappeared."

9. William Wilberforce had a house at Kensington Gore, where MF met him in the winter of 1812. She was drawn to him as one of the affluent leaders of the evangelical Clapham sect who were dedicated in the House of Commons and the political arena to the liberalization of anti-Catholic laws, the abolition of the slave trade, and ultimately of slavery itself.

For Wilberforce, see HLP to Sophia Byron, 29 June 1788, n. 10.

10. TSW on 22 July described Lutwyche's condition: "Poor dear Lutwyche puts his best Leg forward, to shamble about the confined Walks, at Buxton! . . . A few Bathings have fixed his wandering pains in his Hands. Buxton Doctors call this local Pain and swelling by the noble name of gout. But I suspect that it is of an illegitimate kind, and then Bastard of Rheumatism."

11. John Randolph died unexpectedly on 28 July "of apoplexy, whilst on a visit to his son, at Hadham, in Hertfordshire, aged 64." See *GM* 83, pt. 2 (1813):187–88.

12. John Fisher (1748–1825) had become bishop of Salisbury in 1807, HLP expecting him to move higher in the ecclesiastical hierarchy through court favor, which began as early as 1780.

In 1805 George III, e.g., appointed him to superintend the education of Princess Charlotte of Wales. Although he performed his obligation conscientiously, he was not translated from his bishopric.

13. In 1785 John Fisher went to Italy, where he met the Piozzis. On 14 July 1786 he was called home by George III to a canonry at Windsor.

14. For William Cleaver, bishop of St. Asaph, see HLP to LC, 11 October 1806, n. 2.

15. Sometime during the spring or early summer of 1813, Louis XVIII was shown about Oxford by William Cleaver who, as master of Brasenose from 1785 to 1809, had come to know the university well. For a fuller account of the incident, see HLP to Q, 9 August 1813, and "Harvard Piozziana," vol. 5.

TO CLEMENT MEAD

Brynbella Fryday
6: August 1813.

Dear Mr. Mead's Letters are enough to make one Wild. Why must the hot houses tumble down after all this Ocean of Money spent on the Place? and why must Potatoes sell for nothing at Streatham, when they bear a good Price every where else?

How can You think of my sending Leak to London *now* just before Harvest and Planting Season?——Must I be ruined in Wales and Surrey both? and both at the Same Time?

I had not Confidence in my *own Life* to give Bills for such a remote Time;—
You know that Streatham is to *me* a Life Estate only: go to Mr. Windle, and tell
your Story to him: and take him the enclosed Letter, and act by his Advice:
which you may tell him I will abide by./ Who am Your true Friend and his/
Faithful humble Servant/ H: L: Piozzi.

I don't want Gillow to get on, I have written to him to stand still; I do not
want *more* Expences.

Text Hyde Collection. *Address* Mr. Clement Mead/ Surveyor &c./ Upper Charlotte
Street/ Fitzroy Square/ London. *Postmark* DENBIGH 22<4>.

TO LADY KEITH

> Brynbella Monday
> 9: August 1813.

I waited so long to Thank dearest Lady Keith for her kind Letter, that I might
tell you the Success of my Petition for a poor Seaman's Heirs. I do begin to
think Some Money will be got for them—Mr. Jackson has been so very kind
and polite.[1] The Extracts I made from the good Lad's Letters seem to have struck
his fancy; as indeed they did mine; provoking Tears and Laughter by Turns,
thro' many a dirty, many an ill spelt Page.

Apropòs to *Pages:* The Bishop of St. Asaph told me an odd Thing the other
Day, without appearing to intend it. He was shewing Oxford to Louis dixhuit
he said,—and when they came to the Bodleian Library—reached down an old
curious Virgil; which the King Opened at this Line

> Quæ regio in Terris nostra non plena Laboris?[2]

and Ah Monsiegneur exclaimed his Majesty—Fermons vite; j'ai eu assez de ça.
Were you looking professedly for Sortes Virgilianæ said I my Lord?[3] On the
contrary replied our Diocesan, such a Thought never crossed my Mind. Why
then replied Your H:L:P. it must be confessed a very strange Combination; because I believe no Crowned Head has tried that Trick in that Place, since Charles
the 1st: of England walking there with Lord Falkland before the fatal Battle
where *his* Son was killed,[4] suffered that Nobleman to perswade him——to pull
down that *very Book,* and Search his Fortune in it. The result is well known.
Charles opening the Virgil read aloud

> ————jacet ingens litore Truncus,
> Avulsumque humeris Caput, et sine Nomine Corpus.[5]

Doctor *Johnson,* (who told me the Story) as I dare say you remember; added that
when Lord Falkland saw the King change Colour, he instantly endeavoured to

laugh off the Impression; and shutting up the Book—said he would try *his own Fate* and convince his Majesty such Things were all mere Accident. He opened however at the pathetic Lamentation of Evander over his Son Pallas slain in Aeneas's Cause

Haud ignarus eram &c. &c. Book 11th:[6]

and felt his Voice falter as Evander's did

Et via vix tandem Voci laxata dolore est.[7]

And now can you tell me where one may read this Anecdote? I have searched Clarendon over and over in vain:[8] and am inclined <to> think the Bishop believes it all my own Invention. Pray *pray* bear me Witness to the Tale, I am convinced <you> cannot have forgotten it.

If Mrs. Mostyn is with You, or near You, give her my best Regards: and say how much She is wished for in Wales—where a fine house will make none of us Compensation for her Loss—and least of any—Hers and Your own/ Affectionate/ H: L: Piozzi.

<I *say*> and I pretend to believe, that Lord Keith is at home <now>; and that my Letter goes free of Course. I'm glad you <like the> Concur Story, tho' I certainly have told it you before.

Text Bowood Collection. *Address* R: H: Baroness Keith.

1. Randle Jackson (1757–1837), parliamentary counsel of the East India Company and the corporation of London.
2. See HLP to JSPS, 11 April 1813, n. 6.
3. At least as early as Hadrian (A.D. 76–138), reference has been made to the *Sortes Virgilianae*, a method of divination effected by opening the works of Virgil at random and noting the lines covered by one's thumb in order to predict the future.
4. Henry Cary or Carey (d. 1633), first viscount Falkland (1620), lord deputy of Ireland and a favorite of Charles I.
His son was Lucius (1610–43), second viscount. At first a supporter of the Parliamentary Party, he switched sides by 1641 and became a secretary of state to the king from 1642 to 1643. Present at the battle of Edgehill and the siege of Gloucester, he was killed in the first battle of Newbury on 20 September when he undertook a suicide mission.
5. *Aeneid*, 2.556–58, wherein Charles saw in the destruction of Troy the destruction of his kingdom and himself. HLP records this incident, ca. 6 September 1813, in "Harvard Piozziana."
6. *Aeneid*, 11.154.
7. *Aeneid*, 11.151. This line and that in n. 6 are part of a larger passage (lines 139–80), which describes Evander's grief as he falls prone on the bier of his son, Pallas.
8. HLP refers to Edward Hyde (1609–74), first earl of Clarendon (1661) and *The History of the Rebellion and Civil Wars in England, begun in the year 1641*, 3 vols. (Oxford: Printed at the Theatre, 1704).

TO CLEMENT MEAD

Brynbella
Monday 16: August 1813.

Mrs. Piozzi has at least found in Mr. Windle a Friend who *pities* the Enormous Expences She has been perswaded to go to, for Repairs of Streatham Park;— where he says the Rain is now raining *in* after 1250£ has been paid, and the new Cielings damaged!! Oh dreadful! and Mr. Mead calling for Money——when the Front of the House is discoloured even before *all the Ladies* have Seen it.

I did not tell Mr. Windle that Your Estimate was 1700£ only, and cannot *now* find out how much You would wish to exceed it. For God's Sake do not fright me out of my Senses, as well as out of my Money; but recollect that it is Inhuman to force me on Spending so for an Estate I have only my Life in.

Pray send Word what Cows and Horses are on the Park, and how much they pay a Week. I shall expect 500£ for my Hay before this Year is out: and the Potatoes *must* bring *Something.*

Assure yourself my good Mr. Mead that there is not a Man or Woman in England who could bear so much, with the Patience shewn/ by Yours Sincerely/ H: L: Piozzi.

Horses pay more than Cows; do they not? Pray write either to Leak or to me.

I am excessively sorry too about Gillow: but hope my Furniture is safe.—Ask him, and send me word how *little* Money—not how *much* is absolutely necessary to make the Place *profitable* for you know I do not want it to be dressed up for a House to spend Money *in*——but to make the Estate such as I may get Money *from*—to clear me of these Miseries.

Surely, *Surely* You will *repair* the House——into the old 1250£——Oh Mr. Mead! I little thought to have heard that Rain could enter such *costly* Roofs as *mine* and spoil my new Cielings and Beds, even *before* they are *used.*—Oh *poor* H: L: Piozzi!!

Text Hyde Collection. *Address* Mr. Clement Mead Surveyor &c./ Upper Charlotte Street/ Fitzroy Square/ London. *Postmark* DENBIGH; 18 AU 18 1813.

TO SAMUEL LYSONS

Brynbella
22: August 1813.

Mrs. Piozzi presents her most respectful Compliments to her old Friend Mr. Lysons as Governor of the British Institution; with an earnest Request that he will protect her Portraits from being copied, as She was strictly promised before She could consent to lend them.——it would break *her* Heart, and ruin the Value of the Pictures to Posterity: and now some Artist living at No. 50, Rathbone Place who spells his Name So that she cannot read it——unless 'tis Joseph:[1] writes to her begging he may copy the Portrait of Doctor Johnson——when She was hoping all the four were by this Time restored to their Places at old Streatham Park.

Mrs. Piozzi wishes Mr. Lysons Joy of his Brother's Marriage,[2] but hopes he himself is not now at Hemstead Hall, as She knows not where to apply.

Text Hyde Collection. *Address* Samuel Lysons Esq. / Keeper of the Records &c. &c. &c. &c./ Tower of/ London.[3] *Postmark* DENBIGH 224; 24 AU 24 1813.

1. 50 Rathbone Place was occupied by G. Jackson, "composition ornamental manufacturer."
2. Widowed for five years, DL married on 2 July 1813 Josepha Catherine Susanna, née Cooper (d. 1868). The marriage was a matter of convenience. In a conversation with Joseph Farington, 7 May 1811, DL "said he had no prospect of Domestic Comfort but in another marriage, & that He had seen a Lady . . . who appeared suited to Him. He required for His Children, a Superintendant of His Family, & shd. wish for a woman of from 30 to 35 years of age." See Farington, 11:3925.
3. In December 1803 SL had been appointed keeper of the records at the Tower of London. With that appointment, he ceased to practice law.

TO CLEMENT MEAD

Brynbella
4: October 1813.

Mr. Mead says, and I confess my last Letter written under the Impression of very disagreable feelings. Can you tell me any Thing to lighten that Impression?
My Bankers Book tells me

	£
That you received on the 26th of August 1812.	100:0:0
Leak paid you on the 28th of October 1812.	150:0:0
Leak paid you again upon the 13: January 1813.	110:0:0
Leak paid you again on the 15th January 1813.	100:0:0
and to Southey he paid	20:0:0
Leak like wise paid to Mead	
and Southey 8th February 1813.	200:0:0
Draft on the 23d March Ditto	100:0:0
Draft for Southey 30th March Ditto	100:0:0
Draft on the 9th of May	100:0:0
Draft on the 28th of May	100:0:0
Draft 7th June	100:0:0
Draft 14th June	100:0:0
Draft 12th July	100:0:0
Draft 26th July	100:0:0
Draft 21st August	100:0:0
Draft 28th August	300:0:0
	£ 1880:0:0

already paid: and pray how much more is to go? The Estimate is already exceeded 200£ and *do* my good Friend—*be* my good Friend; and do not try to make me believe you are suffering Hardships from so true a Wellwisher to you and yours/ as is/ H: L: Piozzi.

Text Hyde Collection. *Address* Mr. Mead/ Streatham Park.

TO THE REVEREND REYNOLD DAVIES

Brynbella
7: November 1813.

My dear Mr. Davies
  I came home but last Night from a Visit to Lady Williams at Bodylwyddan where I often spend my Time when Salusbury is away at Races or Hunts, or whatever calls him from me; at my Return Your excessively kind Letter was the first I opened: Parsons has done well to pay at last, for I really must have *coerced* the Gentleman:[1] You are most welcome to the 10£ <for> the School in May, and very merciful You do not take it sooner. It is a foolish thing to confess, but I know not very perfectly what Money is due to me from him,—or how it becomes due at all; or how I could get quit of all Transactions with him, which is much to be desired——Charles Shephard I dare Say could tell the whole of it, and we shall at last have him to consult I greatly fear, for Things of still more Importance. Do you know whether he is in London?—or gone to Ireland (as Leak thinks) about my Lord de Blaquiere's Affairs? Wherever he is, he has Possession of Dear Salusbury's Letters of Denizenation signed by *Yourself,* by Lord Coventry, Lord Kirkwall, Sir Walter James, and The Rev. Doctor Gray Prebendary of Durham, in the Spring of the Year 1809.[2]——When I say Signed, I only mean that the Petition for Privilege of being Denizen was so signed; and it expressed that it was requested the Child should by those Letters be empowered to take certain Estates expected from Me—as well as I remember—but I forget whether I was *described* or not: it was since Mr. Piozzi's Death. No Naturalization was accounted necessary. My Salusbury is The Second Son I *think*—of Mr. Giambattista Piozzi, who was one of 14 Children, younger than my Husband and bred a Merchant at Brescia in Lombardy—but I fancy had more taste of Gayety than Knowledge of Commerce. He married Theresa Fracessi of a great Mercantile House at Venice and a near Relation (I believe Niece) to the noble Lord Count Lewis Fenerole—but the French Revolution destroyed all hope of Success to Trade, and its subsequent Tyranny having ruined both their Families—My Husband sent for the Boy who was bred up by yourself and who had been previously baptized by Name of My Father John Salusbury—under the Notion probably that I might patronize his little Nephew on A Future day. I am now so sincerely attached to the Young Man that it is my Intention to give him The Estates I possess here in Wales as soon as he comes of Age—meaning on

the 9th Day of September next——and am desirous that he should have *legal* Title to my Name and Arms——The more so, as he has made Choice of a Lady whose Character and *Family* I cannot but approve. The Deeds are however *not drawn* because I thought it was better have this Business settled first but I have made my Will in his Favour giving him the said Estates by Name of John Salusbury Piozzi commonly called and known by the Name of John Piozzi Salusbury. Now for Your Question of Who my Father was? to answer which demand it will be best to go back to Sir John Salusbury of Lleweny

Text Ry. 533.30; a draft.

1. John Parsons (fl. 1784–1819). From 1804 to 1806 he rented land in Streatham from the duke of Bedford. In the latter year his name disappears in the "Land Tax Assessments" only to reappear again from 1812 to 1819. In this seven-year period he himself owned land in Streatham, but he also sublet small tracts from RD and Max Kymer. These two men rented land from HLP, so that in a sense Parsons was a tenant of HLP once removed. See the Streatham "Land Tax Assessments," C.R.O., Surrey.
2. See HLP to JSPS, 1 May 1809 and 30 May [1809].

TO LORD LIVERPOOL

[7–16 November 1813].[1]

If Lord Liverpool knew the Friendship that subsisted between his good Father and Mrs. Piozzi who presents this Memorial—it would not lye long forgotten in the Office[2]——as her heart is deeply interested for its Success; and the consequent Advantages of Denizenation to a Baby snatched fom the Cannon's Mouth when Revolutionary Rage devoured the North of Italy: when We know not whether his Parents remain alive or not.——He has now no Friend but the presenter of this Petition, who whilst her Name was Thrale could have asked few favours which the late Lord Liverpool would have hesitated to bestow/ on Your Servant/ [H: L: Piozzi.]

Text Ry. 533.35; unfinished draft.

1. This letter may be dated between 7 and 16 November 1813 when HLP worked to have JSPS bear "*legal* Title" to her name and arms. Once so named, he was legitimated as her heir.
2. For Robert Banks Jenkinson, second earl of Liverpool, and his father, see HLP to JSPS, 6 May 1809, nn. 3 and 4.
At this time Liverpool was first lord of the treasury, or premier.

TO THE REVEREND THOMAS SEDGWICK WHALLEY

Brynbella
17: November 1813.

My Dear Doctor Whalley

Shall have a Letter as soon, and as many Letters as he pleases; La Conversation des Amis ne tarit pas; And we have Subjects that we like well enough—public and private. I am glad Louis dix huit is at Bath: he will see how we live in our *tight little Island* as Moreton calls it,[1] and I half wish he had heard Siddons read Macbeth at Your House in the Square. All Foreigners are deeply impressed with the Night-walking Scene——and he is really worthy of such Amusement.[2] I think very often Your kind Heart will feel that sweet Duchesse D'Angoulesme's melancholy Charms presenting themselves before you perpetually.[3]

Buonaparte will not now long dishonour the Throne of the old Bourbons. He just was reaching to the Summit of His Ambition, but the Way was so slippery as he went you see,—so wet with human Blood; that he missed his Foot quite *foolishly* at last; and now

> Down, Down the Precipice in haste he goes,
> And sinks in Moments what in Ages rose

Doctor Randolph did not use to be like the High Priest in Homer a denouncer of Mischief and Prophet of Plagues;[4] but we shall see him in another Humour soon.[5] I am glad dear Hannah More is well; We shall no Two States—and Scarce Two Individuals agree what Terms of Peace we shall approve; but every Individual,—and I dare say many States will agree in Subscribing to her superior Merit. And I love her the better for listening to our charming Siddons. I wish I was among you, and must tell Miss Williams so very *soon;* or She will be angry enough, tho' She knows how true it is, without more Repetition.

Poor Mr. Lutwyche's Blow was a very heavy one, and these overcharged Clouds and heavy Rains will add to the Weight—he might recover if he was to Winter at Bayonne under Protection of Lord Wellington.[6]

My runaway Boy has made Shrewsbury Hunt an Excuse to go and get a kind Look from his Harriet, but he comes home to morrow: I really flatter myself Dear Sir, that you would like *her,* and that She would love *you.* Her Form and Figure reminds me always of Lady Kirkwall, but the Expression of her very black Eyes is timid and tender rather than sparkling;—and "Gentleness and Joy make up her being"[7]——I know Dear Dr. Whalley would take her to his heart.

She comes of Age in January next, but Salusbury must go on counting the Moons till September: I think there are no fewer than Nine of them.

And now who will repeat the old Observation that People living in the World—London or Bath—never complain of the Tardiness they find in Country Correspondents; while the Rusticated Rogues of 200 Miles distance, are always—and with Reason lamenting the few Letters they receive from Friends at

London or Paris?—I can always contradict *this* Maxim by shewing Your flattering Commands to me to write away, and not wait for Answers or Requests.

We Country folks are well inclined to think that Style is like Hay; that which gives most Trouble, and takes most Time in making—is sure to be the *worst.* So here's a good Rick of hasty Stuff—which I have just found out is put together on a torne Sheet of Paper too—no additional Recommendation: but must be pardoned. Will you Dear Sir do me the honour to claim a Remembrance for me from our common Friends, and ask Chevalier Boisgelin if it be true that Buonaparte once walking over Versailles with Abbe Sieyes: the last mentioned said, I *think* this was the *Tyrant's Bed.*——Ay Sir, replies the other, and had it been *mine;* I should have slept soundly in it to night—While you were Saying Mass.

These Things are probably made for the People, but it was given me as authentic. Are Stories of Princes *ever* authentic? not I hope those we heard from Langford Court.[8] The Damsel spoken of *then,* lives (I find) in close Amity and voluminous Correspondence with a Lady I just know by Sight, of the Name and Family of her who (I believe) slept in my beautiful Room at Mendip Lodge when I left it. Dear Mrs. Whalley will recollect the Three Syllable Name beginning with an E.[9] Meanwhile here is a tremendous Land and Sea Storm, the noisiest Weather I ever heard so early in the Winter: We begin planting the Mountain to morrow: Those who live to see the Trees grow up will find this House charmingly sheltered by them; and Salusbury's Titmice may reap Profit from them beside. I must leave Things as neat and compact for him as I can—— and as pretty Siddons used to say of her Children: I must pray for them, and then leave them in the hands of God. It delights me to hear so much Good of her Cecilia. Adieu my dear Sir, and pray that I may continue to deserve that unvaried Friendship with which you have/ so long honoured your much Obliged/ H: L: P.

Text Berg Collection +. *Address* Rev: Doctor Whalley/ Queen Square/ Bath. *Postmark* DENBIGH 224.

1. Although HLP attributes the phrase to the dramatist Thomas Morton, it was coined by Thomas John Dibdin (1771–1841) in his song "The Snug Little Island."

2. *Macbeth,* 5.1.

3. For Marie-Thérèse-Charlotte de France, see HLP to LC, 27 December 1795, n. 5.

In 1799 the princess was married to her cousin, Louis-Antoine de Bourbon, duc d'Angoulême. She served as "symbole vivant des horreurs de la Révolution, statue de la douleur figée dans une éternelle mélancholie." See Jules Bertaut, *La Vie aventureuse de Louis XVIII* (1949), 147; *Journals and Letters,* 7:373.

4. The couplet is probably HLP's. For the high priest in Homer, see Pope's translation of the *Iliad,* 1.127–32: "Augur accurst! denouncing Mischief still,/ Prophet of Plagues, for ever boding Ill!"

5. For the Reverend Francis Randolph, see HLP to PSW, 29 August [1791], n.9.

6. HLP uses the city of Bayonne and its citadel to symbolize the anticipated invasion of France by Wellington's troops moving northward from Spain.

7. Nicholas Rowe, *Jane Shore,* 2.1.149.

8. Langford Court in Burrington parish, Somerset, was part of the inheritance of TSW's first wife Elizabeth (Sherwood), née Jones. After her death in 1801 it belonged to TSW, who rented it out before its sale in 1804.

9. The name was probably Errington and the "Lady" therefore a relation of Mrs. Fitzherbert, whose mother was an Errington.

TO JOHN WILLIAMS

Brynbella
20: November 1813.

My Dear Sir

If you have forgotten that you begged me to work You a Butterfly—I have *not* forgotten:—and The Ladies at Bodylwyddan said you made Choice of Black and blue *Ulysses*. He is gone home today—more like the Insect than the Coloured Drawing is; for I looked very lately at him in Bullock's Musæum: but one can make but very mean approaches to the Colouring of Nature.

How short our Lives are! and how sudden our Calls away! Is what I see in the Papers true concerning your Regius Professor? who was once an Acquaintance of mine—or I dream so.[1]

Salusbury is just returned from visiting his Shropshire Friends, with whom he proposes going to spend Christmas and enjoy the annual Festivities of Tredegar, invited by his and Pemberton's College Friend—Young Morgan.[2] We hear that Myddelton delights in his University Life,[3]—no Wonder;—pray make Him accept my Kind Regards: and believe me Dear Sir ever most faithfully yours/ H: L: Piozzi.

Text Ry. 6 (1813–21).

1. Joseph Jowett (b. 1752) received his LL.B. from Trinity College, Cambridge, in 1775 and his LL.D. in 1780. Two years later he was appointed regius professor of civil law. He died on 13 November 1813.
   2. Tredegar, Monmouthshire, was the seat of Charles Morgan (1760–1846), second baronet (1806), M.P. (1787–1831), who had married ca. 1791 Mary Margaret Stoney (d. 1808).
   JSPS was a contemporary of Sir Charles's eldest son, Charles Morgan Robinson Morgan (1792–1875), later Baron Tredegar (1859), who had matriculated at Christ Church, Oxford, 8 May 1811.
   3. The eighteen-year-old Robert Myddelton was at Clare Hall, Cambridge, where he would receive his B.A. (1818) and M.A. (1822).

TO JAMES DISNEY CATHROW, SOMERSET HOUSE

29: November 1813.

Sir[1]

I am sorry to think that Your kind Packet being *Missent* to Chester, reached me but just now: You have made me Very happy by your so obliging Attention, and I shall be most glad to see the Name *properly Gazetted*.[2]

No need to mention Mr. Thrale's Family at all except just as it now stands in the Paper I have the honour to return to you.[3]

The Dates of My Father and Uncle's Births I have corrected by a Manuscript in the Hand Writing of my Grandmother Lucy Salusbury of Bachegraig;[4] the others are right I believe.

My Maternal Great Grandfather and his Wife Hester Salusbury of Lleweney, both lived to a prodigious Age:[5] I have heard my Mother relate that She saw her Grandpapa crack a Peach Stone with *his Teeth* the Day he was 80 Years old; and he died not till many Years after—Your Date is probably correct.

If Mr. Piozzi Salusbury was at home, he would unite in a Thousand Compliments and Thanks with her who has the honour to be [Your faithful Servant/ H: L: Piozzi].

Copy of The Formulary for my Inspection

His Royal Highness the Prince Regent has been pleased to give and grant unto John Salusbury Piozzi Salusbury Esq. second Son of Giambattista Piozzi of Brescia in Lombardy Merchant and Nephew of Gabriel Piozzi late of Brynbella in the County of Flint Esquire deceased, who married Hester Lynch Salusbury only Child and Heir of John Salusbury late of Bachegraig also in the Said County of Flint Esquire deceased: and Relict of Henry Thrale late of Streatham in the County of Surrey Esquire—also deceased: His Majesty's Royal Licence and Authority that he and his Issue may continue to use the Surname of Salusbury in Addition to that of Piozzi: and that he and his Issue may also bear the Arms of Salusbury *only;* out of grateful and affectionate Respect towards the Aforesaid Hester Lynch Piozzi the Widow of his said late paternal Uncle Gabriel Piozzi deceased: such Arms being first duly exemplified according to the Laws of Arms, and recorded in the Herald's Office, otherwise his Majesty's Royal Licence and Permission to be void and of none Effect.

And also to order that his Royal Concession and Declaration be registered in his College of Arms.——

Copy of the Paper sent for my Signature

I do hereby signify my Consent and Desire that John Salusbury Piozzi Salusbury Esq. Nephew of my late Husband Gabriel Piozzi Esq. deceased, and who hath hitherto assumed and used the Surname of Salusbury, with my Approbation, do forthwith apply for his Majesty's Royal Licence, authorizing him and his Issue to continue to use the Surname of Salusbury in Addition to that of Piozzi: and that he and They may also bear the Arms of my Family of Salusbury.

I am the more desirous that the said John Salusbury Piozzi Salusbury should obtain such Royal Licence; as I am about to settle certain Estates and Property upon him: and am anxious that he should legally bear the Surname of Salusbury previously to the Execution of such a Settlement.

Given under my Hand and Seal this 29th day of November 1813./ Hester Lynch Piozzi.

Text Ry. 554.20.

1. James Disney Cathrow (ca. 1778–1854) was rouge dragon pursuivant of arms (1797–1813) and then Somerset herald of arms (1813–54). See Walter H. Godfrey, Sir Anthony Wagner, and H. Stanford London, *The College of Arms . . . being the 16th Monograph of the London Survey Committee* (1963), 163.

2. According to HLP's manuscript note, JSPS "Took the Surname of Salusbury in addition and

the Arms of Salusbury only by Royal Sign Manual bearing date 4 Dec: 1813" (see n. 3 below). But "such Arms" had first to be "duly exemplified according to the Laws of Arms and recorded in the Heralds Office otherwise His Majesty's Royal License and Permission to be void and of none effect." The arms were exemplified 17 December 1813, the document having been signed by "Isaac Heard Principal Garter King of Arms, George Clarenceux King of Arms, Ralph Bigland Norroy King of Arms" (MS., N.L.W.).

3. The "Paper" was an elaborate "Pedigree devised by [HLP] to allow [JSPS] to assume the name of Salusbury by Royal Patent." The manuscript, written in anticipation of the Royal Patent granted on 4 December, was designed for the above three heralds of the College of Arms. The "Pedigree" is now at the N.L.W.

4. For Lucy, wife of Thomas Salusbury of Bachygraig, see HLP to Q, 23 July 1805, n. 8.

5. HLP's "Maternal Great" grandparents were the following: "Sir Robert Cotton of Combermere in the County Palatine of Chester created a Baronet by King Charles the 2nd Knight of the Shire for the said County died 18 Dec: 1712 buried at the Buried Place of the Family near Nantwich." He married "Hester only daughter and at length sole heir of Sir Thomas Salusbury of Llewenny in the County of Denbigh Baronet and a Colonel in the Army; Died about 1710, buried at the Buried Place of the Cotton Family near Nantwich." See the manuscript described in n.3.

TO THE REVEREND JOHN ROBERTS

[November–December 1813][1]

With a Thousand Compliments to Mr. Roberts, his Old Friend obeys his Commands however awkwardly—but he may introduce it *how* he likes, or burn it *when* he likes, only concealing the ˙Writer.——

---

*In case the underneath should be inserted in a periodical work, the Writer's name was hereby enjoined to be concealed.—

Perhaps the Characteristic of our Nation—as of its Individuals—may be impartially confessed to be pride: and indeed we have within these few Years formed to ourselves a new Phrase when Battles have been gained, or Dangers escaped.——as——This was a *proud* Day for England &c.—Let us see however if there is nothing we ought to be *ashamed* of,—even now that we no longer buy and sell the African Negroes, and sweeten our gentle Ladies' Tea with Sugar drawn from *their* Blood and Tears.[2] A gentler Nation than the Hottentots, a People sprung as it should seem from Abraham and Keturah—Brahma and Kiettery.[3] Tender to Animals, Temperate in their Food, Fearful of dishonest Gains, and seeking rather to bury the General Corrupter Gold in his Native Earth, than use it to ill Purposes—are at this Hour encouraged by our Government in gross Idolatry, of the most horrible and hateful Species: encouraged I must say with *Cruelty* by those who should endeavour to propagate the Religion of the Parent Country—not remain wholly absorbed in the Desire of enriching her. If Britain cannot grow Wealthy without taking Money *Abroad* for Crimes punished by Death *at home*, will her Prosperity be a Thing to be *proud* of?

The Females who strip Children in London Streets, (abandoned as they are) would start I trust at Sight of Infants exposed to Sharks, and tied to Mouths of Crocodiles: nor could the Mob who pelted the last poor Rascal in the Pillory be easily persuaded to believe that the same Government which punished *him*—took Money for conniving at similar Practices in a distant Division of our Empire—and that a Part of our Revenue is derived from permitting Murder, Infanticide and Abominations—not to be named.

I remember a Book called *Rome a Custom-house for Sin:*[4] and there were the Sums specified for obtaining Dispensations to commit such and such Offences against God and Man—*under the Papacy;*—our virtuous Protestants exclaimed and justly—and some said how proud we ought to be of having shaken off a Mode of Worship disgraceful to Human Nature. But of what Christian Sect are those in Hindostan? who at this Hour make the Monstrous Vices of our Subjects *there*——a Source of the Revenue? Oh what a Farce it is to drive from Britain, Gay Gentlemen of the first Rank, first Fortune, and first Figure for a Propensity in Asia deemed *meritorious*—when if they would but fill their Purple Sails, and float in all their Elegance to *that* warm Climate!

> Joy to the City of great Jaggernaut
> Joy to the Seven-headed Idols' Shrine

might resound thro' our Dominions: close to Calcutta Walls, whilst our grave Governors might look with Admiration or Contempt: and send their Clerks and Servants to the Gate, to take the Money from presiding Priests

> While calling on their God
> These self-devoted Bodies they might lay
> To pave his Chariot Way;
> On Jaggernaut they call,
> The ponderous Car rolls on and crushes all.
> Thro' Blood and Bones it ploughs its dreadful Path
> Groans rise unheard, the dying cry
> Of Death and Agony,
> Are trodden under foot by yon mad Throng,
> Who follow close, and thrust the deadly Wheels along.[5]

So sings our Laureate! and so speaks Buchanan![6] one in the warm Phraseology of his Indignant Muse, one speaking forth the Words of Truth and Soberness. The Idol is mentioned in Parkhurst as a Sort of Moloch—Page 394—and he applies it (as he applies every thing) to Elementary Worship.[7]—Be the Intention of his Worshippers what it will; We know that 400 Youths and 300 Girls are devoted to this Monster annually: and that they pay Money to the British Government for Permission of Debaucheries practised of Old by the Aegyptians as says Herodotus in his Euterpe[8]—and as the Prophet Ezekiel complains when, he censures the Jews for imitating them.[9]

The Historian mentions the Car drawn along by People, 60000 at least attending the Ceremonies; which few survived, so great was the Slaughter, and so terrible the Crowd—I think the Idol was concealed from View.

Text Victoria and Albert Museum Library. *Address.* Rev. John Roberts/ Bryn Gronu/ Dymerchion.

1. The letter can be dated November-December 1813; i.e., shortly after Robert Southey became poet laureate in October 1813.

2. On 25 March 1807 the king signed into law "the bill for the abolition of the slave-trade." See *AR* 49 (1807): 110–20.

HLP derived the image of sugar and slavery from Voltaire's reference in *Candide:* "C'est à ce prix que vous mangez le sucre en Europe." For her indebtedness, see *Retrospection,* 2:483.

3. A nation gentler than that of the Hottentots was Hindostan, as HLP called it. She explains the equation between biblical and Hindu figures in her Bible (1811) as a gloss of Genesis 49:9—"Judah is a lion's whelp." She wrote: "Abraham however died not till he was 175 Years old—having had after his Wife's Death Six more Sons by Katurah; Mother to the Hindostanee Casts—who seem to recognize their male Progenitor in *Brahmah.*"

HLP would have read of the Hottentots in William George Browne's *Travels in Africa, Egypt, and Syria, from the Year 1792 to 1798* (see her letter to LC, 1 May 1799, n. 2) and in John Barrow's *Account of Travels into the Interior of Southern Africa,* 2 vols. (London: Cadell and Davies, 1801–4).

4. *Rome a great custom-house for Sin; or, Table of Dispensations and Pardons with Sums of Money given for them,* 3d. ed. (London, 1715). The pamphlet was twenty-four pages.

5. See Southey, *The Curse of Kehama* 14.1.5.

6. For Claudius Buchanan and the Juggernaut, see HLP to Q, 18 February 1812, n. 1.

7. See John Parkhurst, *An Hebrew and English Lexicon Without Points* (London: W. Faden, 1762), 395; and especially his *A Greek and English Lexicon* [1769], 4th ed. (London: G. and J. Robinson, 1804), 441, where he describes the brass idol, made burning hot by a fire within, and the sacrifice of children to it.

8. *History,* 3.27–29 ("Thalia").

9. Ezekiel 20:7–8.

TO LADY WILLIAMS

Brynbella Saturday Night
4 December 1813

I return Dear Lady Williams The Naturalist's Magazine with a Thousand Thanks[1]—DeFoe's Plague of London came Safe home,[2] and I hardly dare open it while confusion is so near us as the Mediterannean, to which this new opening Commerce will be leading Ships now every Day.

What says Dear Sir John to his Six Pence? I think it in very great Danger; Your Ladyship may see by every Newspaper that Buonaparte means to negotiate: keep what he *can;* and hope for Opportunity of regaining the rest (or somewhat as good) upon a future Day. Oh! You will find that the Allies after securing what they fight for, will leave Great Britain to indemnify the Enemy for *French* Losses, by *our* Islands at a Distance, where the Americans will assist him to insult and injure us: and a Seven years Peace which may just serve to *lull* the *English,* will give time to Buonaparte for whetting his Vengeance and Desire of falling on us again.[3]

Meanwhile our Folks will be contented while Corn is cheap; and whether the Farmer—can pay his Rent or no, will not interest Ministers who think only of the Commercial Interest; and who are sure to be Huzzaed about his Friends to the Community, when Bread and Beer are to be had at Low Prices.

So Your Ladyship sees I am still a Croaker; but ever Dear Sir John's and your truly attached/ as Obliged/ H: L: Piozzi.

A Thousand kind Remembrances to Your Darlings.

Text Ry. 4 (1812–18).

1. *The Naturalist's Pocket Magazine; or, Compleat Cabinet of the Curiosities and Beauties of Nature*, 6 vols. (London: Harrison, Clusp, and Co., 1799–1802). It describes various "Birds, Fishes, Flowers, Insects, Quadrupeds, Shells, and other Natural Productions." Each verbal description, preceded by a colored print, is short and designed for a popular audience. Authorities—Linnaeus, Pennant, Buffon, Ray, Goldsmith, Edwards, etc., are casually mentioned.

2. The book was HLP's. According to a "Catalogue of Books at Brynbella, 18: October 1806," it was listed as "De Foe's Plague—1 Vol." It was not listed among the books from Brynbella sold 17–19 September 1823. See *Sale Catalogue* (2).

3. Implicit in the paragraph are certain facts and HLP's interpretation of newspaper reports: e.g., the Opposition's unwillingness to impose a harsh and humiliating peace upon Napoleon; and the continuing war between Great Britain and the United States, with the latter maintaining cordial diplomatic relations with France.

The idea of a negotiated peace was drawn from "various reports . . . upon the authority of letters from Paris. Some mention the intended departure of a Minister with proposals of peace to the Allies; others, that Buonaparte's Speech to the Legislative Body, which meets to-morrow, will be very pacific. . . . One letter has been received, and . . . has been communicated to the high authorities in this country, containing two lines . . . 'The Government is almost at its last gasp: the most important events are preparing'" (*Courier*, 1 December).

TO JOHN WILLIAMS

Brynbella
12: December 1813.

My Dear Mr. Williams

flatters me no little in requesting a Letter; and I am most happy to send him the Compliments of the season. It is a very old fashion. *Our* Ancestors used to send Misletoe to each other, The Romans presented Dates and dried Figs to their Friends, and the modern Italians make up little elegant Boxes of Sweetmeats for the Purpose.

We keep our Oaks as clean as we can from all Parasitical Plants—We leave the Sugar plumbs to the Children, and send empty Wishes of a merry Christmas and a happy New Year. Even *that* good Custom is going out apace.—Well! Ovid's Line to Germanicus was the prettiest—Di tibi dent Annos, a te nam Cetura sumes.[1] Buonaparte doubtless thought such a Speech would suit *him* Some Months ago, but he must renounce all hope of being *Germanicus*.[2] Sir John Williams and I have a Wager on his Conduct; and if he *Treats* or *Re*treats according to my Expectation, Your Father will be Loser—Six Pence.

He will be Loser more than Six Pence—by this Fall in the Price of Wheat.— Our Tenants will break like Ice in a hard Frost and we Farmers shall tumble in, every Day some.

It was a kind Thing in You dear Sir to write me that nice Cambridge Intelligence. To shew You I deserve it, and that my old Pate has not yet ceased to interest itself about what *can* concern me but a short Time——let me beg you to bring me Word home whether 'tis true or not that in Emanuel College may be seen a Copy of Tully's Epistles illuminated with a Head of our King Harry the 8th and Faust's Name, in Faust's own hand Writing—prefixed to it.[3] You know better than I do, that Faust, and his Clerk Schaffer, were the first Inventors of the Art of Printing;[4] and that when by their new discovered Method, they had found means of multiplying Copies of the same Work; People believed they must necessarily be *Necromancers:*—and we have not yet done coupling *The Devil and Doctor Faustus.*[5]

Adieu Dear Mr. Williams! we shall soon meet at Bodylwyddan, I hope *now:*— The shortest day is coming, the *happiest* Day not far off.

My Salusbury sets out tomorrow on a long Tour through South Wales, Bath, Enborne &c. He unites with me in every kind Wish, and I remain Yours and your amiable/ Family's ever/ H: L: Piozzi.

Text Ry. 6 (1813–21).

1. *Epistulae ex Ponto,* 2.1.53–54.
2. Germanicus Caesar (15 B.C.–A.D. 19), a Roman general to whom Ovid in the lines quoted wishes many years so that his virtues and worth will be vouchsafed.
3. Since no record exists of HLP's visit to Emmanuel College, she is recalling (somewhat inaccurately) what was told to her perhaps by SJ, who visited Cambridge in February 1765; or Michael Lort, regius professor of Greek at the university; or even Clement Francis, now a pupil at Caius.
   HLP refers to *De Officiis & Paradoxa* (Mainz: Johannes Fust . . . Sed arte . . . Petri [Schoeffer] . . . effeci finitum, 1465). The volume was printed in red and black on vellum. It originally belonged to Prince Arthur, elder brother of Henry VIII, and the first page of each of *De Officiis's* four books was decorated ca. 1500 with the prince's coat of arms and with flowers. How it came to Emmanuel remains a mystery but it is still there with the shelf mark—MSS., 5.3.11.
4. Johann Fust, or Faust (fl. 1440–66) and Peter Schoeffer (fl. 1449–1502), both of Mainz.
   "Hansard, in his *Typographia,* awards to Gutenberg the high appellation of Father of printing: to Schoeffer that of Father of Letter-founding: and to Faust that of Generous Patron, by whose means the wondrous discovery, 'The Nurse and Preserver of the Arts and Sciences,' was brought so rapidly to perfection." See C. H. Timperley, *Encyclopaedia of Literary and Typographical Anecdote* [1839, 1842], intro. Terry Belanger, 2 vols. (New York and London: Garland, 1977), 1:107–8.
5. HLP's association of Fust or Faust with Dr. Faustus was usual, causing Timperley to note that "John Faust or Fust, is by many supposed to have derived his name from *Faustus,* happy; and Doctor Faustus seems to carry an air of grandeur in the appellation; but very erroneously so; for *John* Faust, or Fust, is no more than *John* Hand, whence our word *fist.*—Nichols' *Origin of Printing*" (ibid., 1:107n).

TO HARRIET MARIA PEMBERTON

Brynbella
15th: December 1813.

Oh what tedious Letter Carriers! what sullen *Posts* are those between your Longnor and our Brynbella! My charming Correspondent's agreeable Letter arrived not till this Evening, altho' written last Fryday——Why Intelligence from Edinburgh would come quicker by half! Even Our Brace of Inestimables will travel faster than *so*——with a lame Horse and new-built Gig—really[1] to break under them. It will really be a happy Day when we See them once again, and my Thanksgiving on the 13th of February will come more sincerely from my

Heart—if they *do* return safe—than the Political one ordered for the 13th of January tho' no one wishes Prosperity to their native Land more truly than Myself.[2]

I hope you will like your Fly;—it was Linnæus's Favourite among all the Papilio Tribe; and I was fortunate in having so fine a Specimen to copy from——but 'tis no small Undertaking to present *Work* of *any* Sort before such a Painter and Colourist as our lovely H: M: P. Besides that the Tints of every Bird and Insect are So heightened by the Heats of Amboyna, where this *King Priam* displays his Green and Gold Glories to the Sun, that one is hopeless of equalling its Brilliancy.——The other Side of Your Ridicule will exhibit The Sphinx Moth of Malta——considered by Naturalists as the first Ornament of the *Night:* I threatened to do a Dead Leaf—but Salusbury did not approve the Device; and I was glad to be hindered from attempting what I could not have executed to please myself.

You are very obliging Dear Madam in expressing Concern for my Solitary State——The Toothach, Swelled Face and broken out Lips have employed me ever since Monday;—but a Letter from Llangollen just arrived, will give me a good Night, and I shall write to my Darling with his four Names *to morrow.*—The Gazette has given him Permission and Authority—nay *Command* to assume my Arms Name &c. *now;* and Mrs. Mostyn *must* change her Style when She directs to him again.

I have no Frank; our Bishop is so *fussy,* and makes such Difficulties if one asks him, that 'tis better not think about such Nonsense. The Dear Bodylwyddan Family are all at Chester, where Mrs. Jordan at Threescore Years old is getting 30£ o'Night[3] for acting Miss Peggy and Miss Prissy and my Lady Teazle &c.[4] I will endeavour to let my Run-away know when I leave *his* House for Sir John Williams's;—but really they make such a Ramble of it, it will be proof of a good Marksman to shoot Letters at Them with any Hope or Prospect of Success.

The *first* must of Course be aimed at Tredegar; and God knows whether he will not now have left his favourite Sophia before mine of tomorrow Morning reaches Longnor. Give my true Love to the Rogues however; and beg Your Brother to remember the Fun we had at Bath upon his Birthday once, when I gilt the Letters of his Name *Edward* and hung them on the Epergne for a Streamer. Oh if he should but fall in Love with one of my Cousins—Sir Robert Salusbury's Daughters![5] how pretty and curious that would be! And I recollect his Saying—that very Day—that he felt as if *I* was *his Relation.* Mr. Thelwall[6] who called on me Yesterday, says that one of the Miss Salusburys is an accomplished Girl, and he is sure to meet her at Sir Charles Morgan's.

Make my truest Respects and Compliments acceptable to Mr. and Mrs. Pemberton, and assure them that they have a faithful Servant/ in Dear Miss Harriet's very/ Sincere and Obedient/ H: L: Piozzi.

The Drawing is delightful, I cannot praise it half enough.

Text Ry. 592.3. *Address* Miss Harriet Maria Pemberton/ Longnor/ near/ Shrewsbury. *Postmark* DENBIGH 224.

1. Ready. Perhaps HLP was anticipating "really" in the following sentence.

2. A thanksgiving was announced for 13 January 1814 for "'the increased prospect which recent events have afforded, of the complete deliverance of Europe from a yoke most disgraceful, galling, and oppressive'; on the freedom of Holland, the recovery of Hanover, and the exploits of the Marquis of Wellington."

On the appointed day, the Prince Regent drove in state to divine service at St. James's Chapel. In addition to several members of the Royal Family, other distinguished guests included the archbishop of Canterbury, the bishops of Salisbury and Carlisle, and Lords Liverpool and Bathurst. The bishop of London preached from Isaiah 14:7.

See *GM* 84, pt. 1 (1814):86, 87.

3. According to H. Hughes, *Chronicle of Chester* (1975), 198–99, Dorothea Jordan, at the age of fifty-one, appeared in *The Soldier's Daughter* and *The Belle's Stratagem* in December 1813.

On 10 December the *Chester Chronicle* wrote: "The performances of Mrs. Jordan have proved most attractive at our [Chester] Theatre, and seldom have we seen such highly respectable and crowded houses.—She is, truly, a wonderful woman; and her appearance is still interesting, although she is loaded with the weight of above 50 winters. She concluded her unrivalled performances on Tuesday night [7 December], in the part of *Letitia Hardy* [in Mrs. Cowley's *The Belle's Stratagem*]." See the *Chester Chronicle*, 10 December 1813.

4. Miss Peggy appears in Wycherley's *The Country Girl* (as altered by Garrick); Miss Prissy or Priscilla Tomboy in T. A. Lloyd's *The Romp;* and Lady Teazle in Sheridan's *The School for Scandal*. These were all parts in which Dorothea Jordan excelled.

5. For Sir Robert Salusbury and his wife, Catherine, see HLP to Q, 20 September 1803, n. 9.

Their daughters were the following: Sarah Catherine (1782–1866); Charlotte Gwendolen (1786–1861); and Elizabeth Jane (b. 26 June 1787). See Henry Cotton Salusbury and Stephen Gibbon Salusbury, *The Salusburies of Lleweni* (undated and unpaginated).

6. The Reverend Edward Thelwall of Llanbedr Hall. See HLP to Q, 6–7 March 1805, n. 2.

TO HARRIET MARIA PEMBERTON

Brynbella
23: December 1813.

My charming Correspondent has drawn herself into a nice Snare by writing to *me* so kindly. She will be quite *pelted* with Letters,—ask Salusbury else;—but continue to write notwithstanding, and hang the Materials: no Pen can seem bad, that traces good Words of those we Sincerely esteem.

Meanwhile I have written Twice to Tredegar—to clear away all Apprehensions concerning my Health. Would not You have been sorry for me my Sweet Lady? when I could neither eat nor speak, and was even forced to feel glad that my dearest Salusbury was at Distance, because he would have been calling the Medical Folks, of whom my Terror is greater than of Disease itself——even tho' under the *agreeable* Form of Doctor Cumming. Well! Well! Bessy Jones and I got thro' very cleverly, and She behaved perfectly,—and deserves her high Favour at Longnor.

And now accept my truest Wishes of Happiness in this next New Year—— when if I mistake not, You are to come of Age. Will you condescend to listen if I say it is a *Serious* Moment tho' a *Merry* one. Do not take it Ill if I offer one Piece of Advice—It is that you will *do* nothing, and *engage* to do nothing that is *likely* you should *repent*, when you shall have longer employed your Discretionary Powers.

In Eight Months Time I shall make a similar Speech to Salusbury, from whom I do confess to expect, all that his high Sense of Religion and Honour will prompt him to; They have kept him *poor* in Comparison with the Rich and Gay, but in his *State* of *Competence* he may be *prosperous;* and to deserve Success, is better than to enjoy it. I would have thrown him into the bustling World, Lucrative or Political; and I would have supported him in any Profession, but such were his Scruples, and such his Indolence—he could find none that suited him. What then remains? but to give him all I *can* give, and grieve that it is no more. My Name and Arms are his *own* now, and in no one's Power to wash off his Carriage when he keeps one; a Trick which Malice *might* have plaid to give *me*— more than *him*—Mortification——but he *is* my Son at last—in true Earnest; my Son by Adoption, inserted into the Pedigree of my Descent, and registered in the Herald's College—so there's an End of such Designs if there were any.

The avoiding Oxford, Enborne &c. is delightful——Bath was not so formidable to me; Salusbury would have seen his Guardian *there,* Sir Walter James; and my Friend Dr. Whalley: but all is best as it is. The Weather is beautiful, and what you tell me of the Horse is cheering. They will be back to Your Birthday on the 1st and to mine the 27th of January. I felt very sad tho' I said nothing, to think of my dear Runaway—running *quite* away so, from the *last* Anniversary I shall ever enjoy at Brynbella——and besides *my own Feelings,* The *People* think so much of those things, that it is better on all Accounts he should be here.

Your Moth——The *wrong* Side of Your Ridicule, kisses Your fair Hands with this Letter: I fear tis *drawn,* puckered as we Females call it, a little in one Place; but I would not unpick it for fear it should arrive too late for New Year's Day, and nobody but Critical Salusbury will see the Fault.

Farewell lovely and kind Correspondent; and pray let no bad Pen hinder Your writing to your So/ much obliged and faithful/ H: L: Piozzi.

When you send a Letter to The *Inestimables,* put my Love into it.
Compliments and Kind Remembrances *at home.*

Text Ry. 592.5.

TO JOHN SALUSBURY PIOZZI SALUSBURY

Brynbella
23: December 1813.

What will my Dearest Salusbury say when I tell him I have been writing all Evening to Miss Harriet Maria Pemberton, presenting her Moth as a Birthday Present, and giving her *good Advice.* She has been excessively obliging with her Sweet Letters and Soft Words——and seems *so* Thankful to her kind Brother for promising to return and make her happy—pretty Creature! it was charmingly done of our inestimable *Pem*—That it *was.*

Well! how will this Moth *fly* to her? I shall write to Doctor Thackeray and beg him to forward it——he is a *sad Forwarder* I find, but no matter:—Every thing is best as it *is* always, except our own Crimes and Follies. I should have tried to satisfy myself with that Speech, had you *forborne* to be here on my *last* Birthday,—last at Brynbella certainly; but am happy to think you will be able to *run home*—even if You *run back* again when so near as *admired Salopia.* Apropos you never bring me even a Cake from Shrewsbury.

Mercy on us! What Times my Darling comes of Age in! I shall repeat my *good Advice* to *You* when the Day arrives, and so I shall to *your Friend:* but the Post of honour will soon be a private Station, I'm sure it will; The Plot is Thickening towards the 5th Act; and whilst others see *Sunbright Prospects,* I am apt to believe that the Mist we live in, magnifies them.

My Household is all sick: Leak's Wife shrieking in Hysterics, The Cook come home—"with a burning Fever and a broken Heart" like Varanes,[1] and ne'er a Guinea got from the dead Mother, who broke *her* heart *too.* A pretty World to launch into! And so says Sir William Cunningham, whose Son was drowned in the Canal just above Pultney Street Bath last Week[2]——I'll pledge my Life there's not an Atom of Danger—says Mr. Moore always; whilst I see and hear nothing *but* Dangers, whence nothing but *his* Providence who was born for us just 1813 Years ago, protects a few favoured Individuals. Among *them* may my Salusbury be ever found!——Oh that fine Mr. Lloyd Hesketh who does not know the Difference between Good Friday and Christmas Day, is one of your merrymaking Companions at Tredegar I find[3]——taking it for *Passion Week* perhaps.—

Billy Williams[4] called on me this Morning and will dine and sleep here next Wednesday to *bag* a few Wood Cocks, Pheasants &c. for the Bodylwyddan Birthday.[5] John Williams is expected home tomorrow; He went up with the Cambridge Address, so did Doctor Myddelton——They give a splendid Ball at Gwaynynnog next Tuesday. Who says I send you no News? The best is that I am got well myself, and shall give my one Pound Note at Church next Saturday——The Children have all had Clothes, poor as I am, and their Parents have had Beef——Was it wicked to hope their Prayers *so purchased*——might benefit my dearest Salusbury? Sir William Jones (the learned Orientalist who died young in India,) composed a private Petition (which Lord Teignmouth published)—beseeching the Almighty to pardon all his foolish and improper Requests to the Throne of Grace for Temporal Blessings on *himself,* his *Wife* &c.[6] He was a good and a Wise, and a rich and a learned Man; and *he* did not disdain to know when his Saviour was born and when he died for us; nor disdain to consider the first as a Season of Rejoycing—The other of Mourning. I do hate such Affectation of Impiety, and have never liked that Mr. Lloyd Hesketh since. Farewell! I should not wonder to see a Letter before the Week is out. Continue to love me, and I shall continue to live for you and be daily more and more Your Affectionate/ H: L: P.

Give best Remembrances to Edward—when does he tumble his other Names about! You see there was no need to be of Age.[7]

Text Ry. 587.207. *Address* J.S. Piozzi Salusbury Esq./ Sir Charles Morgan's/ Trede-gar/ Monmouthshire. *Postmark* DENBIGH 224.

1. Varanes was a character in Nathaniel Lee's *Theodosius*. Unable to realize his love for Athenais, Varanes soliloquizes in 5.2: he suffers from "a burning Fever, and a broken Heart."
2. HLP refers to a tragedy of 6 December "Drowned, whilst skaiting on the Kennet and Avon Canal, near Bath, a son of Gen. Sir W. Cunningham, who had just finished his education, and was on the point of accepting a desirable situation in the East India service; a son of Dr. Briggs, of Worcester, who was on a visit at Sir Wm. C's; and Felix, son of —— Mogg, esq. of Wincanton. The youngest of the three, Master Briggs, fell in first; and his companion, in endeavouring to rescue him, shared the same fate. Anxious to render assistance to his unfortunate friends, the third youth hastened to the spot;—the fragile surface again gave way, and he also sunk to rise no more." See *GM* 84, pt. 1 (1814): 95.
3. For Lloyd Bamford Hesketh, later Lloyd Hesketh Bamford-Hesketh, see HLP to MW, 6 March 1811, n. 1. Educated at Eton and Christ Church, he was on 25 October 1826 to marry Lady Emily Esther Anne Lygon (d. 1873), youngest daughter of first earl Beauchamp.
4. Sir John and Lady Williams had an eight-year-old son, William, who seems a bit young for these activities.
5. JW was born on 9 January 1794. In honor of his son, Sir John gave "an annual dinner and ball . . . on the 10th instant." See the *Morning Post*, 17 January 1814; HLP to Ly W, 16 February 1804, n. 3.
6. See John Shore, Lord Teignmouth, *Memoirs of the Life, Writings, and Correspondence, of Sir William Jones* (1746–94) (London: Sold by John Hatchard, 1804), 357–59. The prayer was written by Jones on 1 January 1782 about fifteen months before he went to India and more than twelve years before he died.
So popular had the prayer become since its publication that SS, e.g., copied it into a notebook for ready reference. See "MS. notebook" (Access No. 37; 737—Class No. 091.56) in the Bath Reference Library.
7. Edward William Smythe Pemberton assumed the surname Owen in lieu of Pemberton in 1814 upon inheriting Condover Park, near Shrewsbury. See HLP to JSPS, 20 August 1808, n. 1; 16 July 1810, n. 10.

TO JOHN SALUSBURY PIOZZI SALUSBURY

Wensday
29: December 1813.

My truly Dear Salusbury's kind Letter is come at last——I did expect Cathrow's Account of our Expences by this Post,[1] and I did think Davies of Streatham would have written to thank me for Mutton and a Peacock which I sent for his and Mr. Embry's Christmas Dinner:——and partly I did expect a Line from Longnor, saying that Miss Harriet liked her Moth; which went by the Mail of last Wednesday 22d of December—(This Day sennight)——but *your* Letter makes amends for every one else's Neglect. God keep me the Love and Esteem of my *own Son* and God keep him worthy of *mine*; The rest must go as it will.

Pleasure may be found at Tredegar, or at Twenty Places—Happiness at *none*—except in *Prospect:* and we must look at the *Prospect* thro' Religion's Telescope, or it will be *all a Mist*.

Have you Time to read Letters, tho' not to write them? This is the fourth I send. John Williams was here Yesterday and calmed my Impatience by his Account of cross Posts, bad Roads &c. I was indeed very, Oh *very* anxious—Come, Come; a Young Man who has *such* Friends fretting about him, is *nearer* to Felicity than those he sees drinking, Dancing, and Singing in the same Room. I understand there is a Miss Wood among you—very beautiful and very rich—a Baronet's Daughter——She must make *Pem's* Mother and Sister amends for his not returning to wish Miss Harriet Joy on her 21st Birthday—and She—pretty Creature!—*must learn* that Promises are precarious, and Hopes fallacious in *this World*.[2] Boys and Girls both hate to be *told* so, but Men and Women *feel* that so it *is*:——and *should* turn their Eyes and Hearts——to where Performance is *sure*, and Hope is swallowed up in *certain Enjoyment*.

I have lived wholly in one Room since you left me. The first Week passed in Pain and Apprehension on *my own* Account: The second in restless Agitation for your Safety,—The Third or fourth I will try to spend at Bodylwyddan. If I get any Excuse from Longnor to trouble them with a Letter, assure yourself I will write—and that in the Tenderest Terms—to wish Miss Pemberton a happy Opening of the next New Year.

You lose all the *North Wales* Wit now, but I can't help copying out *This*[3]—It is a pretty Compliment to Southey—before his Ode is printed:[4] Maybe some of Your Frolickers have seen it.

Dialogue upon Parnassus Hill

Musa loquitur ----- A Horse! A Horse!—Dear Pegasus be ready,
        The Laureate calls, and We've no Time to lose;

Pegasus-------------- I'm here: but will Lord Wellington be steady?
        And fear we not some sad Reverse of News?

Muse ----------------- What Scruples! you shew'd none when Buonaparte
        Thunder'd at Lodi Austerlitz and Jena;[5]

Pegasus-------------- Ah Muse! and were not You all warm and hearty
        To celebrate his Conduct at Vienna?[6]

Muse ----------------- Heroic Deeds on Clio here have Claim
        Tho' in a Tyrant's Cause, or Madman's Quarrel;
        But when true Friends solicit our Applause
        See to what Hands our Care commits the Laure[l]

        Nor need we back to distant Times refer;
        Bourbon to eulogize, what Wits conspire!
        Fred'ric the Great was sung by gay Voltaire,[7]
        And Marlbro' prais'd by Addison and Prior.[8]

Pegasus-------------- Well then, I wait Your Call; The Year fourteen
        Shall feel the Trump of Fame by Fate blown larger;

Britain's bright Glories shall of All be Seen,
And Britain's Laureate mount the Classic Charger.

Do you not wonder I can be amused with such Stuff while Silence and Solitude surround me so? but here's such heavenly Weather for walking out—I sit within only the dark Hours: and Lord bless me:—pulling up the Blind this Moment to get Light for finishing my Letter, I perceive the *Sash* has been opened by some *Ninny;* and if I have *not* caught an Immense Cold—Why 'tis a Wonder sure—but I did not perceive it.

Upon what Slender Strings one's Life and Happiness do hang!!

Adieu! be well, be wise, and remember with what cordial Kindness, Love, and Esteem I wish your next Year a happy one. If it proves such to my own Salusbury, it *shall* not be deemed otherwise to/ his Affectionate/ H: L: Piozzi.

Direct as usual when You *do* write; I shall not go to Bodylwyddan till Saturday the 8th of January Hughey's Birthday.[9]

Text Ry. 587.208. *Address* J: S: P. Salusbury Esq:/ at Sir Charles Morgan's/ Tredegar/ Monmouthshire. *Postmark* DENBIGH 224.

1. Behind HLP's statement is the following letter by Cathrow, dated 23 December 1813 (Ry. 554.21): "Madam/ I have to acknowledge the favor of your obliging Communication of the 17th Instant and beg to advise you of my Intention of sending by tomorrow's Mail Coach the Instruments relative to Mr. Salusbury's Confirmation of the Name and Grant of the Arms of Salusbury, which are now completed and recorded. In the Case you will find a Notification of the Fees and Expenses attending the same agreeably to your Request but which I beg you will not trouble yourself to discharge until it is more perfectly convenient."

2. Anne (d. 1863), the daughter of Francis Lindley Wood (1771–1846), second baronet (1795), and Anne, née Buck (d. 1841). In 1824 she was to marry John Walbanke Childers (1798–1886), of Cantley, Yorks.

3. "The Dialogue upon Parnassus Hill" was written by HLP on 27 December. See a manuscript called "Select Manuscript on Various Subjects and Several Occasions" (Ry. 647.62). It appears also in "Harvard Piozziana," where there is a statement: "The following Dialogue on Parnassus is an old-fashioned Jeu D'Esprit—imitated from the French of an Anonymous Panegyrist on Louis 14. 'Tis among les Pensées Ingénieuses de Bouhours—and is I fancy *his own*——one reads it nowhere else, and I believe the Thing itself is known to very few Writers or Readers of the present Day" (vol. 5).

4. Robert Southey, poet laureate since October 1813, was expected to write an ode in celebration of the New Year. But see particularly *Ode Written during the Negotiations with Buonaparte, in January, 1814* (first published in the *Courier,* 3 February 1814).

5. The Bonaparte victories at Lodi on 10 May 1796, at Austerlitz on 2 December 1805, and at Jena-Auerstädt on 14 October 1806.

6. HLP refers to Bonaparte's humiliating defeat of the Austrians, a defeat formalized in the Peace of Schönbrunn on 14 October 1809 after the battles of Wagram and Znaim.

7. See the following works by Voltaire: his dedication to Frederick, or Friedrich II, which prefaces *Mahomet,* first produced at Lille in 1741 and at Paris in 1742; *Voyage à Berlin;* and especially the letters exchanged between the king and Voltaire.

8. See Addison's *The Campaign* (1705) and Prior's *An Ode, humbly inscrib'd to the Queen. On the late glorious Success of Her Majesty's Arms* (1706).

9. Hugh Williams, soon to be twelve.

TO HARRIET MARIA PEMBERTON

Brynbella
1st January 1814.

I feel mortified Dear Miss Harriet to find myself beginning a Letter of Condolence when it should be Congratulation: but don't be discouraged, I'm sure it was not Salusbury's fault; he wrote me a Sheet full of Lamentations to think he was delayed from Longnor, by any Gayeties going forward in South Wales. I have heard from him but once, and that once he wrote with a Croud of People round him all busy in some Frolic or another.——*Perhaps* my Maternal Feelings on his Account ran somewhat against yours: *perhaps* I thought it was not much amiss, that a Young Mind should learn (without my teaching,) that Pleasure is not Happiness. You too,—my amiable Friend and Correspondent will see that Disappointment hovers over all Hope of Earthly Enjoyment like these Fogs which spoil our Comfort in this the very finest Weather that Winter ever exhibited.

It is very flattering to me that you like your Moth; The Colours are completely different from those of the Butterfly; Let me never lose that obliging Partiality you are pleased to express towards *me;* for I have had Disappointments *enough* in my long Passage thro' a Thorny World; and could not bear to be Scratched with Briars at the End of the Avenue. From Dear Salusbury I expect a kind hand to conduct me *Safe home;* and a Promise of Endeavouring to obtain the best Apartments for *himself* in our *Father's House.* If you shew him this Letter, he will cry out "Oh it's my Aunt's *way;* She is always moralizing somehow or another, but She is very good-humoured notwithstanding."

My Hours of Silence and Solitude will end when the Gayeties of Tredegar do; The 8th of January is my Godson's Birthday at Bodylwyddan, and I shall spend a Week there if *pretty well.* Salusbury had better however not change his Direction, nor confuse himself about such Nonsense any more; but send me word that *he* is happy, and I will try to make myself so. My Affection for him is not *Selfish*—and so you would say if you saw the Box which came to hand an hour ago with all the Documents of this Name-Business, the Account of *Costs* &c. but never mind; by Dint of living the whole Year in perfect Retirement as I do, all will at length come round; and in seven Years as I told your Mama, I shall be as *sleek as a Mole,* notwithstanding my Intentions towards his Worship—who really grows dearer to me every Day than he was the last.——And I am just now going to tell him so, and to say how I drank Your health to *myself* to day; and wished You a Thousand happy New Years, and assured myself that you would shew your Sweet Temper by not fretting that your Brother and your Friend were absent, when I dare say our Dear *Pem* could not have helped it— or have come away without exciting Wonder, or Curiosity, or something You Yourself would not have liked.

So now pray do smile on their Return, and make both *them* and *me* ten Times more your Admirers.

I am, as I am sure you must plainly perceive, with most sincere Regard Dear Madam Yours, and your Papa and Mama's/ faithfully attached/ H: L: Piozzi.

Let me hear you are well *sometimes; often* if you can find Spare Moments.

Text Ry. 592.6. *Address* Miss Harriet Maria Pemberton/ Longnor/ near/ Shrewsbury. *Postmark* DENBIGH <22>4.

TO LADY KEITH

Brynbella
17: January 1814.

I wish you a happy New Year dear Lady Keith—and thank you Sincerely for making mine begin agreeably by reading such an Interesting Letter.

The Weather is Cold beyond all Thought, beyond all Precedent I believe: tho' five or six Years back we had more Snow, it was not of this *minute* Canadian Kind, which penetrates even into strong-built Houses.[1]

The Accidents and Offences—which my Friends tell me is all I ever read of a Newspaper;—multiply this Sharp Season, so as to give me full Employ. With regard to Public Affairs—those of the present Time, resemble the Poetry of the present Time—loud and boisterous one Moment, and at another—gloomy and obscure.

> Pump'd with incessant Toil and strange Success,
> Forth from th' unfathom'd Gulphs of Emptiness.[2]

I have no Means of guessing how 'twill End, or whether we *Should* or Should *not* wish the Extinction of Buonaparte.[3]

The Armies now on foot are very numerous,[4] and If they are all armed like the Dragon's Teeth by Cadmus[5]—with Swords and ne'er a Shield, they will in the same manner compleat each other's Destruction and their own; and then— we will shut the Temple of Janus.[6]

Meanwhile Cecy tells me that She dreads a Peace, because her Sons are to make their Fortunes by the War:[7] and my Neighbours—all Country Gentlemen—dread the Peace because it will bring down the Price of Corn, and Value of Land &c.

The Pokers into Prophecy dread Peace as Physicians dread an Interrupted Pulse——Precursor of the one long Pause, preceding the Sound of the Trumpet.[8]

That Apoplexies should be frequent, shocks more than it amazes me;—Constriction drives the Blood rapidly to the Head or Lungs; and naturally brings forward Sudden Death, or Pulmonary Consumption. They will be common if the Weather does not break Soon.

I am glad Dear little Bertie is where he *Should* be; his lovely Cousin is a Sweet Thing I doubt not:[9] Lady William's Daughter born the November before her, is a famous Lass—Sir John punished her with a frightful Name Ellen Ursula— because She frighted him with her Tediousness on the first Appearance; but She is nimble enough now, and he rejoyces that he did not as he threatened— call her *Bridget*.

I wish there was a Book made out of the Bons Mots of Babies—but People would say none of them were genuine.

What an odd Performance is Lord Byron's Giaour![10] very fine tho', the beginning and the End. Il ne manque que la Pauvreté pour etre Poete.[11]

But how People's Minds are altered Since Pope's Time! who says

> What woeful Stuff this Madrigal would be,
> By some starv'd hackney Sonnetteer—or Me:
> But let *a Lord once* own the happy Lines,
> How the Wit brightens, and the Style refines;
> Before his sacred Name flies every fault,
> And each exalted Stanza teems with Thought.[12]

Now on the contrary, every Eye is watching, and every Heart hoping for a Mistake, merely because the Writer is a Nobleman: Was he a starved Sonnetteer, I suppose they would shower Money and Praises upon him.

Mrs. Montagu's Letters however are delightful, and every body says so—*I* devour them: the Names of all one's Contemporaries do *so* interest one, There is no Possibility of laying down the Book.[13]

The Bride of Abydos is a Cold Thing after the Giaour:[14] Lord Byron resembles the Almond Tree which puts the *Flowers* out before the *Leaves*. We are all on Tiptoe for the Wanderer,[15] and for Miss Edgeworth's Patronage.[16] Staal's Allemagne I have not yet seen:[17] and now is my Paper finished before I can express half my Concern for your Domestic Griefs, or tell how Lady Keith's Band was admired at Tredegar. Accept and dispose properly of every good Wish and every Affectionate Compliment from Yours and Lord Keith's H: L: P.

Text Bowood Collection. *Address* R: H: Baroness Keith.

1. Almost until the end of January the frost was severe.
2. See "Harvard Piozziana," 5:16:

"I was called upon at Bodylwyddan to read Lord Byron's Giaour—a new Poem which I had never seen: It is a fine wild Performance, difficult to comprehend, and most untowardly awkward to read at Sight: I was applauded however, and applauded the Writer in my Turn, tho' Such Verses are by no means to my natural Taste, where

> Words heap'd on Words in Piles confus'dly rise,
> Half lost in Fog:—and seem to touch the Skies;
> Pump'd with incessant Toil and strange Success
> From forth Th'unfathom'd Gulphs of Emptiness."

3. As late as 9 March (see the terms of the treaty of Chaumont), the Allies were prepared to deal with Napoleon, agreeing that he should be offered traditional French frontiers in exchange for

Elizabeth Montagu. Portrait by Sir Joshua Reynolds (1776); engraved by Ridley. (Reproduced by permission of the Henry E. Huntington Library and Art Gallery, San Marino, California.)

a general cease-fire. Should he refuse (as he did), the Allies agreed to wage total war against France and to restore the Bourbons.

4. The allied armies had invaded France from different quarters but chiefly through Switzerland. "Other armies passed the Rhine at Dusseldorff and Coblentz. The whole force amounts to at least 300,000 men; and the route which they took through Franche Compte and Lorraine, is the most vulnerable part of France. The Emperor of Russia, with the last of his reserves, crossed the Rhine, at Basle, on the 13th of January." The Russians, aided by the forces of the various German states, have laid open "the whole extensive plain, from the frontiers of Lorraine, Champagne, and Burgundy, to Paris."

In addition, Wellington's forces were on the offensive, having in October and November crossed the Pyrenees into France. And the Austrians had reached Verona.

See *GM* 84, pt. 1 (1814):81–83.

5. When his sister disappeared, Cadmus—a figure in Greek mythology—was sent to seek her. At Thebes, to get water he slew a dragon, the offspring of Ares, and suffered a period of servitude. Upon the advice of Athena, he planted the dragon's teeth, from which arose a harvest of armed men whom he killed by setting them to fight one another. Only five survived to become the ancestors of the Theban nobility.

6. Janus's temple in the Forum had two doors facing one another. In war the doors stood open and in peace they were shut.

7. Harry Mostyn was now at the Royal Naval College. His younger brother, Bertie, was on a three-year tour of duty at sea.

8. Revelation 8:1, 2.

9. Georgiana Elphinstone, now aged almost five.

10. John Murray had run off a few copies of *The Giaour, a Fragment of a Turkish Tale* in March 1813, a poem in couplets Byron had started in the autumn of 1812. The poem was based on the episode of a Turkish girl whom the poet, while he was in Athens, had saved from being thrown into the sea.

The first edition of the *Giaour* was advertised in the *Morning Chronicle* of 5 June, Byron having increased the poem by some 300 lines after its private printing. Through July and August he kept adding and emending passages which the printer accepted because the public was buying copies as quickly as they appeared. Before the end of August a total of five editions had appeared. See Leslie A. Marchand, *Byron. A Biography*, 3 vols. (New York: Knopf, 1957), 1:408.

11. See "Harvard Piozziana," vol. 4. "I saw a new Book this Year written by Lord Byron, he is a cleverer Fellow than one expected—in some Respects a real Poet; and loves—as they all do—to thicken the Gloom of Life.—Well! no matter; Poussin said of some Italian Amateur Nobelman: non gli manca chi Solamente la Necessità. And Lord Byron wants only Poverty to make us acknowledge him a Wit,—perhaps a scholar; but he is a Lord—and the People do so hate him."

12. *Essay on Criticism*, lines 418–23.

13. *The Letters of Mrs. E. Montagu, with some of the letters of her correspondents.* Published by Matthew Montagu . . . her nephew and executor, 4 vols. (London: Cadell and Davies, 1809–13).

14. *The Bride of Abydos* was published on 2 December 1813, and sold even more quickly than *The Giaour*: about 6,000 copies were bought within a month of publication. See Marchand, 1:423–24.

15. See, e.g., the advertisement in the *Morning Chronicle*, 17 March 1814. "On Monday the 28th instant will be published, dedicated to Dr. Burney. *The Wanderer: or, Female Difficulties.* In 5 vols. duodecimo. By the Author of Evelina, Cecilia and Camilla. Printed for Longman, Hurst, Rees, Orme and Brown, Paternoster-Row; and at the British Gallery, 54, New Bond-street."

16. Maria Edgeworth's *Patronage* in 4 vols. appeared in February 1814, going through two editions in 1814 and a third in 1815.

17. On 27 September 1813 *The Times* announced that "speedily will be published" Mme de Staël's *De L'Allemagne* in three volumes. The work appeared in October with its English translation, *On Germany*. According to the "Preface," the work, completed in 1810, "preserved a studied silence on the existing French Government. . . . and after 10,000 copies had, with [the censor's] permission, been printed, Savary, the Minister of Police, seized and destroyed the whole impression, compelled Madame De Stael to give up the original manuscript, and ordered her to quit France, her native country, within 24 hours." See *GM* 83, pt. 2 (1813): 461.

TO CLEMENT FRANCIS

Brynbella
Monday 17: January 1814.

My dear Mr. Francis

It was very kind in You to write so attentively from Kensington Gore,[1] and very prudent to tear yourself away, and return to College; since you will persist in working at these Demonstrations, instead of prosecuting Studies more cogenial to Your Humour, tho' less profitable to your Fame—perhaps to Your Purse.[2] That God may bless your Endeavours is my true Wish and Prayer; and I have lately been conversing with some Young Cambridge Men, who respect your Character though unacquainted with Your Person. Mr. Williams however,—Son to Sir John Williams, protests he *will* know you, and when Lord Massey hears you are *My* Friend, he will desire to be Yours.[3] I begged him to enquire for me where Pilpay's Fables are to be found in Your University; he is called Bidpay sometimes and there is a little Shade of Mystery over the Work—leaving one in Doubt whether they were written in Arabic or no;——if any such Edition exists, 'Tis at Cambridge.[4]

Tell me what the World says of Lord Byron's Poems? I think the Giaour has much Wild Sublimity: and the beginning—(The Proem I mean,)—beautiful;— So is the End. Bride of Abydos made no Impression on me after the other: Lord Byron is like the Almond Tree which puts out its *Flowers* before the *Leaves.*

Dear Marianne is become a tardy Correspondent, and I court her all I can— too. But is it not a Shame to have written so many Lines as *here* are, and not a Word of Public Events; which in *Wonder* surpass all that ever occurred I think, since the World kept any Register of what happened in it. Nor are private Accidents and Offences—in the Newspaper Phrase—less worthy of being Chronicled. Sudden unlooked-for Deaths fright one with their Frequency; This Violent Cold Weather occasions such Constriction, The Blood is driven forcibly to the Head, and produces Apoplectic Fits in *full* Habits, Consumption in Sangwineous Constitutions; sending the vital Stream too hastily to the Lungs. Pray be careful,—This is no Season to live freely in.

My dear Salusbury has passed his Holydays at Tredegar in South Wales, he is now among the proud Salopians,——I write every hour begging him to stay away *somewhere;* for Travelling this Weather is dangerous on every Side.

Your Aunt is happy sure to have escaped France: I dare say *She knew* what was coming.[5] We shall have her Book out *anon;* but here are no flaming News from Lord Wellington: It seems as if the French Generals *there* were in desperate earnest; does Soult I wonder, fight so for *his own Glory* alone? or is he the only Man who defends Buonaparte?[6] Write to me—that's a kind Friend; and cheer my Solitude with some Intelligence out of the living World,——which has been long *remotely viewed,* as through a very faulty Telescope by Dear Sir/ Yours ever most faithfully/ H: L: Piozzi.

I hope poor little Dolph is well by now.[7]

Text Yale University Library. *Address* Clement Francis Esq: Caius College/ Cambridge. *Postmark* DENBIGH <224>.

1. William Wilberforce's house, where MF was now a guest.
2. Clement Francis at Caius College worked—he said—"for a Wrangler's Degree, the greatest Honor in the Senate House" (*Journals and Letters*, 7:196n.). In time he would be ordained a priest, but while at the university he had an intense interest in geometry, in "Demonstrations" (ibid., 7:32).
3. Hugh Hamon Massy (1793–1836), fourth baron Massy of Duntrileague (I., 1812), had matriculated at Trinity College, Cambridge in 1813 and received his M.A. in 1815. In 1826 he was to marry Matilda, née White (1799–1883).
4. HLP refers to a collection of tales known variously as "The fables of Pilpay or Bidpay," "The book of Kalilah and Dimnah," "Anwāri Suhailī, &c." "Each chapter forms a story, which is supposed to have been related at the request of a king of India by his philosopher Bidpai, in order to enforce some particular moral or rule of conduct. . . . In many of the tales the parts are played by animals, and that as if they were men and women."
This collection of stories, part of Buddhist literature, originated in India but passed into Persia ca. 570 A.D. About this time, it was translated into Syriac and about 750 into Arabic.
"A Hebrew translation of the Arabic, of uncertain date and authorship, was the parent of a Latin one, made between A.D. 1263 and 1278 by John of Capua. . . . This Latin version" was subsequently rendered into various European languages. See *Kalīlah and Dimnah or The Fables of Bidpai*, ed. I. G. N. Keith-Falconer (Cambridge: At the University Press, 1885), xiii–xv.
5. FBA and her son had traveled to France in the spring of 1802 to join M. d'Arblay, planning to return to England in October 1803. But by May 1803 war between England and France resumed. Mother and son remained in France until 13 August 1812.
They came back to England because FBA believed her health to be imperiled and because she wished to see her family again, especially her father, now eighty-six. Moreover, she feared that Napoleon's plans for conscription might affect her eighteen-year-old son. Ultimately, she came home to sell *The Wanderer*, whose unfinished draft she had carried to France.
6. Nicholas-Jean de Dieu Soult (1769–1851), duc de Dalmatie (June 1808), maréchal (1813).
On 12 July 1813 he assumed command of the remnants of all French forces in Spain, which he reorganized so that they could fight the campaign of the Pyrenees against the Allies, winning the Maya and Roncesvalles actions but losing those at Sorauren and Vera in his efforts to avert the fall of Pamplona and San Sebastian. He then worked futilely to forestall the allied advance onto French soil.
7. Ralph "Dolph" Broome was so ill that his mother had removed him from London. On 9 November 1813, MF wrote HLP: "Poor little Dolph still keeps his alarming cough, which is always worse in London; so Mama comes to Richmond for good air . . . [for] a twelvemonth." The boy seemed to improve for a while but by 18 March, she wrote that neither "Mama nor Dolph are well, both invalids nursing through this desperate winter" (*Journals and Letters*, 7:208–9n.).

TO THE REVEREND LEONARD CHAPPELOW

Brynbella
18: January 1814.

The Dear Ladies of Llangollen—who do every Thing that is kind, have procured me at length a Letter from Mr. Chappelow:[1] The Wonder is how the Mails travel this Canadian Weather,[2] it is colder I think than in the Winter of 1794 or 1806—
Lady Keith says such a Snow was scarce ever seen in the Southern parts of Devonshire;—She says too, that *her* Lord's eldest Daughter, Miss Mercer Elphinstone, has caught a severe Cough and Pain in her Side with the Intenseness of the chill Air[3]—Indeed I see Apoplexies and Consumptions in every News Paper according as the Blood drives to the Head or Lungs.

My Young Man, dear Salusbury; will I hope escape both: he has passed the last four or five Weeks at Tredegar, and witnessed the Festivities of South Wales, I expect him home now towards Wednesday next.

I direct this to Mouse Trap Hall because I conclude you will get soon to London now. Your Quality Friends must all be at the Birthday,[4] and I hope Lady Bradford will be happy in *all* her Children.[5]

Lord Wellington seems to find no small Resistance on *his* Part,[6] while the Allies are proceeding (We are told) to dictate Peace at Paris.[7] Is Soult the *only* General I wonder, who is attached to Buonaparte; or does he fight for his own Glory alone? Some one was saying Soult was once in England Valet or Butler to one of our Noblemen—Is it so?—Do tell me some News now and then, remembering I live in Solitude and Snow here in my native Mountains.——But I do mean to come into the living World again; a *Revenant* as the French call a Ghost——and then I shall reproach you with Unkindness if you have not been a better Correspondent.

Mrs. Mostyn is in London—No. 10 Seymour Street; her eldest Son at Westminster, her Second at Portsmouth, her Third—in America.[8]

How the Time flies! And the Young Folks grow up!

Are you acquainted with Lord Byron? I knew his Grandmother and loved her dearly[9]——The World won't hold his Fame in a few Years, unless *as you say* Repulsion follows quick upon Attraction. What do our Llangollen Ladies say to the Giaour, and Bride of Abydos? They are watching—so am I;—for Madame D'Arblaye's Wanderer.

But Adieu! My Comfort is, that I have called out the *Vital Spark,* and whilst alive I am sure You will not quite forget Dear Mr. Chappelow's/ Ever Obliged and faithful/ H: L: Piozzi.

Text Ry. 561.146.

1. HLP responds to LC's letter, dated 5 January from Longleat (Ry. 563.101).
2. So delayed were the "Mails" by frost and snow in January that Francis Freeling, secretary of the General Post Office, was to send out a circular letter, dated 21 January:
"It being matter of great importance to the country to get the roads cleared for his Majesty's mails, you will apply to the Overseers of Parishes, and to the Surveyors of Highways, as well as to other persons concerned, and urge them to employ all the means in their power to make the roads passable for carriages with as little delay as possible." See *AR,* "Chronicle," 56 (1814): 9; also the *Evening Mail,* 24–26 January.
3. For Margaret Elphinstone, see HLP to MW, 17 February 1808, n. 4.
4. From the *Morning Post,* 19 January:
"Yesterday being the Queen's Birth-day, the morning was ushered in with the ringing of bells, as was customary when it was celebrated with the pomp of a birth-day Court; the flags on the steeples were displayed, &c. The King's Guard at St. James's Palace mounted in white gaiters, the same as on Court days; the state colours were carried with them, and the men had their usual allowance of porter. At one o'clock the Park and Tower guns fired a double royal salute. In the evening their Majesties' trades-people illuminated their houses, and the Theatres were illuminated as usual upon similar occasions, C. R. a crown, and various devices."
According to *The Times* on 20 January, the queen, to celebrate her birthday further, "had a party at [Windsor] to tea, cards, and a concert."
5. Lady Bradford had been, according to LC's letter, "in great agitation, till she learned that Orlando was safe—he was slightly wounded at the storming of St. Sebastian—but was not in the Last Battles which continued five days. . . . Orlando will soon come home, for Promotion as well as Charles the Sailor—whom we expect here this very day."

For Lady Bradford's children, see HLP to LC, 2 May 1814, n. 8.

6. HLP refers to Soult's actions to delay the allied movement on French soil: particularly to the battles of Nivelle (10 November 1813), the Nive (9–12 December), and St. Pierre (13 December), etc. See *GM* 84, pt. 1 (1814):71–75, for the lists of dead and wounded among Wellington's troops.

7. HLP refers to the peace conference at Châtillon-sur-Seine, which opened on 5 February 1814. On 7 February the Allies (the English delegation headed by Castlereagh) stated their terms to Caulaincourt: France was to surrender Belgium, the Left Bank, Savoy, and Nice, and to retire within her 1791 boundaries. By 8 February Napoleon had rejected these initial terms, although the allied conferees continued to meet until 18 March. See *The Times,* 4 April.

8. Involved in the War of 1812, the ship on which Bertie Mostyn served had been ordered to intercept all shipping along the Atlantic coast from Block Island to Cape May, to pursue and capture all American ships she met, commandeer them with their cargo, or destroy them.

9. For Sophia Byron, see HLT to Q [15 July 1784][a], n. 5.

TO HARRIET MARIA PEMBERTON

Brynbella
Wensday Night 19 January
This Letter goes tomorrow 20: January 1814.

A Thousand Thanks Dear Madam for your kind Letter—it but confirms Suspicions long entertained by me, that Salusbury was unwell—How should he or his Friend be otherwise?—heating their Blood with drinking, Dancing &c.—and then; rushing into this Cold Air, enough to kill a Gyant. The best Way is to live *low* while this Weather lasts——and keep the Body open: those who *cram* themselves will find bad Consequences, such as befall Ladies who draw their Stays so tight they scarce can breathe, and then sit down to a *good* Supper as they call it: but the Blood so driven must go *somewhere,* and its most natural Course is to the Lungs whence Coughs arise——not to be cured by Currant Jelly *Lozenges.*—But I shall fright, without convincing you: let us then change the Subject, and for the fiftieth Time—admire the *Posts,* which brought me this last obliging Letter in *Two* days, when mine to you from Bodylwyddan took up *five,* and the Snows then not half as deep.——Give my best Love to our Inestimables, and tell your Brother I congratulate him on coming off so easily as with a *broken-out Face.* Dear Salusbury shall have a half-sheet *all his own* full of Reproaches for never telling me how he does: it was exceeding kind in you my sweet Lady to let me know the Truth——I could get no Intelligence from Joseph, any more than from his little Dog, or rather Dog*ess;* who would be a Beauty I think, but for her long Ears and Tail. Does Salusbury like your Ridicule I wonder? and will our dear Edward acknowledge that I can work as neatly with my Needle as the most Illiterate Woman alive?

You do not tell if he has brought his Heart home. My London Letters Say North Wales cannot be colder than the Metropolis——where nothing seems to draw Attention from Political Subjects, except the Indian Jugglers;[1] and the Duke of Kent; who seeing them swallow their own Swords with Impunity, challenged them to swallow *His:* and so the Man *did,*—Yes, and brought it back bloody, and the Duke was deeply affected, but the Fellow suffered nothing in Consequence.

Perhaps however you have heard this before;——You have I am sure *often* heard before what I repeat with the Sincerest Pleasure that I have the honour to be Dear Miss Harriet's much *Obliged* and faithful/ H: L: P.

I enclose Mrs. Whalley's Letter, (for such I believe it;) in Consequence of Dear Salusbury's idle Curiosity, or Curious Impatience——if he is gone you will send it back to Brynbella.

Text Ry. 592.10. *Address* Miss Harriet Maria Pemberton/ Longnor/ near/ Shrewsbury.

1. The Indian jugglers had been performing in London since the summer of 1813 at 87 Pall Mall. The price of admittance was 3s., or 2s. for an upper seat. As the *Morning Post* for 27 July 1813 described them: "These celebrated Orientals continue to exhibit . . . to the astonishment of the curious, and to the great gratification of the public. The swallowing of the sword is now no longer doubted. . . ." They continued their London performances through the early winter of 1815. See HLP to Ly W, 3 February 1815.

TO JOHN SALUSBURY PIOZZI SALUSBURY

Thursday 27: January 1814.

This Moment comes a Letter from my Dearest written long before that which arrived Three Days ago: This is the one in which you mention the Bonfire made on the Bosom of pretty Sabrina. Old Thames has had Fairs and Carriages and every thing—but Ships,—these three or four Weeks.[1] I am sitting by a good Fire waiting for Doctor Cumming and Major Pilkington[2] and Mr. Moore to come and console me for being deprived of Your Company——but while I write, The News of our poor Physician's being confined to his bed comes to hand——never was there so sickly a Time. *You* always say the Weather is just like every Weather at the same Season, but few are of the same Mind;—and my last Year's Pocket Book mentions The Birds singing on this Day:——They have little Fancy to sing *now*, but our Servants say that Joseph is to sing tonight—*instead* of Them.

No dancing will be attempted.[3] There is very little Snow left Towards the Sea, but never were Newspapers so crouded with Accidents and Offences are[4] these are, now We have got them. London appears to be in a frightful Condition, and Paris will soon be in a Worse from *other* Causes, if I mistake not.

We that reside at Distance from the Metropolis are best off perhaps, and I am happy to hear Mr. Pemberton is so much better;[5] you never by any *Accident* mention your *own health,* but as you say of me—No Complaints are made, and perhaps that *does* imply no Occasion for complaining. We have a fine bright Sun today, and I took a good Walk, and did not feel it too Cold. The poor Women at both Lodges are very seriously Ill; and Leak's Wife has never been out of Bed for a Fortnight——I think *his* Health has not been improved by Matrimony, the wretched Man looks as if he were quite exhausted,—and so I suppose he *is*.[6]

Mr. Charles Shephard says he is going to the West Indies—assure yourself dear Salusbury I have no *War* with him:[7] I am a miserable Combatant, and to Triumph over *me* is small Victory to any one——My hope is to escape the Streatham *Coal* Bill, as I have a Letter to shew—under Mr. C. Shephard's own hand—saying he discharged it:—and *this* is so modest a hope,—one may be permitted to indulge it. Mrs. Whalley has written to me very politely indeed: The Bath People are those who I depend on for my *Social* Comforts in future, not the London ones. Doctor Whalley will last me out I dare say; and while he lives, Mrs. Siddons will never be my *open* Enemy.—My Fears from them all, are as cold as my hopes: They will do me neither good nor harm. My Business is to keep a Watch on my own Thoughts, and whilst I am solitary, not to be *idle.* An empty House is every one's Property[8]—and bad Fancies will occupy a Mind untenanted, unless the Centinels are awake to repel Them——

Here come my Dinner Companions: Poor Souls! but Major Pilkington accepts the Offer of *your* Bed where two Maids have lately slept every Night. I was quite sorry for the Men, coming half on foot half on Horseback thro' Snow and Ice to dine with *me*; but I never *did* since I can remember, spend a Birthday in *complete Solitude,* and had no Wish to pass *this* so——Therefore sent for these Friends to break the Gloom.

Singing or Dancing—or scarce *Breathing* was about the House to be heard; because Mrs. Leak was too ill to be disturbed with Noises—so Good Night Dearest, and let us thank God for this soft Rain which will carry away some Ice and Snow, and leave the Commerce of the World more open.

Major Pilkington I see has no Notion of the Cossacks going to dictate Peace at Paris; but so many strange Things *do* happen one cannot much wonder— happen what *will.*[9]

It is surely *somewhat* strange that after saying (most truly no doubt) how ill you were: I should receive Three or four Letters from you, never naming your health at all. I am however always glad to see your handwriting, as I am/ always most anxiously and most/ Affectionately Yours/ H: L: P.

Pray make my proper Compliments.

Text Ry. 587.218. *Address* John Salusbury Piozzi Salusbury/ Longnor/ near/ Shrewsbury.

1. "The Thames, between Blackfriars and London bridges, continued to present the novel scene of persons moving on the ice in all directions, and in greatly increased numbers. . . . The whole of the river opposite Queenhithe was completely frozen over; and in some parts the ice was several feet thick, while in others it was dangerous to venture upon; notwithstanding which, crowds of foot passengers crossed backwards and forwards throughout the whole of the day." See *AR,* "Chronicle," 56 (1814):11–12; *The Times,* 15, 16, 20–22, 26 January 1814.
2. Robert Pilkington (1765–1834), ultimately a major general, was an engineer in the royal artillery.
3. HLP was having a small birthday celebration.
4. As. Perhaps HLP was anticipating "are" later in the sentence.
5. For Captain Edward Pemberton of Longnor, see HLP to JSPS, 20 August 1808, n. 1.
6. AL and Ann Glover were married on 9 October 1813.
7. Charles Mitchell Smith Shephard was to take up residence on the Windward Islands. He died on St. Vincent, leaving behind him a common-law wife, named Maria Bail, and four "natural"

children—Harriet, William, Caroline, and Thomas, all minors in 1839. For a copy of his will, see C.R.O., Berkshire (D/EX 360/16).

8. Matthew 12:44–45. She recollects SJ's warnings on the dangers of idleness in moments of solitude. See HLP to PSP, 30 August 1802, n. 5.

9. The Cossacks were so feared as a military power that *The Times* on 17 March could write of the Russian victory at Laon: "If Blucher, if the Cossacks, get to Paris,—to Paris, the seat of Buonaparte's pride and insolence,—what mercy will they show to it; or why should they show it any mercy? . . . Perhaps, the famous city of which we speak may even now be laid in ashes." HLP assumed that along with military might went political prowess so that the Russian envoys could dictate peace terms not merely to the French but to the Allies. See also *The Times,* 9 and 22 January 1814.

TO HARRIET MARIA PEMBERTON

Brynbella Fryday
4: February 1814.

I am sincerely grieved my Dear Miss Harriet,—*indeed* I am; to think of these odious Posts, which will perhaps retard the joint Letter written by Salusbury and myself the moment of his Arrival,—and keep you another Day in Agitation of Spirits.—We sent the strangely-written Performance by the Postillion who brought him hither, that not a Moment might be lost:—and now yours shew but too plainly that they have not reached Longnor at the Hour one had a right to expect.

But 'tis Time to calm all Apprehensions. Our Inestimable is so near, so *close* I may call it to *quite* well, that I allow him a Minced Pye to day.——Oh never fear my *shewing* up Meat at Breakfast; I value him too much——and for Seven Months more—I *will* take Care of him. With regard to The Friends he tells me I am then to resign him to; I well know how high he has always stood in their favour: and have every well grounded Hope of my Place being well supplied. They shall find me *ready* to fulfill every Promise I have made Him, in the fullest possible Confidence that he has repeated them with Accuracy——and am only concerned to Think my Power is so limited. Your Mama and Your Brother have often heard me say that I would give Salusbury my Paternal Estate here in Wales: He knows its Extent to a Tittle, and I hope has never led you, (I'm sure he has not:) to fancy it more than it is. Every Day makes me wish it were more, the nearer I am to parting with it; and every hour adds to my anxious Desire of living till he is of Age, that by *giving* it—instead of *leaving* it: he may escape the Legacy Tax, and be enabled to provide for the dear Lady of his deliberate Choice. And now God bless charming Miss Harriet, and let us agree to love this Dear Fellow as he deserves; and as I really do believe He will always deserve from You and from Your Affectionate and/faithful/H: L: Piozzi.

Text Ry. 592.12.

TO HARRIET MARIA PEMBERTON

Brynbella Thursday Night
10: February 1814.

My sweet Harriet—no longer *Miss*—but my Niece elect; has written me just the prettiest Letter in the World, and I sincerely hope and trust we never shall be worse Friends than we are to Day. On our own Dear Salusbury's Promises I have the firmest Reliance; he does indeed possess the very Soul of Honour, and will make us both happy by an exemplary Conduct. If the Money-Stuff falls short, it is only to be lamented on your Account and His: You both deserve larger Fortunes, but as You both intend being prudent and careful, It may be made *do* as the People say; and I will leave Wine, Plate, and House-Linnen, so that there shall be no need——no *Immediate* Necessity,—of purchasing; because my Heart *does* approve his Choice: I should *not* have done so for a richer, if to me a less amiable Lady. For the rest——He is my Nephew, my *Son* and *Heir*; and when I have *given* him my Estate, it shall be my Study to *leave* him as few Debts as possible. I *have* none, except for the Repairs of Streatham Park; which if I live will be wiped off in Two or Three Years, and the continued Assurances of your mutual Happiness will keep me alive Two or Three more I hope. 'Tis a sweet Comfort to think that since I have had this dear Child under my Care, I never did cause him a Tear: and that I can at 16 Years End or more—contribute to his Well-being, according to the Mode he makes Choice of——placing *Himself* among the Friends he has invariably preferred to every other Set, every other Circle, he has been introduced to——How then can I doubt their Kindness towards *him?*

Meanwhile I wonder that Your Brother don't write to me, Do you know that I think it very odd/ With Mr. Pemberton I was *always* a favourite,—and expect to be more so, when he and Dear Mrs. Pemberton see what an Affectionate Aunt their darling Daughter possesses in her *Sincere* Friend/ Hester Lynch Piozzi.

There is not an Atom of the Cough or Cold remaining.

Text Ry. 592.13.

TO SAMUEL LYSONS

Brynbella
17: February 1814.

Dear Mr. Lysons

I was desired by some Disputants to obtain correct Information, and felt immediately that I could be *Sure* of it from no one but yourself. The Question is— What Authority can be produced for an Account given in some public Print of a Frost on the River Thames—equal or nearly equal to this last——in the Second or Third Centuries?[1]

Do me the very great Kindness to let me know:[2] and *where* you read the Fact, whether in Holinshed, Stowe, Speed, or Strype's Annals[3]—and from what Record the Incident is taken——it having been averred that no Records could then have been kept——I mean in 260 or 270 A.D.

Having now discharged my Commission, I take the Opportunity tho' *late* of wishing you and your Brother a happy New Year; and full Enjoyment of the Felicities which People seem in such strong Expectation of. Your living World is so remote from *us here;* and the Intelligence so limited——that I know absolutely nothing of what is going forward. My Correspondents always begin their Letters with——"You have *heard so much* of &c. &c., that I am precluded hearing *at all.*"

Come now, do send me a kind Letter and tell me if Madame D'Arblaye gets 3000£ for her Book or no:[4] and if Lord Byron is to be called over about some Verses he has written——as the Papers hint.[5]——And tell me how the Peace Makers will accommodate the Pope[6] and the little King of Rome too[7]—and the Emperor of Germany[8] beside, whose second Title was King of the Romans.—— And how all this and Ten Times more is to be settled—before St. David's Day.[9]——Wonders! Wonders! Wonders! Why Katterfelto and his cat never pretended to *Such* Impossibilities.[10] What says your Brother to *these* Days,——He used to feel amazed at the Occurrences of 21 Years ago: but if everything we Saw so tumbled about *then,* can be so easily and swiftly arranged *now*——much of our Horror and Surprize might have been saved.

The Fire at the Custom House must have been very dreadful; I Hope you suffered nothing but Sorrow for the General Loss.[11]

Devonshire Square is a Place the Situation of which is unknown to me, but I have Friends there, who I should grieve for, if they came to any harm.

Adieu dear Mr. Lysons; *If* I *live*—which no other old Goose does I think; thro' this Winter; We shall meet at old Streatham Park, and I shall once more tell you truly, and tell you *personally* how faithfully I am yours/ H: L: Piozzi.

If you ever see Captain James and Lady Flaminia, tell *him* that one of the Pleasures I look forward to, is Introduction to her Ladyship[12]—which I hope for thro' you and thro' Lady Kirkwall.

Text Hyde Collection. *Address* Samuel Lysons Esq./ Tower/ London. *Postmark* DENBIGH <2> 24.

1. See *Bell's Weekly Messenger,* 30 January:
"In the year 220 a frost in Britain lasted five months. In 250 the Thames was frozen nine weeks. 291, most rivers in Britain frozen six weeks. 359, severe frost in Scotland for fourteen weeks. 568, the rivers in Britain frozen for two months. . . . 695, the Thames frozen six weeks, and booths built on it. . . . 908, most rivers in Britain frozen two months. 923, the Thames frozen thirteen weeks." *Bell's Weekly Messenger* carries its statistical and historical survey of frosts, British and Continental, up to 1795, and gives as it source the *Encyclopedia Perthensis.* It concludes, as does *The Times,* on 26 January with a detailed description of the frost in London, 1739–40. See also *GM* 84, pt. 1 (1814):142–44, 239–42.
2. SL replied 26 February 1814 (Ry. 552.24):

"I never heard of the great Frost, you enquire after, nor if such a one happened, is it at all likely to have been recorded in history. Many no doubt there have been from the earliest times, and probably some may be recorded by our early monkish historians; the first that I recollect to have seen mentioned is that of 1149 when Holinshed tells us on the 10th of December 'it began to freeze extremely and so continued 'till the 19th of February, whereby the river of Thames was so frozen, that men might pass both on foot and horseback over the same.' In the 28th year of K[ing] Hen[ry] 8 Hall (in his Chronicle) says 'This year in December was the Thames of London all frozen over, wherefore the King's Majesty with his beautiful Spouse Queen Jane rode throughout the City of London to Greenwich' but the greatest Frost mentioned in history, I believe was that of 1683, it began in December and lasted till February . . . [when] 'The Thames was so frozen that there was another City, as it were, on the ice, by the great number of booths erected between the Temple and Southwark, in which place was held an absolute fair, for above a fortnight, of all sorts of trade. An ox was likewise roasted whole, bulls baited and the like.'" SL went on to describe the frozen Thames in 1708–9, 1740, 1754, 1771, 1777, 1784, and 1788–89.

3. Raphael Holinshed (d. 1580), *Chronicles of England, Scotland, and Ireland* [January 1587], in 6 vols. (London: J. Johnson, 1807, 1808), 2:99, 455; 3:802–3; 4:228.

John Stow (ca. 1525–1605), *A Survey of London* [1598, 1603], reprinted from the text of 1603, ed. Charles Lethbridge Kingsford, 2 vols. (Oxford: Clarendon Press, 1908), 1:24.

John Speed (ca. 1552–1629), *The Theatre of the Empire of Great Britaine* (London: J. Sudbury and G. Humble, 1611).

John Strype (1643–1737) reprinted Stow's *A Survey of the Cities of London and Westminster . . . Corrected, Improved, and very much Enlarged . . .* 2 vols. (London: A. Churchill, 1720), 1:56.

4. According to the "Articles of Agreement" (Yale University Library), FBA was to receive from Longman, et al., £1,500 for the first edition of *The Wanderer* (£500 on the delivery of the manuscript, £500 six months after publication, £500 a year after publication), and another £1,500 for five subsequent editions (£500 for the second and £250 for the third to sixth editions). Since the novel went through two editions (with difficulty), FBA earned £2,000. See *Journals and Letters*, 7:passim.

5. Early in 1812, Princess Charlotte in a public quarrel with her father had been reduced to tears. Within a few days, the *Morning Chronicle* printed an anonymous poem that began, "Weep, daughter of a royal line,/ A Sire's disgrace, a realm's decay. . . ." In 1812 little attention was paid to the poem, but two years later, in the second edition of *The Corsair*, Byron acknowledged the poem as his. By the middle of February newspapers charged that Byron's lines offended royal privilege and the sanctity of a father-daughter relationship. See John Drinkwater, *The Pilgrim of Eternity* (London: Hodder and Stoughton, 1925), 187–91.

6. By 22 January Napoleon ordered that Pius VII be removed from Fontainebleau (before he was rescued by the advancing Allies) and be taken indirectly to Rome. By 16 February, he had reached Savona and within a month the Allies at Châtillon were to demand as part of their peace proposals the full freedom and independence of the Pope. Napoleon, however, had anticipated the Allies' demand: on 24 May the Pope "made his public entry into Rome . . . attended by the Ex-King of Spain, his consort, the Queen of Etruria, the King of Sardinia, &c. His Holiness has interdicted Cardinal Maury from his functions, and summoned him to Rome." See *GM* 84, pt. 1 (1814):611.

7. For François-Joseph-Charles, styled king of Rome from his birth, see HLP to Q, 22 March 1810, n. 2.

8. HLP refers to Napoleon's father-in-law who in January acceded to the will of the Allies. Thus, "a preliminary Treaty between Great Britain and Austria has been signed by the Earl of Aberdeen and Count Metternich; by which the Emperor of Austria engages to employ all his forces against the common Enemy, and the British Government to support his exertions by every means in its power; and both parties are pledged not to enter into any separate negotiation, or to conclude any peace, armistice, or convention, unless by mutual consent" (*GM* 84, pt. 1 (1814):83).

9. At this time HLP shared with other Britons bewilderment about peace plans. Thus, *The Times*, 7 February, editorialized:

"We must frankly own, that we have derived more alarm and anxiety from a perusal of the German papers to the 26th ult. which we have just received by the way of Holland, then we could have felt from a series of lying French bulletins. . . . We learn from these papers, that the Allies, with the concurrence of Lord Castlereagh, had resolved *to make new overtures to* Buonaparte!! . . . we trust that the Allies will at once declare that they can recognise and treat with no other Sovereign of France than Louis XVIII."

By 12 February, *The Times* reported that Bonaparte refused to submit to the terms worked out by the Allies and that peace negotiations stood still.

10. Gustavus Katterfelto (d. 1799) was a well-known London quack who announced his forthcoming appearances in advertisements headed "Wonders! Wonders!"

11. On the morning of 12 February, "a fire broke out in the Custom-house, in Lower Thames-street, which burnt with great fury, and in a few hours destroyed that old but useful pile of building." Many barrels of gunpowder lodged in the custom house exploded so that the fire spread to adjoining warehouses and tenements. The actual loss to the government in pounds sterling and in documents was incalculable. See *GM* 84, pt. 1 (1814): 191–92.

12. George James II (fl. 1775–1840) had been commissioned in the Second Dragoons or R.N. British Dragoons as of 16 June 1807. By 1812 he had become a captain in the same regiment and as of 3 December 1818 he was promoted to the rank of major. He remained in the army until April 1820, when his name disappeared from the army lists.

On 6 April 1809 he had married Lady Flaminia Hay (1775–1821), youngest daughter of the fifteenth earl of Erroll.

TO CLEMENT FRANCIS

Brynbella
9: March 1814.

You are all of you too kind dear Mr. Francis; a most obliging Letter from Young Williams lies before me now, and must be acknowledged——I am much flattered by, and very proud of my Cambridge Friends. Do not plague Lord Massey or yourself about the Fables; *Your* Account of them is quite satisfactory, without the Book.[1] Addison and the Author of Gil Blas have culled the best I doubt not.[2] The Two Owls is to be found in more Places than one, but I can't exactly say where. Oh when You come to my Age You will see much of the Learning which made the Solid Care of your *first Course* in the Dinner of Life——hashed up, and warmed in various Shapes for *the Second*. Doctor Johnson told me the Story you relate from that Repository of Anecdote Howell's Letters[3]—a long Time ago—he had (he said) been *poaching in Suidas for unlicensed Greek* as Pope expresses it,[4] and found the Passage you so good-naturedly transmit to me. There is much curious Matter quaintly expressed in my Countryman's obsolete Epistles,[5] but one grows fonder of such Sort of Literature as Life advances——It is surprizing that your *Esprit precoce* should feel any Taste for them——but you were always running against Time and winning. The *Dot and go one* was happily set aside I hope. See what a good Mark Charles Shephard has carried his Talents to; Pemberton tells me he has 1500£ o'Year——My Heart is exceeding glad, because one hates to see Abilities rusting for want of proper Exercise—— and he pays a heavy Forfeiture in giving up the full Flow of London Conversation, so that Envy will not mingle in the Sensations such good Fortune is calculated to excite. Your Sister is more tardy than She used to be in her Communications: Your Aunt is among the Lucky People who take up Praise and Pelf beforehand, Every body rejoyces that She is to get 3000£——every body feeling sure that her Book will deserve it. A Work descriptive of *Manners*, a Pen that is skilled to shoot Folly as it flies,[6] will produce pleasing Contrast to these odd Performances—which hiding their heads in a Mist of Unintelligible Sublimity, make us *believe* they touch the Skies——whether they do or no. There is however Truth enough in what Burke says of Obscurity being a *Source* of the

Sublime[7]—Our Fancy has been sadly *let down* since Truth *illuminated* our Political Prospects. A new Fog arising would perhaps be better than the Certainties which are likely to follow soon.—They will deeply affect our Old Acquaintance *Dot and go One*. I hope to see Streatham Park as an *Inhabitant* the hot Days of next Summer; but will Summer or its Precursor Spring ever come to Great Britain again? They never moved forward so slowly.

Salusbury sends you his best Compliments; I rather begin to fancy that he and his *Friend* Pemberton may possibly write *Brother* before this Year will be expired: but Multa cadunt you know, so the least said is best I believe:—certainly when said by Dear Sir/ Your truly faithful—/ H: L: Piozzi.

Text Berg Collection, m.b. *Address* Clement Francis Esq./ Caius College/ Cambridge. *Postmark* DENBIGH 224.

1. At least six editions of Pilpay or Bidpai in English were available to HLP. A Joseph Harris (fl. 1690) did the first, using the "fourth" or "Persian" version: *The Fables of Pilpay, A Famous Indian Philosopher: containing many useful rules for the conduct of humane life* (London: Printed for D. Brown . . . Charles Connigsby . . . T. Leigh, 1699).

It is difficult to know what version of *Pilpay's Fables* interested HLP. That she continued to be interested is evident in a note in "Minced Meat for Pyes": "I have *found* at last where I *may find* Pilpay's Fables. There is a beautiful Copy in the British Museum among Sir Hans Sloane's MSS. This I learned in the Life of S[ir] W[illiam] Jones."

2. There is no direct recorded evidence that either Joseph Addison or Alain René Le Sage used Pilpay, although the former in *Spectator* 293 tells a Persian fable of a drop of water and an oyster. HLP may have associated this with Pilpay. For its actual source, see Bond, 3:46n.

3. James Howell (1594–1666), *Epistolae Ho-Elianae: Familiar Letters domestic and foreign. . . . Upon emergent Occasions* (1645), 11th ed. (London: R. Ware, J. and P. Knapton, T. and T. Longman, C. Hitch and L. Hawes, J. Hodges, J. and J. Rivington, et al., 1754).

The anecdote SJ borrowed from Howell's *Letters* is missing with Clement Francis's letter.

4. *The Dunciad*, 4.228.

5. James Howell traced his pedigree to Tudwal Glôff (fl. 878), son of Rhodri the Great.

His father was Thomas (d. 1632), curate of Llangammarch, Brecknockshire, and later rector of Cynwil and Abernant, Carmarthenshire. The place of James Howell's birth is uncertain, although the matriculation list of Jesus College, Oxford, in 1610 give it as Carmarthenshire.

6. See Pope's *Essay on Man*, 1.13–14.

7. HLP alludes to the "odd Performances" of "modern" poets—particularly Byron and Southey.

See Edmund Burke, *A Philosophical Enquiry into the Origin of our Ideas of the Sublime and the Beautiful*, ed. J. T. Boulton (London: Routledge and Kegan Paul, 1958), pt. 2, secs. 3, 4, etc.

TO JOHN WILLIAMS

Brynbella
13: March 1814.

How kind you are! my very dear Mr. W[illiams] and how happy it makes me to feel that my Conversation can still be agreeable to Young People of good Sense and good Taste. Such Partiality will encourage me to a long Chat with you concerning the atmospheric Stones which have attracted much of my attention. I do believe that Diana of the Ephesians was no other than one of These and it was thought you know that She fell down from Jupiter[1]—but I have heard a

Cambridge Man maintain that it was possible the *Moon* might produce them, an Idea best befitting a *Lunatic* and about as good Philosophy as that of poor Langford and his alternate Revolutions of the Earth and Sun.[2] Doctor Milner's Joke on such Immechanical notions is the very best I know—the ready furnished House.[3] They must I think go *up* before they fall down.—And certainly there are more Volcanoes at Work than we are watching, which fill the air with Substances of an attractive kind which for the most part assume Conical Shapes, as Nature when alone always appears particularly to delight in.

The Dea Pessinuntia or Cybele of Classic Mythology was I fancy a mere Meteroic Composition.[4]—They washed her with much Silly Reverence you may remember, and Heliogabalus's Black Stone that he drove into Rome with four white Horses was nothing better—only the form happened to be perhaps a more elegant and perfect Cone. He was a *Syrian* you know, and this dropping hot from heaven as they believed—served excellently to represent their Bel, or Baal, or lost Thammuz—The *Sun* in Short—of which Divinity he was *Priest;*— as a Pyræum of aspiring Flame.[5]

I'm glad you are a Reading Man Dear Sir, it is the best Thing after all. "Eruditio inter prospera Ornamentum, inter Adversa Refugium"—is an old Saying of old Lactantius, and cannot be too often repeated or recurred to.[6] What would have become of me These last Years at Brynbella had I not loved Reading?

The French Ladies when they cease to attract Notice by their Wit or Beauty— confess that they must turn either fausse Devote, or vraïe Valetudinaire. My good health Thank God protects me from the last; and to insult the Heaven we hope for—by Hypocrisy, in the final Stage of our Journey thro' Life—would be *too* bad.

The present Winter has been the longest and severest I have known; and some Accounts give one to fear it has had serious Effects upon the London, as on the Dublin Poor-folks. Oh God forbid that the natural World should in its Concussions keep Pace with the Political World! I should then be tempted to think the Dissolution of all Things was approaching[7]—if the *Elements*—meaning the *Constituent Parts* of whatever has hitherto been binding on us, were let loose in *La Physique* as the French term it: as for *La Morale*—They were first to cut the Cables, and now seem at a Loss to know whither they are driving.

I think Your Father wins his Wager of me concerning Buonaparte: Salusbury is gone with his Young Friend Pemberton to Bodylwyddan at this Moment. Lord Massey is most obliging in not forgetting me—No matter for the Fables: I have a clear Account concerning them, from Francis of Caius College, and do not want to possess the Book.

Mrs. Mostyn is in London among the Gay Mortals that walk and drive *upon* the Earth just now; and I suppose are *Superficial* enough in every sense: Quere whether She will not have forgotten Tales and Spars before you are become an Adept in her *once* favourite Science, Geology.

Let me hope my dear Sir that you will not pursue that Study till it leads you into Doubts destructive of all Comfort in this World and all happiness in the Next.

I am not afraid of Gibbon.[8] Whoever has a true taste of Cicero's Sweetness and

Virgil's Majesty will not take *his* Modern Terseness of expression, or neatness of quick finish—so completely French—for Perfection. But I am myself taking unauthorized liberties. Let not the freedom deprive me of your engaging correspondence so flattering and delightful to your/ old and sincere friend/ H: L: P.

The Gentlemen are just come home and send best Remembrances—They found and left every Thing well at Bodylwyddan except Miss Blackburne.—[9]

Text Ry. 6 (1813–21). *Address* John Williams Esqr./ Trinity College/ Cambridge. *Postmark* DENBIGH.

1. See Acts 19:28, 35. In the margin of her Imperial Family Bible (1811), HLP glossed these two verses. "This Diana was a black Stone in a Conical Form, an Aerolyte *I* fancy; and the People fancied She fell down from Jupiter. Her Temple was the finest piece of Work in those days; and called one of the 7 Wonders of the World. The Cybele Pessinuntia was a Duty of the Same Sort—a *Stone* or Piece of Basalt——generated in the Clouds as Some say; and Some believe it sprang out of a Volcano. . . ." See also HLP's marginal gloss of Genesis 28:18.
2. The priest and geologist William Langford (b. 1745) was "poor Langford" because he had died on 21 January 1814. See *GM* 84, pt. 1 (1814): 202.
A graduate of King's, Cambridge (B.A., 1767; M.A., 1770), he was associated most of his life with Eton, serving as assistant master (1766–75), lower master (1775–1803), and fellow (1803–14).
3. Essentially a chemist, Isaac Milner (1750–1820) was a Cantabrigian, who served as president of Queen's (1788–1820), Jacksonian professor of natural philosophy (1783–92), and Lucasian professor of mathematics (1798–1820); F.R.S. (1776–1820).
Since JW's letter is missing, we cannot determine "Dr. Milner's Joke" although his reputation as a wit—sometimes a cruel one—was well known.
4. Cybele or Magna Mater, originating in Phrygia, appeared in Rome as a black meteoric stone (appearing as the face of a silver statue).
5. Heliogabalus was a sun god of Emesa in ancient Syria and worshipped in the form of a black cone. In this paragraph, HLP's mind moves from association to association. Cybele, symbolized as a black meteoric stone, recalls Heliogabalus and other semitic deities—Bel and Baal. Then her mind and its associations come full circle as Cybele evokes the recollection of her son/lover, or Tammuz.
See also Bayle, 1:306, whose sources were Diogenes Laertius, 2.10; Pliny, 2.58; Plutarch's "Lysander," in *Lives*.
6. See HLP to JSPS, 28 January 1808, n. 4.
7. See 2 Peter 3:10.
8. HLP associates Edward Gibbon with the promotion of skepticism, primarily because of his chapters on the growth of Christianity in the *Decline and Fall of the Roman Empire*.
9. The daughter—either Elizabeth or Harriet—of John Blackburne (1754–1833) of Orford Hall and Hale, Lancs.

TO CLEMENT MEAD

Brynbella Wednesday
23d March 1814.

Mrs. Piozzi earnestly wishes to hear that Mr. Mead has finished with Streatham Park, where She hopes to send Leak very soon in the next Month and follow herself the first Week of July.

When Mr. Mead's Account is made out and carried to Mr. Windle, It will be the happiest Day She has seen many Years—when She reads his Name at the bottom of a Receipt in full of all Demands from his/ humble Servant/ H: L: Piozzi.

I neither can nor will send any more Money till the *whole is over*—which God speed, for I am weary to Death on't.

Pray write to me or to Leak immediately.

Text Hyde Collection. *Address* Mr. Mead Surveyor &c./ Upper Charlotte Street/ Fitzroy Square/ London. *Postmark* ST ASAPH.

TO JOHN SALUSBURY PIOZZI SALUSBURY

Put in—Thursday 28th
April at St. Asaph 1814.

My dearest Salusbury

should not have been plagued with a Letter merely to say L'*Erba cresce*, but Jones of Bryntirion tho' he Sends no Money, has at *least* and at *last* written to say The Money is safe, and will come one of these Days:[1]

I thought You would be glad to hear it.

Meantime The Intelligence from Streatham Park is such that I have written this Moment to say I will *begin* June with them, instead of *ending* it——and 'Twill be best for you to get quit of me, and my *fellow Devourers.*

I have indeed only lived on picking the Bones left by Servants these Three or four Days; and am on my Road to Bodylwyddan at *present*——I never light a Candle till 8 o'Clock, and go to *Bed* tho' not to *Sleep* at 10.——So *my* Expences are not much: but *do* bring me some *Pens*, for those Leak sent are wretched Things, and *you know the Use* I make of them. If Oldfield comes whilst I am away——just between Thursday 28th and Saturday 30th—The *last* Will must do; for I shall inevitably hang myself.[2] To prevent such a Finale however, a Letter goes this Day to Bettwys[3]—Lady Williams's Invitation came but Yester Morning by Accident, so I could not write before to him. Your Bed is lain in every Night— so is the Bed Mrs. and Miss Pemberton slept in when they were here last.

The Park looks as green as an Emerald, and

The Rain it raineth every Day.[4]

The *Condover Brook* I suppose runs famously indeed now. Pray tell the young 'Squire he purposed being a good Correspondent, when *we parted;*[5] but his pretty Sister is worth Twenty of him: and Pray tell *her* how much and how sincerely I rejoyce in the Thought of seeing her and dear Mama next Monday.

Miss Thrale writes a World of Chit-Chat; London really seems quite distracted with Joy:[6] You will have a *fashionable* Correspondent soon in your Affectionate H: L: P, You have long had a *very fond* one. Your Dear Ladies will be cruelly fagged coming 50 Miles to Dinner[7] so—We will not think of sitting down till six o'Clock. *Pray* do not fatigue them about hours; You know I never regard such Nonsense. People that *must* have their Dinner at such and such a Moment, have

been my Scourge many a Time: but I never teized anybody about that Stuff—
on *my own* Account.

God bless my precious Creature, and those he loves best: and bring them all
safe well and happy to *his own*/ Brynbella.

Text Ry. 587.220.

1. For Thomas Jones of Brynterion, Bangor, see HLP to AL, 12 March 1812, n. 3.
2. HLP made a new copy of her 1813 will, merely changing the date to 19 April 1814. (It is now
at the Pierpont Morgan Library.)
3. The letter went to her lawyers, John and Thomas Oldfield. Her 1814 will was witnessed by
the latter.
4. *Twelfth Night,* 5.1.392.
5. For "Pem's" inheritance of Condover Park, about four miles south of Shrewsbury, see HLP to
JSPS, 23 December 1813, n. 7.
6. HLP refers to the following events in London, all of them related to the restoration of the
French Bourbons.
On 20 April "the inhabitants of London were gratified with the extraordinary . . . spectacle of
the solemn entry of a king of France." The streets of London were crowded at noon with "persons
of the first distinction" although Louis and his train did not arrive until some time between five
and six o'clock.
On 22 April "The Right Honourable the Lord Mayor, the Aldermen, Recorder, Sheriffs, City
Officers, and Common Council of the city of London, waited upon his majesty XVIII. . . . at Grillon's
Hotel, in Albermarle-street, with an Address, which was read by John Silvester, Esq. the Recorder."
The next day, 23 April, "about eight o'clock, his most Christian Majesty, the Duchess of An-
gouleme, the Prince of Condé, and the Duke of Bourbon, left London to embark at Dover for France.
An immense concourse of people had assembled in Albemarle-street at an early hour" to wave
farewell to the Royal Family.
See *AR,* "Chronicle," 56 (1814):32–35.
7. HMP and her mother.

TO ALEXANDER LEAK

Thursday 28: April 1814.

I received your welcome Letter from Streatham Park—my very good Leak; and
am only *Sorry,* not at all *Surprized* that Things go no better. I was very anxious
indeed for Your Arrival, and am impatient to be gone from hence——Not so
poor Andrew:—he lingers like Buonaparte at Fontainebleau,[1] because he must
Sell up his little Property before he departs—Poor Creature! I will send him
and Sophia together if 'tis worth the Trouble and Expence——but my Purpose
is, to set out myself the Fryday 27th of May—exactly a Month hence; and indulge myself with the Cathedral Service on *Whitsunday* at *Lichfield* 29th of
May——and so get home on Tuesday to Dinner.

My Dear Mr. Salusbury is at Condover Hall whence he brings his Ladies on
Monday next——and they will stay a Week or so. Till Then I shall enjoy myself
at Bodylwyddan, among *real Friends;* soon to be changed for flattering and de-
vouring *Acquaintance* in Surrey, but do not you engage Horses and Coachman
for me: I will do as I do here, take Horses from Tooting—*The Wheatsheaf there:*

and pay my Guinea a Time for being carried to London. If I go *four* Times o'Week (which God forbid;) and stay 12 Weeks at Streatham Park: one 50£ note will clear my Expences, and I will *not* as (I used to do) keep a Streatham Diligence for eaters and drinkers, and Censurers, and fault-finders.

Ah Leak! You little know my Sufferings in the Sweet Place I give you the Care of; but God made the *Places*, and the People make *Themselves:*—at least make themselves *what they are*——and poor dear Louis the Eighteenth is gone *home* to a Nest of Hornets[2]——so why should not I? I will bring my best Looks, and best Spirits with me, and live as *cheap as I can.*

Remember my *private Commission* and send me some Biscuits, and tell dear Mr. Hugh Hammersley He is among the few I shall be *sincerely* happy to entertain,[3] so will Sir Lucas Pepys be.

Mr. Davies is a funny Man, and I suppose his Butcher is like another Butcher; He *has* kept the 10£ I promised him for the School. Pray learn how much there is at the Bankers, and how much is likely to content Mead and Gillow.

Dear Salusbury gets no Money from Bryntirion, only Excuses: but it will come, only *lingers* like Andrew.—And that is *a bad Thing this Year.*

The Weather is *wet* rather than *warm;* but seems likely to mend, and the Glass rises. I don't remember any Barometer at Streatham Park.

My Abode will be in the *Library* and my own Bed Chamber, no more—— except when I call *Company* round me. Meanwhile my Neighbours will be kind and goodhumoured, and I shall be glad to see *them* at Tea &c. Mr. Hill seemed very amiable,[4] and so did those Friends I met at Mr. Davies's.——*New* Acquaintance are best; They *can* have no *old Malice.* Lord and Lady Coventry have been *uniformly* and on *every Occasion* kind and consoling to their and/ *Your* old Friend/ H: L: P.

—Cyodevant Glover has behaved beautifully to bear her Journey so well: She deserves to be *Leak now.*

Pray write again very Soon, and say you applaud my *Intentions.*

I suppose You *must* give your Rascally Gardiner a Month's Wages or a Month's Warning——and I will not be a Month longer away from Streatham Park.—— We never knew where the Spring of the Carriage was left—and you never *told.*

Miss Bridge walked here and back the other Morning,[5] She is sorry to see Mrs. Ray *so broke* She says;[6]——and I may be Sorry to see Miss Bridge no brighter: one old Fool pitying the other!!!——while the Young laugh at us all.—

I fear Mr. Windle is but too right.

Text Hyde Collection. *Address* Mr. Alexander Leak/ at Mrs. Piozzi's/ Streatham Park/ Surrey. *Postmark* 10 o'Clock AP 30 1814; E 30 AP 30 1814.

1. On 29 March 1814 the allied armies came before Paris and the next day engaged the French massed on the heights of Fontenoy, Romainville, and Belleville (to the allied right) and Montmartre (to the allied left). But by 30 March the capitulation of Paris was signed. On 31 March the allied armies entering Paris were welcomed as liberators, despite the large number of French dead.

The Times (20 April) reported that "Buonaparte was still at Fontainebleau [as of 14 April]; after several nervous attacks, he had fallen into the greatest depression." By 26 April *The Times* announced the departure of Napoleon from Fontainebleau on 20 April.

2. The "Nest of Hornets" involved not merely Louis's own family (like the *ultra*, comte d'Artois) but also large sections of the French population who had suffered during the last months of the military struggle. Many resented the armistice signed in the middle of April, feeling that they and France had been sold out. See Jean Orieux, *Talleyrand ou le sphinx incompris* (Paris, 1970), 568.

Moreover, the Bourbon restoration represented a compromise that might be shaken further by the already-scheduled Congress of Vienna. Ultimately, Louis had to concede that morale among professional French troops was so low that a pro-Napoleonic takeover by the military in 1814 might be possible. See Bertaut, *La Vie aventureuse de Louis XVIII*, 188.

3. When Thomas Hammersley died in 1812, his place in the bank was filled by his elder son, Hugh (d. 1840).

4. Herbert Hill (1750–1828) had matriculated at St. Mary Hall, Oxford, in 1768, receiving his B.A. from Christ Church in 1772, his M.A. in 1774. He became chancellor of the choir of Hereford Cathedral and in 1810 the rector of St. Leonard's, Streatham. An uncle of Robert Southey, he was largely responsible for establishing a school for the education of the poor of the parish of Streatham.

5. For Frances Bridge, see HLP to JSPS, 16 July 1810, n. 6.

6. For Elinor Ray, now eighty-two, see HLP to JSPS, 16 July 1810, n. 11.

TO THE REVEREND LEONARD CHAPPELOW

Brynbella
2: May 1814.

I am sorry you complain so of your health dear Mr. Chappelow: very sorry *indeed*, but complaining People always outlive those who appear stronger. My Health was never to be lamented much, tho' bad enough five Years ago, when You met Sir Lucas Pepys consoling me at Morin's Hotel. Did you enjoy a gay Dinner at Mrs. Merrik Hoare's? I hope you did, and that the vile Cough will Yield to the warm Breezes we may surely expect *next* Month if not *This*.[1] Don't you remember our listening out of Two different Windows at Otricoli to hear the Cuckow? and agreeing that he sung stronger in England? We will hearken for him at Streatham Park if you please *this* Year;—Tho' I am half afraid he is quite *built out* by now in all the Environs of London. He sings all *June* don't he?

There have been famous Rejoycings round your gay Metropolis certainly— and with Reason. I hope the Temple of Janus will now keep *shut*, as long as it has been *open*. When will the Property Tax be removed?[2] I shall like *that* as much as the Sight of Alexander.[3]

> And so the Dragon burst insunder; Then Daniel turned to the People and said; *Lo! these be the Gods ye worship!*[4]

I think Clergymen never take Texts from Apocryphal Books—or this would be a good one; while Buonaparte continues to be remembered;—but that will not be long if He dies, or lives quietly at Elba.[5]

Lord Byron has bestowed his Book very properly:[6] Lord Bradford makes himself amends in his gay Moments for the Depression he feels in the melancholy ones.[7] The hot Fit is more than proportionate to the Cold One always in Agueish Patients—and to *young* People what is Life but a Fever?

I am glad Lady Bradford is so blest in her children; She deserves all the happiness She *can* receive from them——The Gentleman who writes those beautiful Letters was my little Friend *Henry* I fancy: he was a nice Boy.[8] You say nothing of Mrs. Clay—*pretty* Mrs. Clay as She was for a long Time. The Ladies of Llangollen are ever charming——You should not lose their Correspondence, it is really very valuable.

My dear Salusbury will be calling on them as he comes home from Condover Hall I suppose: were he at my Elbow he would dictate respectful Compliments: You must accept *my* best and truest Wishes, and don't be lowspirited and read Medical Books; and fancy Your Lungs endangered. If it is in earnest a Bronchial Catarrh as You call it—The Lungs are safe enough; and Youthful as you and I are Dear Mr. Chappelow, Our *Consumptive Days* must have been past 40 Years ago at least.

Come now, be merry and good humoured, and write me one more Letter, before I tell you truly and *personally* how much/ I am Yours/ H: L: Piozzi.

Text Ry. 561.147.

1. According to LC's letter from London, dated 29 April (Ry. 563.103): ". . . I was in my bed and almost dying at Lord Baths at Longleat—never did a poor wretch suffer so much as I Felt from the dreadful, and as the dethroned would have said, frightful Country. . . . 6 weeks did I labour under a dreadful Cough, bilious complaint and ultimately I was plagued with a Rheumatism. . . . My complaint, which must end me is an hereditary complaint . . . bronchial Catarrh—which I have had 7—and may have 5 years longer.—But I have no peace with my Lungs—except in very warm weather. I shall I hope spend my next winter under the Rock at Hastings which keep[s] off the N.E. Wind—unless I run to earth sooner."

2. HLP anticipated agitation for the removal or reform of the property tax, which began seriously in December 1814. According to the *Morning Chronicle* for 16 December, one of the first groups to organize their demands was "about 200 of the inhabitants of Westminster" meeting at the Crown and Anchor Tavern, "to take into consideration the propriety of petitioning Parliament against the continuation of the Property Tax."

Londoners saw themselves as the instigators of reform and believed their example would "be followed throughout the Kingdom. It will then be seen whether any man will dare to force the continuation of this hateful measure against the opinions and feelings of the whole country . . ." (*Morning Chronicle,* 17 December).

3. At this time Alexander was in Paris. He would arrive in London on 8 June, remaining in England until 23 June.

4. See HLP to LC, 18 June 1801, n. 3.

5. On 13 April Napoleon ratified the treaty of Fontainebleau, which banished him to self-chosen Elba, possessed in full sovereignty, with an annual revenue of two million francs for himself, with a reversion of one million to the empress. The treaty further allowed a revenue of two millions and a half to be distributed among the members of his family; a capital sum of two millions to be spent for his followers; sovereignty over the duchies of Parma, Piacenza, and Guastalla for the empress, with succession to her son and his descendants.

6. *GM* for May reviewed Lord Byron's *Ode to Napoleon Bonaparte.*

"Common rumour and strong internal evidence attribute this anonymous Poem (which has already reached a Fifth Edition) to Lord Byron; and this supposition is not derogatory to his acknowledged talents." The poem is a denunciation of Napoleon as a "throneless Homicide." See *GM* 84, pt. 1 (1814):477.

7. In LC's letter of 29 April: Lord Bradford "whose finances entre nous—are by no means in a flourishing state, has been at the center of the Earth—Lower he could not go—he is now and has been for some time, in the Moon—in the highest spirits, at head Quarters—with Lord Castlereagh &c. &c.—he is now at Paris, emptying the Champaigne bottles—and I hear this morning, but I hope Lady B—— will not hear of it—giving Dinners to forty people at a time—notwithstanding he has been so depressed, and distressed in mind body and Estate."

8. Lady Bradford had four sons: "George Augustus Frederick Henry, now twenty-five; Charles Orlando, twenty-three; Orlando Henry, twenty; and Henry Edmund, nineteen."

LC in his letter reported: "Orlando is just returned for promotion, and almost so young—that he carries his Eggshell, on his head, has already ten Lieutenants below him, and consequently will be on full pay on the peace Establishment. Charles the sailor is first Lieutenant on board the yatch, which carried over the King of France—in a fortnight he brings over Alexander the Good as well as the great . . . and he will certainly be promoted—so that both having escaped bullets, will be on full pay in the time of peace—Lady B—Angel of a Son is upon his Travels—with Mr. William Clive and Lord Herbert—he continually writes to Lady Bradford his mother the most delightful Accounts of what he sees—. . . His Letters might be printed without correction. . . . Orlando— i.e.—ci devant—Little O—has had his hair breadth Escapes—he was wounded slightly at St. Sebastians."

TO JOHN SALUSBURY PIOZZI SALUSBURY

[ca. 2 May 1814]

My dear Salusbury will not wonder to see these Pages ill and unsteadily written; He has assisted me in My Work of sorting old Papers the most uneasily impressive Occupation upon Earth.

May *My* past Sorrows afford *Your* joyful Horrors some pleasing Amusement on a future Day![1] But let my Name——now Yours,——be too dear to You for endurance of *censure*, from Strangers to my Story, my Person or my Character. I leave you with the utmost Confidence that you will never cease to love my Memory—however distant your Time may be past from me, or from any one whoever took interest in my Concerns—as Friend or Enemy. Farewell! You have all I can do for You: what You can do for *me* is, so to act, as to do honour to my Choice of a Son, as your *dear* Uncle acted to make People (who had most blamed our Connection at beginning),—most ready and vehement to applaud it in the End.

Once more Farewell! and gain the Love of those for whose Company you are in Haste to change *mine;*—so That it may be *Sincere,* disinterested, and/durable, like that of/ Your/ H: L: P.

Text "Harvard Piozziana" (Harvard University Library, MS. Eng. 1280).

1. This letter marks HLP's presentation of the five leather-bound volumes of "Harvard Piozziana" to JSPS. The dating of this letter is dependent upon that of the last entry in the manuscript on 2 May.

TO FRANCES WHALLEY

Brynbella
2d May 1814.

My Dear Mrs. Whalley is unspeakably kind in sending me those sweet Verses—pray *pray* accept my truest Thanks, and believe me among the Sincerest of them that rejoyce.

It was really and apparently the finger of God, because We might have had Peace with this strange Mortal——had he not been inspired to reject Terms which no Man in his Wits would have rejected[1]——and for my own Part I doubt his Sanity——Let us see how he behaves at Elba with his Title of *Emperor* so odly continued to him: The Island cannot I think be bigger than our Anglesey.

From Buonaparte to the *Dog* is a Step *higher* certainly: let me request you Dear Madam to send him immediately to Streatham Park—where I have Servants *now*—and will be myself if it please God before the Whitsun Holydays are over.

My Dear Salusbury will probably call me to Witness his Happiness early in September;[2] and when all that Nonsense is over, I shall hope at Old *Bath* to find Lodging-houses much the Cheaper, for the immoderate Emigration to Paris.[3] What a Grand-Merci it was, that the Usurper did not get *in* there before the Allies! He would most infallibly have blown the Town up.

We have reason now to expect them all in London for a short Time, and a mad Moment it will be no doubt—a *short* one I sincerely wish it may be;[4]—— having no Taste to Crouds and Crush, and no desire to die like the Parish Clerk of Sittingbourne:[5]

> Yet not incurious, feel inclin'd
> To know the Converse of Mankind.[6]

Adieu Dear Madam! present me most kindly to Dear Doctor Whalley and give my tender Love to the fair Queen of Mendip. I wish some of these noble Strangers could see the beautiful Lodge and Veranda——They have no private Property like it—no, not *one* of them.

Farewell! and forget not *her* who will be ever/ Yours while/ H: L: Piozzi.

Text Berg Collection +. *Address* Mrs. Whalley/ Queen's Square/ Bath. *Postmark* DENBIGH <224>.

1. Peace terms were offered to Napoleon during an armistice in the late spring and summer of 1813 when a congress was held at Prague. There, Austria proposed the following: the French Empire was to return to its natural limits; the Grand Duchy of Warsaw and the Confederation of the Rhine were to be dissolved; Prussia was to return to her frontiers of 1805. Napoleon did not reject these terms but waited so long before accepting them that Austria declared war against France on 10 August 1813.

2. JSPS was to marry 7 November 1814.

3. For the rush of English visitors to France immediately after the Peace of Paris, see Marcel Moraud, *La France de la restauration d'après les visiteurs anglais . . . 1814–1821* (Paris, 1935), 15–17.

4. By 14 May *The Times* was to provide specific dates for the arrival of the allied sovereigns and their parties.

"By the most recent advices from Paris, we learn that tomorrow is the day fixed for the departure of the Emperor Alexander and the King of Prussia from [Paris], on their proposed visit to England. . . . [They] were to be preceded by Marshal Blucher and General Platow. The Prince Royal of Wurtemberg, and Generals Von Essen and Oppen, are already arrived."

5. "On Louis XVIII.'s triumphant return from this country in 1814, to ascend the throne of the Bourbons, multitudes thronged to congratulate him as he passed, and the street at Sittingbourne being very narrow in parts, a man, not the clerk of the place but of the neighbouring village of Bobbing, was driven over by the royal carriage, and killed. Louis XVIII. granted a pension to the

widow and children, which, much to the credit of the French Government, malgré the various subsequent changes in the reigning powers, still continues to be paid" (Wickham, 2:372n.).

6. Swift, *Cadenus and Vanessa*, lines 314–15.

TO JOHN WILLIAMS

Brynbella
7: May 1814.

I was just wishing for a Letter from my dear young Friend when this last very agreeable one arrived. In return to your *Congratulations*, I send you my *Invitations, cordial ones*, and hope to see you at Streatham Park as early in June as possible.

I leave this Place on Friday 27: of May—meaning to treat my ears with Cathedral Music at Lichfield on Whitsunday and then home to dinner the *last* of this Month—*Can* the word be repeated without Seriousness? *ought* it? when such Changes of Place and Vicissitudes of Company, Connections &c. force the mind upon reflecting that *The Last* Hour is at hand to us all—

At dear Bodylwyddan however I suppressed my feelings, and forbore to take any leave. The *Enormous Occurrences*, the strange Circumstances that surround us all, contribute to hide lesser Objects from one's View, and in some Measure to diminish the Power of Impression which would otherwise be formidable to weak Spirits—A general Topic of Conversation precludes all private chitchat—as a general Mourning hinders any one from displaying their taste in dress.—We are all of one Mind and stare with Wonder at Events of which the Cause is scarcely visible.—The immediate one we must look for in Buonaparte's Madness, and to speak correctly—I feel some doubts now concerning his being of *Sound Mind*—but why does Francis the 2nd content himself with the awkward Title bestowed upon *him* when Napoleon was conqueror? If he is Emperor at all, he is Emperor of *Germany*. If he is satisfied with *Austria* he is Duke not Emperor.[1] The Sovereigns of Europe should be careful not to make Titles ridiculous, when there are so many Jacobins ready to ridicule them.

With regard to *our own* Nobility and People of Fashion getting into these horrid Scrapes of Swindling and forging and Stock jobbing and the Lord knows what.[2]—They fright *me* to read of them—we need no longer say with Captain Macheath

> I wonder we h'ant better company
> upon Tyburn Tree![3]

The Executive power should really address them now in the official Phrase of
My Lord and Gentlemen!
I never heard of such fellows.—

Dear Salusbury contents himself with a private Station: he has got his favourite Ladies here with him, and is the happiest of human creatures. Pemberton will see the Knot tied, and then, (after coming of Age) he will go to the Continent in February next where I dare say you will meet him; though I really think Travelling would be wiser, safer, and more advantageous two years hence when things are settled and that *Swell* which always Succeeds *such* a Storm is come down to the natural Level.

If you will turn the figures which compose my Age, making me 47 years old instead of 74, I will go *too*—not otherwise.

Farewell! and let me find a Letter on the Library Table at Streatham Park, saying what Day you will be with me there, and dear Lord Massey if he has not forgotten his obliged servant and my own Mr. Williams's ever attached Friend and truly faithful/ H: L: P.

Text Ry. 6 (1813–21). *Address* John Williams Esqr./ Trinity College/ Cambridge. *Postmark* HOTWELL 208.

1. The Napoleonic campaigns that brought about the treaty of Lunéville (9 February 1801) virtually sealed the fate of the Holy Roman Empire. The Habsburg monarch therefore worked to prevent the subordination of his family and the loss of territory. On 11 August 1804 he assumed the title of Franz I, hereditary emperor of Austria (what HLP called "The awkward Title"). On 6 August 1806, after the defeat at Austerlitz and the treaty of Pressburg, he put aside the title and functions of the Holy Roman emperor.

HLP would recognize him as emperor of Germany because he was a descendant of Rudolph (1218–91), the founder of the house of Habsburg, and the first of his family to ascend the German throne.

HLP wants the title of archduke for Franz since the members of the imperial house are archdukes (or archduchesses) of Austria; later princes (or princesses) of Hungary, etc.

2. Toward the end of 1813, Thomas Lord Cochrane's uncle, Sir Alexander Cochrane, became commander in chief on the North American station. He left his flagship, the *Tonnant*, to be equipped by his nephew, who was also nominated his flag captain. At this time Lord Cochrane came to know a French refugee, a Captain de Berenger. On 20 February 1814, the Frenchman sent word to Deal (and from there to London) that Napoleon had been killed, the allies were about to take Paris, and peace was imminent. The funds rose suddenly and then fell. Another one of Lord Cochrane's uncles (who had assumed the alias of Johnstone) made a sizeable profit from the fluctuations in the market. Cochrane (despite a lack of evidence), his uncle (Johnstone), and the swindler were placed on trial. Lord Cochrane was sentenced to pay £500 as a fine, stand in the pillory for an hour, and be imprisoned in the King's Bench for a year. See *The Times*, 9–11 June.

3. Gay, *The Beggar's Opera*, 3.13.air 67.

TO ANN LEAK

Brynbella Sunday Night
15: May 1814.

This Morning while I was thinking how I had forgotten to mention Mr. Salusbury's Dog, and while I was looking out an Excuse for writing again to Streatham Park—comes Leak's Letter. Let me now before I answer the Particulars, beg of You to receive the Animal kindly, and pay the Expences if there are any:— When Mr. Pemberton returns to Shropshire, he will convey him Safely home. It is the Spotted Dane from Dr. Whalley's That I mean, and you may expect him every Day—

Peggy is not only willing, but eager to come to be near London I suppose, and Near Mrs. Leak: and She will manage with Two Cows well enough, and keep as much House clean as I use; and 'tis better shut the rest up, till Accident calls it into use. But airing the Rooms &c. You will *know* to be necessary, and see that it is done. I told her I would keep no Ten Guinea Maids, and would treat them with no Doctors as I have done *here;* but nothing will keep Peg from following——so you will act accordingly.——If She leaves me in Surrey She must find her way back to Wales as She can: I pay no more Journeys for her—which I made her clearly understand.

I sent your Husband a Draft on Hammersley for 50£ by this Morning's Post—at *Seven* Days only: and when You read this Letter, it will be just *Ten days* and no more till You see at Streatham Park if it please God/ Yours ever/ H: L: Piozzi.

Text Hyde Collection. *Address* Mrs. Leak/ at Mrs. Piozzi's/ Streatham Park/ Surrey. *Postmark* DENBIGH <224>; 10 o'Clock MY < >.

TO ANN LEAK

Sunday Night
22: May 1814.

This is my last Letter to Streatham Park,——at least my last Letter during May 1814. My *last* Appearance at poor dear Dymerchion Church was made Three Hours ago—in Company with my *Successors;*—my *next* Entrance will be to the Vault where repose my *Predecessors:*——and by then, there will have been made many Changes. Mary Laundry was asked in Church this Morning, Doctor Cumming came with his Bride and took Sandwiches at Noon:[1] Mrs. Mostyn of Segroid is Said to be going with her eldest Son to France——so the World does not stand still you see.

Mr. Roberts looks like very *Death itself,* and Mr. Lloyd's Mother is dead they say,[2] and I read Prayers tonight for *the last Time,* and the Sweet-hearting Folks will be interrupted for one half hour. Mrs. Ray and Miss Bridge I should think good for a Year to come; but Sally Cook is poorly, and has had Doctor Cumming.

My Purpose is to sleep at Chester next Fryday—at Lichfield next Saturday: pass the Sunday there, and get to Dunstable on Monday Night whence the Drive to Streatham is nothing; I shall be at home by Two or Three o'Clock.

Here is a hot Sun with a Sharp Wind enough to destroy all Vegetation: yet we see Pease, and we eat Asparagus. The Fruit is very promising; but I see no Grass long, and waving as it used to be——and the Milk is wretched, and the Mutton lean.

Four more Dinners however are all I shall ever witness again in *this* Place; and Leak's Wife made my Welcome at the *other* Place dependant on the *Money* I remember——So Heaven have Mercy upon poor H:L:P: A cold Chicken however is all I want or wish——and a clove of Garlick with it.

Doctor Cumming pronounces Cook's Complaint to be Love, and he *must* be a judge of *that* Disorder I suppose.

I hope some Rain is coming soon to lay the Dust. We shall turn out 11 Mouths next Fryday from/ Brynbella.

Adieu for a short Time, and give my Compliments to merry Mr. Davies.

Text Hyde Collection. *Address* Mrs. Leak/ at Mrs. Piozzi's/ Streatham Park/ Surrey. *Postmark* DENBIGH <224>; MY 25 < >.

1. George Brownlow Cumming had married Lucy Margaret Yorke (d. 1819) of Erdigg and Dyffryn Aled, Denbighshire.
For Dr. Cumming, see HLP to Ly W, 9 February 1810, n. 11.
2. The widow of Thomas Lloyd of Denbigh and mother of David. There is no burial record for Mrs. Lloyd at Denbigh or the neighboring parishes (C.R.O., Clwyd).

TO ANNA MARIA PEMBERTON

Dunstable[1] Monday Night
30: May 1814.

The Dear Ladies did seem to wish so kindly and sincerely for a Letter, that I will not even wait till the End of my Journey, to say how perfectly well it has been performed to *this* Place: once as familiar to me as Salop to Yourselves. My earliest—and of Course my happiest Hours were past within Ten Miles of it at my Uncle's Seat Offley Place in Hertfordshire;——where, and of which I was Heiress—*Presumptive* apparently, for he married again, and gave it away by his second Lady's Directions.[2] I find the Country wonderfully improved——so is *every* Country, but no Pease are forward like those we left at Brynbella, and I see no Grass better than Dear Salusbury's; even in Cheshire, where one might expect rich Pasturage. His Spirits—somewhat depressed in the Morning of Fryday the 27th rallied I dare say after he found it necessary to depend wholly on *himself.*

My Bessy Jones being really ill at Chester made me forget myself to think of *her*——She had parted with her Parents at Holywell, and was very low indeed, but we are all bright again now; and I shall find a Letter on the Library Table at Streatham Park to say our Darling 'Squire is well and *busy.* Let me request his Harriet to take the only Method of driving away anxious Thoughts by *Employment* of any kind She can perswade herself to think *Important*——The Cold was half of it Nervousness, and is I flatter myself vanished away by now.

My old Gardener Andrew who never was in England before, says he looks in vain for Lleweney or Brynbella; but the Roads astonish him with their Breadth and Beauty.

Adieu dear Ladies, and accept the true and tender Regards of Your most Faithfully/ Affectionate Servant/ H: L: Piozzi.

You know I always help Mama first, but the next Letter shall be Directed to H: M: P.——

Text Ry. 594.2.

1. In Bedfordshire.
2. See HLP to SL, 23 April [1787], n. 3.

TO JOHN SALUSBURY PIOZZI SALUSBURY

Tuesday Night
31: May 1814
Streatham Park.

Without waiting for Frank or anything else—I hasten to assure my dearest that I am come safe home, and have read his Letter—his kind,—*sweet* Letter, for which accept my Thanks.

Andrew is beginning to recover his Amazement at Sight of the numerous Carriages which above all other Things attracted his Notice, and Confounded his Understanding. And I found myself well enough to walk round the Grounds this Evening after Dinner, which has been *Chicken* and Asparagus so constantly, I feel as if *Feathers* were growing out of my Arms &c. The Meat was no cheaper at Coventry than here, and Poultry at a *mad* Price. Leak buys cheap Corn and feeds ours at home. He asked for you with apparently deep Interest. We had a Cow calved today, and our Grass looks better than other People's Grass——but none looks well——and our Pease are podded, and will go shortly to Market. But you had rather be told how I found a Letter here from Mrs. Pemberton saying that her pretty Harriet had an inflamed Eye, but Mr. Wynne would soon set all to rights.[1]

I dare say all *will* soon come to rights—when She is out of the *Way* of *Inflammation;* and *your* Health will be better too.

Mind your *Business* my precious Creature, and drive away Thought by *Employment.* Time flies fast enough; as I perceive by the Changes in this Place, indeed in *all* the Places I past by to come hither. Let *us* so fill up our hours as not to fear the Motto of a Dial that stared me in The Face driving along; and said to *me*—speaking of the Minutes, *Pereunt sed Imputantur.*[2]——

How many has your poor H: L: P to answer for! but those I have spent with *You* were always pleasingly, sometimes I hope usefully employed; if anything I was happy enough to say or read—tended to encourage my Darling to tread the path of Salvation. Here comes Abbé Davies, who asks for You tenderly, and says young Dicey is gone to Paris on a Frolic, but means it for his last Flash[3]—— then marry—like dear Salusbury—The Girl of his heart; and settle in the Country.

Mrs. Mostyn has sent her eldest Son to finish his Studies in Edinburgh, where less Money will be spent, and more Literature, and more Vice avoided—than in the heart of London, and Top of Westminster School.[4]

Davies thinks this is Lord Keith's Advice,—it is *good* Advice certainly; and probably Scotch Advice—her Second Son is with her I understand.[5] I suppose I must announce my Arrival to all the Ladies——must not I?—No Haste though: I dine at the Streatham University tomorrow,[6] and will seal up this Letter tonight for my *Shadow* to carry in the Morning before 8 o'Clock that it may not miss the Post.

I like my little Shadow very much: 5 Guineas o'Year, with ten Times the Activity and Good Sense of Joseph; 12 Years old they tell me he is, and his Name *Charles*. Like Master Slender I keep only a Man and a Boy now, but what They? I will *live still like a poor Gentleman born.*[7] Well! dearest Angel! you see I can laugh yet; and pray pacify my poor Folks, and tell them I shall not forget them, and give my good Wishes to *black* Nancy, and the *White* Duck: who ought to be come off her Nest now with a little Train of 11 Young ones after her.

Your Dog is a beautiful Creature, but Leak sighs after Tinker——"Te Phyllida O Piozzi; trahit sua quemque Voluptas."—Is that a good Verse! I think not— The female Name should have ended in *n*, but I could not find one. Farewell till Fryday Evening when you shall have another Letter from your fond and faithful/ H: L: P.

Text Ry. 587.223. *Address* John Salusbury Piozzi Salusbury Esq./ Brynbella near/ Denbigh/ North Wales. *Postmark* PM JU 1 1814.

1. Probably the surgeon Hugh Wynn (fl. 1794–1828), of Pride Hill, Shrewsbury. See Tibnam's *Salop Directory,* 1828.
2. Martial, *Epigrams,* 5.20.13.
3. Thomas Edward Dicey (1789–1858) of Claybrook Hall, Leics. Although he had matriculated at Oriel College, Oxford, in 1806, he was admitted to Trinity College, Cambridge, whence he graduated B.A. (Senior Wrangler) in 1811 and M.A. in 1814. He married in 1814 Anne Mary, daughter of James Stephen, a master in chancery. Dicey was to become an important railway entrepreneur.
4. John Salusbury Mostyn had been admitted to Westminster School on 18 June 1810 and left in the spring of 1813. By 1817 he was to become a cadet in the East India Company service (Bengal) and by 1819 a lieutenant in the 5th Extra Regiment, N.I.
5. Henry (Harry) Meredith Mostyn.
6. That is, with RD.
7. *The Merry Wives of Windsor,* 1.1.275–76.

TO JOHN WILLIAMS

Streatham Park
1: June 1814.

My dear Williams's kind Letter followed me to Wales—by Leake's zealous Care; so I was without it longer than I should have been. How flattering are your obliging Attentions! and at such a Time too, when every Thought must have been Literature, I am convinced,—and every Care—Employment. You will deserve a Wife "beautiful as the Houries and wise as Zobeide" (which is the Oriental Compliment to a Lady) for being so diligent:[1] but do not scorn to cultivate the *Modern* Languages which—just now—will be particularly useful; as I feel persuaded *nothing*, nor *nobody* will long delay you in our Island—Well! My advice is, Go: The moments are interesting, and you will know how to make advantage of them. The same conduct no more suits two different Men, than the same coat does;—nor would I counsel You for the world to take dear Salusbury's Method of making Yourself happy—but he poor fellow is un vrai Solitaire— nothing to lean upon but an old blasted Oak which the next Storm must de- stroy——and which *must* perish by Decay if no Tempests continue to tear it.— Since then he likes the new Family he connects with——why with all my heart——There are so many Cross Roads in our Journey thro' Life, and they are so dirty and so dangerous—one is contented to see a young Man make Choice of a clean and a straight one; however unadorned by Flowers, and however undiversified, (is there such a word?) by Elegant Turns, and sometimes *too serpentine* Windings.

I staid longer in Wales than I thought for—there was So much to be done at parting; so I saw Mr. Cumming, and heard of Mrs. Heaton's Death,[2] and Rector Clough's Danger——he was very near following his Lady.[3]

Mrs. Mostyn is in London with her Second Son—The Eldest is gone to Edin- burgh they tell me, but I have as Yet seen none of the Ladies; Little Bertie is in America.

The hope of Peace does not yet operate either on our Funds or on our Provi- sion: Nothing cheap but Corn, and Quartern Loaves—for Horses, Posting &c. continue costly as ever——House rent at Bath will fall however, if all the Families run away to the Continent and few will stay at home.

Lady Williams, dear Lady Williams neither called nor sent; I knew She would not.

Mrs. and Miss Pemberton were with me at Brynbella for the last Three Weeks——and *we* all left Salusbury the same Morning. If you write home tell your Mama that She shall have a long Letter when I have anything to relate worth hearing. It is *no* News to tell her how much I love and respect her—but I shall grow like Your Aunt who never tires when talking of Bodylwyddan. Farewell, and remember how short our Distance is grown, and never pass through London without calling.

If I should ever arrive at the Happiness of seeing my Debts paid and half a crown in my pocket I will come to Cambridge. I am certainly upon Short allow- ance *just now* but as Master Slender says—

"What tho' I will yet live like a *poor Gentleman* born"—

Once more and twenty times/ Adieu my dear Sir; and let nobody you love, forget how faithful a Friend, and how/ Affectionate a Servant/ You possess in H: L: Piozzi.

Text Ry. 6 (1813–21). *Address* John Williams Esqr./ Trinity College/ Cambridge. *Postmark* JU 1 814.

1. Zobeide, or Zebi-el-Khewatin, was an Abyssinian princess who died in 831 A.D. Celebrated for her piety and generosity, she is said to have founded the city of Tauriz, or Tabriz, one of the most important in Persia, ca. 791. For SJ on Zobeide, see *Idler* 101.
2. Sarah Heaton of Plas Heaton, near Denbigh, had died 21 April. See also HLP to Q, 28 January 1795, n. 3.
3. Dorothea Clough of Grove House was buried on 30 April, aged fifty-nine. Her husband, Thomas, rector of Denbigh parish, was buried 7 September, aged fifty-seven. See the "Denbigh Burial Register," C.R.O., Clwyd.

TO JOHN SALUSBURY PIOZZI SALUSBURY

begun Monday Morning
6th [–7] June 1814.

My Dearest's Letter—speaking well of his new Servants—came this moment, since our Friend Pem: drove from the Door: if you do not wish to have the Dog, *he* will have him. Young Men's Resolutions often change, and indeed it would have been odd enough to *leave* London when every body else is flocking *into* it——Edward therefore resolves to stay and see—like Catherine—the End of this Ado.[1] There is Ado in Plenty, and more than will end well I fancy. To me no matter tho', who resolve to sit still. The Ladies were here Yesterday, Mrs. Mostyn and Mrs. Hoare; and made our Dinner *Roast Beef only.* Their *Second* Luncheon. Cecilia looked divinely: Ten Years at least younger than her Sister, There are seven Years between them as I remember. I shewed them a Tree that was tearing the House down faster than I can build it up——Oh cried Sophia, The Place would be *frightful* without that Tree—I shewed them a *dead* one, and begged Permission to cut *that,* which they graciously afforded. Lady Keith is in France with her Husband. Our Talk (like that of all the World) was about Princes and Princesses——The only People said I, of whom one may speak ill with certain Impunity and some Chance for Applause. And without being called on to recapitulate our Words a Year after as I was by Mrs. Fitzhugh.[2] Oh! I was cross and spiteful enough, and the Visit has given Me the head Ach and a bad Night's Sleep. The continual Laugh and *Te he* of fine Ladies, possesses a Power of depressing my Spirits beyond all telling. They admired the Fire-screens prodigiously, and the Portrait of pretty Brynbella. Mrs. Mostyn was amazed to see a Pianoforte so *like* that in Wales. It *is* that my Dear said I. Good Lord! and did Salusbury consent to part with *That*? The less unwillingly (was my Reply,) because wanting the additional Keys, it can be plaid upon by none but Professors, and is incapable of executing Modern Music at all.

This was the only Time Your Name was mentioned——and the Talk stopt there.

Our Weather here is mournful, but mending; The Foreigners will have real Cause to inveigh as all Foreigners do, against the English Climate: Never, no never was such a Season seen.

What a fine Fool should I have been to wait another Week or fortnight for Mr.

Oldfield!—encumbering *Your* House, while wanted at *my own.* I *suspected* that he would not bring the Deed with him, and *felt* that its Signature was *frivolous.*

Pem: shewed me some beautiful and expensive Lace which is probably meant as his Nuptial Present. Leake's Wife—conversant enough in such Matters, admired it much; and Bessy Jones was delighted of course: we forgot shewing it to the Ladies: he was so desirous of looking over Massinger's City Madam[3] with me in order to Settle the Merits of Mr. Kean,[4] who I imagine is an Actor like Cooke.[5]

Tuesday Morning 7 *June*—Weather like *November.* I am better today, quite well indeed; recovered my Visit from the Ladies—which however must be returned;—I will go to London tomorrow, my Horses being just come. If I thought Walter Scott's beautiful Verses would drop into your hands by any other Means, I would not double the Price of this Letter by inclosing them——but they are *so gay,* and at the same time *so tender,* that I—who am no Tear-dropper by Profession, felt my Nose all-of-a-tingle, as I read them to myself for the first Time. Southey our Laureate is a married Man it seems, and resides among the Lakes of Westmoreland;[6] he is not Yet come to Town or to its Environs. An Invitation to The Rehearsal of Vauxhall Festivities[7] where I should have been a principal Person thro' Andrews, Topham[8] &c. was refused by Me this Moment on Pretence of Weather——but it might have driven me into *a Stream* I could not easily have escaped *out of,* so Prudence said—"Stay at home you old Fool" and I do stay—Tho' never was any home so dull and gloomy——The Ladies said "don't you find Streatham Park *charming?* I should perhaps find it so replied I,—were its Charms *Visible,* but one is so shut within

This close Dungeon of Innumerous Boughs

Milton[9]

that nothing can be seen at all.

And now—Darling of my true Heart Farewell!

It gives me great Delight to hear that you employ yourself——and sometimes in the midst of Your Employments, that You Think of her/ Who is Entirely Yours and Yours/ alone/ H: L: Piozzi.

Now don't fancy I praise these Lines for their *Originality,* because my Memory can tell whence *the Manner* and *Manufacture* of them was taken. I praise the Tenderness which in the 4th Stanza took me by sudden Surprize.[10]

Lord Coventry is not in the Country so no Chance for a Frank.

A mighty pretty Letter from *Your Bella* is just arrived—I have written to her <mama>, and shall soon do so again.

Text Ry. 587.225. *Address* John Salusbury Piozzi Salusbury Esq./ Brynbella/ near Denbigh/ North Wales. *Postmark* <   > Unpaid Streatham; <7>o'Clock JU<   >1814; JU 7 1814.

1. Katherina in *The Taming of the Shrew* (5.1.142) says: "Husband, let's follow, to see the end of this ado."

2. For Charlotte Fitzhugh, née Hamilton, see HLP to PSP, 22 May 1802, n. 5.

3. Philip Massinger's comedy *The City Madam* was first acted "at the private House in *Black Friers* with great applause" in 1632 and then performed intermittently until the closing of the theatres in 1641. For the stage history of *The City Madam*, see *The Plays and Poems of Philip Massinger*, ed. Philip Edwards and Colin Gibson, 4 vols. (Oxford: Clarendon Press, 1976), 4:10–15.

4. Edmund Kean (1787–1833) had performed at the Haymarket and Drury Lane, as well as in the provinces, as a strolling player before he made his first major appearance as Shylock at the Drury Lane theater on 26 January 1814. During this first season he also played successfully such roles as Richard III, Othello, Hamlet, and Iago.

William Hazlitt, in the *Morning Chronicle*, 26 May, reviewed Kean's brilliant performance of Luke in *Riches*. See *The Complete Works of William Hazlitt*, ed. P. P. Howe, 21 vols. (London and Toronto: J. M. Dent and Sons, 1930–34), 18:195–96.

5. George Frederick Cooke (1756–1812) began his professional career in Brentford, spring 1776, when he acted in *Jane Shore*. Two years later, at the Haymarket, he appeared as Castalio in *The Orphan*. Primarily a Shakespearean, he proved his versatility on 13 November 1800 when he played Sir Archy Macsarcasm in *Love à la Mode*.

HLP's association of Kean and Cooke is apt, since Kean thought that Cooke had never been surpassed as an actor.

6. Robert Southey had married Edith Fricker (1774–1837), while Samuel Coleridge had married her sister Sara. Ever since 1803 the Southeys had lived in Greta Hall, Keswick, a house they shared with the Coleridges.

7. On 13 June 1814 *The Times* carried an advertisement for Vauxhall: "Under the patronage of his Royal Highness the Prince Regent. The Public are respectfully informed, these Gardens, highly improved and beautified, will open for the season on Wednesday next, June 15, with a splendid Fete, in honour of the Peace. Admission 4s. Doors open at seven and the Concert begins at eight o'clock." The fete, which opened on 15 June, was repeated on 17 and 20 June.

The Times, 20 June, printed a laudatory review of Vauxhall's opening as a "captivating place of public amusement."

8. For Miles Peter Andrews and Edward Topham, see HLP to SL, 17 November 1787, n. 5.

9. *A Mask* ("Comus"), line 349.

10. Preoccupied with JSPS's forthcoming marriage, HLP seems to have been receptive to sentimental tales of young love. A reasonable speculation is that the lines to which she alludes are in the fourth of the introductory stanzas of Sir Walter Scott's *The Bridal of Triermain, or the Vale of St. John, a Lover's Tale*, published in March 1813. The subject, derived from Arthurian legend, incorporates fairy tale elements of Sleeping Beauty and of magic. She seems to have hoped that JSPS, anticipating his nuptials, might be moved, as she had been, by the "Tenderness" of poetic secret emotion, the bashful "hues of pleasure and regret," the "crimson glow" of love.

TO HARRIET MARIA PEMBERTON

Streatham Park
Fryday [ca. 8] June 1814.[1]

It is to thank the lovely Harriet a Thousand Times for her kind Letter that I write this——for though I now have seen the London Shops and the London Fashions—my Correspondence will not be worth a Pin.——The first of these exhibiting *Velvets* at the Windows for Ladies Wear, on what was for much of my Life esteemed the longest Day; and the fashionable Fair ones I *saw*, close wrapped in Furs as they would have been in November.

Not so the gay Lass whom the Men call galloping Moll. A beautiful Young Courtezan dressed in the most becoming Manner, who watched the coming of these Foreigners to Town,[2] seated on her particularly fine Horse; and rode Side by Side with Old Blucher thro' the crowded Streets—increasing *his* Admiration

Brynbella. 1814. Watercolor by Harriet Maria Pemberton Salusbury. (Hyde Collection, Four Oaks Farm. Reproduced by permission.)

and that of the Populace.[3] I kept out of the Throng of Course; but going to Town on Business the Day after, heard every one talking as much of *Miss Russell* as of the Emperor or King.

Meanwhile there is not a Head painted, engraved, or made in China Ware, or in *any* Ware; that has not the Emperor's Name written under it——nor can one hear a Word said—on any other Subject.[4]

I fancy the Cold Weather combining with People's Passion for the Prince of Orange is likely to bring in a Warmer Mode of Clothing than has been lately worne.[5] Dutch Sleeves puffed out to make Ladies look broad as they are long, have been seen on our Elegantes; and if that Taste takes, There will be a famous Alteration in the Dresses.

One would indeed be surprized at the Effect produced by such Nonsense: I went to see an Exhibition of Pictures, and felt myself quite struck by the Portraits of many old Acquaintance—Men in Laced Wastecoats, Women in long Ruffles— as they wore them half a Century ago——*trying* one should Suppose, to make remembering them impossible.[6] The landschape Painters are happier. Nature is always the Same; and I think this is the proper Place to mention how much my charming Friend's Brynbella has been admired by those who have, and who have *not* seen the Place itself.

It is difficult to imagine any two Situations so unlike each other as are Dear Salusbury's and my own.

This House is really so bosomed in Wood; it is tho' white, scarce visible from the private Road that runs by it—and from my Bed chamber Window one can see neither Earth nor Sky: so closely the Trees and their various Foliage intercept all possibility of View. Your Brother and I were noticing the Difference last Sunday when he dined and slept here, and met Two of my Daughters: Mrs. Mostyn and Mrs. Hoare—Lady Keith is said to be in France with her Husband.—Sophia enquired most *Affectionately* for Mrs. Pemberton, but Your *Futur* was not mentioned at all—except once by Cecy—as wondering he permitted the Removal of the Piano a forte——on which said I, none but Professors can play for want of the additional Keys, and no modern Music can be executed.

The Conversation was not renewed.

You can scarcely imagine how odd it seems to me *never* by any Accident to hear *his* Name, who for 15 Years was a constant Topic——but when your Brother comes, (and he kindly says that shall be often;) I make myself good amends, by talking of nobody else.—My Letters from Wales convince Me he is very well now, and If Discipline will cool his favourite Lady's feverish Complaints, I think they must be over by this Time. Adieu Sweet Lady, and present me Most kindly to Dear Mama; and pray read Mrs. Pemberton what I said about galloping Moll——believing me ever most/ truly and tenderly Yours/ H: L: Piozzi.

Text Ry. 592.19. *Address* Miss Harriet Maria Pemberton/ Condover Park/ near/ Shrewsbury. *Postmark* Two Py Post/ Unpaid/ Streatham; <1>o'Clock JU 9 1814; JU 9 1814.

1. HLP misdated the letter 11 June 1814 (Friday was the 10th): it was in fact written ca. 8 June and postmarked the next day.
2. According to the *Courier*, 8 June, the "Foreigners" were as follows: "the Emperor of Russia; the King of Prussia; Prince Henry of Prussia; the sons of the King of Prussia; the Prince of Orange; the Prince of Mecklenburgh; the Prince of Bavaria; the Prince of Wirtemberg; the Princess of Oldenburgh; Marshal Blucher; the Hettman Platoff; General Barclay de Tolli; Generals Bulow and Yorck; Prince Metternich, &c. &c."
3. Field Marshal Gebhard Leberecht von Blücher (1742–1819), created Prince (Furst) Blücher von Wahlstadt (1814), commander in chief of the Prussian armies in the field against Napoleon in 1815, had arrived in London on 7 June 1814 and did not leave for home until 11 July. Of all the visiting dignitaries, he attracted the greatest public affection. See *The Times*, 8 June.
4. That is, Czar Alexander I.
5. After Napoleon's defeat at Leipzig in 1813, Willem Frederik (1772–1843), only surviving son of the late stadtholder, Willem V, was recalled by the Dutch as Prince Willem VI, Hereditary Sovereign Prince of the Netherlands. In 1815 he was to take the title of King of the Netherlands and Duke of Luxembourg in order to affirm the reestablished unity of the Netherlands.
6. According to an advertisement that first appeared in *The Times* on 27 April 1814: "British Gallery, Pall-mall.—This Gallery will be re-opened on Thursday, the 5th of May, with a selection of the best works of Hogarth, Wilson, Gainsborough, and Zoffani, with which the proprietors have favoured the British Institution for the purpose of evincing the merits of those eminent masters. By order./ John Young, Keeper." The exhibition ran until mid-June.

TO JOHN SALUSBURY PIOZZI SALUSBURY

begun Saturday Morning
11 [–13]: June 1814.

Yesterday afforded me much Amusement purchased by some Fatigue. I went to see the Morning Preparations for their Grand Evening Shew in London;[1] and found few things equal to the Glass Shop near the Mews—Where Peace was written up in Sparkling Materials—bearing at Night I'm sure,—The complete Appearance of precious Stones. From Pall Mall (where I bought some *Blucher* Ribbons Mrs. Pemberton's Colour;) I walked up Bond Street with them, and meeting with a most *singularly* fine Piece of Cambrick on my Way, carried both to Mr. Smyth's—the Perfumer[2]——Who undertook to send them directly to You accompanied by the Coffee I promised—and directed by your own *Dear Hand* on two bits of Parchment that you may remember I put in my Pocket Book on Purpose——at Brynbella Two Days before we parted.

The People at Blake's Hotel were so civil—inviting me to send Parcels there, or be of any possible use to me &c., when I called on their Waiters to ask for a Footman; that I am led to *hope* they will get me a nice one for You:——at this *Moment* no Man or Woman quits London who can thrust themselves into it by any means,[3] but this mad Moment will soon be over; and the People's Purses *so* lightened by Pick Pockets—besides paying Ten Guineas for Window Seats whence nothing can be seen and so forth—that Things will drop to Their regular and natural Level sooner than was expected. You have often said what a Country this *is*—prompted by Admiration. I felt so when reading the Article of Condemnation passed on Possessors of Millions in a Kingdom filled with Money-seekers, Money-lovers &c. No Shelter is however found for the Guilty.

My Lords and Gentlemen must suffer like other People.[4]

The Duke of Wellington was not of my Mind probably, he wanted to make the Spaniards eat *Force*meat, and they gave him Poyson.[5] I have had an Antipathy to compulsive Measures public and private ever since My Mother told me that She was severely whipped once o'Year because She would not eat *Melon* when a Child—and Why should one human Creature compel another human Creature to eat *Melon*? Had She pretended an Aversion to Bread or Beef—rough Treatment had been provoked; because one might live to *want* Bread and Beef; but to be flogged into eating *Fruit* was too foolish.—And if the Spaniards really felt averse to Freedom, and fond of Restraint——why should we *lash* them into Love of it?——If they come and threaten me tonight I will put a Dozen Candles in the Window, but as for dirtying my pretty clean house for their Wars and their Peaces—*I will not*. Mrs. Mostyn gave me an Invitation for her Sunday Breakfast——after Church——so you shall hear how it *goes off;* The Visits must be returned, and this is the best way. I *did* call on Sophia Hoare.

Oh Stupid! I have left the Blank Place for a Seal *on the wrong side the Paper. Saturday Night 11th June still.*

Here comes Pemberton—nerve shaken and terrified at the Crowds he has driven his Gig thro', among shrieking Women, and Hackney Coaches trying to tear his Wheels off.—A Child *was* killed he Says; and the open Place about Whitehall, not half open enough for the Multitudes of People. I was much amused myself in the *Morning* by the Device at the Admiralty. A Sailor—saying——Every Man *has* done his Duty—Old England; to Britannia who replies, Thank You my Lads, so you have. But Oh my poor Peg! and Andrew, how will they ever come home alive!! Bessy Jones refused to *go* a long While, but they had her out at last. Sunday Morning brings *her* safe in again; but Thomas left the Girls and Andrew, and when *they* will arrive Who can tell? Pem goes with me to Mrs. Mostyn's, and will take Care <we come> back at Night. Here is the first warm Day: Sunday 12th of June 1814. Doctor Gray goes to Durham tomorrow, so I lose him.[6] The Pennants who I met upon the Pavè of Bond Street leave London this Morning[7]——Mr. Este Father to pretty Mrs. Wells of Piercefield,[8] will come to see me here I hope——he was a true Friend when so many proved false ones. We have walked round the Grounds and when the Carriage comes to the Door—away for Seymour Street.

The Sports went happily off—and Mrs. Siddons invited my Beau and myself for a Dinner next Thursday: Pem: however feels *low* this Morning—Monday 13th and protests he will hasten home—Thro' Enborne——He will be better tomorrow tho', at least I hope to see him so and then I shall coax him to remain where he is till *Fryday.* Lord Kirkwall looked frightfully ill and ugly at Mrs. Mostyn's Dejeunè, *every* body grown older; Mr. Chappelow most so. The Talk was all about the Regent's going to a *Front Box* prepared for him and his illustious Visitants at the Opera.[9] He sate between the Emperor of Russia and the King of Prussia and after the Huzzaeing for these Was over—Enter the Princess of Wales to her *own Box* attended by Lady Charlotte Campbell who fainted away from Fear of Consequences and Flutter of Spirits.[10] *No* Consequences happened after all—except that the *Three* Sovereigns all made her Royal Highness a low Bow, which She returned with a Curtsey——I think there was no Need of *Actors on the Stage.* They were in Dear Uncle's Phrase—*Superfluous.* People now say the long-parted-Couple are to be reconciled, and *Peace* proclaimed in private as in *public Life.* Never was so *noisy* a Pacification——our John Bulls shout for Joy whenever they see the Allied Princes, and that is whenever they think proper.

Somebody said that the Mob called for them as the Keepers call their Beasts at Exeter Change: crying come out, come out, and out they all come——but This Letter is only a bad Epitome of a good Newspaper so I will end it and say how truly and Affectionately/ I am your/ H: L: P.

Text Ry. 587.227. *Address* John Salusbury Piozzi Salusbury Esq./ Brynbella/ near Denbigh/ North Wales. *Postmark* JU 13 814.

1. The allied sovereigns were to go in state on the evening of 11 June to the opera but not before they "made their appearance in Hyde Park on horseback, to gratify the curiosity of the public. The number of people assembled there seemed to surpass all calculation; but, notwithstanding the crowds which were there collected on the occasion, we did not hear of the slightest accident" (*The Times*, 13 June).

"In the evening the earl of Liverpool entertained the Prince Regent, the Allied Sovereigns, and the other illustrious characters who shed such a lustre on the British Court, at dinner." At seven, the Prince Regent in his carriage, Alexander and the Grand Duchess with their escort, the king of

Prussia with his family, the dukes of York and Kent, General Platof, etc. all proceeded to the opera where they arrived about ten. See *GM* 84, pt. 1 (1814): 614–15.

2. James Smyth and Nephews, perfumers, at 117 Bond Street.

3. The crowds in London are described in the *Courier,* 13 June:

"The week that has just passed, the week just begun, and the week that is to come, will be the most brilliant, the most animating, and the most joyous period recorded in the history of the British capital. . . . The exultation is common to all classes. . . . Never was London so full—and all her population seems to live in her streets. Business, study, almost sleep, seem to be forgotten. It is one universal scene of bustle, and animation, and noise. But the clamour is without confusion, the exultation without riot. During the three nights' illuminations we have not heard of a single accident."

4. HLP refers to the fact that Lord Cochrane "was, on the 8th of June, placed in the prisoner's dock at the Court of the King's Bench on a charge of conspiring with his uncle, Mr. Cochrane Johnstone, with De Berenger, and with some other persons, to defraud the Stock Exchange. Lord Ellenborough, who presided at the trial, delivered a charge which was even more virulent and more marked by political spite than was his wont, and the two compliant jury brought in a verdict of 'guilty,'" denying Cochrane the right of appeal.

For the causes of the trial and Cochrane's punishment, see HLP to JW, 7 May 1814, n. 2; also Thomas [Cochrane], eleventh earl of Dundonald, and H. R. Fox Bourne, *The Life of Thomas, Lord Cochrane, Tenth Earl of Dundonald, G.C.B.,* 2 vols. (London: Richard Bentley, 1869), 1:26–33; Anon., *The Calumnious Aspersions contained in the Report of the Sub-Committee of the Stock-exchange, exposed and Refuted, in so far as regards Lord Cochrane, K.B. and M.P.,* etc., 2d ed. (London, 1814).

5. In the *Courier,* 10 June: "A report was circulated . . . to turn our rejoicing to mourning, our milk to gall. It was rumoured in one of the Evening Prints, that the Duke of Wellington in his journey to Madrid had been way-laid and assassinated with two of his Aide-de-Camps."

6. RG was on a visit to the bishop of Durham, Shute Barrington.

7. David and Louisa Pennant were returning to Downing in Flintshire.

8. For Harriet Wells, daughter of Charles Este, see HLP to LC, 1 May 1802, nn. 2, 3.

9. See *The Times,* 13 June 1814:

"Last Saturday night made a memorable night in the history of [King's Theatre]." The opera performed was *Aristodemo* and present were the allied sovereigns, their entourages, and the English dignitaries. "Shortly after the entrance of the Prince Regent, the Princess of Wales came into the house, magnificently habited in black velvet, with a diadem and plume beaming with diamonds. She was loudly applauded. The Prince Regent immediately bowed three times towards the box wherein her Royal Highness was situated; an immense applause followed these indications of attention, to which her Royal Highness made a suitable return. The Emperor Alexander also bowed twice in the same direction, and continued to look for some time through his glass towards the Princess's box."

10. Charlotte Susan Maria Campbell (1775–1861), youngest daughter of the fifth duke of Argyll, was reputedly one of the most beautiful women of her time. When her first husband, Colonel John Campbell, died in 1809, she became lady-in-waiting to the Princess of Wales. Lady Charlotte married the Reverend Edward Bury (d. 1832) in 1818.

TO HARRIET MARIA PEMBERTON

Streatham Park
Wednesday Evening
15: June 1814.

I never suffer Letters truly dear to me to remain very long unanswered. *Yours* shall of Course be *instantly* acknowledged. Mr. Pemberton had scarcely driven from the Door I think, when it was delivered me;—He came hither in his Gig last Saturday Night, when London was in the height of her Delirium; glad to escape from Some Degree of personal Danger in passing thro' Crouds of which 'tis really very difficult to form any Idea;—and the Gig was *damaged.*

Nervous Patients are not well calculated to struggle among such noisy and numerous Throngs—and he was afraid of *doing* Mischief perhaps more than of suffering it; when circled by shrieking Women, and Children clinging to the Wheels &c.

In short he slept here, and has only been to Town since in my Company, who he knows will run no Hazards. We passed one Day at Mrs. Mostyn's,——but *her* Party was too large for him; tho' 50 People dispersed up and down four Rooms, can scarcely feel any Inconvenience from each other. The Conversation You will easily believe was all about past, present, and future Gayeties.—The Ball at Whites[1]—to be held now in a few Days was the favourite Topic and as a Ticket *may* be obtained for 20 Guineas—a *Man's* Dress—for 30 more; many will go that have fewer Claims on Society than your Brother; he however came prudently *home hither,* and finding his Health less and less to his own Liking—— Tho' *I* saw nothing to alarm me:—we sate together reading the new Novel called the Wanderer, till Yesterday, when as he seemed to wish a Medical Interview— I drove him to Dr. Pemberton who protested him perfectly safe,—only suffering nervous Irritation:[2] and This Morning he left me for Enborne, where he may have more Skillful, but not more tender, or assiduous Attentions. It was merely the Distraction of London which had shattered him: Such Guns firing, such Rockets rising, such Numbers shouting, such Lamps blazing, would discompose any but the Veterans of Pleasure—And the Bustle not over yet. I saw a Lady's Petticoat which cost 60 Guineas only Silver Gauze and She confessed it was to wear *one* Night only, no more—so you see how mad the People are all grown.

Meanwhile *my own* Matters here at Streatham Park must and shall be kept quiet. The ill Usage I have suffered leaving me neither Pot nor Spit as I told dear Mrs. Pemberton,—I am beginning the World anew; and surely you and Mrs. Morris[3] would laugh if I told you as Leak and his Wife shewed *me,* that the People had even taken the Feathers out of my fine Pillows, and filled the Ticks with worne-out and dirty Dusters. Was it not high Time to come home and see at least what was going forward? Salusbury Is I hope going on prosperously with *his* Reformation Plans; It is *very* necessary that both he and I should be *very* prudent; and you will find us so—I dare say: My heart loves him too well to indulge *myself* much, at his future Expence. The Haymaking—Mowing at least, is at length begun; but 'tis a miserable Crop: they have *scraped* the poor Park that nothing can grow on it; but something will be made by grazing Cattle after Harvest, and as I said to your Mama,——If I can but *live* Three or four Years, *I will yet be as sleek as a Mole.* Your Brother will tell you what *he* Thinks.

The Princess of Wales (by going to the Opera when *they* did,) forced a profound Bow from her Husband who was seated between the Emperor and King of Prussia who could not—and did not wish I suppose—to forbear returning her Salute from a distant Box. The Regent was so applauded, that when they all went out, *he bowed again;* and Reconciliation has been talked of ever since. You will be sure I speak merely from hear-say.

And now dear charming Harriet Adieu! Our kind Edward as you call him, invited me Very cordially to Condover Park, when we will have many a chearful

Hour, and renew the pleasant *Laughs* that kind Mrs. Pemberton Said She enjoyed so well in the Company of Her and your H: L: P.

I have seen a successor for simple Joseph—compleatly *his* Reverse, and not simple at all. Salusbury must send me word whether he will give 23 Pounds o'Year for an active Waiter, and I dare say no bad Valet, a true London Servant——I think a good Salopian might have been a Safer and a cheaper Inmate, but he knows *best.*

Text Ry. 592.20. *Address* Miss Harriet Maria Pemberton/ Condover Park/ near/ Shrewsbury. *Postmark* JU C 16 1814.

1. Established ca. 1698 as the original White's Chocolate House in St. James Street, the subsequent rendezvous for wits, aristocrats, and literati became White's Club in 1736. It continued until 1871. The ball was given on Monday, 21 June. See the *Morning Chronicle,* 22 June:
"The *Fête* given by White's Club on Monday night, was splendid in point of female beauty and elegance. The whole world perhaps could not display such an assemblage of handsome women; and in point of decoration it was as well as mere temporary erections can be—that is to say, it was pretty rather than beautiful. . . ." Nonetheless, more than 2,500 persons were able to sit down to supper at two in the morning and to continue their dancing until long after sunrise. "The Emperor of Russia danced with different Ladies; with Mrs. Littleton, Mrs. Arbuthnot, Lady Jersey, and others. The King of Prussia did not dance; but enjoyed himself in mixing familiarly with the company; and all the illustrious Foreigners spoke with admiration of the unparalleled assembly of beauty."
2. Christopher Robert Pemberton (1765–1822) attended Caius College, Cambridge, receiving his M.D. in 1794. By 1800 he was physician at St. George's Hospital, London, where he remained until 1808. He served also as physician extraordinary to the Prince of Wales, the duke of Cumberland (1806), and to the king.
3. The Pembertons' housekeeper.

TO LADY WILLIAMS

Streatham Park Saturday
18th: June 1814.

I take no Small Share of Shame to myself dearest Lady Williams, for not having written Sooner——but Public Matters are best detailed by News-writers who know how to Set Things off advantageously—and besides that; I have taken more Care to keep out of the Bustle than others to get into it——and I think they take enough:—giving 15 Guineas for a Window to see the Sovereigns pass to Guild hall this day[1]—after seeing them all day long at their Own Windows— or in the park or somewhere——for they never refuse themselves to view—— their Backs are I believe never tired of bowing, nor their hands of being shaken.

The Emperor Alexander enjoys the Sport so much—his Companion must appear to like it[2]——He cried with Sensibility at sight of the Six thousand Charity Children occupying the Dome of St. Paul's;[3] and sung the 100th Psalm with them in Unison——He likewise joined the General Chorus of God save the King sung at one of the Theatres—and the People clapped their hands sore with Applause.[4]

A Prussian Officer I met at Mrs. Mostyn's seemed Enchanted with our Reception of the Allies; and said Blucher felt Quite in *the Skies* at the Particular Favour *he* stood in with the vast Population of England. Population *indeed*! To the regular Million of Inhabitants—it is said that 100000 Visitants are added——one has real Difficulty in passing the Streets any where about the Neighbourhood of Pultney Hotel.[5]

My domestic Affairs keep me very much at home, and the Invitations I have rejected, refused, and avoided, would make you laugh if you saw the heap.— One Gay Day at Mrs. Mostyn's where I met Lord Kirkwall, and one other Gay Day at Mrs. Siddons',[6] near whose Cottage lives as I am told——his sequestered Lady,—I *did* indulge myself with;—but all Endeavours to see the Charming Viscountess—were vain.—

We had two flaming hot Days, which we must call Summer I suppose;—That Season is over now, and this house, the coldest in England I believe, wants fires in every Room. The Hay smells sweet however, and tho' a light Crop, is particularly *fine*. Brynbella Pease have twice the flavour these have, but there is Prospect of many Strawberries. The Hothouses can bring nothing in this Year, because the Surveyor has neglected to mend them—having spent my Money for other Purposes:—It was high Time to *come home*.——

Mean while the Appearance of Wealth displayed, is beyond my Comprehension. People think nothing of Paying 20£ for a Ticket to White's Ball; and 50 Guineas for a Dress—which they consider as impossible ever to put on again—— 75£ was offered Yesterday for a Ticket, but Eber who sells 'em, waited to get 100£.[7] All Sunday will be employed in canvassing to obtain one.

I met Dear Mr. Pennant and his lovely Lady on the Pavement in Bond Street— just as they were meaning to return into Wales. If their Son and Yours are not in Town now, They are the only good Young Men who can come, and do not.

My Eldest Grandson is at Edinburgh his Mama says; The Youngest in America.—Harry is with *her*, a fine tall young Naval Officer; but when I *saw* him,—with a Swelled Face.

Colds were never so common certainly: This ranting up and down will demolish many a fine Lady, and Men are still worse off—as they must protec[t] the Women, who will run where no Protection can save them. I am convinced that many Valuable Lives will be lost. Young Pemberton said the Death of a Child from the throng of People in his Street, Sickened him so completely, that he ran hither for Refuge; and was nervous and could not eat. I recovered him however in some Degree, and he is gone home thro' *Enborne*—Mr. *Shephard's;*—without having seen above half the Shows.

Adieu Dearest Madam and do not wholly forget—though distant;/ Your Ladyship's and kind Sir John's/ ever true and faithful/ H: L: Piozzi.

How do you like the Wanderer?

Text Ry. 4 (1812–1818). *Address* Lady Williams/ Bodylwyddan/ near St. Asaph/ North Wales. *Postmark* 7 o'Clock JU B 18 814 <Penny> Post Streatham.

1. See the *Courier*, 16 June 1814:
"The procession to Guildhall on Saturday [18 June] will be the same as on the first visit of a King to the City after his Coronation; and the whole Fete is to be conducted on the ancient precedents. The Prince Regent is to go in the state carriage, with eight cream-coloured horses. . . . The two Sovereigns go with his Royal Highness in the state carriage. . . ."
The high point of the visit was a dinner. The "Regent with his Royal Guests and attendants proceeded to the Hall; the Regent, Emperor of Russia, and King of Prussia, taking their seats under a grand state canopy in the centre of the table, at which were seated 21 personages of the Blood Royal, including the Grand Duchess of Oldenburgh." Most of the guests remained at the feast until three in the morning. See *GM* 84, pt. 1 (1814): 685–87.
2. Catherine Paulowna (1788–1819), the fourth daughter of Czar Paul I, had married in 1809 Georg, grand duke of Oldenburg (d. 1812).
She was the favorite sister of Alexander and one of his few confidantes. Arriving in England on 29 March, she was the first of the foreign dignitaries to appear in London, where she became a dominant and controversial figure.
3. "At half past 11 [on 16 June] the Emperor, attended by Lord Yarmouth, proceeded to St. Paul's Cathedral. Here his Majesty witnessed the annual assemblage of some thousands of the clarity children belonging to different parishes of the metropolis; an interesting sight, which does so much honour to British benevolence, and which cannot fail to make the most affecting impression on every beholder. His Prussian Majesty, and the Princes, his sons, were also present; and the august party were every where greeted, both on going and returning, with the cheers and acclamations of the people" (*The Times*, 17 June).
4. The allied sovereigns on 16 June were at the Drury Lane, expecting to see Kean in *Othello*, but arrived too late for the performance. "At 25 minutes before 11 the curtains of the boxes were drawn, and the two Monarchs entered amidst the general shouts of the audience. The curtain then drew up, and about two hundred of the performers appeared, and sang God save the King. The Emperor joined most cordially in the chorus" (*The Times*, 17 June).
5. According to *The Times*, 23 June:
"From the arrival of the Emperor, Escudier's Hotel [Pulteney's Hotel] became one continued busy scene both day and night. The interior of the house was almost constantly crowded with ladies and the juvenile branches of our distinguished families, who filled the great hall, the passages, and staircase, in constant succession, to have a glimpse of the Emperor. A curious scene always took place on his passing in or out of the Hotel. On such occasions he very condescendingly shook hands with some of the females, and would put his hand between the rails of the staircase to shake hands with others. This caused such an emulation with the fair sex to obtain this honour, that some actually came a considerable distance from the country to experience the gratification."
6. SS lived at Westbourne Farm in Paddington.
7. Joun Ebers, bookseller, stationer, and librarian, at 23 Old Bond Street.

TO ANNA MARIA PEMBERTON

[Streatham Park]
[21 June 1814.][1]

I am always ready and willing to write to Dear Mrs. Pemberton and her amiable Harriet, and if alive, Shall be ready to attend her kind Call to Condover when the Month of August shall be ended. Do not be in earnest uneasy about Your Son, valuable as he is to his Parents and Friends: he is in no more Danger than we all are—all Day long. A Short but comfortable Letter he wrote me from Enborne, set my heart wholly at rest; he wanted nothing but a good Appetite, and said he had regained that.

London is enough to distract any Head but those accustomed to the delirious Whirl of Dissipation, and tear any Nerves to Pieces that are less strong than Cart

Ropes. To the regular Million of Residents 100000 Visitants have been added, as People tell me, and I suppose they will go home hoarse with making such an Incessant Noise—leaving the others with their Hands *so* sore with clapping the Allied Sovereigns, that they will not be able to work again for a Month. Business indeed does stand nearly still; The common Routine of Business: because if you send a Packet or Parcel by anybody *but* such a trusty Creature as fat Thomas; 'tis sure to be lost or stolen. Bessy Jones got *one* View of the Illuminations *one* Night:[2] but would rather have Seen the Dressed Ladies adorned for White's Ball I dare say, than all the Transparencies in the Town. They are scarcely come home *Yet* from that gayest of all gay Scenes,—when I have received and thanked Dear Mrs. Pemberton for her obliging Letter, and all her sweet Partiality to her/ Affectionate Servant/ H: L: Piozzi.

[The rest of the Paper is devoted to Harriet only.]

I reply to my dear Niece-elect immediately—though I have little to Say besides thank you, and Thank You again, for your very kind and obliging Expressions. The showy Footman's Character was exactly what *you* feared, and I wished to *avoid* for Salusbury. He must wait as patiently as he can Poor fellow! till I have received an Answer from Sir Denzil Cope's Widow concerning *another* Man who has applied for the Place.[3] *He* seems of a less active Sort, but has the *Appearance* of more honesty—and what a difficult thing it is to find Virtue and Abilities combined in *one* Person, every body can Witness:——how indeed should such a Man be purchased for 20£ o'Year?——I suppose the Sovereigns we are running after would be glad to get such a Servant for 2000£ o'Year? We must do as *well as we can.*

Mr. Leicester seems perfectly polite,[4] and correct no doubt with regard to the beautiful Girl I mentioned. Your Shrewsbury Illuminations did well to make their own Heroe their own Object; I dare say they were very pretty:[5] ours which shewed Buonaparte in disgrace, were I think the principal Favourites:—and the Anagram which makes out L'*Ile d'Elba* into *Le Diable* is admired too.

Our dear *Pem* is at home with You by this Time, heartily tired I doubt it not of the Distracted Scenes he left behind, which have been much increased since his Departure. 80,000 People trampling each other is to any rational Creature a dreadful Thought; and altho' the Streets were lined with Military during the grand Procession to Guild Hall——some were Crushed so as to exhibit no Trace of who or what they had been. I have as Yet heard nothing concerning White's Ball—indeed it is scarcely over I suppose, though this is written at 12 o'Clock Tuesday Morning—or call it Noon as you please, The 21st of June 1814 and *Cold* as in March, and the 1st Week of April.

Our Hay Making goes on *some*how; not very well, nor very ill: The Men run from their Work if not watched, to catch a Glimpse of Soldiers which were collected from all Quarters Yesterday, to be reviewed by the Princes.——The noise of Drums, Cannons, Plateau-Firing, and a long Et cetera of clamourous Merriment which reached to Streatham Park Yesterday, is quiet this Morning; and Cuckoo sings again——but we have no Roses. A few Strawberries and immense Quantities of Pease I send to Market, Tho' exposed to gross Imposition, and hopeless of not being cheated. My beautiful Pond too is full of Fish, but if the neighbouring Rogues can get at them no other way,—They *shoot* them: Tell your Brother so,—he will be very angry. When the Rascals see them leaping as they do now of an Evening,—and can catch no more of them;—I dare say They cry *Whattt* a *Pittty*?

I have had one or Two Young Ladies to see me since I began this Letter, who tell me they were more Entertained with visiting the Don Cossacks in their Barracks——conducted thither by Mr. Wilberforce;——then in shaking the Emperor by the Hand——So Curious was their Management of the long Spear measuring 12 Feet, and so tender the Treatment of their Horses, which they behave to,——exactly by their Account——as some Men here do to a *favourite* Dog. Platoff has given his Charger to our Regent;[6] but the Fellows while fondling the Creature, are ready to cry over him: because they say—Poor Dear! he will have no one that can *talk Russian* to him; nobody to speak *his own* Language.

10 o'Clock on Tuesday Night I receive Intelligence that White's Ball went off very finely indeed——and the Place did *not* take fire, which many apprehended it would do, The Decorations being all of Muslin dyed of Various Colours. Miss Lyddel had the Offer of a Ticket but refused, because She was not *half well*:[7] Dr. Baillie praised her,[8] and said that 50 Girls more Ill than She—would go at all hazards, and that he expected 40 of them would die in Consequence of such Ardour after Amusement. So now Farewell, and praise for a *ready* Correspondent at least, my Dear Salusbury's Affectionate Aunt and his best-loved Lady's ever faithful H: L: Piozzi.

Make my best Compliments to Papa and beg your Brother to write to me: never mind Franks——I suppose You will see the 'Squire of Brynbella in a Fortnight.

Text Ry. 594.3. *Address* Mrs. Pemberton/ Condover Park/ near/ Shrewsbury. *Postmark* <7> o'Clock JU 23 <1814>; Two Py Post Unpaid Streatham; JU 23 1814.

1. The letter may be dated 21 June, since White's ball, held on that day, was still in progress.
2. "The illuminations on account of the late Treaty of Peace, which commenced on Thursday [9 June], concluded this night [11 June]. The allegorical transparencies were extremely numerous; and the illuminations were very general and brilliant. The Custom-house, the Excise-office, the Bank, Somerset-house, and all other public offices, were particularly distinguished for tasteful arrangement and magnificent display of light." See GM 84, pt. 1 (1814):694; *The Times*, 10, 11, and 13 June 1814.
3. Elizabeth Dorothea Francis (d. 1840) had married on 13 September 1810 Denzil Cope (1766–1812), tenth baronet (1806), of Bramshill Park, Hants.
4. Henry Augustus Leicester (1756–1816) had married on 16 February 1791 Letitia Owen Smythe (d. 21 November 1812), second sister and co-heir of Nicholas Owen Smythe Owen, of Condover.
5. The Shropshire hero was Rowland Hill (1772–1842), cr. Baron Hill of Almaraz and of Hawkestone, Salop (17 May 1814); cr. Viscount Hill of Hawkestone and of Hardwicke, Salop (22 September 1842), about three months before he died.
   Entering the army 21 July 1790, he advanced steadily to the rank of general (1825). He distinguished himself particularly during the Peninsular War. From 1828 until 1842 he served as commander-in-chief of the British army.
6. Count Matvei Ivanovich Platof, or Platov (1751–1818), the hero of the Moscow campaign, had arrived at Dover early in the morning of 6 June and remained in England until 16 July.
7. Henry George Liddell (1749–91), fifth baronet (1784), of Ravensworth Castle, country Durham,

married in 1773 Elizabeth Steele. At this time there were two unmarried daughters: Anne (d. 1843) and Charlotte Maria (d. 1850).

8. Matthew Baillie (1761–1823), a specialist in thoracic and abdominal medicine, had in 1795 published his innovative *Morbid Anatomy of some of the most Important Parts of the Human Body*. Four years later, his practice had grown so large that he gave up teaching and resigned his post at St. George's Hospital. After helping to attend Princess Amelia in her last illness, he was made physician extraordinary to the king.

TO JOHN SALUSBURY PIOZZI SALUSBURY

[Thursday 23: June 1814.]

And now my dearest Salusbury set your honest honourable Heart at rest; and do not take fright because You owe the Bank of Denbigh 50£—assure Yourself beside, that it was This Morning only *Thursday 23d* of *June* that I *received* your agitated Letter, and replied to it *within the hour*: sending the Two poor Ten Pound Bills which I had kept to buy myself a new Gown and Cap for Your *Birthday &c.* which Mrs. Pemberton and her Son have so often and so kindly invited me to, at Condover Park. The Lady You emphatically call Your *Darling*, has a Letter from me oftener than enough: and full of Fashions, Fal lals, and Stories of White's Ball. I send you a Newspaper quite crammed with such Stuff, because you will see it There just as it really was: and do dear Soul amuse Yourself with reading it, and don't be seriously alarmed, but rest perswaded that no Man resolved as you are to be prudent, and live within your Income, will ever be distressed in earnest—'Tis Impossible. If one Year is bad, another Year will be better; if Corn is low prized; Horses, Poultry, and 1000 other Things will get low-prized too:——and the Level will most certainly be found. I cannot however send you Money, and will not deceive You with Expectation of any. A little Box with Salts and Candles you will receive, and such trifling Presents I *may* spare from Time to Time; but cannot think of giving my Estate away, and sending Money besides——least of all *now* when I am myself hard-prest beyond all bearing; but that I don't *tell* because 'tis useless——and 'tis better *not*——Let me but live three Years, and you shall see me *Sleek as a Mole*, and never a Debt in the World: my Spirits are not easily cast down, I have Suffered so much in my Life—and got thro' so much: nothing now shall make me wretched—— while you keep good and wise and well——a little pinching perhaps we must both endure for the first Year, but Courage dear Salusbury!

> All is best tho' oft we doubt
> What the unsearchable Dispose
> Of highest Wisdom brings about,
> *Ever perfect in the Close.*[1]

Milton.

Lady Frances Wilson has got the Man's odd Will established that left her 3000£ o'Year because he liked her Looks at the Opera;[2] and you remember a Woman of Colour at Bath covered with Diamonds, a Mrs. Robinson the Admiral's Widow, *her* Will is established too.[3]

Poor Lord Dundonald! *There* is true Misery——Having an eldest Son sentenced to the Pillory after Expulsion from Parliament and Loss of his Spurs and Honour as Knight of the Bath. I pity *him* much more than I do Lord Cochrane.[4] Here comes the Character of your new Footman, 'tis a *very* good one as Men go now; and I have much Hope in him: he seems gentle and good humoured, and very willing to please. Why don't you go to Bodylwyddan as usual? Sir John Williams is your Guardian till next September, and could give You Advice and Comfort, and tell you what hope there is from Caernarfonshire—*he* knows The Country, and knows Jones of Bryntirion, and all about them. I think his Son will dine with me today——meaning Young Williams,—Mrs. Mostyn brings him, if he *does* come. Ah my Dearest Salusbury! can you make me believe that a Fellow bent on his own Business, and residing closely like yourself on his own little Income, while other People are flashing and flareing, and borrowing, and spending their last Guinea in dissipation of such Thoughts as must arise when reflecting on their wild Conduct: can you I say, make me believe that *such* a fellow will ever feel real Distress? I must then *dis*believe that Book which tells us To seek *first* the Kingdom of God and his Righteousness;—and all other Things shall be added unto us.[5]

So poor Mrs. Ray is packing up for the last long Journey;! I wish her an easy Passage over the broad River, and such a Reception on the opposite Shore as I desire for myself—tell her so.

Your kindness shewn in *that* Quarter will not pass unrewarded by him who accepts even a Cup of Cold Water given to his poor Brethren.[6] I was a Blockhead and a Monkey to write you that Nonsense about my Right to the Pew in this Church—or to trouble my head about Burial Places of People who have not *my* notions on the Subject at all——who think one Place as good as another, and who only *laugh* excessively at my antiquated Ideas concerning Life, Death, and above All Things *Burial* Places!!! I shall think no further of the matter.——But I will get myself some old-fashioned Spouts to carry off the Water—That I *will* do. For these Pipes that go down the Sides of Modern Houses, choak with the dead Leaves in Autumn; and bursting by the next heavy Rains ruin all I have been doing and force me to do it over again—and that is vexatious beyond all telling, after such expence,——The Expence not yet *half* discharged. My *Linen* Bill came Light, under 20£ and is paid. The Coppers and Kitchen, and Laundry Utensils *Must* be paid——and I cannot *raise or borrow a Guinea*, so all is Trust on the Tradesmen's part;——and finely am I entangled——Yet not dismayed. Steady Resolution will do everything. My hothouses bring in never a Penny: Mead never repaired them in Time to bring Fruit for this Year, they are *putting together now*——and may possibly pay their Expences *next* Year,—*certainly* the Year after——if I can but keep alive, and *un*-vexed; and not be writing in the Night and as I am now, but lie still and sleep, and *dream* of Dear Salusbury, instead of fretting about his little Difficulties.

Our Pictures increase in Value, and when I look on the beautiful Lanschapes round this Dining Parlour,[7]——and see Two Cannalettis like those in Your *Break-*

fast Room selling now for 100£ each:[8] my Spirits rise, tho' I *did* sell my Stock at 69½ and here they are up again at 72. But then the Debt to Gillow has been lessened by 150£ and that to Mead, by 200£ since I *came home*. For Things must be done by Degrees.

The Weather is surprizing meanwhile, and the Hay spoiling: I will get Moore's Almanach[9] today if possible, and I will send you a Three Days o'Week Paper such as I take myself.—*The London Packet*—so that we may have *one* Book or *Readeable* in common with each other.

When our Rascally Workmen are gone, Leak can keep Pigs for me, and lessen our Expences Twenty ways; but whilst *they* stay, 'tis all Wrong, and Robbery and Vexation. My Carthorses are useful, amiable and excellent; and were bought cheap even at a dear Moment. Come now, have a good Heart; and rest convinced that when an old Woman feels hope in every Vein, a Young Man needs not be sorrowful. I dined with our Rector and met *Doctor* Southey the Laureate's Brother:[10] and read his Odes.[11]

They will be much Criticized, and are certainly written *Invita Minerva* but fine in a certain Way.

Adieu! It is very cold, so I will go to Bed again and get myself warm: Good morrow tho'. The Man will come—John Bowen for this Letter, when I am at Breakfast Fryday 24th of June 1814. Till when and ever/ believe me most Affectionately yours/ H: L: Piozzi.

Text Ry. 587.231, 231 +.

1. *Samson Agonistes*, lines 1745–48. HLP has altered l. 1748, "And ever best found in the close," and underlined it for emphasis.

2. Sir Henry Wright Wilson (d. 1832), of Chelsea Park, had married 9 August 1799 Lady Frances Elizabeth Brudenel Bruce (d. 1836), daughter of the first earl of Ailesbury.
William Wright, also of Chelsea, had died 13 February 1814, "having on the 5th of August, 1800, made his will, appointing Lady Wilson and the Honourable Charles Abbott executors, and bequeathing to the former the residue of his property, after payment of his debts, and some specific legacies." See *AR*, "Appendix to the Chronicle," 56 (1814):284; *The Times*, 28 February.

3. Ann Robinson (d. 1814) of Pulteney Street, Bath, "Wife of Mark Robinson, Esquire, a rear Admiral in H.M.N."
She was the widow of Thomas Shirley (d. 1797) "of Coleman Street, merchant in the City of London," from whom she inherited a large fortune on condition that upon remarriage she would leave no more than £2,500 to her second husband. She therefore left this sum to Mark Robinson as long as he did not "at any time dispute, question, controvert, or otherwise interfere with or disturb my Executors in the performance of the Trusts of this my Will." The will was signed 17 December 1810 and proved at London 29 November 1814. See P.R.O., Prob. 11/1562/625.

4. For Archibald Cochrane, ninth earl of Dundonald, see HLP to Ly W, 1 May 1809, n. 3.

5. Matthew 6:33.

6. Matthew 10:42.

7. On the third day of the sale of Streatham Park's contents (10 May 1816), the following landscapes, which had hung in the dining room, were sold: lot 73, Barrett's Windermere, sold for £22.1*s.*; lots 74 and 75, two landscapes by Pether, sold for £42; lot 76, Ruysdale, Canal of Dort, sold for £29.1*s.*; lot 77, Pether, Rocky Landscape, sold for £28.7*s.*; lot 78, his Morning, sold for £13.2*s.6d*; and lot 79, his Evening, sold for seventeen guineas. See *Sale Catalogue* (1).

8. For the work by Canaletto, which the Piozzis brought from the Continent in 1787, see HLP to SL, 30 April 1785, n. 3; 11 May 1786, n. 12.
They remained at Brynbella through most of 1817, but they were sold by JSPS before the auction of HLP's property at Manchester in September 1823.

9. Francis Moore (1657–ca. 1715), astrologer and almanac writer, began publishing in 1699 a

compilation of predictions designated *Kalendarium Ecclesiasticum: . . . a new Two-fold Kalendar.* The name was soon changed to *Old Moore's Almanac* and then *Moore's Almanac.* Among those responsible for continuing the long-lived serial were Tycho Wing (1696–1750), Henry Andrews (1743–1820), and Charles Hutton (1737–1823).

10. Henry Herbert Southey (1783–1865) studied surgery at Norwich under Philip Meadows Martineau (d. 1828). In November 1803 Southey entered the University of Edinburgh, where he graduated M.D. in 1806. Finally, establishing his practice in London, he became a licentiate of the College of Physicians on 22 December 1812. For his later career, see *DNB.*

11. Robert Southey, *Odes to His Royal Highness the Prince Regent, His Imperial Majesty, the Emperor of Russia, and His Majesty the King of Prussia,* published by Longman [etc.].

TO THE REVEREND THOMAS SEDGWICK WHALLEY

Streatham Park
Monday Night 4: July 1814.

Ah my Dear kind Friend! my ever faithfully attached Doctor Whalley! And must we really part *so* without any well founded hope of meeting again in this World?——Your sweet Letter would have taken my Breath quite away, had not our beloved Siddons prepared me for its Reception. Neither She nor I however can say a Word against your very rational Plan: Health is the first Thing to be considered, and as You say—*our* Lives are of Consequence to our Successors. I am glad I saw Mendip in its full Beauty and Glory—*very* glad: I have now seen the most beautiful Place in England; under Possession of a Friend I must forever love and respect.

Let me hear often from You,—how else shall I hear *of you* when in France?[1]

Dear Salusbury is not here; his Letter of last Week said he was to be at Shrewsbury on Wednesday to see the Illuminations and join in the Processions made there for my Lord Hill the Shropshire Heroe. To be *frantic with Joy is* become Characteristic of English People; London has borne the Appearance of a *mad Town* these last Weeks since I have been in its Neighbourhood; and Rejoycing is not yet at an End: altho' I suppose Money must be at an End, and that very soon, if half is true which I am told concerning the Expences of these truly voluptuous Festivities. The Dear Lutwyches called here, and took an early Dinner and pitied me, and admired my Gilded Millstone. I am yet undetermined about it; but my Desire and *Hope* is to keep it in my own hands: spending the Winter Months at Bath—The Summer Months here *if possible.* No one can *guess* the Expence of my Dilapidations and Repairs: I will tell *you* honesty that Mead's Bill is 4160£ Sterling, of which he has had already 2550£—All this beside the Furniture. Never mind: I will endeavour to get thro' all, with the Help of a faithful Steward, but there must be a little pinching the first year. House rent will probably be cheaper than usual in Great Towns, when so many People are flocking to France——I expect the Bath Folks must lower their Prices, but *nous verrons*——and you know how little my Heart leans to the despairing Side of Things.

The Spotted Dog has lived happily here this long Time, and is at last sent off to his Dear Master with a new Footman; so he will be taken Care of upon the Road; and in Eight Weeks I expect A Call to witness the *beginning* of Felicity to my Darling Boy.[2] There is no Reason why those Young Creatures should be otherwise than happy, except that Happiness is not the Growth of this World, nor *should* be Sought in it. That panting after future Enjoyment which starts out in the first Germ of Life, and continues even while that Germ is withering——was certainly intended to push still further than this Globe admits;—or Fancy would not *cruize* when quite incapable of raising Wind enough to change her Place. No matter; You and I, (whatever we may say to others or ourselves,) still feel a Possibility of *clearing out* from every Difficulty even *here;* and a Hope of dying *at home* undisturbed by outward Circumstances: May it be so to both of us! and May our Successors be contented with what we have done for them! conscious that we could do no more. *I do think* The very Air of France will lighten the Oppression on Your Spirits, and that my first kind Letter will be a chearful one. Do not stop nearer than Lyons or Grenoble; it is scarcely worth while to change for a less Southern Latitude; and *seriously I do think* such another horrid Winter as the last, would separate us more than a Sea Voyage will. Be of good Cheer!—remembering how among many, *many* Friends you leave behind,—Thousands of Prayers and Wishes for your safe Return are sent daily to the Throne of Grace; and none more/warm and true than those/ of Dear Dr. Whalley's Forty Years attached/ and ever obliged Servant/ H: L: P.

Make my best Compliments to Mrs. Whalley.

I *could* not write a longer Letter, still less could I write a *pretty* one. May the God you have never ceased to trust and to believe in, send you safe home in his good Time.

Farewell!!

Text Berg Collection +. *Address* Rev: Doctor Thomas Sedgwick Whalley/ Mendip Lodge/ near/ Bristol. *Postmark* JY B 5 1814.

1. HLP responds to TSW's letter, 2 July (Ry. 564.30), in which he announces his impending flight to France, his poor health, and by implication his unhappy marriage.
". . .This once darling Place [Mendip Lodge] is become a *gilded Millstone* for *me.* As it would be a Folly and a Sin, to keep at a great Expence, what I can no longer hope to enjoy, I am looking out sharply, on all sides for a Purchaser, of a Place and Property, highly attractive and eligible for a Person who has good Health, fine Taste, and a large Fortune. All the Furniture is to be sold with the House &c. . . . The Malady of my Chest, and, as wise Doctors say, of the bottom of my Wind pipe, increases so much and made such a miserable Creature of me the whole of last Winter and Spring, that I have determined to . . . seek a milder and more settled climate somewhere in *France.* . . . Mrs. Whalley cannot leave the Charge of her poor Brother; nor indeed would she like the Journey, and Voyage, or the accommodations and mode of living on the Continent. Her Habits of Life, and turn of Mind are peculiar, and *new ones* even with *bonne Volonté,* are not easily adopted, at 58:—Your old, and true Friend, therefore, is to become a Wanderer at *68.* . . ."
2. On 9 September 1814 JSPS was to have his twenty-first birthday.

TO CHARLOTTE BARRETT

Streatham Park
Saturday
9: July 1814.

My dear Mrs. Barrett[1]

Our Marianne plays us very false—does She not? I begged her to make the Engagement for me to dine at Richmond—after She had left Kensington Gore and returned to her Family: but not a Word does She write, so I will make my own Engagement—and name next Monday Sennight——or Tuesday Sennight, which *You* like best, 18th or 19th of July: and bring her home with me to stay a Week or fortnight—or till You come and fetch her away.[2] She *must* stay over the 22d because 'tis pretty Mrs. Hoare's Birthday and I *keep it accordingly.*

Make my proper Regards—Those are sure to be my *best* Regards, to Your good Husband and Mother and Young ones[3]—and believe Dear Madam/ Yours Sincerely/ H: L: Piozzi.

Text Berg Collection, m.b. *Address* Mrs. Barrett/ Richmond Green/ Surrey. *Postmark* Penny Post Unpaid Streatham; 7 o'Clock <9 JY 1814>.

1. For Charlotte Barrett, see HLP to Clement Francis, 28 July 1810, n. 10; and 13 November 1810, n. 10.
2. HLP visited the Barretts in mid-July. Much of the talk had to do with Charlotte Barrett's aunt, FBA, and *The Wanderer.* On 19 July (Berg) FBA heard from her niece.
"My dear Mother told you of my having faithfully delivered your message to Mrs. Piozzi. . . . she received it as she ought, very kindly—and she was so good as to dine with us a few days ago. . . . When she was here she enquired very much and earnestly after your health. . . . Shall I tell you what she said of your sweet Juliet [the heroine of *The Wanderer*]?—she said she had been reading it. 'So have *we* at the Wilberforce's,' said Marianne. 'Well my dear,' cried Mrs. Piozzi, 'and did you *breathe* till you had finished it? because *I* could not—and to be sure, if it is a principal merit, in a work of fiction, to excite an ardent interest and to keep it up and increase it to the end of the tale, *this* work surpasses *all* that have even yet been written. I *never* was in such an agony, as this book put me in, till I could see a termination for Juliet's misery.'"
3. Charlotte Barrett's eldest child was the six-year-old Julia Charlotte (HLP to Clement Francis, 13 November 1810, n. 10). In addition, she had Henrietta Hester (1811–33); Richard Arthur Francis (1812–81). In October she was to bear Henry John Richard (1814–29).

TO SAMUEL LYSONS

Streatham Park Monday
11: July 1814.

Will Dear Mr. Lysons like to take a *mere* Family Dinner with his old Friend H: L: Piozzi. tomorrow at poor Streatham Park so long neglected.

I am sorry for the short notice, but I live quite retired as my fair Daughters can Testify; and you will be ill amused, unless by enlightening her who Always had a just Value for Yours and Your Brothers Conversation and/ who is ever faithfully/ Yours/ H: L: P.

Text Hyde Collection. *Address* Sam: Lysons Esq./ Keeper of the Records/ Tower.

TO JOHN WILLIAMS

Streatham Park
13: July 1814.

My dear Mr. Williams

What is become of your kind Mamma that She never writes? I am very jealous of her good Opinion, and would not lose her Friendship for I don't know what myself. You had a Loss in not dining here that Day with the Lutwyches; Mary Mayhew *did* look like one of the Daughters of Paradise and here was Florentina Mackay too, a very nice Girl and my Cousin:[1] as for Mrs. Siddons's Heart, You have got that Safe enough—Why don't Your Cambridge Men call her to make Readings at Your University? The Oxford People flattered her very much, and She *so* liked the Employment.[2]— Oh and Cecilia Siddons is an exceedingly pretty Girl,—I forgot *That:*[3] but you ran away as if the Town was on fire—of which there will be more Danger on the Tenth of August.[4] I am very apprehensive of a Riot, and the Day chosen is *such* a fatal one Le Dix d'Aout! Lord Cochrane forever meets your Eye on every Wall, and Measures are taken every day to reelect him when expelled The House.[5] I who remember Wilkes supported for so long a Time by the Mob against the Government must necessarily feel anxious[6]—and you see they have thought it proper and prudent to acquit Lord Waterpark's Brother.[7] Nobody thinks it either proper or prudent to set up that nonsensical Sea fight on the Serpentine River.[8] I would have little Bertie be *Admiral*, for *my* Part; and made Sir *Hyde Parker*[9]—if he is not outgrown the Employment.

Your horrid Story was strictly true after all, and a fearful Tale it is; but I find it attested by Accoucheurs and Surgeons of all possible Eminence, and can hesitate to believe it no longer.[10]

So much for the Wonders of the *Natural World.*—There is a wonder talked of today in the Civil or we may call it the *political World*—equally unprecedented I believe, but by no means *physically* improbable. One dares not speak out yet; tho' there was A Mob round the Door of the Lady's Father this Morning as I passed through Pallmall who were all talking, and looking, and expecting to hear how it goes.[11] Shall we praise or blame Dear Salusbury's utter want of all Curiosity concerning any one Thing but the pretty Girl he is attached to? *That* Disposition appears to me among the odd Things one stumbles over—but I really have Individually much Reason to rejoyce that he has taken Shelter (tho' in a Shed,) from the Storms that seem gathering round in every Direction. *I* should at his Age have felt inclined to go out and look at the Lightning,—by which Means I should have got blinded;—and he, *will keep his Eyes.*

Mrs. Mostyn seems much amused with the Variety of Strange Reports passing up and down: when I expressed my Alarm concerning the 10th of August— Her Expression was, "Oh! they will have something else to think on by then."

You will always have much to Think on; Yet I really do *wish*—and sometimes entertain a *Hope* that my Dear Williams will now and then think of his very old Friend/ and Obedient Servant/ H: L: Piozzi.

Text Ry. 6 (1813–21). *Address* John Wiliams Esq./ Bodylwyddan/ St. Asaph/ Flintshire/ N. Wales. [Forwarded from Trinity College/ Cambridge.] *Postmark* 12 o'Clock JY 13 1814. Two Py Post Unpaid Streatham. CAMBRIDGE <32>. JY <C> 15 8<14>.

1. For Clementina Mary Mayhew, see HLP to Ly W, 30 January 1802, n. 7; for Florentina Mackay, see HLP to PSP, 26 April 1793, n. 9.
2. The readings of SS at both universities "were given at what were called private parties; but which included very numerous audiences, and all the distinguished individuals of the colleges." She and Cecilia travelled to Oxford in the spring and to Cambridge ca. 20 July. See Campbell, 2:352–54.
3. Cecilia Siddons was now twenty.
4. "The Tenth of August" recalled the massacre of the Swiss guards at the Tuileries in 1792 (HLP to Charlotte Lewis, 18 August 1792, n. 4). It also anticipated mob reaction to Lord Cochrane's standing in the pillory, scheduled for 10 August (That part of his sentence was remitted; see *The Times*, 12 August).
5. HLP summarizes the response to the guilty verdict handed down in the trial of Lord Cochrane; see her letter to JSPS, 11 June 1814, n. 4.
The *Courier* (6 July) reported that "After a long debate, the House of Commons last night, by a majority of 140 to 44, ordered Lord Cochrane to be expelled." By the eleventh the *Courier* wrote an editorial, first admitting its sorrow over Cochrane's fate but emphasizing that "no sorrow for him can make us remain silent, when attempts are making to render the country dissatisfied with those venerable institutions to which we owe the liberty we possess, and to induce the people to look with suspicion, if not with hatred, upon the Judges and the Trial by Jury."
On the same day, the *Courier* announced the report of the electors of Westminster, who had met on 8 July at the Crown and Anchor. There it was unanimously decided that Cochrane "is a fit and proper person to represent the City of Westminster in Parliament."
6. For the response of Wilkes's constituency to his being denied a seat in parliament, see HLP to LC, 3 June 1796, n. 8.
7. Second baron Waterpark (I., 1807) was Richard Cavendish (1765–1830). His youngest brother was Frederick (1777–1851), who was charged with forgery. On 8 and 9 July the *Morning Post* reported: "We learn from the Dublin papers which have reached us this morning, that the trial of the Hon. F. Cavendish, who stood capitally indicted for forging a power of attorney, by which the Bank of Ireland was defrauded of 1250*l.* terminated on Monday afternoon [4 July].—He was acquitted."
8. In Hyde Park the Serpentine river was allotted for the spectacle of a naumachia, in which a British and French fleet, represented by barges brought from Woolwich, and fitted up to resemble men of war of the line and frigates, were to exhibit the manœvers and circumstances of a naval fight. See *AR*, "Chronicle," 56 (1814): 68. Most newspapers treated the naumachia with tolerant contempt. See the *Morning Chronicle*, 7 July.
9. Hyde Parker (1739–1807), knighted (21 April 1779), vice admiral (1794). He served in American waters during the War of Independence, later commanded in Jamaica, the Mediterranean, and the North Sea in the French Revolutionary and Napoleonic Wars.
10. An early allusion to the "impostor" Joanna Southcott. See HLP to John Williams, 24 July, and to TSW, 19 November, both in 1814.
11. Because Princess Charlotte wished to break off her engagement to the Prince of Orange, to remain in England, and to be with her mother, the Prince Regent, accompanied by the bishop of Salisbury and four ladies, on 12 July entered Warwick House. There he told his daughter that her servants were dismissed, that she would be confined at Carlton House for five days, and then taken

to Cranbourne Lodge in Windsor Forest, where she was to live in virtual exile. On the same day, she escaped to her mother's house at Connaught Place. Advised by Henry Brougham, she returned to Carlton House early on 13 July, having first signed a document that nullified her engagement to the Prince of Orange. See *AR* 56:218; for the notoriety attached to the incident, see the 121 quatrains by Peter Pindar, *The Royal Runaway; or C—tte and Coachee!!* (1814).

TO HARRIET MARIA PEMBERTON

Streatham Park
Saturday 23: July 1814.

The franked Letter from a Sweet Lady who promises soon to be my dear Niece Harriet,—never came till Two Days after that written by her own True Love——and I was glad it happened so; because *Yours* mentioned his having a Pain in his Head or Stomach; and his own dated Three Days—or at least Two Days after—seemed as if dictated by Health and Good humour. It is the Mind which affects the Body in almost all Cases, and I really do weary Heaven with Prayers that I may once see the 9th of September past; and my Darling out of all Fears concerning the Legacy Tax, and Twenty Things which my outliving that Hour will obviate. Meanwhile I had a Fright as I told *him*, and my Bowels are paying for it now. Windle, my Attorney, who settles with Mead—wrote me Word very cooly that there was 384£—never brought to Account besides all the monstrous Sum which I told Salusbury and his brother Elect I was obliged to pay. Oh that *did* terrify me indeed—and till Leak returned from some Errand he was gone upon——my Uneasiness increased every Hour. The Money was however clearly accounted for by the Surveyor himself, who was obliged to recant his further Claim, and all stands exactly as it did——Leak found it in the Fellow's own handwriting.[1]

Lord bless me my Dear ! what a World full of Hazard, Fraud, and Folly are you going to *plunge* into! Yet I wish the first *Dip* was over, and we could see you shaking your Ears, and writing your new Name——Tell Dear Salusbury that Lady Williams of Bodylwyddan is poorly——and Miles Peter Andrews—dead. Mrs. Mostyn saw him gallanting Girls up Bond Street *Two* Mornings only before he was a Corpse——and he had sent 200 Cards out to invite us for the Grand Fête and Foolery in St. James's and Green Park which his House looks into.[2] I had refused of *Course*. My Refusals are Innumerable. Except this one Day when I hoped for the Company of my Daughters and their Friends to drink Mrs. Hoare's health on her Birthday—My House has been a perfect Nunnery,—and my Kitchen,—cool as my Grotto.—

Salusbury will wonder when I say The Wind never blows here, but 'tis very *very* nearly true; and *that* I perceive, is the Cause of so much Fragrance all about these Places—The Atmosphere is so heavy; and seldom if ever, brushed by a quick Current of Air. I did not recollect how *still* the Environs of London were, till coming strait from Wales it struck me forcibly.

You have but to command us My Dear concerning Your Shoes, or any other little Parcel we can bring down. I bid your Sweetheart ask You if You would like to have me *bring* or *send* the pretty Muslin which I hope you will be pleased with.

Did dear Salusbury guess what *his* Present was?—that is gone to Brynbella. May God preserve him from wanting it! 'Tis a nice, well-furnished Medicine Chest with a Book inside, to tell the uses, Weights, Measures, &c. and an elegant Pair of Scales.

Tell him I have made a new Conquest of a handsome Young Physician—*So* like *his own* saucy Father—when I knew him abroad—that I can't keep my heart out of his Hand—but I *do* keep my Health out of all their Hands as yet, tho' my Inside is crying even now for Rhubarb and Chamomile Tea.

Mr. Kynaston Powell shall be plagued with this Heap of Stuff, not worth Postage:[3]—It serves however to assure You how much I am Yours and your Familys/ Affectionate humble Servant/ H: L: Piozzi.

Text Ry. 592.22. *Address* Miss Harriet Maria Pemberton.

1. For the happy outcome of this contretemps, see Windle to HLP, 15 August (Ry. 601.93) and HLP to Windle, 19 August, both in 1814.
2. Miles Peter Andrews had been ill for only a few days when he died in Cleveland Row on 18 July 1814. "His death was so unexpected, that he had sent out above 200 cards of invitation to ladies to see the fireworks in the Green Park from his windows." See *GM* 84, pt. 2 (1814):190.
3. John Kynaston (1753–1822) of Hardwick, Salop, was a member of a leading Tory family in the county. After succeeding to the estates of his material uncle John Powell in 1797, he assumed the additional name of Powell. On 3 October 1818 he was created baronet. As M.P. (1784–1822), he was a follower of Pitt and consistently voted with Government.

TO JOHN WILLIAMS

Streatham Park
24: July 1814.

That I am so kindly remembered by my truly dear *friends* at Bodylwyddan is better than all the flash and false Fire of *Acquaintance* in the Environs of our still crowded Metropolis.

Some anecdotes however one does pick up, and some strange things one hears—witness your now well-authenticated Story of the pregnant Boy.[1] Does it not fill Lady Williams with just wonder? For my part I do think our common Parent is provoked by the Insults she daily is receiving so that—as Milton says—

> Great nature breeds perverse;
> All monstrous, all prodigious Things
> Abominable, unutterable &c.[2]

There is a tale about the Town now of Joanna Southcote—The pretended Prophetess, which for Impiety surpasses all We have Yet heard but till I know more I will say nothing.[3] Did my letter directed to Cambridge follow you all across the Island I wonder! Oh it was ill worth the paying for. "Ne craigner pas amasser de la Rouille."[4] *Gold never rusts.* It has likewise another property in common with my amiable Young Friend and Correspondent—It unites easily and kindly with other Metals—where Silver, a second best Character is saucy, and resists all Incorporation.

You have read Douglas's little Tour through Greece I dare say—if *not,* you *must* read it.[5] The people are all mad after Grecian antiquities and 'tis a very good taste I am glad on't.

My residence here gives me pleasant Opportunities of hearing and seeing &c. but the [o]dious purse has been so drained by Surveyors, Upholsterers and all the rest of those Bloodsuckers that I shall be forced to let poor Streatham Park for awhile at least—if to be dirtied by Babies—how it will vex me! When all is settled I will let you know how we managed.

Meanwhile the Emperor deserved much of the Bustle we made about him. When a child it seems, his Grandmother Katherine the great Autocratrix, took an English Boy out of a Merchant's compting house at Petersburgh; and put him about the young Czar as a Playfellow and to teach him our Language:— when she had done with him[6]—he was sent off of course, and Alexander confessed that his Companion was forgotten. One day however in the crouds of London, The Emperor recognized a Face he knew and made the Man come up and say in what way he was *now* and how he could be served—after which Interview no time was lost till the Prince Regent had not promised only but actually provided this old companion of his new friend with a place in the Treasury valued at 500£ a Year.

Such actions are like those related in our novels and acted on the Stage.

But it is Time to talk of Dear Lady Williams—and her Bird Cage. Cripps of Piccadilly calls it an *Aviary.*[7] My old Acquaintance the Canaries who helped me to deafen the kind Mistress of the Mansion will I hope find themselves very happy in so large a habitation and it will stand on the Balcony if too big for the Dressing Room.

Meanwhile her Ladyship must be blooded again—and be blooded in the Hand too—as She was in the Foot; There is no difference in Her Disorder only the mere Situation. Pray assure her and dear Sir John of my continued Affection. I think he will like the Joke of Lord Cochrane—quitting the *Stocks* to mount the Pillory well enough:[8] but the People were so resolved to make his Punishment a Triumph to him, I feel heartily rejoyced that it has been remitted.—Such an Experiment would have been too dangerous in these extraordinary times.[9] The Naumachia upon our Serpentine River will do no harm—it only sets People laughing—and the *Pacific Ocean* as Lord Coventry calls the Scene of their amusement will not endanger them with a *Lee Shore* engagement. But adieu! I have written this bad greasy Paper quite to the End, without saying how your handsome Cousins graced my Table on Mrs. Hoare's Birthday. The eldest says he is going to Vienna. Once more adieu! and love/ Your/ oldest and truest friend/ H: L: P.

Text Ry. 6 (1813–21). *Address* John Williams Esqr./ Bodylwyddan/ St. Asaph Flintshire N. Wales. *Postmark* 12 o'Clock JY 25 814.

1. See, e.g., the advertisement in *The Times*, 11 July: "Extraordinary Phenomenon.—Shortly will be published, by Subscription, in 4to, price 10s. 6d. accompanied with appropriate engravings, an accurate Description, &c. of a Foetus, recently removed from the Abdomen of a young Man, 16 years of age. By Nathaniel Highmore, Sherborne, Dorset; and Member of the Royal College of Surgeons, in London. This preparation is now in the possession of the Royal College of Surgeons. Subscribers' names will be received by the Publishers, Messrs. Longman and Co., etc."

2. *Paradise Lost*, 2.624–26.

3. At the age of sixty-four Joanna Southcott began to ail in March, having announced the previous October that her son, Shiloh, was to be born. The news of her pregnancy, earlier dismissed, was in July and August being debated. On 2 August the *Morning Chronicle* wrote: "Our readers have probably often heard of an impostor, of the name of Johanna Southcote . . . who has lately given out that she is pregnant with the true Messiah, and expects to lie in in a few weeks. It is a positive fact that a cot or cradle, formed of the most expensive and magnificent materials, has been bespoke, by a lady of fortune, for Mrs. Southcote's *accouchement*, and has been for some days exhibited at the warehouse of an eminent cabinet-maker in Aldergate-street. It is surmounted with a dove, and inscribed with texts of Scripture, most grossly and blasphemously perverted."

4. Probably HLP's alteration of Pope's *Imitations of Horace*, Epistle, 2.1.35: "Authors, like Coins, grow dear as they grow old;/ It is the rust we value, not the gold." See also his epistle, "To Mr. Addison, Occasioned by his Dialogues on Medals," lines 35–36.

5. HLP refers to *An Essay on Certain Points of Resemblance between the Ancient and Modern Greeks*, published on 13 June 1813 for John Murray. The *Essay*, consisting of 198 pages, sold for 7s.6d.

HLP's interest was spurred by its author, Frederic Sylvester North Douglas (1791–1819), a son of Sylvester Douglas, first baron Glenbervie, who toured Greece in 1810 while he was a student at Christ Church. Indeed, the *Essay* is dedicated to Charles Henry Hall, dean of Christ Church. For Hall, see HLP to JSPS, 22 February 1810, n. 2; for Baron Glenbervie, HLP to Q, 31 January 1810, n. 2.

6. Biographers do not mention the boy but seem to agree that Alexander learned English from his nurse, Pauline Hessler, an English woman married to one of Catherine's footmen. See, for example, Alan Palmer, *Alexander I* (London: Weidenfeld and Nicolson, 1974), 7.

7. The "*Aviary*" was custom made by John Cripps, wireworker and sieve maker, at 204 Piccadilly.

8. For Sir John's interest in puns, see HLP to Ly W, 16 February 1804, n. 3.

9. Of the various punishments suffered by Cochrane, only his standing in the pillory before the stock exchange was remitted because Sir Francis Burdett, his fellow member for Westminster, threatened to stand with him, and the government feared a riot.

TO JOHN WILLIAMS

Streatham Park
[ca. 10 August 1814][1]

My dear Mr. Williams has every possible Claim to a quick return of Correspondence. Lady Williams's bird cage set out on the 27th of July last by the Holy Head Waggon from the Castle and Falcon Inn, Aldersgate Street, carefully packed: and the Man who sold it wonders it is not yet arrived:—I thought your Letter would have Said it was on the Balcony inhabited by ½ Dozen Darlings. I'm glad Mr. and Mrs. Pennant are well and happy; they deserve all the Felicity this World can give. Doctor Myddelton was beforehand with us all in detecting this blasphemous Imposture which now stares every body in the face and draws whole Shoals of Fools and Knaves after it in a most daring and offensive manner.[2]

The Scripture tells Men that there is but one Sin which *cannot* be forgiven—

so now they are all in haste to commit *That*.[3] I refused every Invitation for the Shews in the Park; and saw the red glare over London so plainly from my own Gate that every Moment added to my rejoycing that I was no nearer the Crush and the Croud where so many *unnamed* Human Creatures perished. Miles Peter Andrews the rich and the Gay sent out 200 Cards of Invitation to see the Festivities from his Windows, Verandah &c. in the Green Park—but Miles Peter Andrews (his Friends say) *went off* before the *Fireworks*: so his Heir removed the Body—and received the Company *himself*.[4] You and I have read of a Golden Age, a Silver Age and an Iron Age—<is> not that we live in The *Marble* Age? So smooth—so *Cold*—and so *polished*.

Mrs. Siddons will be enchanted with her new Conquest—She was in Love with you before She knew that it was *reciproque*: but indeed we Women seldom fail of knowing when the Arrow is aimed aright. She and her *very* pretty Daughter are going next Month to Paris under Convoy of Mrs. Mostyn of Segroid—— If dearest Dear Salusbury had not attached himself to more agreeable—though not truer Friends than myself;—I would have gone too: but 'tis foolish to be without a Male Protector in a foreign Country, and I wonder those Three handsome Women are not afraid to venture; They do not feel a Consciousness of their own hazards, but Ladies have fewer Fears than they used to have.

I am however going to leave my beautiful Mansion for a Twelvemonth: The Russian Ambassador Count Lieven wishes for it;[5] and The Expence of living here is too much for me— coming as it does upon the *Enormous* Demands of Mead and Gillow: Bath was always my Second Choice; and like the *second* Character in a Novel, sometimes is more pleasing tho' it strikes you less than the First.

After I have paid my expected Visit at Condover Park in September, I shall retire to Bath and wash away the Remains of Worldly Care—at the Pump. Meantime 'tis really curious to hear the different opinions of those who live at the Fountainhead of Information. London at this moment exhibits Bills stuck up on every Post with Murder in large Letters on it—soliciting the Apprehension of a Fellow who has killed his Sweetheart;[6] and the Lawyers all declare That the Annals of Newgate are *disgraced*—comical enough!—by the proceedings of the Common People these last Three Years.—Whilst we all witness the Profligacy of *higher* Orders, and the Women of Pleasure complain That the Tradesmen's Wives and Shopkeepers Servants help to ruin their Profession by intruding on it—in the *Streets—Per Contra*—as Shopkeepers would express it: You may hear The *Good* People (I visit many of those who style Themselves the Evangelicals:) congratulating me and each other on the Diffusion of Religious knowledge, and consequent virtuous Behaviour. Jews—say they, are converting,—Slaves releasing, and heathen Nations obtaining Instruction by means of Missionaries warm in the Cause of Piety, and useful in Researches for bettering the General Condition of Mankind.[7] Preachers no longer supine, vye with each other in Eloquent Persuasion of their Hearers, who Twenty or Thirty Years ago would have run after anyone of those who now adorn our Pulpits—and are—as far as I can observe, very cooly listened to.

Such is my Survey of London for the Year 1814. I think dear Lady Williams will explain all these Wonders into Proofs that the concluding Scenes are not above a Century or a Century and half's Distance from the present Day.—But I have omitted one strange Thing. You remember a Miss Beffin—who wrote a beautiful Character,—we must not call it *Hand* for she had no Arms below the Shoulders, and no Legs below the Knee,—her Landschapes were neatly drawn and her fine Needle Work deservedly prized—but She has done a greater—at least a more marvellous Thing than any of these: She has married and brought into the World a well formed healthy Infant! Mrs. Mostyn is my Authority. I *think* She saw the Child.[8]

And now my Dear Williams adieu! Present me most Affectionately to all my true Friends at *happy* Bodylwyddan, and when you are kind enough to write, Ask Salusbury for Direction,——He has for 16 years guided/ the Destiny of Your most faithful and Obliged/ H: L: P./ and for *his* Sake alone—She quits her sweet Residence at Streatham Park.

He is at Brynbella *now* I am *sure*. The Weather is delightful. Mrs. Hoare's Birthday gave us the first Sunshine—It has lasted ever since.

Text Ry. 6 (1813–21). *Address* John Williams Esqr./ Bodylwyddan/ St. Asaph Flintshire/ N: Wales. *Postmark* 12 o'Clock AU 10 1814.

1. This letter may be dated from its postmark, 10 August 1814.
2. Joanna Southcott's "Imposture."
3. For the sin against the Holy Ghost, see Matthew 12:31, 32; Mark 3:28–30; Luke 12:10.
4. Frederick John Pigou (d. 1847) was Andrews's residuary legatee and chief beneficiary of his cousin's great wealth. See the latter's will, P.R.O., Prob. 11/1558/386–87, signed 7 August 1813, and proved 17 July 1814.
5. Prince Christophe-Andréiévitch Lieven (1777–1839) had been Russian minister of war, ambassador to Berlin (1809–12) and to the Court of St. James's (1812–34).
6. HLP refers to the murder of Mary Anne Welchman, a dressmaker in Mount Street. On 5 August, she had been shot twice in the head by James Mitchell, a rejected suitor. Having made his escape, he was apprehended on 10 August at Salisbury and subsequently executed. See *The Times*, 6 August; *GM* 84, pt. 2 (1814): 184.
7. Through MF, HLP met several members of the Clapham sect, a group of evangelical Anglicans, active from 1790 to 1830. Many of them (nicknamed the "Saints") served in Parliament and worked for the abolition of the slave trade and slavery. They supported the Church Missionary Society, the British and Foreign Bible Society, and the Religious Tract Society. They financed the *Christian Observer*, which Zachary Macaulay edited from 1802 to 1816 and which HLP read regularly.
8. From *AR*, "Chronicle," 51 (1809): 322–23: "*Wonderful Production of Nature, now exhibiting at the house of Mr. Polley, No. 17, New Bond-street.*—Miss Beffin, a young lady who was born deficient of arms and legs—she is of a comely appearance, 24 years of age, and only 37 inches high; she displays a great genius, and is an admirer of the fine arts; and what renders her so worthy of the public notice is, the industrious and astonishing means she has invented and practised in obtaining the use of the needle, scissors, pen, pencil, &c. . . . all of which she performs principally with her mouth."
    She was Sarah Beffin, or Biffin (1784–1850). According to one contemporary report: "Her landlady says she is married to a handsome young man [a Mr. Wright] who takes care of her money & lifts her about, but she preserves her first name, like madame de Stahl, because it is the most celebrated." See *Journals and Letters*, 11:395, n. 12.

TO JOHN SALUSBURY PIOZZI SALUSBURY

Stratham Park
Saturday 13: August 1814.

My dearest Salusbury must not be offended—tho' perhaps he may be displeased, at my begging him to excuse my *Presence* on the ensuing Occasion at Condover Hall.[1] My Embarrassments and Perplexities——to call them by no *harsher* Name;—are such as will not admit of my coming down to Shropshire. That it is no Disrespect to your new Friends, every Word I speak, write, and mean, will evince. That my Affection for you is such as no Young Man ever possessed, or deserved, beside Yourself; will be proved by my ready Signature of whatever Papers or Parchments Mr. Robert Pemberton shall prepare and Send me to Bath:[2] and I will make Mr. Ward give me a *Sketch* for a Will to be made after you come of Age, nominating You and Mr. Robert Pemberton as my Executors because the Guardian and Trustee Stuff will then be over:——besides that my Distance from Shrewsbury and my truly Solitary Condition will act as future Proofs that the Testamentary Disposition was not made under Influence. I shall indeed have nothing to leave *Then*——but these beautiful Pictures and *Books*——more valuable than I thought them; but you are always right——you *said* they were worth 2 or 3000£ and so I understand they are. The Paintings old Wilson estimated three Years ago at 2000£[3]——and said they would double their Value in 4 Years.

Catalogues and Inventories have been all my Labour and Study: and I will ensure the House and Contents for Twenty five Thousand Pounds, so that if the Ambassador and his Suite set it on fire, you may not be left wholly on the *Pavè*. My Furniture is very elegant certainly; and I bought a new Sideboard since Dear *Pem* was here, and an Octagon Table of British Oak,[4] which as Count Grimani said of the roasted Rabbet—shall have no Companion.[5] The last Tenants took my fine old Sideboard, and left me a filthy Second-hand one in the Place.

But Language is weak to describe my Torments: and the Robberies, *Insults* and Afflictions heaped on your poor H: L: P.

Well no matter: May I *but* live to see or hear of your coming of Age: May I *but* hold a Pen to sign this Deed of Gift, and save your Legacy Tax:—*then* make my own new Will, and take Chance for the rest—Long Life or short. God knows my Heart, and that I would rather go to Prison for my own Salusbury and the sweet Girl of his deliberate Choice;——than I would possess Blenheim and be Parent to any of the Reprobates I see around me——Their Conduct is detestable and their Deaths dreadful.

Why do you never go to Bodylwyddan? Young Williams is an amiable Creature—and particularly partial to *me*. In these Days when England is divided between gross Infidelity—and blasphemous Fanaticism, what a Happiness it is to deal with People who are in their Wits! Mr. Heaton is among them, as we have always heard; and Dr. Cumming—exemplary.[6] If any of my Neighbours yet remember me—say I have been much harrassed, and that my Health and

Spirits *require immediate Bath Water.* The Assertion is *strictly true;* but there are *other Reasons* which you shall one Day be told—not *now.*

Meanwhile do you recollect a Story of a Coal heaver that left large Sums of Money behind him, after having wanted a Pair of Breeches, and when he got a Pair—saying—God Almighty sent them: for no one else knew his Measure? Well! This Fellow set up for a Preacher——in *a Room*——and such is the Veneration his hearers have Shown to his Memory, that The Arm Chair he taught them out of—Sold last Week for 60£ Sterling, to A *Broker;* who will get 80£ for it from some of the Dupes that swore by him. He was buried if you remember with much Pomp, and *SS* written on His Escutcheons meaning a *Sinner Saved.* What is come to the People?

Have you seen my Working Spectacles? in a $\left. \begin{array}{l} \text{Shagreen} \\ \text{Chagrin} \end{array} \right\}$ Case? I used to

keep them in the Wings of the Back Gammon Table, and certainly never brought them away. When The Papers come to be signed, you may send *Them,* and the Scrap-Book if You have done with it. I *expect* to leave this sweet Place on Saturday next for Blake's hotel——whence I go to Bath—but after you have answered *This* Letter, direct to Hammersley's, till contrary Directions arrive from my dearest Salusbury's true and *tried* and/ tender Friend, Aunt,/ and Parent/ H: L: Piozzi.

I have written my Excuses to the Ladies at Condover Park:—I *cannot* go thither, *so it don't signify*—as We Women express it——but don't you grieve about it; It shall be exactly the same Thing to *You.*

Text Ry. 588.241. *Address* John Salusbury Piozzi Salusbury Esq./ Brynbella/ near Denbigh/ North Wales. *Postmark* Two Py Post Unpaid Streatham; 7 o'Clock AU 13 1814; AU C 13 814.

1. JSPS was to come of age on 9 September and marry HMP two months later, on 7 November. For the announcement of the wedding, see *GM* 84, pt. 2 (1814): 600.
2. Robert Pemberton (1764–1816), an attorney of Shrewsbury, was a cousin of HMP's father.
3. When the Streatham Park "Pictures" and prints were sold 9–10 May 1816, they brought over £1,900.
For John Wilson of the European Museum, see HLP to JSPS, 28 April 1813, n. 5.
4. In the library was an octagon table, made of the root of oak, inlaid and banded on stout pillar and claws, and brass socket castors. It was to sell on 11 May 1816 for £6.
In the dining room was a mahogany sideboard, over seven feet wide, with drawer in the center, and handsomely carved on reeded feet. It also sold on 11 May for £8.5.
5. For Filippo Vincenzo Grimani, see HLP to Q, 19 December 1794, n. 11.
6. HLP refers to John Heaton (1787–1855) of Plas Heaton, Denbighshire, lord of the manors of Wereham and Bryncaeredig. On 1 August 1814 he had married Elizabeth, née Jones (d. 1822), of Cefn Coch.
For Dr. George Brownlow Cumming, see HLP to Ly W, 9 February 1810, n. 11.

TO THOMAS WINDLE

Streatham Park
Fryday 19: August 1814.

My Dear Mr. Windle
  was troubled with a Visit from me Yesterday, to deposit in your kind hands
every Letter and Paper received by me from that Mr. Mead which has cost *me*
such intolerable Anguish. The Receipt you sent me is *among* them of course;
and Three very Important Letters from Mead acknowledging Monies at various
Times for which I have by some Accident no Stamped Receipts.[1] All Mr. Charles
Shephard's Letters relative to Streatham Park are there also; and your Clerk
gave me Credit for tying and sealing them up so very neatly.
  My Dear Mr. Salusbury was in the Carriage with me; he came to London full
of Anxiety and Alarm at my apparent Distress: resolving to extricate me by any
means in *his* Power.[2]
  I am however quite safe to all appearance. The Russian Ambassador has
signed Agreements to take this House and give me 600£ o'Year for it: and I will
go directly to Bath, where I can live cheap and pay all my Debts——dismissing
all *Horse Equipage*, an Expence I am not at present able or willing to Support.
  —If we could meet before I leave the Environs of London it would be a great
Consolation to Dear Sir/ Yours ever/ H: L: Piozzi.

  I leave this House on Monday Morning for Blake's hotel in Jermyn Street,
whence I take Wing for Bath:—and Mr. Salusbury——for *Shropshire.*——

Text Hyde Collection.

  1. What prompted HLP's visit to Thomas Windle, a lawyer of Bedford Row, was the receipt of
his letter, which explained her present financial relationship with Hammersley's and Mead.
  On 15 August Windle had written (Ry. 601.93):
  "Hammerleys have nothing to do with the Bills drawn on you by Mead, but pay them when due,
which with Money in their hands, they will *not dare to refuse*, and here I cannot help expressing my
astonishment, that, Mrs. Piozzi should have laid herself open to the insults of that Mead, or the
refusal of her Bankers when in truth she wanted no favor from either, certainly not from the latter
and only an imaginary one from the former—
  "I shall settle with Mead in the course of the day and send you his receipt. . . ."
  On the cover of this letter, HLP had written: "Windle's sweet Letter saying he settles with Mead—
and the Receipt from Mead came by the same Post and I return it safe to Mr. Windle."
  2. For the source of JSPS's "Anxiety," see HLP to HMP, 23 July 1814.

TO JOHN WILLIAMS

Steatham Park
22: August 1814.

My Dear Williams's
  Letter added greatly to my Distresses and I have Suffered much from per-

plexing Occurrences since We met last. Our truly excellent and amiable Salusbury left every Thing, and every Thought to come flying hither, and when we had settled in some Measure *My* Plagues and Torments he told me *Yours*—and I forgot the rest—Poor dear Sir John! but he is better now, and will be better;— he must however be careful; for if the Disease is a true Angina—There is always caution necessary for Fear of its Return. Long live our friend Dr. Cumming! always respected among us—now *beloved.* Aye and long live the memory of Doctor Johnson who said to me once so wisely when my heart was apprehensive for the safety of a friend:

"Why Madam if Death comes against us rapidly, presenting his Scythe, an active and skillful Physician may give him a Turn but when the Dog shakes your sand in the hour glass—you must wait the end in hopeless Inactivity."[1]

The last my dear Williams knows to be *my* Case. The first is your good Fathers.—As to my charming friend Lady Williams I wonder not that her nerves have been disturbed; this world's vexations are such that our *Fibres* ought to be *cart ropes:* I will go so far out of it as to remove from this Neighbourhood at least, and swallow my Sorrows washing them down with Bath Water: happy in my beloved Salusbury's continued attachment and in my own power to say "non faciam vitio, culpâve minorem."[2] Streatham Park is from this day the Country Seat of Count Lieven, the Russian Ambassador.

You will be kind enough to direct Post Office Bath; and let me know your hopes and fears that you may be sure of a sympathizing friend/ in your very much Obliged and/ faithful H: L: P.

Lady K—— is gone to Ireland.[3]

Text Ry. 6 (1813–21).

1. HLP had attributed a similarly phrased statement to SJ in *Anecdotes*, p. 188. Even earlier, furthermore, and in her own voice, she had told FB: "A physician can sometimes parry the scythe of death, but has no power over the sand in the hourglass" (12 November 1781: *Diary and Letters*, 2:82).
2. See Horace, *Satires*, 2.6.7.
3. Lady Kirkwall had gone to Ireland to attend her father.

TO ALEXANDER LEAK

Sunday
28: August 1814.

I begin to have a Notion that Leak,—and perhaps his Wife too, will be glad to hear of my safe Arrival at the Place of my Destination. They will not however rejoyce—as indeed I cannot,——in the present Prosperity of Bath; where every house either *is*—or expects to be occupied. I have at length fixed on a complete *Nut Shell* in old Pierpoint Street, for 3 Guineas per Week all the Year round.

You will not Suspect me of giving *Dinner* Parties, when I assure you *faithfully* and *seriously*, that my best Parlour is not an Atom bigger than *yours at the Lodge:* It is clean certainly—as I hope yours will be; but for 150£ o'Year I could not find a Dwelling for my little Family, unless in the Streets where the Poor Players, and Dancers, and Mrs. Sharp are living.[1]

Pierpoint Street is not *very grand* you'll say;—but I am close to both Parades, and the Pump, and Dear Upham's Library:[2] and I must not feel ashamed of the Reduction in my Circumstances—for it proceeds from no Fault committed. You would laugh tho' (or cry) to see the Tradesmen pressing for my Custom; and offering me Houses up and down Pultney Street, Johnstone Street &c. of 300£ o'Year Rent—Thinking everything the Same with me as usual. But *my* Two little Drawing Rooms would Scarce contain Three Card Tables, and one Forte Piano would fill the whole Apartment,—so the Lords and Ladies have no Chance for Diversion at the Expence of Your poor Friend H:L:P. It would have been less offensive to have lived *more out of Sight:*—but my Dear Salusbury, for whom alone I wish to live at all, likes to have me at Bath he says, because it is but 90 Miles from Condover Park; and he fancies me safest here on Account of the best Physicians being round me.

God keep me out of their hands. The dirty Lodging No. 11 North Parade, which he and I occupied last Year in our Way to Mendip; lets at 220£ the whole House, and miserably furnished. I was amazed indeed; but Laura Chapel was crouded this Morning till the People fainted away; and Thomas came home Sick with the Heat in middle of Service from St. James's Church.

The Markets are very reasonable; best Joynts of Mutton, Beef, and *Veal* at 7d. 1/2, Fish in plenty, and no Fowl or Chicken is beyond 2s.6. Butter 16d.——Wine at the old War Prices; Claret 14s. the Bottle, and People enough to drink it.

My Cellar is stored with 3 Bottles of Port and 3 of Madeira; I hope they will last 6 Weeks. My Cellar is a Cupboard of Course—no Servant's Hall in the whole Mansion.

This Moment brings a Letter from Mr. Windle: It does not tell me what I am impatient to learn, the Extent of Mead's *After-Clap*—as I call it: nor whether Dorman[3] and he have settled their Dispute yet.——Pray let me hear soon, and direct Post Office Bath.

Do my Letters escape paying Postage because you live at *The Ambassador's?*

Blake[4] says we shall have Demand on us for Taxes when the Count *leaves;* but I think the Agreement Secures us.

The worst House in Johnstone Street is 260£ o'Year.

Southey[5] is here in a very dashing Style.

Text Hyde Collection. *Address* Mr. Alexander Leak/ Streatham Park/ Surrey. *Postmark* BATH <AU> 29 1814; 10 o'Clock AU 30 1814; E 30 AU 30 1814.

1. Elizabeth Hopkins Sharpe (1756–1821) was the widow of the oboist Michael Sharp (d. 1800) and sister of Priscilla Hopkins Kemble.

She had two talented children: the painter Michael William (d. 1840) and the musician Elizabeth (see HLP to PSP, 26 April 1801, n. 4).

2. John Upham (fl. 1805–34) was the owner of a bookstore and circulating library, Lower Walks, Bath. By 1819 he was listed in the Bath directory as librarian to his Majesty, "his shop the most valuable in Bath . . . especially for books of reference." See Randall Mainwaring, *Annals of Bath*, 219.

3. John Dorman, glass manufacturer and potter, 9 Rathbone Place, London.

4. B. Blake, proprietor of Blake's Hotel.

5. Possibly James Southey. See HLP to AL, 12 March 1812, n. 1.

TO ALEXANDER LEAK

> Bath 31: August 1814.
> written at Night

It was foolish enough in me to lament *my* Difficulties while you are so much occupied with Your own and Mrs. Leak's. I wrote however to Penning[1] immediately to expedite the Scheme you yourself came to Blake's Hotel on purpose to resume,——and which was all along *My favourite Project*. It is a Shame if the Blakes should not be most willing to receive your Wife on very moderate Terms for a Temporary Residence——and you said you would not be <needing> *Personal* Accommodation.

Our Newspapers Shew that Count Lieven is still at Brighthelmstone; and his Servants——if they partake at all of his polite Disposition,——would I should think be happy to leave you in your Room till his coming home to settle.

I am very sorry indeed to think you are so much Incommoded, and all upon my Account: but certainly to let the House was our great Concern; and now it *is* let, the best is to make oneself happy: I have particular Reason to rejoyce in the Thoughts of getting Such good Interest for my five or six Thousand Pounds laid out on Streatham Park, and getting it from the *House* too, which was so long considered as A mere Incumbrance upon the *Estate* from which I was naturally led to hope the best part of my Profits. Profit however, and Friendship too, sometimes comes from a Quarter least expected.

Miss Williams came and offered me a 50£ Bank Note for my Journey, when She heard that Mr. Salusbury and his new Friends requested, and even *required* my Presence at his Marriage; and when She saw by my Countenance the Distress it will put my Purse to.

You may be sure I refused her; but round Opulent and Prosperous London, I had no such Offers.——The Mouse Trap Hall in dirty old Pierpoint Street I have been perswaded to relinquish: it [costs] 164£ o'Year. My hope is now to have fixed on one in The Bristol Road, quite new and clean: under the Royal Crescent, *far* beyond Mrs. Sharp's,[2] but in the same Line:—paying 150£ and I am to save my Coach-standing beside, which costs 6£ 10s. per Annum here at Arnold's——and *There*, The LandLord throws me in a wretched Stable, which I can let to a Man close by—who will in Exchange keep my Carriage in his Places, whatever we call them;—Coach houses.

There is a little Garden besides, which we can keep Mint and Sage in, with Andrew's help: but a Sick Child prevents my taking Possession——so I live in this odious Two Guinea Lodging; and write this Letter by *one Candle*, never having lighted Two at once since we parted.

Our Things are not come yet which were sent by the Canal, and God knows where we shall put them when they *do* come: My Intended Habitation is no bigger than an Acorn Cup; and I live besides *that*, in cruel Suspense to think when I shall be called to Shrewsbury. The Glovers are at Weymouth; but their House and Establishment is gay and grand: and they are as much *higher* in Style than they were formerly,—as I am *lower*.[3] The Art of falling without hurting one's Mind, is however to be learned;—and I am a very good Scholar in learning it.

May You and Yours notwithstanding, escape for many long Years such a Tumble-down; as has been Experienced by your/Old Friend/ H: L: P.

I should be happy to hear Mrs. Leak was fixed at Blake's hotel till She can get to the Lodge;——They would not I am convinced be unreasonable in their Demands: and I cannot bear her suffering Inconvenience on *my* Account. It would certainly be none to live at Blake's Hotel, where so many find comfortable Apartments.

In short We must end as Dearest Dear Mr. Piozzi ended—with

Trust upon Leak, and he shall do for the best.

My Life is all that's wanted, to get through every Embarrassment, and perhaps the Journey may do my *Health* good.

I hope you put my Letter for the Count, giving Characters of all the Literary Friends round the Library—into his Hand or His Steward's.

Write once again Post Office Bath, after *that*, Condover Park near Shrewsbury.

Text Hyde Collection. *Address* Mr. Alexander Leak/ at/ Streatham Park/ Surrey. *Postmark* 10 o'Clock <   > 1814; E 2 SE 2 1814.

1. Possibly John Penning, later of 6 Holles Street, Cavendish Square. He was an upholsterer and auctioneer who at this time was to appraise the contents of Streatham Park not only for insurance but for possible sale.
2. For Elizabeth Hopkins Sharp, see HLP to PSP, 26 April 1801, n. 4.
3. John and Frances Glover lived on fashionable Pulteney Street, Bath.

TO HARRIET MARIA PEMBERTON

Bath
1: September 1814.

This Moment brings me the joint Letter of my truly amiable and beloved Ladies. I hope so to arrange my little Matters—after all; as not to shrink from Mr. Pemberton's Challenge, but to come and dance with him as we at first intended. Dear Salusbury must be called the *Irresistible* as well as the *Inestimable:* I thought he had let me off——but No:——he holds me to a Promise made many Years past to accompany him at The Altar, and I *will* accompany him. Your kind

Brother too gave me the most cordial Invitation when we parted, and You are all so kind and so Charming——That you will pardon my Change of Mind, and receive me graciously on Wednesday or Thursday The 7th or 8th of this new Month, and when I return home I will carry the Skreens, Purses &c.

The beautiful Weather and perpetual Change of Air will drive away the slight Cold I caught on my first Arrival, and the Sight of Salusbury's Happiness and yours will do me Service.

Expect me therefore in the best possible good-Humor, unless some thing very serious indeed should happen, to destroy this *last* Pleasure wished for by dear Mrs. Pemberton's and our Sweet Harriet's/ Sincerely Affectionate/ and faithful Servant/ H: L: Piozzi.

I have got a Place for My little Possessions, and shall defer all other Arrangements till my Return; bringing no one with me but happy Bessy Jones. When Dear Harriet says so kindly I think more of hers and her Husband's Comforts, than of my own;—She does me Justice:——but *my* Felicity *now* depends on Theirs—God preserve it!

I hope this is my *last* Letter to *Miss* Pemberton.

Dear Caroline is very good and I think will be very pretty.[1]

Text Ry. 592.27. *Address* Miss Harriet Maria Pemberton/ Condover Park/ near/ Shrewsbury. *Postmark* BATH 1 SE 1 814 109.

1. For HMP's fourteen-year-old sister Letitia Caroline, see HLP to JSPS, 20 August 1808, n. 1.

TO ALEXANDER LEAK

Bath Monday Morning
5: September *1814*.

I think with Leak entirely, that if the Count should not come—no bad Consequences need ensue: With Regard to Taxes our Agreement says *He* will *exonerate* H: L: Piozzi; and to his Honour we must trust——my heart tells me we *may* trust implicitly. People are expecting the Ambassador *here* with his Lady;[1] who if She resembles an English Lady, will like any Place better than a House taken by her *Husband* without consulting *her.*

I want to hear the Result of the Battle between Mead and Dorman; because on *that* partly depends the Extent of Mead's further Demand, his *After-Clap* as I continue calling it.

My best Method of rendering the Journey to Shropshire *less* heavy on my empty Purse, is to go *directly*: because there is a Sick Child in the new Habitation which prevents my taking Possession, and I shall escape a fresh Week in these vile Lodgings—and save the Wages of a Maid, and save Housekeeping, Washing &c. My hope is to return by the first Week in October[2] and I leave Thomas to take Care of Andrew and the Packages——when they arrive; and the *unpacked* Imperial, Plate, Chest &c. Miss Williams will take Care of them all.

She is very, *very* far distant even from *hope* of being *rich* I believe; but something tells me She is further from being *Poor* than She once was; because her health is established, her Looks bright; and we walked Three Miles together last Saturday by the River's Side.

My Garden is a narrow Gravel Walk down to the Stable with Two Brick Walls and a Border of Earth. I should think Six Pence o'Year very ill-bestowed on it.

Grapes and Vines are not high-prized even *here;* and the Vines upon the Crescent Houses, and those of the South Parade are covered with natural Bunches now: *Un*ripe You may well suppose, but bringing forward by Bell Glasses; which sparkle and glisten so as to distress my Eyes when walking near them: I know not how they answer to the Proprietors.

The Wheat looked ill coloured as we came along a Week ago, but very heavy Crops: Weather most unseasonably hot, and the Sunshine clear beyond Example; We have neither Smoke nor Cloud. Two Guineas per Week do I pay for these dirtiest of all dirty Apartments, which I am going to change for Splendid ones at Condover Park, and clean ones at my Return.

The new Mansion is not further from the Pump after all, than the Pump in Streatham is, from our own House and Park:——not so far the Servants say; They reckon it not much more distant than Mr. Davies's, and *no Hill*: 'Tis on *this* Side the beautiful new Range of Buildings called *Norfolk* Crescent, with the sweetest View in the World, and The Crescent Gardens to walk in;[3] and I am promised plenty of Nightingales to delight my Ears in the Spring. Mrs. Lutwyche's hospitable Table is within a very short Walk indeed;[4] and they all know I can give nothing in return *but* Tea and Talk. The Glovers lament my Distance,[5] and none but such Friends as come for Kindness alone, will do anything but knock *once* at my Door, and say how *far* it is.

I am delighted with its *Smallness* and *Remoteness;* My Time and Money will be Spent only on *myself.*

How happy I should be now with the old Secretaire you were accustomed to use at Brynbella! My Study at the new house is more luminous than *that* Room, and The Hon. Miss Hay teaches me how to turn my Packing Cases into Book Shelves. She has done hers very neatly: for She is a distressed Gentlewoman like myself, and put to her Shifts how to live——tho' you may remember her with Bishop Bagot—his Lady's Sister, and in a high Style[6]——Scotch and Welsh People are not easily dejected however,——and to use a Scripture Phrase—"He who now goeth on his Way weeping (and bringeth forth good Fruit;) shall doubtless come again with Joy, and shall bring his sheaves with him."[7]

That you may live happily, and see me *clear of Debt;* is the Sincere Wish and Prayer of yours ever/ H: L: P.

My Foot is on the Step of the Chaise. God send me safe out and *home* to my new Dwelling.

Text Hyde Collection. *Address* Mr. Alexander Leak/ at/ Streatham Park/ Surrey.
Postmark BATH SE 5 1814; 10 o'Clock SP 6 1814.

1. Daria Khristoforovna Lieven, née Benckendorff (1784–1857) had accompanied her husband to
his diplomatic posts in Berlin and London. In 1834 she was to serve as *dame d'honneur* to the Russian
Empress, but by 1837 she settled in Paris, which she left temporarily in 1848 for London and in
1854 for Brussels. Her salon in the hôtel Talleyrand functioned as a rendezvous for the diplomats
and aristocracy of Europe.
For a portrait of the Princess Lieven, see *The Greville Diary,* 2 vols. (London: William Heinemann,
1927), 1:542–43.
2. HLP was not to settle into Bath until ca. 11 November 1814.
3. Construction of Norfolk Crescent, designed by John Palmer (ca. 1738–1817), began in 1798 and
eventually consisted of nineteen houses, four stories high and three windows wide. The facade is
plain, relieved by ground floor rustification and iron balconies off the first floor.
4. William and Mary Lutwyche lived at 12 Marlborough Buildings in Walcot parish, as did HLP.
5. The Glovers lived in Bathwick parish, virtually across the city from HLP.
6. For Margaret Hay, see HLP to JSPS, [13-] 14 May 1813, n. 4.
She was the sister of Mary Bagot (d. 1786), wife of the late bishop of St. Asaph, and niece of the
ninth and tenth earl of Kinnoull.
7. Pslams 126:6.

TO ALEXANDER AND ANN LEAK

Condover Hall
Sunday 9 [-10]: October 1814.

My good Leak is better acquainted with poor H: L: P's Finances than he is with
her Heart, if he thinks She would suffer herself to be extricated by *any Single*
Hand. To solicit the Public is no Disgrace, and no Individual can be hurt by
Subscribing to a Book which they may amuse themselves by studying, by ap-
plauding, or by *condemning;*—as best will compensate them for their Subscription of a Pound Note or a Guinea.[1]

I am in haste to get home, that I may Set to work; tho' God knows it will be
Sharp living on 80£ till January, and I must pay my Rent with Parsons's Money
and Davies's.[2]

Dear Mr. Davies! I dare say he is half sorry for me, isn't he?

Lady Keith is at Heath House near Bristol,[3] from whence you may remember
She once paid me a Visit in Pultney Street for a Night or Two, and slept in the
Back Parlour when dear Mr. Piozzi was alive; She will perhaps do so again, tho'
I have had no Letter from her since last March or April[4]——but Miss Williams
loves a Bustle and a Wonder. Thomas and Andrew are on Board Wages, so they
will not Entertain old Jacob with anything *but* Gossip;[5] and my Packages are
safe arrived, and that is a good Thing at any Rate, and the Expence of seeking
them saved.

Oh Pray get Parsons's 22£10s.0 for me, because such is Mead's After Clap, I
have not one Shilling beyond actual Necessity——and Mr. Windle has received
only a 200£ Draft for him, and the *Threatening* Letter he was cruel enough to
write me last Thursday after I sent you his Bill franked by Mr. Lyster.[6] I thought

it best enclose *That* to No. 1: John Street Bedford Row, and tremble to think what Expences I am incurring *there* again.

Be that as it may, the Account of all that Work should most certainly be examined, because I can be no judge of the Demand at all; only so much Postage to pay, and so much Mortification to endure. But I believe this is your Wedding Day, and I wish not to sadden it by my Sorrows. Your Expressions are very kind to me, and I am convinced you are doing the best you can for the Estate.

Hay is at 6£ 10s. now in Shrewsbury Market, and will be dearer. The Weather smiles on us, tho' Fortune frowns: and you see as every Thing does happen unexpectedly, some good Turn may be hoped for.—

A British Heart should be like a British Oak, not apt to swell and bud out with the earliest Breath of Spring and Prosperity,——nor yet fade and lose all its Honours with the *very first* Rough Winds of Winter.

I shall be willing to be assisted in promoting the Sale of my Book by Lady Keith; and shall feel vexed if I am delayed here till her Holydays are over. She always passes some Weeks every year with her old Friend Mrs. Smith of Heath House; and I should be most glad to consult her upon *literary* Business as no one knows it better.

Give my Love to your Wife and say how well I wish her.

Mr. Cox is found;[7] so now these young People will have only to wait till he has signed and sent the Deed hither.

Monday Morning 10: October——

Dear Leak's very good natured Letter is just now arrived, and claims my kindest Acknowledgements. Do not believe it a Disgrace to print my Book by Subscription: The ill thoughts that attach themselves to such Conduct arise from Swindling Fellows having taken that Method to fill their own Pockets, and then run away without publishing the Work. I shall not cheat my Subscribers; In the mean time however, if I *should* want 50£ between Christmas and January, I will promise to accept it from no one but Your Husband and yourself to whom I hope and trust it would be speedily repaid. Not one Guinea further would I stir for the Universe, because of the dreadful Risque you would run on account of my worne out Life. The Tradesmen I am less scrupulous about. *They* would be Sure of their Money——and I shall have 500£ in January you know.

I wish Leak would *not* pay Gillows People nor promise them more than what my last Letter agrees to. He must get me a little Statement from Hammersley— and the 22£ 10s. from Parsons. I have 100£ at the Banker's *now*——or I dream so; after the 200£ is gone to Mead. The Dividends pay Gillow their 100£ making 600£, and the remaining 80 I keep for Bath.

We shall get thro' even clear *if I live*, but it is very mortifying to pay those who deserve *least*, at their expence who deserve *most*: and I cannot bear that it *should* be so. Leak and Lonsdale[8] to wait while my Money goes to Mead and Gillow! makes quite enraged your Affectionate/ H: L: P.

Text Hyde Collection. *Address* Mr: Alexander Leak/ Streatham Park/ Surrey. *Postmark* SHREWSBURY 10 OC 10 1814 165; 10 o'Clock OC 12 1814.

1. HLP believed that children were often misnamed. Familiar with Edward Lyford's *The True Interpretation and Etymologie of Christian Names* (1655), she began her version after GP's death. Her "Lyford Redivivus or a Grandame's Garrulity," consisting of some nine hundred names, was ready to be marketed.

2. For the land that John Parsons and RD rented in Streatham, see HLP to RD, 7 November 1813, n. 1.

3. For Jane Smyth of Heath House, near Bristol, see HLP to Q [23 May 1801], n. 14.

4. HLP's last letter to Q was dated 17 January 1814. Another eighteen months were to elapse before her next recorded letter to Q on 12 July 1815.

5. Jacob Weston, HLP's former steward at Streatham Park, now lived in Bath.

6. Richard Lyster (d. 1819), of Rowton Castle, Salop, a lieutenant colonel in the 22nd Light Dragoons, served the office of high sheriff in 1812. He represented Shrewsbury in Parliament (1814–19).

7. See HLP to Ly W, 2 November 1814.

8. William Lonsdale, cabinet and furniture maker, at 7 Broad Street, Soho.

TO LADY WILLIAMS

Condover Park
Wednesday 2d: November 1814.

My dear Lady Williams
shall know every thing that I can tell her, in return to Enquiries which I know are dictated by Friendship and not by mere Curiosity.

Mr. Oldfield left every thing smooth and indisputable on the 26: of last September,[1] when the Deed of Reconveyance was ready to be signed could my own Dear Piozzi's last Surviving Trustee be found, or his Representative——*he* was far away however;—meaning the Representative: for Old Cox of Quarley—*The real Man* has been dead long enough ago.[2] And when we found the present Gentleman he refused his Signature under a Notion that tho' Heir at Law to the Trustee, he was *no more:*[3] and that the Executors ought to be responsible—This they denied; his Father's Will making the Business *Special,* Counsel's Opinion became necessary; and it was at last agreed that I should Sign first: so the Deed came down hither, and I executed it in due form, and it was dispatched to London last Wednesday.

Mr. Cox was however gone to his Seat in Wiltshire by *That Time*—and *our* Solicitors now promise to make *his* Solicitors send it after him—and so the Time goes on, and so is our Patience put to Tryal. Letters coming every day to wonder what is the Matter, Salusbury fretting himself till it frights me; and *my own* Affairs running to Ruin while I am delayed here looking after *his.*

No Vexations however have kept me from making incessant Enquiries after the Health of Dear Sir John: and my last Accounts from Chester were so favourable I was in high Spirits at least on *that* Side my heart, when Your Ladyship's kind Letter came Yesterday Morning.

I am delighted that my amiable Young friend has decided so wisely: and more than delighted to think I have a Chance of seeing him to cheer the Spring of my Year of Penance 1815.[4] He will Stare to see me fixed in an *Acorn Cup*—a complete *Nutshell,* after leaving me so apparently settled at Streatham Park:——

but the Repairs and consequent Expences have been such at *that Place* that they have half ruined me; and I am going to try what Resources may offer themselves in the *Writing Way,* when I can once Wash my head clear of these Darlings, and their present Perplexities. Indeed they are too amiable not to be sincerely pitied.

Your Ladyship's Letter coming freed by the Bishop's *firm hand,* gives me opportunity of sending my Respects to him and Mrs. Cleaver with this Reply enclosed.

Our Dear Sir John will understand and explain the Nature of our Delay most perfectly, altho' awkwardly enough expressed by/ Your Ladyship's most Obliged/ and faithful/ H: L: Piozzi.

How happy Miss Williams will be to see her Niece and Nephew! And how desirous am I to hear better News of Sir John!

Let me have a Letter soon and accept our united Regards.

Text Ry. 4 (1812–18). *Address* Lady Williams/ Bodylwyddan/ St. Asaph.

1. HLP refers to the legal transfer of Brynbella to JSPS's possession following his twenty-first birthday.
2. Richard Cox (d. 1803) was a banker who had witnessed the marriage settlement between HLT and GP, along with Augustine Greenland. See Ry. Ch. 1239; HLT to Q, 12 July [1784], n. 3.
3. Richard Cox had married in 1747 Caroline Codrington, who bore three children: Caroline, Mary, and Richard Bethell. It was the signature of the last named which was required for the "Deed of Reconveyance." See the relevant parish registers for Quarley, C.R.O., Wiltshire.
4. JW had planned to go abroad but instead continued his studies at Cambridge.

TO ALEXANDER LEAK

Direct Post Office
[11 November 1814]

Leak really does me great Injustice if he thinks me Insensible to *his* Vexations, whatever my *own* may be.——Pray write or make *Some* body write; *any* body who will say you and yours are *alive* at least.

I am arrived at my *Nutshell* after a Run of 54 Miles this 11th day of *November* 1814, having Slept at Ledbury in Herefordshire last Night, and you will not wonder that I now wish to go to bed when I shall have indulged in the tub of Bath Water which Thomas has kindly provided for my weary Limbs. Farewell, and let me have *Some* Account from poor Dear Streatham Park if all there have not forgotten/ Theirs and your old Friend/ H: L: P.

Better make Mr. Davies write.

Text Hyde Collection. *Address* Mr: Alexander Leak/ Streatham Park/ Surrey. *Postmark* NO 11 1814; E 14 NO 14 <1814>.

TO THE REVEREND THOMAS SEDGWICK WHALLEY

Bath
19: November 1814.

My dear Doctor Whalley—both absent and present, ever-highly-valued by his oldest and best judging Friends; must at length receive the Intelligence he expressed himself kindly desirous to read—The Marriage of my good Boy with the Girl of his heart. After a hundred frivolous and teizing Delays——occasioned by the Wish of dear Piozzi's surviving Trustees——we at last prevailed on Mr. Cox, his Heir at Law, tho' by no means his Executor;—to sign the Deed of Reconveyance—which he wished to avoid doing, and *did* avoid till the first Counsel in England said he *must* do it:——because being Freehold Property, He made himself amenable when he took his Father's Landed Estate. We therefore went to Church on the *seventh* of this Month, and the happy Younglings jumped into their Carriage and away to *their own Brynbella*, leaving me a while to comfort Mrs. Pemberton at Condover Park Salop for Loss of her Harriet Maria. From that Magnificent Dwelling I drove hither in a few Days—-

> From Apartments of Eighteen Feet high where they dine
> To a Chair-lumber'd Closet just Twelve Feet by Nine

as Goldsmith says:[1] but 'tis big enough for my little Establishment, and Straitened Income: Straitened by the Surveyor and The Furnisher of Streatham Park— always a gilded Millstone round my Neck, while you will acknowledge 6500£ a dreadful heavy Debt on any Dowager——much however is already paid, and the rest *shall* be paid if God lends me Life: for I will leave nothing for my Executors to discharge of *Expences* on *my* Account, except Funeral ones, and they shall carry me home to Dymerchion—die where I will.

Your running to France was a cruel Stroke on me: I applaud the Deed however, and only marvel why you do not go further towards the South——Lyons and Grenoble are *such* Places to pass a Winter in; a very few Considerations restrain me or I would go myself.

Siddons is come home I hear, but not from *her:* What She has done with herself and Mrs. Mostyn during the Course of their Tour, remains in Darkness— but they are Dear Creatures all the Party of them, and no doubt delighted with their Frolick.

Sir Walter James too is gone,[2] and Bath looks very empty when I go anywhere,—but 'tis only to the Lutwyches, and to Church that I *do* go. Pray tell whether our Anglican Church is openly tolerated since the return of the Bourbons.

There were always Calvinists about Grenoble, but those who are fluttering about Paris know nothing but the Dimensions of the Gallery at the Louvre, and the Price of good Dinners chez les *Restaurateurs*.

Nevers is an Interesting Place, to *me* as Birthplace of *Maitre Adam* whose Chevilles nobody reads but myself.[3] The Entrance to The Town is however famous for its striking Beauty: and the Duke of the District! Oh how well do I remember the thin, tall, slight-made—but very elegant Person, coming over here to settle as Ambassador,[4] what was called The Peace of Paris.[5] Charles Townsend to whom all Bons Mots in those Days were ascribed, sayd humorously,—Why here are the actual Preliminaries of a *Man* sent over to dictate to us the Preliminaries of a *Peace.*[6] If however this airy Figure did actually survive the Horrors of Robespierre's Reign, remaining unsuspected and untouched thro' a Revolution effected by Assassins, and ended by a Superior Dæmon who crushed them all at once he was indeed a wondrous Mortal; and *deserved* at least to see the rightful Family restored. My heart tells me however that Le Duc de Nivernois died about Two Years ago——You will *not* die abroad I am confident. Like your excellent Mama's,[7] *Your* Constitution will with Care outlast hundreds who appear strong and well-bodied——but we *un*complaining Creatures live only because never attacked by Illness: like

> The Friend that is true—because none will confide,
> And The Nymph that is chaste who has never been tried &c.[8]

The Moment I am taken seriously hold of by Disease, *I* shall despair of my own Life; and that disposition will give more Power to the Enemy: There was a Mr. Hay an Apothecary here at Bath who said that was the natural Feeling and Conduct of all the *Welsh* People he had known and so it certainly is.[9]

Have you heard how our English World is improving? Marianne Francis tells me that by Dint of perpetual Teaching and Learning, we make rapid Approaches to a *happy Time.*[10] She does not give Instances; but I shall ask her this Evening whether 'tis in Religion or Morality that we are getting forward so: If Lady Roseberry and Sir Henry Mildmay are mending the *Manners* of our Nation,[11] Surely Mr. Howston's Pamphlet,[12] and Mrs. Joanna Southcotes Advertisements do no less in the Cause of Religion.[13] I never felt my Ears tingle as they do of late with these Stories, which even at 74 years old, are actually *new* to my Dear Doctor Whalley's ever Obliged/ and faithful/ H: L: Piozzi.

Text Berg Collection +. *Address* A Monsieur/ Monsieur le Docteur Whalley/ a la Poste restante/ Nevers/ France. *Postmark* E PAID 21 NO 21 1814; FOR < > 131 1814; Nov 26 1814; ANGLETERRE.

1. *The Haunch of Venison, a Poetical Epistle to Lord Clare*, lines 67–68.

2. Sir Walter James was at his country seat, Langley Hall in Berkshire.

3. Adam-Billaut (1602–62), commonly styled "Maître Adam," a French poet, and a joiner by trade, wrote *Les Chevilles de m^e Adam, menuisier de Nevers* (Paris: chez Toussainct Quinct, 1654).

4. Louis-Jules-Barbon Mancini-Mazarini (1716–98), duc de Nivernais, held a number of ambassadorships: to Rome (1748–52), to Berlin (1756), and to the Court of St. James's (1762–63). In 1787 he was minister of state in Necker's cabinet. Refusing to leave France in 1791 with the *émigrés*, he was later imprisoned.

For his obituary, see *AR*, "Chronicle," 40 (1798), 35; for his poetry and criticism, see the catalogue of La Bibliotheque Nationale.

5. The Peace of Paris was in fact concluded in February 1763 by the French secretary of foreign affairs (1758–70), Étienne de Choiseul-Stainville. Ending the Seven Years War in Europe and overseas, it also established Britain and Spain as the greatest colonical powers in the world.

6. HLP refers to Charles Townshend (1725–67), chancellor of the exchequer in the Pitt-Grafton ministry. He was well-known for his wit and perception.

7. Mary Whalley died at Winscombe Court, the seat of her second son, Francis, in 1803, at the age of ninety-six.

8. HLP's variation on Congreve's *Love for Love* (1695), 3.181–82. (See the "Song" set by John Eccles beginning "A Nymph and a Swain to Apollo once pray'd.")

9. For Alexander Hay, "an eminent apothecary of Bath," see HLP to Elizabeth Lambart, 19 February 1788, n. 3.

10. For MF's learning, see HLP to JSPS, 26 September 1808, n. 2. She also gave up company and society, the theater, and music; "rejoicing"—as she told her sister Charlotte Barrett—"in going after the poor, & teaching children &c. the society of religious people, reading & exercise" (Barrett, Eg. 3704A, f. 89); *Journals and Letters*, 7:31n.

11. Archibald John Primrose (1783–1868), fourth earl of Rosebery (1814), important in Scottish political circles, had married in 1808 Harriet Bouverie (d. 1834), niece of the earl of Radnor. Their marriage ending in divorce, she then married Henry St. John Carew St. John-Mildmay (1787–1848), fourth baronet (1808), the husband of her late sister, Charlotte (d. 1810). The marriage was performed at Stuttgart by special permission of the king of Württemberg.

12. A mistaken designation for the Reverend Frederic Thruston, author of the pamphlet: *An Original View of the Night of Treason; shewing in this Night When the Rebellious Jews Rejected the Truth, that Pilate was a Traitor to Caesar; Judas Guilty of the Most Complicate Treachery; and that Peter, After the Three Denials, according to a Distinct Prediction, Three Times Apostatised* (Coventry: Printed for F. C. and J. Rivington . . . London, by Merridew and Son, 1813).

13. The *Morning Chronicle*, e.g., advertised on 22 October: "An Address of Mrs. Joanna Southcott. To the Public.—To-morrow the Sunday Monitor will contain an Address from the above Lady to the Believers and Public in general, which she sent to the Proprietor last night. It will alleviate the Public anxiety respecting the Birth of the Child, and will give many interesting particulars not before known."

Her "Address" appeared as scheduled in the *Sunday Monitor* on 23 October. On the same day and in the same newspaper appeared another advertisement for Joanna Southcott as prophetess: "*The Holy of Holies Unveiled*!! by Philadelphicus."

The skepticism is summed up in a jingle printed in the *Morning Chronicle*, 3 September: "A *pious fraud* you know's no sin,/ So pray prepare your lying in;/ Thou art a shrewd old jade, I swear,/ If thou canst bring *the thing* to bear!"

TO THE REVEREND ROBERT GRAY

Bath
27th: November 1814.

Streatham Park was worth anyone's seeing six months ago. Upon some threats concerning dilapidation, I set heartily to work, new fronted the house, new fenced the whole of the 100 acres completely round; repaired stables, outbuildings, barns which I had no use for; and hothouses which are a scourge to my purse, a millstone round my neck. 6500£ sterling just covers my expenses, of which 4000£ are paid; but poor old dowager as I am, the remainder kept me marvellous low in pocket, and drives me into a nut-shell here at Bath, where I used to live gay and grand in Pultney Street. Direct, however, Post Office, when you are kind enough to write, and I shall get your letter. Count Lieven is my tenant, and pays me liberally but so he should; for his dependants smoke their tobacco in my nice new beds, and play a thousand tricks that keep my steward, who I have left there, in perpetual agony. I am famous for *tenants* you know. So much for self.

Lord Byron was such a favourite with the women. We all agreed that he might throw his handkerchief; and I rejoyce so pretty and pleasing a lady picks it up.[1] I knew his grandmother most intimately, Sophia Trevanion, Admiral Byron's Lady; and she was a favourite with Doctor Johnson.[2] He would have been glad that her grandson was a poet, and a poet he is, in every sense of the word: 'au moins il ne manque que *la pauvretè* pour l'être,' as some one said of a gentleman painter in France many years ago.

Text Hayward, 2:269–70.

1. On 2 January 1815 Byron was to marry Anna Isabella Milbanke (1792–1860) at Seaham, county Durham. She was the daughter of Ralph Milbanke, later Noel (d. 1825), sixth baronet, and Judith (d. 1822), daughter of Edward Noel, first viscount Wentworth.
2. See Hyde-Redford, 3:208, 211–12, 216, 241, 372; 4:250. In each of his letters, which run from 7 November 1779 to 27 November 1783, SJ writes of her as a woman distressed and worthy of compassion.

TO ALEXANDER LEAK

Bath Tuesday
13: December *1814.*

Don't make yourself so wretched my good Leak——all will at length go well: and God will bless our Endeavours; *he* knows that I wish for Life and Money on *other* People's Accounts——*not my own.*——You will see how *I* can live in a Nutshell when you and I meet next——and I want your Advice about forty Things.

Beg your Wife to bring my Bill from Dyde and Scribe's with her,[1] and my best Cap—which was made for the Wedding, but I never got it: and do you get Cobbe's, and Price's, and Smythe's Bills,[2]——likewise my Balance of Account from Mortlake[3]—(I paid him 15£ in the Shop)—and the Balance from Hamlets too,[4] and bring them all in Your Pocket——likewise my Green Book settled by my favourite Clerk Mr. Pearce at Pall Mall.[5]

I hope We have 100£ of Savings to add to the 500£ Dividends, if Parsons has paid in his Money:—*I hope so.*—And then these Tradespeople shall have their just dues, and we will go on scraping and scratching here till April——when I hope to make Gillow up his 1000£ and discharge Lonsdale's long Account—— to the Year—from his Goods coming for Streatham Park.

My little Book now in London under Examination by Longman of Paternoster Row, will perhaps pay the four Lawyers; Ward, Windle, Robinson, and Oldfield. Salusbury writes me word poor Oldfield is very Ill, and you will be sorry to see Doctor Bowen and his gay Lady so little like Themselves.[6]

This Weather is enough to kill us all. Our River floods the Country round; and even *my* Health feels the Pressure of so heavy an Atmosphere. I think it is a new Thing for me to complain of tightness across the Breast like Consumptive Misses; but a sore Lip is *not* a new Thing, and I am just going to have one.

Bessy Jones always said, and I now see She was in the right: that one of these half-out-of-Town Houses was the foolishest thing in the World. My next-door Neighbour is making a Hothouse to poyson me with the Smoke and Choke, and take away the Comfort of my pretty Back Window——and if one *was* to be ill——The nearest Doctor is too far off, but I am in high Spirits about my Book. We hope to make it match the *Anecdotes* in Size and Shape. 300£ the Price; and *more* if We can make it run a Second Edition. I could have got 500£ by Subscription I dare say; but then there would have been printing &c. to pay for, and canvassing for Subscribers, and being cheated at last by People you must make a Curtsy too—beside;——so I shall be very contented to end all no worse than *this*; and will go hard to work when Upham returns——if the Work is approved of.

It is a blest Thing at any Rate that we are quit of Mr. Briggs,[7] and of the Terror he *caused me*; Oh that Report did alarm me no little: I think he would have set the Place on Fire. Your Living in it will be a great Security doubtless, both to Count Lieven and myself.

Mr. Parsons will be *sure* to pay when he sees the Hand of an Attorney—— The Money must have been due when Mr. Davies's was due—the 10th of November last. By *that* Time next Year, I shall hope to get into a *Walnut* Shell; and no creditor but Mess. Gillow and Co. Mead's last Receipt as per Installment is in November and he will be humbler by then.——So will our Lodging-House People. Hancock of Pultney Street No. 17 already expresses his Wishes that we had taken his House at 200£ for the whole Year[8]——But if I had given only *150£* it would have been dearer to *me* than *this*——where I *cannot* entertain any body; and where nobody *can* expect it.

Leak and his Wife w<ill> be my only Guests, and they shall be very welcome. I think *She* has been reading the Book I used to teach Lady Keith out of,— concerning Solid Glory and real Greatness:—but it <was not> Her *Ladyship* who had in future Times to recall its Precepts—-but her Affectionate Mother/ and Your true Friend/ H: L: P.

I am *so* glad Mrs. Mostyn is come safe home.

This Moment 6 o'Clock <in> the Afternoon—Tuesday, comes dear Mrs. Dimond to in<vi>te me to see the *French Players* from her Box[9]——and if I had <not t>aken a little Rhubarb and <Alum> in the Morning, I would have gone. The People are most excessively kind; that they are:——how foolish it was to take the Physic.

Text Hyde Collection. *Address* Mr. Alexander Leak/ Streatham Park/ Surrey. *Postmark* 10 o'Clock DE 15 1814; E 15 DE 15 1814.

1. Located at 89 Pall Mall, Dyde and Scribe (later Harding, Howell, Ashby, and James) sold "Furs, Haberdashery, Jewelry, and Perfumery."

2. William Cobbe of the Haymarket was a chemist; for Edward Price, who took over Badioli's Old Italian Warehouse, 5 Haymarket, see HLP to AL, 13 January 1813, n. 2. For Cobbe's bills, see Ry. 598.92; for Price's Ry. 598.66; for Smyth HLP to JSPS, 11 [-13] June 1814, n. 2.

3. John Mortlock, Colebrook-dale China manufacturer, at 250 Oxford Street.

4. For Thomas Hamlet, jeweler and silversmith, see HLP to JSPS, 27 October 1811, n. 1.
5. A clerk at Hammersley's.
6. For William Bowen, see HLP to PSP, 14 April 1803, n. 2. William Bowen was to be buried in the Bath Abbey on 4 April 1815, his wife, Sophia, in 1830. See the "Abbey Burial Registers," C.R.O., Somerset.
7. HLP confused the name Briggs for Trigg. From 1804 to 1813 a Richard Trigg rented property from HLP. See the "Streatham Land Tax Records," C.R.O., Surrey.
8. According to the "Bathwick Poor Rate Books," the Reverend Richard Hancock lived at 17 (renumbered as 16) Pulteney Street from at least 1814 to 1822, when his name was replaced by that of William Hancock. See the records at the Guildhall, Bath.
9. For the "French Players," see their advertisement in the *Bath Herald*, 10 December. William Wyatt Dimond's widow was Matilda Martha, née Baker (ca. 1757–1823) of 17 Norfolk Crescent. See "Bath Abbey Burials," C.R.O., Somerset.

TO ALEXANDER LEAK

No. 17 New King Street
Shortest Day 20: December 1814.

Your Letter Dear Leak comes in a melancholy Moment, and is a very melancholy Letter.[1]

My Book is returned upon my hands by Longman just as Hathchard returned it to you——Kind Words but no Money, and Upham dares do nothing without *Them*.[2]

Mr. Salusbury has referred the Tax People to me *here* for my Establishment of Servants &c. at Brynbella for *a full Year*. I cannot pay what I do not understand, and beg of you for Gods Sake to stand between me and further Misery.

I sent you Word that Mead demands his 77£.15s.11 two Days ago, I now send you Word that Walker of Denbigh has sent me in *his* Bill for 30£[3]——Your Wife said he would do so, and you know Count Lieven said She was a Witty Woman.

I will have more Wit than to despair Yet——Lord Keith will find us good Stewards I doubt not. From her Ladyship I have not heard these 9 Months—— but hope Thomas will live to tell you, and you to hear and to contradict what She said *of You*,/ when at the House of your poor/Friend/ H: L: P.

The Post waits.
Keep up your Spirits for *all our* sakes.

Text Hyde Collection. *Address* Mr: Alexander Leak/ Streatham Park/ Surrey. *Postmark* BATH DE 20 1814 109; DE 21 1814, 10 o'Clock.

1. AL's letter, which is missing, anticipated that of 22 December, which is reproduced as the next letter.
2. HLP, supported by new friends JF and EM, would make yet one more attempt to market "Lyford Redivivus" in 1815.
3. Samuel Walker, linen draper, of Vale Street, Denbigh (C.R.O., Clwyd).

ALEXANDER LEAK TO HESTER LYNCH PIOZZI

Streatham
December 22, 1814

Madam,

Every thing go badly. I have been this Day to Windle with Your Letter of Yesterday but he gave Me no comfort, but say Mead has produced His Vouchers to Him and satisfied Him of the Debt being a just one, and that You did promise payment in January, and in short He seem determined to defend Mead, instead of you. So I fear the Money must be paid, or we shall have the Lawyers to contend with, as well as Mead. You made a Wretched choice of Friends indeed. On my Return Home I found Your other Letter containing Mr. Salusbury's Demand. I think His Conduct not at all better than Meads. Indeed His want of Gratitude make it less excusable, this is the return you meet with from Him for whom You have made Yourself, and so many others Miserable. I am not I think in general vindictive, but I hope this Young Man will be rewarded as He deserve. He ought to have paid the Taxes, and not in Your present circumstances, have even carried them to You, they cannot make You give an account of Your establishment after this length of Time, they must go by the old returns, the paper is signed by no Name, it is only a Trick of Mr. Salusbury to shuffle of[f] the Payment, which he ought to have made Six Months since. Let Him settle it as well as He can, do not trouble yourself about it. Walker You must pay, so You must other Tradesmen in Wales, if Mr. Salusbury is ungrateful enough to refuse them, which I expect He will do. Was his poor Uncle but alive to see His conduct. I dare say neither Tradesmen nor Taxes have ever been Paid at Brynbella since I paid them. I am sorry but not much disappointed about Your Book.—What has Parsons usually paid? I know nothing about His Rent, have no papers that relate to it, shall I pay Mead His demand, Windle has all the Bills &c. relating to them. I have nothing to refer to. Do nothing about the Taxes at Brynbella to make others suffer for Mr. Salusbury,/ I am Madam Your/ Obedient Servant A. Leak.

Text Ry. 609.4

TO ANNA MARIA PEMBERTON

Bath
[ca. 24 December 1814][1]

And now my Dear Mrs. Pemberton, who is so comically afraid of not *giving Satisfaction* to her own Son, in the House of her own Nativity;[2] must console *me* who have reason enough to fear:——not for my beautiful Doe, which is both cheap and Excellent; but for the more beautiful Lamb, which I durst not send now, lest it should get injured by its Companion and by the Weather: The Weather is wretched for Meat—as you see.—But what will *My* Partner Dear Mr. Pem: say? who knows what Sheep are; when I protest Solemnly and Seriously—The Lamb will cost five Guineas. 'Tis the Time of year which so raises the Price——Roasting Beef sells at *one* Shilling o'Pound—Veal at 13 Pence; it was not so Two Months ago, and will not be so Two Months hence——nor will You be able to get a Mouthful of Seafish for Your gay Day, unless strange Changes happen; The News from Plymouth is dreadful;[3] all the small Vessels wrecked, and Lives lost, which *last,* is to our Bath Bon-vivants, and professed invalides—quite a secondary consideration: for no Selfishness equals that of a Sick Man. Nothing however keeps People from giving *Parties:* Sir Drummond Smith who is *considered* as dying,[4] and Mrs. Whalley who is left under *Care* as I may Say, of Servants She is *obliged to retain* till her *Lord's return:*[5] both saw Company yesterday, and both look chearful this Morning. Such is the World——and there is a new Man come to Bath, of whom we all are talking; that means to give public Lectures on the form and Shape of all our *Heads*——from whence to tell how the *Contents* are arranged, and he calls his Science *Craniology.*[6]

The Epigram I promised Salusbury may accompany this Intelligence: It is at least as Witty as the Mottoes for Your Dessert Supper, which cost 3s.6 the Dozen; I have got 12 Dozen for you.

Epigram on two Jews

Between these Jews we scarce can know
A Difference in Degree;
For one appears a Jeu de Mots,
And one—a Jeu d'Esprit.

a Cambridge Joke and was sent by Young Williams of Bodylwyddan to amuse his Aunt. My favourite Verses about Mr. *Van* bringing up the *Rear* that I told Salusbury I would get for his Scrap-Book; are I am afraid quite lost in the Whirl of newspapers that tumble up and down these public Reading-Rooms, Libraries &c.

If I can hear any more good *Small-Talk* you shall have it with the Lamb.

That Sir Thomas Mostyn[7] is going to be married to The Daughter of Montague Burgoyne[8]—who is Son of Sir Roger Burgoyne by Lady Frances, Sister to the last Earl of Halifax; you probably heard before I did[9]——likewise of the Fire in Llangollen Vale, destroying the new Manufactory.[10]

Here therefore shall end my Letter; but not my Wishes of Health, Joy, and increasing Happiness to all at Condover Park who possess a very faithful Servant/ in Dear Madam Yours ever/ H: L: Piozzi.

Text Ry. 594.6.

1. The letter may be dated ca. 24 December when the *Bath Herald* first advertised the sixteen lectures of Dr. Sputzheim "on the propensities, sentiments, and intellectual Faculties of the Mind."
2. See HLP to JSPS, 16 July 1810, n. 10; 23 December 1813, n. 7.
3. Under date of 14 December from Plymouth, newspapers reported "the French brig Jeane

Adelle, Capt. Laval, from Oporto bound to Havre de Grace, laden with oranges" was wrecked on 13 December. "The mate and two of the crew were washed on shore and saved; but the Captain and three seamen were drowned. . . . The Swedish galliot, Sophia, Capt. Siegen, from Liverpool for Hamburgh, is still in Whitsand Bay totally dismasted. Pilots will attempt towing her into this port the moment the gale abates, which now blows furious.

"The brig Providence, Captain Craig, which went on shore yesterday, at Feat's Hill, still remains there, on the rocks, full of water: about half the cargo has been got out, and nearly the whole expected to be saved, but in a damaged state.

". . . The Anne of London, G.S. Browne, master, fired several guns this afternoon, which appeared to be for assistance; several pilots went off, when they were informed it was for the master's amusement: such conduct is highly blameable during a gale of wind" (*Courier*, 16 December). See also *The Times* and the *Morning Chronicle*, 16 December.

4. After the death of his first wife, Mary, née Cunliffe in 1804, Drummond Smith (d. 22 January 1816) was created baronet, 11 June, in the same year. In 1805 he married Elizabeth, née Monckton (d. 1835), eldest daughter of William, second viscount Galway, and widow of Sir Francis Sykes.

5. For Frances (Horneck) Whalley, see HLP to JSPS, 18 April 1812, n. 1.

6. For the craniologist, see n. 1; and HLP to JSPS, 15 May 1812, n. 11.

7. HLP reports Bath gossip since Thomas Mostyn (ca. 1776–1831), sixth baronet of Mostyn, died unmarried. He was M.P. for Flintshire (1799–1831), sheriff of Carnarvonshire (1798–99), and sheriff of Merionethshire (1799–1800).

8. Montagu Burgoyne (1750–1836) had two daughters: Frances Elizabeth (d. 1818) was to marry on 13 January 1815 Sir Guy Campbell (d. 1849), C.B.; Elizabeth (d. 1833) married 15 August 1818 Christopher Blackett (1788–1847) of Wylam, Northumberland.

9. Roger Burgoyne (1710–80), sixth baronet (1716), M.P. for county Bedford (1735–47), had married in 1739 Lady Frances Montague (d. 1788), eldest daughter of George, fourth earl of Halifax (1715).

10 "This morning [8 December] the cotton-mills of Messrs. Turner and Co. at *Llangollen*, Denbighshire were totally destroyed by fire. The romantic situation of the buildings, and the vast column of flame, which 'shook its red shadow o'er the startled' Dee, and illuminated the castellated mountain and along the Valley, formed a picture terribly sublime." See *GM* 84, pt. 2 (1814):598.

TO JOHN SALUSBURY PIOZZI SALUSBURY

> Parish of *Walcot*
> Bath
> 6: January 1815.

I received Dear Salusbury's Letter with the more Delight as I began to think it long in coming, for altho' surrounded like yourself with Attentions and Compliments——My Heart *will* turn more than it ought to do,—more at least than I wish it to turn to those for whom I am leading this out-of-the-way-Life;[1] which others are Striving to soften by Civilities. Oh when Spring comes, that I can *walk* to their Parties, Dinners &c. I will not be so tardy of Acceptance——but Chair hire ruins me, my Habitation is so distant:—and as to keeping Invitations and Caresses *away*!——Why they would follow me to Petty France.—So would Duns and Bills I believe: Mr. Williams of Chester, and the Newspaper Man there dispatch long Accounts after *me* for Plum Puddings you and I eat together last April[2], and Articles of Intelligence which are probably adorning Your Red Book *now*. But as I said in a former Letter—*They* shall wait, and be last paid *certainly*. Why—my Water Cart will never get lightened, if these Fellows follow with Pailfulls to pour in at the Top, while it is passing by small Holes drilled on the

Sides. These January Dividends all go to the London Tradesmen; meaning *all* which Mead and Gillow leave me,——except a wretched 100£ which I keep to buy Potatoes till April; Mr. Windle, who wrote me a Letter I received at Condover saying what A Rascal Mead was—I shewed it you:—now takes his Part openly, and I must submit to the gross Impositions of which Leak *convicted* him, or be dunned by Windle for Sums far beyond my Power.

Well! as Baretti used to say at Back Gammon, These are *cursed bad Dice*—— but we must play them as We can.

My Book is still a Resource: but Subscription is accounted *So* degrading, that if I cannot sell it by private Contract, I will even try to starve it out, and not despair even then.

Now for Something we shall both like better. I met Sir Alexander Grant—a Red-Ribboned Scotch Man, at a Dining Party; and he asked me for *You*. Said You were the *prattiest* Lad that Eyes ever looked on;[3] and that Lady Caroline Castle Stuart thought so too;[4] Lady Sarah is going to be married very well *indeed*[5]——so is Lady Catherine Annesley:[6]—all *That* Family remembers you with Affectionate Admiration.[7]

But 'tis Time to wish you a happy New Year among the amiable Friends that you preferred to *all of us*: I hope the Lamb arrived safe, and was liked; and that you gave Dear Williams my little Godson's Present.[8] Oh do be so very kind as to recollect my Misery for want of my dear Mother's Spectacles, that Misery increased now by the Loss of my own. Put them into the Pocket of the Young Heir, and future Baronet of Bodylwyddan—he will be careful of them for his H: L: P. John Octavius Glover gave me a very pretty Bridal Dinner, shewed me the Books I once presented him with—and protested they had Accompanied him into Three Continents—He is A fine handsome showy Fellow, tall and stout: his Lady *Whiter* and *fairer* than Poet's Descriptions, her Hair immense in Quantity, and just the Colour of your Mahogany Doors at Brynbella; soft smiling Blue Eyes——but wretched Teeth—and 25–000£

These are unadorned Truths.

What else have I to tell you? That Doctor Bowen's Life is despaired of;[10] and that poor dear Mrs. Stratton went home to Bed when She had been with me to the Play, and has never quitted it since:——but Dr. Parry has hopes that She *may* live.[11] He is a good *Hoper.*

I have purchased nothing from an Apothecary's Shop since we parted, but a Lump of Camphor which cost me 6d. and tho' I converse with *many* Physicians, *never have fee'd one.* My orders are however to call Doctor *Gibbes* when Thomas and Bessy see me dying—so you find *he* is the favourite;[12] and George on the Parade has my Promise for the *burying*——I had an old Bill of Seven Pounds with *him*, but he never asked for the Money, *So he's paid.*[13]

Adieu dearest—and present me properly—which is very affectionately to all you love: and all who love *you* and don't forget poor/ H: L: P.

I feel sorry you never got that Letter which Lord Gwydir franked to Miss Moore because of what was enclosed in it.[14]

<I prevent tax> gatherers from injuring us—I referred 'em to Lake and he

says they can't demand any thing from *me* but the 50£ Penalty frights me.[15] I am going to Dinner at Lady Bayntons.[16]

My Neighbours were *so* kind when I was *Drowning*——for I forgot to tell you that lying so near the River the flood broke in, and played the very Duce with us all.[17]

It was a horrid Sight when Corn and Carts and Horses and Pigs were to be pulled out by Boats—a horrid Sight indeed! but all's *over now,* only the People catched colds, and many of them died.

Text Ry. 588.254. *Address* John Salusbury Piozzi Salusbury Esq./ Brynbella/ near Denbigh/ North Wales. *Postmark* BATH.

1. HLP had taken lodgings at New King Street shortly after her arrival in Bath, ca. 11 November 1814.

2. The bills of Bowdery and Kerby, Jr., London, and John Williams, the grocer of Bridge Street, Chester, were among the many that confronted HLP at this time. For the stationer's bills, see HLP to AL, 21 January 1813, n. 1; for HLP's long-standing trade with Williams, see her letter to Q, 23 February 1796, n. 1.

3. Alexander Grant (1775–1825), seventh baronet (1780) of Dalvey, county Elgin, resided at 29 Great Pulteney Street. See the "Bathwick Poor Rate Book" (1818), Guildhall, Bath. Grant was wearing the crimson ribbon of a Knight of the Order of Bath.

4. Lady Caroline Castle Stewart (1784–1864) was on 16 January to marry James Bathurst (1782–1850), an army officer who was knighted 28 September 1831 and attained the rank of lieutenant general in 1837.

5. Lady Sarah (d. 1871) was the sister of the above and the younger daughter of Andrew Thomas Stewart-Moore (1725–1809), first earl Castle Stewart (I., 1800).

Lady Sarah was married only in 1836 to the Reverend George Crimstead (1800–39), of Redburne, Herts.

6. Lady Catherine (1793–1865) was the elder daughter of Arthur Annesley (1744–1816), eighth viscount Valentia (1761) and first earl of Mountnorris (I., 1793). On 4 December 1814, at Brussels, she married Lord John Thomas Henry Somerset (1787–1846), an army officer and a son of the fifth duke of Beaufort. See *GM* pt.2 (1814): 674; *GM*, n.s. 19 (1865):258–59.

7. Having married twice, the earl of Mountnorris had a large family. His first wife, Lucy, née Lyttelton (1742–83) bore George (see HLP to JSPS, 19 February 1810, n. 7); Juliana Lucy (d. 1833), now married to John Maxwell Barry (1767–1838), fifth baron Farnham (1823); and Hester Annabella (d. 1844), the wife of Norman Macleod (d. 1830), a major general.

The children of Mountnorris's second wife, Sarah, née Cavendish (1763–1849) were Henry Arthur (1792–1818); Catherine (d. 1865); and Frances Caroline (d. 1837), the wife of Sir James Webster Wedderburn (1789–1840).

8. 8 January 1815 was Hugh Williams's thirteenth birthday.

9. John Octavius Glover (HLP to JSPS, 22 March 1808, n. 6) married on 22 November 1814 at Bognor, Sussex, Eliza (fl. 1795–1832), only daughter of the late John Ewing, of Macedon, county Antrim. See *GM* 84, pt. 2 (1814):600.

10. William Bowen died on 27 March. See the *Bath and Cheltenham Gazette,* 29 March; *GM* 85, pt. 1 (1815):378.

11. Mary Stratton of 13 Camden Place, Bath, was to die on 19 November 1828, aged eighty-four. See HLP to PSP, 5 April 1801, n. 3. So grateful was she to Caleb Hillier Parry that she remembered him in her will, leaving him £50. See P.R.O., Prob. 11/1749/738, signed 24 September 1828, and proved 24 December 1828.

For Dr. Parry, see HLP to PSW, 1 September 1789, n. 7.

12. Dr. Gibbes was to attend HLP on her deathbed. When he arrived at Clifton from Bath, "she had just enough strength left to trace with her fingers the outline of a coffin in the air" (Clifford, 456). For George Smith Gibbes, see HLP to Roberts, 20 March 1807, n. 6.

13. Thomas George of 6 North Parade was a haberdasher and undertaker. HLP's "Pocket Book" entry of 6 January records: "Paid George's Bill 7. 6s. 0d" (Columbia University Library).

14. For Miss Moore, set HLP to Q, 3 April [1795], n. 1. Peter Burrell (1754–1820), first baron

Gwydir (1796) franked HLP's letter. See Wraxall, *Memoirs*, 3:352–55 for an account of the rise of the house of Burrell.

15. See HLP to AL, 20 December 1814 for her scuffle with "the Tax People."

16. Sophia Bayntun, née Mayhew (d. 1830) was William Lutwyche's niece and the wife of Rear Admiral Sir Henry William Bayntun (1766–1840), K.C.B., G.C.B. The Bayntuns lived at St. James's Square, Bath.

17. According to the *Bath and Cheltenham Gazette* (4 January 1815): "In consequence of the incessant fall of snow and the sudden thaw accompanied with heavy rains, last week, our river overflowed its banks to a considerable height. A butcher of Tiverton lost several sheep in the flood; and on Tuesday night a chaise and horses were driven into the river at Frome Bridge."

TO ANN FELLOWES

Tuesday Night
10: January 1815.

My dear Miss Fellowes[1]

I have been confined till today, and now called only to say how much I feel obliged—by yours and your Brothers Partiality. He has been good enough not only to amuse, but to prescribe for me.[2]

> And don't you account it a horrible Seizure
> As cruel Misfortune could make;
> That the Face should give *Pain,* which no
> longer gives Pleasure,
> And the Teeth which can't eat—Should
> still ache?
> Yet Kindness so flattering is sure to
> avail me
> That soft Paregoric I find;
> If applied to my Cheek it should happen to
> fail me,
> 'Tis sure to succeed—*on my Mind.*

H: L: P.

Text Ry. 533.32.

1. For Ann Fellowes, see HLP to JSPS, 18 April 1812, n. 10.

2. James Fellowes (1771–1857) received his M.B. (1797) and M.D. (1803) from Caius College, Cambridge, and served thereafter in the army medical corps until his retirement in 1815. From 1804–6 he worked in Santo Domingo to treat an epidemic there. Returning to England, he was knighted in 1809 and subsequently worked at Cadiz as chief of the army medical department.

On 1 January 1815, HLP noted in her "Pocket Book" their first meeting at the Lutwyches. Two days later, she saw him again at his sister Ann's. The friendship between HLP and JF grew rapidly, so that he became her adviser, confidant, and literary executor.

TO ANN AND ALEXANDER LEAK

Bath Wensday
18: January 1815.

My good Leak and your good Wife.

Oh come; *do* come,[1] We have so long been hoping for this little bit of Pleasure—I cannot deny myself and You the Comfort of meeting, and bring the Cap, and bring the Bills, and let us see what *can* be done, and what can be *hoped*.

Streatham Park must pay the trifling Expence of the Journey; and to every thing *here* you and your Wife shall be *more* than Welcome:—and we will plan a meeting for my *Wedding Day* the 25th of July;[2] and You shall find unaltered, and unalterable by any Circumstances, her who was ever Your/ Obliged and true Friend/ H: L: P.

The Post is waiting.

I shall think you *dead* if you don't come, but indeed I quite depend on seeing you both. I have so much to say which I cannot write.

Text Hyde Collection. *Address* Mr. Alexander Leak/ Streatham Park/ Surrey. *Postmark* BATH <   >; 10 o'Clock JA 19 1815; E 19 JA 19 <1815>.

1. On 15 January, HLP "Received a melancholy Letter from Leak, and answered it with an Invitation"; on 18 January, "Letter from Leak—wanting as it appears a warmer Invitation—I sent one directly"; on 19 January, "wrote to Leak out of *Fear now*: I had written out of Kindness before." See the next letter, below. A depressed AL and his wife were to arrive for breakfast on 26 January, the day before HLP's birthday, and remain in Bath for four days. Since HLP did not wish to "spend a birthday in *complete Solitude*" (HLP to JSPS, 27 January 1814), a visit at this time would have been especially welcome.

In an undated note to Sir James Fellowes about this time, HLP reflected on her birthday: "Yet will I not, (like Dr. Johnson) quarrel with my Birthday.—To have been born in this World is our only Claim for some sort of Place in the other: and surely to have gained Attention and Friendship from Dr. [Arthur] Collier in my early *Days* when the Hour of Female Attraction was scarce arrived; and from Sir James Fellowes in my latter Scenes,—when that bright Hour was over—might well Compensate for Three busy Acts of a much more Tragic Drama than has been played in, by poor H: L: P. through a fatiguing Part enough——Though sometimes sweetly supported, sometimes cruelly thwarted by her Companions on the Stage" (Ry. 533.40).

2. From 23 to 25 July (her wedding anniversary) HLP was in London attempting to ease her financial problems by the sale or rental of Streatham Park. On 24 July she visited Merrick Hoare, who offered her "*Hopes* again." The next day she wrote: ". . . came home and met Dagliesh, he gives me good Advice, but small Hopes of Lord Keiths purchasing.—Mr. Anderdon came; but is Proof against every Attempt towards ensnaring him into a promise. Oh what an Anniversary of my second Wedding Day!—Oh poor *poor* H: L: P." ("Pocket Book," 1815).

TO MRS. LEAK

> Bath Wendesday Night 12
> o'Clock
> 18: January *1815.*

Dear Leak

This Morning I wrote to your good Husband in the best possible Spirits; and I begun my Letter oh come, *do* come, and let us *enjoy* this little Comfort of Meeting on the 27th.

I now write again, and repeat my Request of *Oh come, do* come: for poor Jones and I are in sad Trouble indeed. My Letter was scarcely sent away, (Thomas was too drunk to carry it—) when after a Short Visit from some Literary Friends—— I called for Dinner, and Thomas set it on; but bursting into a Passion of Tears, said it would be the *last:* for he must go to London directly and go to Prison— all on his Mother's Account. When I told Bessy Jones——I fear said she 'tis something *here* that drives him. The Man behaves so oddly——and tho' She has a good Spirit enough, I plainly saw *Fear in her Face.*

We neither of us pull off our Clothes this night; and either She or I shall carry this Letter to the Post Office in the Morning. The Plate is all safe so far, and We have the Keys——and the Boy is *locked out* who he in a Manner forced in upon the Females last Night, of which I knew nothing: he says he will go directly to Streatham Park, so I gave him a little twisted up Note for your Husband; and if The Story he tells is *True*, about his Mother and the Mortgage of her Shop; *I pity him.*

Now don't you believe *we keep a Boy*——for none of us knew the Youngster who spent last Night here, and 'tis *that* which keeps me in *Alarm*; but I never mentioned the Circumstance to Thomas, for to say Truth——*I durst not.* Till we know he is actually off, I think Sleep will not visit No. 17 New King Street, and *glad at heart* shall I be, when I can tell you all the plague this Affair has been, and still is to your/ poor/ H:L:P.

God keep you both well till we meet. I count the Days and the hours, and am most earnest to see you both.

The Morning of the 19th is come, and Thomas is gone; our Girls asked him what they were to say if any Man called for him—-he replied that the Man would meet him at the White Lyon——and that he believed him to be a Bow Street Officer—gone now to fetch some other Man from Bristol.

He parted from *me* respectfully and kindly, and with many Tears: he never went to his own Bed all Night——I gave him his Great Coat and feel sorry for *him:* for *ourselves* much more.

I shall be happy to see and tell you all and am impatient for the Time.

Thomas says Leak knows his Affairs and how he owes 132£ but we who know *nothing* think it a mysterious Business, and feel much perplexed; I shall not be happy till you come. He carries a Note for you.

Text Hyde Collection. *Address* Mrs. Leak/ Streatham Park/ Surrey. *Postmark* JA 19 1815; 10 o'Clock JA 20 1815; 20 JA 20 1815.

TO LADY WILLIAMS

Bath
3: February 1815

My dear Lady Williams's Hand writing is ever most welcome to me: and how good Sir John and You both are to my Children! Accept my best Thanks, and grateful Acknowledgments. I had a letter from Brynbella Yesterday—full of the Kindnesses they receive, 'tis a cruel Thing to think I can repay no Attentions in the little wretched Nutshell I inhabit; but by strict Care and Frugality, I shall get out of my Confined Situation by this Time Twelve Month,——at least in some Degree:—Could I hope to see the Year 1817, I might see it at Streatham Park, and have a House of my own over my own Head once again[1]——but Man proposes, and God disposes;——With his disposal it is best to acquiesce chearfully——We know not what we wish for; and except to grow wiser and better—The most rational Plan is, not to wish at all.

Some of these Philosophers tell me that a Famine is within Sight: Farmers will not grow Corn, and other nations will withhold it, when they see us distressed; and when John Bull is hungry—how dreadfully he will roar![2]

Meanwhile do not my dearest Lady regret, or suffer our dear Sir John to regret—That his Son will go abroad. Let him learn to value home by seeing how differently other Nations carry on the Commerce of Life——I hope our Country is still the best——bad as it is:—and as to Temptations, he need not pass *Bath* without encountering *Them:* We have more Gaming here than anywhere because We have more Money; and because Money will do more for a Man in England than elsewhere, more people are rapacious to get it *The nearest Way.* We were saying how rich the Indian Jugglers grew: Yes, replied a friend, but let them be as Rich as they Please——Still they must be Jugglers; They can neither quit their Profession, nor change it—nor associate with any *but their own Cast.*[3]

There is however one perpetual Reason for giving a Young man Permission to do as he desires; Those who give leave *sleep better,* and blame themselves less whatever may befall. I was shewn a handsome Man the other Day, who is of a good Family, and was left in charge of a fond mother—She had but *him,* and he would go into the Army. But dint of Tears and mingled Threats She obtained a solemn *Oath* from him that he would not be an Officer: In Three Weeks after, There was Talk of Peace; but *he* was run away, and is a strolling Player now on this Stage under a fictitious Name.

I am just come from visiting Miss Williams——her Wrists appear to me as if turning all to Bone——enlarging at least, and gradually stiffening; but her Head and her Spirits are much better.—She was very low indeed last Week, but always friendly; and her Feet don't fail her, for She outwalks every body. The Sight of her Niece and Nephew will contribute greatly to her Restoration. Here is soft warm mild Weather; and I have seen a Honeysuckle coming into Leaf quite in the open Air, but This is the last Month of Winter.

Dear Hughey is a good Fellow and will always feel a kind Feel towards poor God Mamma. I hope the Solicitor is well too, and old Kitty, and the Birds, and every thing at dear Dear Bodylwyddan. The Salusburys lament some Disorder among their Servants, but Sir John's kind Recommendation of Mr. Hughes will be a good Thing for them.

Young Pennant must get well of his Fits, or his poor Mother will suffer more than He.[4] How clever Doctor Cumming is! He is a prodigious Acquisition to the Country. Does his Lady bring, or propose to bring him a Baby?[5] Doctor Myddelton is got home by *now;* I hope he left his London *Cold* at Shrewsbury, from whence he wrote me a very kind Letter.

Sir Thomas Mostyn's intended Marriage is talked of more and more. The Lloyds of Pengwerne will dance at that Wedding with Lead in their Shoes sure.[6]

Miss Ormesby's Acceptance of Colonel Gore[7] must have been a delightful Thing to Lady Maurice;[8] but here is Chat enough for one Letter, and I will tire you no longer than to request Your Ladyship's recommendation of me to dear Sir John's Remembrance; with True Love to all the Ladies, and unfeigned Friendship and Affectionate Respect from/ Your own/ H: L: Piozzi.

I feel sorry for Mr. Hesketh—We have passed many pleasant Days at Grywch, and that lame Young Man will have a sad Loss[9]——The others will all do well enough. Adieu Dearest Lady Williams! and do me the honour to write now and then. I do love a Letter.

Text Ry. 4 (1812–18). *Address* Lady Williams/ Bodylwyddan/ near St. Asaph/ North Wales.

1. HLP's financial obligations were eased when she auctioned off the contents of Streatham Park in May 1816. She consequently leased a house at 8 Gay Street, where, according to her "Pocket Book" entry of 1 January 1817, she hosted a New Year's Day party for fifty guests (Ry. 616).

2. Two years of falling corn prices had forced a number of English farmers to relinquish their leases, while those who held on could not afford to produce crops. See *AR* 57 (1815): 144. Parliament tried to remedy the difficulties of farmers by the enactment of a corn bill, which excluded foreign grain from English markets until domestic corn reached a "famine price" of eighty shillings per quarter. The objections to the bill centered on an artificially elevated price of bread, which would hurt the poor.

3. For the Indian jugglers, see HLP to HMP, 19 January 1814, n. 1.

4. For young David Pennant, now at Christ Church, Oxford, see HLP to JSPS, 10 March 1811, n. 9.

5. On 23 March Lucy Margaret Cumming would bear her only child, George Brownlow (1815–82), who later assumed the name of Wynn before his surname on succeeding to the Garthewin estate after his cousin Robert William Wynn's death.

For Dr. George Brownlow Cumming, see HLP to Ly W, 9 February 1810, n. 11; for his wife, see HLP to Ann Leak, 22 May 1814, n. 1.

6. The Lloyds of Pengwerne were planning to inherit Sir Thomas Mostyn's title and property, plans that would be frustrated if he married and produced an heir.

Specifically HLP referred to Mostyn's sister Elizabeth (d. 1842), wife of Edward Pryce Lloyd. (See

HLP to Charlotte Lewis, 20 September 1789, n. 11.) Moreover, their eldest son, Edward (1805–84), in compliance with his uncle's will, was to assume the surname and arms of Mostyn, becoming second baron Mostyn (1831).

For Sir Thomas's will, see P.R.O., Prob. 11/1788/407, proved in London 14 July 1831.

7. On 11 January Mary Jane Ormsby married Major William Gore of the Dragoon Guards, who assumed the surname Ormsby-Gore, M.P. for county Leitrim (1806) and for Carnarvon Boroughs (1830). See HLP to PSP [ca. 26 July 1800], n. 5; to Q, 26 May 1806, n. 3.

8. HLP refers to the mother of Major Gore. She was Frances Jane Gorges Gore (d. ca. 1829) of Barrowmount, county Kilkenny. On 23 July 1772 she had married Haydock Evans Morres (ca. 1740–76), second baronet (1774), and on 10 February 1778 William Gore (1745–1815) of St. Valerie, county Wicklow, and of Woodford, county Leitrim. See "Prerogative Wills Index," P.R.O, Ireland, for the death date of Mrs. Gore.

9. Robert Bamford-Hesketh of Bamford Hall, Lancs., and Upton, Cheshire, had died on 16 January; for his son, Lloyd Hesketh Bamford-Hesketh of Gwyrch Castle, see HLP to JSPS, 23 December 1813, n. 3.

TO [HARRIET MARIA SALUSBURY]

Monday Morning
6: Februay 1815.

A Thousand Thanks wait on the lovely Lady of Brynbella for her kind Letter and polite Invitation——My Mind is not very changeable, nor does my declining the Pleasure of such a Journey—depend upon *Caprice*. Surrounding Circumstances, and Dear Salusbury's own Preference of this Place for me—have combined to send me hither,—*and here I fix*. It is the Place I can really be most private in, and yet not lead the Life of a Hermit—Young Williams will assure you Bath is admirable for *young* People, and I aver it is the best Situation for old ones. He has caught a famous Cold, and coughs worse than an Old Woman today.

There was a Supper tho' for 400 People which he did not partake:[1] Your Namesake was the happy Girl who got the Ticket.[2] Mrs. Wynne of Llewessog is here, and curtsies to me at Church.[3] Doctor Myddelton writes word what a gay Dinner You had, and every body agrees in Saying how happy you make Your excellent Husband——Long may your Felicity last! my Comfort is in Thinking what a Short Time we were kept waiting for it; Tho' mutual Impatience made it appear a long one.

Your Brother says,—If I read his Letter correctly;—That he has to lament the not having been Christened before he was 8 Months old;——he has however to rejoyce in keeping his Parents to attest his Birth and Baptism.

I am sorry Mrs. Myddelton is become Such a complete Wreck of ruined Beauty.[4] Mrs. Mostyn's last Letter says The new Actress Miss O'Neil is very like The Eldest Daughter of Guaŷnynnog.[5] We have not had Mr. Kean: and People tell me he is dying;[6] so is my new Servant The Man I took in Thomas's Place.[7] He will be a sad Loss, for when There is a *Footman*, one can save chair hire by running to Dinner at a Friend's as I am just going to do now, when I have said how much and how Affectionately I remain Yours and your Husbands/ ever/ H: L: P.——

Eliza O'Neill as Belvidera. Artist unknown. (Reproduced by permission of the Henry E. Huntington Library and Art Gallery, San Marino, California.)

Dear Williams is so hoarse he can now hardly sing the Praises of Condover Park with which he is nearly as much enamoured as I am——and I have seen no such Butter, no such Cream, no such Cheese.

Text Ry. 594.9 [two letters under a single cover, one to Anna Maria Pemberton and the other to Harriet Maria Salusbury]. *Address* Mrs. Pemberton/ Brynbella/ near Denbigh/ North Wales. *Postmark* BATH <   > 18 <   >.

1. A "Dress Ball" was held at the New Assembly Rooms on 4 February, in honor of the "Anniversary of King Charles's Martyrdom." See the *Bath Chronical*, 2 February 1815.
2. That is, Harriet Williams of Bodylwyddan and JW on a visit to MW, their aunt.
3. For Anna Maria (Mostyn) Wynn, see HLP to LC, 30 March 1795, n. 1.
4. For the Reverend Robert Myddelton and his wife May, see HLP to LC, 15 September 1794, n. 1; to JSPS, 20 August 1808, n. 3.
5. The Irish actress Eliza O'Neill (1791–1872) made her London debut at Covent Garden on 6 October 1814 as Juliet to WAC's Romeo. Playing to packed houses as a "younger and better Mrs. Siddons," she left the stage in 1819 to marry William Wrixon-Becher (1780–1850), cr. baronet (1831).
  For Caroline May Myddelton, the eldest daughter of Gwaynynnog, see HLP to JSPS, 4 March 1812, n. 1.
6. The exaggeration of Bath gossip. According to *The Times*, 14 January, Kean, while performing at Drury Lane, suffered an "indisposition"; i.e., hoarseness. By 21 January, however, he was able to act Romeo.
7. In her "Pocket Book" for 1815, HLP indicated that she interviewed candidates on 20 and 21 January, "preferring James Smith." She also noted (ibid., 19 January 1815): "There is some Strange Thing we know not what—happened to *Thomas*, but 'tis some thing dreadful as it appears: The Man is gone away half distracted,—but he is gone."

TO ANNA MARIA PEMBERTON

Monday Morning
6: February 1815.

My dear Mrs. Pemberton was extremely obliging to add her Invitation to that [of] her amiable and Interesting Young People. I must assure you all at once that no Caprice or Unkindness has any Share in my Resolution of denying myself the Pleasure of a Journey to Brynbella. I feel myself *compelled* to suffer the Denial of *many* Enjoyments;—and when Mr. and Miss Williams return to Wales they will convince You that I do not remain here out of Preference to the Vale of Llwydd or even Streatham Park.

Bath is however a Place which always agrees with me—and People here are so kind,—so much kinder than I deserve, who have never given even a Cup of Tea to any human Creature but my own Servants; that I should be graceless indeed not to love them: and it is a *safe* Place too, compared to any other—— They will always respect the Residence of Invalides, and when the Head-cuttings which they threaten London with, come forward;[1]—Sick Old Grandames here will be playing their Cards in Peace. Your Cold has I hope long ago taken its flight—The approach of Spring will soon drive such Complaints before it. Our crocuses &c. are numerous and beautiful, The Markets filled with Violets and

Primroses every Saturday Morning; but I have heard no Birds yet—The Surrey Groves are full of Thrushes I hear, They make the best of their Time now, for the Nightingales will soon draw all Attention from their Audience quite away.

What a curious Choice Young Mr. Mytton has made—by the Account in your Letter:[2]—I had wholly forgotten that silent Man, rich as he is![3] and nobody ever named him in my Company since I left Condover Hall: tho' Mrs. Leighton and I were chatting together for an hour Yesterday.[4] She will however bring Children enough after four and Twenty Years old surely. Mr. Wynne of Plas Newydd at 18 Years old married a Wife of 36, and She brought him Three Girls.[5] Mr. Greatheed married a Lady 11 Years older than himself for Love,[6] and She produced a Son who was their mutual Felicity for Three and Twenty Years[7]—and Then died, leaving a Daughter, or a half Daughter or a natural Daughter——or some charming Thing that delights them *all* to this Day.[8]

Dear Mrs. Pemberton Adieu! I had a kind Letter from Mr. Smythe Owen Three Minutes ago, which I will answer and Thank him for: but must work hard at my Book, to finish it for These People's Inspection[9]——remaining meanwhile/Your old patched Poetess, but/truly faithful Servant/ H: L: Piozzi.

1. On 28 January London mobs protested the pending corn bill by attacks on the residences of the M.P.s who supported the measure. Petitions against the bill were pouring into London. See the *Bath Herald*, 28 January.

2. A relative of Anna Maria Pemberton, John Mytton (1796–1834) of Halston, Salop, was educated at Westminster and obtained a commission in the 7th regiment of Hussars. His "curious Choice" involved his remaining in that unit while it formed part of the army of occupation in France and his putting off until 21 May 1818 his marriage to Harriet Emma, née Tyrwhitt-Jones (d. 1820).

3. When only two, John Mytton inherited the family estates: the manors of Halston and Habberley, Salop; the manors of Bicton and Monk Meole, near Shrewsbury; the ancient mansion of the Vaughans in the center of that city; the extensive manor or lordship and estate of Dinasmowddry, in Merionethshire, etc.

4. For Louisa Margaretta Anne Leighton, see HLP to JSPS, 18 April 1812, n. 4.

5. For John Wynne and his wife Sarah Anne, see HLP to LC, 1 February 1798, n. 8. They had three daughters: Caroline Sobieski (b. 1799), Augusta Eliza (1800–69), and Madelina (1807–10). See Warren Derry, *Dr. Parr: A Portrait of the Whig Dr. Johnson* (Oxford: Clarendon Press, 1966), 200–205, 249–50, 280–83, and 344–46.

6. For Ann Greatheed, see HLP to Q, 26 July 1785, n. 7.

7. For the death of young Bertie Greatheed at Vicenza, Italy, see HLP to Q [31 December 1804], n. 8.

8. Young Greatheed, who had married in France, left a child, Anne Caroline (1804–82). In 1822 she was to marry Charles Percy (1794–1870), a son of the first earl of Beverley, who in 1826 assumed the surname and arms of Greatheed-Bertie before Percy.

9. "Lyford Redivivus."

TO ANN LEAK

Bath
Tuesday 14th: February 1815.

Dear Leak

I write to you because I am not quite sure that your good Husband may be at home. He must do me a favour, or a Service——whichever he pleases to call it: he must take down the 2d: Volume of British Synonymy——It is near the Chimney—between it and the Door——and under the Letter N he will find this Article—Name, Nominal Distinction &c. &c.[1] Then he must copy out for me those Jewish Names of the Generations before the Flood.

Adam——Man.

Seth——Set or placed

Enosh——in Misery;

I have forgotten the rest——but they end with *Consolation.*—I will insert them in my New Book. There is no harm I suppose in borrowing a Guinea from one's own Bureau, to put in one's own Purse. Since it is Now—*new* to People,—they may as well be reminded.——The Thing is in [its] own Nature very extraordinary.[2]

I hope the Jewish House mentioned in our News Papers—is not our Friend's who dined with us.[3] One dares not name Names.

Miss Flora Macleod has dropt into a Down Bed at last[4] if 'tis true that She marries Young Hesketh, so handsome and with such a fine unencumbered Estate:[5] but there are People who say he is engaged to Lady Acton, a gay Widow.[6]

Pray tell me who comes and goes, and particularly how you are coming on Yourself, as you have all the best possible/ Wishes of your/ H: L: Piozzi.

[Ma]ke your Husband send me the *Stuff* as soon as ever he can.

Text: Hyde Collection. *Address* Mrs. Leak/ Streatham Park/ Surrey. *Postmark* BATH FE 14 1815; 10 o'Clock FE 15 1815.

1. In *British Synonymy* (2:50–51), HLP presents a list of names: Adam, Seth, Enosh, Kainan, Mahaleel, Jared, Henoch, Methuselah, Lamech, and Noah. Arguing "that they contain and mystically exhibit a concise and wonderful scheme of prophecy, in their own Hebrew tongue, of the restoration of fallen mankind by a bleeding Messiah," HLP comes up with the following: "Man, / set or placed, / in misery, / lamenting: / blessed *God*, / shall come down, / teaching, / that his *death* will send, / to humbled smitten man, / consolation."

2. HLP includes the list—Adam to Noah—under *Methuselah* in "Lyford Redivivus," 126–27. She gives as her source "Rowlands"; i.e., Henry Rowlands, *Mona Antiqua Restaurata . . . In Two Essays* (London: J. Knox, 1766), 203–4. Rowlands presents the same chart and refers to Genesis 5:29.

3. The *Bath Herald* on 11 February 1815 reported from London (9 February) that "Two Houses in the City, we regret to state, stopped payment on Saturday last. One of them, a Jewish house, Messrs. L. & C. failed for not less than 300,000£."

The "Friend" was Angelo Levy, a diamond merchant, of 12 Devonshire Square (HLP to JSPS, 2 March 1810, n. 2).

4. A daughter of Julia, née Macleod, and Olaus Macleod of Bharkasaig, Flora married Dr. George Baillie of Edinburgh.

5. For Lloyd Hesketh Bamford-Hesketh and his marriage on 25 October 1826 to Lady Emily Lygon, see HLP to JSPS, 23 December 1813, n. 3.

6. Mary Anne Acton (ca. 1785–1873) had in 1799 married by papal dispensation her uncle, John Francis Edward Acton (1736–1811), sixth baronet (1791) of Aldenham, county Salop. She never remarried.

TO JOHN SALUSBURY PIOZZI SALUSBURY

No. 17 New King Street Bath
Tuesday 21: February 1815.

My Dearest Salusbury never waits a Moment for my Answers to his Letters, and This last shall have its most Important Part replied to,—*first.* When I left Condover Park I told Your Brother Smythe Owen that altho' I willingly signed the Testamentary Disposition which Mr. Robert Pemberton drew up for me—I hoped it was not the *last* Will of H:L Piozzi, because being drawn at *their* House, and witnessed by their Family; It bore an Appearance of Influence which I considered as not according to the Notions I had of either The Pemberton Honour or my own:[1] and I proposed executing another Instrument to the same Effect, when in my little Independent Nutshell——at half a Year's distance of Time from seeing any of the Family. It was therefore I asked when Mr. Oldfield would send his Papers, Agents &c.—That I might be ready, and every thing might be done (as the Servants say) *under one.*[2]

Your Invitiation is the kindest possible, and I am glad it comes so early, that you may not *say* you were ever disappointed by poor Aunt. Every possible Reason that can be suggested By Pride, Prudence, or Common Sense is against my going;—and indeed it would be cruel to urge me. Young Williams is of my Mind; he sees I have taken this wretched Place for a Twelvemonth certain; and I will not live again as I did at Condover—(most happily of Course)—but paying so dear for it——House Rent going on 40£ a Quarter—Board Wages 15£ for the Time, and Thomas running me in Debt as far as he was able. No Œconomy can keep Pace with such Conduct, nor will I expose myself any more to the Insults I received at Streatham Park—if by any Labour or any Privation I may be enabled to escape them. My Dividends are as you well know Sequestered to Mead thro' this whole Year 1815—leaving me a bare Subsistence. The Count's Payment of his Rent is sequestered to Gillow: and till they are satisfied,—*both of them*—— and Your *Felicity* Bill paid to Ward,[3] and my own *Infelicity* Bill paid to Windle, I will not stir.[4]

Doctor Myddelton was obliging enough to ask me to Gwaynynnog, and Lady Williams says every kind Thing about coming down to her Neighbourhood—— so as I am a Young Woman, and as nobody ever dies——You may get my Room aired against *July* or *August 1816,* but certainly not sooner.[5]

Now for other Matters.

Lady Callender is at London in her own House, hearing I suppose all the gay Talk.[6] Oh truly did my dearest Salusbury say to me once—"Why Aunt you know You and I live retired here like Old Puddles,—and so you wonder when you hear of a Man breaking his Leg, and the Bone piercing his Stocking—but *in the World* People think nothing of such Matters." True indeed! The Duke of Dorset has Broken his own Neck,[7] and Colonel Disney has had his Arm *broken for him;*[8] and both are forgotten in a Week: newer stories giving The Turn and the Ton to Conversation.

Our handsome Friend Lloyd Hesketh is said to be already married or solemnly engaged to a beautiful Widow—Lady Acton: very young, and very charming; who was married to Sir Richard by Papal Dispensation, he having been Husband to her own Aunt before——but She is considered as a Model of Elegance; how She will like Gwrych remains to be Seen. Mr. Shute and his Bride were at Laura yesterday,[9] but did not recognize H: L: P of Course;—and I had no Ambition. The Glovers describe her as very Timid and Shy;[10] She was not the Lady I took her for: She is an Officer's Daughter without Pretension to Beauty,[11] or Possibility of Fortune, and looked exactly like all the Girls,——that were not pretty Girls;—at Laura Chapel.

I rejoyce to hear Mrs. Pemberton is coming to Brynbella, hope change of Air will be found good for her Health: and I'm so glad Mr. Heaton is happy, and his fair Lady so well liked.[12] Poor Mrs. Wynne was once an Acquisition to the Neighbourhood, and justly admired for her Elegance and Beauty: She is now I think to be *approved* at least for her Appearance of Content——and her tranquil Manner: so well-bred, and indeed so philosophical.[13] Doctor Myddelton says She quits the Castle very soon.

Poor Mrs. Wynne! and She visits at Plâsnewydd with such Apparent Cordiality; so unlike her immediate Successor I am Thinking.[14] Mrs. Mostyn is not yet at Segroid Doctor Myddelton says; and Charles Wynne of Course not at the bottom of her Table in the Country: perhaps London is a Place that suits him better.[15] Sir Watkin's Marriage[16] and that of Sir Thomas Mostyn must surely be Very Interesting to the Dwellers in the Vale of Llwydd——I wonder that my Letters neither from Gwaynnynog nor Brynbella mention a Word of them. The Accounts from Town concerning this new Actress Miss O'Neil, make me confident She resembles The eldest Miss Myddelton; I *think* somebody said She did— but She runs away with immoderate Applause; and in that only—resembles Mrs. Siddons.[17]

Adieu! Present me most kindly to your agreable Ladies——Your fair Consort and her charming Mamma. But do not believe me *now*—as of old Time—restless about dear Salusbury, and apprehensive for his Safety and Happiness. He is as Safe I think as this World permits a Man to be,—and as happy in his Companions as he himself wished to be. I can only pray for a long Continuance of his Comfort, and Delight in the Road he chalked out for himself.

Sir Nathaniel Wrax<all> had nothing at starting into Life except Talents and Education: but in India they were serviceable to him, and he married to Advantage as I remember; and he has been a Writer for Government and they seldom fail rewarding their Friends by Place or Title or something.[18] I heard the other day that Cecy's Cast-off Lover James Drummond is come from abroad rich and prosperous; and is married to Lady Emily Murray the Duke of Athol's Daughter.[19]——I suppose Miss Castle—his first Wife who went with him, Soon died.[20]

Tell dear Doctor Myddelton that I will write him a Letter of most unmerciful Length very soon: and ask him if he thinks our Agreement with the Count (which he never saw,) will cover the poor's Rates. His People buy Garden Stuff from < but> are most tardy in paying for it.

Once more Adieu says your/ most truly Affectionate/ H: L: P.

Text Ry. 588.256. *Address* John Salusbury Piozzi Salusbury Esq./ Brynbella/ near Denbigh/ North Wales. *Postmark* BATH FE 21 1815.

1. See HLP to JSPS, 13 August 1814.
2. HLP's 1815 will (duplicating that of 1814) is missing. The binding instrument was written on 26 March 1816 and witnessed by Joseph and Hunter Ward and Edmund Pepys. See P.R.O., Prob. 11/1645/356, proved 22 June 1821.
3. The *"Felicity* Bill" involved the solicitor's "Expences concerning Salusbury's Marriage"; see HLP to JF, 31 July 1815.
4. HLP's *"Infelicity* Bill" arose from the expenses of repairing and refurbishing Streatham Park.
5. According to her "Pocket Book," 1816 (Columbia University Library), HLP left Bath for Wales on 2 August, arriving at Brynbella four days later. She began her return journey on 10 September.
6. Margaret (Kearney) Callender, or Callendar, née Romer (d. September 1815), was the widow of Sir John; see HLP to JSPS, 19 February 1810, n. 2.
7. George John Frederick Sackville (1793–1815), fourth duke of Dorset (1799), was killed on 14 February when he fell from his horse during a hunt near Dublin.
8. According to the *Bath Herald* (18 February), James Edmund Cranstoun (ca. 1784–1818), ninth baron (1796), shattered the arm of a Colonel Disney (aged twenty-two) with a pistol shot. Cranstoun had found the officer "in the most indecent situation" with his wife, Anne Linnington, née Macnamara (ca. 1791–1858).
9. Thomas Deane Shute (1793–1855) of Bramshaw Hall and Burtonhouse, Hants., had married on 24 January Charlotte, née Cameron (*Bath Herald*, 28 January). See *GM*, n.s. 43 (1855): 222.
10. For Colonel John Glover and his wife, Frances, see HLP to MW, 21 May [1807], n. 9.
11. Charlotte Shute's father was William Neville Cameron (1755–1837), a major general in the East India Company.
12. For John Heaton and his new bride Elizabeth, see HLP to JSPS, 13 August 1814, n. 6.
13. For Anne Sobieski, née Dod, widow of Robert Watkin Wynne of Plas Newydd near Denbigh, see HLP to Q, 27 April 1796, n. 2.
14. That is, Sarah Heaton; see HLP to Q, 28 January 1795, n. 3; to JW, 1 June 1814, n. 2.
15. HLP reports gossip of a possible association between CMM and Charles Wynne (d. 1851), a son of the late Robert Watkin Wynne.
16. Sir Watkin Williams-Wynn was to marry on 4 February 1817 Henrietta Antonia, née Clive (1786–1835), eldest daughter of the first earl of Powis.
17. Eliza O'Neill's performance of Mrs. Haller in *The Stranger* (a role often played by SS) was praised in *The Times* (6 February). She repeated the role on 16 and 18 February 1815.
18. Wraxall had traveled to Bombay in 1769 in the service of the East India Company and was appointed judge-advocate and paymaster of the forces in the Guzerat and in the Baroche expeditions. Leaving the service in 1772, he returned to England. Wheatley observes that "It has been generally supposed that he returned with some sort of fortune, but Sir Lascelles Wraxall speaks of him at this time as unknown and friendless." See the preface to *The Historical and Posthumous Memoirs*, 1:xiii; also HLP to JSPS, 30 [March 1811], n. 6.
19. More Bath gossip. Emily Jane Murray (d. 1896) was the daughter of Henry (1767–1805), the fourth son of the third duke of Atholl (see HLT to FB, 20 May 1784, n. 11). She was to marry in 1829 Lieutenant General Sir John Oswald (1771–1840), G.C.B.
20. For James Drummond's marriage to Harriet Castell, see HLP to LC, 4 September 1795, n. 11.

TO ANN LEAK

Tuesday Night
7th: [March] 1815.[1]

My dear Leak

must not mistake me: I am not looking to Streatham for *Returns*——I neither expect nor hope, nor *think* of such a Thing. I am shocked only for Your poor

Husband——to whom I can *now* make *no* suitable Return: and feel grieved lest he should distress himself about the Improvements of the Place. Let the Place but pay its own Expences, and pay *him* when it is able to pay;——and I am content;—If I *die* he shall be contented too.—

My best Plan is to live as I do, and I cannot live closer; and stay quite quiet till I can afford to move: but the Count should send his Money into Hammersley's[2]—or how am I to keep my Word with Gillow? for he must have his 150£ next Month. And I can't bear to draw for my Quarters Rent *here* till there is some Money at the Bankers.

Meanwhile poor little Jones makes Man and Maid and all;[3] and the Sick Footman *cries*: and gets a tiny bit better; and would open a Door and shut a Window if he was able—out of Gratitude.

Doctor Brown-Mill however says the Man will live:[4] he called here one Morning and I lamented my Fate [to] *him* and he took the [poor] Mortal under his charitable Care—[He I] think set the wretched Creature quite up again——out of pure Good nature.

Doctor Brown Mill is a Man who travelled with a Sick Friend, and brought him home *Well* about a Dozen Years ago. On their Return, The Gentleman sate down—made his Will,—and left *a large* Estate to his Physician——disinheriting the Heirs whose conduct had half broken his Heart. *In* Three Years more The recovered Friend was *too lively*, rode an unsteady Horse, fell from him, and died; and the Heirs disputed the Testamentary Disposition of Course. It was given against Them however, and Doctor Brown took the Name of Mill with the Fortune annexed to it.[5]

He is the Man who gave Advice to poor French People without Fee or Reward, and Lewis the 18th is perpetually sending him Presents from abroad[6]——and he has undertaken James Smith.

Thomas is a sad Fellow after all: took my Money to pay Bills which he never discharged; and made a Supper for his Friends some Night and now charges Bessy Jones to pay for the good Cheer he gave Them. Then goes and coaxes Mr. Smythe Owen out of Money and a Character——God forgive the Man! he has no Principles at all I think.

But here comes Old Jacob Weston! I told you he sent me two Hares, and now he comes to offer me 47£.[7] My obligation to him is the same as if [I] took it—— which nothing would tempt me to do. I told him that all the Laudanum at The next Apothecary's Shop would not put Me to Sleep if I did take it—and so he declined the Conversation——but he was in true good Earnest.

Mr. Mangin has undertaken to dispose of my Book which *he* likes better [than I] do;[8] and says he will *Threaten* to publish [by] Subscription if the Man he applies to, does not propose giving a handsome Price. Somebody has written Verses here in praise of the Bath Favourites, and speaks much of

> The Wit that illuminates Piozzi's bright Page:
> Which charmed the great Scholars of Centuries past,
> And *will* charm while the Land and the Language shall last.[9]

Mozaib is I believe no *proper Name* in the old Testament, but in the 4th Chapter

Edward Mangin. Mezzotint by J. Saxon; engraved by W. Say. (Reproduced by permission of the Trustees of the British Museum, Department of Prints and Drawings.)

of Ruth and the 15th Verse—it is said, "He shall be a *Restorer* of thy Life and a Nourisher of thy old Age".———And in the Hebrew Bible this *Mosheb* or *Mozaib* means *Restorer*———I was very glad of the Name.

Mr. Smythe Owen said you were very civil to him, but it was too bad a Day for him to see any thing; he will go again however.

Doctor Myddelton writes word that the Salusburys are very happy &c.: I wonder Oldfield is not come yet with his Fine and Recovery Nonsense[10]———he wrote me word his Brother would be here in nine Days———but what I want most is the Count to pay his Quarterage———They said he was punctuality itself.

Mrs. Mostyn never wrote again, after I accounted to her Seriously for my obscure Manner of Living, which She appeared to Think worthy of Blame or Ridicule———like the People who say Lord Ma'am I wonder you should *like* to live [as I live now]. I should wonder indeed if I did.

Smythe Owen said Mrs. Mostyn looks older than any of her Sisters unless 'tis Lady Keith who looks very well too he says———and dresses particularly gay. I am most desirous of contributing to their Gayety and Happiness—but wish they *saw* as Jacob Weston says *he* did: that Streatham House nor Streatham Park *ever* looked in such <order> since he first knew them in 176<8>. He remembers Mr. Thrale granted Ray the Bricklayer a Lease of that Land Mr. Parsons pays Rent for,[11] in the Year 1770—a Fifty Years Lease, and I think that very likely; but it should be looked into. Perhaps Mr. Robinson of Carey Street could tell; but in the first Place he hates me, and in the second Place I owe him Money.[12]———Mr. Davies *must* know I should imagine without further Search.

Do not *you* be frighted at the Mobs———They will only make a Noise; and an Ambassador's house is the Safest of any.[13]

Dear Leak how the Time flies! here's Easter coming directly, and then April will come and I shall have some Money———and *Then*———What then? You will see.———But the Count must pay or I forfeit my Honour to Gillow: no room to say how much I'm yours/ H: L: P.

Write soon again, and tell if Leak has got his 18£———and if he can guess my Debt to Mr. *Windle*.

Text Hyde Collection. *Address* Mrs: Leak/ Streatham Park/ Surrey. *Postmark* BATH <   >; 10 o'Clock MR 9 1815.

1. Misdated February for March; see postmark.
2. Count Lieven was at present renting Streatham Park.
3. For Bessy Jones, see HLP to JSPS, 24 [-26] April 1813, n. 2.
4. George Gavin Browne-Mill, originally Browne, or Brown (1748–1842), M.D. (1779), was a fellow of the Royal Society of Physicians, both in London and Edinburgh. Practicing in Bath as early as 1792 at Brunswick Place, he moved in 1809 to 27 Marlborough Buildings, where he lived until his death. See "Bath Abbey Burials," C.R.O. Somerset.
5. That is, David Mill (d. 1807) of Bath. Having written his will in 1791, Mill added a number of codicils: in 1792 he left £3,000 to his physician for "attention and kindness . . . experienced for several years past"; in 1799 he gave his doctor and his four original beneficiaries equal shares in a West Indian plantation on Cariaron; in 1802 (the fourth codicil) he disinherited two beneficiaries in favor of the doctor and requested that he "take upon himself . . . the name of Mill in addition to his" own. See P.R.O. Prob. 11/1472/47, proved in London, 29 January 1808.
6. Louis XVIII, who had been treated by Browne-Mill in 1813, created him on 7 April 1820 a

baron of France and a chevalier of the Legion of Honor "pour services rendus aux Français." See the *Bath Chronicle*, 20 April 1820; the M.I. (west-end door and screen) Bath Abbey.

7. Ann Leak on 19 March (Ry. 609.7) commented on Weston's offer: "I am glad He is greatfull tho it was not likely that you would accept of his Money and I don't know how he could offer it to You but We hear that He is become a rich Man now by the Death of some relation so I sopose that gave him courage."

8. Edward Mangin (1772–1852), who took his B.A. (1793) and M.A. (1795) from Balliol College, Oxford, was descended from an Irish-French Huguenot family. Ordained in the Irish church, he served as prebendary of Rathmichael in St. Patrick's, Dublin (1800–1803); thereafter as prebendary of Rath in Killaloe until his death. A miscellaneous writer and fluent conversationalist, he became one of HLP's Bath "Cavaliers," who was eager to help her "dispose" of "Lyford Redivivus."

9. The lines (slightly altered by HLP) are part of EM's anonymously issued *An Intercepted Epistle from a Person in Bath, to his Friend in London* (Bath: Gye and Son, 1815), 39–40. The poem, describing various Bath personalities, was read as a "squib which exploded with considerable brilliancy. It has made a great deal of noise, without doing the smallest injury" (*Bath Herald*, 11 March).

10. For John Oldfield's "Fine and Recovery Nonsense" (which involved HLP's right to bequeath her Welsh estates to JSPS), see her letter to JSPS, 19 April 1813, n. 1. For Edward Oldfield, see HLP to JSPS, 5 March 1809, n. 1.

11. For the wealthy Richard Ray, "wood mason," see HLP to Q, 7 July 1787, n. 2. According to the extant "Land Tax Assessments," Streatham, Ray was renting Thrale land in 1780, paying at first £20 annually and in 1795 an additional £10 (C.R.O., Surrey). For John Parsons, see HLP to RD, 7 November 1813, n. 1.

12. For Edmund Robinson of 1 Carey Street, Lincoln's Inn, see HLP to JSPS, 11 April 1813, n. 11. HLP had not yet paid him for drafting her will of 19 April 1813.

13. Although opponents of the corn bill were peacefully gathering petitions in large numbers against the proposed legislation, HLP anticipated the outbreak of violence in London. Between 6 and 9 March, as the bill neared a final reading, there was house-breaking and vandalism as mobs shouted "No Corn Bill!" They were to attack the homes of the bill's parliamentary supporters. Troops were called to restore order, and *The Times* (10 March 1815) advised all "Noblemen and Gentlemen . . . to insist that their servants should stay at home in the evening during the present disturbances." The bill was to receive the Royal Assent on 23 March.

TO JOHN SALUSBURY PIOZZI SALUSBURY

Thursday 9: March 1815.

My dearest Salusbury may assure himself I keep up my Health and Spirits as well as I can. Every Account from Brynbella has breathed Happiness and Gayety; and Mr. Oldfield is I suppose on the Road to execute *Your* Wishes by my Hands. The Trees were well worth 10000£ Three or four Years ago—The Timber must naturally fall in Value when none is wanted for Shipping; and every Country able and willing to send Loads of it—if it were wanted. I wonder it is worth any thing for *my* Part.

My Hot Houses and Green Houses are to pay *Treble* Tax; other People who are so taxed, can tear their Hothouses and Greenhouses away; but I am bound by Law to keep mine up—so much for *my* Causes of Felicity.[1] I am glad yours— as you deem them such—are increasing.[2] My Footman is sick poor Creature! or he would be useful;—We do as well as We can, and live as close as we can; I can live no closer, and what's more I *will* live no closer. Poor old Jacob Weston hearing how hard pressed I was, came to see me; and offered me his little Money that he had saved, and cried when he looked over my house and Garden.

It was not so his Mistress *used to live* he said—but Plymmer Arrian?[3] is the Question with us all——When I have any, I will send you some: but Mead and Gillow cut my Dividends *so* short, and the Count has not paid his Quarterage *this* Time; and Leak is forced to pay my Poor Rates and Tythes out of his own Money by selling out[4]——They come to 80£ and I had Hamlet to pay you know, an old Bill: and Price and Cobbe and a long &c. So I am run as dry as a Chip. Meanwhile Dear Sir James Fellowes who has this Moment walked home with me says—Why Mrs. Piozzi you will live to be a hundred. Why so? because you are so careful of your Health——come now do tell me what is Your Dinner to day? A Calves Foot.—Nothing else! *Nothing.* And what Yesterday? a Bason of good Veal Broth—But what do you drink? Why Two, or sometimes *Three* Glasses of the best Wine Money can buy;—Madeira or old Hock which Mr. Salusbury of Brynbella gave me. Oh! *You'll* not want Physick—or Physicians; and when you do—*Here am I.* was the Answer: but Doctor Browne Mill takes care of my sick Footman, for very Charity to the Man, and to *me*; and will I do Think save his Life—so poor as H:L:P is become, She has some Friends—and some Flatterers, witness these Lines in a Pamphlet——which if you did not profess hating Books, I would send you by Oldfield.

> Now Thompson or Goldsmith my Studies engage,
> Or the Wit that illuminates Piozzi's bright Page:
> Which adornd and delighted the Age that is past,
> And will charm while the Land and the Language shall last.

I have not the Original near me so I quote by Memory. Well! Dear Salusbury! don't you recollect little Walmsley who repeated Stories to me out of my own Writings,[5] and put The Archbishop of Tuam out of Countenance in the Crescent?[6] He is now driving his Barouche and four up and down at a famous Rate, and would dash his Father's Fortune completely to pieces; but that it has received help from an Advantageous Match.[7]——Mr. Shute (young Williams tells me) will have *some* Money, or some Diamonds of Value with his Lady *some* Time or other——he has at least got a very pretty young Mother with Flowers in her Hat. Quite a Gay Dresser in the Front of the Fashion.[8] Mr. Smythe Owen writes me Word that Lady Keith makes a brilliant Figure in the London Circles; Her Health and *Life* are interesting to You who seem to see the Clouds that are coming forward; tho' I hope at a Distance.

The Uproar in London makes Impression here—where we worship the Echo of the Metropolis;[9] perhaps You are no believer, probably no Reader of the Accounts our Papers swarm with. Does your Brother in Law write to his Mama and Sister the Things he tells *me*?[10] Miss Williams, once the least, is now I do believe the *most* happy Woman in Bath. Her Nephew is so kind and so attentive, and fondles her about, as She never was fondled since I knew her, certainly: Her Niece is very obliging too, and particularly amiable, Every body likes, but her Aunt quite adores her.—

As I walked up Belmont Hill last Week, a very handsome Man riding on a very handsome Horse attracted my Attention—when seeing me look earnestly at him—Is it says he Mrs. Piozzi that I have the honour to recognize? tho' 'tis 15 Years since We met—and that only for an Hour at such a House? It is Sir; and very blind or very ungrateful must Mrs. Piozzi be grown, if She doesn't acknowledge her Dear Friend's Son—Captain George James. We then shook hands, and he said he would bring his Wife Lady Flaminia to see me the Moment She came into the Town.[11] They were in Quarters now at Trowbridge he said, and his Sister with Them,[12] who made the fine Drawing of Atalanta's Head over the Door in Your Wing Room on Blue Paper: I was rejoyced to see him. What else shall I tell you? That poor dear Abington is dead will *not* interest You;[13] that Siddons is alive you will not care much about. That Lady Kirkwall deserted and indebted,[14] is skulking about London in Wretchedness and sorrow is very grievous to Think on

> Deserted at her utmost Need
> By those her former Bounty fed:[15]

how dreadful!

I would in her Place make Artificial Flowers for my Living, and sell them rather than starve *so*—*That* I would. The Report however *may* not be true, so 'tis better say nothing about it.

Mrs. Glover has been very ill since her Son and his Lady left Pultney Street: John Octavius has got some Appointment at Farnham in Kent: his Family will be increasing, and he thinks it necessary I suppose to do something now the Profession of a Soldier is getting as useless as Chimneys in Summer Time.[16]

I have not heard a Bird sing yet; but then I have not walked in Sydney Gardens, where The Tacamahacs are coming out apace. *Yours* I dare say are very forward, and the Mazercon Bush by the Kitchen Garden out of Bloom before now.

Farewell! and be as happy as wished you by Your *true* Wellwisher/ and ever Affectionate Aunt/ H: L: P.

Give my best and sincerest Regards where *all* your own Regards are fixed.

I wrote my Letter over Night to take to the Post Office in the Morning. When Oldfield arrives, I will ratify your Settlement by A new Will made in The Parish of Walcot Bath. The Bishop of Meath and Mrs. O'Beirne have asked me to Dinner however, and I go.[17]

God bless *my only* Dear, and Adieu.

Text Ry. 588.257. *Address* John Salusbury Piozzi Salusbury Esq./ Brynbella/ near Denbigh/ N: Wales. *Postmark* BATH 9 MA 9 1815.

1. According to HT's will, HLP was responsible to his heirs (i.e., his daughters) for maintaining all buildings at Streatham Park, including hothouses and greenhouses. (HLP's lease with Lieven also confirmed this obligation.) Hence, her anxiety about the chancellor of the exchequer's announcement in the Commons on 28 February of new taxes "to be substituted for the Property Tax"; e.g., "New Duties [on] Windows in Shops, Warehouses, and Green and Hot Houses," at 3s. 6d. per window (glass surface of eighteen square feet). See the *Bath and Cheltenham Gazette,* 1 March.

2. HMS was to bear her first child, Hester Maria, on 25 August.

3. HLP had used the term earlier in HLP to JSPS, 17 March 1811, n. 8.

4. Writing to HLP on 24 February from Streatham Park (Ry. 609.5), AL reports Windle's opinion that the estate's "Property Tax must be Paid by You. . . . It is near Fifty Pounds for the last Half Year, and there will be another Payment to be made at Midsummer. I have also £30 to pay for Poor Rates. I must therefore go sell more of My Little Property out of the Stocks to pay it. Those accumulated distresses have made Me almost beside Myself, in the mean time I cannot help thinking it is a little hard on those who are obliged to suffer, that Mr. Salusbury is to be rewarded, at their expense, after having been the source of all the distresses they suffer, but so it is in the world, those who behave worst are the most rewarded."

5. John Walmesley (1798–1832) was to matriculate in 1816 at University College, Oxford, where he would receive his B.A. (1820) and M.A. (1824). He became a barrister at the Inner Temple and died unmarried at Boulogne-sur-Mer. See *GM* 102, pt. 1 (1832): 382.

6. William Beresford (1743–1819), first baron Decies (1812), became archbishop of Tuam in 1794.

7. The elder John Walmesley (1775–1867), of the Hall of Ince, Preston, Lancs., and 14 the Circus, had taken as his second wife Ellen, (fl. 1790–1860), daughter of Richard Godolphin Long (1761–1835). The first Mrs. Walmesley was Hannah, née Conron (1775–1808); see *GM* 78 pt. 2 (1808):955 for her obituary.

8. Thomas Shute was the son of Samuel (d. 1806) of Fernhill, Isle of Wight, and Breston Lodge, Hants., and Henrietta Anna Margaretta, née Gwynn (d. 1795). The elder Shute had married secondly Anne, née Ricketts, by whom he had four daughters. See *GM* 76, pt. 1 (1806): 481.

9. On 7 March, HLP wrote in her "Pocket Book": "Riots real in London, Threatened, and threatened loudly here in *Bath*." For the phrase "worship the echo," see HLP to SL, 1 March 1786, n. 4.

10. Edward William Smythe Owen of Condover Park.

11. For Captain George James and his wife, Lady Flaminia, see HLP to SL, 17 February 1814, n. 12.

12. Either Frances or Gertrude James.

13. Frances Abington, whom HLP had met in London, died on 4 March 1815. See HLP to SL, 1 March 1786, n. 12; *GM* 85, pt. 1 (1815): 284.

14. See HLP to Q, 17 October 1807, n. 1, for the Kirkwalls' separation.

15. Dryden, *Alexander's Feast*, lines 80–81.

16. Captain and Mrs. John Octavius Glover were to have a daughter, born 15 September 1815, at Farnham, Surrey. See *The Scots Magazine*, 77, pt. 2 (1815): 872.

17. Thomas Lewis O'Beirne had married in November 1783 Jane Stuart (1755–1837), a granddaughter of the seventh earl of Moray. In her "Pocket Book" on 9 March HLP thought the "Dinner" to be "a very good Party and pleasant Chat." For the bishop of Meath, see HLP to PSP, 16 December 1802, n. 3.

TO ALEXANDER LEAK

Bath Thursday Night
16: March 1815.

I could not write sooner to my good Leak—because I was making my Will. Mr. Edward Oldfield has been here with that foolish Fine and Recovery, and I have signed the Acknowledgement, and all is settled. I am to make the Will again after the Business has been done in Wales, but you know how little I regard personal Trouble.

A worse Misfortune threatens; I received a Letter this day directed and franked by Lord Keith——with these Words inside the Cover "Report runs that the News from France is unfavourable, No Activity among the People, too much among the Troops. K."[1]

The Letter contained in this dismal Envelope, was from Count Lieven; He had I suppose sent it to Lord Keith. It states that he is so immersed in Business, he can no longer enjoy Streatham Park; and has sent me Word that Tho' he might have delayed letting me hear till 3 Months nearer the Time, he chose to let me know *Now,* that I might go home and *Enjoy it myself.* Fine News indeed! it puts me completely out of Breath. Not a Word about Payment, except to say what an Uneasiness it will be to *him* to pay for a Place he cannot be living in.

Mr. Edward Oldfield says nothing has been well done at Brynbella since Mr. Leak left it[2]——Oh Dear! I am ready sometimes to wish a little of the Money I spent there, was in my Pocket now;—but no: When all Accounts are carried in to the great Chancery of Heaven, neither mine nor Yours will be found dictated by *Selfishness* I believe——and the World goes on so rapidly to its own Ruin, more People than Mr. Faber will be found steady in a Perswasion of its short Continuance: It vexes me that I left Faber's Books in Wales, Every body here is buying and reading them: They were out of Fashion while Buonaparte was boxed up in Elba:[3]

But Books and Timber rise and fall like Stocks, depending like them upon Opinion.[4]

I am going to write the Count a long French Letter in answer to his *very polite* but *very afflicting* Communication. You must apply under hand to Mr. Parnell,[5] and get all *we can*: and lament the Loss of the rest.

Mr. Windle will not tell me what I owe him, and fighting in the Dark is to me dreadful: Let us know the worst of every Disaster, because Fear—which is emplanted in us as a Preservative—ceases when it can preserve us no longer; and Courage comes of its own Accord——when Escape is out of the Question.

What a Mercy it is I did not as I once felt inclined——run with the rest of our Folks to Paris—and what a *double* Mercy that Mrs. Mostyn is come safe home!

I must write my French Letter so farewell.

Keep up Your Wife's Spirit [as well as that]/ of your poo[r]/ H: L: P.

Text Hyde Collection. *Address* Mr: Alexander Leak/ Streatham Park/ Surrey. *Postmark* BATH <MR 17 1815>; 10 o'Clock MR 18 1815.

1. Having been exiled to Elba in April 1814, Napoleon, accompanied by eleven hundred followers, escaped on 26 February, and landed on 1 March near Cannes. He then proceeded through Grenoble to Lyons (8 March) as the soldiers of both cities shouted "Vive l'Empereur!" See *GM* 85, pt. 1 (1815): 267. News of his escape first reached England on 10 March (*The Times,* 11 March).
2. Writing to HLP on 19 March (Ry. 609.7), Ann Leak corroborated "what Mr. Oldfield says conserning Brynbella . . . great Alterations [have been] made since We was there." Among these was the conversion of "the Poor Old Library" into a maid's room and the felling of trees.
3. For Faber's *Dissertation,* see HLP to Q [25 January 1806], n. 22. In the revised fifth edition (2 vols.), Faber argues, e.g., from Revelation 16:10–11 to maintain that after Napoleon's exile to Elba, France's condition was "precisely such as is described in the remaining part of the prophecy of *the fifth vial,*" which precedes "the vial of vintage . . . the catastrophe of the great drama" of Armageddon (2:xx–xxi, 407). The following works by Faber were among the books sold from Brynbella 17–18 September 1823: lot 150, "Faber on the Mysteries of the Cabiri, MS. learned notes, 2 vol plates 1803"; lot 353, "Faber on the Prophecies, 3 vol MS. notes 1808"; and lot 395, "Faber on the Origin of Pagan Idolatry, MS. notes 1788." See *Sale Catalogue* (2).
4. HLP responds to a statement made by AL on 12 March wherein he lamented that while HLP was working on "Lyford Redivivus" to make money, "Mr. Salusbury go an easier way to work to get it by cutting down a Thousand pounds in Poor Old Bachagrag Woods" (Ry. 609.6).
5. Hugh James Richard Parnell (ca. 1784–1862), a solicitor who practiced at 32 Church Street, Spitalfields, acted often as an estate agent. On 19 March, Ann Leak told HLP that "aplying to Mr.

Parnell . . . is likely to be of very little use (unless it is to get you another tenent) but as to Mr.
Parnells power over the Counts purse I fancy is very small, and is much afraid to offend him. . . .
Leak is *now* writing to Mr. Parnell and intends going to London to Morrow to make inquiries for
another tenent." See *GM*, n.s. 12 (1862):107.

[TO COUNT LIEVEN]

[16 March 1815][1]

Lord Keith's melancholy Envelope covered a Letter from the Russian Ambassador particularly afflicting to H: L: P. who takes the Freedom of returning her
Answer by the same obliging Conveyance.—[2]

Pendant que la Lettre de Monsieur Le Comte de Lieven m'accable de Politesses,
le Malheur qu'elle m'annonce—me desole. J'ai donné ma Maison a Louage seu-
lement parceque les Circonstances Tyranniques ne m'ont pas permis d'y de-
meurer; et perdre ma Peine enfin! apres ces Depenses enormes, et perdre encore
Monsieur le Comte de Lieven qui me faisoit tant d'Honneur. Ah! que ces Mo-
mens sont terribles! J'esperois qu'au moins les gros Vents qui arrachent les
Chênes voudroient bien Epargner les pauvres petites Saules qui se plient [prê-
tent] a L'Orage.
   Eh! Monsieur le Comte! votre Excellence a dejà payé (au moins c'est comme
ca que je l'espere [l'attend])—deux Quarts de L'Année:[3] elle me <pense> digne
de Compassion, et elle ajoutera ses egards payera encore les deux Autres.

> Et je dirois fort bien si je n'etoit pas sage
> Si pour vaincre l'Effort de leur Injuste Rage
> Sur les Bords de lateine et du Rhin et du Tage
> Il falloit mes quize Cens Ecus
> Je ne les demanderois plus.
> Mais sans ce secours tout suivra votre Loi,
> Et vous pouvez en croire Les Muses sur leur Foi.

   Ah puisqu'il vous promet Mirachels sur Miracles, Faites vivre votre Sibylle
et voir tout ce qu'elle prevoit.

Text Ry. 893.9; a draft.

   1. For the date of this letter, see HLP to AL, 16 March 1815.
   2. HLP drafted her response immediately to Lieven's note, dated 14 March, that threatening
circumstances in France forced the cancellation of his lease.
   3. HLP recorded in her "Pocket Book" on 18 March that she received Lieven's "Quarterage £150."

TO LADY WILLIAMS

Tuesday
21: March 1815

Dear Madam

My amiable young Friends tell me Your Ladyship has a Mind of a long Letter from me, and that I am not yet forgotten at Bodylwyddan: where Mr. Williams's Account of the Licentious Amours to which the great Cage has seduced Your Canaries—made me laugh in the Street as we came home from Chapel together. How must you now be rejoycing—and Dear Sir John,—to think the French Journey was deferred! and how ought I to thank God that Mrs. Mostyn came safe home before the Troubles broke out.

She professes to like a Busy Scene—but this would have been too serious: Lord Exeter is said to have paid 500£ in fees up and down for purpose of getting away early.[1]

Oh Madam! what Times are we living in; yet what thoughtless People one does meet, and what strange Silly Speeches one does hear—but so it is, and must be.

A Fire, a Jigg, a Battle and a Ball,
Till one great Conflagration bury all.[2]

I was a sad Blockhead to leave Faber's Books upon the Prophecies behind me at Brynbella: they are so sought for now, Your Ladyship would wonder. While Buonaparte remained in Elba nobody thought of them: it must be very gratifying to the Author—That *He* should be immediately looked up to when all the Folks are wondering, and thinking What will come next? What will come next?

But France is not the only Theatre of Present *Marvels:* a Shower of Fish and Frogs fallen in the Streets and on the House Tops at Inspruck calls the Attention of many, and is certified by every creature in the Place. A Tornado did certainly whisk up these poor little Animals which carried *out of their Element* for some Miles,—fell where least expected, bruised and breathless; terrifying beholders, and raising Astonishment in all. When Mr. Williams and I were chatting about these uncommon Events I begged him not to name them at Brynbella, where I understand the Lady of the Mansion is pregnant; and should any thing wrong happen: *our* Nonsense,—*mine* particularly;—might be charged with the Mischief done.

Your Ladyship protests against acting in *that Character* any more: So I may tell *You* all I know (which is nothing) of a frightful Person in London who has a Head or Face at least like a Pig, and who having lost her Companion by Death, has now lately been seen by divers Females applying for the *Post:* as the *Snouty Lady* is very rich, and offers a large Stipend for a Friend to keep her Company.[3]

As I am very poor, and Piggey wants one who can speak French and Italian; my Sport was to say that I would offer *myself,* but Music being insisted on, I lose the Place for want of Accomplishments: so I cannot according to the old Proverb make a *Silk Purse of a Sow's Ear.*

Truth is, I can make no Purse at all: but by resolutely living in a mean habitation and keeping no Servants &c. I shall escape Arrests, and pay all the Debts incurred *at* Streatham Park and *for* Streatham Park by the Time Two Years are out. But while I am saying so, and hoping so,—comes a Letter from cruel Count Lieven the Russian Ambassador, to say that such is the Pressure of these dreadful Times, he shall never be able to Enjoy my beautiful Place again; and as he does not like (of Course) to pay for what he has not, begs to be *off* &c.

Fine News indeed! These are bad Dice Baretti used to say when playing at BackGammon; but we can't change the Throws.

Mr. Oldfield's Brother has been here for Two Days, came on Dear Salusbury's Business: I fancy he will tell his Friends what a fine Place Bath is, for he seemed to like it no little, and I hope his Employer will approve of all that was done— as it had no Object *but* his Approbation.

I'm sure I have every Right and every Reason to like Bath when People pay me as many Civilities—*more* if possible—than they did when I was able and willing to entertain them with Parties and Musick.

Miss Williams's Health is much mended by the Arrival of her Niece and Nephew, whom She follows in and out of every Assembly with most adoring Fondness. We have few Welsh here I think, the Morgans of Golden Grove I saw but once[4]—A Showy Mr. and Miss Griffith were thinking of the Continent, but this News will keep every body in our Island.[5]

How is Miss Catherine Griffiths of Caerhen?[6] Miss Williams has left off raving about *her* Health, since these Darlings came from Bodylwyddan; but She was quite in Haste for that Young Lady and her Mama to fly to the Madeiras!!

Adieu Dearest Madam! keep yourself well and Dear Sir John: and do me the honour to retain in your Ladyship's Memory/ The most true/ and tenderly attached of your Servants/ and Friends/ H: L: Piozzi.

Text Ry. 4 (1812–18). *Address* Lady Williams/ Bodylwyddan/ near St. Asaph/ Flintshire/ N. Wales. *Postmark* <BATH> MA 2<1> 81 <5>.

1. Brownlow Cecil (1795–1867), second marquess and eleventh earl of Exeter (1804).
2. Pope's *Dunciad*, 3.239–40.
3. In February and March, a hoax had circulated about a woman in London "with a strangely deformed face, resembling that of a pig, who is possessed of a large fortune, and . . . wants all the comforts and conveniencies incident to her sex and station" (*The Times*, 16 February; also 9 February). Punning on the story, the *Bath Herald* printed an elaborate biography of one "Anna Maria Wilhelmina *Bacon*." HLP also records the story in her "Commonplace Book" under "Face," commenting: "I incline to believe the Tale a mere Invention."
4. Edward Morgan (1759–1831) of Golden Grove, Flintshire, lieutenant colonel of the Flintshire militia, a deputy lieutenant and magistrate for forty years, and high sheriff in 1792. In April 1792, he had married Louisa, née Griffith (d. 1835), of Rhual. See P.R.O., Prob. 11/1844/185; N.L.W., Register 4, Folio 749 (probated Court of St. Asaph, 1831).
5. Probably the Griffith family of Garn, Denbighshire; specifically, the barrister John Wynne Griffith (1763–1834), who was politically active in Denbigh, and his sole surviving daughter, Harriet (1801–59). His wife, Jane, née Wynne, had died 8 March 1814.
6. Catherine Griffith (1794–1816) was Sir John Williams's niece. She was the second daughter of

the Reverend Hugh Davies Griffith (d. 1802) and Emma, née Williams (1769–1858), of Caer Rhûn, Conway, Carnarvonshire.

TO JOHN SALUSBURY PIOZZI SALUSBURY

Good Fryday Night
24: March 1815.

My dearest Salusbury

cannot avoid remembering the Agreement he *witnessed;*—it *is as you say;*——but the Count wishes to get off his Bargain: and every Friend to whom I have shewn his Letter, *feels* that I have no Chance of obtaining my Money by any *serious Demand* of it. He is *a privileged Man.* I have written him a Sort of gay Supplication——filled with Compliments and Predictions of Success against Buonaparte, but still *pressing my Suit* that he will *pay his Fortune-telling Sybil* the whole Years Rent; to which I receive no Answer. Mr. Hammersley says he has a Tenant ready for me—but *that* Man will have the whole Estate, and pay nothing beyond what Count Lieven agreed to give for the house only——no more will anyone;——Indeed when the House is *let,* you can't make use of the Farm Yard at all, to feed Pigs or fat Cattle or feed Poultry——Those who inhabit the Dwelling will not bear that you know, and tis a manifest Disadvantage. If he quits, I must do the best I can for a Year or so. Every adviser says—*Let* it; my Heart says *Nay:*——and now and then a Thought crosses my Mind that it is *possible* he may be a *Man of Honour* who won Your Affections and mine that Morning at Streatham Park; where I put up *Ten Beds* new on purpose to accommodate him——and sequestred the 600£ he promised me—to Gillow.

Bad Dice indeed! as Baretti used to say at Back Gammon—but we must not call our own Throws.

The King of France suffers worse than I do, and deserves better: he is wise and worthy, and pious and grateful—and we will hope God may be pleased to shorten his Afflictions by taking away his Life.[1]

People here are so agitated they cannot wait to read News: Placards are pasted up at every Bookseller's Door telling what the last Mails say: and this has gone on for a whole Week.

Young Williams seems amused with the Bustle, and the pretty Girls say, Passion Week would have been *duller* than *ever* if it had not been for Buonaparte.[2]

The High Winds however made *Noise* enough:[3] I was forced to make Bessy Jones walk with me to Church every Day since Sunday, lest the Gusts of Air at the Corners of Queen Square should fairly blow me down: and we saw Heads of Lamps, and broken Slates in Plenty lying on the Pavement all about—very dangerous.

Meanwhile the Pease in my Garden are very forward. Mr. Oldfield saw them with much Delight, and now we have done Signing and Sealing this Nonsense said I; You had better dine with me and go to the Play: and pass your Evening

Mr. Oldfield,—and *then:* jump *into* the *Stage* and away to Wales again. I will (replied the Man with invincible Gravity) go to the Play: but I will not *jump* there upon the *Stage.* He kept his Word I am positive—or I should have heard of the new *Harlequin.*

The little Trees on the Bryn are good little Trees for growing so; Timber will again rise in Value and Corn again be at a proper Price. The Uncertainties of Life give Hope as rationally as they give Fear; and those must be wise People indeed, who in the Month of *March 1815* can make a reasonably good Guess at what may happen before *May.*

Sir Stephen Glynne's Death will bring on Elections in Wales I suppose, and Election Quarrels[4]——but perhaps he is no more *Dead* than the other great Baronets are *married,* who I expected you to tell me about; and you either laughed or wondered what I could mean most likely.—But one does hear such Rumours and Contradictory Reports, it is impossible to keep one's Wits from Wandering. I'm glad Mr. Oldfield found me looking so well—My Fear is of growing too fat: which better becomes Mrs. Pemberton and Mrs. Merrik Hoare than it would Your ever/ Affectionate Aunt and/ True Old Friend/ H: L: P.

This Part of the Paper must be devoted to Loves, Compliments, best Wishes, and most perfect Regards to your amiable Inmates at Brynbella, and its much-admired Lady. Happy Fellow are You in Your Exchange of Domestic Society.

Here come Talkers, and Tellers with their Eyes full of Fire, Their Tongues full of Argument, and their Pockets full of Pamphlets:—such an Easter Eve did I never witness.

There is however one Joke going, which you will like better than Political Disquisitions. Old Coutts the Banker at 78 Years old married pretty Miss Mellon The Young Actress a Month ago. He is now seriously Ill says one, Ay replies the other his Wedding was *Comical*——so the whole is a *Mello* Drame.[5]

Adieu!—no Letter from the Count. Many think he will be recalled home, and that we shall try to make Peace with Buonaparte: never mind. Tis *Your* Business as it is your Pleasure I am sure, to present none but *agreeable Images* before the Eyes of your most *valuable Possession* and no other shall you receive from hers and yours most Tenderly/ H: L: P.

Text Ry. 588.259. *Address* John Salusbury Piozzi Salusbury Esq./ Brynbella/ near Denbigh/ North Wales. *Postmark* BATH MA <   > 18 <   >.

1. In his last days in Paris, Louis XVIII seemed to the Prussian minister to have a "calme" tantamount to "mertie." But on 18 March Louis decided to leave Paris and travel north to Lille the next day. He made this decision, kept a secret until the evening of 19 March, because of the calamities of the preceding two days: Ney's defection, the collapse of Berri's army, Napoleon's arrival at Auxerre, and his rapid march on Paris.

On the night of 19–20 March, the various companies that constituted the Maison du Roi moved in confusion toward the Belgian border (*The Times,* 6 April). According to the *Journal de Gand* of 29 March, Louis had arrived in Bruges from Ostend on that day. He then went to Ghent, where on 30 March he was welcomed by the comte d'Artois and the duc de Berri. The king settled in the townhouse of the comte d'Hane de Steenhuyse in the rue des Champs. See Edouard Romberg and Albert Malet, *Louis XVIII et les Cent-jours à Gand,* 2 vols. (Paris: A. Picard, 1898–1902), 2:196; *Journals and Letters,* vol. 8.

2. *The Times* seemed astonished by the amount of news from France. On 18 March it commented: "If the subject were not of so momentous a nature, we could almost be tempted to derive amusement from the various and contradictory rumours."

3. Bath was experiencing windstorms that lasted through the first week in April. See the *Bath Herald*, 1 April; the *Bath and Cheltenham Gazette*, 5 April.

4. Stephen Richard Glynne (1780–1815), eighth baronet (1780) of Hawarden Castle, Flintshire, had died suddenly on 5 March at Nice. See *GM* 85, pt. 1 (1815):373; *AR*, "Chronicle," 57 (1815):124.

5. Thomas Coutts (1735–1822), cofounder of the banking house that bears his name, married on 1 March Harriet Mellon (1777–1837), a former actress. The first Mrs. Coutts—Susan, née Starkie—had died in January Rumor had it that Coutts had been intimate for some time with his second wife. See *GM* 85, pt. 1 (1815):274.

TO ANN AND ALEXANDER LEAK

> Bath
> [26: March 1815][1]

Well! here is Easterday——a Dismal one; but it *is* Easter Day, and the Count has not written; and Sir James Fellowes to whom I shewed my Letter, says——That his taking so much Time to deliberate is *a good Sign*, for the Man who deliberates about obliging a Lady——is *lost*——I suppose however the Lady must be a *Young* one. This is the Translation of what I wrote to him.

> Count Lieven's Letter while its Politeness does me honour, goes near to break my Heart.——I let my House to your Excellency only because tyrannic Circumstances surrounding me, took from me all possibility of Inhabiting it myself. And now to lose my Pains at last, after Expences so enormous! and lose my Tenant too who did me so much Honour.—Dreadful Moments! I hoped that these Political Storms which tear up the strong Oaks would at least have spared the feeble and worne-out Willow, which bends before the Wind. Ah My Lord! your Excellency has already paid Two Quarters—you will think me worthy Your Care——You will pay the other two.—And I might say if I had not too much Discretion:
> That if my poor Three hundred Pounds were necessary to tame the Fury of These terrible Foes——they should be yielded up at once——but without *Them* The World will soon obey *your* Command; and the Muses will be bound for *me*—*this once*. Fortune has no Oracles against Victorious Russia:[2] but you must give Life to your Sibyl that you may hear her Predictions in Your Favour./ H: L: Piozzi.

A Friend of Jones's going to Town I sent you the Book—which pray read—especially *Page 39*.[3] Every body is buying it:—The Author is the Gentleman who transacts *my* literary Business. May *that* be as lucky! This little Pamphlet has run thro' Three Editions in Three Weeks, and another is preparing.

The End of my Letter to the Count which I marked on the Side in your Translation enclosed was written in Verse. I fancy he don't know how to get rid of me.

Text Hyde Collection. *Address* Mr. or Mrs. Leak/ Streatham Park/ Surrey. *Postmark* [obliterated].

1. The year is 1815, HLP waiting on the word of Count Lieven and his continued rental of Streatham Park. In that year Easter Sunday fell on 26 March.
2. On 13 March at the Congress of Vienna, Russia and other signatories of the First Peace of Paris declared that Napoleon was "an enemy and disturber of the tranquillity of the world" who has "placed himself without the pale of civil and social relations." They therefore committed themselves to defend "any . . . government or people that shall be attacked" by him (*The Times,* 28 March). Russia, whose military might had already been proved in 1812, now promised to maintain a large force in the field.
3. EM's *Intercepted Epistle.*

TO LADY WILLIAMS

Bath
March 29. 1815.

Oh my dearest Lady Williams!
What Times are we living in! Your Ladyship is certainly perswaded not without good Cause of The Explanation your Dear Mamma and yourself were ever partial to: The Events come forward as Scripture says they will do, like Pangs of Parturition;[1] every Pain sharper than the last;—and now while the other Powers are *Threatening,* Buonaparte is *acting:* If Haste is not made, The Attempt to dethrone him will be vain. Here comes a Friend however, to say that Sir Walter James and his Family are safe at Dover.[2] Great Anxiety has been felt on their Account and they put to Sea in that particularly high Wind which snapt off the Top of our fine Obelisk here in Queen Square,[3] and was near blowing our chairs about in no pleasant Manner—a Coachman was carried off his Box by the Gale, and run over by the Carriage he was driving. It is entertaining to hear the Varieties of Opinion, and very amusing to see the Crouds round *those* Libraries who get the earliest Intelligence.
Your Dear Son makes the best Use of his Situation; hears, talks, *learns* what passes in the present Day, and studies when alone,—what past in preceding Times:—he is a nice Fellow, and every one delights in him. We go to Miss Wroughton's together next Saturday.[4] I have renounced all Parties; but for the Pleasure of introducing Mr. Williams, I *did* break my Rule to wait on Lady Willoughby,[5] and shall do so *once* more for Miss Wroughton's Concert.—
Salusbury relinquishes all his old Acquaintance—but who can pay too high a Price for Happiness? may his present Passion continue! I should not be much astonished if Mr. and Mrs. Lutwyche and pretty Miss Mayhew were to take a Flight to Wales this Year—They cannot go to France. My Destiny is fixed by the Side of this beautiful River, and the Somersetshire Hills round me; but what can be come to Denbighshire and Flintshire, that such horrid Crimes should take Place among Cambro Britons. It was comical enough, the fancy was of seating dear Sir *John* next a Man, who he would disapprove of *to touch his Horse*

as he said to some horrid Fellow that once lived at the Mill—Davies I think his Name was. All those stories however are best kept quiet; writing Letters, and demanding an Investigation does more harm than good. The Sickness at Cambridge grows more and more serious They say:[6] What a Mercy Mr. Williams has left it.

Our Dear little Solicitor will make his Way well at School,[7] but your Ladyship will really have a cruel Loss, and so will Sister Ellen. These young Creatures—Objects of our Care for so many Years, must and will desert *us* for Objects of *their* Choice, Conjugal or Professional; and then we fancy we lose their Hearts, which in reality we never possessed. It is a fearful Thing meanwhile to see how Wickedness does spread itself——Forgery and Murder are Crimes which never used to be heard of, 200 Miles from Hyde Park Corner; and now there is a *Yorkshire* Gentleman who has maintained an excellent Character for 17 or 18 Years under Sentence of Death—unless the Regent pardons him, for making and using false Stamps &c.[8] Our good old King never did remit Punishment for Forgery—because he said no Commerce could be carried on in a Country, where that Offence had hope of Forgiveness;[9]—and he half broke his own heart I remember hearing, when he sentenced his favourite Drawing Master.[10] This Mr. Blackburn is however expected to escape;—Such Sort of People have *Such powerful Friends.*

The Spring is a very forward one; I see Tulips quite common in the Market, but have no Money for Luxuries of any sort;—They are always expensive: and it is only by spending nothing on myself, that I can hope to pay my Debts if—which would be very surprizing; I should yet live a Year or two.

Some Suggestion of Dear Salusbury's new Friends sent Mr. Oldfield hither Two or Three Weeks ago; they were *so* earnest I should live till March!!! He told me Dear Sir John was looking very well. No wonder he grows fat: It is the common way with every body after a sharp Illness. My Date of this Letter is 29th: but it does not go till Fryday 31st. I kept it open in hope of News, but none arrives: We are all on Tip-toe to see if Louisa Maria goes home to Paris—If She does; Why the Game's up—That's all.[11] Her Return will prove the defection of Austria from the Allies—and the Emperor Francis's secret Wishes in favour of Buonaparte. Your Ladyship and I will then read our Bibles and watch the Event. If I had thought on it, Oldfield might have put Faber's Books in his Green Bag. There is a set at Brynbella all filled with Notes[12] by her who has the honour/ to be ever Dear Lady Williams's/ true and Affectionate humble Servant/ H: L: Piozzi.

I keep the Secret safe, It is prudent enough so to do. The *less* is said about *any* Correspondence *the better.*

Give my best and truest Regards to Dear Sir John and all who remember their poor but ever faithful H: L: P.

What became of Sir Thomas Mostyn's Marriage? and Sir Watkin's? I am so glad of a Letter from Bodylwyddan—without it, I hear *nothing.*

Text Ry. 4 (1812–18). *Address* Lady Williams/ Bodylwyddan/ St. Asaph/ North Wales. *Postmark* BATH MA 31 109.

1. See, e.g., Isaiah 26:17; Jeremiah 22:23, 49:22, 50:43; Micah 4:9–10.
2. Sir Walter James, his wife Jane, and his two unmarried daughters—Frances and Charlotte Elizabeth—had visited France where their plans were interrupted by Napoleon's return. As HLP was to learn later from TSW (Ry. 564.31): "I fell in with Sir Walter and Lady James and their daughters at Montagris—all looking ill and scared. He terrified beyond measure! and fancying that Bonaparte could fly like the Eagles whose Effigies grace all his standards. They hurried to the Hague, the day after their arrival at Paris." For Sir Walter James and his family, see HLP to PSP, 27 March 1798, n. 2.
3. Erected by order of Beau Nash in 1738 in honor of Frederick, Prince of Wales, the obelisk was originally some seventy feet high with a sharply pointed top. This was trimmed by a windstorm on 28 March (*Bath Herald*, 1 April).
4. For Susannah Wroughton, see HLP to PSP, 21 [November 1792], n. 8.
5. Priscilla Barbara Burrell, née Bertie (1761–1828), *suo jure* baroness Willoughby de Eresby (1780) and her husband Peter Burrell, first baron Gwydir, lived at 30 Royal Crescent, Bath, during the season.
6. For typhus at Cambridge, see HLP to TSW, 2 April 1815, n. 23.
7. HLP's godson, Hugh Williams, was about to matriculate at Rugby.
8. Born in Leeds, Joseph Blackburn was tried for forgery at the Yorkshire Lent Assizes on 18 March 1816. He was a respectable and respected attorney, who specialized in the preparation of legal documents such as deeds and mortgages. Blackburn was found guilty of having forged stamps on deeds as early as 1810. Despite the testimony of some twenty character witnesses and an appeal to the Prince Regent for mercy, he was executed at York Castle (*Leeds Mercury*, 27 March). See also *The Times* and *York Herald*, 12 April).
9. On 10 March 1775 "A discovery was made of a very uncommon kind of forgery, carried on for some time past by Robert and Daniel Perreau, twins, the former an apothecary in high practice in Golden Square; the other living in genteel life in Pall-Mall. The two, in confederacy with a Mrs. Rudd, who cohabited with Daniel, have, from time to time, raised considerable sums of money by means of bonds forged in the name of the well-known agent, William Adair, Esq., which they have imposed upon several gentlemen of character and fortune as collateral securities with their own notes for the payment of the said sums."
    The trial was held in early June and both men were judged guilty and sentenced to death. The trial elicited petitions "signed by 78 capital Bankers and merchants of the City of London on behalf of Daniel Perreau." Nevertheless, they were hanged at Tyburn, 17 January 1776. See *GM* 45 (1775):149–50, 278–84; 46 (1776): 22–24, 44–45.
10. George III's favorite "drawing master" was William Wynne Ryland (1732–83), king's engraver, who was tried and executed for forgery.
11. HLP responds to two news reports in *The Times*, 27 March:
"We are assured that the Empress Maria Louisa and the Prince her son, will arrive in Paris on the 4th of April." And in another report:
"On Tuesday, the *Duke of Wellington* packet, from Dieppe, brought over sixty passengers, several of whom had recently left Paris. The Austrian Ambassador left that city on Saturday night [25 March]. This circumstance does not much tend to confirm the *Morning Chronicle*'s 'very curious fact' of a deep intrigue between the Emperor Francis and the scoundrel whom he has publicly proclaimed 'to be out of the pale of civil and social relations.' Even the Paris papers admit, too, that the Archduchess Maria Louisa has forbidden any mention of Buonaparte's atrocious undertaking to be made in her presence" (*The Times*, 30 March).
    As early as 27 March, Napoleon tried to cover up his embarrassment over Marie Louise's continued absence. Thus, he distributed posters that promised her return to Paris by way of Rambouillet. But his announcements failed to convince the royalists, who sang mockingly: e.g., "Ah! dis donc Napoléon / Ah! n'vient pas ta Marie-Louise." See Jean Thiry, *Les Cent-Jours* (Paris: Berger-Levrault, 1943), 140.
12. See HLP to AL, 16 March 1815, n. 3.

TO JOHN SALUSBURY PIOZZI SALUSBURY

Bath Sunday Night
2: April 1815.

I thank you for your Letter Dearest Salusbury and have the Pleasure to say that Your Opinion is everybody's Opinion——*I must let Streatham Park.*—They who give me the Advice do not know as You must necessarily know—the Evils which possibly,—nay probably—may result. Leak will leave me; I shall have no Person on the Spot to guard those Pales from being plucked up and burned, which have cost me such Thousands putting down. The Trees may again (for ought I know) be lopt and topt; and the Ladies justly enraged.[1] The Catalogues and Inventories, made with such Care, who is to keep them? and upon my Decease where is my Successor to look for what was there in the Year 1814?——not to little Bessy Jones, who knows no more of Streatham Park, than of Condover hall;——She lived there Two or Three Months.

Well! The Count makes no Reply to my *Request* that he would fulfill his Contract; and some say that looks well, some say not;—Whoever says it looks *polite,* stands single. That 600£ o'year is better than nothing I not only know, but feel; and Mr. Gillow's Advice for me to let the Place is not quite disinterested.[2] Leak feels sorry to leave me I suppose, but if his Wife dies,[3] who I trust cannot live this Year out, he will be a free Man again;——and I understand by no means a rich one.——Nothing can be done at any Rate till Count Lieven determines what he *himself* shall do: I will then write again, and tell you my own Opinion. Bath is very amiable indeed, and very kind. The *only* Place I should imagine where dressing like a Pauper, and living like a Hermit—my Self-Love is never offended by Negligence or disrespect.

Dear Young Williams made me *present* him at Miss Wroughton's Concert last Night; you know Miss Wroughton's House is the Court of St. James's in *our* Town.[4] When I had done my Duty—I ran from the Music——which only reminded me of happier Hours, and talked Politics with Sir Robert Wilmot till 1/2 past Ten.[5]

Are you too happy to care about the Matter?—So is Mr. Davies; He finds it *all good Fun.* Doctor Bowen is Dead at last; what! not till *now* I hear you exclaim; no Poor Fellow! not till now. 16 long Weeks has that wretched Man lain—his Life despaired of.—A happy Release say his Wife and Attendants, and so indeed it is.[6] Sir Walter James and his Family are lying sick at Dover, to *rest* themselves: They travelled Eleven Days and *Nights* without taking their Clothes off; and came over in a Cockle Shell of a Ship at last, in that tremendous Storm of Wind which blew off a very large Piece of our pointed Obelisk in Queen Square here, and the Pillar looks ten Times better without it.

I should have been very much afraid in my Chair going to Lady Willoughby's that Night, but that Beaux are never wanting to take Care of *me*; a Coachman was blown off his Box at Lansdown while stooping to pay the Turnpike the same Evening, but our Weather is now settled into a warm Summer, and the Pease in my Garden are most prosperous.

Doctor Whalley is gone to Mons in Flanders; fine Mr. Almons leaves him,[7] Mrs. Lutwyche says;[8] and he is under the sole Care of handsome John: his Lady his quitted her charming House in the Square and resides in a Cottage in sight of Mendip Lodge. Poor! *Poor* Mrs. Whalley.[9]

Sir R. Hill is gone to battle Buonaparte;[10] The Ladies who have Sons and Husbands seeking Promotion are delighted with the War——among them is Mrs. Mostyn.

The Report here is, that our Allies have required a Sum so enormous from England to regain what was lost (they say) by her Fault; that Lord Liverpool refuses to ask it of us;[11]——and the Marquis of Wellesley is to take his Post.[12]—— *He* will have no Scruples concerning our Money taken to enrich and aggrandize his Brother, of Course.[13]

So we are to fight away and spend the last Guinea and the last Life say some sulky Fellows, for Purpose of Setting a Man upon a Throne he cannot keep; and from whence he would fall of himself if there were no Buonaparte breathing. The French hate a quiet, decent, pious and peaceable Sovereign, who makes them go to Church and shut their Shops on a Sunday:[14]——They would rather have *Drouet* the Postillion's Son,[15] than *him.* What then (say another Set) shall we have a Hornets Nest of this dreadful Kind in the Bosom of Europe, and not try to blow it up? Why every Nation will be governed by its Army if this goes on; and the Russians will have Platoff for Emperor,[16] and the English will have Duke Wellington or Sir R. Hill for King;——or what think you of my Lord Combermere?[17]—My Lady has fine Lace Trains, whilst her Papa is starving.[18]

Mr. Greenfield preached a Sermon to day so pious and so pathetic that many Tears were shed[19]—his own amongst them——I never heard Politics so tenderly touched upon, and with such general Approbation. Your Friend Welstead is in Bath too;[20] don't you remember saying at Cheltenham that if Nicky himself, had heard *him* preach, he would have burst out o'crying? Lady Castle Stewart is coming with the unmarried Daughter back to our Market——Dr. Crawford will be very glad.[21]

Oh I was wrong about Lady Acton: It was her own Uncle, her Father's *own* Brother that She was married to: Sir James Fellowes knew them very well in Spain; She always called her husband Mon Oncle in conversation: I wonder if Hesketh and her Ladyship are Married or no.[22]

Did Williams tell you of the Sickness at Cambridge?[23] It is very severe indeed—but Medical Men hoped much from those high Winds.

When does dear Oldfield write? and set me to make my Will again? I wait his Orders.

Little Bessy Jones does not grow mouldy for want of Work; but I give her no Trouble about my Health; which cannot easily be better: and you see I have lived *till March.* Adieu, and present me most Affectionately to your Dears and Darlings; assuring yourself that I am ever most truly Theirs and/ your own/ H: L: P.

Text Ry. 588.260. *Address* John Salusbury Piozzi Salusbury Esq./ Brynbella/ near Denbigh/ North Wales. *Postmark* BATH 3 AP 3 1815 109.

1. HLP had not forgotten her daughters' anger when, in the course of renovating Streatham Park, trees were cut. See, e.g., HLP to Mead, 16 and 20 May 1812.

2. Gillow, the upholsterer, was waiting to be paid for his work on the furnishings of Streatham Park. HLP cleared her debt only in January 1816. See her letter to JF, 26–27 [January 1816].

3. Ann Leak was pregnant and given to hysterical anxiety.

4. In an obituary, Susannah Wroughton of Catherine Place is described as "an extraordinary character, that for upwards of half a century was the *cynosure* of [Bath's] world of fashion." See *GM* 95, pt. 1 (1825):477.

5. Robert Wilmot (1765–1842), third baronet (1793), high sheriff of Derbyshire (1803), and lieutenant colonel in the Derbyshire Yeoman Cavalry. He owned a mansion in Harley Place, Bath, until November 1818, when he sold it and moved to 1 Rivers Street (*Bath Herald*, 7 November 1818; "Walcot Poor Rate Book," Guildhall).

6. William Bowen was fifty-four when he died 27 March in his home on Gay Street. He was to be buried 4 April in the main aisle of the Bath Abbey (in time with his wife, Sophia, née Boycott, who died in 1830 and his sisters Rebecca and Hester, who died respectively in 1827 and 1833). See Bath Abbey Burials, C.R.O., Somerset; also HLP to JSPS, 6 January 1815, n. 10.

7. TSW's friends—e.g., Hannah More—faulted "Amans for quitting his kind master in a distant land and in bad health" (Wickham, 2:408). But TSW corrected this impression in a letter to HLP, 29 April: "Amons, my old and *still* faithful Friend, has left me with my entire approbation to settle independently among his very respectable Relations. I cannot express how much I miss him" (Ry. 564.32). The friendship continued, TSW leaving Amons £300 in his will. See P.R.O., Prob. 11/1752/ 117, proved 7 February 1829. For William Walter Slade Amons, see HLP to TSW, 11 May 1808, n. 2.

8. Mary Lutwyche had received a letter from TSW, 30 March (Wickham, 2:393–94) and relayed its information to HLP.

9. No longer able to live with his third wife, TSW fled to France in the summer of 1814. See HLP to TSW, 4 July 1814. Frances (Horneck) Whalley, who did not hear often from TSW, was forced to vacate her expensive house at 16 Queen Square for a less costly cottage.

10. Within a few hours of learning that Napoleon had returned to France, the government sent General Sir Rowland Hill to Brussels, where he arrived on 1 April. He advised the Prince of Orange, fought at Waterloo, and was made commander of the 2nd Corps of the British army of occupation in France and the Netherlands (1815–18). For Sir Rowland, see HLP to Anna Maria Pemberton [21 June 1814], n. 5.

11. The Tory ministry had pledged £5,000,000 in subsidies to Britain's allies. While the precise amount of the pledge was not widely known, a small group of the opposition—e.g., Samuel Whitbread—questioned the aims and costs of the alliance against Napoleon. Whitbread argued that "it was not our interest to make a fresh crusade for the French throne." But Whitbread's amendment of the Prince Regent's request for financial support of allied preparations was defeated on 7 April by 220 votes to 32 (*The Times*, 8 April 1815).

For Robert Banks Jenkinson, second earl of Liverpool, first lord of the treasury (1812–27), see HLP to JSPS, 6 May 1809, n. 3.

12. HLP reports speculation. The marquess of Wellesley, who almost became first lord of the treasury of a coalition ministry in 1812 but yielded to Liverpool, was out of office. He assumed no political obligations until 1821, when he accepted the post of lord-lieutenant of Ireland.

For Richard Colley Wellesley, see HLP to JSPS, 15 May 1812, n. 5.

13. Arthur Wellesley, duke of Wellington.

14. Even before the Napoleonic return, Louis XVIII's hold on the French throne was rendered shaky by unrest in his country. In the salons of the Bonapartists, generals and other high-ranking officers, ignored by the Bourbons, sneered at their successors, the aging *émigrés* who had done little fighting for about two decades.

There was unrest too among the leading members of the Liberal Party, who would usually meet three times a week at Mme de Staël's home in Clichy. For them, the Bourbon regime was reactionary.

A real danger to the Bourbon dynasty came from the *ultras* and the royalist newspapers. *La Quotidienne* and *Le Journal Royal*, e.g., denounced not only the people and principles of the Revolution but anyone associated with liberal causes. Such journalism provoked open discontent among most of the general public. Shopkeepers and workers had other grievances. They felt their ability to manufacture and sell was hampered by church decrees that prohibited work on Sundays and certain holy days.

So unstable in fact and future was the Bourbon monarchy that Thomas Creevey, then in Brussels, recorded in his journal for 22 April Wellington's opinion that "a Republick was about to be got up in Paris by Carnot, Lucien Bonaparte, &c., &c., &c.," and that Napoleon would be assassinated. See *The Creevey Papers*, ed. Sir Herbert Maxwell, 2 vols. (London: J. Murray, 1904), 1:215; Helen

Maria Williams, *A Narrative of the Events which have taken place in France, from the Landing of Napoleon Bonaparte, on the 1st of March 1815, till the Restoration of Louis XVIII* (London: J. Murray, 1815), 42.

15. Jean-Baptiste Drouet (1763–1824), best known for his part in the arrest of Louis XVI at Varennes, was the son of the postmaster of Sainte-Menehould.

16. Count Matvei Ivanovich Platof, or Platov (1751–1818), the Russian general and hero of the Moscow campaign.

17. HLP refers to her relative Stapleton Cotton (see her letter to Q, 4 January 1801, n. 3). He had become well known when, as a lieutenant general in the cavalry during the Peninsular War, he "made a most gallant and successful charge against a body of the enemy's infantry, which they overthrew and cut to pieces" (Farington, 12:4187).

18. Stapleton Cotton had married as his second wife in June 1814 Caroline, née Fulke Greville (d. 1837).

19. An Oxonian, Edward William Grinfield (1785–1864), B.A. (1806) and M.A. (1808), of Lincoln College, was minister of Laura Chapel (1815–29). Ordained in 1808, he favored an extreme orthodox Anglicanism.

20. Henry Welstead (1775–1819), who received his B.A. (1799) and M.A. (1802) from Caius College, Cambridge, was ordained deacon and priest at Chester in 1804. At this time he was curate of Culworth, Northants.

21. For Dr. Stewart Crawford, see HLP to PSP, 6 August 1802, n. 7. His wife, Eliza, seriously ill, was to die in December 1815. See the *Bath and Cheltenham Gazette*, 27 December.

HLP implies that Lady Sarah Castle Stewart was of marriageable age and that Dr. Crawford would be an unlikely widower. (By November 1817, he was to marry Caroline à Court, or A'Court (ca. 1782–1848) of Heytesbury, Wilts.). For Lady Sarah's marriage, see HLP to JSPS, 6 January 1815, n. 5.

22. For the marriage of Lloyd Hesketh Bamford-Hesketh of Grwych Castle to Emily Esther Anne Lygon, see HLP to JSPS, 23 December 1813, n. 3.

23. Pupils of two colleges at Cambridge suffered from "remittent and low nervous Fevers," attributed by a local surgeon to "a morbid constitution of the atmosphere generally: but aggravated by unfavourable local situation" (*The Times*, 31 March 1815). Jackson's *Oxford Journal* (25 March) identified the disease as typhus, which some believed "was caused . . . by opening a long-closed drain in the neighbourhood of Jesus College [producing] mortality among its students." See Charles John Shore, second baron Teignmouth, *Reminiscences of Many Years*, 2 vols. (Edinburgh: D. Douglas, ca. 1878), 1:67. By early June, the fever had disappeared from Cambridge, having caused seven or eight deaths since the first of January. See *GM* 85, pt. 1 (1815): 295, 559.

TO THE REVEREND THOMAS SEDGWICK WHALLEY

Bath
8th: April 1815.

Whether in England France or Flanders, my Dear Doctor Whalley is ever the same kind Friend and agreeable Correspondent.[1] I like your Residence at Mons extremely, for tho' you did run away from Buonaparte, there will be no Need to run away again I dare say: The French will be convaincus de leur Erreur, et le Tout will perhaps soon be over. We are here all on Tip-toe for Intelligence: Every Eye full of Fire, every Tongue full of Argument, every Pocket full of Pamphlets.——There will be little else I do think in any of our Pockets.——My poor Income already sequestered to the Surveyors and Furnishers of Streatham Park &c. so as to leave me but 600£ o'Year;—is to undergo further Taxation they tell me;[2] and our Mutton is 9d. the Pound, while you are paying only 2d. 1/4.

The Country is beautiful beside, and the Spring forwarder than usual. Brussels—where we spent such pleasant hours in Each other's Company, is not far from your present Place of Abode;[3] and if you would write those charming Long

Letters often, I would shew the Activity you tell me of, by running down Stairs most swiftly to meet the Post. Dear Salusbury's Correspondence is now not worth a Pin,——he is thinking of nothing but his little Wife; and She is thinking of nothing but the little Child She intends to bring in the Course of this next Summer and Autumn.[4]

There has been a Sort of Contagious Sickness at both our Universities; I rejoyce my Boy is no longer a Boy—and at neither of them. We had a curious Account of the Duke D'Aremberg's Family in our Public Prints lately:[5] Is it true that they have all been so marked out by Misforturne? and was the charming Lady You made Verses on—which Verses my poor Husband set and sung—— Was She Guillotined?[6] I never knew it till lately——Lord bless me! what Things has France done and suffered within these last 25 Years! and not weary yet!

Oh Yes, I hope these are the last Convulsions of her Lunacy, and that Restoration to common Sense is at hand. It is exceedingly disagreeable meanwhile to hear our own People say that Louis dixhuit is too good a Character for the present Times: when more *Energy*, meaning more *Wickedness* is necessary to Royal Wellbeing. He is right however in saving his Soul, if he cannot save his Country;——but if the Usurper is brought to him, (which would not now much amaze me;) he must not let him go, as the Fools did who had him in their Power last Year about this Time:[7]

The Sandal Tree which perfumes the Axe that cut it down,[8] is the best Emblem of Lewis the 18th's Behaviour to his Marshals.[9]

Mrs. Lutwyche has really suffered pungent Sorrow on this Occasion, and Doctor Browne Mill: but we are all reviving, and hoping, and half expecting good News every day. If you have any Compassion for our Earnestness write Dear Sir, and tell what Conjectures we may form, and what Glimpse of Clear Sky may be seen through the present suddenly-raised Fog. We have no Occurrences to relate: Bath goes on as it used to do: now a Coffin pushing you off the Pavement, and now a Base Viol Case.

Poor little Doctor Bowen was buried last Week after a miserably long Illness of Sixteen Weeks——I think *that* an unhappy Fate indeed.

Whatever Door is opened for our Departure, let us pray to God that it may not *hang o'Jar*—as the vulgar Phrase is, for 16 Weeks!!! Doctor Murray too is very Ill;[10] but old Harington, Immortal Doctor Harington, still lives, and still composes good Musick: his setting Shakespear's Words of "Look Love Look—It is the Nightingale,—no 'Tis the Lark.—"for Three Voices has really an admirable Effect—as a Glee.[11]

We have the Roscius too, Mr. Betty; a Good Actor:[12] and Dear Miss Williams has got her Niece and Nephew Mr. and Miss Williams of Bodylwyddan in the Town: They will add Ten Years to her Life I do think.

May yours Dear Sir be long and happy! And may we once more meet to rejoyce in the final Comforts accrueing from this fermentation in the best Spirits of Europe—ever and truly Yours/ H: L: Piozzi.

We have now received the Newspaper with our Regent's Resolution to *arm*— it will I hope be followed by his Resolution to *act*.

SECOND NIGHT OF

MR. BETTY's

ENGAGEMENT.

This Present THURSDAY, MARCH 30, 1815.

Will be performed Shakespeare's TRAGEDY of

OTHELLO

THE MOOR OF VENICE.

Othello .... Mr. BETTY

(The Second time of his ever performing that character)

Duke of Venice	Mr. EGAN	Roderigo	Mr. CUNNINGHAM
Brabantio	Mr. CHARLTON	Montano	Mr LEY
Cassio	Mr. ASH	Lodovico	Mr. COMER
Iago	Mr. BENGOUGH	Officers, Mess. ORREBO, LODGE, &c.	
Desdemona	Mrs. VINING	Emilia	Mrs. WESTON.

To which will be added the Grand Chinese SPECTACLE of

ALADDIN

OR THE WONDERFUL LAMP.

Aladdin, a Friendless Orphan Lad, will for that night be attempted by Mr. ORREBO

(IN CONSEQUENCE OF MR. WARDE'S INDISPOSITION,)

Tahi Tongluck, Cham of Chinese Tartary,	Mr. EGAN
Kien Tupac, the Grand Vizier	Mr. COBURN
Kerim Azac, the Vizier's Son	Mr. COMER
Haroun	Mr. HIGMAN
Alfajah } Officers of the Cham {	Mr. HODDESON
Kosrou	Mr. LEY
Hamet	Mr. LODGE
Abenazac, a Wicked Magician	Mr. CUNNINGHAM
Kazrac, his Dumb Slave	Mr. CHATTERLY

Princess Badreulboudour, the Cham's Daughter, Mrs. VINING

Zobeide	Miss GIROUX—The Widow Mustapha, Aladdin's Mother, Mrs. EGAN		
Amrou	Miss SHEENE,	Gulnare	Miss WHITE
Zora	Miss HAGUE	Uli	Mrs. LODGE
Dinarzarde	Mrs. DAVIDGE	Zelis	Miss RAWLINS.
Genie of the Ring, Miss E. CUNNINGHAM		Genie of the Lamp, Mr. DAVIDGE.	

☞ TURN OVER

Playbill for William Henry West Betty as Othello. (Reproduced by permission of the Henry E. Huntington Library and Art Gallery, San Marino, California.)

I will not grudge my last Guinea.[13]
Miss Williams comes in and bids me add her Compliments.

Text Berg Collection +. *Address* A Monsieur/ Monsieur Le Docteur Whalley/ Mons/ Posterestante. *Postmark* BATH 8 AP 8 1815; E PAID 10 AP 10 1815.

1. On 4 April 1815 in her "Pocket Book," HLP recorded the receipt of "a long Letter from Doctor Whalley at Mons" (Ry. 564.31). Mons was an important allied base during the *Cent Jours.*
2. Among other forms of taxation, the property tax, which was to be terminated with the end of the war, was continued at one shilling per pound.
3. When the Piozzis arrived in Brussels during the first week of February 1787, they were welcomed by TSW and his first wife, Augusta Utica, née Heathcote (1742–1807), a "maiden Lady of large fortune" (Farington, 6:2133).
4. JSPS's first child, Hester Maria, was born 25 August 1815.
5. The newspapers reported that the duc d'Aremberg's son had been killed on 7 March in a horseback riding accident in Vienna. See the *Bath Herald,* 1 April, which commented on the misfortunes that pursued the family. "The father of the young prince received, when hunting, a gunshot in the eye, by which he was deprived of his sight; his mother was guillotined; his brother was forced to banish himself in consequence of a duel, in which he had the misfortune to kill his adversary; and finally his sister perished in the fire at the house of Prince Schwartzenberg, at Paris."
6. Much of the newspaper account is accurate; see HLP to Q, 31 July 1810, and nn. 11, 12, 13, 15. What is untrue is the death of Pauline, duchesse d'Aremberg. As TSW was to explain on 29 April (Ry. 564.32), "the amiable Dutchess died quietly in her Bed eighteen Months ago. It was *her Mother* the Countess de Lauragois, who was guillotined."
7. HLP refers to the conference at Châtillon-sur-Seine, which had opened 5 February 1814. For the Allies' conciliatory gestures to Napoleon, see her letter to LC, 18 January 1814, n. 7.
8. For the Indian proverb, see *Oxford Proverbs,* No. 1853, 699.
9. On 1 April, the *Bath Herald* reported that three marshals of France had joined "the list of perjured traitors . . . who have all gone over to the Tyrant." Each of the three, made maréchal by Napoleon, became reconciled to the Bourbon regime until the *Cent Jours,* when they rallied to the Napoleonic cause. They were the following: Michel Ney (1769–1815), prince de la Moskowa; duc d'Elchingen; Louis-Gabriel Suchet (1770–1826), duc d'Albufera; and Edouard-Adolphe-Casimir-Joseph Mortier (1768–1835), duc de Trévise. Of the three, only Ney was to be executed for treason on 7 December, having declared to his troops on 14 March in the Place d'Armes at Lons-le-Saulnier: " . . . la cause des Bourbons est à jamais perdue . . . je vous ai souvent menés à la victoire; maintenant je vais vous mener à la phlange immortelle que l'empereur conduit à Paris." See Henri Houssaye, *1815, La Première Restauration,* 3 vols. ([1892–1905] Paris: Perrin, 1911), 1:318.
10. J. T. Murray (1768–1818), M.D., ran an "infirmary and Dispensary" at 2 Fountain Buildings, Bath.
11. Between 1780 and 1800, Henry Harington published four collections of glees in addition to many single glees, catches, and duets. On 27 February HLP noted in her "Pocket Book" that she dined out, enjoying "Music, beautiful Catch and Glee Singings, Dr. Harrington's Look Love Look from [*Romeo and Juliet,* 3.5.6–11]—very fine." The song was entitled "Look neighbours look" and first was printed in Harington's *A Favorite Collection of Songs, Glees, Elegies & Canons* (London, ca. 1780.)
For Dr. Harington, see HLP to SL, 15 November [1788], n. 6.
12. William Henry West Betty began on 28 March an eight-night repertoire at the Theatre Royal, Bath. On his first night he played Selim in John Brown's *Barbarossa* to "the most cheering applause" (*Bath Chronicle,* 30 March). HLP saw him in Othello and "liked it." Again on 11 April, her "Pocket Book" indicates that she saw Betty once more, and that he was "greater than ever."
For Betty, see HLP to LC, 17 November 1803, n. 2; to Ly W, 29 December 1804, n. 3.
13. On 6 April, Eldon, the lord chancellor, read to the Lords while Castlereagh, the foreign secretary, delivered to the Speaker of the Commons the Prince Regent's message that French affairs "have induced [him] to give directions for the augmentation of his Majesty's land and sea forces" (*The Times,* 7 April).

TO MR. LEAK

Bath
11 April 1815.

Till your Letter of yesterday arrived, I felt perswaded that you wished Me to get quit of Streatham Park chiefly because thinking that a Person who brought 25000£ to one Husband, and twice as much to the other——was living here a Life unworthy *both* and that I ought by any honest Means to encrease my Income, and live Grander; for *happier* I do not want or wish to live.

I have already paid for my fine Bible; and our Week's Bills, including the Beer, the Butter, the Grocer, the Butcher, Baker, etc. seldom pass 7£ or 7£ 10 if my own little Pocket Expences are not *very* particular, because even they are included——This we will say comes to 30£ o'Month or 360£ per Annum.

I shall send you a Hundred Pounds in November *of Course*, poor as I *now* am; and after this 1815 is out, I must get richer whether I will or no. It were better send *Two* Hundred every Year than lose *for ever* the Place which has been my Pleasure, my Plague and gilded Millstone now for 52 Years and *Dear* Doctor Myddelton! *he* respects no Prejudices, he is ready to Sell Mother and Grandfather——every Thing and everybody, for my sake. And how will the Ladies like such a Step?

Oh Lord! I would not offend them in the last Years of a long Life spent in admiring their Persons, Talents and Characters——no, no; I would rather live in a Garret, and die in a Cellar, than give *them* Cause of Offence.

Mean while do not suppose me unfeeling to Mortifications; The hapless Book is returned with the same Speech you brought it back——last Summer; and Walker of Denbigh sent me So pressing a Letter today, that I felt *constrained* to send him a Checque for his 30£.

It is to my Credit however, that the Intelligence *his* vexatious Epistle brought, concerning poor Henry Moore's Dangerous Illness; did not fail of giving me serious Grief, tho' tormented by Cares of my own.—

I sent a Copy of Doctor Myddelton's Proposal and your Letter to Brynbella——without much Comment; I wonder what Salusbury will say to it! His new Friends will probably urge him to persuade me to sell the Place, and every thing in it; and vest my Money in the Funds, now Stocks are so very low. My Heart however does not much feel as if the Stocks were Safer than the Pictures, which would likewise lose Value by quitting the Library for any other Place.

Tell Doctor Myddelton I say so: for I did not remember *that* Objection; and consult him (he is not far off) whether we had not better offer the Place to the Ladies as a Present; They to pay Taxes, and Stand to Repairs——I to *give* them the use of Pictures Furniture etc.—for my Life——retaining still the Power to dispose of them, at my Demise. If they refuse, I should have less Scruple to sell *Stock and Block* as Mr. Thrale used to call it.

For your own Part——do not let me be your Hindrance, if I cannot be your Help; for I am with all my Heart yours and your good little Woman's sincere/ Friend and Well-wisher/ H: L: Piozzi

I will write to poor dear Mr. Moore and enclose a Letter for Salusbury with this *new* Proposition——Speak to Mr. Davies about it, or Mr. Dalgliesh, or both; but pray write to Dr. Myddelton directly. I have written myself but omitted this new Idea of giving the Place away——Indeed it came into my head afterwards:

The Box went by the Wednesday Morning Coach 5 o'Clock. They could not get some one of the Things done before then.

Poor Doctor Bowen is dead at last after 16 weeks dreadful Illness: he has left 2000£ to the Bath hospital.

Text Hyde Collection. *Address* Mr. Alexander Leak/ Streatham Park/ Surrey. *Postmark* 10 o'Clock AP 15 1815.

TO JOHN SALUSBURY PIOZZI SALUSBURY

Bath Wensday Night
12: April *1815*.

My dearest Salusbury

I reply to the last Part of your Letter first: You have certainly not had the Small Pox, Measles, or Hooping Cough since I first saw you here at No. 43 in Pultney Street Bath, Sixteen Years ago last November:[1] but there are Letters at Brynbella from your Parents saying that you had gone through all the Three Disorders, *and were quite fit for your* Journey to England: That I recollect was their Expression: and more than that I know not.

Doctor Cumming is a happy Man; a Man is I believe never so happy as when he first embraces his first Son.[2] Mr. Oldfield has written, and I have obeyed Orders—The Duplicate of my last Will is probably by now in his Possession. It was executed last Monday.

We will now talk if you please of my *last* and *only* Possession, poor Streatham Park! built for me by my first Husband, as Brynbella was by my Second.

I took large Paper that I might have room to copy out a long, and *intentionally* a very kind Letter from Doctor Myddelton upon the Subject——He dates from some Place in Surrey, I cannot read the Name;—but the Post Mark is Croydon.

My Dear Madam

Having this Morning had a long Conversation with Leak upon the Subject of your Affairs at Streatham, and under your Roof; and having well weighed all the Circumstances of your Situation, I am perswaded that the best Mode you can adopt, is to offer your Life-Interest in the House, Premises, and Park with all the Pictures estimated at 5000£ and the Furniture 3000£——to your Daughters for 6000£[3]—after the Refusal of the first Proposition—The Second should be to any one of them Separately.—Should this Second be rejected, which is very probable, allow me to recommend to you to remove all the Pictures to some Auction Room in London for Sale; with the Exception of Mr. Thrale's Portrait, and advertise the House, Premises, Park and Furniture to be Sold with your Life-Interest in the same. Rely upon it, you will *thus*, dispose of the whole to advantage. If you form the Resolution I will endeavour to learn for You from any Auctioneer, the probable Expence of his Visits to Streatham, with every Concomitant Expence attending his Visits to Streatham and the Sale. You will fix the Minimum or lowest Price—I imagine at 4000£. The Books to be considered as a Separate Article. Leak has done all in his Power to serve you, and has got 18£ from the Count for Garden Things—He offered him *12 shillings* in *the Pound*, and most of his Creditors have been able to get no more.

The House looks well, and The Duke of Orleans wants a Residence; but I trust you have had enough of Foreign Tenants.[4]

Any Tenants, would to confess the Truth, bring on in the Course of Three Years, such Dilapidations, as would be a heavy charge upon Your Purse again; and This is an additional Reason for my Unqualified Recommendation of Selling the whole.

So far Doctor Myddelton: The rest of his Letter tells only how Mrs. Hill of Streatham has another Son[5]; with goodhumoured Chat concerning Indifferent Matters, with the News of the Day——in Regard to his Proposal concerning Streatham Park, You will doubtless take Advice from your Friends: and will communicate to me what is Your own Opinion after having consulted them. Dear Dr. Myddelton may be deemed officious—but certainly not Interested: The low Price of Stocks may likewise operate upon Advisers,[6] and the Improbability of my Pictures now rising in Value, if I should be unfortunate enough to live Seven Years;—looking out new Habitations, and Canvassing for new Friends.

When Clem: Francis asked the City People, what my Life was worth four Years ago, they said Two Years;—and offered 1000£ for Streatham you may remember. But Streatham Estate is sunk to half its Value, and the Property Tax is sure to be laid at 15 1/2 in future. Turn it in Your Mind, and let me know; who only wish to offend *none* of my Successors. Leak has improved the Estate and put the Gardens in order, which were in a State of sad Distress indeed——I guess not why the Ladies hate him so, he has done them nothing but Good and had he been more *accommodating* to the Count, I must have been amenable for the Deficiency. I suppose his Excellency will pay me 12 shillings in the Pound for Rent, I suppose he will:—and think me much too happy. But my Creditors will not be *so* contented.

Meanwhile was I to employ a professional Man, Windle methinks should have the fairest Claim; without whose Interposition Mead would never have accepted the Payment by Installments—and in whose Hands *You* and I left all the Receipts and Papers concerning Streatham Park—A Place of, and about which, Mess. Ward and Knox are wholly ignorant;[7] while Windle knows every Gate and Platt, and Post and Rail that have been put upon the Premises. I have written to ask both of them what I am indebted, but they think it polite to delay the Answer; and Windle said he would wait till my Book came out.——I fancy that will scarce appear at all, till it passes through more fortunate fingers, than those of my Dearest Salusbury's ever Affectionate/ H: L: P.

I will tell Mr. Williams as much of this Prosing-Stuff as he will listen to, but fancy he will take a deeper Interest (as most Men would at this Age,) in a new Fashion. I saw the Young Roscius[8] last night from Mrs. Dimond's Box,—where he came up and chatted after the Play was over; He enquired for *Miss Pemberton*—and I told him *Mrs. Salusbury* was well, and married. He seems a true Salopian,[9] and is happy in Lord Hill's Fame—his Mother appears a good Creature, and says her Son is unspoiled by Prosperity—so indeed say everybody.[10] The Play represented the Distresses of Charles 2d and his concealment in the Oak: our Audience took it up, as appropriate to the Distresses of Lewis the Eighteenth, and the Applause was violent. Accept and dispose of my best Love and truest good Wishes my Dear Salusbury: and confess that no one can more *desire* to do what you will approve, than your/ poor/ H: L: P.

Dear Doctor Myddelton you see, thinks not of the Offence all this must give the Ladies: and *My* Prejudices are alike out of his Head.—Sell away, Sell away—is all his Notion: My Mother and Grandfather,[11] every one except Mr. Thrale.[12]

Don't be in a hurry to decide, There is Time enough.——And you will have Mr. R. P's *Advice.*[13]

This Moment brings me by Post the enclosed Letter from Leak, and in a dunning Letter from Denbigh the Account of Henry Moore's Danger—Pray tell his good Father that I grieve for *his* Cares, tho' I *have so many* of my *own.*[14]

Text Ry. 588.261. *Address* John Salusbury Piozzi Salusbury Esq./ Brynbella/ near Denbigh/ North Wales. *Postmark* BATH AP < > 109.

1. For JSPS's first meeting with HLP and GP at Bath, see HLP to LC, 26 December 1798, and [ca. 6 or 7 January 1799].

2. See HLP to Ly W, 3 February 1815, n. 5.

3. The idea that her daughters buy out HLP's life interest in Streatham Park was not new but conceived first in 1811 by TSW. See HLP to TSW, 20 February 1811.

4. Louis-Philippe (1773–1850), duc d'Orléans, king of the French (1830–48). The eldest son of Philippe Égalité, he fought in the revolutionary army, deserting to the enemy with Dumouriez after Neerwinden. Exiled from France, he returned only in 1814 with the Bourbons, who restored his immense family fortune. During the *Cent Jours*, he took refuge in England.

5. Catherine, née Bigge (1773–1818), who in October 1808 became the wife of the Reverend Herbert Hill of St. Leonard's, Streatham, bore her fourth son, Alfred, baptized 9 April. See "St. Leonard's, Streatham, Baptisms," Greater London Record Office. For Hill, see HLP to AL, 28 April 1814, n. 4.

6. For falling prices between January and April, see *GM* 85, pt. 1 (1815): 96, 384.

7. Joseph Ward had long been one of the Piozzis' many solicitors. He had practiced with James Knox (fl. 1770–1840) until 1815, when Ward is listed alone at 44 Bedford Square, and Knox at 98 Great Titchfield Street, Marylebone. See HLP to Jonathan Sterns, 30 October 1790, n. 3.

8. Betty acted in Walter Aston's *The Restauration of King Charles II. Or, The Life and Death of Oliver Cromwell. An Histori-Tragi-Comi-Ballad Opera* (ca. 1732).

9. Betty was born at St. Chad's, Shrewsbury.

10. The widow of William Henry Betty (d. 1811), Mary, née Staunton (fl. 1770–1840), originally of Hopton Court, Salop, is described as "a lady of good education and high accomplishments, who had a great predilection for the amusements of the Theatre, and in private often recited plays and poems." See the *Era*, 30 August 1874; *Eddowes Shrewsbury Journal and Salopian*, 2 September 1874.

11. HLP alludes to Zoffany's portrait of Hester Maria Salusbury, done ca. 1766. Not offered at the Streatham Park auction in 1816, the portrait is now at Bowood House.

She refers also to "a Print of old Sir Robert Salusbury Cotton—my Mother's Grandfather," which was "among the Rubbish at Streatham Park when all was selling up: but I lost Sight of it, and Leak protests he never saw it . . . it vexed me to have it stolen or destroyed——but I was too near Destruction myself to care then—as I care now." See HLP's "Commonplace Book," under *Remarkable*, dated 15 November 1818.

12. HT's portrait by Reynolds was not presented for sale during the auction of 1816.

13. For the lawyer Robert Pemberton, see HLP to JSPS, 13 August 1814, n. 2.

14. The dunning letter came from the apothecary John Moore, whose elder son, Henry, now a surgeon and a burgess of Denbigh Borough, was ill. See also HLP to PSW, 15 September [1792], n. 3.

TO MR. LEAK

Bath Sunday
16: April 1815.

Well! Dear Leak! here has been young Williams with me, and as a Friend to Mr. Salusbury I consulted him. His first Cry was Sell it, Sell it; but when He was led to reflect how much *local* Value the Pictures would lose by removal to an Auction Room out of the *Place* they were made for: and when he saw how much of Life and its Comforts I should lose, by existing under the Weight of having disobliged Mr Thrale's Daughters——he desisted from urging me: and said how he should like to marry and live at Streatham Park himself, and how happy it would make him if Leak lived there too. Talking *on*,—he recollected Lord Massey[1] that they used to joke for liking *me* so much at Bodylwyddan:—his Mother (exactly my Age) and his Sister are coming from Ireland, and will want a habitation.

At any Rate he hopes Leak won't leave me. My Reply was, that I would not repay Leak's Friendship with Injury——nor hinder him from doing better for himself, than I can do for him. Indeed if I know my own Heart, I would rather live upon 600£ o'Year for six years to come, than give a painful Hour to the Representatives of *either* of my Husbands,——whatever they may think of *me;*——much more the faithful Adherents of my fallen Fortunes: and suppose I should live till the Streatham Lease is out; Jacob Weston thinks four or *five* Years at most are wanting——and then the additional Hundred Pounds annually received from that which now is Parson's, will come in Aid towards keeping up Streatham Park and Gardens in high Order——for the Ladies,——preserving Pictures Bronzes Books etc. in *their Places* for Mr. Salusbury.——Now don't you *wonder* at my Hopes of living four or five Years; because Stranger Things than *that*, are passing before your Eyes every Day. And to confess a Truth—The Strangeness of many late Occurrences, gives as good Room for Hope in many Cases, as for *Fear*.

I must live however so as to meet Death, (The only Certainty,) with light Burdens on my Conscience; and to do so, *I must not sell Streatham Park*.

Doctor Bowen is dead at last, leaving 30,000£ to a Wife who scarcely brought him *one;*—and 2000£ to our Bath Hospital.

Mr. Greenfield[2] urged us all to give—*while we could*—a doing that the *richest* of his Hearers could not in these Days tell how soon he might want the Assistance of a Place he was now solicited for Subscriptions to.

Farewell! and write to me when at Leisure, and give my true Love to your Wife from hers and yours/truly H: L: P.

Old Simon Foulkes of the Bryn is dead—and poor Henry Moore of Denbigh dying——Those who take Wing now, will escape seeing,—*perhaps participating* [in] dreadful Scenes.

Perhaps Streatham Park may be *useful*——if if—if—You guess what I mean——and if you think that Event *impossible,* as many do:—you and I are not of a Mind./ Farewell!

Find out when the Lease expires.

Text Hyde Collection. *Address* Mr. Alexander Leak/ Streatham Park/ Surrey. *Postmark* 10 o'Clock AP 17 1815; 17 AP 17 1815.

1. Hugh Hamon Massy, fourth baron Massy of Duntrileague (1793–1836), who was almost exactly the same age as JW. See HLP to Clement Francis, 17 January 1814, n. 3. Catherine, née Taylor, who had married Hugh, the second baron (1733–90), in 1760, would have been close to HLP's age but had died in 1791. The fourth baron's mother, Margaret, née Barton, wife of Hugh, the third baron (1761–1812), did not die until 1820 and must be the mother referred to here. He had five sisters.
2. Reverend Edward William Grinfield of Laura Chapel. See HLP to JSPS, 2 April 1815, n. 19.

TO JOHN SALUSBURY PIOZZI SALUSBURY

Wensday
19: April 1815.

My dearest Salusbury

Half Measures are the fashion with Princes and Ministers; half Measures shall be adopted by Me. *I will not give* the Place; and I *cannot* bear to sell the Place.

Make my truest and tenderest Regards to Your very amiable Wife and Mother, and explain to them how *kindly* I take *their* Feeling for my Tranquillity of Mind;——which I should forfeit for ever—if I was led to sell poor dear old Streatham Park—The Residence of my Youth, The Pride of my Age.

You are welcome to *all I have*——except my Honour and Conscience; The Loss of *them* would deservedly shorten my Life.[1]

Leak and Parnell are letting it, or endeavouring to let it——but I will (like the Wench in the Jest Book) be *let alone:*[2] for no Sleep have I enjoyed since Dr. Myddeltons Letter arrived.

Now do not fancy that the Ladies ever write or express any Tenderness towards *me,* They have none to express:—but it is my own Prejudice in favour of the Place——and the Impracticability of my living or dying in Peace was I to *sell* my Husband's Gift,——His Childrens old Streatham Park.

We must Think no more of it.

The Welsh Post is so pressing I have no more Room and no more Time: if I *had*, it should be employed in Compliments to Your Ladies: of whose very polite Desire to oblige me, I am really very Sensible.

We shall do well enough *Someway*: and you must be as contented as you *can*, with my out-living my Debts, and leaving you the Personalty as it stood when you saw and admired it——but do not urge the Sale; It would *afflict* if not *offend*/ Your very Affectionate Aunt/ H: L: Piozzi.

Text Ry. 588.263.

1. HLP responds to JSPS's advice, as recorded in her "Pocket Book" on 19 April: "Salusbury says—Sell Streatham Park: and give me the Money. I *will not.*"

2. "A Gentleman, inspecting lodgings to be let, asked the pretty girl, who shewed them, 'And are you, my dear, to be let with the lodgings?'—'No,' answered she, 'I am to be *let alone.*'" See W. Carew Hazlitt, *Jests, New and Old*, 96.

TO ANN LEAK

Wensday
[19: April 1815][1]

I have Patience enough my dear Leak, if your Husband will add some of his own. There is no doubt of our getting thro' our Troubles by mere *Living on;* if these sudden Storms do not arise to shake me as I go forward.

As to the Laughers, and the Consolers; Those that *pity*, and those that *grin:*——I care nothing about them.

My Desire is to keep Streatham Park as *my own* during my Life; and I will neither part with my House or my Steward whilst I can hold them.

Your Residence *must* be an Article if the Duke of Orleans takes it;[2] and I *must* have a *Banker's Security*——or where shall we look for our Money.

Dear Mr. Williams goes to London next Week; I recommend him to Blake's Hotel: he will gallop over to Streatham Park I am sure, if it is but to see and comfort *you.*

Take Care of Baby;[3] 'tis a lucky House for bringing young Things:[4] and I feel sorry you tell me nothing of Pigs and Poultry: I wish some body would take the house *only*—and leave the Land Gardens &c. to your Care.

I have written Mr. Salusbury Word that I *will* not give away the Place—which I see frights *him,*——and that I *cannot* sell the Place, which would I'm sure— kill *me.*

The Tenor of my Letter is such,—*He will Think no more on't.*

I have no Letters from him but upon *Business*, and none from the Ladies at all——It is not who is *deserving* of my favour that I think about; All five are *deserving* young People, with regard to their *Conduct in Life*——and as to Affection towards *me*. All are *alike* Affectionate!!!

I feel *your* Kindness the more Sensibly as it is the less bestowed——except by

Those who have lived in my Service.——But perhaps They see in a more favourable Light, what the others deem Faults and Follies.

With Regard to my living close I am respected for it by People of Sense and People of Birth: and Leak has read in some of my old Books I dare say, that "Those who want least, are most like the Gods who want nothing."[5] By the Time I *do* want Delicacies, I shall be able to afford them honestly:——and every Body paid *Twenty*, not *Twelve* Shillings in the Pound——but Bessy Jones *crams* me as it is; I am in no Danger of losing any real Comforts of Life:—and God forbid that *you* should lose any for the Sake/ of Your truly sincere and/ attached/ H: L: P.

When does Little one purpose to increase our Cares? I'm glad you like his Things.

Text Hyde Collection. *Address* Mrs. Leak/ Streatham Park/ Surrey. *Postmark* 10 o'Clock AP 20 1815.

1. The letter was written 19 April, HLP noting in her "Pocket Book" for that day: "Received and Answered Salusbury's Letter and Leak's—they hope the Duke of Orléans will take Streatham Park."
2. In England by March, Louis-Philippe had several meetings with the Prince Regent, beginning as early as 5 April. Then they talked for several hours in the presence of Louis' special envoy on how best to bring about a new restoration in France with the duc d'Orléans as the moderates' solution to a choice between Louis XVIII and Napoleon. See Romberg and Malet, 1:157–61.
3. According to "St. Leonard's Baptisms," Alexander Piozzi Leak was born at Streatham on 29 May and baptized 12 June.
4. Eight of the twelve Thrale children were born at Streatham Park.
5. The saying is attributed to Socrates, *Memorabilia*, 1.6.10 (*Johns. Misc.*, 1:329, n. 2). SJ cites it as the theme for *Adventurer* 119, and HLP uses it in the *Anecdotes*, 275.

TO MR. LEAK

Tuesday
25: April 1815.

Why do I hear *nothing from* Streatham Park? No harm is happening to Leak or his Wife I hope.

Doctor Myddelton writes with such Eagerness I half suspect *some* of my *Deserving* Successors are earnest with him to press me to sell the Place.——I will listen the *less* to any Overtures that may be made; tho' till I received his last Letter, I had resolved to write to Miss Thrale giving them a hint that I was advised to part with the House, and bidding them if they liked it, apply to Dr. Myddelton. However I hoped before now to have heard that the Duke of Orleans[1] was about *taking* it; and *that* is what I should like best; a Tenant for the *house*, who would suffer you to Inhabit the Cottage: They say The Duke is a very worthy man, but I remember Mr. Ward of Bedford Row saying when Count Lieven took it, we ought to have asked his banker's Security.

Why does not that good Mr. Knox make out his Account? I fear he is (like Mr. Moore in old Times) sitting up every Night to write the Articles; If you ever go to Town ask him. I have not seen the house advertised, tho' I have looked diligently, and never seeing any thing like it; My hopes are, It will be *Lett.*

Poor Dear Siddons seems by the Death of her Son[2] to have been deprived of *every Hope* on this Side the Grave: but her Heart is happily set on the *other side* the Gulph which All must pass:

May her Example be followed by Your Old Friend and her unceasing Admirer—H:L:P.——whose *last* Words are and shall be

I will not Sell my Life in Streatham Park.

Text Hyde Collection. *Address* Mr. Alexander Leak/ Streatham Park/ Surrey. *Postmark* 26 AP 26 1815.

1. For Louis-Philippe, duc d'Orléans, see HLP to JSPS, 12 April 1815, n. 4.
2. SS's son, Henry, manager of the Theatre Royal in Edinburgh, died 12 April 1815. See LC to HLP, 23 November 1815, n. 7.

TO LADY WILLIAMS

Bath
30: April 1815

My dear Lady Williams

I hasten to Thank You for your very kind and friendly Communications. The poor Philosopher will be missed in Wales, but more deeply mourned in London; where his Talents and Knowlege were more valued and better appreciated—— I heard him much lamented by Gentlemen of whom I knew nothing, till we agreed in being sorry for Moussey Lloyd as they called him.[1]

Your Ladyship will have a Loss at Grwych too: do these Young Ladies marry?[2] I should have expected fair Ellen Hesketh to have left Miss Margaret Heaton far behind:[3] but the Man who takes *her* will have a rational and pleasing Companion for 20 or 30 Years; and love her as well the last Day of their Union as the first. Now Long live my Dear Lady Williams; and see the Prediction prove true—— remember you never said Who the Man was.

Oh! well do I recollect the Fun about the Fat Cheek: and glad am I, that Sir John is so chearful and hearty. His Son is a very nice Young Man, of whose Acquaintance every body seems desirous; but whoever attracts Notice, is sure to have a Spiteful or at best a Silly word said of them. Never encourage People to tell you such nonsensical Things, and they will soon have done.

Mr. Williams talks of going next Week to London, and I shall then know more concerning poor dear Streatham Park——which some Friends wish me to part with *intirely,* by selling my Life Interest in the Place——a Step I cannot bear to take—unless it was to Mr. Thrale's Family; and they will not purchase what is so soon to be their own without buying——why should They? You are all very kind to be thinking of it.

We will not trouble Mrs. Wynne of the Deanery,[4] nor dirty the white Fingers at Brynbella by reaching down the Book:[5] I can borrow it now at any Library, and there is a newer Explanation by Mr. Frere, which the Town runs after.[6]

Believe me dear Madam the wisest Men are bewildered by the strange Circumstances which surround us. One hears forty different Opinions in a Day;—and the next Day 40 other Opinions. What I like *least* is the Democratic Spirit of our own Folks—high and low.——The Walls exhibit inflammatory Words in every Street of London and of Bath;—and wash them out tonight as you please—The same Words or Worse, appear again Tomorrow.[7] Buonaparte himself feels Limitation of his Power, and fears of Course—further Limitation. I should not wonder if the Traytors who called him from Elba should betray him to the Allies; and then go to cutting each other's Throats as in the Times of Terror, The Reign of Robespierre. Nothing shall make me believe that the Conduct of France for these last 25 Years, has deserved—or will be permitted long to enjoy, Peace and Quietness under the paternal Care of their lawful Sovereign: No, No; if he will not revenge his Brother's Murder—Heaven will avenge it—and the Hour is I believe hard at hand. As to Great Britain her best Policy is to remain quiet at least for a while: Raising Supplies to Destroy Buonaparte, may raise Confusion and Mischief at home: and who would tear the Props from a Building—to put Cudgels into the Hands of its Defenders?

'Tis a wild World indeed; but I should be very sorry pretty Mrs. Pennant left it before her Time: She is so amiable; and does so sincerely love Dear Bodylwyddan. I suppose it is of the Lying In 20 Years ago, that She now feels the Effect. Lord bless me!. how Thankful should I be who have gone thro' the Business 13 Times with so little remaining Inconvenience. I suppose the fair Lady of Brynbella will be taken double and treble Care of; being such a *Petted* Darling both of Mother and Husband. Salusbury's Vaccinating himself is comical enough—I never knew he was afraid of the Disorder; which Dear Mr. Piozzi never *had*, nor ever thought about——Once when I recommended Caution to *him*, he said perhaps he might have taken the Small pox when at the Breast, but his Parents never observed it—and as for *Inoculating* himself or his Nephew, I suppose no Sum could have bribed him to it——It was accounted a Sinful Action in those Days—So it was *here* in Old Time: My Uncle never had it, nor I fancy my Father, unless they Vaccinated themselves accidentally by rubbing their Horses, or handling their Cows: your Ladyship knows *that* was the Way by which Doctor Jenner discovered this new Method.[8]

There has been an unmerciful Wind, which filled our English Air with Typhus, and destroyed many very promising Young People: I am sorry for those you mention——but a Meeting is to be called for purpose of contriving Means to keep London free from it. Adieu dearest Madam: I have scarce Room to say how much and how sincerely I remain/ Your Ladyship's ever respectfully and tenderly attached/ H: L: P.

Text Ry. 4 (1812–18). *Address* Lady Williams Bodylwyddan/ near St. Asaph Flintshire/North Wales. *Postmark* BATH 1 MY 1815; BATH AP 30 1 <815>.

1. John Lloyd of Wigfair, M.P., F.R.S., etc., had died on 24 April 1815.
2. The sisters of Lloyd-Hesketh Bamford Hesketh of Gwyrch Castle were Frances (d. ca. 1860), who was to marry Thomas Hudson (ca. 1772–1852), M.P. for Eversham (1831–34), and Ellen (d. 1864), who on 20 September 1819 was to marry James Robertson Bruce (1788–1836), second baronet of Downhill, county Londonderry (1822).
3. Margaret Heaton (d. 1851), sister of John Heaton (HLP to JSPS, 13 August 1814, n. 6), had married on 24 April Joseph Venables Lovett (d. 1866) of Henlle Hall, Salop.
4. Mary Wynne (ca. 1755–1818) ("St. Asaph Burial Records," C.R.O., Clwyd).
5. The book that HLP wanted was Faber's *A Dissertation on the Prophecies.* See HLP to Q [25 January 1806], n. 22; HLP to AL, 16 March 1815, n. 3.
6. For James Hatley Frere and *A Combined View of the Prophecies of David, Esdras, and St. John, Shewing that All the Prophetic Writings Are Formed Upon One Plan* (London: J. Hatchard, 1815), see HLP to Ly W, 10 May 1816, n. 10.
7. Through petitions and placards, many Britons were protesting their nation's involvement in French affairs. On 27 April the Livery of London held a huge assembly at the Guildhall and dispatched a petition to the Commons. Denouncing the House's "marked disregard" for "the Petitions from the City and those of the Nation at large" and "total want of sympathy [for] . . . the People," the Livery members protested the "determination . . . [of] the Ministers . . . again to plunge this devoted Country into . . . War." They further claimed "it to be an imperious duty . . . to use every constitutional means towards averting from the Nation the overwhelming calamities with which it is menaced." See, e.g., the *Bath and Cheltenham Gazette*, 3 May 1815.
   Protests were aimed also against passage of the corn laws. By 9 March the different petitions against them "are supposed to have been signed by not fewer than 800,000 individuals." See *GM* 85, pt. 1 (1815):358.
8. Dr. Edward Jenner, who discovered in 1796 the efficacy of Cowpox vaccine against small pox.

TO JOHN SALUSBURY PIOZZI SALUSBURY

Saturday 6: May 1815.

As Dear Salusbury's last Letter consists almost wholly of Reproaches—mine should be filled only with Apologies: but indeed *indeed* I cannot perswade myself to confess the Offence. Miss Glovers[1] were making Baby Linen for their Brother who was married Three Weeks after You—so much for my being premature in my Attentions, and as you say Mal a propos; as to my *Expressions*—they shall be more guarded in future—They do not speak my heart if they give You or Yours a Shadow of Displeasure. I had acknowledged even with Grateful Affection the Goodness of both your dear Ladies when they were kind enough to say—"Please yourself about Streatham Park;" and no Letter I ever had from Brynbella lay a whole Day unanswered: Come, now, tho' You will be so soon a Father, and I suppose a Grandfather too:——do not be a captious Old Man before your Time; but leave Suspicion of Offence where none was meant, to Age and Peevishness and to Her who has been for Sixteen Years/ Your truly Affectionate Aunt/ H: L: P.

I never knew You were afraid of the Small Pox, so never thought of recommending Vaccination; Your Dear Uncle who said he never had it, certainly never feared it; and I suppose would not have been Inoculated for the Universe.

Come again and correct *Your* Expressions my good Sir! You cannot be *disappointed* at my not going to Wales this Summer; You could not *expect* it: I told you at Condover Hall I could not come, I told you so in every Letter since.

Ah! Dear, cruel! *cruel* Salusbury! Is *this our* Correspondence? Well! but I think I shall creep half way into favour again—for I have put my Cause into the *Whitest* and *softest* Hands. So Adieu.

Bessy Jones said She heard a Cuckoo this Morning—The Swallows came just as Buonparte entered France; I saw Three skimming our pretty River on Lady Day.

Text Ry. 588.265. *Address* John Salusbury Piozzi Salusbury Esq.

1. For Anna and Henrietta Glover, see HLP to MW, 21 May [1807], n. 9.

TO HARRIET MARIA SALUSBURY

Bath
Sunday Night 7 May 1815

I am delighted once more to see the dearly loved Handwriting of our charming Harriett, and more than delighted to think you like the Christening Things. If I am to choose the Name—and She should be the wrong Sort call her Hester-Maria and let our Names be united.[1]—but don't ask me to appear in Person; I *cannot*——excuse me my Dear, Indeed I *will* not come to Wales till July Twelvemonth: I have unanswerable Reasons, and will explain them when I *do* come. I wrote to Salusbury under Cover to Mrs. Pemberton Yesterday Morning——You will probably open the Letter. It is of no Consequence.

What you tell me of Your Brother does indeed look like Settling——but perhaps the Complexion of Things abroad and Things around have an Effect upon *his* Serious and Judicious Mind; They are certainly such as never were seen before.

Our Weather is beautiful, and the Country wears a most smiling Appearance indeed, Yet I daresay Your amiable Namesake Miss Williams,[2] will not rejoyce exceedingly in the Exchange of Pultney Street for Bodylwyddan——*Your* Society will however be a Solace to her.

It has been somewhat an unhealthy Season this Year though a fine one; and certainly young Williams either *was* or *thought* himself very far from well the first Weeks he spent among us——but do not tell his Mama so, for She will be wild with Apprehension; and every bad Symptom was removed so long ago, that he has probably forgotten it.

Your Complaints dearest Madam can have but one Cause, and That an agreeable one, soon besides to be removed. No one is so *Safe* as a Woman with Child: they are well known in the Medical World to be beyond all other Mortals—out of Danger:——and the savage buyers and Sellers of Life-Annuities, consider

Pregnancy as a *Security:* They do indeed; so have a good Heart, and be as well after going through it 13 Times; as is Yours and Your good Husband's/ Affectionate Aunt and truly faithful/ H: L: P.

I should have seen more of Miss Williams but we are a measured Mile and half apart. We do however meet now and then.

Text Ry. 592.32.

1. Hester-Maria unites the names of HLP and HMS, but it was also the name of HLP's mother, Hester Maria Cotton Salusbury.
2. Harriet Williams, daughter of Sir John and Ly W.

[TO SIR JAMES FELLOWES][1]

Bath
Tuesday 9th: May 1815.

My poor luckless Book—like a rejected Lover with second Proposals,—comes creeping to request Your Patronage: be kind Dear Sir, and get it as *happily settled* in the World as you can. If Subscription was likely to be more successful than private Contract, I would comply——when you see Streatham Park That Gilded Millstone which weighs me completely down; and when You have spoken to my Steward Leak—no Distress of mine will Surprize You. *Such a Place* to keep in Repair!!

Mean while Mrs. Lutwyche has asked me to Dinner for tomorrow to meet Chevalier Boisgelin just arrived from France:[2] I hope you will have a Card—— and if you do Retrospection the honour to buy it when in London, send it hither to me, and I will correct it neatly and put Manuscript Notes to it in Twenty Places, to make it as worthy as I *can* make it of a Place on Your Shelves.[3]

Look at my Portraits of all the deceased Worthies, and you shall see them again in *Verse* Characters[4]——a Literary Curiosity known to none but to her who feels happy in considering herself as Yours and your charming Sisters/[5] Ever faithful as Obliged Servant/H: L: P.

Text Hyde Collection.

1. That JF is the recipient is indicated by the entry in HLP's "Pocket Book" for this day. "I committed my luckless Book to its *new* Patron Sir James Fellowes:——poor Mangin had no Fortune with ["Lyford Redivivus"], or I fear without it."
2. For Boisgelin, see HLP to TSW, 20 December 1811, n. 9.
3. JF bought a copy of *Retrospection*, which HLP received by 20 June. See her "Pocket Book" for that date.
4. That is, "Characters of the People who are intended to have their Portraits hung up in the Library here at Streatham," in fourteen stanzas. See *Thraliana*, 1:470–76; Hayward, 2:170–80; Ry. 647.29.
5. JF's elder sister was Ann. His other sister was Lucy (1780–1837), who on 6 March 1800 had

married Francis Hill (d. 1828), a factory owner in Wiltshire. See *GM*, n.s. 7 (1837): 556; "Register of Baptisms and Burials," C.R.O., Wiltshire; Kenneth H. Rogers, *Wiltshire and Somerset Woollen Mills* (Edington: Pasold Research Fund, 1976), 72–73.

TO MR. LEAK

Fryday
12th of May 1815.

With Leak's Letter of to Day comes one from Gillow's Clerk Mr. Penning; Offering me a Tenant for 7 Years, or for 3 Years, or for my Life——paying I *think* 600£ o'Year for the whole——Farm Garden and all I suppose: but do not quite understand his Figures——or he will *buy me out*——which no Human Creature shall do——except my own Daughters, or their Husbands or some Friends of theirs.

No other Mortal shall *possess* my Pictures China etc. or the Place itself indeed: If *they* wish it, I will consent, but Consent is not Intreaty.

Tell Mr. Dalgliesh so; I have referred Penning's proposing Tenant to *him* and to *you*/ and am ever Yours and Your Wife's/ Sincere friend/ H:L:Piozzi

Text Hyde Collection. *Address* Mr. Alexander Leak/ Streatham Park/ Surrey. *Postmark* BATH MY 12 1815; 10 o'Clock MY 17 1815; 18 MY 1815.

TO MR. LEAK

Bath
Thursday 18: May—1815

Well Dear Leak!

I told you I sent Penning's Letter to Mr. Dalgliesh, and begged him to make Enquiries after Gillow's Tenant: The Return of Post brought me a long Letter of Advice——politely written——but clearly wishing I would *offer* the Place for Sale to Lord Keith.

Now there was an Expression in a past Letter of yours, which helped to hinder my doing so——Lord Keith (say you) may *refuse* having to do with it. Lord Keith shall never *refuse* me any thing, thought I; for I will never *ask* him any thing——much less to buy Streatham Park House and Grounds for 6000£ when *you* know, and Hammersley knows, (By his Books;) and *Windle* knows that the Repairs alone—Mead's Bills come to that Money, besides Pictures valued by Wilson at 2000£ long ago; and The unpaid for Furniture from Gillows. Friendless I am, sure enough—and hard pressed; and liable to have advantage taken—— but whilst I can walk home with my half Pound of Butter in my hand,—from

Market in the *Morning*, and find every agreeable House open to me in the *Evening*, I need not shrink from my present Situation; and probably it will not get worse.

What Hope is there of Count Lieven's payment? He is used to send his Money in by *now*; and what say Mr. Parnell and Mr. Penning to that Business? and who is the proposed Tenant?

I am sadly in the Dark at this Distance, and cannot afford to come nearer.

How is little Wife? Give her my Best Wishes. My Heart hopes She will do very well. She has at least/ the Prayers of/ H:L: Piozzi

Text Hyde Collection. *Address* Mr. Alexander Leak/ Streatham Park/ Surrey. *Postmark* 10 o'Clock MY 19 1815; 19 MY 19 1815.

TO MR. LEAK

> Bath begun Tuesday Evening
> 23d May 1815.

I wonder more at Leak's Compassionate Kindness, than at his hasty Expression when irritated beyond all bearing.——Endurance,——*Power* of Endurance—I should call it,——is a Gift from Heaven; and has been most mercifully bestowed upon poor H:L:P.—After a completely Sleepless Night, I was amusing Three Literary Friends in the Library; when Doctor Gibbes joining us, I told *him* the State of my Mind, and begged him to feel my Pulse——They were all Three much more affected than the Present Inhabitants of one of my Houses, and the future Inhabitants of the other would have been.

Who *will* be the Inhabitants of Streatham Park? does Lord Keith buy it for his Lady and Daughter?——and will he pay for it when he has bought it? and will he pay in Time for me to discharge my Debts?——Count Lieven does not do So——

I am now at his Mercy——The Offer was carried to Post yesterday: The Answer is an Honour I perhaps must wait for, but great is my Fear it will be more Honour than Advantage.

Walker of Denbigh wrote so *pressingly* I could not avoid in complying with *his* Demand: he has had his 29:13:0——Make no Reply but such as I can tell Mr. Salusbury; I am willing he should know how hard the Burden falls on me, and how *heavy*: but *you* do not need *Enemies* in Addition to the Plagues I have brought upon you; and 'tis better not to make him such.

Dear little Wifey will bring a seven Month's Baby no bigger than a Mouse if we worry her so——but if She does,——I can take my oath that Susanna Arabella Thrale was *not* carried seven Months in *my Inside;* and She is a Stout Woman now of 45 Years old. The King of England is a Seven Months Child, and see to what an Age he lives!

No Answers from Wales, neither from Brynbella nor from Gwayryrnog.

Yes, Yes, here come both the Answers Wendesday 24th. They advise me to sell and must never in future blame me for having sold——so 'tis all over, and you must take the enclosed to Mr. Dalgliesh.

Mean while think if I have not had Cause for *Irritation*——Bills from Broster the Chester Beau; for Books bought *for,* and left *at* Brynbella,——Two or Three Years ago. I know your Sentiments on that Subject——Poor old Jacob Weston is a Contrast——he sends Leverets and Rabbits and Enquiries perpetually. I hope I pacified (by Promise of Payment) *Mr. Lionel Thompson,* for whom I had always a Sort of Partiality——so God bless you and Adieu. My Fingers will be steadier when I have had Lord Keith's Answer.

Give my Love to your Wife and assure her that her Body suffers little less than does the Mind of/ Hers and Yours/ H:L:P.

Salusbury objects to my taking an *Annuity:* is not he even comically in the right?

Text Hyde Collection. *Address* Mr. Alexander Leak/ Streatham Park/ Surrey. *Postmark* 10 o'Clock MY 25 1815; 25 MY 25 1815.

To ANN LEAK

written Saturday 27th
will be sent Sunday 28th: May 1815.

I am much relieved by hearing you go *safely on* Dear Leak—and wonder not a little when The Time is to come, that we shall all be *out of our Pain.*

My Friends Sir James Fellowes and young Mr. Williams of Bodylwyddan will I hope come and See Streatham Park——while it is Yet mine——but since Mr. Dalgliesh named Lady Keith in his last Letter, I have less unwillingly laid the whole——without Reserve——at *her* Feet;[1] and hope She will not *kick it away.*

I have perhaps foolishly set my heart on a Small house in Gay Street, smaller than this, at exactly *Twice* the Rent;[2] but the Situation is more than *Twice* as good, The Coming-In and Staircase *beautiful;* My Bed Chamber as handsome, and *larger* than that at *home*——meaning foolishly again,—Streatham Park. The Furniture quite elegant, and the Prospect from my Window upstairs, and from the Drawing-Room under my Bed Chamber—truly *delightful.*

No spare Bed however; nor no Parlour but the Spacious Eating Room where Indeed I shall be glad to give my Library Friends who have contributed so much to my Comfort——a Bit of Fish and a Glass of Wine now and Then.[3]

The Drawing Room has folding Doors and a dainty nice little Reading and Writing Room—*to The Street* behind it.

Now if I *buy the Lease* I must pay 130£ o'Year Rent, *besides* for this sweet pretty Nut Shell: The People *here* say I had better give the 300£ per Annum for Three Years *certain,* and see how I like it *then.*

My Bed Chamber has seized on my own Imagination, and on that of Bessy Jones——hers communicates with it, so that She can hear if I stir or move.

The Kitchen no Rarety.—But a good Garden and Key out to the Crescent Fields, whence I am but a Step from Mrs. Lutwyche's, Lady Willoughby's or Mrs. Holroyd's.[4]

Your Husband has I dare say often noticed the House, No. 8 in Gay Street; with an Ornamented Front unlike its Fellows and a Bow Window *back* to the Country.[5]

Callan and Booth are the Proprietors for 9 Years[6]—People that Leak used to buy old China of——for me——when We had Money to fling away. They live here in Westgate Street, and I hope do *not* know how much I like their house.

Sunday 28:

Just come sick from Church—and have lost my best Lace Veil in the Street [and] find a Letter on my Table from Windle asking me in Lord's Keith's Name and his Attorney's——to be more *explicit* in describing my *Offer*: whether it means to give up the Pictures——and Davies and Parsons's 50£ o'Year or no.[7] Dear Mr. Windle never knew of the 50£ o'Year:—I begged him to Manage *his best for me:* but remembering *Your Advice*, requested him not to let that part us. They will perhaps make me some trifling Compensation.

Call on Mr. Windle some Day, and get a Talk with Him, and let me know his real Mind.

This Part of my Letter is to your Husband whose I am very sincerely as/ Yours/ H:L:P.

They are to have Pictures and Bronzes and *everything* to be sure, The House and its *Contents.*

Text Hyde Collection. *Address* Mrs. Leak/ Streatham Park/ Surrey. *Postmark* BATH MY 28 1815; 10 o'Clock MY 29 1815.

1. On 22 May HLP recorded in her "Pocket Book" that she sent an "Offer to Lord Keith through Mr. Dalgleish"; she "repeated [the] offer to Dalgleish enclosed to Leak" two days later.
    For Robert Dalgleish, see HLP to JSPS, 24 [-26] April 1813, n. 6.
2. HLP was to sign the lease for 8 Gay Street on 22 June 1816. See her "Pocket Book" for 1816 (Columbia University Library). For a photograph of the exterior of the house as it appears now, see John Tearle, *Mrs. Piozzi's Tall Young Beau, William Augustus Conway* (Rutherford, NJ: Fairleigh Dickinson University Press, 1991), 59.
3. The friends she usually met at John Upham's bookstore and circulating library, Lower Walks, Bath.
4. Mary Lutwyche of the Marlborough Buildings, at the west end of the Royal Crescent; Priscilla, Lady Willoughby de Eresby of 30 Royal Crescent; Sarah Martha Holroyd of 3 Queen's Parade (see HLP to PSP, 7 March [1803], n. 1). The addresses of the three ladies represented Walcot parish at its most fashionable.
5. Designed by John Wood (1704–54), 8 Gay Street, "called 'The Carved House' . . . had a different and unusually elaborate treatment on the ground and first floors." See Charles Robertson, *Bath: An Architectural Guide* (London: Faber and Faber, 1975), 64.
6. In *Robbins's Bath Directory* (1800) and the *New Bath Directory* (1812), Callan and Booth are listed as cabinet makers and brokers at 16 Westgate Street. By 1819 (*Gye's Bath Directory*) the business was conducted by their wives.
7. For RD and John Parsons, who rented Streatham land from HLP, see HLP to RD, 7 November 1813.

TO LADY WILLIAMS

Bath Thursday
June 15th. 1815.

My dearest Lady Williams
is excessively kind and her Letter quite delightful; It would be droll enough
to come and live so as you describe, for Two or Three Months next Summer,
but what Plate and Linen and China would They find me? for my poor little
Store must be left here at my Winter Residence;—and I suppose my real Possessions at Streatham Park must all be sold to my Daughters if I am so urged and
forced to part with them.—Dear Salusbury and Doctor Myddelton—who saw
that Place when he was in Town, do nothing but press me to get rid of it—and
a Neighbour in the Village of Streatham wrote to me Two Months ago or more,
to say that if I would offer it to Lord Keith *he* would purchase for 6000£ the Sum
Dr. Myddelton valued it at.—

The Valuation was certainly *hasty;*—but since they were all so warm in the
Cause—*I did offer it*—and received nothing for my Offer but Silent Neglect. Why
good Gracious! The very *Repairs* have stood me in more Money than *that* besides
the Furniture all new and beautiful, and——my Life (which they are shortening
among them) in the Estate.

Meanwhile Leak who lives there, says, The Gardens &c. *do* make no adequate
Return; and that the House and Estate are Taxed so high with Tythes &c. and
Hothouses and Greenhouses—and *Out* Houses of all sorts, that it will be a
Millstone round my Neck to ruin me: and *He,* and everybody is wishing me
well rid on't. So if they will purchase—*let them:* but the Suspense would be
dreadful, if these dear Bath People did not comfort me, and amuse me as they *do.*

Sir Nathaniel Wraxall is got in a fine Scrape with his entertaining Book, but
it sells the better; and will I hope pay the Expences of his Law Suit with Count
Woronzoff. I do fancy you will be diverted with the Stories it contains—many
of which passed under my own Eyes.[1] The favourite Novel is Discipline,[2] but
Guy Mannering has a great deal of Merit.[3]

Miss Williams's Health was much mended by the Sight of her Niece and
Nephew. Mrs. Hughes of Kinmel will surely not be perswaded to marry again—
She must be 70 Years old.[4] The Changes in Your Ladyship's Neighbourhood are
numerous indeed, and the Loss of Grwych a great one.

Our Brynbella Folks are in much Care for that Mr. Leicester, They best know
why:[5]—If any Income died with him it is bad indeed, because there are Nine
Children, but I know not what they were living on before—If upon *Sir John*[6]—
he is no particular Loss—10 People are easier kept than 11.

Mrs. Mostyn always loved France and French Fashions. The Expectations of
our Talkers and Tellers run high indeed, and we are all jostling each other to
get sight of the *now* empty Newspapers; *hoping* these Allies may strike the first
strike;[7] and *fearing* lest Buonaparte should get before hand with them.

Has Your Ladyship seen any of the very pale Pink Candles?—beautiful in
their light Tint of the very faintest possible Red?—I am told they are composed

of *Human Fat* meaning human Flesh converted to a fatty Substance by putting it in running Water—and that—not being able to Manufacture it up to the Brilliant Whiteness required from Spermaceti; they give it this Pink Cast, and sell the Candles *cheap*. Is not this a new-fashioned Method of *Illuminating* one another.[8] I think dear Sir John will laugh, and Miss Emma will shudder—but we learned it from the French; who at Ostend have salted down a Dozen Hanoverians *for Winter Store*. Oh Me! what a World does this grow! but I shall be the less discontented to leave it.

Mrs. Salusbury is to lay down her burthen at Chester they tell me; Indeed that charming Mr. Rowlands is deservedly a Favourite with every one[9]——I wish pretty Mrs. Pennant's Case were in *his Power*—how is the young 'Squire David?—I heard he was very Nervous.—[10]

Poor Mrs. Wynne of Garthuin is here, and very agreeable—and her Husband *seems* to ail nothing—but I suppose he is on the Invalid List: his Mother not altered at all.[11]—Mrs. Stothard of St. Asaph was delighted with her Frisk; had they said She meant to return so soon, Your Ladyship would have had an earlier Account of yours and Dear Sir John's ever obliged and Faithful H: L: P.

Does dear Mr. Williams go abroad or no?—He must mind what he eats and drinks.

The Majendies are all charming,[12] and good Reports go before your new bishop.[13]

Did you ever steep your Hands in hot Grains? hot as you could bear them? I have heard it strongly recommended.

Mr. and Mrs. Willet have a pretty little Place here, and hope to get out of their Penance in Seven Years: A long Time to look forward to, even for the Young and Gay.[14]—

The Two Tureens are Very fine; We brought them home from Dresden.—[15]

Mr. Williams will shew you the Intercepted Letter from Bath—a Thing much admired: it had been thro' 3 Editions, and is now out of Print—very kind it is to Your Ladyships poor H: L: P.

Adieu!——I give but 3 Guineas o'Week *where I am*.

Text Ry. 4 (1812–18). *Address* Lady Williams/ Bodylwyddan/ near Denbigh/ North Wales. *Postmark* JU 15 <1815>.

1. Wraxall's *Historical Memoirs of my own Time . . . from 1772 to 1784*, 2 vols. (London: Cadell and Davies, 1815) had appeared on 14 April and in a second edition by June. Shortly after publication, General Count Simon, or Semen Romanovíc Voroncov (1744–1832), Russian ambassador to the Court of St. James's, brought Wraxall before the Court of King's Bench on charges of libel. In his book, Wraxall credited Voroncov with the imputation that Catherine II had ordered the poisoning of George III's niece, Augusta Carolina Frederica Louise (1764–88), Princess of Württemberg. This imputation helped to exonerate the Princess' husband, Friedrich who on 18 May 1797 married the Princess Royal of England.

The Court of King's Bench found Wraxall guilty and sentenced him to a fine of £500 and a six-month prison term. The latter had been cut in half through the intervention of the Prince Regent, who had been persuaded by the Russian ambassador that his honor had been satisfied. The objectionable passages were expunged from the second edition. See the *Edinburgh Review*, 25 (1815):178–

220; *AR*, "Appendix to the Chronicle," 57 (1815):290–93, and 74 (1832):208–9; the *Morning Post*, 2 September 1816.

For those events that Wraxall reported and "which passed under [HLP's] Eyes," see her marginalia in the *Memoirs*, cited by Hayward, 2:89–122.

For the marriage of the Princess Royal to Friedrich Wilhelm Karl of Württemberg, see HLP to the Ladies of the Williams Family, 3 May 1797.

2. [Mary Brunton], *Discipline: a novel*. By the author of "Self-control," 3 vols. (1814). By 1815 it had reached a third edition.

3. [Sir Walter Scott], *Guy Mannering; or, The Astrologer*. By the author of "Waverley," 3 vols. (Edinburgh: Printed by J. Ballyntine and Co. for Longman, Hurst, Rees, Orme, and Brown, London, etc., 1815).

4. The Reverend Edward Hughes of Kinmel Park had died on 1 June. His wife, Mary, now seventy-two, remained a widow until her death in 1835. For the Hugheses, see HLP to LC, 21 April 1800, n. 9.

5. Charles Leicester (1766–1815) was a son of the fourth baronet of Tabley House, Cheshire. He had died in London, leaving nine children. In 1798 he had taken as his second wife Mrs. Pemberton's sister, Louisa Harriet, née Smythe (ca. 1774–1862). See George Ormerod and Thomas Helsby, 1:626.

6. For Sir John Fleming Leicester, see HLP to LC, 4 August 1798, n. 9.

7. Even as HLP was writing this, Napoleon surprised the Allied forces mobilizing on the Belgian border. On 15 June the Armée du Nord attacked Wellington and Blücher at Charleroi and began the chain of events that culminated at Waterloo on 18 June. News of some of this activity reached England only on 22 June with the publication of a *London Gazette Extraordinary*. See *GM* 85, pt. 1 (1815):357–58, 627–29.

8. Writing about *Farthing Candles* in a "Commonplace Book" entry dated 1815, HLP says: "Well! my Candles are better sure *(in a litteral Sense)* than these fine Pink-coloured Spermaceti ones sold in the Shops; which I am now told are composed of Human Fat;—Human Flesh I should Say: exposed to a quick running Stream, which in due Time turns it to a Substance making excellent Candles, but as the Manufacturers cannot get them to wear the finer White Hue we are accustomed to admire in Spermaceti, They give them this Elegant but Artificial Colouring of a beautiful pale Pink. "A famous Method *indeed* of *Illuminating* each other; and leads me to be less incredulous of the Tale told concerning a French Innkeeper at Ostend who salted down some dead Hanoverians this Summer, for Winter's Use!!"

9. John Rowland (fl. 1785–1841), surgeon and accoucheur of Chester, and a member of the Royal College of Surgeons of London.

10. It is difficult to know if young David Pennant was "Nervous" because of his mother's illness, which she survived, or because of his studies at Christ Church, Oxford, which he began in January 1814.

11. Letitia, née Stanley (1776–1832) was the wife of Robert William Wynne (d. 1842) of Garthewin, a lieutenant colonel in the Denbighshire militia. His widowed mother was Elizabeth, née Dymock (ca. 1741–1816).

12. For Henry William Majendie and his wife, Anne, see HLP to JSPS, 27 September 1812, n. 13.

13. A Cantabrigian, John Luxmoore (1756–1830), D.D. (1795) had recently been translated from the bishopric of Hereford (1808–15) to that of St. Asaph.

14. John Willett Willett (ca. 1744–1815) of Merley House, Dorset, and Upper Park Street, Bath, and his second wife, Frances, née Wilson, whom he had married in 1805. See P.R.O., Prob. 11/1575/629 for Willett's will, proved 20 December 1815; for his marriage, *GM* 75, pt. 2 (1805):676; John Hutchins, *The History and Antiquities of the County of Dorset*, corr. William Shipp and James W. Hodson, 4 vols. (Westminster: John Bowyer Nichols and Son, 1861–73), 3:306, 310, 311.

15. The two soup tureens with covers and stands that were to be sold on 10 May 1816, the third day of the Streatham Park auction, as lots 5 and 19.

TO SIR JAMES FELLOWES

Sunday
18th June 1815.

My Dear Sir James Fellowes,
   Left me but ill that Saturday Morning, and I have never been very well since. Cramps and Pains all over the Epigastric Region which our Ladies call Spasms, and the Spaniards Flatos——I finished your Book notwithstanding,[1] 'till it came to the Nuns' Part;[2] and then made me my own Dissertation. Apropos your charming sister tells me that I may send heavy Pacquets by this Conveyance, and so I will too——but if you will read Faber's last pamphlet——a half-crown work, 76 Pages only,[3] you will see that it is France not Buonaparte——except as Agent for her——against whom the Prophecies appear to present Commentators, as originally directed: and I have of late years been inclined to think with them, tho' bred in a different School.[4]
   Miss Fellowes followed me to the Play last night with your kind Friendly Letter[5]——how good you all are to poor H. L. P. I must not complain with so much reason to be thankful, but you remember the Italian Proverb:—[6]

Aspettare, e non venire,	To waste whole Days in vain expecting,
Stare in Letto e non dormire,	Consume the Night in sad reflecting,
Servir amici, e non gradire,	On friends forgetful or neglecting,
Son tre Cose a far morire.	Must of all ills be most dejecting.

I never could translate those Lines tolerably till this Streatham Business was pending——as we have learned to call it from the Lawyers——but the ladies have taught me.
   I am delighted that you have seen the Park and my Mother's incomparable Likeness: when I thought myself dying last Week, I tied up your Paper in her Spanish Bible and gave it my Maid to take care of for you. She, like yourself, was a Proficient in all languages, and like you prefer'd la Verdadera Castellana—— a Bible by Cyprian de Valera is the only thing I possess worthy your acceptance by which you may remember me.[7]
   The portraits in the Library are alive with strong Resemblance all of them—— and I——only am left a poor dejected solitary thing, like the Old Woman in Goldsmith's *Deserted Village*.[8]
   Leak is an excellent Creature: You know I am much beloved by my servants, old Jacob Weston and Young Betsy Jones——We used to call Leak the General down in Wales——General Lake; because he conducted all things, and made that Estate twice the Place it was when he came to it——but Salusbury and he never liked one another.
   Write to me, Dear Sir, you shall know whether I am to live in this Fret-work or get into a plain Place——before I know it myself; Leak shall call and inform you——but when you have Leisure send me a Letter——because if in the Dark Flint there does lie a spark of concealed Fire, it will starve there, without the

polished Steel strikes it out[9]——and send the Retrospection in Boards from Stockdale, That I may correct the gross and numerous Mistakes. I believe at my Heart that in the 1000 Pages there are more than 1000 Errors[10]——May your Book have better Fortune! I was going to say how I hated Scotsmen and McGregors in particular,[11] when comes a Letter from that dear generous Mr. Dalgleish—wishing to offer to lend me Money——Astonishing! I really never spent six evenings in his Company and shall I be low-spirited when endued by God Almighty's peculiar Mercy with Power to endure such Enmity——and excite such Friendship as in this extraordinary Year 1815——have been offered to dear Sir James Fellowes's obliged and grateful./ H. L. Piozzi.

Leak is selling out his own Stock now to pay my Taxes—Poor Thing![12] I do hope Sir James F. will fancy some of the articles and save from hands of the profane. Perhaps the family will be zealous to secure some Things—— perhaps an Offer will arrive of taking the *Tout Ensemble*. People see me live as I do and think I mean a long Continuance in the same Course of Wretchedness——but I am the more Tired of it, as I see so little Pleasure given to those who should render my situation more Comfortable by at least affected Assiduity——but neither real daughter nor adopted Son have ever dropt a hint as if I was living beneath myself——only Salusbury just said once, Why did I not keep a man servant? My Reply was——because I could not afford it? This Sale will make me rich in my old Age; and I see everybody selling, so why should not I their Example pursue, and better my Fortune as other Folk do?

Text Broadley, 55–58. *Address* Sir James Fellowes at Lord Gwydir's, Whitehall.

1. *Reports of the Pestilential Disorder of Andalusia, which appeared at Cadiz in the Years 1800, 1804, 1810 and 1813; with a detailed account of that fatal epidemic . . . at Gibraltar, during the autumnal months of 1804 . . .* (London: Longman, Hurst, Rees, Orme, and Browne, 1815).

2. In the appendix (p. 421 n.) dealing with the victims of the plague in Seville, JF enumerates "912 nuns" among the 42,463 females stricken.

3. *Remarks on the Effusion of the Fifth Apocalyptic Vial, And the Late Extraordinary Restoration of the Imperial Revolutionary Government of France: To which Is Added a Critical Examination of Mr. Frere's Combined View of Daniel, Esdras, and St. John* (London: F. C. and J. Rivington, 1815). The pamphlet, published in June, sold for 2s. 6d.

4. Faber concentrates largely on the Book of Revelation to anticipate events in Napoleonic France, adding a *caveat* (pp. 4–5):
"Let me not . . . be here misunderstood as asserting, that, because the transfer [of imperial power] took place during the reign of Napoleon Buonapartè, that *single individual* henceforth becomes the exclusive scope of prophecy until the awful retributory day of Armageddon. He is no further the subject of it, than, as his actions form a *part* of the *general* actions. . . . Prophecy does not so much treat of *individuals*, as of *communities*. . . . It matters little, whether Robespierre, or Buonapartè, or any other ruffian . . . be for a season at the head of affairs; the *revolutionary government* . . . is alone the subject of prophecy."

5. At the Theatre Royal, Bath, HLP saw as the main piece *The Fortune of War. A comic Piece in two Acts*, translated from the French by James Kenney, which had been first performed at the Covent Garden on 17 May. See the *Bath Chronicle*, 15 June.

6. As cited by Giordano Bruno, in his *Candelario*, 4.1 (S. vittoria Coq.). See HLP's "Commonplace Book."

7. Cyprian (Cipriano) de Valera (ca. 1532–1625) was once a Sevillian monk who, emigrating to England, became a Fellow at both Oxford and Cambridge. Thereupon he began his twenty-four year project of revising Casiodoro de Reina's version of the Spanish Bible. The result, known as "C. de Valera's Version," was published in Amsterdam in 1602.

8. The "wretched matron" is described in lines 131–36: "She only left of all the harmless train, / The sad historian of the pensive plain."

9. HLP's variation on the proverb "in the coldest flint there is fire." See, e.g., *Timon of Athens*, 1.1.22–23; *Rambler* 25.

10. For an account of the errors in *Retrospection,* see HLP to Q, 21 June 1801.

11. HLP implies the famous act of the Scottish parliament (3 April 1603) by which it was ordered that the name of McGregor be abolished forever. See *Boswell's Johnson,* 5:127–28, n. 3; SJ's "Life of Mallet," *English Poets,* 3:400 and n. 2.

12. On 15 June HLP wrote in her "Pocket Book": "Received a querulous Letter from Leak—he is selling out his *own* Stock to pay my Taxes."

TO HARRIET MARIA SALUSBURY

Bath
Wednesday [5:] July [1815][1]

Your Letter my lovely H:M:S. was a very obliging one—I am glad you are fond of Brynbella, and find the Place pleasing to you:—Doctor Cumming was always friendly to me, it is comfortable to think he is so happy.

Dear Salusbury did behave very sweetly to some People—of the name of Batley I *think,* but am not sure.[2] They were delighted with his Politeness however;—and *their* Friends—will be the more civil to me in Consequence. One never knows how far a Chain of good humoured or ill-humoured Conduct can extend.

The high Bonnet (in your Letter,) for I never saw one any where else, except once in London for a Joke;—made me laugh: pushing things to such extremes must always be comical.——The short Petticoats and Flesh-Coloured Legs I *have* seen, but they are dying off;[3] our grave Men would not permit their Wives and Daughters to go any further with that Frolick.

You are rioting away now in nice Bread and Butter and Milk and Cream at Condover Park:—I never saw them in such Perfection as there. Grass will be growing scarce again except at Condover very soon however—The Sun has such Power. I hope you keep yourself from being Tanned, for certainly Brynbella is a famous Place for tearing a good Complexion to pieces—the Sea Air is so very drying. The Babies at Gwaynnynog meantime defy all Weathers: Their Skins are the finest I ever saw.[4] Our Town here is hot and dusty, I seldom go into it; The River side is much more alluring: but when the Mails come in, People run to hear what has happened, and every body looked displeased this Morning to think that Buonaparte has escaped again,—Although no one took Care to keep him from escaping.[5] Your Father and Husband are the least interested in Public Affairs of any Friend or Acquaintance I have in the World. How they would laugh to see blinking Old Men, and tottering old Women——dispute for a Newspaper at the Libraries; or Struggle in the Street for a Sight of what is written in great Letters at the Booksellers Doors!! They would Think the Folks mad, and mad indeed We are.

Mr. Henry Burton would have pleased his Fancy however had he been of our

Water Party——for we got out at Claverton tell him, and saw the old House where he went to School:[6] and poor Graves's pretty Church all new done up,—[7]and the great Ralph Allen's Tomb &c.:[8] Some of our Company were so charmed with the Situation, they resolved on being buried in Clavertons Churchyard——a complete Flower Garden:—*I said I was engaged to Dymerchion.*

These troublesome and officious Business-Makers at Streatham Park will send me thither before I'm wanted: with their Tenants and their Purchasers, and their Plagues. I was quiet enough till they disturbed my Retirement with Hopes and Fears, and Letters and Vexation. I wish they had let me alone——but they never did *that* till now, that I want to hear how all is settled; and now the Post passes the Door.

Be happy whilst you can My Dear, and assure yourself that Age is nought but Sorrow——I amuse myself indeed with the Reading Wraxall's *Memoires* of my own Time and his[9]——Salusbury remembers my Visits to Sir Nathaniel Wraxall's Lady; and my making him laugh when we met, by showing him how the Father and his Son kicked one another's Shins under the Table,—hoping I did not see—at the Tea-Party. Oh pray tell him that Mr. Hopkins Northey and his Wife, with whom we made Acquaintance the same Year, are parted—and the Lady means to apply to her Cousin Duke Wellington for Reparation of her Wrongs real or Supposed.[10]

Farewell! and love your Husband, and keep yourselves happy *in* Yourselves. When that's over, All's over. Salusbury says you know that Friendships are false, and so I'm sure they are; but what else remains for his and your poor Affectionate/ H: L: P?

Give my best to Mr. Smythe Owen——I never comprehend whether Papa and Mama are at Condover or Ryton[11]—They have my best Regards and good Wishes.

Text Ry. 592.36. *Address* Mrs. Salusbury/ Condover Park/ near/ Shrewsbury. *Postmark* BATH 6 JY < >.

1. Postmarked "6 JY < >," the letter can be dated 5 July, a Wednesday, in 1815; see e.g., Whitbread's suicide; Louis XVIII's second restoration.
2. HLP refers to a Salopian family named Bather of Meole Brace; specifically, to Martha Hannah, née Halifax (d. 30 August 1824), the widow of John Bather (1751–1796), vicar of Meole Brace, and their son John (1781–1839), a barrister of Lincoln's Inn, who was infatuated with HMP before her marriage. See also HLP to JSPS, 9–10 November 1816, n. 13.
3. See HLP to PSP, 27 March 1798.
4. The Myddelton babies: Mary Anne Charlotte (1800–1861), Charlotte Maria (1802–20), Louisa Dorothea (1804–23), Henrietta Augusta (1807–66), and Hugh (1811–23).
5. After his defeat at Waterloo on 18 June, Napoleon, along with a small staff, was for a while virtually invisible to the Allies. On 8 July *The Times* queried: "The first question which suggested itself to every one was what is become of the prime cause of all these evils? Where is the Arch-Rebel Buonaparte?"
6. Henry Burton (1775–1831), a Salopian, had been educated at Richard Graves's school at Claverton and then at St. John's College, Cambridge. Ordained a priest in 1779, he held the vicarates of Madeley (1786–1831), Atcham (1799–1831), Holy Cross and St. Giles's, Shrewsbury (1804–25), all in Salop.
7. HLP refers to the small church of St. Mary, which went through a series of restorations in

the nineteenth century. As a matter of fact, it was overrestored so that it lost its historic interest. The wall paintings of St. Michael and the Crucifixion on the south wall were erased during a restoration. Noteworthy in the church is "the taking of Christ" (north transept), an early fourteenth-century panel; an ogee arch with heads in the spandrels; and a chalice and cover, ca. 1572. East of the church stood the manor house, built ca. 1580. What survives are the spectacular terraces, with openwork panels, leading down to the main road. The gate-piers are topped by openwork obelisks.

8. Ralph Allen died 29 June 1764. An M.I. to his memory was placed in the south aisle of the Bathampton church. His remains were buried in the churchyard of Claverton. The tomb is a square structure with three arches on each side and crowned by a large vaulted pyramid.

9. HLP and JSPS met Nathaniel William and Jane Wraxall in March 1811. See her letter to JSPS, 30 March 1811. For Wraxall's *Memoirs*, see HLP to SL, 21 July [1789], n. 4.

10. For William Richard Hopkins Northey, see HLP to TSW, 28 March 1811, n. 10. Northey had married Anne Elizabeth, née Fortescue (d. 1864), a granddaughter of Elizabeth Fortescue, née Wellesley (i.e., Wellington's aunt). The young couple remained married and had six children.

11. A hamlet on the river Worf in Salop.

TO EDWARD WILLIAM SMYTHE OWEN

[Bath]
[9: July 1815].[1]

My Dear Sir

As you have honoured me with Your Friendship and were kind enough to mention the Subject in Your last Letter—I take the very great Liberty of enclosing these Letters to *You* because your charming Sister said She and Salusbury were going to Condover, in the last I received from Brynbella.

You will see that every Expectation of Purchasers at Streatham Park is completely over: and I should have been better prepared for the Disappointment, had I understood—that one Party was endeavouring to buy with Money from the other Party——The Solicitor Mr. Windle however always assuring me—and truly—that the Price was Not the Cause of Objection, I went on hoping, and expecting—and talking of a good House in Gay Street &c.—till Yesterday's Account from Lord Keith's Attorney sent from Him,—(Robinson)[2] to Mr. Windle; gave me the finishing Blow, and I am now in Treaty with a Tenant Mr. Anderdon the Bank Director—whose Name you see among the Subscribers of 200 Guineas to those who suffered at Waterloo.[3]

So they have had their Hoax—and I am where I was: and here is enough on a Subject so uninteresting, compared to the Wonders which salute one's Ears at every Street-End.

The Report of Two Great Men sent to the tower of London[4] makes us even forget Kean's acting,[5] and Whitbread's Suicide;[6] which two Articles occupied us all Yesterday, nor can a House burned down and two valuable Lives lost in the Fire, which cannot be called extinguished in *Union Street* here at Bath—[7] divert our Attention from Paris captured, Louis proclaimed again,[8] and Two Great Men—God knows who—sent to the Tower.

If Salusbury is gone to Chester or any where You will convey the enclosed to him, in kindness to her who is ever very Sincerely/ Dear Sir/ Your faithful Servant/ H: L: Piozzi.

Pray present my best Regards to all My Friends round the Wrekin[9]—particularly Mr. and Mrs. Pemberton and Miss Fanny,[10] and Mr. R. Pemberton and his agreable Son.[11]

Text Ry. 533.33. *Address* Edward William Smythe Owen Esq./ Condover Park/ near/ Shrewsbury. *Postmark* BATH 9 JY 9 181[5].

1. Postmarked 9 JY 181< >.
2. For Edmund Robinson, the attorney, see HLP to JSPS, 11 April 1813, n. 11.
3. For John Proctor Anderdon, see HLP to JSPS, 28 April 1813, n. 3. Anderdon not only subscribed to the Waterloo fund, created to assist the wounded and the relatives of those killed in battle, but he also became a nominee to the committee for conducting the Waterloo subscription. See the *Courier,* 4 July; *The Times,* 5 July.
4. The unfounded "Report" stated what HLP noted in her "Pocket Book" on 9 July: "Lord Grey gone to the Tower." But even as one of the Opposition, he spent no time in the Tower nor did the other "Great" man at this time.
5. When Edmund Kean ended his engagement at Drury Lane on 4 July, he arrived at Bath for the first time to perform "Four of his principal Characters" between 8 and 15 July (*Bath Chronicle,* 6 July). HLP's "Pocket Book" shows that she saw three of his four performances: on 8 July Shylock; on 14 July Richard III; on 15 July Macbeth. She missed Othello on 13 July.
6. Samuel Whitbread (b. 1764, according to the "Cardington Baptismal Register," C.R.O., Bedfordshire) was M.P. for Bedford (1790–1815). On 6 July he cut his throat at his London home, 35 Dover Street. As a leading Opposition spokesman in Parliament, he suffered a bout of depression in the late spring, believing that his political career was over. On 26 May, e.g., he delivered a vehement but unsuccessful attack on the Second Treaty of Paris, the Quadruple Alliance, and the war (*The Times,* 27 May).
The coroner's jury declared that his suicide was provoked by "mental disquietude" caused by "the great mass of business, national and private" and by "a local pressure on the brain, discovered on dissection." See *AR,* "Chronicle," 57 (1815):127–28.
7. On 9 July, the premises of a Mr. Dimond, a hairdresser of 2 Union Street, caught fire. The chief fireman and a servant, who had returned to retrieve her possessions, were killed. See the *Bath and Cheltenham Gazette,* 12 July 1815.
8. Allied troops under Wellington and Blücher "occupied the Barriers of Paris on the 6th, and entered the city" the next day. See *GM* 85, pt. 2 (1815):75. Louis XVIII returned to the capital on 8 July.
9. Wrekin is a parliamentary district of Salop.
10. For Smythe Owen's half-sister Frances, see HLP to JSPS, 20 August 1808, n. 1.
11. The lawyer Robert Pemberton of Shrewsbury had an only son, Robert Norgrave (1791–1848). An Oxonian, he took clerical orders and in 1818 became rector of Church Stretton, Salop, where he remained the rest of his life.

TO CECILIA MOSTYN

Bath Thursday
12th: July 1815.

My dearest Cecilia

I take large Paper because I cannot write across as You do, though I read Your Writing in that Way very well.—The Pens &c. are all shocking bad, and *this* Stuff fit for nothing—but ones' Will. You are right enough in laughing at me for troubling Doctor Myddelton about my pecuniary Affairs; but Solemnly do I protest to you that not contented with volunteering his unsought Services—he all but *forced* them on me, and *what could I do?* He and a Neighbour of mine at

Streatham—Mr. Dalgliesh,[1] never let me rest all Winter till sometime in May they persecuted and perswaded me to offer Lord Keith my *long* Life and *large* Possessions for 6000 Pounds or Guineas—The latter as I remember. Then came Letters from Solicitors, and House-Agents, and Histories of Tenants turned away, and an infinite deal of Disturbance—till last Week came a Release from some of the Lawyers employed—saying Lord Keith knew nothing of the Place or its Value, and Mrs. Piozzi might do what She pleased with it.——So much for Facts; and I hope as mine Hostess Quickly says, *here be Truths.*[2]

Sir N. Wraxall's Book sells all the better for the Bustle made by Count Woronzoff—mine would not attract any such Notice I fear: My Patrons have been unlucky, not unkind; and Times are much changed with me since I could patronize any one. *Your* Arithmetic alone can make my Income 3000£ and *Your* Imagination alone, turn my wretched Habitation into a good House. My Income Is simply *this.*

	£
Interest of Money in the Consols—pd. in Jan: ------	700 = 0 = 0
Do. in the Reduced pd. in April ----------------------	180 = 0 = 0
Newton's Rent pd. in April----------------------------	180 = 0 = 0
Interest of Money in the Consols pd. July ------------	700 = 0 = 0
Do. in the Reduced pd. in Octr. ----------------------	180 = 0 = 0
Newton's Rent pd. in Novr. ---------------------------	180 = 0 = 0[3]
	2120 = 0 = 0

Out of this Income I am to pay Gillow and Mead		
now owing --	1500 = 0 = 0	
Ward, Windle, and Lonsdale[4]——Three People--	450 = 0 = 0	—not one House.[4]
Beside petty Debts scarcely less than ---------------	150 = 0 = 0	—at the least
	2100 = 0 = 0	Debt.

Taxes of Streatham Park forgotten.

And Whatever Surplus of Riches you can find me; must buy these Annuities and Mansions that you tell me of—till then I feel happy in not being Threatened (*as I have been*) with Arrests. Count Lieven did take Streatham Park, and did say he would pay me 600£ per Annum for it. He *has not paid,* and I cannot make him pay. He made me put in 10 or 12 Beds for his Family, which I must pay for; and because he did not take the Estate; forced me to keep Stewards, Gardiners, &c. at an immense Expence, beyond what the Ground produced. I shall now endeavour to let it for almost *anything*—and so it will go to *Ruin* again, if I don't get a *famous* Tenant. I have spent 6500£ on the *House* and Paling; 500£ more on recovering the Garden, Park &c. from Destruction; and making it—as every one

says now—a beautiful Place, inside and out. You saw it This Time last Year——
in its State of Improvement.

I hope once more *Here be Truths*.

Text Bowood Collection.

1. For Robert Dalgleish, see HLP to JSPS, 24[–26] April 1813, n. 6.
2. Spoken by Pompey, servant to Mistress Overdone, in *Measure for Measure*, 2.1.127, 133.
3. Thomas Newton, the tenant of Crowmarsh Farm; see HLP to John Gillon, 18 November 1799, n. 2.
4. William Lonsdale, a cabinetmaker, 7 Broad Street, Soho. For her long-standing debt to him, see HLP to AL, 13 December 1814.

TO ALEXANDER LEAK

Bath
Fryday 14: July 1815.

I write to Thank Leak for his less-agitating Letter than any I have received from him a long Time. That dear Mr. Dalgliesh behaves to me like a Brother. I have repaid his kindness with *Confidence*——What else has poor H: L: Piozzi to bestow?——and have assured him of my own good Spirits and Resolution to bear what God sends; and free myself as *soon*, but as *quietly* as I can.

You shall see me in a Poor-house, before you see my Streatham Possessions swept into an Auction Room: The Ladies shall not have that to say of me.

Meanwhile if Mr. Anderdon should take to the Place, and like it well enough to purchase my Life and the Contents of the House,—I would not refuse them to *Him*: and then he might cut down the Windows and do his own Way; and I should say like the Irish Poor—Long Life to your Honour, and your Honour's sweet face.

I knew the Breast would recover—how should it help recovering? Letting Matters alone is so good a Method! Your Wife will have better Health than ever She had—and what Nonsense it was to send all that back upon the Mass of Blood! but Providence withstood the Perverseness of the Physicians.

God Almighty will I feel certain, provide for you better than I could have done; and every *real* Friend I have will surely assist *you*. My Abilities are Small indeed, but shall be exerted to get our Accounts settled—*whilst I live*—and when I cease to do so, you will find yourself a Legatee.[1]

Old Jacob Weston is at the Greyhound Richmond, and will I dare say try to see Streatham Park once again.

My Desire is to see it in Mr. Anderdon's *Care* for Three Years at least;—and then if he pleases—in permanent Possession——God send he may like it well enough to buy.

I am so disposed to be a good *Hoper* that as Mrs. Dimond has invited me to her Box to see Mr. Kean tomorrow, I shall most assuredly go. You scarce can think how kind these dear Bath People are. If I were to win the Golden Prize in this Lottery—I would never spend my Winters out of Bath.[2]

Give my Love to your *little* Wife, and your *great* Boy.[3] Andrew leaves us next Week, which will lessen our Expences——Poor Bessy Jones has had more plague than comfort with him.—He must however take new Clothes, new Shirts, and a 5£ Note with him, or what will he *not* say to Mrs. Mostyn? who so oddly persists in my having an Independent 3000£ o'Year and a *fine House.*

It makes me laugh instead of crying: *so strange a Fancy.* Salusbury's Letters *only* complain of my Ill humour,[4] and he is the *only* Person who does complain of it. Give my best Regards to Sir James Fellowes, and assure him that in assisting *you* any way,—he will most oblige his Obedient Servant H: L: Piozzi.

Text Hyde Collection. *Address* Mr. Alexander Leak/ Streatham Park/ Surrey. *Postmark* 10 o'Clock <JY> 15 1815.

1. HLP left "to Mr. Alexander Leak one hundred pounds, to his Son Alexander Piozzi Leak one hundred pounds" (P.R.O., Prob. 11/1645/356, proved in London 22 June 1821).
2. The "Grand Golden Lottery," contracted by Richardson, Goodluck, and Co., was to begin drawing on 19 July for three main prizes of £40,000, £30,000, and £20,000, "besides 12,000 Guineas, which will be paid in Gold without Deduction (*Bath Herald,* 15 July 1815).
3. In her "Pocket Book" for 30 May, HLP recorded that AL's "Wife has brought a Boy"—Alexander Piozzi.
4. See, e.g., JSPS's letter to HLP, dated from Condover Park on 8 July (Ry. 591.3):
" . . . you seem so determined to misunderstand the meaning of my Letters that really I am quite at a loss how to express myself. It has been my grand object during the whole of this unpleasant business respecting Streatham to write such letters to you as I thought would prove to you my desire to assist you . . . —but how vain have all my hopes been——so far from thinking me your friend, you have considered my advice given from interested motives. . . . In short the kinder my letters have been, I have observed your answers to be more spiteful."

TO LADY WILLIAMS

Bath Sunday Evening
16: July 1815.

It was sweetly kind in my dear Lady Williams to write me such a long, such a *nice* Letter, expressing so much Desire too—of seeing me again. How far is your Marine Villa from Grwych? and how near to Abergeley?—It is monstrously high-prized.—The Hut I now inhabit stands me but in three Guineas o'Week; and I have no need of *Horses* or Carriage. Indeed I shall (if I take it for another Year certain) have the Place I am living in for *Two* Guineas o'Week 110£ per Annum instead of 150£. Mr. Williams knows it *is* a wretched Hut, but still 'tis Bath you know,—or close to it—and I should have expected a Welsh Cottage about the Same Price of those at Sidmouth, Devonshire, where no body thinks of giving more than Two Guineas and a half.

My dearest Lady's kind Head is upon *past* Times, when her now poor H: L: P—thought little of 3 Guineas the Week. A little Independant Spot however, where I could breathe my Native Air, and dip in the Sea, and visit my Young Friends in my Old Neighbourhood, and see Lady Williams very often—— has its Temptations; Meantime I cannot stir from this Place be it how it will till next July 1816 after *the Dividends* are paid; and God send me clear of Debt even *then*—for I much doubt it. So we will make no Bargains, and indulge no Hopes for a long while to come.

My own Family pretending an Inclination to buy my Life in old Streatham Park, and take the Furniture, Books, Pictures &c. giving me 6000£ at once—— made me believe I should pay all I owed, and have some Money loose for an Excursion—my Income being by that means set free. But after increasing my Lawyers bill with Letters &c. relative to This Transaction, here am I left worse than I was before; and if I do not get a good Tenant for that Place—it must infallibly eat me up. Mr. Williams can inform your Ladyship how large an Estab- lishment it requires——but I *do* hope Mr. Anderdon the Bank Director is going to inhabit it directly. Count Lieven never pays, nor can I make him. Lord bless me! They *did* say *He* had cut his own Throat at one Time, but it was only a Mistake. Mr. Whitbread's Suicide is a frightful Event—and strange Surmizes follow; the Party have however hushed all up, by saying how his Skull was Thickened.

I think all our Skulls are thickening for my own Part. What Folly it is in the Allied Sovereigns to foster those horrid Jacobins! and tye up Blucher's hand from giving them the Correction they so justly deserve[1]—but Indulgence always ends in Severity,[2] and the *next* Time they provoke us to arm against Them—I do think Paris will blaze. But we forget even Wellington and Blucher in our Bursts of Admiration when Mr. Kean appears. I have seen him now in Shylock, Macbeth, and Richard—and nothing can exceed the Applause he gains, or the Crouds that follow Him. There are so many new Devices to obtain Notice—we must not wonder if Faults are found in some of them. But old Macklin used to say[3]—The Treasurer of the House—is the best Critic; and if so, Kean is the best Actor. Our Theatre here is said to hold only 300£ and there was 309£ paid in at the Doors last Night—large Sums of Money turned away.[4] Miss Williams wished to be among us—but was wholly unable to bustle in such a Throng: her Wrists are sadly swelled—but her Spirits good:—I am convinced that Visit from her Niece and Nephew have done her all the Service possible, and when the pain is in her Hands and Arms,—The Head and Stomach are free. She is delighted at the Schemes of Pleasure offered to her Relations at Caerhèn, but seems anxious concerning the Health of the Youngest Son.[5] Your Ladyship has every Reason to account Yourself a happy Mother, and it is natural that I should rejoyce to hear Mrs. Mostyn is so. *She* will doubtless be one of the first to revisit France, which really will want some English Guineas to restore her Power——of flying at us again. As for Buonaparte his Part is not yet played out;[6] We shall hear of him when least expected—he will be on the Stage once more I doubt not: coming up a Trap Door like a Devil in a Dance. People said the other Night that Kean resembled him[7]—but I should expect more Grace and Dignity from *his* Military Habits:—for Expression of Cruelty and determined Unforgiving Spirit, either in

Duke of Wellington. Portrait attributed to Sir Thomas Lawrence, date unknown. (Reproduced by permission of the Henry E. Huntington Library and Art Gallery, San Marino, California.)

Eyes or Gestures;—I defy Fouché, Roederer, and Carnot to exceed our new favourite Actor.[8]

Your Ladyships Anecdotes, and Accounts of Letters from the Hills, are very welcome to me indeed, and exceedingly well worth attending to: I should never have known them but from you. Our Shropshire Friends are not communicative——The Advice—concerning an Event common to all, was wise and good: Will they follow it?

Dear Lady Williams, accept my Tenderest and most grateful Regards—and share them with kind Sir John. He was ever most Obliging and Friendly to his and to/ Your Ladyship's firmly attached/ H: L: Piozzi.

Compliments and Loves to the lovely young ones.

Mr. Williams's Admirers Lady Bellmore and her Sister[9]—have a cruel Loss in his departure.

Text Ry. 4 (1812–18). *Address* Lady Williams.

1. Louis XVIII on 8 July announced his new ministry, which included as minister of the interior the regicide Joseph Fouché (1759–1820), duc d'Otranto, or Otrante. *The Times* (12 July) consequently declared that "the Allies ought to insist on a policy of exclusion of the Jacobins. It is an insult to loyalty . . . to see the crime of regicide triumphant."

There was, moreover, no unity of opinion as to France's fate among the representatives in Paris of the Allies: the Russian, Prussian, and Austrian sovereigns, along with Castlereagh and Wellington as the British delegates. Thus, the British and the Russians advocated a period of conciliatory occupation. The Prussians, however, demanded that France cede territory while General Blücher argued further that "mistaken lenity has cost already . . . more than a hundred thousand of lives" and that the city be "blown up if the Parisians failed to pay a hundred million francs" (*Bath Herald*, 15 July).

2. For SJ on indulgence, see HLP to Q [21 June] 1801.

3. For Charles Macklin, see HLP to SL, 31 December 1785, n. 5.

4. According to Belville S. Penley, the Theatre-Royal at Beaufort Square "held between £250 and £300, but £200 was considered a very good house." See *The Bath Stage: A History of Dramatic Representations in Bath* (Bath: Bath Herald Office, 1892), p. 98. Period playbills for the theater show that seat prices were 5*s.* for boxes (reduced to 3*s.* after the third act of the main attraction), 3*s.* for the pit (likewise reduced to 2*s.*), and 1*s.* 6*d.* for the gallery (likewise reduced to 1*s.*) (Bath Reference Library, playbills from 1806 to 1820).

5. The younger son, Walter· Davies Griffith (1802–47), who was to enter the Royal Navy. For the Williams's continuing concern over the boy's health, see HLP to JSPS, 30 April 1820.

6. Although Napoleon had surrendered to Captain Frederick Maitland (1777–1839) on board H.M.S. *Bellerophon* on 15 July, the English public was not to learn of the event until 21 July "by means of a dispatch from Viscount Castlereagh, dated Paris, July 17, and published in a Gazette Extraordinary" (*Bath and Cheltenham Gazette,* 26 July 1815).

7. Both Kean and Napoleon were short, about five-and-a-half feet each. They were said to have large heads with classical features.

8. HLP refers to three revolutionaries: Joseph Fouché, Pierre-Louis Roederer (1754–1835), and Lazare-Nicholas-Marguerite Carnot. The last two became *pairs des Cent Jours.* For Carnot, see HLP to LC, 18 June 1804, and n. 3.

9. HLP refers to Juliana, née Butler (1783–1861), the wife of Somerset Lowry-Corry (1774–1841), second earl Belmore (1802). Her sister was either Sarah (d. 1839) or Anne (d. 1831).

TO ROBERT DALGLEISH

Bath
Sunday Morning
23: July 1815.

Dear Sir

My Letter did not *quite* answer, as I wished it; but Mr. Anderdon made me a very polite Reply—and I hope he will do me the Honour to call at Blake's Hotel, Jermyn Street, on Tuesday next—day after tomorrow, and settle every thing. I do long to see and converse with you about that Purchase-Business, which my Thoughts have hardly dismissed from a Notion of Possibility; I will have a clearing up of The Mist it is enveloped in: for this odd Uncertainty is a wretched Existence, and Every Body now is so bursting with Happiness about the Capture of Buonaparte, that no one is out of Fashion/ except Dear Mr. Dalgliesh's/ Much Obliged/ H: L: Piozzi.

Text National Library of Wales 13936C. *Address* Robert Dalgliesh Esq./ Streatham/ Surrey. *Postmark* BATH JY 23 1815; 10 o'Clock JY 24 1815.

TO SIR JAMES FELLOWES

Blake's Hotel
Monday July 31st *1815*.

My dear Sir James Fellowes's friendly Heart will feel pleased that the Spasms he drove away—returned no more: altho' you were really scarce out of the Street before I received a cold short Note from Mr. Merrik Hoare who married one of the Sisters, to say that Lord Keith—who married the other wished to decline purchasing: so here I am no whit nearer disposing of Streatham Park than when I sate still in Bath——Money spent, and nothing done——but Bills thronging in, every Hour. Mr. Ward[1] the Solicitor has sent his Demand of 116£:18:3 I think, for Expences concerning Salusbury's Marriage. I call that the *Felicity* Bill:

Those which produce nothing but Infelicity, all refer to Streatham of Course. But you ran away without your Epigram translated so much apropos.

> Créanciers! maudite Canaille,
> Commissaire, Huissiers et Recors;
> Vous aurez bien le Diable au Corps
> Si vous emportez la Muraille.[2]

> Creditors! Ye cursed Crew,
> Bailiffs, Blackguards, not a few;

Look well around, for here's my All:
You've left me nothing but this Wall,
And sure to give each Dev'l his Due
This Wall's too strong for them or You.

I must make the most of my House now they have left it on my Hands, must I not? *may* I not? and like my Countrymen at Waterloo—Sell my *Life* as dear as I can.[3]

Oh terque quaterque beati![4] Those who fell at the Battle of St. Jean, when compared to the Miseries of Cadiz and Xeres.[5] And Oh happy Sir James Fellowes! whose Book well disseminated will save us from these Horrors——or from Accumulation of them;[6] when the Cambridge Fever shall break out again among the Lincolnshire Fens, if we have unfavourable Seasons.

The best Years of *my* temporal Existence——I don't mean the happiest; but the best for Powers of Improvement, Observation &c., were past in what is now Park Street Southwark, but then—Deadman's Place; so called because of the Pest Houses which were Established there in the Great Plague of London.[7] From Clerks,—and *Black Guards not a few,* I learned there; that Long Lane, Kent Street, and one other Place of which the name has slipt my Memory—were exempt from Infection during the whole Time of General Sickness,[8] and that their Safety was imputed to its being the Residence of Tanners. I am however now convinced from your Book, that it was Seclusion, not *Tan* that preserved them.[9]

And do not Dear Sir despise Your Sibyl's Prediction: for that God's Judgments are abroad, it is in vain to deny; and tho' France will support the heaviest Weight of them till her Phial is run out; our Proximity, and fond Inclination to connect with her, may, and naturally *will* produce direful Effects in many Ways upon the Morals, the Purses, and the Health of Great Britain.

Do you observe that there is already a Pretender started to the Bourbon Throne?[10] You cannot, (as I can,) recollect in the very early Days of the Revolution, that Abbè Sieyes declared he had saved the *real Dauphin* from Robertspierre, substituted another Baby of equal age, to endure the fury of the Homicides.[11] Some of us believed the Tale, and some—the greater Number—laughed at those who *did* believe it——but an Intelligent Italian since dead, assured me that the last Pope—Braschi believed it; and marked the Youth in Consequence of that Belief, with a Fleur-de-Lys upon his Leg. Whether the young Man described in the Newspaper as teizing the Duchess d'Angoulesme,[12] is that Person or another: or whether some Fellow under the Influence of National Insanity *imagines* himself the Dauphin; he is likely enough to disturb them and divide their Friends. Such Times, by the Violence of Fermentation produce extraordinary Virtues; but your incomparable Don Diego Alvarez de la Fuente,[13] would never have had his Excellence of Character properly appreciated, had you not been the Man to hand his Fame down to Posterity——Æneas would have been forgotten but for Virgil.

I am not yet aware that any Suspicion of promoting Contagion during the fearful Moments you describe, lighted on the Jews:[14] The Propensity they shew to deal in Old Clothes makes it very likely that they should now and then propagate infectious Diseases among their Christian Persecutors—but I hope those Days are coming fast to an End; when France has been disposed of—— *Their Turn will come.*

You will find a kind Word or two for Them in the first Chapter of my 2d: Volume,[15] but *the last Chapter in the first Volume* is my favourite, and should be read before the short Dissertation on the Hebrews for Twenty Reasons.[16] I hope you like my Preface, and find it *modest enough,* tho' the Critics had no Mercy on my *Sauciness.*[17]

Well! now the rest of this Letter shall be like other People's Letters; and say how hot the Streets are, and how disagreeable London is in the Summer Months; and how sincerely happy I should have been to pass the next Six or Seven Weeks at Sidmouth, but that,——Oh such speeches are *not* like other Peoples Letters at all:——but that,—I have not (with an Income of 2000£ o'Year) five Pounds to spend on myself, So encumbered am I with Debts and Taxes.—

Leak says he must pay 40£ Property Tax now this Minute. He is a good Creature and will be a bitter loss to his poor Mistress whenever we part, altho' the keeping him and his Wife and his Child——is dreadful——Is it not?

Since however in Mental as in Bodily Plagues, Despondency brings on Ruin faster than it would come of itself——

> What yet remains? but well what's left to use,
> And keep Good humour still, whate'er we lose.[18]

Give my best Love to Dear Miss Fellowes, compliments to Mrs. Dorset if with you,[19] and true Regards to Your venerable and happy Parents, beseeching them all to remember that they have/ A true Servant in Dear Sir Your infinitely Obliged/ H: L: P.

The Battle with Anderdon will be fought tomorrow.—I make sure of losing the *Field*; My Generals are unskilful.

Direct Mrs. Piozzi Bath.

Text Hyde Collection. *Address* Sir James Fellowes.

1. For Joseph Ward, see HLP to Jonathan Sterns, or Stearns, 30 October 1790, n. 3.

2. HLP found the quotation in *Carpenteriana* [1790] in Garnier's collection of *Ana*, 7:184–85: The quotation is preceded by this statement:

"Le baron Descoutures, ayant appris que ses créanciers avoient obtenue une sentence contre lui, & qu'ils avoient dessein de faire exécuter ses meubles, les fit enlever une nuit, sans que personne s'en apperçût. Un huissier vint un jour après, & ne trouvant personne, il fit ouvrir la porte par un serrurier, en présence du commissaire: mais ils furent très-étonnés de ne voir que quatre murailles, sur une desquelles etoient écrit de quatre vers . . . " [HLP's quoted French lines follow].

3. A dispatch from Wellington estimated "between 12 and 13,000 British and Hanoverian non-commissioned officers and soldiers . . . killed, wounded, and missing" (*The Times,* 4 July 1815). Modern estimates of British total losses at Waterloo run to 15,000.

4. Virgil's *Aeneid,* 1.94.

5. The "Battle of St. Jean" is Waterloo.

JF's *Reports of the Pestilential Disorder* (p. 50) states that the plague at Cadiz in 1800 struck 48,688 persons, killing 7,292 between August and November. During the same year, the plague was responsible for nearly 10,000 deaths in a population of 35,000 at Xeres de la Frontera, a town near Cadiz (p. 440).

6. JF's book advocated quarantine, good ventilation, and cleanliness as methods for preventing and controlling the plague and other pestilential disorders that HLP feared all her life.

7. Deadman's Place, Bankside, later called Park Street, Borough Market, Southwark, was on the east side of the Thrale brewery, at the entrance to which stood the Thrales' townhouse. Although pest-houses were established during the bubonic plague of 1665, Deadman's Place was so named for having been a burial ground.

8. HLP's information is contradicted by Evelyn and Pepys, who maintained that the plague of 1665 swept through and killed many of the inhabitants of Kent Street. See Wheatley, 2:332.

9. In his book (pp. 440–43) JF describes a tannery near Xeres, where the thirty-eight tanners remained free of the contagion. Some people attributed their immunity to "the friction of the oil" with which they worked. But JF tended to believe that such immunity stemmed from the fact that the tannery "stood on an open area outside the town and [was] well ventilated."

10. The *Bath and Cheltenham Gazette* (26 July) tells of the arrival in London of a person "who insists that he is no less a personage than the Dauphin, who, according to all accounts, died in the Temple." Having applied for an interview with the duchesse d'Angoulême, the claimant was "refused on account of the want of such proofs as are thought necessary to support his extraordinary statement."

11. HLP mentions twice in *Thraliana* the myth that Sieyès had saved the Dauphin (2:1003, n. 6; 1006, n. 2).

12. The duchesse during the *Cent Jours* was to move between England and Louis' court in exile. In the first place she worked to gain support for the royalist court but in the latter place—according to rumor—she tried to dissociate herself from her royal uncle, who remained indifferent to most things except court protocol and his own prerogative. See Marie-Antoine, vicomte de Reiset, *Souvenirs du lieutenant-général, vicomte de Reiset*, 3 vols. (Paris: C. Lévy, ca. 1899-[1902]), 3:195–97.

13. In his *Reports* (pp. 316–22), JF told of the selfless work of a Spanish physician, Don Tadeo Lafuente, inspector of public health in the army camp at Gibraltar, who personally attended the sick during the fever contagions of 1804, 1811, and 1812, and who effected "wonderful cures" of yellow fever "by the early administration of bark . . . in much larger quantities than were ever . . . given before."

14. Discussing the progress of the yellow fever contagion in Gibraltar in 1804, JF writes (pp. 108–9) that the Jews, "who were very numerous in Gibraltar . . . were not generally attacked by the prevailing disorder until after the 18th of September, the day of atonement. . . . " Previously, "the Jews had cautiously kept to their own families at home, and not one of them was . . . ill of the prevailing disorder." But their congregating in their synagogues on the feast day and admitting "strangers amongst them" led to "the propagation of the malady, and afterwards occasioned" a high mortality rate.

15. HLP writes in *Retrospection* (2:10–12) of "that selected people, who, on the first grand muster of mankind, stood foremost in the ranks of Humanity. . . . He who has seen a Jew, has seen a gentleman, if ancestry can make him such, unaided by education."

16. "To the Sacking of Constantinople, A.D. 1455, and its immediate Consequences" (*Retrospection*, 1:442–61).

17. In the "Preface," HLP had indicated that "half a moment will suffice to prove that whilst the deep current of grave history rolls her full tide majestick, to that ocean where Time and all its wrecks at length are lost; our flashy *Retrospect*, a mere *jet d'eau* may serve to soothe the heats of an autumnal day" (p. viii). This statement was singled out by the *British Critic* and the *Anti-Jacobin* as symptomatic of the "Preface" as a whole. The latter, e.g., found it "flippant and light, pert rather than pertinent."

18. Pope's *Rape of the Lock*, 5.29–30.

19. Julia Fellowes (1774–1850) was the wife of JF's brother, William *Dorset* (1769–1852), formerly an officer in the naval packet service and now secretary to Lord Gwydir. (William Fellowes and his wife lived at this time in Sidmouth.) See the *Bath and Cheltenham Gazette*, 24 July 1850; "Bath Abbey Burials," C.R.O., Somerset.

TO SIR JAMES FELLOWES

Monday Morning
Blake's Hotel
7: August 1815.

My dear Sir James Fellowes
    will wish to hear how all ends, with his much agitated Friend and her trouble-
some Business; I think all ends in mere Smoke at least for the Present. The
Anderdons neither take nor buy——but were excessively civil at last, and invited me to a famous Dinner indeed, worthy of old Streatham Park in its best
Days——and *I played the Company* in my own House, and the Gentleman who
Sate next me was an Admirer of our Dear Miss Fellowes, and an Acquaintance
of yours—. We could not I think want for Chat. His Name is Casmajor,[1] Brother
to the fair Lady of the Mansion,[2] and knew you in Spain or Portugal.
    I was sorry to break with them, but Mr. Anderdon wanted a Place where
he could make Improvements—and my Successors would have considered no
Alteration as Improvement——he wished to cut Trees, and throw down some
little Wall, and cut the Windows down——Why good Gracious! The Girls would
cut my head off.
    [Purchase] did not suit him he Said—as a temporary Residence was all he
required.——So I must exert my Powers of patient Endurance—till next London
Season, and then proclaim an Open Sale, and if the Ladies are offended who
can help it?
    Merrik Hoare never called to ask if I was dead or alive; so to Day I set out on
my Way back to Bath—where every body will ask me about Buonaparte, and I
shall have nothing to tell.
    When in the Library at Streatham Park yesterday I just looked into an old
Book of my Writing—now completely out of Print, and found these long-
forgotten Lines.—The Date 1792.[3]

Shall impious France tho' frantic grown
Drag her pale Victims from the Throne?
    Shall Royal Blood be spilt?
Yet think neglectful Heav'n will spare,
And by conniving seem to share
    In such Gigantic Guilt.

No: tardy-footed Vengeance Stalks
Round her depopulated Walks,
    Waiting the fate-ful hour;
When human Skill no more can Save,
But hot Contagion fills the Grave
    And Famine bids devour.

Rise Warriors rise! with hostile Sway
Accelerate that dreadful Day,

Revenge the Royal Cause:
Exerting *well-united* Force,
Tear all Decrees that would divorce
True Liberty from Laws.

Is it not very odd I should so predict what is sure enough likely now to befall *them*, and yet never predict what has befallen myself. But I do not even now repent my Journey. The Offer to my Daughters was not only made, but in Person *repeated*; so my Conscience is clear of Blame if we sell——there are however those who Think nothing but an Acre of Land will in Two or Three Years be worth a Guinea. The Funds do fall so strangely, and so fast.[4]

Should these Explainers of the Prophecies prove the wise Men We take them for, and should the Call of the Jews be at hand—*Their* taking out such monstrous Sums would break us down at once; but The Turkish Empire must give way before that hour approaches;[5] and rapidly as the Wheel does run down the Hill, increasing in Velocity every Circle it makes;[6] I can't believe that Things are coming so very forward, but that poor H:L:P. may by the Mercy of God escape those Scenes of Turbulence and Confusion.

Your Book however helps to alarm me: I had no Notion that Such Pestilence had been so near, and you can have but little Notion how little we were impressed by Newspaper Accounts of what You Yourself not only witnessed but endured.[7]

From all future Ills that Heaven may protect *you* is the sincere Wish and Prayer of yours and your charming Family's/ truly Obliged/ H: L: Piozzi.

I mean to sleep at Speen Hill tonight,[8] dividing the Journey more equally.

Text Hyde Collection. *Address* Sir James Fellowes.

1. Lewis Duncan Casamajor (1786–1820) had been a Cantabrigian who left without taking a degree. He served in Portugal as secretary of legation (1809–15) and chargé d'affaires (April–July 1814). In October 1815 he was to be promoted to secretary of the embassy at the Court of St. Petersburg, where he would also serve as plenipotentiary until his death there on 3 March. See P.R.O., Prob. 11/1633/464, proved in London, 29 August 1820; *GM* 90, pt. 1 (1820):474.

2. For Frances Anderdon, née Casamajor, see HLP to JSPS, 28 April 1813, n. 3.

3. From *British Synonymy* (2:340), the lines form part of a discussion concerning the verbal distinction between *victim* and *sacrifice*.

4. England suffered a postwar depression, wherein export trade was reduced by 16 percent and import trade by nearly 20 percent. See *GM* 85, pt. 2 (1815):96, 192.

5. In *A Dissertation on the Prophecies* (2:401–14), Faber states that the pouring of the sixth vial (as remarked in the Book of Revelation) will effect the dissolution of the Ottoman Empire and the restoration of the ten tribes of Israel.

6. For the Horatian image, see HLP to TSW, 20 December 1811, n. 4.

7. For "Newspaper Accounts," see, e.g., *The Times*, 20 October and 28 November 1810; 9, 10 November and 23 December 1813. In its issue of 28 November 1810, *The Times* included a letter from JF, dated from Cadiz on 11 November.

8. On 7 August, HLP spent the night at the Castle Inn, Speen Hill. See her "Pocket Book" for that date.

TO THE REVEREND THOMAS SEDGWICK WHALLEY

Bath
August 13, 1815.

My firm persuasion that dear Dr. Whalley never received a long letter from me at Louvain makes me write again,[1] that we may at least talk over some of the wonders we are living amongst before we part for ever. An odd expression, say you, when we are separated by seas and lands. We are so; but still, inhabiting the same little planet, our feelings are as yet alike, and the consequences of what now passes will, while we stay in it, affect us both, and both in the same manner.

What scenes have you been witnessing! Mrs. Whalley, to whom I sent for fresh directions the other day, tells, you are becoming a connoisseur in firing! skilful to know at distance the different modes of dealing destruction round them, adopted by friends and enemies. Dear sir! what an accomplishment![2] Your ear, so particularly nice in poetry and music, will have had heavy complaints against your feet for marching it into such horrors; but I can easily comprehend how positive the people were, who, like the spectators at Homer's chariot-race, all watched with agitation the coming in of the victors, and all were sure that their conjectures were the true ones.[3] Well, the wonders that I have to relate are, that this Man, this Buonaparte, whom to dethrone such torrents of blood were willingly spilt; whom to depose, such treasures of money had been willingly spent, no sooner surrenders himself than we make an idol of him, crowd round for a glance of his eye, and huzza him as if he were our defender; officers revering *him* as emperor, who had pronounced his own abdication; and sailors protesting him a fine fellow, &c.[4] Had not Government prudently prevented his touching shore, hundreds, nay thousands, would have drawn him up and down in triumph; they were waiting in wild expectation of the sport.

But, as I went over Westminster Bridge last week, I saw we were building a new mad-house twice as big as old Bethlehem Hospital; and sure no building could be so wanted for Englishmen. And now to what carried me over Westminster Bridge.[5] You have, my dear sir, frequently advised me to make an offer of Streatham Park, my life and interest in it, with the contents, books, pictures, &c., to Mr. Thrale's four daughters; and two months ago a Scotch gentleman in that neighbourhood said he was sure my Lord Keith would give 6,000*l*. for it, if I would speak first and invite his acceptance. I did so, but none of the ladies ever writing a syllable on the subject, and the negotiation having dropped from Mr. Dalgleish's hands into those of two attorneys, it seemed dying away, and I feared my solicitor might have given offence by considering a copy-hold of 50*l*. per annum up in the village, as a separate article, so I resolved to go myself, and drove suddenly up to Mr. Merrick Hoare's in Baker Street, who married Sophia Thrale. She was ten miles out of town, at her maiden sister's cottage; but he received me with cold civility, said my offer was a very liberal one; and when I assured him that money should not part us, for that they might take the 50*l*. a year, giving me something or nothing, as they liked best, he promised to write Lord Keith word, and I entreated an early answer, because a Mr. Anderdon, the bank director, had talked of making overtures, which, if they refused, I must accept, because I am in something too much like real distress. So he lent me his arm, and I walked down to Jermyn Street, Blake's Hotel, where my maid was; and nothing more did I ever see or hear of any of the family, except a cold dry note, saying Mrs. Piozzi was at full liberty concerning Streatham Park, with which Lord Keith would have nothing to do.

This was after Mr. Anderdon had got another house.[6] All my scruples and delicacies are therefore at an end; and if you hear, when in Italy, about May or June 1816, that H. L. P.'s house is advertised for public sale, believe it; for I will get all I can now, unless such taxes are imposed as will break down the very dividends; and if so, it will be best to keep a spot of earth out of which one may dig potatoes.

Meanwhile, here are public reports abroad such as to make one consider private calamities as nothing. God's judgments are most certainly falling at last on sinful France;[7] and this odd retardation of Buonaparte's departure,[8] his letters picked up by one of our Bath tradesmen,[9] and the frantic fondness of our unaccountables here in England for the person of a man they sought so sincerely to destroy at Waterloo, fill the mind by turns with terror, admiration, and surprise. I almost wish I was nearer the source of intelligence; but that is like wishing oneself nearer the crater of the volcano, when one hears Vesuvius roar.

My health I say nothing about. After running seventy-five miles without stop or stay, and then walking from the top of Baker Street to Blake's Hotel, complaints would come with an ill grace; and 'tis no matter if they hear I am able to live and see to my own affairs. They deserve that mortification at least.

Your triumph of mind over body is delightful; dear Dr. Whalley has no enemies to vex by his superiority over common mortals, but many friends to render happy. The Lutwyches are at the Lakes just now; pretty Mary Mayhew making drawings, and I trust making conquests up and down.[10] Chevalier Boisgelin looks well in the face, but is more than ever, I think, *perclus de tous ses membres.* Our best joke going is how the Bellerophon has once more taken Chimæra Ah me! that vile chimera was *Ante* Leo, I remember, *retroque* Draco,[11] and I am so afraid he will slip his long tail out of whatever confinement they put him in; but many who have been at St. Helena say 'tis impossible.

Well! now here is a long letter, and not one word of dear Salusbury in it; but he is safe, well, and happy, and will soon be a father. He was in too much haste, but security from vice, and its consequent evils here and hereafter, is such a thing! No purchase was deemed costly that bought such a treasure, at least by a mind constructed after the old fashion as was that of, dear sir, your ever obliged, and grateful, and faithful,/ H: L: Piozzi.

We have a beautiful harvest here in England, smiling and copious. In France, next year, there will certainly be famine. How can any nation maintain half a million of foreign troops without feeling it most severely?[12] It alarms me, because, though I wish them punished, I don't wish them starved; and, besides all the rest, there is a danger of contagious fevers following scarcity, which Sir

James Fellowes' new book has put into my head, and makes me very glad you are going to dear Italy. It is the safest place at present; but before you go, write to me, dear sir. 'Mrs. Piozzi, Bath,' is sufficient.

Text Wickham, 2:403–7. *Address* [Rev: Mr. Whalley/Louvain.]

1. TSW had written to HLP from "Louvain Pays Bas" on 29 April (Ry. 564.32). Having spent eighteen weeks there, he went on to Ghent (TSW to HLP, 31 August [Ry. 564.33]).
2. On 19 June, still in Louvain, TSW wrote to his niece, Marianne (Maria Anne) Wickham, née Dawe (d. 1834), telling her that he was within earshot of the battles of Quatre-bas, Ligny, and Waterloo.
"Though distant above thirty miles from the field of battle, I distinctly heard the roar of the artillery for twelve hours, and could perceive that it advanced and became louder on the left, where the Prussians were so far defeated as to fall considerably back."
TSW continued on Waterloo: "The field of battle, not being more than five little leagues from Louvain, the thunder of artillery and musketry shook the windows at which I stood . . . all ear for the tremendous contest. From three to five the momentary roar of war grew louder and louder; from five to seven it neither increased nor diminished; from seven till half-past nine it became, to my great joy, fainter and fainter." From the sounds of the artillery, TSW could predict an Allied victory at Waterloo. See Wickham, 2:399–403.
3. See the *Iliad*, bk. 23.
4. Many of the English were angered at the cordial reception accorded to Napoleon by Captain Maitland and his crew, who called him "a devilish fine fellow" (*The Times*, 27 July).
5. The Bethlehem Royal Hospital (i.e., Bedlam) was begun in 1812 and completed in 1815 at a cost of £122,572. Located on a twelve-acre site in St. George's Fields, Lambeth Road, Southwark, the new hospital could accommodate almost two hundred patients with room for expansion. It replaced the original hospital at Moorfields that dated from 1676.
6. On 5 August HLP noted in her "Pocket Book": "The Andersons very obliging, but have taken Mr. Cator's House in Beckenham Place."
7. According to newspaper accounts: France is in "an unsettled state at present, and not holding forth the promise of speedy or radical improvement. . . . " And again: "The appearance of affairs in France, as described both by private letters and public journals, becomes every day more dark and lowering. Commotions . . . are confidently foretold and expected." See *The Times*, 9 and 10 August.
8. With the defeat of Napoleon at Waterloo on 18 June, HLP expected immediate reprisals to be taken against him. But it was not until 7 August that he was transferred to the *Northumberland*, which carried him to St. Helena. See *The Times*, 25, 29, 30 July; 5, 10, 11, 21 August.
9. Crowds gathered at Plymouth to catch a glimpse of Napoleon on the *Bellerophon* anchored in the harbor. One Mr. Mulligan, a Bath silk-mercer, secured a boat and was permitted to approach within fifty yards of the ship. Seeing Napoleon throw fragments of paper through his cabin window, Mulligan retrieved them. They included "a letter from an American to Buonaparte . . . MS translations of the Speaker's and Prince Regent's speeches at the close of the last session. . . . [and] part of a letter from Buonaparte to Maria Louisa, evidently written immediately after his late abdication." See *GM* 85, pt. 2 (1815):518; *The Times*, 14 August.
10. For Clementina Mary Mayhew, see HLP to Ly W, 30 January 1802, n. 7.
11. "As soon as an august personage was informed of the capture of Buonaparte, he communicated this important intelligence to a Prince of his family, observing—'The ancient fable is at length realised: the *Chimera* is in the power of *Bellerophon*, and will not this time escape again'" (*The Times*, 25 July 1815). According to the *Iliad* (6.219–25), Bellerophon slew Chimera, a fire-breathing monster with the head of a lion, body of a goat, and tail of a dragon. Hence, HLP's references to Leo, the Lion, and Draco, the Serpent or Dragon.
12. By November 1815, France was occupied by 150,000 allied troops under the command of the Duke of Wellington.

TO SIR JAMES FELLOWES

Monday 28: August 1815.

Retrospection too much crouded with Figures; Anticipation—in *every* Sense a *Blank!*——and thus it is Dear Sir that the World runs away. Mrs. *Flint* and *Dun* (where you bought the bitter Horehound,)[1] *hard* as one of her Names——and dreadful as the other, told me our lost Fortune on Saturday Night; I send it you inclosed to Miss Fellowes, who will accompany it with pleasanter Tydings I hope. Do the Friends for whom you are sacrifizing Health, make you large Compensation by trying to be happy themselves? I hope they do.——If *more* Inducements are wanting, they will surely think on *that*.

I have been plagued with a Gum boil—a Mouth Abscess—Punishment upon the Peccant Part for all that Rattling Nonsense it poured out on Fryday Morning when you met Miss Williams here. But we had been talking gravely before; and my Mother used to repeat a Spanish Refrain, which *you* know I dare say,—but I do not—expressing—"from a Companion that knows but one Book, and can relate but one Story—Good Lord deliver me"[2]—and sure enough Monotony will always tire, whether the Talk be of Mutton or of Metaphysics.

> One charm display'd, another strikes our View,
> In quick variety ever new——[3]

as some among our Streatham Wits used to say, was *her* forte.

Well! but Leak thinks I see, that Necessity will compel me to dispose for ever of *that* Place——and Lady Williams invites me strongly to quit *every* Place; and purchase a beautiful Cottage near my own native Sea with sublime Mountain Scenery, and good Convenience for Bathing——20 or 30 Miles from Brynbella (where by the Way there is a Baby born,)[4] and Two or Three Hundred Miles from London or from Bath. The Place is to be hired, or sold with its Fairy Furniture, and you would laugh to see little Betsy Jones's Fear lest I should accept the Offer, and as *She* says, bury my self completely alive——She knows well enough what North Wales is in the Winter.

Shall I try the Book of Names first?[5] and with out further Care concerning Money after the Debts are paid—venture on No. 8 Gay Street? I should like that better. This East Indian War however will keep the Property Tax on most certainly,—perhaps increase it; and that will affect all our Purses.[6] The Cambrian Heiress passed an Hour here this Morning——She is really a very rational Girl, and her Father says Cobbet's last Performance is beyond all Measure Inflammatory.[7] We shall surely have a *Storm* literal or figurative; and the first would do least harm. But here's the bit of Paper quite exhausted, without a Word of the Portrait[8]——my Letters give the truest Portrait after all—and this is a *Miniature* of/ Dear Sir James Fellowes'/ exceedingly Obliged Servant/ H: L: P.—

Text Pierpont Morgan Library.

1. Dunn and Flint, pastry-cooks at 39 Gay Street, are listed in the *New Bath Directory* (1809), but do not appear in *Gye's Bath Directory* (1819).

2. An Italian proverb, "Da matto attizato, da uno che legge un libro solo, da villan riffatto, da Recipe de Medici, da etcetera de notari guardici dio," translated as, "From an angry fool, from one that reads but one book, from an upstart Squire, from the Physicians recipe, and the Scrivenors etcaetera, the Lord deliver us." James Howell, "Morali Proverbiali," *Proverbs; or, Old Sayed Sawes & Adages in English (or the Saxon Toung) Italian, French, and Spanish whereunto the British, for their great Antiquity, and weight are added* (London: [Cornelius Bee], 1659), 7 (paginated separately by language). The *Proverbs* is subjoined to *Lexicon Tetraglotton* (1660).

3. For the commonplace, see, e.g., *Spectator* 470.

4. Hester Maria "Missey" Salusbury was born 25 August.

5. "Lyford Redivivus," which neither JF nor EM could place with a publisher.

6. Britain was fighting the Rajah of Nepal in a rugged border war. By autumn the British gained "favorable peace terms." See *GM* 85, pt. 2 (1815):358–62, 449, 456, 550–54; *The Times*, 21 August, also 9 and 11 September.

7. In "Five Letters to Lord Sheffield, On his Speech at Lewes Wool-Fair, 26 July 1815" which appeared in *Cobbett's Weekly Political Register*, 28 (26 August):225–87, William Cobbett (1762–1835) disputed Sheffield's advocacy of a bill to restrain the importation of wool. While admitting the financial troubles of sheepherders, the journalist protested that higher wool prices would only burden other classes. He thereupon observed in "Letter V" that the "situation of England, compared with that of the United States of America, is such as to induce every man to emigrate to them . . . " (p. 262).

8. HLP had a miniature of herself painted by Sampson Towgood Roche (1759–1847) of Pierrepont, or Pierrepoint Street. She gave it to JF "when *He* professed a Sentimental Attachment to poor H: L: Piozzi." See her "Commonplace Book" under the entry *Oughts and Orts*.

TO LADY WILLIAMS

Monday
28th: August 1815.

My dearest Lady Williams was excessively kind in writing so about that pretty Cottage—but do not let us make engagements for *next* Summer, while this still remains so warm. Besides that my Intentions are to die at Bath if it so pleases God—and then—how little Time have I to pass at pretty Cottages!! If I *should* live till next July indeed, (when the Dividends are paid you know,) I would drive down to Wales certainly: and see the dear Brynbella People and their Baby; and thank my kind Friend Sir John Williams and his charming Lady for retaining their Regard thro' so long an Absence. I *did* hope too the Pleasure of seeing pretty Mrs. Myddleton once again and the Doctor: but Hope is a good Breakfast as some wise Man says—*a wretched Supper*:[1] and when Doctor Myddleton is sick one must feel alarmed,—because he never was Sick before Since I had the Pleasure of knowing him.[2] The best is to hear good of the Younglings who have long Life in expectation. My dear Godson was always a fine Fellow, and his Woodcock will be a welcome Present.

Poor Harriet Salusbury had a rough Time I hear, but a very Safe one, Some one told me that Cecy Mostyn had her eldest Son with her, and I was glad of that.—God keep them out of crazy France![3] 'Tis idle not to *see* what we shall soon be obliged to *feel*—that God's Judgements are falling heavy upon all Europe——heaviest on that impious Kingdom. Buonaparte is sent—*apparently* to

Extinction. He has made the World his Pedestal long enough; Himself the Sole Figure, and Mankind the Lookers-on——There will be nobody to look at him in Saint Helena but Rats; with which the little Place so swarms, that they can Grow no Corn; We send them Wheat from England.——A Lady here——who passed Three Months upon the Island,[4] says he will be horror-stricken at his first Arrival, and either kill himself or die distracted. Does not your Ladyship remember our dear little *Solicitor*—now a Pulpit Critic[5]—saying when we forbore to admire at his Jumps any longer: Look Flies; Look I say Flies, how I jump—— Buonaparte may say Look Rats, for other Admirers will soon be weary of wondering at his Prowess. I think he will plague us no more.

Mean while do not Dearest Madam engage this pretty Cottage; I may die 20 Deaths before next Summer, See but how few of our Friends are left alive! I *may* too get out of Debt next July, and then I might be tempted (with a freed Income) to take a comfortable House *here* and end my Days—an old *Bath Cat*—Snappish at the Card Table, sullen at the Conversation Parties——and passionate With the Maids at home——following them up and down Stairs with a Cambrick Handkerchief in hope of finding Dust on the Mahogany Bannisters.

Ah dearest Lady Williams! [tear] what a wretched Flavour do the Dregs of any Life leave behind them! It is Cruelty not Kindness to wish such Life prolonged: Let me entreat your Friendship not to desire it for Your Poor/ H: L: P.

Thousands and Ten Thousands of Loves, Compliments and Respects wait on all. I love to see a Letter.

Mrs Pennant seems recovering by her Visit to Bodylwyddan, I feared She was in a worse Way: poor Mr. Lloyd of Kefn, is miserably broken up, but will I think go a while: he must have a < > Miss of his Neighbour at Wigfair.

Text Ry. 4 (1812–18). *Address* Lady Williams/ Bodylwyddan/ near St. Asaph Flintshire/ North Wales. *Postmark* BATH AU 28 181<5>.

1. Francis Bacon, *Apopthegms* (1625), no. 95: "Hope is a good breakfast, but it is a bad supper."
2. For Myddelton's fatal illness, see HLP to Ly W, 4 December 1815 and n. 1.
3. Because of the various armies of occupation throughout France, the Bourbons were reviled for having returned "in the foreigners' baggage." Moreover, the tension between the royalists and Napoleon's supporters was so intense that "the South of France has been in a state of great agitation: at Nismes, Montpellier, Toulouse, and Marseilles, there have been violent tumults" with massacres and assassinations. See *GM* 85, pt. 2 (1815):266–67.
4. In her "Pocket Book," 28 August, HLP identified the lady as JF's sister-in-law, Julia Fellowes. See also HLP to JW, 9 October 1815.
5. Hugh Williams.

Boney's meditations on the Island of St. Helena—or—The Devil addressing the Sun. *Paradise Lost* Book IV (August 1815). Caricature by G. H[umphrey]; engraved by George Cruikshank. (Reproduced by permission of the Henry E. Huntington Library and Art Gallery, San Marino, California.)

TO ANNA MARIA PEMBERTON
AND
JOHN SALUSBURY PIOZZI SALUSBURY

Bath Thursday
31st: August 1815.

Nothing can exceed my Thankfulness dear Mrs. Pemberton—for the admirable Account I heard this Morning in Your united Letter. Lord Crewe's Accident on Llangollen Hill so filled my Heart with Fears for Salusbury:[1]—but You are all *safe, well,* and happy and I am sure the Baby will have a beautiful Nurse in her own pretty Mamma.

She must do Aunt the honour to accept the enclosed as my *Old fashioned Christening Fee:*—for though the Draft is drawn for her Husband, at least in *his Long Name;* The Present is to Harriet.

I think Mr. Smythe Owen has taken the Safest Time to go to Paris; The Allied Armies will keep all steady, and he will see the fine Pictures before they are removed[2]——but nothing he will admire more I suppose, than at his return— The little Niece. She will be a stout Lass by the Time I add to the Number of those who never saw such a Charmer: but the head of Hair her Father mentions, will come off—won't it?—and change for a Shade lighter. Nobody mentions her Eyes, I hope they are black as *Sloes.* But I shall release *Your* Eyes Dearest Madam, which have certainly been held waking quite long enough, and now do go to Sleep and to the warm Bath afterwards, and be quite well.

Dispensing Mercurial Medicines to new-delivered Women is A Thing so wholly novel to me, that I seemed quite Surprized when I read that Line of your Letter; but 'tis because Matters were managed so differently in old Days from what they are now;[3] People have improved on past Practice; and we do *so* well anyway, if it so pleases God. I have no Doubt of The Titmouse's Health and long Life—her Parents will give her no hereditary Disorders.

So Adieu dear Madam and make Salusbury just say the Draft is arrived safe or I shall be fidgetty about *That*——I write to him on t'other Side the Paper—— and only beg you to accept my best Regards and give my True Love to Your Daughter and *Grand* Daughter assuring them I/am Ever theirs and Yours/ H: L: Piozzi.

Bath Thursday 31: August 1815.
My dearest Salusbury was a good Creature for writing me word you were got Safe to Salop——I really felt alarmed about the Journey, but you seem to have managed very well between Riding and Mail Coach and all.

What Agitation the little Lady has already occasioned! and of how much more will She be the Cause 16 or 17 Years hence! Could my Prayers or Wishes produce her any additional Happiness She would be very sure of it——but Happiness is a Commodity hard to be purchased—Pretty Creature! She will probably *bestow* more than She *Enjoys*——I think that is commonly the Case with Females.

Oh! I tried to laugh you know, about poor Mr. Lloyd of Kefn being a Bath

Beau; but there is no Joke; he is completely a Bath Invalid.[4] Lady Williams writes very kindly to me, and has a Mind to tempt me to end my Days among my Native Mountains in Caernarvonshire——but I feel most at Home *here*, and *you* feel that tis the best Place for me: and when I can get my Embarrassments all disentangled, I shall like to make Bath my last Home in this World. Mrs. Pemberton will *shew* you the Draft I have enclosed for Christening Fee—as we used to call it. And now Dearest Dear Love Farewell, and write directly to your ever Affectionate H: L: Piozzi.

Text Ry. 594.14.

1. John Crewe (1742–1829), first baron (1806) of Crewe Hall, Cheshire, had "lately sustained a great injury" upon being thrown from his carriage in North Wales. See the *Bath Herald*, 2 September 1815.
    2. By August, reports had reached England that "the pictures and statues that [had] been plundered from" Austria, Spain, Prussia, Parma, Rome, Milan, Modena, Florence, Verona, and Venice by Napoleon's army were in the process of being returned to their owners. Field Marshal Blücher, the emperor of Austria, and the king of Spain were supervising the removal. See *GM* 85, pt. 2 (1815):170; HLP to LC, 21 July 1796, 3 July 1797.
    3. The use of "Mercurial Medicines" after pregnancies was not so common as to be listed in the detailed article "Pharmacy" in the 1797 edition of the *Encyclopedia Britannica*. It does, however, list numerous forms of mercurial prescriptions, popular as an emetic and a stimulant (particularly to aid blood circulation).
    4. Edward Lloyd (1750–1830) of Cefn, near St. Asaph, had been active in North Wales as sheriff of various counties and as a commissioner of peace. See the *Bristol Mercury*, 8 June 1830.

TO THE REVEREND JOHN ROBERTS

Bath Monday
18: September 1815.

I feel glad to be remembered by old friends Dear Mr. [Roberts][1] and think your letter both agreeable and useful. If by the most amiable Character in F[lintshire] you mean my Successors at pretty B[rynbella], your Letter becomes still more delightful to me. But why must Family Prayer be a *new* thing in our Vale of Clwydd? I don't recollect ever sleeping from my own House except at Lleweney, Gwaynynog and Bodlewyddan, and there were *always* Family Prayers—in my time. Of poor Mr. A[nwyl],[2] who used to read them at the first named Place, I hear a bad Account, but tho' Death shakes the fatal Dart over him,[3] he forbears to strike hitherto; and Time given—will I hope be Time used. The difficulty is in using it efficaciously. Those *Trappists* you inquire about, condemned themselves to dig a portion of their own Graves every day; and never met at their silent melancholy meals—but with a *real* not *painted* Death's head on the Dinner-Table. If encreased horror and detestation of this Life, be the best Preparation for that to come—These People are best prepared.[4] If to instruct the Poor be the best employment of the Rich: our Folks at Bath here, are the best employed. Schools frequent as Streets, and Ladies devoting whole days to teaching Children are *our boast*,[5] yet we have hard hearts here *too*; and little Tradesmen are arrested by great Tradesmen to the complete ruin of many a family—but the next Generation will be better, if learning proper answers to sometimes difficult questions—will make them so——Ah dear Mr. [Roberts] will *anything* make us better?—nothing I fear but the grace of God, which must be long prayed for and late obtained.

Meanwhile here are three large Receptacles for Public Service in a less space than that between B[rynbella] and D[ymerchion]—not crowded but *crammed* every Sunday and twice a'week beside. I know not the Tenets of half the Sectaries, but all *except the Socinian Chapel*—which increases every day—do certainly preach *Christianity* in some mode or other——and when I talk of *three;*[6] I only mean close round my own Lodging—out of the windows of which I plainly now hear them singing Psalms. You will not however easily believe that I think the world mends because such efforts are made towards mending it. Never were the Annals of Newgate *disgraced* by such crimes as have under cognizance of the Legislature this year says an intelligent Writer: Never were there as many Offences committed against the Spiritual Court in *Seventy* Years, as in the last *Seven,* said a Doctor of the Commons but last Week. And what say you does my old [Parish] friend infer from all this? Why my Inference is merely—that the Word of God is accomplishing: that many run to [and] fro and Knowledge is increased[7]—that as Eternity has been compared to a King and represented by a Serpent with the Tail in his Mouth[8]—so Christianity will end as she began, zealous and active and spreading over Nations long obscured by ignorance. [I know] that notwithstanding all this, there shall come *Scoffers* walking after their own *lusts*—despising *Government*, Presumptuous, Self-willed being not afraid to speak evil of *Dignities*—to whom (as St. Peter says) The Mist of Darkness is reserved for ever.[9] From such false Teachers "Libera nos Domine".[10] I find the Parish Churches and Chapels the safest places for *my own part*; when I cannot go I read my own fine Bible at home with Notes by Locke and Waterland and my Lord Clarendon. 3 Vols Folio and a beautiful Type.[11]—It is the only expensive purchase I have made, and cost me ten guineas—second hand.—Death at my Age can't be unexpected or I might tremble at the sudden seizures within my hearing of—but as Dr. Johnson said Supineness after *fifty* is as a Man snoring in a besieged City; but Supineness after *seventy* is as a Man sleeping—on an attack from the Assailants.[12]

When Maria Theresa, the Empress Queen we called her,—arrived at her last moments, after receiving the viaticum and having endeavoured to prepare herself for the last awful leave-taking of life, some of her Attendants proposed to her to try for a Quarter of an hour's Repose. No, No, said she. Death shall have no Advantage of me that I can help or hinder; I will meet him waking and with my best Powers of Mind——the best will scarce suffice perhaps.[13] If I could have gotten a frank I would have enclosed you what I received this day. Yesterday I mean; to show you how busy the People are converting Sinners up and down with little Tracts of their own writing—and 'tis but Justice that they *do* so, for when they have drawn all the Congregations from their appointed Ministers—(far as they are able) it is but fair to minister to them themselves. Indeed never were Clergy-men accounted of so little use or Value. Gentlemen and Ladies preach and pray at these schools, and I see Lord D. at the head of a Bible society.[14] By the time the Hierarchy and Tithes are abolished, you shall find a new [obliteration] order of things coming forward; So that nobody will miss 'em.

Farewell! You tell me nothing of Mr. L[loyd] or of Mrs. R[oberts][15] but I hope both are well and will accept the best wishes of dear Sir Yours and theirs faithfully/ H: L: Piozzi.

Your Book will have good success I dare say.[16]
I was afraid of Scott's Bible:[17] I have got a New Testament by Theodore Beza.—[18]

Text Victoria and Albert Museum Library. A copy.

1. For the Reverend John Roberts, see HLP to PSP, 31 July 1803, n. 4.
2. For the Reverend Robert Anwyl, "the chaplain of Lleweney hall," see HLP to JSPS, 13–14 March 1809, n. 2.
3. Cf. *Paradise Lost*, 2.672.
4. Much of what HLP writes about the Trappists (Cistercian monks) is confirmed by William Dorset Fellowes' book *A Visit to the Monastery of La Trappe in 1817* (London: Stockdale, 1818). He describes them as the most penitential order in the Catholic Church. During their meals, they interrupted their silence only to read aloud "passages from scripture, reminding them of death" (p. 13). Whenever an interment occurred, a new grave was at once opened "for the next that may die" (p. 16). And their small cells contained only "a bed of boards, a human skull, and a few religious books" (p. 21).
5. Among such institutions active in Bath at this time were the free and charity schools, fourteen societies to relieve the poor, and several Bible and missionary societies, including the Society for Promoting Christian Knowledge and the Female Bible Association. See R. S. Neale, *Bath 1680–1850: A Social History or a Valley of Pleasure, Yet A Sink of Iniquity* (London: Routledge and Kegan Paul, 1980). In the "Commonplace Book" under *Learning*, HLP comments that "Lady Willoughby . . . teaches School with more Success than any of the Women who in these Days delight in Educating Young People."
6. Living in New King Street, HLP was in the immediate neighborhood of at least three dissenting chapels: the Socinian Chapel, where the Unitarians met, was on Trim Street; the Moravian Chapel was on Monmouth Street; and the Methodist Missionary Society met at the New King Street and Walcot chapels (*Bath Directories*).
7. Daniel 12:4.
8. In Far Eastern terminology, "Eternity" has been used to signify "Your Majesty." The Gnostic symbol of the Ouroboros represents eternity by a snake biting its tail.
9. See 2 Peter 2:10, 17.
10. See especially the first and second epistles of Paul to Timothy; John 4:1; Romans 16:17.
11. William Dodd (1729–77), *A Commentary On The Books Of The Old And New Testament. In Which Are Inserted The Notes and Collections of John Locke, Esq.; Daniel Waterland, D.D.; The Right Honourable Edward Earl of Clarendon, And Other Learned Persons. With Practical Improvements*, 3 vols. (London: Printed for R. Davis, in Piccadilly; L. Davis, in Holborn; and T. Carnan and F. Newbery, junior, in St. Paul's Church-yard, 1770). The copy at the Rylands contains numerous notes in HLP's hand (Ry. 698.76). The third leaf bears an inscription also in HLP's hand, dated 23 August 1820, Penzance, Cornwall, requesting that JF accept the Bible after her death and stating that it had been "Bought of Upham Bath,/ 27: Feb: 1815/ and paid 10£: for."
Along with Dodd's Bible, HLP also left JF a copy of the Apocrypha (1813), "Bought at Bath 27: May 1815."
12. See *Rambler* 78: "To neglect at any time preparation for death, is to sleep on our post at a siege, but to omit it in old age, is to sleep at an attack."
13. The anecdote about Empress Maria Theresa is long-lived and repeated by C. L. Morris, who states that when on her deathbed, she told her son: "I do not wish to be overtaken by death. I wish to see it come." See *Maria Theresa: The Last Conservative* (New York: Alfred Knopf, 1937), 332.
14. Possibly the very rich Francis Basset (1757–1835), cr. baron de Dunstanville (1796) of Tehidy, Cornwall. He was closely associated with Bath through his first marriage on 16 August 1780 to

Frances Susanna (d. 1823), daughter of John Hippisley Coxe of Stoneaston, Somerset. Also possibly George William, Viscount Deerhurst, a former Streatham resident.

15. HLP refers to the vicar's wife, Anne (who was to outlive her husband) and his curate, John Lloyd, at Tremeirchion. For the latter, see the parish registers for that year (C.R.O., Clwyd).

16. In 1814–15 Roberts was publishing a bilingual periodical, *Cylchgrawn Cymru*, which was to end with its fourth number. He was, however, also working on a Welsh version of the Homilies of the Church of England, which was to be published in 1817.

17. Thomas Scott (1747–1821), a self-educated commentator on Scripture and an ordained priest, prepared what is known as "Scott's Bible," i.e., *The Holy Bible . . . With Original Notes . . . to which are added a Concordance, General Index, and Tables,* 4 vols. (London: Bellamy and Roberts, 1788–92).

18. Theodore Beza, Théodore de Bèze (1519–1605), John Calvin's chief assistant and successor as leader of the Reformed Protestant Church in Geneva, annotated several editions of the New Testament using the Greek Codex Bezae, a manuscript that Beza had freely translated into Latin and given a Calvinistic interpretation in his extensive annotations. HLP's *Sale Catalogue* (1) includes two editions of Scripture by Beza: one with the date of 1642 (8 May, lot 241) and another dated 1632 (9 May, lot 35).

TO JOHN SALUSBURY PIOZZI SALUSBURY

Bath
20: September 1815.

My dearest Salusbury is now learning by cruel Experience what every Book on every Shelf could have told him long ago: that Life is full of Cares, and that all our Pleasures however short lived—and however imperfect, are purchased and paid for by bitter and severe Pains. What You are Suffering, is Suffered—popularly speaking—by *every*body. It is not I believe One Person in 40000 who rears all their Offspring; and those which are brought up, cost their Parents much health, much Peace, much Time and much Money. I have myself lost Eight at various Ages:—some within the Month, some within the Year; one at Three Years old, a *Son*; and one Son at 11. From those that remain, I have as You know four Grandchildren——and their turning out Well must compensate.[1] I fancy the eldest Mostyn will be something of a Scholar, and the other two good Officer-like Fellows;—I hope So.

The World is not favourable to Virtue, less so than ever indeed; and 'tis difficult to find Parents who are trying to Secure it for their Progeny.[2]

Beauty to the Girls, Situation in Life to the Boys,—are the Wishes of Fathers, Mothers, and Friends who cross *my* Path, and I live with People of all Sorts.

Some of those among whom the Currents of Life have driven me, are connected by Marriage with the Abdys:[3] The Elopement of Sir William's Lady with Lord Charles Bentinck gives much Concern of Course.[4] She is Sister to pretty Mrs. Wallhouse Lyttelton, who must behave better, and not follow bad Example——*her* Husband is probably more amiable (you knew him) than the Baronet:[5] and it behoves Gentlemen to make themselves beloved——when no stronger Tye than mere Preference restrains the Lady.

We grave Folks say these are the Consequences of French Principles, and I say the whole Army will come home completely freed from any Principles at all. If such Men marry—'tis to gratify a momentary Appetite (Passion is too sentimental a Name:)—if they baptize their Children, 'tis to assure them a Register,—if they take them to the Altar, 'tis to comply with custom, and prove themselves no Papists:——and if they choose a Profession, 'tis to get them as the Phrase is off their own hands.

Such you will find the World in its State of Improvement—nor is that Word misplaced: The Powers of Mechanism are so extended, that You will soon hear of the new Mode adopted to manage Air Balloons,[6] and make our crossing the Channel still easier than it is now: but I will not anticipate; You may however if it will amuse dear Harriet, tell her how the Tambour Work is now done all without hands, and by Enginry alone in the prettiest and most expeditious Manner possible; but you are nearer the Scene of Action than myself, and have most likely witnessed the beautiful Machinery.[7] I know not whether Count Linois was here in Your Time: he was so loved and liked and Fêted that poor Uncle used to be enraged with us for inviting him so constantly——The next is—he will be hanged——and most deservedly.[8]

I think my Darling that I resemble the Rake in Clarissa who after he has rattled away Nonsense for half an Hour to a Man in deep Affliction—says, and "so I comforted and advised him."[9] *Your* best Consolation however, will be Baby's Recovery; of which I entertain no small hope. The Spirit of Vegetation, the Vis Vitæ is so strong in Infancy, nothing can Surprize one which results from it.

Adieu! and may Your next Letter be more chearful. Meantime assure yourself of my truest and tenderest Wishes, and believe me most/ sincerely and faithfully your Affectionate/ H: L: P.

Let me intreat you dearest Salusbury to make my Affectionate Respects to Mrs. Pemberton with every feeling of Sympathy for her and our charming Harriet——I shall be glad to see a Letter again, tho the Postman's knock makes me start yet.

Text Ry. 588.290. *Address* John Salusbury Piozzi Salusbury Esq./ High Street/ Shrewsbury. *Postmark* BATH SE 20 1815 109.

1. CMM's three sons and Q's daughter.
2. CMM's eldest son, John Salusbury, abandoned scholarly ambitions to become in 1817 a cadet in the East India service. Harry was promoted to commander by 1830, but Bertie's naval career was shortlived, when in 1827 he retired to Brighton with CMM.
3. JF's youngest brother, Captain Sir Thomas (1778–1853), R.N., had married in 1813 Catherine Mary Abdy (d. 1817). For her brother William, see n. 4.
4. On 5 September 1815, Anne Abdy, née Wellesley (1787–1875), seventh and natural daughter of the marquess of Wellesley and wife of William Abdy (1779–1868), and last baronet (1803), of Felix Hall, Essex, had eloped with William Charles Augustus Bentinck (1780–1826), lieutenant colonel in the army and a son of the third duke of Portland. The Abdys' marriage, which took place in 1806, was to be dissolved in 1816, Anne and Bentinck marrying in July of that year. For the case brought by Abdy "to recover damages [£30,000] for criminal conversation between his wife and Lord Charles Bentinck," see *The Times*, 4 December 1815 and the *Bath Herald*, 3 February 1816.
5. Hyacinthe Mary Wellesley (1789–1849) had married in 1812 Edward John Walhouse Littleton (1791–1863) of Teddesley Park and Hatherton, Staffs., cr. Baron Hatherton (1835).
6. HLP had in mind a "Grand Aerostatic Exhibition" that opened in Bath on 22 September. It

featured "the Ascension of a Silk Balloon, which in a few seconds will be succeeded by . . . A large Montgolfier, 24 feet high" (*Bath and Cheltenham Gazette*, 20 September).

7. The machine lace trade was enhanced by John Lever's construction in Nottingham of point net and warp lace machinery during 1812–13. See William Felkin, *A History of the Machine-Wrought Hosiery and Lace Manufactures* (Cambridge: W. Metcalfe, 1867), 271–78.

8. The comte de Linois had been a prisoner of war from ca. 1806 to 1814. At the first Bourbon restoration, he was appointed governor of Guadalupe. As such, he was accused of inciting a rebellion there against Louis XVIII in June 1815. Two months later, the British took Guadalupe and Linois was returned to France, again as a prisoner of war. Charged with disobedience and revolution, he was to face a court martial in March 1816, at which he was acquitted and granted a pension. See *GM* 85, pt. 2 (1815):270, 357–58; and 86, pt. 1 (1816):266; *The Times*, 13 and 16 March 1816. See also HLP to LC, 4 June 1806, n. 4.

9. On the night of Clarissa's death, 7 September, Richard Mowbray writes to Belford, giving him a description of Lovelace's reaction to the event. The letter concludes with "And thus we comforted and advised him."

TO SIR JAMES FELLOWES

Bath
Wednesday 27th: September 1815

Why Dear Sir James Fellowes! Peter the Cruel was surely *Your* Ancestor instead of *mine*. After the Thousand Kindnesses You and your charming Family—Hombres y Hembras had heaped on your ever obliged H:L:P;—to run out of the Town so, and never call to say Farewell.[1] Ah! never mind; I shall pursue you with Letters, and they shall be more Serious than You count on. Los Flatos visited me again on Saturday—attended with a new Symptom—*Nausea*: lequel m'obligea par force de rendre L'Estomac, tho' I had dined *solely* on Cold Chicken. I took Rhubarb and Laudanum in a little Pepper-mint Water, and passed the Night, under a strong Perswasion that these Spasms would be fatal *some* day—and *so they will*. Recollecting mean while little Bessy's Responsibility towards my Executor, I took your Spanish Bible *myself* to Linten's (the Man in Hetling Court,) on Monday Morning;[2] and thither the Wraxall shall follow, when I have finished cramming it with Literary Gossip:—Your Name on the first Page Secures it for the present.

Now do not wrong me by Suspicion of low Spirits: All the Absurdity consists in making you an Offer of Such trifling Remembrancies.[3] But with Regard to *my Life* which has already past the Portion of Time allotted to our Species—Forgetfulness of Danger would be Fatuity, not Courage. You would not think highly of a Soldier who hearing The Enemy's Trumpet tho' at a Distance, should compose himself to take another Nap:——but what would *he* deserve who should be found sleeping on an Attack?[4]

I have lived to witness very great Wonders; and am told that Bramah the great Mechanic is in Expectation of perfecting the Guidance of an Air Balloon so as to exhibit in an almost miraculous Manner upon Westminster Bridge next Spring.[5] I saw one of the first,—the *very* first Mongolfier I believe; go up from the Luxembourg Gardens at Paris——and in about an hour after, expressing my Anxiety whither Pilâtre de Rosier and his Friend Charles were gone[6]——meaning of Course to what Part of France they would be carried; A grave Man made Reply. "Je crois Madame qu'Ils sont allès—ces Messieurs là, pour voir le Lieu ou les Vents se forment."

What Fellows Frenchmen are! and always have been: I long for your Brother's new Account of them,[7] and if I could turn the Figures from 74 to 47, I would certainly go and See them myself, in a less hazardous Vehicle than an Air Balloon. Abate Parini.[8]

Text Harvard Theatre Collection, Pusey Library, TS 941.5; a draft.

1. HLP's joking comparison of JF and Czar Peter I (1672–1725), infamous for his cruelty.
   In a letter to her, dated from Sidmouth on 1 October [1815], JF reported his hurried departure from Bath while suffering "from a pain in the face" (Ry. 555.78).
2. The stationer Lenten at 3 New Westgate Buildings, near Hetling Court (*Gye's Bath Directory*, 1819).
3. HLP had turned over to JF Wraxall's *Historical Memoirs* by the summer of 1816. In his letter to HLP, 31 August 1816, he comments: "I value all your 'Scraps' and shall take care of them" (Ry. 555.73).
4. An allusion to SJ's *Rambler* 78. See HLP to the Reverend John Roberts, 18 September 1815, n. 12.
5. HLP did not know that Joseph Bramah (b. 1748), an engineer, had died on 9 December 1814 at Pimlico. See *GM* 84, pt. 2 (1814):613.
6. The incident is recorded in *Observations*, 1:22, as having occurred in 1784, probably 19 September when an ascent was made from the Tuileries. For the Montgolfiers, see HLP to SL, 30 April 1785.
   HLP's recollection of details is uncertain. Not only does she misdate the "first Montgolfier" ascent, but she also appears to telescope unrelated flights of Pilâtre de Rozier (HLP to LC, 16 August 1802) and Jacques-Alexandre-César Charles (1746–1822).
   See Charles Coulson Gillispie, *The Montgolfier Brothers and the Invention of Aviation* (Princeton, N.J.: Princeton University Press, 1983).
7. William Dorset Fellowes, *Paris; during the interesting Month of July, 1815. A Series of Letters Addressed to a Friend in London* (London: Gale and Fenner, 1815).
8. Giuseppi Parini (1729–99), a cleric and poet, was a member of the Della Cruscans. HLP's cryptic allusion is probably to his "Sonetto . . . Sopra Il Pallone Aereostatico," which was followed by her "Imitation of the Foregoing Sonnet on an Air Balloon" (*Florence Miscellany*, 58–59).

TO THE REVEREND JOHN ROBERTS

Bath
27th: September 1815.

Dear Mr. [Roberts'] letters are very kind, and perfectly agreeable to me; It is indeed a flattering circumstance to be remembered by Old Friends thro' such severe changes of Fortune; but though poor, I will not as you say turn my back on the Missionary Society, for which no one can feel more sincere Respect, or from which no one can form more ardent Expectations.[1] That Great should be the Company of Preachers—in savage and distant countries where by hearing alone God's holy Word must be promulgated till diligence and dutiful Attention have multiplied Translations without End—is most *desirable*——I am only old fashioned enough to think that where we have the Advantage of a <pure>

Establishment, these *Volunteer* Instructors claim more than is their Due:—and take too much upon them——altho' *no Sons* of Levi.[2] If Saul lost his Kingdom by taking the Priests Office on himself, surely these unordained Gentlemen do take a heavy Responsibility on *themselves;*[3] when administering the blessed Sacrament in their unconsecrated Conventicles—but I will say no more upon the Subject nor Judge too rashly, when so near being Judged.

My Bible has notes by Doddridge, by Warburton, by Michaelis, by every body.[4] My business is with the Text—it teaches me to forgive Injuries and to owe no Man anything but to love one another.[5]

One Year and half is past and gone however; and in as much more time I shall be free; if before then I am not called myself from all such cares and torments—tho' I trust that in giving Account of our Stewardship—correct discharge of lawful Debts will be required from many who drive such thoughts far away.

The finest possible Weather, and the longest Summer I ever witnessed is at length giving way to Autumnal Rains and Equinoctial Winds. The Planet Mars has shone with uncommon brightness, tho' we are making ourselves believe that War is now distant—and a peaceful order of things coming forward. Mr. Faber will look Sharp towards Turkey I suppose; and hoping that the Phial poured out on France is exhausted, will be straining his Sight for the Kings of the East to come in.[6]

I saw a Gentleman from Benares the other day, he seems to think Matters are ripening for Improvement there about—only we should not he says press the Business forward with imprudent Zeal——They may be led, but not driven in that Country.[7] So here is Prattle enough for one Post dear [Sir] and pray present me to your respectable Lady with all due esteem and think as favourably as you can of your assured Friend &c./ H: L: P.

Text Victoria and Albert Museum Library. A copy.

1. What in part prompted this letter was HLP's receipt on 26 September of "A Letter from Mr. Roberts begging Money for Missionaries—God knows I have it not to give" ("Pocket Book").
The growth of the missionary movement kept pace with the evangelical revival that began in the late eighteenth century. By 1815 there were several missionary societies—particularly strong among the Methodists—with representatives in China and in South and West Africa. Active too was the British and Foreign Bible Society, which hoped to make and distribute translations of the Bible in non-Christian countries, such as China.
2. One of the twelve tribes of Israel, the Levites were set apart as priests and their assistants to do the work of God. See, e.g., Numbers 1:50, 8:23–26, especially chap. 18.
3. See 1 Samuel 13:8–13; 15:22–26.
4. Those commentators singled out by HLP were Philip Doddridge (1702–51); William Warburton (1698–1779); Johann David Michaelis (1717–91).
5. See Matthew 6:14; Romans 13:8.
6. In *A Dissertation upon the Prophecies,* Faber predicted that the dissolution of the Turkish empire would prepare "a way . . . for the kings from the East . . . [who] are most probably the ten tribes of Israel" (2:xxi).
7. See HLP to JF, 28 August 1815, n. 6.

TO SIR JAMES FELLOWES

Bath
Tuesday Night 3: October 1815.

It was very sweetly kind in Dear Sir James Fellowes to write so; and if the Man that brought me the Letter is a wise Man and a safe Man &c. he shall have Your Bible to carry back—The Wraxall is not completely made up yet.

I am as well as possible just now: so was poor Mr. Willett,—Willet of Dorsetshire, who dined in Park Street here last Week,—four hours before he was a Corpse.[1] Miss Williams had a sad Loss of him——but I think You and I never met there.[2] Lord Keith is going to enfranchise the Copy-hold Property at Streatham—for which I receive about 50£ o'Year;[3] and my Solicitor Mr. Windle is indignant, because my Consent or Concurrence has never been asked—tho' they can do nothing without it.

That good-natured Mr. Dalgliesh however, who was so kind to me offering his Security if you remember——advises me not to resent their Behaviour, because he thinks if there was no Intention of purchasing, they would scarcely think of freeing the Land. *His* Advice is to advertise *before* Christmas, that *after* Christmas will be set to Sale such and such Property,——and he feels a Hope that the Ladies will not suffer the Auctioneer to enter.—Tell me your own Opinion.

With Regard to public Matters, I think Maximilian the witty Emperor of Germany was not far from right when he Said that *He* like Agamemnon of old, was Rex Regum;[4] The King of France Rex Asinorum, The King of England Rex Diabolorum (tho' he had not heard of the Irish Mutineers of *our Day*:); The King of Spain Rex Hominum—I hope They will verify the Appellation and behave like Men and Gentlemen.[5]

Of dear Cervantes' Merit you must know *most*,[6] and those who do so must *most* value him. I believe there is no Writer in Europe as popular——no not Shakespear himself, who is justly the Idol of his own Country——while the Spanish Hero, is Hero of *every* Country—No Nation that does not swarm with Prints, and resound with Stories out of Don Quixote——and 'tis very likely I am quoting my own Book when I say so; but there is no remembering the crouded Figures clustered together in Retrospection.[7] We will talk of the Name Book when I am grown rich: It will do nothing for me till I don't want it. And *that* Day I purpose to *see* on the 25th of next July——If not hindered by Los Flatos—and *Cramped* in my noble Exertions. 9 Months is not it to July? Well! I have carried many a heavy Burden for 9 Months,——and why not a Load of Debt? 'tis a new sort of Burthen, but Leak writes me Word that Gillow's Bill has many Charges in it that cannot be supported—so if he can heave off a *Hundred* Weight, Things will run better——and 'tis only following your Example about the vexatious Tooth,—bearing, and forbearing, and wearing the Misery out.

Our Theatre is open, and I saw the new Opera Dancers from Mrs. Dimond's Box.[8] La prima Donna is the smallest Creature I ever saw, That was not a Dwarf;—her Husband a Colossus of a Fellow, and The Waltze they dance together just the very oddest Thing I ever saw in my Life.[9] We were talking here one Morning if you recollect—with Miss Williams—of these Baylerinas, and the Ideas they intended to excite. The present Set excite *no* Ideas except of dry Admiration for the astonishing Difficulties they perform; and some serious Fears lest they Should break their slender Limbs in the Performance——Holding out one Leg and one Arm in a parallel Line is destructive of all Grace, and when after springing up to a prodigious height, they come down on the Point of one Toe——nothing can exceed our Wonder at its Possibility, except one's Joy that they escape in Safety. Music and Dancing are no longer what they were, and I grow less pleased with both every Hour.

> Year chases Year, Decay pursues Decay,
> Still drops some Joy from with'ring Life away—[10]

but Do not let us teize Dear Miss Fellowes to write, it only worries *her* and whilst I am conscious of it, cannot delight *me*. While Secure of a Friend's Affectionate Regard, I abhor dunning them for Letters: When my Heart tells me that their Kindness is growing cold, and feels weary of keeping up an uninteresting Correspondence,—'Tis then that Silence is a *Mute* that *strangles.*[11]

I am enchanted to think of your Brother and Sister's Felicity——They are the most amiable and most deserving of Happiness that can be found; and how Wise they were to discover the Value of Happiness in Time, and fling no more of it away![12]

We have an old Beauty come here to Bath——you scarce can remember her one of the very *very* much admired Women, Lady Stanley—Poor Thing![13] She went to France and Italy early in Life, learned les Manieres, and les Tournures, and how gay a Thing it was to despise her Husband——who was completely even with her—

> In Youth She conquer'd with so wild a Rage
> As left her scarce a Subject in her Age:
> For foreign Glories foreign Joys to roam,
> No Thought of Peace or Happiness at home.[14]

Her Fortune however as an Independent Heiress She held fast;[15] and her Wit and Pleasantry seem but little impaired—but the Loss of Health sent her here, and She wonders to see mine so good, so indeed do I; but we were no puling Family—my Father both my Grandfathers—and Three Uncles all died *suddenly*—which renders me more watchful of Course, Never mind; Pope says Act well your Part, there all the honour lies.

> Nos sumus in Scena—quin et mandante Magistro
> Quisque datas agimus partes: sit longa brevisve
> Fabula, nil refert.[16]

I hope You will come to Bath soon, and give me some good Advice: I *do hope* you will: nobody will be more observant of it—as nobody ever could esteem it more than does Dear Sir James Fellowes's ever Obliged and Faithful H: L: Piozzi.

You have made all *Your* Friends—*my* Friends; Pray tell them what a grateful Heart *that is,* which they have been so kind to.

Text Harvard Theatre Collection. Pusey Library, TS. 940.6.

1. The M.P. for New Romney (1796–1807), John Willett, died in Bath on 26 September of apoplexy. See the *Bath and Cheltenham Gazette,* 4 October; *GM* 85, pt. 2 (1815):379.
2. MW lived at 43 Park Street and was a neighbor of Willett.
3. The legal confirmation of HLP's lifetime right to Streatham Park and its reversion after her death to the Thrale daughters.
4. The "Rex Regum," Maximilian I (1459–1519), Holy Roman Emperor (1493–1519), in likening himself to the most powerful king in Greece, recognized that he was the second founder of the Habsburg house and its great empire.
5. HLP uses these various epithets to comment on contemporary affairs.
Louis XVIII was the king of asses because his subjects were scornful of his conservatism and he accepted the *Ultras'* influence.
In making the English monarch king of the devils, HLP alludes to disturbances in Ireland over the tithe system that required "military aid and extraordinary magisterial powers." By 25 September the insurrection act was reinstituted there.
Fernando VII (1784–1833) had returned to the throne of Spain in 1814 and allowed the establishment of ministerial despotism. HLP "hoped" that the secret societies of liberal revolutions, newly re-formed, would dissolve themselves, that the partisans of the constitution of 1812 ("deceañistas") would cease insurrectionary activity.
6. JF on 1 October had written: "I have been reading Don Quixote through in Spanish—it is most truly diverting" (Ry. 555.78).
7. See *Anecdotes* (pp. 281–83), where HLP recalls SJ's judgment that the book was "the greatest in the world . . . as a book of entertainment." Noting that *Don Quixote* "is a sort of common property, an universal classic," she adds "Shakespeare himself has, till lately, been worshipped only at home . . . while engravers and translators *live* by the Hero of La Mancha in every nation" (p. 282). See also *Retrospection,* 2:287–88; *Thraliana,* 1:3, 354–55.
8. Bath's Theatre Royal opened for the season on 30 September 1815 with WAC playing the lead in Nathaniel Lee's *Alexander the Great* (1677).
9. On opening night, the drama was followed, according to the *Bath and Chelenham Gazette,* by a "Grand Divertisement," consisting of "a Grand Pas de Trois . . . and a Grand Pas De Deux, by Monsieur and Madame Léon."
Léon was dancing master at the King's Theatre (1814–17), during which time his wife, Virginie Léon, also danced there. Reviewing the performance, the *Bath Herald* (7 October) called her "one of the most agile and graceful little figures we have ever seen."
10. SJ's *The Vanity of Human Wishes,* lines 305–6.
11. Cf. Cowper, *Conversation,* line 352: "The fear of being silent makes us mute."
In *British Synonymy* (1:178) HLP alludes to "the Turkish slave, who in his earliest years had his tongue torn out by the barbarous ministers of despotism to insure silence concerning their intrigues."
12. On 1 October [1815], JF wrote that "the happiness of Julia and Dorset Fellowes at Sidmouth appears to be uninterrupted and they are both delighted with their House, which belongs to Lord Gwydir." Dorset Fellowes was Lord Gwydir's secretary.
13. Margaret Stanley, née Owen (1742–1816), widow of Sir John Thomas Stanley (1735–1807), sixth baronet (1755) of Alderley Park, Cheshire. Lady Stanley's arrival in Bath was announced in the *Bath Chronicle,* 21 September.
14. Pope's *Epistle II. To a Lady.* "Of The Characters of Women," lines 221–24.
15. Lady Stanley was the heiress of Hugh Owen (d. 1742) of Penrhôs, Anglesey.
16. Pope's *An Essay on Man,* 4.194. HLP latinizes two of Pope's sources: Epictetus' *Enchiridion,* c.17, and Seneca's *Epistolae,* 77.17. Cf. *Spectator* 219; Aaron Hill, *The Plain Dealer* 28.

TO JOHN WILLIAMS

Bath
9: October 1815.

My dear Mr. Williams used to write to me; and promised when we parted that he would not forget so good a Custom. But no Letter comes and from here none can be expected to produce Amusement. Bath is a Desart; all your Belles gone—as well as all the Butterflies. *They* lasted longer than usual this year, so did the Swallows, who left us but last Saturday: and 'tis odd enough, but the Autumn is very little if any, advanced here; from what I left it round Streatham Park—9 weeks ago.

No Talk of Buonaparte now—he seems to me as completely forgotten as if he had never been born. When the Ships return—that Conversation will renew of itself.[1] Sir James Fellowes's Sister in Law knows the Island of St. Helena, every Creek of it; She was married there, and resided in the Place Three Months:—her Notion is, that no prison can be safer or more complete; but I have read some old Saying that there is no Pass so narrow but an Ass laden with Gold can get Through,[2] and he has Plenty of Money in his Hands, and in his power too.

I think your good Father rejoyces from his heart to find how the French are forced to refund their stolen goods[3]—It will humble them beyond all Measure, and I shall not for my own Part think their Pride punished enough till the Pillar is taken down from Place Vendôme.[4]

We have got the great Parisian Dancers here at Bath en attendant for the London Theatre, when they will exhibit on the *Opera Stage*.[5] It is a curious sight to see them—standing on the Point of one Toe like Cataleptic Patients, with a Leg and Arm extended quite out in two parallel lines.—But the Pig-faced Lady would to me be quite as good a show[6]—and not a bit more out of nature. Madame Léon is however so pretty, she may be sure to find Admirers—when she sits still.

Do you remember a Miss Nash that sang very pleasingly? Virtue Nash we called her and she was a *good* Girl, and is praised in the *Intercepted Letter* where so few come off well.[7] The London Managers have doubled the salary we give her.

And I hope she will glide off the Stage without blame
And let nobody cheat her of her *Christian Name*.

Have you been to Brynbella and seen our little Baby? *She* will be named like the running Mare Shropshire Lass—I suppose, when She comes to be a Toast, and her Merits inscribed on the Drinking Glasses. I wonder if that Fashion is among the gay Fellows!

Lady Stanley is here to whose honor and beauty so many Bumpers have been swallowed and the empty Glasses thrown over empty heads innumerable. *Poor*

Lady Stanley! And how she looks *now*! We meet tonight at Mrs. Holroyds! but don't you be thinking of

Three Cats sate by the fire side
all in a basket of coal dust &c.[8]

because we intend to be very entertaining and very witty. General Leighton is our regular Beau and General Donkin our Volunteer Visitant.[9] He has just recovered his Hearing at 89 years old; and he has done well as I tell him for he has much Good to hear of his only Son—a charming Fellow, and just now very happily married.[10]

I think the place my kind friend Lady Williams destined for me near Conway might produce Letters less barren of amusement than this.[11] Yet I will send it—a peppercorn Acknowledgement of the Affection I owe my dear Mr. Williams and his amiable Family: to every Member of which present me, with every tender and respectful Wish/ believing me most sincerely and faithfully/ Yours/ H: L: Piozzi.

Text Ry. 6 (1813–21). *Address* John Williams Esqr./ Bodylwyddan/ St. Asaph/ North Wales. *Postmark* BATH 9 0C 9.

1. Escorted by a convoy, Napoleon sailed from Plymouth on 4 August and arrived at St. Helena on 13 October. Among the first ships of the convoy to return was the *Redpole*, which left St. Helena on 22 October. Her captain presented his dispatches to the admiralty on 4 December (*The Times*, 5 December).

2. There are several variations on this saying. See Tilley, p. 20 (A356), and particularly Howell's "There's no fence or fortress *against an Ass laden with Gold*" (*Epistolae Ho-Elianae*, 1:108).

3. The British compelled the return of Napoleon's art spoils to their rightful owners. According to a letter from Paris in *The Times*, 4 October, "The Louvre begins to look extremely vacant for want of the fine specimens of art, which have been carried off by waggon loads under the inspection of artists from the several countries to which they are transporting them."

4. In 1810, a column, with a statue of Napoleon as Caesar, had been erected at the Place Vendôme to commemorate his victory at Austerlitz. The statue of Napoleon was replaced in 1815 by a fleur-de-lis as a token of the Bourbon's return.

5. The Léons were to dance at the King's Theatre on opening night 13 January 1816 (*The Times*, 11 January).

6. See HLP to Ly W, 21 March 1815, n. 3.

7. Virtue Nash (fl. 1795–1816), actress and singer, appeared at Bath's Theatre Royal and the Drury Lane between 1813 and 1816, when she disappeared from theatrical records. She was to make her Drury Lane debut on 28 October as Polly in *The Beggar's Opera* and to receive generally favorable notices, including one from William Hazlitt in the *Examiner* (6 November 1815).

She is fulsomely versified as a singer in EM's *Intercepted Epistle*, 38–39.

For reviews of her performance, see *The Times*, 30 October; the *Bath Herald*, 18 November.

8. HLP likens herself, Mrs. Holroyd, and Lady Stanley to the "three cats" popular in children's verse.

For Sarah Martha Holroyd, see HLP to PSP, 7 March 1803, n. 1.

9. For Baldwin Leighton, whose mother-in-law was Lady Stanley, see HLP to JSPS, 18 April 1812, n. 4; for Robert Donkin, see HLP to JSPS, 20 March 1810, n. 9.

10. In August 1815, prior to his departure from England for duty in Madras, the younger Donkin married Elizabeth Markham (1790–1818). See *AR*, "Chronicle" 57 (1815): 118.

11. In Carnarvonshire.

TO JOHN SALUSBURY PIOZZI SALUSBURY

Bath
Tuesday 10: October 1815.

My dearest Salusbury's kind Perswasion of what I have so long Suffered, is my best Compensation for the Sufferings; and I remember our Harriet saying at Condover this Time last Year—"Why then if you do actually live a Year in the Way you talk of,——We shall *see a New Thing.*"[1] I have indeed exhibited myself wholly in *a new Character* and I *would* have published the Book by Subscription to get sooner out of it——but the People I live amongst would not really *suffer* me to do it; and they are so kind, I could not bear to go against their Advice and even *Consent.* Any other Way of bringing it out—would have cost me 200£ at starting;—and then take Chance for Profit and Repayment. *That* Measure, my Poverty rendered impracticable; and my Fear of involving myself further:—and as to Purchase and Sale in these Times, *They* are out of the Question.

God knows how Streatham Park Furniture will sell second hand—and spoyled as they have spoiled it. Nothing sells well, but advertising can do no harm: I will copy Windle's *last* Letter that you may see his Opinion. Doctor Myddelton and you both seemed to think the Money (almost any Money) better than the Books, Pictures &c.——but if my Life in the Estate does not go *too,* I shall not be disencumbered of my Expence: and 'twere better I kept Streatham Park as it should be, than suffer it once more to run to Ruin. Why Lord Keith wants to enfranchize the Copy hold there, I guess not—hear wise and in *this* Business disinterested Windle on the Subject.

I see I have written on the wrong side the Paper—topsy Turvey, but it don't much matter.——I have scored under the Words as he scores 'em.

7 October 1815.

Dear Madam—

Many Thanks for your favour; but with regard to the Copy hold, I am *far* from thinking that your enabling Lord Keith to enfranchise will induce him to purchase: he has not I assure you any such Idea, neither does he in the least Degree encourage it. And for this Reason I must beg leave to with hold my Approbation from the Agreement until I again receive your Directions. Your own Goodness of Heart induces you to accommodate one who has *no* Inclination to *serve you:* If however it must be so, I shall—with Reluctance comply. As to a Sale, this may be adviseable, and it is probable that the noble Lord may attend and bid; but his Attachment to Money will I am satisfied confine that bidding to no great Amount; and he will rather prefer all Chances. Here however he *may be* disappointed by proper Instructions to the Auctioneer.

I am most happy to think next Month discharges you of Mead; and I am Madam &c./ Windle,

with Regard to Crowmarsh I suppose some Dispute exists about the Quantity of Land——The Rents fall everywhere, and I suppose in Oxfords—

So much for Mr. Windle's Opinion of Lord Keith, and *his* Notion of him as a Purchaser. The Day I saw Mr. Merrik Hoare in London I recollect his saying We are all *at* Lord Keith to make him free the Copy hold—but as I cared not about it I forgot his saying so, and never enquired why they wished it free.

As for myself, whether or no I can shake *every* Debt off by mere privation——is difficult to say *yet*:——when nearer to July, I shall be a better Judge. You know the Dividends this Month are 180£ and Newton pays 200£. Gillow, Mead, and Leak have each my Promise for 100£—Ward, Windle, Lonsdale must all wait till January—and my Lodging must be paid out of the 80£. Poor as I am however, I have put Hester Maria's hair into a Gold Locket, and paid for it honestly—The Bath people will not hurt me I am sure. I pay as regularly as possible, and Thank God our Bread and our Meat are at very reasonable Prices—so is Fish, but I dare not touch it. You must not fancy my Health *unimpaired*, but 'tis better than most People's, and all the Medical Men are ready to lend their Help.

We shall certainly come if we *can* in July, and *I hope we may*. Had the Book Succeeded I had been cleared sooner——but even Upham said "God forbid I should live to see Mrs. Piozzi soliciting Subscriptions"——and then What can one do?—nothing I think but save every Sixpence—and *hope* for lasting Freedom.[2]

Kiss my little God Daughter for me,[3] and tell your pretty Lady how much I love her. 'Tis 9 Months to July——*She* knows one may bear a heavy burden for 9 Months in the certain Assurance of laying it down *then*. Apropòs to Lyings In, John Octavius Glover has got a Noble Girl as big as Two: She tortured her Mother with *heart-sickness* the whole Time of Pregnancy, but the Labour was over in Three Hours; and She says it was the happiest Day of the whole Time.[4]

Mademoiselle's Name is Octavia.

I never will take this Paper for the sake of holding more—again There is no writing on it, 'tis Impossible: I must just say however how sincerely and Affectionately I remain yours and dear Harriet's and little Hester Maria's/ Affectionate Aunt/ H: L: P.

When Windle tells *me*, I will tell *you* about the Map—'tis a happy Thing we have it——They *must* come to us after all for every thing.[5]

Text Ry. 588.294. *Address* John Salusbury Piozzi Salusbury Esq./ Brynbella/ near Denbigh/ North Wales. *Postmark* < >.

1. JSPS had written on 7 October: " . . . indeed dear Aunt I do most sincerely hope that by next July you will be quite clear of all your troubles" (Ry. 591.4).

2. For John Upham, see HLP to AL, 28 August 1814, n. 2. Upham was regarded as having "invincible patience, insinuating manners, and an acute and cultivated mind" (EM's *Intercepted Epistle*, p. 17n.).

3. Hester Maria "Missey" Salusbury.

4. See HLP to JSPS, 9 March 1815, n. 16.

5. In his letter of 7 October, JSPS mentioned his discovery at Brynbella of "the Map of Crowmarsh Estate."

For the contretemps over Crowmarsh, which netted HLP £400 annually, see, e.g., HLP to John Gillon, 18 November 1799.

TO ALEXANDER LEAK

Sunday 15: October 1815.

I thought it long since I heard from poor Old Streatham Park, and when I did hear, one Passage in the Letter surprized me.——Because Mr. Salusbury from whom last Post brought me Intelligence; says, that *He* has the Maps etc. of Crowmarsh Farm, and holds them in Readiness to do whatsoever I please with. Ah *dear* Leak! and how came I by Duplicates of those Maps?——Ladies don't usually possess Maps of Land they have merely a Rent Charge on: Mr. Thrale certainly gave me the Estate, but giving it me Twice, I lost it by some Quirk of the Law. Whilst the Farm brought me in, a dry 272£ o'Year however, the Ladies considered it as mine; when the Rent was raised to 450£—I was only to have the Rent Charge.—And no Arrearage for my four Years of Widowhood. Well! and after all, I feel a Tender Fear of offending them—and if I do quicken my Determination of parting with the Place, it will be more for *your* Sake than for any other Reason; because my heart feels a faint Hope *now* of getting clear from all Incumbrances—by mere Privation—in July next, and if these Things, (thro' your Care)—can sell even for 5000£ I shall be able to replace My Dear Piozzi's 6000£ in the 3 Per Cents and purchase myself a little Annuity, or the Lease of the Gay Street House with the remainder.

This is Sir James Fellowes's Advice, to whom I ran this Moment with your Letter—which he approves most heartily.

Poor Windle! well but indeed he gives me the same Counsel as You do, about being decidedly off or on with Lord Keith; and it will not now be long before we see what his Lordship means in very true earnest.

Mr. Matthew is a wise Man I dare say, and detects Imposition enough: The Beauty of all will be to Escape Payment for being imposed on.

That Mr. Wilmot the Seedsman must have his Money I understand, for he has not been paid I suppose: and that is a Cruel Imposition. I thought you would like Mr. Cotton: he has gone Through a good many Tryals as well as his poor Cousin who is/ Your poor Friend/ H: L: P.

I vex at Mr. Anderdon's having taken that Paper which I wrote for Count Lieven—more than the Thing is worth;—but if we sell—no matter how much such Nonsense is disseminated.

We had better learn whether they will accept the *Stript* House, before we strip it: I would not have it lie *stript* on my Hands for the World: it would be like the Ghost of a departed Friend haunting me Day and Night.

Multiplying Letters is of no Use. Call on Mr. Windle yourself, and shew him this Postscript.

Text Hyde Collection. *Address* Mr. Alexander Leak/ Streatham Park/ Surrey. *Postmark* 10 o'Clock OC 17 1815; 17 OC 17 1815.

TO SIR JAMES FELLOWES

[19 October 1815][1]

The next best Thing to shaking a Friend by the *Hand* is seeing his *Hand* Writing——I am happy to read yours, and most earnestly hope you will keep close to the House till better Days:[2] The Ladies will have Sad Weather to travel in. General Gars<t>in did me a great deal of Honour, and deserved some Amusement In Payment for his Trouble in finding the House.[3]

If it were not for Flattery——I should break my Heart yet——Old Bills not counted on coming against me so——but I don't care as the Children say; I shall out of my Plagues, and out of my Prison too—next July.

Mean while Dear old Doctor Lort the Greek Professor was God Father to the Gentleman you mention and his Surname went to the Bishop at the Font as a Christian Name. You will find Doctor Lort mentioned under the Article Daphne as I remember.[4]

But I have had a nice Dish of Flattery dressed to my Taste this Morning. That grave Mr. Lucas brought his Son here, that He might see the *first Woman in England*——forsooth——So I am now grown one of the Curiosities of Bath it seems and *one of the Antiquities*.[5]

This Evening a Chair will carry me to Mrs. Holroyds to meet Two other Females whom Richardson taught the Town to call old Tabbies,[6] attended says he by Young *Grimalkins*; now that's wrong: because they are young Tabbies, and when grown Grey—are *Gris Malkins* I suppose.

Is not this fine Nonsense for the first Woman—Prima Donna!! in good Time!

If I could detain Your Man to say one Grave Serious Word it would express my Content that your dear Father is arrived to take Care of my Inestimable Friend Sir James Fellowes—whose health is of such Consequence. Mind what he says, and believe me most sincerely/ Your Obliged Servant/ H: L: Piozzi.

Text Princeton University Library. *Address* Sir James Fellowes.

1. Although Hayward (2:307) dates this letter 30 October 1815, its contents, particularly her references to Lucas's visit and the Holroyd party, correspond to HLP's "Pocket Book" entries of 19 October.

2. HLP urged an ailing JF to stay indoors while the weather was either cloudy or wet, as it was for the week of 16 October. See the *Bath and Cheltenham Gazette,* 25 October.

3. John Garstin (1756–1820), an engineer in the Bengal army and surveyor general at Bengal, became a major general in that army in 1811. He was on furlough from the beginning of 1815 to 1818, when he returned to Calcutta.

4. In "Lyford Redivivus," HLP reports Lort as saying: "Why I have been baptizing a Child—Daphne. A foolish Exploit enough; was my too sudden Answer——Why returned my Friend, I did hesitate half a minute—perhaps a whole one; but reflecting that no one scruples calling a Lady *Laura*; I felt that the Woman was as good as the Tree at least, so gave the name our Silly Gossips pitched on—but looking further still, when all was over, I recollected how Daphne was Sybilla Delphica—and sure we *Parsons* must not refuse an Appellation which Pausanias says, belonged to *her* whom he calls *Hierophile* a Friend to Priests.—"
For Michael Lort, see HLP to SL, 7 December 1784, n. 12.

5. Richard Lucas (ca. 1761–1827), rector of Edith Weston, and his recently ordained son, Richard (d. 1846).

6. HLP recalled that Richardson in *Clarissa* referred to "The two antiques [who] only bowed their tabby heads." (The letter is by Lovelace to Belford, "Sunday night, July 9.")

TO ALEXANDER LEAK

Bath
Sunday 22: October *1815.*

I receive Leak's Letter this Minute and am glad my Third Hundred Pound Draft arrived safe—I mean *Third* since August 1814—50£ more in January will make it 400£ and I hope I shall be able to afford it.

As you say it is high Time to determine; and my Determination has not been changed. 'Tis to Sell the Contents of poor old Streatham Park (taking out favourite Trifles)[1]—and unless I can so dispose of the Shell and the Grounds as to bear me quite harmless[2]—and my Residuary Legatee harmless also—from all Dilapidations and Demands:—Then to *give* it by a Deed of Gift to my four Daughters. Do you think they will accept it? I am dubious.

Mr. Windle does not seem to *me* to have any kindness for Lord Keith, nor does he wish me to shew him any.—He is angry Lord Keith does not apply to *me* concerning the Enfranchisement of the Copyhold Property.

If Crowmarsh Estate *does* belong to *me*, I have been very Ill-treated: but that is a dubious Business, and perhaps 'tis better be quiet than go into Investigation. I now receive a Rent Charge of 400£ per annum off it, not the Rents and Profits, which are 450£ o'Year.

I earnestly wish Gillow's Bill may be reduced; and think it very odd in You to say it is of little Consequence, because of the People I intend to give my *Small* Wealth to, when once collected together. Nobody knows who I may give it to; nor can anybody easily say of *Themselves one Day*, what may be the Determination of their Minds *another Day*.

6000£ in the Stocks would bring me 180£ per Annum which would add to my Income and to my *Enjoyment*; and if I could squeeze out 120£ o'Year more as an Annuity, it would pay House Rent for the best Habitation I desire here at Bath; and leave me my 2100£ clear to spend among Friends I have made for myself— when they *must* of necessity have been disinterested in their Kindness;—— because it has not be[en] in my Power to give a Glass of Wine, or even a Dish of Tea to anyone for the Time I have spent away from Wales and Surrey.—— The *Bath People* have best Claim on *my* Gratitude I'm sure, however those may act on whose Gratitude I may have Pretensions; and my Intention—my *present* Intention is to live my Life and die my Death among them.

I see I have taken a Sheet of Paper that was begun to be written on; but tis no Matter.

Do you think Count Lieven would pay his Money to Gillow and not send it in to Hammersley—as due to *me*? I should think that Impossible. And if It had been sent to Pallmall I should have heard of it from Them./ God bless you all Three/ says H: L: Piozzi.

You will see a *good hearty* Friend of mine a Mr. Cruttenden of Bath some Day[3]—he brings you a Letter; pray be civil to him: I suppose Dear Cotton will call often.[4]

Text Hyde Collection. *Address* Mr. Alexander Leak/ Streatham Park/ Surrey. *Postmark* <10 o'Clock> OC 23 1815.

1. The "favourite Trifles" were to include, among other things, the works of Dryden and Descartes; paintings by Cipriani and Domenichino; two carved ebony chairs; "a pair of rare old blue and white bottles, richly mounted in silver, *brought overland from India* in the 14th century"; "two antique Etruscan vases"; "a very curious antique cabinet"; a number of kitchen utensils. See the *Sale Catalogue* (1) for 8, 10, 11 May 1816.
2. After the dispersal of the contents, the house and grounds were let for £260 annually to Robert Elliott, who also assumed payment for repairs, taxes, and tithes.
3. The son of a wealthy Southwark merchant, William Courteney (or Courtenay) Cruttenden (1754–1842) was a Cantabrigian who received his B.A. in 1777 and M.A. in 1780. After a brief stint in the army as a captain in the Coldstream Guards, he settled in Heighham near Norwich but frequently visited Bath and maintained his ties in Surrey, i.e., in Esher and Southwark. He had two sons, both Cantabrigians: Edwin (b. 1784) and the Reverend William Cruttenden (1766–1863), a priest who served in Macclesfield. HLP was particularly interested in the latter.
4. HLP's "Pocket Book" on 3, 5, and 6 October mentions visits by "R: S: Cotton" who, according to the entry for 17 October, had gone to Surrey. Robert Salusbury Cotton (1800–24) was the eighth son of Henry Calveley Cotton. For the latter, see HLP to Q, 15 July 1784[a], n. 6.

TO SIR JAMES FELLOWES

Tuesday Night 24: October 1815.

No Anecdote, nor no Verses, no—nor even *Your Praises*—which so highly I value, can give equal Pleasure to the Account you send me of your health; May God Almighty long, *very* long preserve it for all our Sakes: and inspire you with Gratitude for its Restoration, as he has inspired you with Skill to preserve it.

The Day was so bright and at one Time so fine—I was impelled to make the Rhymes you will read enclosed. Collings promises me the Travel Book on Thursday;[1] which I shall correct for you, and make as clean, and as little unworthy of your Acceptance as I can.

Doctor Fellowes is certainly right; I took my Account of Katherine's Cruelty from Gorani;[2] whose Memoires des Cours D'Italie I left in Wales.[3] Are these Verses in your Margin? they *should* be there.

> Elle fit oublier par un Esprit sublime
> D'un Pouvoir odieux les enormes Abus;
> Et sur un Trône acquis par le Crime,
> Elle se maintint par ses Vertus.

> Her dazzling Reign so brightly Shone
> Few sought to *mark* the Crimes they *courted*:
> Whilst on her ill-acquired Throne
> She sate; by Virtue's self supported.

The Anecdotes of Doctor Johnson were begun at Milan, where we first heard of his Death;[4] and so written on, from Mile Stone to Mile Stone; till arriving at Leghorn we shipped them off for England.[5]

Mr. Thrale had always advised Me to treasure up some of the valuable Pearls that fell from his Lips in Conversation; and Mr. Piozzi was so indignant at the Treatment I met with from his Executors[6]—that *he* spirited me up to give *My own* Account of Doctor Johnson in *my own* way——and not send to *them* the detached Bits which they *required* with such assumed Superiority—and distance of Manner—altho' most of them were Intimates of the House——till they *thought it deserted—forever.*

I think we must not tell your Dear Father that his Friend Bennett Langton was one of them. If we do, he will not say as Dr. Johnson did—Sit Anima mea cum Langtono.[7]

But my Marriage had offended them all, beyond hope of Pardon.

Now judge my Transport and my Husband's, when at Rome we received Letters saying The Book was bought with such Avidity that Cadell had not one Copy left, when the King sent for it at 10 o'Clock at Night; and he was forced to beg one from a Friend to supply his Majesty's Impatience who sate up all Night reading it. Samuel Lysons Esq. Keeper of the Records in the Tower, then a Law Student in the Temple, made my Bargain with the Bookseller, from whom on my Return I received 300£, a Sum unexampled in those Days, for so small a Volume.[8]

And here my Dear Sir is a truly-told Anecdote of Yours and/ Your charming Family's gratefully-attached/ H: L: P.

Pray present them my Verses.

Text Princeton. *Address* Sir James Fellowes.

1. HLP refers to *Observations*, a copy of which was found for her by the Bath bookseller Edwin Collings (fl. 1789–1860).

2. In *Mémoires . . . de l'Italie*, Giuseppi Gorani in the section "Projet atroce presqu'incroyable, mais vrai" detailed Catherine de Medici's cruelty, her evil effect upon Charles IX, and her instigation of the Saint Bartholomew's Day massacre of the Huguenots in Paris in 1572 (1:258–67). See HLP's description of the massacre in *Retrospection*, 2:145–46.

For Gorani, see HLP to Cadell, 26 December 1785, n. 2; to Q, 19 December 1794, n. 15.

3. HLP's copy of Gorani's *Mémoires* was sold at the posthumous auction of her library in 1823 (lot 505). See *Sale Catalogue* (2).

4. See especially HLP to SL, 20 January 1785; 26 February, etc.

5. See HLP to Cadell, 20 October 1785.

6. For SJ's executors, see HLP to SL, 26 February 1785, n. 7.

7. Of Bennet Langton SJ said: "'I know not who will go to Heaven if Langton does not. Sir, I could almost say, Sit anima mea cum Langtono'" (*Boswell's Johnson*, 4:280). See also *Thraliana*, 1:108, n. 3.

8. See particularly, Thomas Cadell to HLP, 24 January 1786; HLP to SL, 11 May 1786; to Sophia Byron, 8 June [1789]; *Thraliana*, 2:639.

TO SIR JAMES FELLOWES

Sunday 29: October 1815

My dear Sir—

Our Friend Leak is but a Blockhead after all: I wrote to bid him send me *Johnson's Letters* of which I understood he had seen a clean copy somewhere—— and which I meant——*for you*——to have explained by marginal Notes, and filling up the Names &c.

He sends me however my own Observations on Italy, which by some Perverseness the People *do* call *Letters*: altho' you see in the Preface (where I fear your penetrating Eyes will observe a Shade of Resentment,) that they were no Letters at all;[1] and *that* is the Reason I condemn their Feebleness; because professing to be written for the Public, more Care should have been taken, and a less familiar Diction adopted. This is very ha<rsh>. Criticism; should not I have made a good *Reviewer*?[2] So if Longman will really sell you a clean Copy,[3] and if you are not *yet* tired of poor faded Floretta, and her Works, send for one: and let me have it to make Explanations in.[4]

Mean while *see* how our *Lives* come to be reviewed in the last Stage of our Journey!——We *know* they will be submitted to Examination when the Journey shall be over.——But our Judge is merciful, nailing our Account of Follies to his Cross. Is it then wise to wish delayed The Hour of Retrospection?

Certainly *not* for one so very near it as is/ Your obliged Friend/ H: L: P.

Give my true Love to the Ladies. I enclose poor< >seemed as if longing to write.

I can tell more of Hogarth——than is known to anyone but it shall be for another Time.

Text Hyde Collection. *Address* Sir James Fellowes/ No. 13/ Vineyards.

1. In the "Preface" to *Observations* (1:vi), HLP comments: "I have not thrown my thoughts into the form of private letters; because a work of which truth is the best recommendation, should not above all others begin with a lie. My old acquaintance rather chose to amuse themselves with conjectures, than to flatter me with tender inquiries during my absence: our correspondence then would not have been any amusement to the Public, whose treatment of me deserves every possible acknowledgement."

2. See, e.g., HLP to SL, 13 August, n. 13; 28 November, n. 3, both letters in 1789.

3. Thomas Norton Longman (1771–1842) had taken over his family's bookselling firm in Paternoster Row, ca. 1792. Expanding the firm, he had taken on a number of partners, so that by 1812 it was known as Longman, Hurst, Rees, Orme, and Brown.

It may be that Thomas Cadell the younger had sold either the unbought copies of *Observations* to Longman or its copyright.

4. Planning *The Fountains*, SJ told HLT, "Come Mistress, now I'll write a Tale and your Character shall be in it" ("Harvard Piozziana" 1:61).

For *The Fountains*, see HLP to PSP, 1 August [1798], n. 4.

TO SIR JAMES FELLOWES

30: October 1815.

If Dear Sir James Fellowes still continues under Discipline,[1] this Anecdote of Hogarth—and of his little Friend may amuse him. My Father and he were very intimate, and he often dined with us. One Day when he had done so, my Aunt and a Groupe of young Cousins came in the Afternoon,[2]——Evenings were earlier Things than they are now, and 3 o'Clock the common Dinner Hour. I had got a then new Thing I suppose, which was called Game of the Goose:[3] and felt earnest that we Children might be allowed a round Table to play at it— but was half afraid of my Uncle's and my Father's grave Looks. Hogarth said good-humouredly, *I* will come My dears and play at it with you: our Joy was great, and the Sport began under my Management and Direction. The Pool rose to *Five Shillings*, a Fortune to us Monkeys; and when I won it—I capered for Delight.

But the next Time we went to Leicester Fields Mr. Hogarth was painting[4]— and bid me sit to him——and now look here said he I am doing this for *you*— you are not 14 Years old yet I think, but you will be 24; and this Portrait will then be like you.

'Tis the Lady's last Stake[5]——See how She hesitates between her Money and her Honour, Take you care; I see an Ardour for Play in your Eyes and in Your heart—don't indulge it, I shall give you this Picture as a Warning, because I love you now, you are so good A Girl.

——In a fortnight's Time after that Visit we went out of Town——*he* died somewhat suddenly I believe—and I never saw my poor Portrait again—till going to Fonthill many, *many* Years afterward I met it there, and *Mr. Piozzi* observed the Likeness——when I was shewing him the fine House then de- serted by Mr. Beckford. The Summer before last it was exhibited In Pall Mall as The Property of Lord Charlemont[6]—I asked Mrs. Hoare who was admiring it, if She ever saw any Person it resembled——She said *No,* unless it might once have been like *me* and we turned away to look at something else.

With regard to *Play*——I have been always particular in avoiding it, so that I scarce know whether the Inclination ever subsisted or not—The Scene he drew will certainly never remind anyone of poor H: L: P. and no one but *yourself* knows the Story.

But I must tell you how well your dear father is, and how heartily I made him laugh this morning at one of my comical stories, true as the day, which I heard a silly lady in my own country two or three years ago ask me quite suddenly before a room full of company, to tell her; "for," says she, "you know Mrs. Piozzi does understand everything; what bone her son broke at the battle of Talavera."[7] This was *too* hard a question; but the lady went on: "No, no," continued she, "not hard to Mrs. Piozzi. Louisa, you lost the letter very pro- vokingly which had the fine word in it; and now you laugh, you ill-natured thing, because I can't recollect it, but Mrs. Piozzi will know in a minute." Turn- ing to me: "It was one of your fine words, I say, and very like fable-book." "I have," said I, "heard that Mr. Morgan's horse fell upon him, and perhaps broke the fibula, or small bone of his master's leg." "There, there!" cries out the lady; "I told you Mrs. Piozzi would know it at once."[8]

[In the hand of Sir James Fellowes:
This picture of *Hogarths Last Stake* is now at Goodwood where I went with my daughter to see it——and I believe to this day, the Duke of Richmond who is the possessor of the picture never heard this anecdote nor could know the real history. J. F. /Pangbourne /[9] September 20 1851]

Text: That in the Houghton Autograph File is lacking the last paragraph (which is preserved in Hayward, 2: 310).

1. JF was confined to his house by a lingering illness.
2. For Sir Lynch Salusbury Cotton and his wife, Elizabeth Abigail, see HLP to Isabella Hamilton, 13 May 1805, n. 2. The Cottons had nine sons and five daughters.
3. The game of the goose was a play of chance introduced from the Continent, ca. 1725. The game itself uses a playing board upon which the participants place their stakes and throw dice to determine the movement of their markers. Its name is derived from the board, which has a goose depicted at every fourth and fifth compartment in succession. If the player's cast falls upon a goose, he moves forward twice the number of his throw.
4. Hogarth's town residence from 1733 until his death was the third house from the end on the east side of Leicester Square, then Leicester Fields.
5. For HLP's account of "The Lady's Last Stake," see HLP to Q, 22 March 1810 and nn. 11–14.
6. Francis William Caulfeild (1775–1863), second earl of Charlemont (1799), loaned the Hogarth painting in 1814 to the British Institution for its exhibition of native artists. The painting remained in the Charlemont family until 1874, when it was auctioned at Christie's in London.
7. The battle of Talavera on 27–28 July 1809 was regarded by Wellington as one of the most bitter and costly he ever fought.
8. HLP refers to a comment made by Louisa Morgan of Golden Grove, Flintshire. Her son, Edward (1793–1861), saw action in the Peninsular War as an officer in the Royal Fusiliers.
For the Morgans, see HLP to Ly W, 21 March 1815, n. 4.
9. A village on the Thames in Berkshire.

TO ALEXANDER LEAK

Tuesday 14th: November 1815.

Now my good Leak let your next Letter bring good news. The Parchment is come,—Is the Estate mine or no? We shall stand on *high Ground* if it is: I am exceedingly anxious.

Mean while Mr. Windle thinks I was a Monkey in sending him 100£ for Mead. He imagines Mead accepted Bills from Hammersley:—*I* fancied George Hammersley refused them:[1] Certain it is however, that I can find no Time in which I sent the Money by a Stamped *Order. Let it be done as it should be.*

Newton will send the rest of his Money another day. Mr. Penning has been here to say what a fine Auctioneer he shall be, and truly do I think he seems made on purpose for it.[2] He says that he shall bring the Marquis of Stafford to see the Pictures, and *that* is the best of his Sayings. The Marquis of Stafford is a real good Judge.[3]

I suppose little Dear[4] and I are both in the Wheel of Fortune still, by your Silence with regard to our Success—Alexander is surely a fortunate Name, and Dear Piozzi was considered as a Lucky Man; far as *I* could, I contributed to make him happy; but this Marriage Settlement! is it a real Estate that I have in Oxfordshire at last? or only a Rent Charge?

Some Italian Gentleman whom you never saw, thought he would be very clever once, and write English Verses on the Anniversary of my Wedding Day with my last Husband—so he said

> Is this a Wedding Day
> Or only a Commemoration?
> Let us merry be; and may
> It long be an *Equivocation.*

My Solicitude about this Parchment is not unlike *this Nonsense* but I hope a good Account will come. In an Auction Room I was at two hours ago—A Pair of *Black blue* Jars exactly like mine with Gold Trailing upon them sold for Six Pounds. Old China bears a high Price *here* and you have some very fine at Streatham Park.[5] Oh *do* go to Windle and see and learn about the Settlement. Make yourself understand all about it and give the best and earliest Information/ to Yours faithfully/ H: L: Piozzi.

Text Hyde Collection. *Address* Mr. Alexander Leak/ Streatham Park/ Surrey. *Postmark* BATH 15 NO 15 1815; 10 o'Clock NO 16 1815.

1. For George Hammersley, see HLP to JSPS, 1 November 1810, n. 1.

2. On 13 November HLP had noted in her "Pocket Book" that "Mr. Penning called; and begged to be Auctioneer." However, George Squibb Sr. (ca. 1764–1831) of Boyle Street, Savile Row, was to oversee the Streatham sale. For John Penning, see HLP to AL, 31 August 1814, n. 1.

3. For George Granville Leveson-Gower, second marquess of Stafford, see HLP to MW, 28 May [1807], n. 3.

4. Alexander Piozzi Leak.

5. HLP visited the auction rooms of S. Nichols, 18 Union Street, Bath. On 14 November were sold "A Most magnificent Collection of China; in Lots; comprising jars, vases, beakers, scent-pots, dishes, &c. of the most splendid description of the finest Japan and Mandarin Ware" (*Bath Herald,* 11 November 1815). On the third day of the Streatham auction, 10 May 1816, "Valuable Oriental China" (lots 1–50) was to be sold, which netted HLP about £159. She kept for herself "A pair of jars and covers, rich mazarine blue ground and gilt" (lot 40) for which her agent paid £5.5. See *Sale Catalogue* (1).

TO ALEXANDER LEAK

Bath
19: November 1815

Prudent Leak! if you will keep your Temper,——and the Word is *Mildly* as his Friends say to Coriolanus in Shakespear;[1] you will manage well about Streatham Park I am sure.

Mr. Penning had the Conversation with me almost wholly to himself; only I told him that Leak was a Man of Incorruptible Honesty, and perfect Honour: which I suppose he has found to be true by this Time; though I daresay he thought me an old Woman easily deceived—Young Men may however be wanting in Penetration now and then, especially such *rapid Gentlemen* as Mr. Penning. I do remember the Letter you speak of, it was very vehemently pressing—— and frighted me; I answered it to his handsome Coadjutor Mr. Wilson, and he was civiller.

To that same Mr. Wilson I sent an Order Stamped Draft this Morning for 100£—because Newton has paid his Rent; so now the Gillowes have had 1400£. Mr. Windle seems to think a Rent Charge of 400£ o'Year is all I can claim upon Crowmarsh, but that it is secured to me by giving a Power of Distress in Case of Failure so that (says he) you have Madam, nothing to *fear*——Very well; but by his account I have likewise nothing to *hope*.

Parnell canvasses my Kindness by sending me a Parcel of Sea Biscuits—and Penning by such Letters as I never yet did see!!! but the Impudence of an Auctioneer is *proverbial*.

Make him show you that only Letter he shall ever have from me; it said that I could not understand Gillowe's Bill and should send it for *your Inspection,* and that of People better skilled in such Matters than myself: who could not be expected to know at a 100 Miles Distance the Justice of his Charges.

Keep your Temper however, and let him bring People to see the Pictures; The more Connoisseurs see them the better.

He says Faulder the Bookseller[2] told him what a valuable Library mine was; That *he* knew how Dr. Johnson collected the Books, and that there would be *such scrambling* for them etc.

I have little more to say than Love to little Dear and God Bless/ You all Three and do the/ best you can for/ poor/ H: L: Piozzi.

I shewed Sir James Fellowes Your Letter: I always liked that Leak says he. I felt he was an honest Man and wished you Sincerely well.

Text Hyde Collection. *Address* Mr. Alexander Leak/ Streatham Park/ Surrey.

1. Cominius warns, "Arm youself/ To answer mildly . . . " and Coriolanus responds, "The word is 'mildly'" (*Coriolanus*, 3.2.138–39, 142).
2. Robert Faulder (fl. 1780–1816), London bookseller.

THE REVEREND LEONARD CHAPPELOW TO HESTER LYNCH PIOZZI

London
Thursday 23: November 1815

My Dear Madam—

I cannot tell how long it is since I sent you in a frank a miserable sermon filled with my usual nonsense, from Babworth in Nottinghamshire[1]—where I was upon a long visit to Mr. Simpson Lord B[radford's] Brother.[2]——You have heard that Lord Bradford is made an Earl,[3] the family title being revived at Last in the Person of the now Earl.—The Regent to whom as a Peer he had a right to demand an Audience received him with the most amiable and friendly manner as the companion of their youthful and early days of merriment when the bottles of Claret and Champaign all ran round the Table at Carlton House as if impelled by magic. When Lord B was going to detail his pretensions to an Earldom &c.—say no more said the Prince, it shall be done immediately, Leave the matter to me, it cannot be in better hands.——The Prince always said that amidst all their jovial doings and sayings—Orlando Bridgeman always kept within the Line that marks the perfect Gentleman.—

Lady B is now at Florence,[4] and by this time nursing her new titled Son Viscount Newport—oh with what maternal feelings would she gladly relinquish her Title for the reestablishment of her Darling's health.[5]—Lord B is in England and in a short time joins his family at Florence.—During the Paroxism of Political arrangements before The Allies entered Paris—Lord B was in the midst of all the <Crowned> heads in Europe—and at many of their Dinners.—I mean at the critical moment, when by a threatened Arrangement, we had the Game in our own hands, and were nearly Losing it, by the odd Trick.—Had at that Period the allies made any thing Like a peace with Buonaparte, the Rascal would now have been on the Throne of France.[6]—But two Quires of paper and a new bunch of Hudson bay quills, would not be sufficient to detail all the political remarks which in these momentous times might be comprised.—History such as Posterity will compose, would fifty years ago be styled Romance.——Nay will be guillotined.

I wrote expressly to our friends at Llangollen to know where You was, et quid agitur but they did not tell me till it was too late, so I wrote in a frank, to you at Brynbella, expecting that Your Nephew would alter the direction, and in that case the frank would have followed you all over the world—I hope you are in it, I should be miserable to have a Letter dated Elysium fields.—

I have been very ill, but am better. I have now no complaints ironically so called—except my winter cough which as I expected is returned with these dreadful North and North East winds.—I dare not quit my Chamber, and must be confined in it all the winter.—I have no Companion but a <   > Cat— but he is very Lively.—

I see Mrs. Siddons is on the Edinburgh stage[7]—to initiate Mrs. Allsop—her Daughter[8]—was Mrs. Allsop originally Little red two shoes, and the great grown up puss whom we saw at Your grand Streatham Feast last May or June.—

Miss O'Neil they say is a Prodigy, acting to absolute perfection in Comedy and Tragedy—and such Warblers, were never before [heard] of as Mrs. Nash—Miss Hughes, and Stephens.—[9] I go not to the Theatres—but I would give the World to go, if I were well enough—all my old favourite plays are reviving at both Theatres. I should think myself young again.

You do not I believe buy books.—If you [do] I entreat you to read Scott's Visit to Paris.—[10]

Adieu Dear Madam—/ Ever yours—but not without you soon answer this Letter/ L. Chappelow.

P.S. If Mr. Salisbury did not take proper care, to forward my Last Letter to You—I will wring off the neck of his new Bambino.—

I have seen nor heard anything of the Streatham Horsestealer nor sweet Dr. Perney.—[11]

As I do not stir out—I know not whether Mrs. Mostyn or Mrs. Hoare are either of them in Town.

Text Ry. 563.106.

1. LC's letter, probably written during the summer, is missing.
2. The second son of Henry Bridgeman, first baron Bradford, John (1763–1850) of Babworth Hall, Notts., had assumed by act of Parliament the surname and arms of Simpson only.
3. Orlando Bridgeman, second baron Bradford, was created earl of Bradford on 30 September 1815. See *GM*, 85, pt. 2 (1815):369.
4. For Lucy Elizabeth, Lady Bradford, see HLP to Sophia Byron, 2 June [1788], n. 7.
5. George Augustus Frederick Henry Bridgeman (1789–1865), styled Viscount Newport, second earl of Bradford (1825). See HLP to LC, 8 May 1814, n. 8.
6. LC refers to the less-than-secret negotiations at Châtillon when, e.g., the Allies were willing to make peace with Napoleon if France withdrew to the territorial limits of 1791 and if he yielded his claim to all influence beyond them. See also HLP to LC, 18 January 1814.
7. SS's son Henry, manager of the Theatre Royal in Edinburgh, died on 12 April of "water in the chest." He left his actress-wife, Harriott, née Murray, and three children in financial difficulty. To raise money for them, SS went to Edinburgh and began on 18 November a ten-night engagement during which she played such roles as Lady Macbeth, Lady Randolph, Queen Katherine, and Constance. See the *Bath Herald*, 22 April; *Bath and Cheltenham Gazette*, 29 November.
8. Fanny Alsop (1782–1821), the natural daughter of Dorothea Jordan and Richard Daly (1758–1813) made her first appearance at Covent Garden on 18 October 1815 as Rosalind in *As You Like It*.
9. LC alludes to the following singers: Virtue Nash; Catherine Stephens (1794–1882); and one unidentified Hughes.
10. John Scott (1783–1821) wrote *A Visit to Paris in 1814* (London: Longman, Hurst, Rees, Orme, and Brown, 1815).
11. For John Anthony Perny, now rector of Pirton, Worcs., see HLP to PSP, 15 [December 1793], n. 3.

TO THE REVEREND LEONARD CHAPPELOW

Bath
Fryday 24: November 1815

From a Place most unlike the Elysian Fields you and I saw near Naples,[1] and still less resembling the Elysium of Classic Story; do I write to return Thanks for Dear Mr. Chappelow's kind Recollection of me. I am glad the Bridgeman Family are Bradfords; and glad the Barons are become Earls; and sorry the beautiful Lady who loved honours, Fortunes &c., at least as well as such Things deserved to be loved; died before She could see the Pleasures that were in waiting for her amiable Progeny.—[2]

My Nephew Salusbury was not in fault, he sent the Letter; *I* only was to blame in not sooner acknowledging it: His Faults are very few I fancy, and it appears that People like him in his Neighbourhood. My Retirement has been a *very close one.*

The enormous Expences incurred by repairing, and new dressing-up old Streatham Park were such as to preclude all possibility of my living there; and You Dear Sir witnessed my last grand Flash. *The Immense Debt*—upon an old Woman's Annuitant Income has weighed me quite down: and The Taxes, Tythes &c. of Streatham Park help to devour me, you will hear of the House being shut up after selling the Contents to defray the Bills of Surveyors, Painters, Plasterers, and Slaters besides a new Fence Two Miles round, and repairing Hothouses, Green houses Boathouses &c. set up by past Occupiers of the Premises.

I fear Mrs. Hoare and Mrs. Mostyn and the other Ladies will not be pleased, but 'tis sufficient their Cousin Sir John Lade should go to Prison, Their Mother will endeavour to keep out.[3]

Mrs. Siddons does not own any Mrs. Alsop for a Daughter I believe. The pretty Baby you remember is Cecilia Siddons still; She dined with us that Day at Streatham Park. Somebody was saying that Henry Siddons—Son to the great Actress—who went on the Stage *Years ago* contrary to her Approbation, has left a distressed Family by his Death; Her Journey to Scotland is most probably for *their* Benefit.

Miss Nash is a Bath Belle, born here; and much a favourite; We have all your great Performers in Turn, and shall I dare say run after Miss O'Neill between now and July. Crouds in this cold Weather will help to warm us, I am told Coals will not be to be had: London consumes in One Day what used in our Time to serve the Metropolis *a full year* they tell me. Such Fires are necessary to these Gas Lights, Steam Engines &c.[4] Are not you delighted with the hope of guiding Air Ballons?[5] and resolved to see these famous Mechanists

Sail thro' the Air
When the Moon shines clear

like Witches in Macbeth.[6] It will be very entertaining; and we need not go out of the World without having witnessed the Wonders of it.

Buonaparte seems forgotten: He made Mankind his Gazers, The sole Figure He—for a long Time; but we shall Measure him now without his Pedestal, and learn his real Height.

The Ladies of Llangollen are very kind to me, but so are many Ladies and many Gentlemen—tho' God knows—I have been pulled from *My* little Footstool very completely; living in Two Rooms, with Two maids for fear of Arrests from Mead the Surveyor,[7] and Wilmot the Seedsman &c.—whose Threats drove me hither,[8] and here will I live and die. You know I was ever partial to dear Bath; and the People here have so petted *Poor* H:L:P.—that if She *does* get a Prize in the Lottery at last, her *Riches* shall be spent among *Them.*[9]

These hot Springs too are so comfortable, they wash away Sorrow and Care.

May you have fewer to Get rid of my kind Friend, from Debts and Dangers ever free is the best Wish of/ H: L: P.

Text Ry. 561.148. *Address* Rev: Mr. Chappelow/ No. 12 or 13/ Hill Street/ Berkeley Square/ London. *Postmark* 25 NO 25 1815.

1. A region near Baia, ten miles west of Naples, known as the Elysian Fields because of its beauty and richness. See *Observations*, 2:12.
2. For Elizabeth, Lady Bradford, who died in 1806, see HLP to LC, 23 August 1794, n. 4.
3. A gambler involved in almost constant litigation, Sir John Lade was imprisoned for debt in King's Bench Prison, Southwark, in 1814. For Sir John, see HLP to PSP, 14 September 1798, n. 2.
4. Since the introduction of gas lighting in London in 1807, its use had increased in the city, with the Guildhall, e.g., being so lighted in autumn 1815.
The steam engine also gained in popular acceptance, *The Times* using steam printing presses in 1814. And in the following year, the first steam vessel was launched on the Thames. For the news-worthy quality of the "Steam-vessel," see *GM* 85, pt. 1 (1815): 639–40.
5. HLP noted the flights of the Sadlers, father and son, at such places as Norwich, Newcastle, Glasgow, and Edinburgh. See *GM* 85, pt. 2 (1815):271, 367, 457; *The Times*, 6 September 1815.
For James Sadler, see HLP to Q, 22 April 1785, n. 22.
6. HLP's variation on *Macbeth*, 1.3.81–82.
7. For the amount of Mead's bill and HLP's current indebtedness to him, see her letter to TSW, 4 July 1814.
8. John Wilmot, nurseryman of Lewisham, Kent.
9. Prizes in the State Lottery, 7 November to 7 December, totaled £314,000 (*Bath Herald*, 4 November).

TO MRS. ALEXANDER LEAK

Bath
Thursday 30: November 1815

Oh God forbid Dear Leak! that your Husband should be going to have a Can-cer!—in his Foot too! the least likely Part of the whole Body. It is a Chilblain I hope; Red, black, inflamed and painful. The Schirrus Tumour, whence a Cancer is inclined to form; begins *small, hard,* and *not discoloured;* with lancinating Pains from Time to Time. Every Surgeon will know the Difference at once; and I beg you will tell him that it is *his bounden Duty* to make early Enquiry, and obtain satisfactory Intelligence——if it were only for the Stilling *your agitated Mind: my own* will not be quite easy till we are sure of his safety, tell him so.

It vexes me to see I have expressed myself so awkwardly about Lady Keith's Metastasio. The Work is in six or seven very, *very* small Volumes bound in Yellow, and the Leaves were gilt once; and I think Mr. Seward's Name in the 1st Page.[1]

I have not had my sore Lip yet this Year, and hope to escape it:—The Cramp was cruel to me during the frosty Weather,—but Bessy Jones would tell you there was no Wonder in *that*: when taking advantage of her being gone to The Post Office, I ran with Mrs. Dimond to see Harlequin one of those bitter Nights.

Sir James Fellowes is at Sidmouth bathing in hot Sea Water, or I should have got myself finely scolded——*I really durst not tell Dr. Gibbes*—at whose House I dined Three Days after; and saw quite the finest old Enamel China I ever *did* see—a whole Table Service. The Lady of the House told me She had been offered 25 shillings a Plate and Two Guineas a Dish for them all together, by a Man who meant to purchase them for Selling again. They were a Legacy to Mrs. Gibbes and She will never part with them of Course.

I worked dear Mrs. Lutwyche a Butterfly last Summer, and when we kept her Birthday this 23d of November She produced it framed and glazed for a Fire Screen; and mounted at a famous Expence in Black and Gold: quite a Gay piece of Furniture.

Mr. Penning would make it a Subject of no small Eloquence I suppose: He is a flashy Fellow indeed! and his *Dreams* of the Marquis of Stafford like all the rest of his Conversation and Letters I doubt not.

Pictures are best *seen* in *Snowy* Weather. Pity no one seems inclined to look at mine in *any* season. Beg of Leak to write soon, and believe me Yours and His and our little Fellow's/ ever/ H: L: P.

I hope Your Husband and his *Partner* whoever he is, will pay up the 18£ because I set *that* against Windle's Bill.

When I have a House and Home if it should please God to give me one, not too fine to live in:—nor too wretched to die in; I *will* keep my Parchments in my own hands.

Text Hyde Collection. *Address* Mrs. Leak/ Streatham Park/ Surrey. *Postmark* BATH NO 30 1815; 10 o'Clock DE 1 1815; 1 DE 1 1815.

1. The Italian poet and dramatist Pietro Antonio Domenico Buonaventura Trapassi Metastasio's *Opere* were published in a seven-volume edition (Venezia: Antonio Zatta, 1782-84) and a six-volume edition (Firenze: Stamperia della Rosa, 1787–89), but no edition of his works appeared in the Streatham sale. Lot 277 on the second day of the sale of the books from Brynbella (18 September 1823) was "Opere del Metastasio, 12 Tom Par. 1780," described as "A magnificent set, bound in white vellum, fine impressions of the beautiful engravings." See *Sale Catalogue* (2).

TO LADY WILLIAMS

Bath Monday
4 December 1815.

My dear Lady Williams

Nothing could have surprized me less—or grieved me—*much* more than the so sudden Death of poor Doctor Myddelton.[1]——There is now *your* House alone remaining in the state I left it when quitting Wales on the 28th: of May 1814— a Year and half only! Is Mrs. Myddelton with Child?[2] such a Circumstance would add excessively to their Perplexities. Deaths—unexpected and unprepared for never were so frequent. A Colonel Somebody here Six Weeks ago—said—at the Whist Table—to a Friend looking on. Hold my Cards for a Moment Sir,—will you? I can't see black from Red. The Gentleman made him some encouraging Answer—but it was not heard, his Friend was already a Corpse.[3] Poor Salusbury seems deeply affected—Young People fancy no one ever dies, but of Old Age, or Sickness long endured. Do they *keep their Bed*? is the regular Question. He will declare to Your Ladyship his Astonishment at my Departure from Life some of these Days I trust; but will not have to accuse me of Negligence in discharging all pecuniary Obligations first.—They will be cleared off completely by my Calculation,—if I can but last out till next July Dividends—and there are now little more than Six Months to suffer as I have been contented to do—since we parted.

Wise People say the Property Tax dies of itself in April, and will not be renewed;[4]—such have been our Successes.

I do long to hear how Buonaparte likes his Rocky Cage; and what probability there is of his remaining in it.

Mr. Salusbury of Galtfunon seems a fortunate Man, and a careful:[5] I'm sorry they, and the Segroids and the Brynbellas do not herd more together—It would make them all happier to be merry and good humoured.

Mrs. Mostyn has written to me at last—but says nothing of her Sons.—Does Mr. Williams—*your* Mr. Williams, like the eldest Mostyn? That Boy is going on to 17 I think—Poor Robert Myddelton's Age I have forgotten, but it can't be far from 20.[6] He will be plagued no more about the Difference between Nunc and Jam; and will I hope take a Profession, and *mind* it; and let the Estate lick itself whole in due Time: There is little to be done in these Days without Industry or Privation—and the first would be pleasantest to *me*—at least I am sick of the other.—tho' my Bath Friends suffer me to lose few Pleasures—and I was invited to pass these dead Months in Devonshire at a Gentleman and Lady's House:[7] but I resolved not to quit my Post, till I left it for a *better* either in this World or the next. Dear Williams will find me writing at the Old Window,—but I suppose we shan't see him till after the Bodylwyddan Birthday.[8] His Aunt *did* seem amused with Your Ladyship's Account of the odd Wedding of the Sick Housekeeper—I never knew anything of the Parties.

Spasms are I suppose in Old and plain English—*Cramps* or Cholick Pains; but Cramps more likely, which seizing on the Head or Stomach—kill without more ado. Such Disorders are not much in the Power of Medicine I believe, and they *are* much more common than in distant Times.

Make my best Good Wishes acceptable dearest Lady to every one of your deserving Darlings: may every old year close happily on your beloved House, and every new Year bring new Felicity where so much is hoped and prayed for/ by Your Ladyships ever/ obliged and faithfull/ H: L: Piozzi.

Mrs. Mostyn says Segroid is very Cold, but I suppose it is very pretty.

Text Ry. 4 (1812–18).

1. The Reverend Robert Myddelton of Gwaynynog had died on 27 or 28 November, aged sixty-four. See *GM* 85, pt. 2 (1815):641.
2. May Myddelton had no other children after the birth of her eighth child, Hugh, in 1811.
3. A Colonel William Manby died suddenly on 27 or 28 October. Although identified in the newspapers as a colonel, he is listed in the militia lists as a captain in the East and West Ham volunteer infantry as of 13 June 1798, a unit disbanded ca. 1803. See the "Death Duty Register" (1816), P.R.O., IR 27/158; the *Bath and Cheltenham Gazette*, 1 November; *GM* 85, pt. 2 (1815):636.
4. The tax was to be repealed on 18 March 1816, upon a motion of Henry Brougham (1778–1868), later first baron Brougham and Vaux (1830).
5. For John Lloyd Salusbury of Galtfaenon, see HLP to Q, 31 July 1810, n. 22; to JSPS, 15 December 1810, n. 5.
6. The heir of Gwaynynog was the young Robert Myddelton, now twenty, a student at Clare Hall, Cambridge. See HLP to JW, 20 November 1813, n. 3.
7. Probably at Dorset and Julia Fellowes's house at Sidmouth.
8. JW's birthday was 9 January.

TO ALEXANDER LEAK

Bath
December 8 1815

Why all this Hurry my good Leak! The Gillows have acknowledged 1400£ in the civillest possible Terms, and I am expecting a Letter to Thank me for 300£ *more* which they will receive in January—six or seven Weeks hence—That will make 1700£: I have *promised* them another Hundred in April, and if I live to July They will have *Three Hundred* again. I told them so long ago, and they were contented with my Mode of Payment.[1]

As to borrowing Money of Gentlemen—*That I never will*, whilst Tradesmen will trust me; when they will trust me no longer I will go *Where They send me*: but Never, no *Never* Shall any Gentleman be asked to lend Money to/ H: L: Piozzi. Turn over.

What I did *hastily* was not *paying* the People, but *promising* to pay them: which I did last Summer in express Terms saying they should have these Payments made them up to *2100£*: when I would Stop (was my Expression,) and leave the rest to my Executors: for that I was convinced That Two Thousand one Hundred Pounds was all I could possibly be called on for—and that they should have the last 300£ in July 1816.

They appeared contented and I believe are so.

My Word is Sacred—and so is my Honour: I have led a hard Life to preserve them, and borrowing Money *now* when every body expects to see me free and living on my Income!

Oh that shall never be.

Text Hyde Collection. *Address* Mr. Alexander Leak/ Streatham Park/ Surrey. *Postmark* BATH 8 DE 8 1815; 10 o'Clock DE 9 1815.

1. Gillow and Company, merchants and upholsterers at 176 Oxford Road.

TO SIR JAMES FELLOWES

Sunday
10: December 1815.

How kind You are and how partial! And what an unspeakable Loss shall I have when you enter on a London Life and London Practice[1]—Dr. Holland who writes about the Ionian Islands is going to London to *practise* and exchange the *Cyclades* for the *sick Ladies*.[3] He has been a Lyon here for Three whole Days. I caught the *Queue du Lion* and passed one Evening in his Company.——But a whole Menagerie would make me no Compensation for Exchange of Sentiment in Friendly Converse——

Oh do make haste to Bath and let me lament my Fate to You personally.

Is that being grateful to Heaven though? when *one* Year's valuable Friendship has been granted, at a Time when so few Years can be expected by/ Poor H: L: Piozzi.

"Let us leave the best Example that we can."[3] I have however much to say to you about the Biographical Mémoires—which are really in some Degree of Forwardness.

Adieu! going to dine with the Lutwyches.[4]

Text MS E. 9. 4P5. Boston Public Library.

1. HLP's "Pocket Book" entry for 10 December indicates that she received "A letter from Sir J: F: proposing a London Practice." After his marriage in March 1816, he was to live briefly at Gloucester Place, London, but he and his wife were to settle at the latter's family home, Adbury House, near Newbury.

2. Henry Holland (1788–1873), cr. baronet (1853) took his M.D. in 1811, publishing in 1815 his *Travels in the Ionian Isles, Albania, Thessaly, Macedonia, &c. during the Years 1812 and 1813.* Serving as physician to the Princess of Wales while she was abroad in 1814, he returned to London the following year. He became a licentiate to the Royal College of Physicians in 1816 and a fellow in 1828. Although more fashionable than skilled as a doctor, he was to be appointed physician in ordinary to Queen Victoria and the Prince Consort.

3. See HLT to SJ, 27 March [ca. 1784] in *Letters*, 2:358.

4. For the Lutwyches, see HLP to MW [ca. April 1808], n. 2.

TO WILLIAM MAKEPEACE THACKERAY

Bath, Wednesday
13th December 1815.

My dear Doctor Thackeray's kind partiality followed me so long and so far upon my journey through life,[1] I think he has enough left even now not to be wearying of hearing how I do, and what I do in a situation very new to me indeed, but rendered supportable by the countenance and conversation of pleasant friends and agreeable acquaintance. The accounts I hear from Wales, too, make me very happy and thankful, and convince me that my tenderness was bestowed on worthy creatures who seem to make themselves much beloved in their neighbourhood. Oh how that neighbourhood is changed! Oh how many sighs shall I have to leave on every house as I pass it, if it should please God that I can come down next July, unencumbered by debts and no longer haunted by vexations which have tormented me for two long years! But you are country gentleman enough to know that a high paling round a park of two miles extent, besides fronting a large house made by my exertions as if wholly new, and then furnishing it in modern style supremely elegant, though I thought not costly, cannot be done but by enormous expense, and, in fact, surveyors, carpenters, and cabinet makers, have driven poor Hester Lynch Piozzi into a little Bath lodging, where Miss Letitia Barnston[2] found her, two rooms and two maids her whole establishment; a drawing of Brynbella, and by the fair hand of Mrs. Salusbury, her greatest ornament.

Meanwhile our town, like yours, takes turn for the fine dancers or fine actors when they have a week to spare; and as for private talent, there never were so many young people so skilled in music as now. I heard a child of ten years old, perform on the forte piano last week like a professor.[3] The winter seems as if it would be a long one, it began early, and many old people sink under the rapid changes. Doctor Harrington, however, kept his eighty-ninth birthday a while ago, and listened with delight to his charming compositions.[4] The last catch and glee are said to be the best he ever produced, and sure he lives a proof that air and exercise are not the preservatives of life which we account them, as he always visited his patients in a chair half a century ago, as he now visits his acquaintance, and always with his mouchoir at his face to keep away every breath of wind; when walking in the abbey with his son-in-law last summer, "Come," said he, "let us choose a spot for my old bones," and recollecting himself suddenly—

"These ancient walls, with many a mouldering bust,
But show how well Bath waters lay the dust."[5]

If you have not heard that impromptu before, you will like it. Adieu, dear Sir! and make my best regards to Mrs. Thackeray, with love to the lasses who were nice babies.[6] Do you remember Selina, she would be Mrs. Piozzi herself? Now write me a kind word, do, and say you will be glad to see me next July, but how unlikely it is there should then be anything left of your poor/ Hester Lynch Piozzi.

Text Hayward, 2:317–19.

1. For Dr. Thackeray of Chester, whom HLP came to know through LC, see her letter to LC, 23 August 1794, n. 7.
2. Letitia Barnston (1754–1835) of Chester was Thackeray's close friend. Her nephew, Roger Harry Barnston (1802–49) was to marry Thackeray's daughter, Selina Martha (1806–35).
HLP in her "Pocket Book" recorded seeing Letitia Barnston on 12 September and on 24 and 25 October, during the latter's visit to Bath.
See Jane Townley Pryme and Alicia Bayne, *Memorials of the Thackeray Family* ([London: Printed by Spottiswood & Co.] For private distribution, 1870), 174.
3. On 7 December, HLP heard "little Marianne Broadhurst a famous Forte-Piano Player" ("Pocket Book"). She was the daughter of Thomas Broadhurst (1780–1851), a Unitarian minister, and Frances, née Whittaker (d. 1864), who kept a boarding school for young ladies at Belvidere House, Bath, from ca. 1812 to ca. 1833.
4. On 29 September, Harington's birthday, HLP attended a "Gala in honor of Dr. Harington—a brilliant Concert indeed—good Company and good Singing Catches and Glees" ("Pocket Book").
5. The son-in-law was the Reverend Josiah Thomas (see HLP to SL, 15 November [1788], n. 4). Dr. Harington was known to be a wit, to which this "epigram in the Abbey Church" attested. See Jerom Murch, *Biographical Sketches of Bath Celebrities, Ancient and Modern, With Some Fragments of Local History* (London: Isaac Pitman and Sons; Bath: William Lewis and Son, 1893), 148.
6. For Elizabeth or Eliza (Jones) Thackeray, née Wilson, see HLP to LC, 18 June 1804, n. 15. The Thackerays had two daughters: Selina Martha (n. 2) and Sarah Jane (1805–72).

TO THE REVEREND THOMAS SEDGWICK WHALLEY

Bath
Thursday 13: December 1815.

My Dear Doctor Whalley is very kind indeed in remembering me so tenderly, and wishing for my Letters——how shall I make them worth his Acceptance?—by saying how glad I am that this *Urticaria has* been; and that it will never be again: Those Irritating Diseases never shorten Life, they are in my Eyes a Promise of Longævity; and tho I adhere to the weak Mutton Broth, my medical Friends *do* make me drink a Glass of Wine or two more than usual,—I tell them 'tis because I tell old odd Stories—and set them laughing—after *Dinner.* Mean while I keep on paying all My Money away, and leaving myself ne'er a Shilling——just like Dr. Whalley: and like him I pick up Friends that help me on,—seldom suffering me to endure much Solitude. I am glad you are at Brusselles, 'tis a Place I know so well, and where we were once happy all together.[2]

Do you remember Mr. Merry that they called Della Crusca? he was of our Society: and *you* said he looked like a Sly Intriguer; And I thought what a *rough* Husband he would make, after having been so *Smooth* a Lover to Ladies of high Quality.[3] Not a bit. A Person who knew his whole Conduct and Course of Life in America and watched his Death too, poor Fellow! protests that he expired a willing Slave to a pretty Wife[4]—Sister of Lady Craven.[5] Are you not sorry our dear Mrs. Siddons had to act again for her Son's distressed Family? It is really a great Pity,—and when a young Successor has possession of the public Favour! that fine Miss O'Neill——Oh how the News did vex me!

Every body is pleased however at the final Destination of Marechal Ney,[6] and the King of France's Ministers if made permanent, seem likely to content all honest Readers of the public Prints.[7] We have had an elegant young Physician here—a Doctor Holland, who was of the Princess of Wales's Suite——and who perhaps inspired her Royal Highness with the modern Passion for a Journey to Greece—because he has seen the Ionian Islands, and has written an Account of them, but is now determined upon pursuing London Practice—exchanging *Cyclades* for the *Sick Ladies,* as say the Wits and Jesters—We have another Equivoque going. Doctor Harington's very respectable Son in Law Mr. Thomas, canvassed our Corporation in hope of being Successor to old Phillot as Rector of Bath.[8] By *one Vote* alone he lost it, to the Young Son of a well known Apothecary; The Joke is therefore that We wanted a Pastor or *Shepherd;* but we obtained nothing but a *Crook.*

I am glad you are on the Continent: these rapid Changes of Weather will not be *so* rapid, nor so Death-doing as they are here.[9] Mrs. Haygarth fell a Sacrifice to them three Days ago.[10] That the blind Duc D'Arenberg who I remember so well should have outlived all the Storms of State and all the Horrors of Ill health—seems strange. My poor dear Venetian Friends have sunk under the French Revolution—to rise no more in this World. Memory-Rogers, as we call the Banker who wrote the Pleasures of Memory, told me when in London that he had himself seen the Foscarini holding her hand out for Charity[11]—and when I asked a Cantatrice just come from Italy last Night—how *She* left them; no Account could be so dismal. All the noble Families swept away; the Literary Friends chiefly deceased; and some, with Circumstances of great Horror.— Want, Cruelty, every Affliction pursuing poor Bertola, Pignotti &c. to the Grave's Edge.[12]——The Pisani House Empty[13]—The Villas on the Banks of the Brenta tumbling down! Oh what a Picture! Oh what a Portrait! I am sincerely grieved for them.[14]

Now the 4th Side of my Sheet of Paper is coming to an End,[15] my Heart assures me your last Letter was replied to; but there was some Mistake in the Direction: Louvaine perhaps, written for Ghent. If Mr. Mullins remembers me— make my best Compliments acceptable to him, Mrs. Mullins's Beauty when Clara Jones, can not be easily forgotten:[16] I never saw her since her Marriage, or could have believed that She had a Son 18 Years old, had You not told me so. Oh Sir! how the *Time* does fly!

Miss Wroughton is not come, She has been less brushed—or less hurt by the brushing of his Wing than most of us: and Mr. Lutwyche has rallied in such a Manner since we parted at Mendip You will be amazed when you see him.[17] He can now walk Seven Miles o'Day. But Walking is all the Mode: and I am so weary of The Pedestrians that I am ready to say Allez promener to them all. Adieu Dear Sir and continue your partial kindness/ for poor H: L: P.

Dear Salusbury and his Harriet and his Hestor Maria are all well and happy— if I live till July, I will go see them.

My Maid is convinced I answered your last kind Letter, She took it to the Office and paid the Sum for foreign Postage.

Text Berg Collection +. *Address* A Monsieur/ The Reverend Doctor Thos. Whalley/ No. 1040 Rue Ducale/ au Parc/ Bruxelles. *Postmark* BATH DE 14 <   >; 197 F 15.

1. TSW wrote to HLP on 2 December, complaining of having suffered for six weeks from an "eruption [that caused] fierce and unappeasable itching all over his body" (Ry. 564.34).
2. In February 1787.
3. For Robert Merry and his onetime liaison with Countess Cowper, see HLP to SL, 27 July 1785, n. 6.
4. On 26 August 1794, Merry had married Anne Brunton. He accompanied her to Philadelphia in 1796. While she triumphed on the American stage, he became the unofficial poet laureate of young American writers until his death in 1798.
5. Louisa Brunton (1785–1860) had appeared as an actress at Covent Garden from 1803 to October 1807. She left the stage to marry in December 1807 William Craven (1770–1825), first earl of Craven (1801).
6. Ney, having switched his loyalties from the Bourbons to Napoleon during the Hundred Days, was found guilty of treason by the chamber of deputies and executed on 7 December 1815.
7. Louis XVIII had appointed Fouché to the ministry (HLP to Ly W, 16 July 1815, n. 1). But the chamber of deputies, with its majority of *ultras*, refused to work with Fouché. Talleyrand removed him, appointing him the king's representative at Dresden (a post from which he himself retired on 22 September). He was replaced in the ministry by the royalist Armand-Emmanuel-Sophie Septimanie (1766–1822), comte de Chinon, duc de Richelieu et de Fronsac.
When Fouché "resigned" as ministre de la police, his example was followed by the entire ministry. In a letter to the king, he attributed his resignation to "a baneful spirit of opposition existing in different members of his Majesty's Family." See *GM* 85, pt. 2 (1815):266.
Despite this letter, Fouché negotiated at this time with Louis whose loyal subject he pretended to be and with Wellington whom he tried to interest in an Orléanist succession (Romberg and Malet, 2:162).
8. James Phillott (ca. 1750–1815), rector of Bath since 1798, died on 11 June. Meeting on 3 July to elect his successor, the Bath Corporation was deadlocked between the Reverend Josiah Thomas and the Reverend Charles Crook (1788–1837), chaplain to the Prince Regent, and son of Charles Crook (ca. 1757–1843), an apothecary, former mayor and Corporation member of Bath. On 3 October the Corporation elected Crook by one vote (*Bath and Cheltenham Gazette*, 4 October).
9. During the preceding week, the temperature had fluctuated between 24° and 40° Fahrenheit, the days ranging from fair to stormy. See *GM* 85, pt. 2 (1815):574.
10. Sarah Vere Haygarth, née Widdens (1752–1815) died on 10 December "after a short illness." See the *Bath Chronicle*, 14 December; "Frodsham Burial Register," for 23 December, C.R.O., Cheshire.
11. The Foscarini had been the first family in Venice. In the "Commonplace Book" under *Foscarini*, HLP remarked: "I was told by [Samuel Rogers] . . . on the 26th of July 1815 that he had just returned from Venice,—where the ancient Nobles Men and Women beg Charity in the public Streets—whence all Mirth and Gayety are banished. Madame Foscarini wore a thick Veil; but threw it up, acknowledging Roger's Companion for an old Acquaintance: She held out her hand, They kissed it, dropt Tears on it, and put a Small Coin in:—some who saw them shouted Viva l'Inglesi!"
12. For Abaté [Severino] Aurelio Bertòla de Giorgi, see HLP to Q, 27 September 1786, n. 7.
Lorenzo Pignotti (1739–1812), associated mainly with Florence, was a physician, historian, and contributor to the *Florence Miscellany*.
13. For Almarò Alvise Pisani, see HLP to LC, 28 August 1792, nn. 6 and 7.
14. Venice had been suffering for almost two decades. In May 1797, France had declared war on Venice, and the aristocracy was abolished. The treaty of Campo Formio gave Venetian territory, as far as the Adige, to Austria. And in 1814 the rest of Venice became Austrian.
HLP had long been impressed by the "celebrated" villas along the Brenta. See *Observations*, 1:221.
15. HLP was nearing the bottom of the *third* side.
16. For William Townsend Mullins, later second baron Ventry, see HLP to PSW, 11 February 1791, n. 5; to PSP, 17 February 1795, n. 4; PSP, 24 March 1795.
On 10 September 1797, Clara Jones (d. 1837) married Mullins. They had one son, Thomas (1798–1817).

In his letter of 2 December, TSW indicated that Mullins had offered him "a commodious *spare* apartment in the large and handsome House which he and his lovely and amiable wife occupied" in Brussels.

17. For William Lutwyche's crippling illness, see HLP to TSW, 3 August 1813, n. 10.

TO JOHN WILLIAMS

> Bath
> Shortest Day of 1815.
> [21 December]

My dear Mr. Williams's kind Letter deserves the earliest and the pleasantest Answer possible.—There is no Saying how comical is his Account of the Lady's odd Mirth and Melancholy: but Six Glasses of Champagne would produce odd Behaviour in most of us Matrons I trust.

Poor Doctor Myddelton's Summons must have been unexpected indeed, if no Will was left: Jam satis,[1] and Nunc est bibendum[2] will be good for the next Electioneering Time, but I really hope every thing favourable from the Young Man's gentleness of Disposition.[3]

Sudden Deaths were never so frequent; Poor Mrs. Crawford only just had Time to say—*I'm ill; Oh Lord God! I'm dying*: and so She was.[4]

Mrs. Haygarth was Ten or Twelve Hours bad,[5] they tell us;—and poor Mrs. Donkin Two Days;[6]—but 'tis very dreadful.

Your good Aunt and Cousin were here this Morning—and how Young Griffiths resembles Betty the far-famed Roscius! Few Brothers are much more alike.

Snow Storms are coming on rapidly just at this Time; and remind me of the full Table and chearful Society of Dear *Dear* Bodylwyddan. May the Birthdays go off happily! and when they are over—may some Wind blow you to Bath!

I should be very sorry not to cherish a *Hope* of seeing Wales next Summer; Sir John will praise my Patience in suffering so *small a Cage* to contain me so *long a Time*; but the Debts die off by Slow Degrees; and I mean to make a bold Attempt at regaining my Freedom in Spring, by offering the Streatham Property—in a public Manner—*to Sale*—since the Ladies will not purchase. Gillowe's Demand was 2482£.

We have Macready the Actor here,[7] and a new Lady—very pretty, and very well approved—She was Miss Fanny Griffiths, a Gentlewoman, with 10000£ which her Husband flung away, and she is now trying to get him out of Prison.[8]

We *had* a fine Doctor Holland among us for *too* short a Moment, he was so agreable: has seen and written about the Ionian Islands—and was (if I understand right,) a Medical Attendant on our Princess of Wales; but has left her, and means to practise as a Physician in London—exchanging the *Cyclades*—say we Wits and Wags—for the *Sick Ladies* of England.[9] We made quite a Lyon of the Man: I was invited to every House he visited at for the *Last* Three Days, so I got the *Queue* du Lyon, despairing of Le *Coeur*.

Morgans of Golden Grove are in Margarets Buildings, The Mother very pretty still—and fair Louisa—beautiful, but it is a prodigious Way off, this cruel Weather; and we meet too seldom.[10]

Sir Henry Baynton and his Lady have left their House in St. James's Square;—but come occasionally to Uncle and Aunt, and bring the Baby—which has—of Course no Equal.[11]

You do not *say* Mrs. Salusbury shews for another little one,—and dear Salusbury says *nothing* but about Gwaynynog; so perhaps she will play the good Huswife, and wait a little—better so, better so, I should suppose.—Doctor Crawford is left with Seven Infants *all* under 8 Years old by his Wife's sudden Departure, Poor Fellow!

Are you pleased with The Peace in remote Provinces? it is the *best* Peace ever made by Great Britain;[12] but one sees few happy Faces: and those who went abroad to find Things better, do not Seem to have attained their Wish. What has been told me of the Venetian State would break a Heart of Stone. The Pisani Palace falling; its Possessors turned out to wander:[13] The Foscarini holding out her pretty White hand for Charity in the Street—Tell Mrs. Mostyn of Segroid so, if you meet her anywhere—She will be much affected, and my Authority is very good indeed. Genoa has suffered least in these Commotions Dr. Holland says; and of Genoa *I* knew nothing but its external Beauties—the dear Venetians were my Friends, Companions—Protectors! I am very sorry when I think how helpless *they* were to bear such changes—as Lord Bulkeley[14] said once at Your House I remember, when a Revolution here was expected.—I *can* (Says he,) clean my own Shoes, and brush my own Coat very well; but what will become of those who *can not*?

Adieu! These are painful Reflexions to end with:—but a Thought of happy Bodylwyddan shall put them to Flight,—and prompt my warm Hope that every Individual of that dear Mansion, may long enjoy the Prosperity wished them by their/ H: L: Piozzi.

If I can get a Frank this Nonsense shall cost nothing.

Text Ry. 6 (1813–21). *Address* John Williams Esqr./ Bodylwyddan/ St. Asaph/ N. Wales.

1. Martial, *Epigrams*, 4.89.1.

2. Horace, *Odes*, 1.37.1.

3. See HLP to Ly W, 4 December 1815, n. 6.

4. Eliza Crawford died in Bath on 19 December. For her husband, Stewart, see HLP to PSP, 6 August 1802, n. 7.

5. For Sarah Haygarth's sudden death "at Lambridge House, near Bath," see HLP to TSW, 13 December 1815, n. 10; *GM* 86, pt. 1 (1816): 87; *Bath Chronicle*, 14 December. For John Haygarth, see HLP to PSW, 29 September 1792, n. 7.

6. Mary, née Collins (1748–1815), had married Robert Donkin in 1772. For the general, see HLP to JSPS, 20 March 1810, n. 9.

7. William Charles Macready (1793–1873) made his second appearance in Bath on 5 December and honored an engagement that continued until the following February. During this stay, he met HLP at Dr. Gibbes's house. For the actor's analysis of her personality, particularly her alleged pride, see his *Reminiscences*, ed. Sir Frederick Pollock, 2 vols. (London: Macmillan, 1875), 1:109–11.

8. Macready opened in *Riches; or, the Wife and Brother*. Three women played leading roles in this and other plays: Mrs. Weston, Mrs. William West, and "the Lady." The last, who performed as

Beatrice in *Much Ado about Nothing*, was consistently referred to as "the Lady." Thus, Macready had the role on 9 December announced as a first performance ever "by a Lady" and the *Bath Journal* on 14 December stated that the role would again be played "by the Lady who was honoured with such distinguished approbation in that character, on Saturday last." She may well have been Fanny Griffiths, HLP picking up the account of her from Macready when they met at Dr. Gibbes's house.

9. Henry Holland was about to open a fashionable practice in Mount Street and a few years later in Brook Street, Grosvenor Square.

10. For the Morgans of Golden Grove, Flintshire, see HLP to Ly W, 21 March 1815, n. 4.

11. For Rear Admiral Sir Henry William Bayntun and his wife Sophia, see HLP to JSPS, 6 January 1815, n. 16. Their "Uncle and Aunt" were the Lutwyches.

12. On 20 November 1815 the Allies signed the Second Peace of Paris, which guaranteed Swiss neutrality and created a new Quadruple Alliance. France was allowed the frontiers of 1790. Prussia received the Saar. The fortress of Huninguen was ordered to be destroyed. France was to be occupied for three to five years by a force not in excess of 150,000, and had to pay an indemnity of 700 million francs.

By virtue of the Quadruple Alliance, the Allies agreed to maintain the Second Peace of Paris, to prevent Napoleon's return, to support the occupation forces, and to supply 60,000 additional troops, if required. For full coverage of the treaty, see *The Times*, 29–30 November, 1 December.

13. For the Pisanis, see HLP to LC, 28 August, 5 September, to PSW, 21 November, all in 1792.

14. For Thomas James Bulkeley, baron Bulkeley, see HLP to LC, 13 May 1796, n. 9.

TO ALEXANDER LEAK

Bath Sunday
14: January 1816.

Why what a comical Story that is—about fat Tom and his late-repenting Bride; She was a wise Girl after all.

Will Gillow's People take the Money or no I wonder! Mr. Windle says—Let them alone.—I have a melancholy Letter from Mr. Chappelow in Hill Street, and a very *provoking* one: Saying how *happy I am living at Bath*:[1] because I do not stun the People with my Cries and my Complaints; they Say how happy I am.

The Truth is I am miserable: Poor Bessy Jones continues to cough incessantly, and so do I.—And *you* know how little Bath can do towards curing *that* Complaint. Sir James Fellowes is gone to Devonshire;[2] and We are Doctor Gibbes's Patients now, as is every body here I think.[3] He gives us Antimonial Wine and Tincture of Squills with Paregoric—and while we are vomiting, we are not coughing—of course. If it was better Weather, or nearer Spring—I would try Change of Air, for us;—but She shall have a Blister put on tonight—and after I have seen the Doctor tomorrow, my Spirits will mend perhaps—they are low enough now.

The Brynbella People seldom write, and always empty Letters, except the last—a Week ago;—to say the Child was in Danger.[4]

Lady Keith wrote to wish me a happy new Year in *1815* since when, I hear nothing of her; but People I meet up and down, tell me that her Daughter is the greatest Wit and Beauty possible, and will have the largest Fortune.[5] I am very glad of it.

I have seen the Doctor; he says Bessy's Cough will mend, and that it is the same *every body* has: only She has no Fever, and he can find no Shadow of Danger, begs me not to be alarmed.

Sir James Fellowes's Father who says he has felt Pulses for Threescore Years,[6] protests that Jones's Pulse indicates no Mischief—but the People all do cough dreadfully; and poor old Dr. Harington will die at last:[7]—Colonel Glover confined to his Bed.

Mr. Windle has written to Say Wilmot and Co. press him for the Money; I told him they *could* not have it till April; perhaps he will advance it himself.[8]

It is a happy Thing that your Dear little Boy keeps so well; I have got the fashionable Cough and Short Breath myself: otherwise well enough.

The Bishop of Salisbury who I have not seen for 28 Years, wondered to find me so little altered: and I thought his Lordship looking very well indeed.[9]

Farewell! and be careful of Sudden Colds—like old Mr. Moore—avoid Cold—guard against Cold &c./ Ever Yours/ H: L: P.

Mrs. Perkins—Wife to Mr. Thrale's Head Clerk, is living grand and Gay at No. 10 Pultney Street: She has a beautiful Grandaughter with her, who is much admired.[10]

She will however *leave her Card* She says; at poor No. 17.[11]

No news yet of my Dividends being received:—They will end in 200£ only. The Gillowes *had* snatched 300£ before these other 200£ were presented to them; and now hesitate—Charming Creatures!—whether they will take 500£ and leave me indebted beside——

Yet 'Spite of Fate, My Water-Cart at length *does draw lighter.*

Text Hyde Collection. *Address* Mr. Alexander Leak/ Streatham Park/ Surrey. *Postmark* 15 JA 15 1816.

1. The letter is missing.
2. JF was visiting Dorset and Julia Fellowes.
3. For Dr. George Smith Gibbes, see HLP to the Reverend John Roberts, 20 March 1807, n. 6.
4. The statement did not move AL, who on 18 January used it to write about the baby's father, whose "conduct is too shamefull (or shameless), I never heard of such Ingratitude before, If he was going to die instead of the Baby, it would I think be a good ridance of a Man who is a disgrace to society" (Ry. 609.8).
5. Q's stepdaughter, Margaret Mercer Elphinstone, *suo jure* Baroness Keith (see HLP to LC, 3 October 1808, n. 6). Her inheritance consisted of the barony of Keith, which was entailed upon her and "the heirs-male of her body." (Since her marriage to the comte de Flahaut was to produce only five daughters, the barony of Keith became extinct at her death in 1867.) For the will of Lord Keith, see P.R.O., Prob. 11/1673/417.
6. For Dr. William Fellowes and his wife, Mary, of the Axford Buildings, Bath, see HLP to JSPS, 18 April 1812, n. 10.
7. Harington died at Bath on 15 January. See *GM* 86, pt. 1 (1816):185–86, 352, 640.
8. AL on 18 January reassured HLP: "I will write to Day to Willmot [the nurseryman in Kent] to come here and receive His Money if Windle has not already Paid Him. I shall pay all other *pressing* demands in London, and the others must wait untill April when the Sale Here will make an end of all Debts."
9. For John Fisher, bishop of Salisbury, see HLP to TSW, 3 August 1813, nn. 12 and 13. He was undoubtedly visiting his brother, Samuel (ca. 1761–1846), M.D., of 13 Johnstone Street, physician to the Bath penitentiary. See *GM*, n.s. 26 (1846):668; *London and Provincial Medical Directory* (1847), 322.

10. For the widowed Amelia Perkins and her granddaughter Amelia, see HLP to Q, 17 January 1806, n. 25; also John Perkins to HLP, 1 October 1811.
11. 17 New King Street, HLP's "nutshell" residence.

TO SIR JAMES FELLOWES

(Jour de Naissance)   Tuesday Night
(27. January)   January 16: *1816*.

My dear Sir James Fellowes

will like a long independent Letter about a Thousand *other* People and Things: when I am one of the *Family Cluster*—we *can* think only of *You*—how should we? surrounded by Effusions of your kind Heart, whether in form of Butter or Eggs, or Letters as nutritious to our Minds as they are to our Bodies.——Yet poor old Dr. Harington *must* be thought of, he will be seen no more. Was it not pretty and affecting that they played his fine Sacred Music so lately? and by Dint of loud and reiterated Applause called him forward as he was retiring— to thank him for their Entertainment—he returned——bowed, went home— sickened and——![1] This was a Classical Conclusion of his Life indeed: like the Characters at the End of Terence's Plays *who cry* Valete omnes, et plaudite.[2]—— But *I* would wish a less public Exit—and say Vale! to my nearest Friend—Voi altri *applaudite* to the rest.

Apropòs did you ever read Spencer's long String of Verses, every Stanza ending with Wife, Children and Friends? I can neither *find,* nor recollect them rightly: but too well does my *then hurt* Mind retain my Answer to a Lady (*one* of the Burneys,) who quoted a Line expressive of Contempt for general Admiration; going on to this Passage which I *do* remember——Away with the Laurel, o'er me wave the Willow,/ Set up by the hand of Wife Children and Friends.[3]

My Reply was *No.* for, said I——

Should Love Domestic plant the Tree
Hope still would be defeated:
Children and *Friends* would croud to see
The neighbring Cattle eat it.

Deciduous Plants will lose their Leaves
With Winter's Provocation;
And ev'ry Sigh That Sorrow heaves
Will sap the slight Foundation:

Till in a Sea of Follies tost
Foes to each fine Emotion;
Our drooping *Willow's* driven and lost
On Life's Tempestuous Ocean.

While true to Time-worn Worth, we View
The Verdant Laurel rising:
Firm-fix'd, and of *unchangeful* Hue,
Each Wintry Blast despising.

Around the late-reposing Head
This faithful Foliage hovers:
Points out the Merits of the Dead,
And many *a Failing covers.*

And should the Berries e'er invite
Some envious nibb'ling Neighbour;
A blister'd Tongue succeeds the Bite
And best repays their Labour——

Did you believe I could ever have expressed myself with so much Bitterness?——but if People *will* break the *Heart* even of an Apricot—sweetest and most insipid of all Fruits; the Kernel will yield a harsh Flavour.

Poor Doctor Harington like myself has found the Kindness that sweetened his Existence, always from *without* doors,—never from *within.*

My Cough is no longer a bad one, but the hoarseness does not go off, and when I tried to tell old Stories last Night to amuse your dear Father, I found the Voice very odious——so Sir James Fellowes is best off now, that has me for a Correspondent. Don't you remember in some of my Stuff, how Johnson sayd if he was married to Lady Cotton, he would live 100 Miles away from her, and make her *write* to him——"Once o'Week"—added he, "I could bear a Letter from the Creature; but it is the *poorest Talker* sure—that ever opened Lips."[4] Well! if you asked the pretty Girls to tell you the Colour of the Wind, and explain to you the Tint of the Storm: They would say the Storm *Rose* I imagine, and the Wind *blew*——We used to spell the Colour so—in very old Days.

Meanwhile the Geological Maps of what is to be discerned *under Ground,* are fine Things certainly:[5]——but *I* feel so completely expectant of going to make Strata myself; that the Science does not much *allure* me, altho' I am *deeply* concerned in it, at 75 Years old.

Bessy Jones is better—Syrup of Poppies and Syrup of Squills and—a timely assistance from Nature, of *Diarrhæa,* have done her good:—and she longs to eat Leg of Pork.

That little Thoughtless Thing Salusbury—has kept me all this while in hot Water about his Baby——wrote the *pathetic* Letter you saw:——and then, never (in answer to all my Enquiries) sent Word whether the Child lived or died——

Dear Me! 'Tis a silly Thing to try to extract Sunbeams from Cucumbers like Swift's Projector in Gulliver's Travels.[6]——Lady Keith has written her *Annual* Letter: rather civiller than the last I think.

She will soon have her hands full I trust with this Grand Marriage: Princess Charlotte has at length made her Choice it seems; of Le Prince de Saxe Cobourg—a handsome Man;[7]—and *She thinks so.*—Without that Power of making Impression,—Beauty in either sex is a complete *Nihility*—find me a better Word, and *that* shall be turned out by her who wishes to keep the *best* in *every* Sense for *you.*——Your faithful H: L: P.

God bless!! and give me an Excuse for writing again soon;——The next shall cost you nothing.

God bless!! once more—*ay 20 Times.* Dispose of my Loves and Compliments.

Text Huntington MSS. 6927. *Address* Sir James Fellowes/ Sidmouth/ Devonshire. *Postmark* JA 17 1816 <BATH>.

1. HLP wrote to AL, on 19 January 1816: "Poor Doctor Harrington is just now Dead—could not *quite* reach 90. He had composed some fine Sacred Music for last Christmas, and heard it performed in Public 1st January. The loud Applauses so violently repeated—called him from his Seat in the Orchestra: he came forward,—bowed; was cheered again and again—went home—rejoyced,—sickened,—and died in a very few Days, lamented by every Creature" (Hyde Collection).
2. Terence's six extant comedies end with the words "plaudite" or "vos valete et plaudite," a commonplace at the end of every Latin comedy whose final scene has been preserved.
3. William Robert Spencer (1769–1834) wrote "Wife, Children, and Friends," a ballad of ten quatrains. HLP quotes a part of the eighth quatrain as she remembers it:

> Let the breath of renown ever freshen and nourish
> The *laurel* that o'er her fair favourites bends,
> O'er me wave the *willow*, and long may it flourish,
> Bedew'd with the tears of *wife, children and friends*.

See *English Songs and Ballads* (B.L., 11630. f. 7/115). The Burney "Lady" was FB.
4. See HLP to Isabella Hamilton, 13 May 1805, n. 2.
5. HLP refers to the "Geology of the Apennines": *Conchiologia Fossile Subapennina con Osservazioni Geologiche sugli Apennini e sul Suolo adiacente*, 2 vols. (Milan, 1814). See the *Edinburgh Review* 26 (1816):155–80.
6. See the third voyage of Swift's *Gulliver's Travels*, chap. 5.
7. During the London summer of 1814 Princess Charlotte Augusta of Wales met *Leopold* Georg Christian Friedrich (1790–1865), prince of Saxe-Coburg-Saalfeld, later king of the Belgians (1831). On 23 January 1816 *The Times* announced their betrothal, "which has been so long whispered." The Prince Regent was to give his official consent on 10 March and inform Parliament four days later. See the *Bath Chronicle*, 14 March; *The Times*, 15 and 16 March, etc.

TO SIR JAMES FELLOWES

Bath
25: January: 1816.

Such a Letter! Can anyone be ever ill again who reads it? Why my dear Sir, I have been living *Mihi Carior* ever since our friendly Correspondence first began.—And poor little Bessy! She is to me all that a Daughter should be, and the Sweet Word you Said of *her*, sunk deep into my heart. I have suffered much from Nervous Irritation, but your kind Father is *so* good to me,—he has promised to Smooth my rough Tongue: I did not tell him that I apprehended Aphthæ;[1]—but the Lady who was afraid of her own Hearth-Rug, could not be more fanciful than I have been—

> Strong and more strong her Terrors rose,
> Her Shadow did the Nymph appall:
> She trembled at her own long Nose,
> It look'd So long against the Wall.

This is no Heroick Disposition certainly; but I will not play *Agnes*,[2] and be frighted into any disgraceful Compliances—assure yourself I will not—and now I feel protected.—"Mais tout ç'a m'echauffe la Bile."

So I'll try to recover my Voice, to talk and laugh and sing and rejoyce on the dear, *Dear* 14th of February, which gave *Life* to *Your* Father, to *mine*, no less a Gift—a *Wife* such as no Man ever deserved except my Friend Sir James Fellowes; and Such as I pray to God he may find, who seeks her not in the Mad Circles of Dissipation.

Now for what the Newspaper calls/Miscellaneous Articles—

Great Report is made of the Gay Festival held in the Hall of Caractacus—A Fandango was danced to a new Tune called la *Frasquita dexada*.[3]

Flying Rumours from Sidmouth perswade us to believe that a Gentleman whose Name must be sought among los *Titulados*, and first on the List of *Liberales*; is likely soon to unite himself in Marriage with a Lady—

> *Flavia* her Name 'mong those of heav'nly Birth
> Tho' called Eliza by the Song of Earth.

according to the Mode of naming Goddesses in Homer's Time.[4]

A Triumphant General[5] is expected to make his Entrance into Bath tomorrow by the Night Coach. The *cheapest* Ribbands are preparing for Ornamental Decorations: Fool's Colours for Penning and Co.[6]

A certain Lady once well-known to Fame,—if not completely *out of her Reckoning*, hopes Deliverance from her heavy Burden now—in Two and Twenty Weeks, She means to Sum up all with Saying

Nil habeo, nil debeo, Gratias Deo.

Debts of Gratitude excepted; and They, pain not a Generous Mind.

Au reste; Your Father bids me drink the Bath Water, and I did do so Yesterday, and eat three Mouthfuls for Dinner, and was more alive—or more resembling a live Person than I have been yet Since you left us—and I tried the Bishop of Salisbury's Party last Night, but made a *poor* Figure—so hoarse!—a mute Piozzi is a miserable Thing indeed, but Health will mend; and we shall do better. It is a Shame to think, to feel, or to tell, how *bitter* my Inside is with Bile and Gall: but I'm sure I have read somewhere that Milk itself will turn corrosive by hard Usage, Ill Keeping etc.

The Bishop[7] is very agreable, and tho' he is a Nobleman now and a Courtier, remembers old Times, and old Jokes: and how he and I sate down together on a Dirty Bench in St. Mark's Place Venice to hear a Domenican Fryar—while Harlequin jumped about unheeded on the other Side the Square.

Your Ladies must see the new Book: tho' the best Thing in it is telling how The Foreigner comes to a Inn at Dover, and finding A Member of the Bang-up Club loitering about The Yard, cries here—Ostler, hold My Horse—Know your Road-Work better you———! replies the other, and challenges him.—Escaped from this Misery—he meets a Lady going to a Party—her Head heaped in the fashionable Way with Flowers: Sell me some Roses pretty Dear, cries the New-arrived Foreigner—laying hold of them. Insulting Fellow! cries the Girl. I'll have you punished for an Assault. A Passer-by relieves him from this Difficulty, and they strike up a Friendship and go Together to the Inn. Pray Sir who have I the honour to be so much obliged to—says the Stranger. I Sir am Captain of the Band of Pensioners. The Spaniard looks in his English Dictionary (Johnson's) for so hard a Word; and finds *Pensioner*—a Man hired for the Destruction of his Country. Oh for Pity leave me directly cries he—I am in Company With a Chief of Banditti—What will become of me? Get out of my Apartments.

Well! Now I will have done with all that <   > Morning Nonsense and with the truest and tenderest Regard—*try* to express my Wishes for your Happiness—'Tis all in Vain however—I cannot find anything but detached *Words*—Friendship, Esteem and Gratitude—to which add Three detached *Letters* likewise H:L:P.

Text Hyde Collection. *Address* Sir James Fellowes/ Sidmouth/ Devonshire. *Postmark* BATH 26 JA 26 1816.

1. Aphthae: a name given to the infantile disease "thrush," and in the plural, to the small specks on the mouth and tongue that characterize it, and that also occasionally appear in adults of enfeebled condition (*OED*).
2. In Voltaire's *La Pucelle d'Orleans* (1755), Agnes Sorel, the mistress of Charles VII, is taken captive by the English and consoles herself in the arms of Monrose, page to an English nobleman (canto 12). Lot 127 on the first day of the sale of the books from Brynbella (17 September 1823) was "Oeuvres de Voltaire, 100 tom boards, uncut Par. 1786." See *Sale Catalogue* (2).
3. In a letter to JW of 21 December 1815 HLP spoke of "the full Table and chearful Society of Dear *Dear* Bodylwyddan," adding, "May the Birthdays go off happily!" Perhaps this is an allusion to some festivities at the seat of the Williams.
4. JF, at the time in Sidmouth, was to marry Elizabeth James on 5 March 1816. See HLP to JF, 26–27 January 1816, n. 7.
5. HLP makes frequent reference to AL as "General." See HLP to JF, 26-27 [January 1816], n. 4.
6. The cheapest of motley ribbons are for John Penning, London upholsterer and auctioneer. See HLP to AL, 31 August 1814, n. 1.
7. For John Fisher, bishop of Salisbury, see HLP to TSW, 3 August 1813, nn. 12 and 13; HLP to AL, 14 January 1816, n. 9.

TO SIR JAMES FELLOWES

Fryday 26–27: [January 1816][1]

My dear Sir James Fellowes,

not contented with heaping kindnesses on his poor little Friend; *Thanks* her for her good Opinion; and *Thanks* her for the Tenderness of her Expressions——when Alas! 'tis only honest Truth that tears the first from my Heart; and relaxed Sensibility makes the other flow spontaneously from my Pen. "But so few People will give *one Leave* to love them" would Doctor Collier say continually.[2] They are always (added he) doing some what to hinder me from feeling or expressing my Regard.

Now nobody can take a more opposite Course from this than Sir James Fellowes, who certainly now stands a fair Chance of being suffocated with Kind

Words Wishes &c. Bear 'em as you may therefore. Your dear Sister who overflows with them, left me at four o'Clock because you once chid her for encroaching on *my* Dinner-hour, who can eat no Dinner at *any* hour——and here 'tis 11 o'Clock and I am waiting for more Accounts and what Accounts would I have? when all is going so prosperously.

I will give God Thanks and go to Sleep after wishing you Good Night in the *only* Language you do not understand better than Yours faithfully/ H: L: P. Nôsdawch.[3]

But Sleep hates Bile, and will not reside near where that Person of *Colour* makes his Abode; so here is the 27th and I expect Leak every Moment to shew his Laurels. Meanwhile Mrs. Perkins, Widow of Mr. Thrale's head Clerk so often mentioned in my Biographical Memoirs, is here at Bath in a fine House Pultney Street. We met by Accident and she said she would leave a Card at my Lodgings; but Bessy let her in: and great was her Amazement indeed at my Small Apartments, and contracted Situation;—She behaved very prettily. People are now and then *better* than one counts upon, if sometimes they are *worse:* We must take this World rough as it runs, and depend only on the next.

Here comes the victorious General.[4]

Leak brings me the receipt in *full of all Demands* from Gillowe and Co. 410£ Abatement, and so ends my Ill Will to their house: He has behaved heroically, and done the whole himself. Windle and his Prussians kept in the Back Ground—in the Rear I should say, merely as Corps de Reserve. They all unite in advising me to draw up Advertisements and offer the Contents of the House for Sale early next April;[5] when I do hope my dear Sir James Fellowes will fancy Some of the Articles, and Save from Touch of the Profane. Perhaps the Family will be zealous to secure some Things——perhaps an Offer will arrive of taking the Tout ensemble. People see me live as I do, and think I mean a long Continuance in the same Course of Wretchedness——but I am the more Tired of it, as I see so little Pleasure given to those who should render my Situation more Comfortable by at least affected Assiduity——but neither real Daughters nor adopted Son have ever dropt a hint as if I was living beneath myself——only Salusbury just said once Why did not I keep a Man Servant? My Reply was— because I could not afford it.

This Sale will make me rich in my old Age: and I see everybody selling, so why should not I their Example pursue, and better my Fortune as other Folks do?

Leak is very Indignant concerning the Trifling Demands from Wales: one Bill's first Article begins Six Months after I quitted the Country——but such Trash shall not make me uneasy.[6]

Adieu! my Dearest, *happiest* Friend! Keep clear of the *Tooth Ach,* and bring your own good Looks and Your Lady's[7] Soon to Bath where all are ready to rejoyce over you and none more Cordially than your most Obliged/ H: L: P.

My Face is raving mad with Pain now.

Text Hyde Collection. *Address* Sir James Fellowes.

1. This letter is dated from contents that correspond to HLP's "Pocket Book" entries during January, particularly her meetings with Mrs. Perkins and the arrival on 27 January of Leak "with Gillowe's Rect: in full."
2. For Dr. Arthur Collier, HLS's tutor and her "truest" and "most disinterested Friend," see HLP to William Wilshire, 26 April [1791], n. 2; to LC, 15 March 1795, n. 4.
3. HLP's phonetic spelling of *Nôs da*, "good night" in Welsh.
4. HLP's pun on Leak and her frequent reference to him as General Gerard Lake (1744–1808), first viscount Lake of Delhi and Laswaree, and Aston Clinton, Bucks.
5. The advertisements for the auction of Streatham Park's contents began as early as 12 February in the *Morning Chronicle* and 15 February 1816 in *The Times*.
6. On 21 January HLP noted in her "Pocket Book" that she received a bill from "the White Lyon St. Asaph demanding" £10.
7. On 5 March at St. George's, Hanover Square, JF was to marry by special license Elizabeth, née James (1794–1843), eldest daughter and heir of Joseph James of Adbury House, Northants. See *GM*, n.s. 21 (1844):106.

TO ALEXANDER LEAK

Bath
Thursday Night
8: February 1816

Leak does make me laugh, when he says What *Sums of Money* I have at Hammersley's: Poor Soul! I have just 197: 7: 9

to which by adding 22: 10: 0

219: 17: 9 will be left.

I *think* indeed it should be 220£—but I suppose we must not stand for Three Shillings.—This must be long my Support; because the *March* Dividends are engaged to Leak with Thanks beside,[1] and Ward and Lonsdale *shall* have their 108£ in *April;*[2] and the poor Bath People are so good about giving Credit, that I will pay them the first Moment I can.

With Regard to the *Great Affair*, I am *Mysterious* only because tho' I tell my own Secrets, it is dishonourable to tell those of another.—I can but only add the Word *Hope*—when Certainty is at such immeasureable Distance; and we have little better to depend on all thro' this Life I think,—and even in our last Passage out of it.

A pretty Lady here, a Miss Shuttleworth was knocked down crossing Gay Street into George Street 10 Days ago,[3] by Dr. Mapletoft's Horse: he was visiting a Patient in the Circus, and had hung the quiet Creature on the Rails—whence some Boys loosed him *for Fun*, and drove him galloping down the Hill.[4] Miss Shuttleworth fell, and the Horse over her; entangled, and at last *enraged*; for he was hurt, and she was *not killed:* but has been trepanned for the Fracture in her Skull, and is said to be *dying now.*

Poor unhappy Soul! and a small Fortune to pay Doctors and Surgeons out of. But the little Boys had their Fun.

Mr. Salusbury's last Letter contains an Invitation to Brynbella. He says nothing of Streatham Park, but expresses Wonder concerning Gillowes.

The Newspaper says There is an Infectious Fever in Wales;[5] It says too, That the Plague is confest to be in poor dear Italy:[6] My *Hope* is the stronger, for my Friends *once* had a Notion of going abroad, which such News will check. I have not seen the Advertisement, and am with/ all good Wishes Yours and your Wife and Childs/ H: L: P.

Our Lodgings are let now: Your Note came enclosed to Lord Coventry and Mr. Davies.[7]

Text Hyde Collection. *Address* Mr. Alexander Leak/ Streatham Park/ Surrey. *Postmark* BATH <9 FE>; 10 FE 10 1816; 10 o'Clock FE 10 1816.

1. AL had been using his own money to pay some Streatham Park expenses; see especially HLP to JF, 18 June 1815.
2. For Joseph Ward, the London attorney, see HLP to Jonathan Stearns or Sterns, 30 October 1790, n. 3; for Lonsdale, see her letter to AL, 9 [-10] October 1814, n. 8.
3. Frances Shuttleworth died on 9 February, twelve days after being struck down by a "horse which had broken loose from the care of a servant." See the *Bath Chronicle*, 1 and 15 February.
4. There was a Reverend Matthew Mapletoft (1760–1835) of 19 Catherine Place, vicar of Yedingham.
5. An outbreak of "typhus fever has for some weeks past proved alarmingly fatal, and is still prevalent in different parts of the principality." See *The Times*, 9 February 1816.
6. For the spread of the plague, see *The Times*, 5 and 12 February; also HLP to the Reverend John Roberts, 5 March 1816, n. 1.
7. HLP's Streatham Park neighbors: RD (HLP to PSW, 5 September [1791], n. 2) and George William Coventry, seventh earl of Coventry (HLP to PSW, 11 January 1791, n. 1).

TO ALEXANDER LEAK

Tuesday 13: February 1816.

Leak will be glad to hear that I have seen Sir James Fellowes, and that *he* will certainly see him during the Course of next Week:[1] Whatever he proposes, *I* shall be sure to acquiesce in; and my hopes are that you will make the Place agreeable to him and his Lady for a Short Residence immediately after their Marriage when I beg of You to shew him every thing, and treat him with the utmost possible Confidence as the truest/ Friend of/ H: L: Piozzi.

Sir James Fellowes seems to say he shall use his own Linen,—Mortlock will provide China Ware at *my* Expence.—It is my particular Fancy.[2]
I cannot find the Advertisement, pray shew the Copy of it to Sir James Fellowes;[3] who wishes *by no means* to hinder the Sale of the Place; as he is desirous of every possible Advantage accrueing to me.
His temporary Residence can not injure the Place or its Sale——on the contrary,—*We Hope to promote it.*[4]
Don't hurry yourself or put yourself out of your way till you see Sir James.

Text Hyde Collection. *Address* Mr. Alexander Leak/ Streatham/ Surrey. *Postmark* 15 FE 15 1816; 10 o'Clock FE 15 1816.

1. On this day in her "Pocket Book," HLP noted JF's visit: "We talked of passing the Honey Moon at Streatham Park—paying me 100£ for the same. It would be a nice Thing after all."
2. For John Mortlock, the china dealer at 250 Oxford Street, see HLP to AL, 13 December 1814, n. 3.
3. See the *Morning Chronicle*, e.g., for 12 February 1816: "Streatham Park/ Late Residence of Mrs. Piozzi/ Mr. Squibb (in conjunction with Messrs. Matthews and Taylor, of Fenchurch-street) has the honour of announcing to the Nobility and Gentry, that in the course of next month will be offered to their notice, by Public Auction, the valuable Contents of the above distinguished Residence; comprising the rare and curious Library of upwards of 2000 Volumes, principally selected by the celebrated Dr. Johnson. A Collection of choice Pictures, the productions of the most eminent Masters of the Italian, Flemish, and English schools, a few excellent engravings, an assemblage of rare old China, a few valuable antique Bronzes, &c. &c.——Also the elegant Household Furniture, the greater part of which is recently new. At the same time will be Let by Auction, the elegant Mansion, with suitable offices, large productive gardens, and about 70 acres of valuable meadow land."

The advertisement also appeared in the *Morning Chronicle* for 16 and 19 February, *The Times*, 15 and 22 February.
4. AL on 15 February did not agree, observing that "His residence here, be it ever so short, will make us liable to pay Half a Years Taxes &c. on the House, which I have so far, avoided paying, in consequence of the House being unoccupied" (Ry. 609.9).

TO ANN LEAK

Thursday 15: February *1816*

My good Dear Leak,

Tell your too hasty Husband from me, that I have seen the Advertisement at length—and confess my Amazement—What! expose a Summer Residence to Sale while Frost and Snow is on the Ground!—Pray let the same Notice be repeated at the same Time next Month, and the Month after; People may *then* be induced to look at it perhaps, but surely not *now.*

The very *Sight* of the Grounds in Winter must check and chill every Wish for the Place; but there is no Danger I suppose, for nobody will go look at it in so desperate a Season.

Stop the further Advertisements Dear Leak for Pity; and stir no Step further till You have seen Sir James Fellowes; who is gone from here, and will be with *You* Monday or Tuesday.

I should like that he should know what Expence I lived at, when *last* an Inhabitant of Streatham Park: and what was our Establishment. Yourself and Husband was it not? a Cook and House Maid, My own Maid and A Footman and Boy: I recollect no more Servants and the House Bills were about 8£ or 10£ o'Week, as I remember; except when we gave the Grand Dinner. Make Leak speak freely to Sir James about *every* Thing——If the Place don't suit *him*, he will recommend it: but Your Advertisement has put me quite out of Breath by its Hastiness.[1] Yours ever/ H: L: Piozzi.

Text Hyde Collection. *Address* Mrs. Leak/ Streatham Park/ Surrey. *Postmark* 16 FE 16 1816; 10 o'Clock FE 16 1816.

1. On 22 February (Ry. 609.10) AL responded to HLP's order:
" . . . I have . . . stoped the advertisement of the Sale about which, I am sorry to find, You think I have acted Hastily. The present measure is I hope according to your Wish. You must however permit Me to observe I do not recommend it, it is a Place not fit for Sir James Fellows, and I fear they will soon find it so, should they leave it in the Summer, and Sir James do not seem to think He shall stay longer. You must of course have the place on Your Hands for another Year, and by that time much Money must be expended in repairs. It will be too late then to sell the Effects, every Body will be gone from Town. The Time I had proposed for the Sale was not at all too early. The People were beginning to be very anxious about it and will be much disappointed, many have been to enquire about the Books and Pictures, and seem to think them very valueable."

TO ALEXANDER LEAK

Fryday
16 February 1816.

Leak is a good Man and true, and wishes well to my Interest I am convinced:—no Fear of liberal Compensation if we fix where I hope and desire.

Sir James Fellowes is a Man of consummate honour and his Regard for me has been shewn in every Shape.—He has likewise a good Esteem for Leak as a faithful Steward to poor H: L: Piozzi.

If you go to Lord Gwydir's when you receive *this*, I think you will find him and his Brother,[1] If they *can* be at Streatham Park on Monday, I'm sure they will; and if not on Monday——*Tuesday*. My Love to dear Wife and Child.——

I am sorry for Mr. Salusbury; but have given my *strict Word* to my best Friend, that I will not involve myself on his Account.

Sufficient if I can outlive my own Debts. I am told there is a Way of disseminating the Advertisement (not expensive at all) by pasting it on a Sheet of Paper and sending it to Gentlemen's Houses—They may miss a public News Print, but cannot *miss that*: as it comes in form of a Letter.

Text Hyde Collection. *Address* Mr. Alexander Leak/ Streatham Park/ Surrey. *Postmark* 17 FE 17 1816; 10 o'Clock FE 17 1816.

1. Peter Burrell, first baron Gwydir, was an only son. See HLP to JSPS, 6 January 1815, n. 14.

TO ANN LEAK

Bath Sunday
18: February 1816.

My dear Leak

I have as yet provided myself no Habitation except *the narrow House* I am hastening to: but you and your Friends will not give my Things away; and if the Bidders do not come up to their real Value, Leak will of Course see that they are *bought in* as is the common Custom. I can then judge better about Furniture or no Furniture in the Place where I mean to Settle.—

Had it pleased God to give me *one* more Taste of Happiness on this Side the Grave, he would have inspired Sir James and Lady Fellowes with a Fancy to *purchase* or *take* the Place: where I should then have visited them from Time to Time;——but 'tis Folly to expect anything further from Streatham Park, but Vexation; which I will prepare to endure.

That from Brynbella is indeed hard to bear, but it shall not be encreased by my own Fault. I left them Pictures, Plate, Jewels, Linen, *all I had* as you know, and to hear they are *poor* and in a *deplorable* Case is shocking.[1] But I will change the Subject.

Let me beg of you to write as soon as You have Seen my Friends, and tell me if there is a *Gleam of Hope* that I shall ever see them in a House of *my own* which I have no Reason to be ashamed of./ Kiss your little Boy for me,/ and believe me ever Yours/ H: L: Piozzi.

What! no Account yet of the *Ladies* coming forward to stop the Sale? I see many People who Think the Advertisement will alarm them.[2]

Text Hyde Collection. *Address* Mrs. Leak/ Streatham Park/ Surrey. *Postmark* 19 FE 19 1816; 10 o'Clock FE 19 <1816>.

1. According to AL, 13 February (Ry. 609.9): "I suppose Mr. Salusbury wish to have you at Brynbella that You may pay His Debts. Mr. Davies told Me the other Day that He had been in Company with a Lady, who was just come from a Visit at Mr. Roberts at Dymerchion who gave a most deplorable account of Mr. Salusbury, just however as I expected."
2. On 22 February (Ry. 609.10), AL dismissed HLP's postscript: "I wonder you should indulge a hope that the Ladys will come forward, I am pretty certain they will not."

TO JOHN SALUSBURY PIOZZI SALUSBURY

Bath Wednesday
21: February 1816.

I am so little accustomed Dearest Salusbury, to be called roughly to Account for my Expressions, and find so few People ill pleased with my Correspondence, that I am at a Loss to answer your Accusation.[1] I seldom keep Copies of any Letter—unless upon Business, or when the Person written to is one I fear to trust;—so that I guess not wherein I am to blame: recollecting nothing but what I deemed inoffensive Chat.

My Temper however may possibly be soured by Time and various Vexations——tho' I now do remember something of a Similar Disposition to quarrel on your Part, last May 1815—when I underwent a heavy Censure for some Omission of Ceremony.[2]

We will if you please beware of the Third Time; and put as Speedy an End to this Controversy as possible, nothing on Earth being so disagreeable as Disputation either Personal, or on Paper/ to Your most Affectionate Aunt/ H: L: Piozzi.

Present me properly to your Family and Friends, none of whom I would disoblige on any Account; and I earnestly beg them to think so.

Text Ry. 588.311.

1. JSPS's letter is missing, but HLP's "Pocket Book" entry of 20 February reveals that she had "received a *strange* Letter from Salusbury, as if he had a Mind to quarrel with me!!! Is he going out of his Mind?"
2. See HLP to JSPS, 6 May 1815.

TO SIR JAMES FELLOWES

Bath Wensday
21: February 1816

And here was I sitting *holding* my Pen——like *holding* my Tongue,—when dying to speak and write: for fear of annoying you with Letters at such a busy Time: And here was I making Excuses for dear Sir James Fellowes; because said I he is plucking the *Turkey,* and forgetting the *Goose* of Course. Amidst these wise Reflexions comes your incomparable Father with such a *sweet Scrap*—Oh I do think you are taking a fancy to Streatham Park; and that there is a little Cordial Drop of Comfort at the bottom of my *Old China Cup* left yet. Could you see Salusburys last Letter you would confess I wanted it;——My hand is still shaking from Anger ill-suppressed——But I fly from the Subject.

Leak's Wife is very amiable, and I hope attached to me: her Husband's Manner is surly, but he has a high Sense of Integrity. His Care of Brynbella made the Place quite a Paradise, and tho' none of the People thereabouts felt as much Love as they did Fear of him,—none ever impeached his Honesty or Honour. Whenever I come to Streatham Park (and never will I see it more unless I see *You* sitting there at Bottom of your own table;) The Room where my Mother's Portrait hangs—*must* be *yours.*[1] The Dressing Room will be for your use you know, and Lady Fellowes will keep Possession of Her own Apartment.

Lord Byron and his Wife are parted we hear,[2] and my truly wicked Cousin

Lord Bective is run off with Lady George Beresford cy-devant Harriet Schutz.[3]
What a World it is!——May I *but* live to see You happy in it—and in a House
of mine.——If it be so,——as old King Lear says,

> It is a Chance that does redeem all Sorrows
> I ever yet have felt.[4]

Dear Mr. Dorset Fellowes is very friendly to take an Interest in my Affairs so;
pray Thank him for me, I am got clear of the Catarrh, and can read this beautiful
Siege of Corinth *with good Effect*.[5]

Do you expect to get free of hearing my own little Drama read? because I was
choked that Day when beginning it? no Indeed Sir.[6] I shall bring it with me,
and read it in the Library, where Lady Derby commended it once so earnestly
and wished to act Gunhilda for me[7]——Oh You have not yet *half* done with
your troublesome but faithful Friend/ H: L: Piozzi.

Do you know that I made a complete Conquest of your Brother Henry before
he left our Town?[8] he called on me at 3 o'Clock and staid so long after 5—one
would have thought it was *Sir James Fellowes*!

Now for bad News—but I told you it would be so;—don't be too much
shocked, but Mary Mayhew has broke a Blood-vessel——She is doing (as the
Phrase is) very well.[9] I am going to dine with the Lees of Burlington Street,[10]
and Bessy is pulling the Pen out of my hand to make me be dressed in Time.
Be quiet Bessy; Who knows but you and I may have an Airing of a Hundred
Miles to take together one of these Days?

See what Spirits your dear Scrap of Paper has given *me*, and write again soon;
and tell the *how* the *when* and the *where*.

The Leaks have never written, I was beginning to muse on Misery alone,
when Doctor Fellowes came this Morning and found my Room full of People:—
Sir William Wynn in particular, who begged for a Friend of *his* Permission to
sell his Service of China as *mine*:[11]

Miss Williams saw by the handwriting it was her Brother Fleetwood's;[12] and
felt offended the Application had not been made to *her* instead of Sir William
Wynne.

Text Berg Collection + . *Address* Sir James Fellowes/ at Lord Gwydir's House/
Whitehall/ London. *Postmark* BATH 21 FE 21 1816 109.

1. For the Zoffany portrait of HLP's mother, see her letter to AL, 8 February 1813, n. 8.
2. On 15 January, one year and thirteen days after their marriage and five weeks after the birth
of Augusta Ada (d. 1852), Anne Isabella Byron left her husband, sixth baron Byron, and went to
her parents' home. Two weeks later, her father wrote to the poet, requesting that he agree to a
quiet separation.
3. Thomas Taylour (1787–1870), styled earl of Bective (1800–29), second marquess of Headfort
(1829), was discovered in a "criminal conversation" with Harriet Beresford, née Schutz (1786–1860),
who was "suffering under mental derangement." Bective was ordered by the sheriff's court, Bedford
Row, to pay £10,000 in damages to the lady's husband, George Thomas De La Poer Beresford
(1781–1839), a lieutenant general and third son of the marquess of Waterford. The Beresfords re-

mained married and Lord Bective was to marry in 1822 Olivia (Tuite-Dalton), née Stevenson (d. 1834). See the *Bath and Cheltenham Gazette*, 3 July 1816.

For Lord Bective's father, see HLP to Q, 25 March 1811, n. 17.

4. *King Lear*, 5.3.267–68.

5. Byron's *The Siege of Corinth* . . . [and] *Parisina* had been published in February by John Murray. See the *Courier*, 12 February.

6. For HLP's "The Two Fountains," see HLP to Charlotte Lewis, 20 September [17]89, n. 12. JF had visited HLP on 4 January 1816 when in her "Pocket Book" she wrote: "we read the original Floretta—I began the Drama, but could not go on for coughing."

7. For Lady Derby, see HLP to LC, 3 February 1796, nn. 7, 8. Gunhilda is a character in "The Two Fountains."

8. Henry Fellowes (1774–1864) attended St. John's, Cambridge, receiving his B.A. in 1804 and M.A. in 1807. He was appointed vicar of Sidbury, Devon, in 1813 and remained there until his death.

9. For the ailing Clementina Mary Mayhew, see HLP to Ly W, 30 January 1802, n. 7; to TSW, 13 August 1815.

10. According to the "Walcot Poor Rate" assessments (Guildhall, Bath), the name of Henry Lee (1759–1821) first appears as the occupier of 13 Burlington Street in 1805 and continues as such until 1821. The name is given variously as Harry, Harry Launcelot, or Henry L. Lee. The family at this time consisted of Harry Lancelot (so baptized), of Coton Hall, Salop; his wife Jane, née Cox (of Oxford); their daughter, Catherine Anne Harriet. See also the "Alveley Baptism Register," C.R.O., Salop.

11. Knighted 2 May 1810, William Wynn (1770–1855) was an officer in the army, rising from cornet in the 1st Dragoon Guards to major at Sandown Fort, Isle of Wight.

12. Roger Hesketh Fleetwood Williams, always in need of money, now lived with his wife, Elizabeth, and underage children in Earl's Terrace, Kensington. For his will, proved 25 November 1826, see P.R.O., Prob. 11/1719/612.

On 17 May 1816, AL wrote HLP that "Mr. Fleetwood Williams China sold for 35 Guineas" (Ry. 609.14).

TO ANN LEAK

Bath
Monday Morning
25: February 1816

Dear Leak

After the good natured Letter you wrote me, and after the Letter Sir James Fellowes wrote me, praising Your Attachment to me;—and wishing for such faithful adherents to *himself:*

You may guess how your Husband's *last* affected me when he complains of Ill Health, but wishes his *Life at an End*——rather as I understand——than not dispose of Streatham Park *immediately*—for I hope we *shall* dispose of it, perhaps to Advantage. God knows I would rather part with it to *dis*advantage than confine him to a Situation he has such an Aversion to, when better Plans are probably opening to your View.[1]

My Life *cannot* now be a long one; The Ladies and Mr. Salusbury are all very ill humored, and Mrs. Mostyn has let Segroid for Three Years, and will go abroad—I dare say without ever saying Adieu Mamma![2] but the Epistle of Yesterday, and our Preacher *upon* the Epistle; said, It was our bounden Duty *not* to seek our own, but enduring all things, patiently to suffer long and be *kind.*[3]

That I may have Grace so to do, is the constant Prayer of yours and your good/ Husband's, and the dear/ little Boy's/ H: L: P.

I shall never see Cecy again; yet how little did I think it when we parted last——at Mrs. Siddons's Cottage.[4]

I dated it *Monday* but have found means to send the Letter—this *Sunday* Evening. 25 February.

Text Hyde Collection. *Address* Mrs. Leak/ Streatham Park/ Surrey. *Postmark* 26 FE 26 1816; 10 o'Clock FE 26 1816.

1. AL in his letter dated 22 February recommended that HLP rent Streatham Park, adding in a postscript: "I suppose I must remove to the Smoaky Cottage again. I am unwell too but no matter all helps to wear Life away—would it were at an end" (Ry. 609.10).
2. In 1816 CMM was to go abroad, living primarily in Italy and returning to England only in 1827.
3. The Reverend Edward William Grinfeld at Laura Chapel used as his text 1 Corinthians 10:24; 13:4. For Grinfeld, see HLP to JSPS, 2 April 1815, n. 19.
4. HLP saw CMM for the last time at SS's Westbourne Farm, near what is now Paddington Station.

TO LADY WILLIAMS

Bath
26. February 1816.

My Dear Lady Williams's Letter is delightful, and Sir John's Joke excellent.[1] I certainly never heard a Breath concerning the Destination of Segroid and its *Doves* till your Ladyship told me; but The People are all going abroad in spite of Plagues in Italy, and Earthquakes at Lisbon;[2] I really wish Government would tax the Absentees, for if Money is really scarce at home, why should that little be carried to the Continent?[3] Among the new Publications, Mr. Williams should provide your Ladyship Paris *re*visited by John—not Walter Scott: It is a great favorite here: and I am never weary of the Battle of Waterloo,[4] one of its Heroes met me at a Dinner the other Day, and I was never tired of making him tell about the Scotch Greys &c.[5]—nor did it appear that he disliked the Discourse. Your Account of the Vale of Llwydd meanwhile dear Madam! is very uninviting: But I mean if Life lasts, and Money suits, to come down on a Visit next July, and stay among you till September: when These Lodgings are no longer mine, and I *must* return to move my few, my *very* few Possessions to a less uncomfortable Place of Abode. Dear Mr. Williams can witness I have never changed my Plan; and to confess the Truth, I believe few People would have held to their Resolution of living as I have done for near Two Years together. Bath is the best Place for Single Women that can be found; and the Friendship I have experienced here, leads me to choose it as a *last*—perhaps a *lasting* Residence. The Water is become quite necessary to my Health, and the Society will grow still more agreeable to me, when I have a less inconvenient Dwelling.

Is Mrs. Salusbury again in the Family Way? Her Husband's Letters seem embarrassed somehow; and appear somewhat *very like very Ill-humoured:* but assigning no Cause, I trust it is because the Child cries. Mrs. Wynne of Llewessog is here,[6] looking I think much as usual, but it is the Fashion to say her Health breaks, and perhaps it may.

This has been a most trying Winter to all Constitutions; the Coughs and Catarrhs have injured many, and frighted more.—Mr. Williams will grieve to be told that pretty Mary Mayhew—Mr. Lutwyche's Niece—has *broke a Blood Vessel* tho' Leeches and Blisters had been applied, and every Method taken to prevent it. Another beautiful Girl—Elizabeth Thomas—I forget whether he knew her;— is but barely saved, *if* saved.[7]

Poor Mrs. Myddelton! If the Doctor did settle (as I hear he did) 1000£ o'Year on her at Marriage; his Loss deserves a Tear or Two: we all saw how attached he was to *her,* and all her Relations.

Mrs. Strong's good Luck comes late, but it *does* come.[8] Miss Williams came to me crying because her Brother had [tear] not the Living; but there is another [tear] now She says, and Hope regiven [tear] again.[9] and when She cries now, it must be for Miss Griffith of Caerhèn—who I hope ails less than her Aunt apprehends.[10] I am sure *She* never forgets *Dear* Wales, and its Inhabitants, particularly those of Bodylwyddan—No, not for a Quarter of an hour. We are to meet at her Relation's Mr. Fornby's next Thursday;[11] who have very obligingly made Acquaintance with *me—on her Account* and seem perfectly amiable in their Manners.

Adieu Dear Madam! The March Winds are come a Month before their Time, and are blowing now most dreadfully. You will have seen poor Streatham Park advertised, some one told me and will be sorry for your poor H: L: P.

I'm glad my Godson goes to Harrow;[12] he takes my best Love with him, and when I come in to the Country in Summer, He shall see I have not forgotten him. Is it true that the Mr. Gryffith I met at Bodylwyddan goes to China?[13]

Somebody told me Mrs. Mostyn's second Son was in that Embassy.[14]

Ah Dear Lady Williams! I should feel as strange in Denbighshire *now* as Dear Sir John—in *Bath.*—a flying Visit in July is all I *can promise,* and all that I *will perform.*

Make my best Loves acceptable to all your Darlings.

Scandal says that Lord Byron has driven out his Lady for Mrs. Mardyn.[15] Lord <Bective> run away with Lady George Beresford: Lord Abercorn's <　　　> by Dint of Money[16]—and the Printers heavily fined <for> defaming Lady F. C. Webster.[17]

Text Ry. 4 (1812–18). *Address* Lady Williams/ Bodylwyddan/ St. Asaph/ North Wales.

1. For Sir John's reputation as a jokester, see HLP to Ly W, 16 February 1804, n. 3.
2. On 2 February the inhabitants of Lisbon were frightened "by two smart shocks of an earthquake," which injured no one. See *GM* 86, pt. 1 (1816): 171.
3. Only inhabited houses were taxed for window and house duties.

4. John Scott (1783–1821), a journalist, was the first editor of the *London Magazine* (1820–21). In 1814 he had published *A Visit to Paris* and had recently published *Paris Revisited*. Later HLP called Scott her favorite author "whose Account of Paris and Description of Waterloo I was never weary of reading." See HLP to JW, 5 March 1821.

5. At Waterloo, the Royal Scots Greys (2nd or Royal North British Dragoons) were part of the main assault on the French infantry: "the Greys, with some of the Royals and Inniskillings, dashed into the midst of two divisional batteries, half-way up the ridge, cut down gunners, drivers and horses, upset the guns into a ravine, and then . . . assailed Napoleon's great battery of eighty pieces." See the Hon. J.W. Fortescue, *A History of the British Army*, 13 vols. (London: Macmillan, 1920), 10:366.

The regiment was commanded by James Inglis Hamilton (1777–1815). Entering the Royal Scots Greys as a cornet, he rose to become its lieutenant colonel in 1807 and brevet colonel just before Waterloo. During the battle itself, after repeated charges against the French, when both his arms had been shattered, Hamilton seized the reins in his teeth and charged again to meet his death. See Charles Dalton, *The Waterloo Roll Call*, 2d ed. (London: Eyre and Spottiswoode, 1904), 58–59.

6. For Anna Maria Wynne, CMM's mother-in-law, see HLP to LC, 30 March 1795, n. 1.

7. Elizabeth Ann (1794–1882) was the eldest daughter of Josiah Thomas, the archdeacon of Bath.

8. Margaret Wakelin (d. 1848) had married in 1758 William Strong (1756–1842), who received from Queen's College, Cambridge, his B.A. in 1779, M.A. in 1782, and D.D. in 1802. He had been ordained a priest in 1782 and since then his ecclesiastical preferments were many. He was, e.g., chaplain to the king and to the bishop of Lincoln; archdeacon of Northampton; and canon of Peterborough.

9. For William Williams-Edwards, rector of St.George's, Denbigh, see HLP to MW, 5 July [1807], n. 5.

10. For Catherine Griffith, MW's niece, see HLP to Ly W, 21 March 1815, n. 6.

11. HLP misspells the name of the Reverend Richard Formby (1760–1832) of Formby Hall, Lancs. His mother was Mary, a daughter of Robert Hesketh (d. 1723) of Meols Hall, Lancs. MW's mother was Sarah (d. 1824), a daughter of Roger Hesketh (1711–91), the son and heir of Robert.

12. Hugh Williams's name does not appear in the *Harrow School Register, 1800–1911*. He did, however, enter Rugby in 1816. See A. T. Mitchell, ed. *Rugby School Register: Annotated*, 2 vols. (Rugby: A. J. Lawrence, 1901), 1:194.

13. For Walter Davies Griffith, see HLP to Ly W, 16 July 1815, n. 5.

14. Henry Mostyn was one of the Portsmouth midshipmen selected to accompany William Pitt Amherst (1773–1857), second baron Amherst (1797), first earl Amherst of Arracan (1826), on his embassy to China on board the frigate *Alceste*. The ship had left Portsmouth on 9 February. See *The Times*, 23 January, 13 February; *AR*, "Chronicle," 58 (1816): 24.

15. About the time Byron departed from England, rumors circulated about his supposed intrigue with the actress Mrs. Mardyn, who was to make her debut on 26 September 1816. See Marchand, *Byron*, 2:602, n. 4.

16. John James Hamilton (1756–1818), ninth earl of Abercorn (1789), first marquess of Abercorn (1790).

17. On 15 February 1816 James Webster Wedderburn (1789–1840) was awarded £2,000 in his libel suit against the *St. James's Chronicle*. The newspaper had placed his wife, Lady Frances Caroline, née Annesley (d. 1837), daughter of the first earl Mountnorris, in "a criminal intercourse with the Duke of Wellington." See the *Bath and Cheltenham Gazette*, 21 February 1816.

TO ALEXANDER LEAK

Bath Tuesday
27: February 1816.

Leak must go directly to Mr. Windle and shew him this Copy of a Letter I received to day from Mr. Merrik Hoare, and my Answer to it and you must act accordingly. I understand nothing concerning it.

My Dear Madam   26: February 1816.
    Pray excuse my troubling you upon a Subject of Business, that need not
occupy your Attention long. In the Summer of 1807 Your four Daughters,—
by Recommendation of the late Mr. Gillon,[1] agreed to purchase of the Duke
of Bedford the Enfranchisement of a small portion of Land at Streatham—
held upon Lease at the Annual Rent of Twelve Pounds.[2] The Conveyance was
made to Mr. Gillon In Trust for Them, and We have in vain Searched and
enquired for the Title Deeds. Will You be so kind as to inform me whether
they were sent to You, to be placed with other Papers relative to the Streatham
Property? Sophia writes in Love to you with/ Dear Madam/ Yours Affection-
ately/ H: M: Hoare.

P.S. The Conveyance was drawn by Mess: Brown and Gotobed of Norfolk
Street Solicitors[3] to the Duke of Bedford; and the Compensation Money paid
early in The Year 1808.

To this Letter I paid immediate Attention as you will read overleaf.
Copy of my Answer to H: M: Hoare Esq.

I never Dear Sir possessed any Papers upon the Subject you mention, nor did
Mr. Gillon ever name it to me. My Steward at Streatham Park, or my Solicitor
Mr. Windle may possibly know something of the Matter: This is the first I
ever heard from *any* of the *Family* concerning such a Business; and 1807 seems
a very long while Ago to Yours/ and Dear Sophias/ ever Affectionate/ H: L:
Piozzi.

Make my best Compliments to Mr. Windle, I will write soon to him but had no
time to Day for the Post. Yours ever/ H: L: P.

Text Hyde Collection. *Address* Mr. Alexander Leak/ Streatham Park/ Surrey. *Postmark* BATH 27 FE 27 1816; 10 o'Clock FE 28 1816.

1. For John Gillon, who had died in 1809, see HLP to LC, 30 August 1798, n. 13.
2. For John Russell, sixth duke of Bedford, see HLP to Q, 15 May 1813, n. 2.
3. The transfer of property never took place, since the names of HLP's "four Daughters" do not
appear in the "Streatham Land Tax Assessments" for the relevant period (C.R.O., Surrey).

TO ALEXANDER LEAK

                                                  Bath
                                                  Fryday 1st March 1816

    My good Leak must learn to love my Friends as well as to hate my Enemies.
I have always promised dear Sir James Fellowes my House for his Honey Moon,
and *he must have it:* and my Hope is to pass one happy Week with him and his
Lady there, before I see old Streatham Park no more. That hope has Sweetened
my Existence, which his Care has prolonged; thro' this horrid Winter.[1] And I

cannot believe People are leaving London, when the Princess is to be married in May;[2]——and a little Put-off will only make Bidders more eager. *The Truth is the best Thing to tell:* and *every one* is *welcome* to *know* my Obligations to him and his Family; which I can repay in no other Manner,—and I am sure, and have every Reason to be *certain* he will not hinder my disposal of the Place——but a Month can make no Difference if the Auction is put off so long. My confidence in you was such that I told you *this very Tale* when you were *here*——as far as I was authorized—not knowing then precisely what Day he would be put in Possession of the Lady——and I was sorry we advertised so early on that account.

Assure yourself we shall *lose nothing by* my keeping my Word—and I have every Reason to believe you will *gain* a Friend, who has been very kind indeed to Yours ever H: L: Piozzi.

I have had Misery enough with Streatham Park—and my Heart is set on *one Week's* Comfort in it.

If you tell Sir James Fellowes how matters stand, he will advise *you* and help us thro' the Difficulties *but I shall always think plenty of Bidders* a good Thing, *not a bad one.*

I have my Reasons for wishing to see London in spring——I *told* you so, and what those reasons were: and my Visit to Sir James and Lady Fellowes at Streatham Park will further *that* Business too—I mean waiting on *Ward* or *Windle*—about *my own* Affairs.

Text Hyde Collection. *Address* Mr. Alexander Leak/ Streatham Park/ Surrey. *Postmark* BATH <2MR 2 1816>; 10 o'Clock MR 2 1816.

1. On 26 February AL had written: "Sir James has not the least Idea of continuing here more than a few Weeks, which will I fear be very injurious to the Sale, it will be too late and People will be Ill Humoured, with being so long kept in expectation" (Ry. 609.11). On 28 February HLP wrote to Ann Leak: "Make my House as comfortable as ever you can for my *Friends*——Friends of my own finding and making, in the Close of Life; when turned adrift by naturally born and kindly-adopted Children——Their Attentions have been *so* tender (indeed they have) I cannot be too grateful. Had it not been for Sir James Fellowes and his Father, I question whether I should now have been here." She adds in a postscript: "The Doctor attends me now as if *I was his Sister*" (Hyde Collection).
2. Princess Charlotte Augusta of Wales was to marry at Carlton House on the evening of 2 May 1816. This information was available in most newspapers by early February. "The third son of the reigning Prince of Saxe-Cobourg . . . was in this country in the year 1814 [during] the visit of the Allied Sovereigns; and was much admired and distinguished by all the Royal Family. . . . As the most fit person to be selected to be the husband of the Heiress of the Crown of Britain, [h]e was accordingly invited to England, and the arrangements have gone forward progressively, to the satisfaction of all the illustrious parties concerned." See *GM* 86, pt. 1 (1816):175.

TO ALEXANDER LEAK

Bath
Tuesday 5: March 1816.

I am broken-hearted indeed my good Leak with *this* Letter; and feel for your Foot as sincerely as for my own Vexations.

There is no Mystery at all: I promised Sir James Fellowes long ago, *if he married* to lend him my House for his Honey-Moon—Could I do less? They offered me last Summer a Gratis Share of their small Establishment at Sidmouth, and actually made up an Apartment for Me and Bessy. They were sorry for my wretched situation here;—and perhaps;—(but I hope not,) a little Vanity and Folly may mingle with my Gratitude; and I might have a Wish that his Family and Servants should see *I had a Place* better than the pityful Lodging they found me living in. There is nothing to *determine* about; if Streatham Park does not suit Sir James Fellowes as a *Residence* he will I suppose only borrow it for a while.

The Money Matter grieves me: but if I make any thing like 6000£ of the Effects—you need not doubt my Desire of compensating *You.*

Who can Miss Colmore be? I remember a Gentleman of that Name rich—and I think—a Roman Catholic who came to a bad End some 20 Years ago.[1] Is this his Heiress?

I have trusted upon Leak as Dear Mr. Piozzi said in every Transaction, and never have had any Reserves from him: and nothing is there *now* to conceal or to express——If Sir James Fellowes invites me, I shall certainly come; and I hope We shall among us settle something to make all happy after so much Misery— *I do hope so.*

Mr. Crabbe the Poet has just left me, and says he expects everything from my Spirits and my Honour: and it would be bad indeed if I disappointed Old Friends.

I would rather at any Time be sinned against than sinning: and if Sir James Fellowes *does* disappoint my Expectations of his Kindness; they will be the *last* Expectations formed by poor H: L: Piozzi.

I would send you a Draft, but I have no Money at Hammersleys but what will barely serve my own Purposes: If Dear Sir James Fellowes does not find the Place suit *him*——he will not hinder its Sale: no Body could wish to *occupy* the Place till after the Auction is over.

Text Hyde Collection. *Address* Mr. Alexander Leak/ Streatham Park/ Surrey. *Postmark* 6 MR 6 1816; 10 o'Clock MR 6 1816.

1. Perhaps "Charles Colemore, esq, of Upper Seymour street" who died 6 February 1795. See the *European Magazine* 27 (1795):143.

TO THE REVEREND JOHN ROBERTS

5: March 1816.
Bath Tuesday

Dear [Mr. Roberts]

It is very kind in you, very kind indeed, not to forget your old Friend in a corner; whence I see many of the follies and Sorrows of this Life—enough I hope to keep me from being *Solicitous* though *willing*, to endure it a little longer. Poor Dr. M[yddelton's] death was surprisingly sudden, a man of his spare habit and pale Complexion is liable to any Disease rather than Apoplexy: but never did Death use his Scythe with such success as within these last 12 or 14 Months. Our Town is very unhealthy still, particularly to Children; and the Newspapers tell us of pestilential Fevers upon the Continent, whither all our Islanders seem hasting.[1] Do you interest yourself in the Report of a new Crusade against Turkey? Undertaken by Russia, Prussia and Austria in strict Alliance.[2] It is at least a very strange thing and wholly unprecedented that the Greek Roman and Geneva Churches should so unite; and I dare say you remember though I do not, a treatize written in 1580 by Harvey who found out the circulation of the Blood—in which there was contained Accounts of a remarkable Turkish Prophecy foretelling that the *second* Attack of Christianity should be fatal to the Ottoman Empire.[3] Mr. Clarke's Travels thro' Greece &c. show us plainly, that Constantinople wants but one Push to annihilate her power and such an Event would produce great changes for you young people to contemplate[4]——

We that are only sticking to Life like the old Leaves of a Beech Tree, shall be too much dried and withered to understand their consequences if we *do* witness them; but I suppose much time is wanting to bring so great an Occurrence to Maturity.—Meanwhile the Account you give of your new Bishop and his Family is cheering:[5] and it would be very unfriendly in me not to rejoice sincerely in whatever Good may befall my agreeable old Acquaintance, Mr. J[ones], if it is the Gentleman who I saw at Oswestry after he had left us, and by your Letter it can be no one else.[6] The charitable English Lady too is a fine Example; and likely enough to be followed. Never no *never* was Scriptural Knowledge so diligently promulgated: and in many Places by People one should not have expected to Stir in so excellent a Course. It appears as if they were *Impelled* to it.

My Lot is cast 18 Miles from the Place Hannah Moore has chosen for her Residence.[7] We used to meet often some few years ago; and She is a Lady who is best loved by those who see most of her. My admirable Pastor Mr. Greenfield contents me as a Preacher of sound Doctrine and pure Morality; but Sydney Smyth a popular Orator, filled every Church and Chapel to hear *him* while he was here.[8]—I liked him better in London Seven or Eight years ago: but seven or eight years will change most People for the worse.—The Physical and mental Powers decay sooner than People are themselves aware of and *Voice* seems to have suffered even more than *Countenance* when long parted companions meet again—&c.—H: L: P.

Text Victoria and Albert Museum Library. A copy.

1. Beginning in Naples and the surrounding area, the plague had moved to Austria, Bosnia, and Constantinople. Corfu was suffering from an epidemic of typhus fever. See *The Times*, 27 January; 8, 12, and 27 February.
2. On 26 September 1815, the Holy Alliance, initiated by Czar Alexander, was formed among Russia, Austria, and Prussia. The countries disavowed any military intention, binding themselves to uphold the peace and to move by Christian principles in all political affairs. The pact was ultimately signed by all European rulers with the exception of the Prince Regent and the Pope.

The rumors circulated that the Alliance was directed against Turkey. On 30 March, consequently, Alexander issued a circular that underscored the Alliance's desire to live in peace with the Ottoman Empire. See *GM* 86, pt. 1 (1816):172; *The Times*, 18 and 20 May.
3. HLP confuses John Harvey (1564–1592) with William, who in 1628 published his discovery of the blood's circulation.

The former, having been granted a license by Cambridge in 1587 to practice physic, published *A Discoursive Probleme concerning Prophesies* (London: Printed by John Jackson, for Richard Watkins, 1588). He discusses the Turkish "prophesie of famous record, which so resolutely presageth, and predestineth the finall overthrow of the Turkish dominions, by the sword of the Christians" (p. 46).
4. Edward Daniel Clarke (1769–1822) published *Travels in various Countries of Europe, Asia, and Africa*, 3 parts in 6 vols. (London: Cadell and Davies, 1810–23). He observes of the Turks that "'their portion is prepared;' and while they remain insensible of the schemes for their downfall . . . the different parts of their vast empire may be said to hang together by a *cobweb* ligature" (part 2, sect. 3, p. 488). He notes further that Turkish "resources . . . are daily becoming more and more feeble," that the government is threatened with "open rebellion," and that Russia wants to hoist her flag "upon the towers of *Constantinople*" (pp. 488–89).
5. For John Luxmoore, bishop of St. Asaph, see HLP to Ly W, 15 June 1815, n. 13. His wife was Elizabeth, née Barnard (d. 1820). They had two sons—Charles Scott (1792–1854) and John Henry Montague (1799–1860)—as well as three daughters—Elizabeth Mary, Mary, and Fanny. See Luxmoore's will, signed 6 August 1829 and proved 11 March 1830 (P.R.O., Prob. 11/1769/209).
6. For Thomas Jones of Bryntirion, see HLP to AL, 12 March 1812, n. 3.
7. Hannah More and her sisters lived in Barley Wood, near Axbridge, Somerset.
8. The Reverend Sydney Smith had recently arrived in Bath to visit his father, with whom he remained until May. See the *Bath Herald*, 24 February; *The Letters of Sydney Smith*, ed. Nowell C. Smith, 2 vols. (Oxford: The Clarendon Press, 1953), 1:260.

For Smith, as a preacher in London, see HLP to JSPS, 14 [-15] April 1810, n. 4.

TO SIR JAMES FELLOWES

9: March 1816.

The Dear Scrap your kind Father brought me yesterday, came so late; I had no Chance of replying to it—The Post Bell was that Moment ringing. How good you have always been to me! How good you still are! Feeling for *my* Vexations tho' surrounded with Comforts yourself.

Ah Sir James Fellowes! 'Tis you that have found *Asheri*: did I never tell you the Rabbinical Story of the four Men that were sent to seek for Asheri אשרי ?[1] Well! It is too long a Tale for such short Paper—and besides I really do mean to avail myself of Lady Fellowes's extraordinary Good Nature and come to You, just for one little happy Week.[2] I *must* come to Town you know, about rewriting my Will &c.—against I *have something to leave.*—And here's Your Father and Mother talking of a *Bird in hand*, and saying what a good Offer Mr. Cope[3] has made; and what heavy Drawbacks there will necessarily be to the Exhibition of an Auction Sale—and here's Colonel Barry[4] saying "Trust the Public Mrs Piozzi, you have been always a favourite with the Aggregate—however Individuals may have treated you."

And here's Miss Williams who got a bit of your nice Cake, has had *nice Dreams;* and says that Mr. Lloyd of Wickwar in Denbighshire,[5] who died the other day, and left his Sister Residuary Legatee[6]—has amazed all *our* Country—with his Collection, which they valued at 1000£ only; and *Two* of his Books (old Black Letter fourteen Hundreds:) fetched 500 Guineas of the Money.[7]

Now you see every day that I have no such extraordinary Possessions: but if *People think so*!!

In short my Mind is convinced that every Thing that can be done for me *will* be done. My inestimable Friend will not lose Sight of my Interest;—and Leak is I believe a truly honest Man, incapable of making Advantages by the Sale &c.—at least I *hope* so—Dear Mr. Piozzi's last Words were, "Trust upon Leak, and he shall never deceive you."

Meanwhile if good solid offers being refused, the Bidders at last prove slack; it will be a *feverish* Moment for all concerned.

And now—contented as you kindly are with your Reception, I am thinking how different in many Respects it should have been, had I been as I *used* to be. But my Mind being young, while my Person is old; and my Heart being open, while my empty Purse is Shut; makes the closing Scenes of Life a Strange *Melodrame*/ to Dear Sir/ Yours and Lady Fellowes's/ ever obliged and faithful/ H: L: Piozzi.

Miss Fellowes protests this Letter will go today tho' 'tis *Saturday*—I can't quite believe it, but in the Gamester's Phrase *Here goes.*

Text Hyde Collection. *Address* Sir James Fellowes.

1. HLP's tale, "Asheri," which she describes as "Virtue, Love, and Friendship—three forms under one radiant head," is printed in Hayward (2:181–87). It includes an endorsement by JF, dated Streatham Park, 3 April: "Mrs. Piozzi gave me this (the foregoing) paper in the Library."
2. Escorted from Bath by AL on 27 March, HLP was to arrive at Blake's Hotel on 28 March. Shortly thereafter, she visited Streatham Park, leaving on 7 April.
3. At the bottom of her "Pocket Book" page for the week of 18 March, HLP wrote "I wonder who Mr. Cope is?" In her "Commonplace Book" under *Eye* she notes: "An Irish Gentleman—Mr. Cope." Working through Hugh Parnell, the solicitor and estate agent, Robert Camden Cope (ca. 1771–1819) was interested in buying HLP's life interest in Streatham Park.
4. For Henry Barry, see HLP to PSW, 11 June 1789, n. 2.
5. John Lloyd of Wigfair had died on 24 April 1815. See HLP to Ly W, 30 April 1815.
6. According to Lloyd's will (P.R.O., Prob. 11/1579/207–8), he left "all [his] Real Estates in the Counties of Denbigh and Flint to [his] sister Dorothea [Clough]." Upon her death (she had in fact predeceased him in 1814), the properties were to be the inheritance of his other sisters in turn: first, Mary Elizabeth Potter, then Phoebe, and finally Susannah.
7. Lloyd had a library of more than ten thousand items: books, manuscripts, maps, clocks, and a collection of scientific apparatus. John Broster (d. 1816) of Chester took almost two weeks to sell this material in 1816. Among the particularly valuable books were those printed by William Caxton, Wynkyn de Worde, and Richard Pynson.

TO ANNA MARIA PEMBERTON

Saturday Night
9: March 1816.

Permit me Dear Madam to address those Enquiries to *you*—which the agitated Parents are I fear scarce able to answer. My last Letter from Brynbella is quite heart-breaking, I shall be very impatient for better Accounts. And the Recollection of Anxiety suffered concerning this Dear Baby some Months ago, which after long Silence ended in pronouncing her perfectly recovered; gives me hope—a *faint* Hope, that nothing fatal will follow this Attack. The numerous Complaints with regard to Children this Winter and Spring, make the Case more alarming than I should otherwise think it, because poor Hester Maria is probably just in Labour of a Tooth, and when delivered will be well again. But somehow or other, *every*body's Babies are disordered: Doctor Browne-Mill,[1] who I saw five Minutes after Salusbury's Letter arrived——cried out Good Heavens! are the Children all out of Health in *Wales* too!!

I will add nothing to my own Expressions of Grief on this Occasion——not even an Apology for this abrupt Address to You Dear Madam, who I hope left every body well and happy at the hospitable Mansion where I last had the honour of Saying with how much Respect/ I must ever remain/ Yours and/ Your amiable Family's truly Obedient/ H: L: Piozzi.

My dearest Salusbury will be better pleased I think, on such a trying Occasion;—with honest Sympathy, than elaborate Consolations:—worne-out Speeches, which every one repeats, and I suppose no one regards.

It is impossible not to be excessively sorry for the Sufferings of an Infant—— who is at last far less to be pitied than the Parents.

I have as you observe, gone thro' the Affliction very often indeed; and my Children commonly destroyed each other, as the Death of those in the Bed, affected them who were not yet got into the Cradle. We will hope more Fortitude and better Fortune to little Hester Maria's dear Mama: and it will be a kind Thing to write a less depressing Letter than your last, if the Danger is nearly over. In the hope of such News I remain most Affectionately/ Yours/ H: L: P.

Text Ry. 594.15.

1. For Dr. George Gavin Browne-Mill, see HLP to Ann Leak, 7 [March] 1815, n. 4.

TO ALEXANDER LEAK

Bath Fryday
15: March 1816.

My good Leak

It is always dangerous to set our Expectations too high—but I have had as many *Civilities* from Mr. Hill as could be reasonably *claimed* from a Neighbour of whom I knew nothing at all, but that he seemed an agreeable Man to converse with.

Of his *good Wishes* I always *doubted*, tho' his Wife made me a kind Offer of a Room in her house on some Occasion—I forget what.[1]

That you are right I firmly believe in all you say; but I *must* do what Honour and Good-breeding requires; and I must *not* come to Streatham Park, till the 1st or 2d Day of April—for *very Shame*. Shall I drive straight to Blake's Hotel on Thursday sennight—*at Night?* sleep there; visit Ward or Windle on Business the next Day or two:[2] and wait on Lady Fellowes to Dinner on Monday, remaining one whole Week *no more* for every Reason. *You* will meet me at Blake's on the Fryday Morning 29th March when much may be *said* that cannot prudently be *written*.

Every Transaction of this Life must bring its Difficulties and Displeasures with it: we must squeeze out the Good Part if there is any—and *I* in particular must console myself that this is my last Earthly Transaction.

I shall like to go to Church at St. James's on Palm Sunday, and you know me too well to *suppose* I would break further than the *first* two Days into Passion Week:[3] so if you approve this Plan, expect me at Blake's hotel at Breakfast (a ruinous Scheme too!) next Fryday sennight 29th March 1816——and expect to take Leave of me at Streatham Park on Monday the 8th of April.

I see Salusbury is Gazetted for Sheriff, and I hear his Baby is safe:[4] Mrs. Pemberton has written very politely: and you nor Dear Leak must not expect the People to *feel* towards *me* as I am now feeling towards *you both*—it would do *them* no Good—and who cares for giving Pleasure to one who cannot stay long enough in the World to repay them?

The Rev. Mr. Henry Fellowes came to see me Yesterday—he hopes much from the Sale of the Library, and he is a bookish Man, of retired Habits—but I suppose little acquainted with Things of *fashionable* Attraction. *My* best Reliance is on the Paintings. Colonel Barry—who *does* know the World, and who knew Mr. Piozzi and me in our Gay Days at Streatham Park; sets the Portraits by *Reynolds alone* at 2000£.

We can but hope and pray;—and try to *deserve* Success: which I will *do*, or *endeavour* to do/ while/ H: L: Piozzi.

Once more be careful of your Boy; The Children are all sick every where.

I should like the Old Parlour Apartments best—but say nothing any where else.

Text Hyde Collection. *Address* Mr. Alexander Leak/ Streatham Park/ Surrey. *Postmark* 16 MR 16; 10 o'Clock MR 16 1816.

1. For the Hills, see HLP to AL, 28 April 1814, n. 4; and to JSPS, 12 April 1815, n. 5.
2. HLP visited Joseph Ward and on 29 March signed her last will, making JSPS her residuary legatee.
3. HLP's "Pocket Book" entry for Palm Sunday, 7 April, indicates that she attended services at St. James's, Piccadilly, with Lady Kirkwall.
4. The "Gazette Promotions" of 9 March include "John Salusbury Piozzi Salusbury, of Bryn Bella, esq. Sheriff of the County of Flint." See *GM* 86, pt. 1 (1816):273.

TO JOHN SALUSBURY PIOZZI SALUSBURY

> Speen Hill—The Old Castle
> once kept by Mrs. Ward[1]
> Wednesday Evening 27: March 1816.

From this once favourite Spot of Dear Uncle's, when pretty Salusbury came bounding over Hill and Dale to enjoy our Company who ran to embrace him;——do I address The High Sheriff of Flintshire and 'Squire of Brynbella, with Fear lest he should find Exceptions to poor Aunt's Letter; and perhaps censure the Business She is going to prosecute;—*Poor* Aunt indeed!

But you Said Tell me what is doing—so I will write and Say that Sir James and Lady Fellowes who are at Streatham Park now, have invited the Mistress of the Mansion to visit *Them* and settle Matters somehow—by public Sale or private Contract: and to morrow I shall meet Sir James at Blake's hotel—if he offers me his Carriage to go about in, I shall wait on my Daughters, and obtain their final Determination,—Their Pardon if possible. Meanwhile Your Approbation will be very dear to me—very highly valued indeed: and I hope the Result may deserve it.

Leak has better Spirits and better Expectations of good Bidding than I entertain, whose heart may well be *low* after the Life I have been leading: I tell him that standing Corn never thrashes out to its appearance on the Field; but he hopes much from the Books and Pictures. You go to the Sales of all the Dead and *gone* Folks; I should scarce wonder to hear of you at mine.

The Advertisement I *read* was in the Morning Chronicle; but it has been in the Times, It is a ruinous Practice to repeat Advertising, but Leak will put it in the same Papers next Week.[2]

We have had much Talk at Bath about the Country Banks Shrewsbury and Denbigh with many Conjectures[3]——such as we make about Princes and Princesses—probably—no Word of Foundation in Truth—and My Lord *this* who cut his own Throat,[4] and My Lady t'*other* who ran away with a Man—next Week informs us—that She never spoke to: and such Gibberish we call Conversation—while Death desolates our Parties, and Report tells how Musical Instruments are to be taxed to make Compensation for the Malt Duty.[5]

Ah Dearest Salusbury! when out of this Window my Eye catches the Scenes we once saw together, in Company with Mr. Smythe Owen—and before that with dear Uncle: and the very Fox still on the Pole where you asked me Can't you see that Fox Aunt? Can't you *indeed!* how many Recollections croud my Mind! and how little my Heart thinks of the Subjects which employ the Tongue or Pen—Princess's Marriage or Property Tax,[6]—or backward Spring; or any *legitimate* Theme of a Letter to be written—like other People's Letters—as you used to say. The Truest Word in any one's Letter, is however not so true as that/ I/ remain most Affectionately/ and Cordially Yours/ H: L: P.

Pray present me most properly to Your fairest Lady and her Mother and her Daughter whose Welfare is close to my heart.

Text Ry. 588.314.

1. On 27 March HLP noted in her "Pocket Book": "Set out from Bath at 12 o'clock and reached *Speen* [and the Castle Inn] about seven; not well, but not very bad."
2. There were to be also two new Streatham Park advertisements in April: one for HLP's life interest in the estate, another for its household effects. See the *Morning Chronicle*, 15, 24, 30 April; *The Times*, 17, 19, 23 April: e.g., to be offered "The Life Interest of [HLP] in that capital Mansion, with numerous attached and detached offices, extensive walled gardens . . . and green-houses, plantations and park, embellished with a fine sheet of water, containing about ninety acres, nearly the whole of which is excellent meadow land. The house and offices [newly refurbished] are planned for the accommodation of a family of rank and fortune, and from their proximity to the metropolis (being only seven miles from the bridges) are particularly desirable for the residence of any distinguished official character, or mercantile gentleman of eminence; to be let to the bidder of highest annual rent."
   The other advertisement, announcing the auction of Streatham Park's contents, lists the thirteen portraits by Reynolds; "a beautiful picture of St. Cecilia, by Domenichino; a fine head of Tasso, by Titian; a study, by Cypriani; canal and shipping, by S. Ruysdael; landscapes, by Barrett, Pether, &c.; fine prints framed and glazed, several valuable miscellaneous articles, consisting of two real ebony chairs curiously carved, a few fine bronzes, some rare specimens of the old japan, enamelled and Nankin china; also an extensive library of near 3,000 volumes . . . chiefly selected by the celebrated Dr. Johnson."
3. During the economic depression of 1816—an aftermath of the war—numerous banks stopped payment, including the Shrewsbury Old Bank and that of Messrs. Clough and Company, Denbigh. See *The Times*, 5 February, 23 March.
4. For example, HLP had been taken in by the rumor that Arthur Hill-Trevor (1763–1837), second viscount Dungannon (I., 1771), "has cut his own Throat because a Man asked him for 500£ which he had no means of paying." Finding out that no such event happened, HLP dismisses all Bath gossip as so much idle chatter. See her "Pocket Book," 18 March; "Commonplace Book" under the entry *Hottentot*.
5. On 20 March the chancellor of the exchequer announced his intention to discontinue the malt tax. See the *Parliamentary Debates*, 33 (1816):457–71. On 27 March the *Bath and Cheltenham Gazette* reported that "nothing has been yet disclosed in what ways Ministers intend to supply the deficit . . . new taxes are spoken of, but the only remedy is to lower our expenditures."
6. HLP refers to the parliamentary debate (and the number of petitions it provoked) in February and March 1816 on the property tax, the chancellor of the exchequer's "proposition to renew the Property Tax at five per cent" for the next two or three years and later "continued, or discontinued, as Parliament might think fit." See GM 86, pt. 1 (1816):164.

TO JOHN SALUSBURY PIOZZI SALUSBURY

Blake's Hotel
Jermyn Street London
Saturday 30: March *1816*.

My dearest Salusbury

I was thinking to wait till I had more to tell——but fancying you might wish to hear—as the people say—all how and about it—here comes a Letter from that everlasting Mrs. Piozzi Who has in Effect very little to relate concerning her own Interests, except what passed this Morning at Mrs. Merrik Hoare's. She behaved neither with Kindness nor Cruelty, but complete Indifference—till the Business I came upon was mentioned——and *that* She negatived according to the Parliamentary Phrase,——without *a Division:* for you know I make no figure as a Disputant. I asked if She could answer for her Sisters—or whether I should apply to Lady Keith, As you please certainly—but——was the Reply.—Then you think Lord Keith will *not* come forward to save poor Streatham Park from Public Sale.——*Most certainly not* was her Answer. Well then said I lightly, "Speak in Time or 'tis going, going *Gone*," imitating an Auctioneer. You have not lost Your Spirits was her Observation——No, 'tis enough to lose my Money and my Peace of Mind I think.

How did Your Russians behave?—Oh *like* Russians; They smoked Tobacco in Bed, and put the Place in perpetual Danger of Fire——to Them succeeded Mess: *Anderdon and Co.* whose *little* Children rubbed their Bread and Butter into my best Carpets, ruined my nice new Mattrasses[1]—like Davies's Schoolbaby Lambton and *worse:*[2] while the bigger Boys wrote on My new painted Walls, and cut the Wainscot with Pen Knives. Oh!—continued poor H:L:P.—my Heart is Sick of the Place and the Tenants and the Torments and the Tormentors; *You refuse* all Connection with it, and mine shall end next Week. Sir James and Lady Fellowes to whom I have lent it for their Honey Moon, will fetch me on Monday to pass a very few days, and then Catalogues shall be made out, and a Public Sale proclaimed.

So ended our Conversation: The rest was about General Chat—Coughs and Catarrhs, Ministers and Opposition[3] &c. beside the Disappearance of Sir Charles Monk's Son from Westminster School—a dreadful Occurrence surely![4] and which ought to throw Me on my Knees even in the Street, to thank God for having escaped such a Calamity. If a Member of the House of Commons, a Baronet of Respectability cannot find his Child, nor escape Censure for having lost him, What would have been My Torments, had dearest dear Salusbury so disappeared. The Archbishop of Dublin lost his Wits in Consequence of such a Trick; What would have become of *me*??[5]

Change the Subject.

I was with good Old Mr. Ward yesterday, he enquired much after *your* Domestick Happiness, and promised not to hurry my Payment of his 58£. Others are not so kind, The Bath Folks are very pressing, all but George of the Parade, to whom I have promised my *Burying*, and hope you will be obliging enough to make the Promise good, should I—(as I wish,) die at Bath.[6]

Sir Robert Salusbury poor Man! is *Gazetted* a Bankrupt;[7] I am very sorry for it, and half angry:——It is a great Disgrace to his and my Family. Lord Carington who you may remember our dining with in Pultney Street, has turned away 47 Servants and hastens to the Continent in a Chaise and Pair.[8] He had 11 Daughters and *one only* Son, who has of Course suffered no Restraint from Expence.——But you have possibly forgot them all long ago. Sevigni says that Letters of Entertainment never Entertain *distant* Correspondents: Their Minds are full of quite other People, and quite other Things.[9] Mine is much occupied by the Ill health of Mrs. Mostyn—tho' *distant*——her Sister says She has undergone much Discipline—Blisters &c. Poor dear Cecy! I am very sorry, tho' She never writes to me——nor probably desires to hear of my Existence. God Almighty *commands* us to honour our Parents, and adds a Promise if we *perform the Duty* he knew we should love our Children without bidding.[10] Poor Lady Collier is now in the deepest Mourning for her Son who died at Bayonne A Year or Two ago.[11] She wants to go there and be buried with him. Meanwhile She has asked me to Dinner to morrow—Sunday,——which was more than I got at Mrs. Hoare's.

But the Post Bell will ring for this Letter in a Minute and I shall not have Time to say how I request You to make my best Regards to Mrs. Pemberton and her lovely Daughter—being ever Theirs and Dearest Salusbury's/ Affectionate/ H: L: P.

Text Ry. 588. 315.

1. HLP refers to her last tenants: Count Lieven and his family, and John Proctor Anderdon and his.

2. For John George Lambton, see HLP to RD, 5 May 1803. For Lambton's later career, see HLP to JSPS, 29 June 1818.

3. On 18 March a parliamentary vote on the motion of a property tax was taken. Although the resolution for the renewal of the tax was substantially defeated, the ministry did not topple. See *GM* 86, pt. 1 (1816):454.

4. The eldest son of Charles Miles Lambert Monck (1779–1867), sixth baronet (1795) of Belsay Castle, Charles Atticus (1805–56) attended Westminister School from 1814 to 1823, when he entered Trinity College, Cambridge.

According to the *Morning Post*, 27 March, the boy had vanished on 23 March from Westminster School. "We understand that the father was very angry with the son for some misconduct, and, as a punishment, ordered him to remain at school on Saturday last; but, contrary to those orders, he came home as usual, and was directly sent back again. As soon as he arrived at school he changed his clothes, left the school, and has not been seen by any of his friends since."

5. For Euseby Cleaver, archbishop of Dublin, see HLP to Roberts, 20 March 1807, n. 2.

The story about the archbishop of Dublin was told to HLP by William Cleaver, the bishop of St. Asaph. While it is true that the former had two sons who attended Westminster and Oxford, his mental breakdown has been attributed to the shock he experienced during the rebellion of 1798, when the bishop's palace in the see of Ferns was plundered and much of his property destroyed. See Canon James B. Leslie, *Ferns Clergy and Parishes* (Dublin: The Author by the Church of Ireland Printing and Publishing Co., 1936), 18.

Euseby Cleaver's sons were William (1789–1860) and Henry (ca. 1797–1837).

6. For Thomas George, see HLP to JSPS, 6 January 1815, and n. 13.

7. For Sir Robert Salusbury, see HLP to Q, 23 July 1805, nn. 7, 13, 14.

Sir Robert's bankruptcy was announced in the *London Gazette*, 26 March (*The Times*, 27 March).

8. For Robert Smith, first baron Carrington, see HLP to JSPS, 13 December 1809, n. 5.

9. Marie de Rabutin-Chantal, marquise de Sévigné (1626–96) wrote to her daughter Françoise-Marguerite (1646–1705): "this letter will appear ridiculous to you . . . —that is one of the misfortunes of correspondence at such a distance." See *Letters from Mad. de Sévigné to her Daughter the Countess of Grignan*, 3 vols. (London: Apollo Press, by G. Cawthorn, 1802), 1:60.

10. Ephesians 6:2–4.

11. For Elizabeth, widow of Sir George Collier, see HLP to JSPS, 18 April 1812, n. 12, and 14 May 1813.

HLP refers to Lady Collier's eldest son, George, lieutenant colonel in the Coldstream Regiment of Foot Guards, who died on 30 May 1814 of wounds received at Bayonne. See *GM* 84, pt. 1 (1814):625.

TO JOHN SALUSBURY PIOZZI SALUSBURY

Bath Monday Night
8–9: April 1816.

Vanity; which sticks to our last Sand,[1] prompts me to hope my Dearest Salusbury will be pleased to hear that We made our 88 Miles, (for such We paid for;) in very good Time: coming to Bath with the Sun Setting before, and the Moon rising behind us.

Never were Roads in finer Order; but the Hedges have an Appearance still of Winter's Death, rather than giving a *hope* of Easter's Resuscitation. Not a Bird singing, not a Flower springing——Some one presented me with Three Violets and a Primrose, as considerable Rarities in the Month of April.[2]—I wonder the Opposition are not quite angry with Ministers for Suffering Things to go on in such a Manner, but when *they* have fetched back Buonaparte,—I hope he will put Weather, and Politics to rights at once.[3]

My Table here is littered with Invitations to *Parties* of every possible Kind: but Miss O'Neil does not come as People said She would, to act all Passion Week, and take her Benefit on Good Fryday. The Amusements are deferred as usual, till Holyday Time. Buonparte will manage that too—when he comes over—— but the pretty Girls and dashing Boys must *wait*, Tho' every Wall expresses their Impatience of old Fashions, in the *broadest* Terms that every Eye witnessed.

I left my Auctioneers and Catalogue-Makers full of *Hope* and full of Promises to send you all possible Notice. If you or any Acquaintance wish to buy— We will set every Thing to open Sale——private Offers (unless something *very* particular was to happen,) we consider merely as a Contrivance to get Things cheaper than open Market: If they will offer, let them come forward in the Day of Competition.

Do you remember how in the Year 1813 when I ran from Brynbella to London, full of anxious Care concerning your Estate,[4] I asked Clement Francis to enquire the Value of my Life? And he said the City People set it at *Three* Years Purchase——We expect better than *that* in the Year *1816* when the Three Years are *out*. Well! Good Night dearest Salusbury: I am very sleepy, and of course very Stupid yet with every Wish and Prayer for the Continuance of true Felicity to you and yours I remain most Affectionately Theirs and Your/H: L: P.

Tuesday Morning 9th April 1816.

Good Morrow dearest; the Post goes out from here at five o'Clock and we did not get into Bath till past Seven; so I kept my Letter open to tell you how pretty poor Dear Lady Kirkwall still looks; and how fondly She still dreams of Happiness to come, in the Society of her ever-beloved Husband.[5]

Are not all Ladies dreaming of Felicities in future?—except those who connected with Salusbury remain possessed of it!—*My* dreams tell me of all Debts paid, a clear Income, and a decent Establishment here on the Queen's Parade among my sister Solitaries; Mrs. Holroyd and a long Et cetera.[6] The Rooms I now occupy are so much worse than any I have been thrust into since I left them, that 'tis Time to change; and when my Fellow Lodger called out to me last Night that I might sit in her Parlour, till my Fire burned up—*I thought so.*

I saw the Fox again at Speenhill yesterday; but we only staid for fresh Horses, and ran forward leaving me no Moments for Reflexion on my past happy Days in that Spot; where Dear lost Uncle and I used to run forward, or wait at the Window in breathless Agitation, to see our precious Lad come skipping over the Meadows to spend a Week with us.

Apropos to those Times, All good has been told me of Charles Shephard, who is in the Receipt of 3 or 4000£ o'Year;[7] and he has given me so many pleasant Hours, that my best Wishes are his for ever:—Altho' he changed his Conduct so completely to his old Friend, and our Dear Salusbury's/ tenderly attached/ H: L: P.

Here is neither Room nor Time now, for *one half* of the Respects and Regards, and Loves and Compliments which I wish always to Send to the Inhabitants of Brynbella; you must make my Sincerest Apologies for any Defect consequent on Fatigue or Hurry!

Text Ry. 589.319. *Address* John Salusbury Piozzi Salusbury Esq./ Brynbella near/ Denbigh/ North Wales. *Postmark* BATH <   >.

1. HLP's interpretation of Matthew 7:26–28.
2. From ca. 20 March through to the days on which this letter was written, the temperature hovered in the mid-thirties Fahrenheit, the days sometimes punctuated by hail storms, sleet, and snow.
3. During the economic depression after the peace, a period of general unrest and political tumult, the Opposition attacked the Liverpool ministry on several fronts: on the ministry's desire to continue the property tax; on the Government's treatment of the agricultural community; on its insistence upon a large peace establishment; and even on its costly maintenance of the Household troops, both House and Horse Guards. See *GM* 86, pt. 1 (1816):353–61.
4. See HLP to JSPS, 19 April 1813.
5. For the marriage of the Kirkwalls on 18 August 1802 and their separation, see HLP to LC, 19 March 1799, n. 4; to TSW, 20 December 1811, nn. 6 and 7.
6. Sarah Martha Holroyd of 3 Queen's Parade.
7. Charles Mitchell Smith Shephard was now attorney general of St. Vincent in the Windward Islands. See HLP to MW, 5 July [1807], n. 2; to JSPS, 27 January 1814, n. 7.

TO SIR JAMES AND LADY FELLOWES

Bath
Wednesday 10 April 1816

My Dear Sir James and Lady Fellowes will like to hear that I got safe thro' the Thunder and Lightning on Sunday Evening by taking Shelter at Salt Hill—from whence I ran *hither* over a Road Watered as if by a Water Cart, the next Day; and arrived at my Smoky Hut on Monday Night 88 Miles in 12 Hours.

Too tired on Tuesday to go up to the Vineyards, I saw none of our dear Friends till today: when I caught your Mama and Sister at Breakfast. Miss Fellowes looking *beautiful*; Ten Years at least Younger than I left her. The kind Doctor has been here, but I missed him.

Now comes bad News. Mary Mayhew has had more returns than one, of Her bleedings at the Mouth—and Wise Men see plainly no rational hope can be Entertained.

Your amiable Family are dying to see *you* and your Sweet *Lady*: and I said next Week would be The Time. I found Lady Keith's *Card* on my Table at Blake's hotel on Saturday Night——and returned the Visit on Sunday, leaving the kindest Letter I knew how to write: I *did more*, I left orders with Leak and Squibb to take *their* Money if they offered: but if they did *not* offer, to hurry on the Sale, and put me out of Pain as soon as possible.

This Morning I went into a Picture Auction here in Milsom Street: and saw sold a varnished-up Performance of Peter Nees for 34 Guineas;[1] This gave me Spirits, so did the Story of these Bank Restrictions, which they say will operate immediately in making Money plenty.[2]

I am a miserable Financier, but you will understand me; as Miss Streatfield's Maid[3] said *I* should, when She asked me to lend her Lady *Milk and Asparagus lost.* I *did* immediately comprehend her meaning, and sent her the Milton's Paradise Lost you saw in Streatham Park Library.[4] Perhaps my *Bank Restrictions* may be as awkwardly worded.

Adieu! This vile Paper tears my worne-out Pens, and my worne out Patience quite to pieces; or I would send *more* Compliments, kinder I could not send; to your Dear Brother and Mrs. Fellowes. Your Fair and excellent *Lady* has the truest and most faithful Servant possible, in Dear Sir/ Your sincerely Obedient/ H:L:Piozzi.

Text Berg Collection, m.b. *Address* Sir James Fellowes

1. Either Pieter Neeffs the elder (ca. 1577-ca. 1661) of Antwerp or Pieter Neeffs the younger (1601–75).

2. After the war, there was a great deal of discussion in Parliament about the best means for raising revenue to retire the debt and to keep the country running. In March 1816 the property tax was defeated in the House of Commons and on 8 April the Chancellor of the Exchequer brought in a bill extending for two years the act restricting cash payments by the Bank of England. See the *Bath Chronicle,* 21 March and 11 April 1816; *GM* 86, pt. 1 (1816):550–51.

3. Sophia Streatfeild (Streatfield), like HLP a former pupil of Dr. Arthur Collier, first met the Thrales in Brighton in autumn 1777 and was a frequent guest at Streatham Park. There are numerous

references to her in *Thraliana* and in the first two volumes of *The Piozzi Letters*. See also Clifford, pp. 168, 172–73, 175.

4. A copy of Milton's *Paradise Lost* was lot 77 on the first day of the Streatham Park sale. Lot 112 was "Milton's Poetical Works, *handsomely bound.*" Lot 149 on the first day of the sale of the books from Brynbella (17 September 1823) was "Milton's Paradise Lost and Regained, &c. 2 vol. Baskerville's beautiful edition, in fine state 1758" and lot 282 on the second day of the sale (18 September 1823) was "Milton's Poetical works, 2 vol Tonson's fine large print edition, plates 1738." See *Sale Catalogue.*

TO SIR JAMES FELLOWES

[18 April 1816][1]

All Dear Sir James Fellowes's Letters are kind ones: but we are wanting to see *You*. A Brother, more like you than any of Your Brothers, makes us small amends[2]—for he goes away soon: Miss Williams ran up to him in the Street tho', and wished him Joy; thinking it was Yourself.

The House in Gloucester Place is that Miss Abdy mentioned I suppose;[3] dear Lady Fellowes will be happy to have a Place She calls home. *My* Home for 50 years, will I hope procure me by disposing of it, a temporary Residence for the Remainder of my Short Term:—and what more ought to be wished? by one who will soon take up a narrower Space?

I am glad Squibb is so sangwine; did you see *real* Squibb—The Father?[4] he is a very good-looking Man. There is an old Story of Balbus when Quæstor at Seville, throwing an Auctioneer to the Lyons in his Menagerie, because a Female Friend who was selling up her Possessions, complained to him that the Auctioneer was so ugly and deformed, he frighted all Buyers away.[5] Our People will lose no Bidders by that fault: but is it not odd that the World with all its *Fluctuations*, should have undergone so little *Change*?

Always Vexations, Disappointments, and inadequate [Answers] for what can hardly be helped: tho' the Mode of expressing that Anger is altered by the different Situations of Society—

Always a *Friend* or *two* perhaps in the World, like Sir James Fellowes; always luckless Ladies enough/ like his Faithful and Obedient Servant/ H: L: P.

The Anecdote is recorded in a Letter *to* Cicero from Asinius Pollio: We might have seen it in the Library at Streatham Park.

Make my truest Regards acceptable to Lady Fellowes.

The Dear Family at the Vineyards are as well as possible. No Complaints but of Impatience to embrace You, and your amiable Lady.

Text Princeton University Library. *Address* Sir James Fellowes.

1. Hayward (2:332) prints part of this letter and dates it 18 April. On this date, HLP wrote in her "Pocket Book": "Went to Dr. Fellowes's with my Letter to Sir James."
2. Probably the Reverend Henry Fellowes, who had visited Bath recently. See HLP to JF, 21 February, n. 8; to AL, 15 March, both in 1816.
3. Harriot Abdy (fl. 1795–1850) was the sister of Catherine Fellowes, the wife of JF's youngest

brother Thomas (HLP to JSPS, 20 September 1815, n. 4). On 4 December 1817 she was to marry George Caldwell (1773–1848), a Cantabrigian (Jesus College), who, receiving his B.A. (10th Wrangler) in 1795 and M.A. in 1798, became a Fellow of Jesus (1796–1817) and in 1841 an unbeneficed deacon.

4. For George Squibb, see HLP to AL, 14 November 1815, n. 2. Squibb had two sons, George James and Francis. See P.R.O., Prob. 11/1793/730, proved 20 December 1831.

5. Writing to Cicero from Corduba in 43 B.C., Asinius Pollio (76 B.C.–4 A.D.), governor of Spain, mentions Cornelius Balbus, his quæstor, or financial officer, who inflicted horrible deeds upon Roman officers. "Bestiis vero civis Romanos, in iis circulatoram quendam auctionum, notissimum hominem Hispali, quia deformis erat, obiecit" (10.32.3). See "Letter 32: C. Asinius Pollio Ciceroni," *M. Tulli Ciceronis Epistulae,* ed. W. S. Watt, 3 vols. in 4 (Oxford: Clarendon Press, 1982), 1:333. "Ciceronis Opera, *Glasgow,* 1749" was lot 34 on the first day of the Streatham Park sale. See *Sale Catalogue* (1).

TO ALEXANDER LEAK

Monday 23: April *1816*

I shall be sorry indeed if poor Leak loses his Mother without running down to Norfolk at least for a parting Kiss—of the *true* Friend which Nature gives to us all, in our Mothers; and which Death alone can possibly take away. Youth and Beauty will not retain Life or nothing would kill Mary Mayhew and Mrs. Myddelton: I question if either of them are *actually dead* tho'; *only in a hopeless State.*

My Indisposition did no good, and no harm I believe; no Doctors were wanted:—and Sir James Fellowes has never been here to Bath since his Marriage.

The very tall, stout Captain Fellowes called on me; said he had seen Streatham Park, where nothing excited so much of *his* Admiration, as the Morning and Evening Landschapes in the Dining Parlour, I hope many will be of his Mind.

What a Spring this is! No Swallow! no Cuckoo—and what is as strange to me, and a great deal Worse; no Account of Newton or even of the Dividends—— within a Week of Mayday! ! dreadful!

With regard to the Advertisement, Mrs. Dimond and I looked over numerous Papers together, and could find none;—no matter.—15 Days I have to endure of Expectation; how many of Disappointment God only knows.

Young Williams[1] is kind to his own Aunt at his own Expence, and so far all is well; but he wishes likewise to provide for her at *My* Expence: recommending it to her to come down to Wales with Mrs. Piozzi, and send her Maid by the Stage Coach.

A fine Charge poor Bessey Jones and I should have of a helpless Lady, who cannot when in the best health put her Hand in her Pocket; it is so swelled and stiffened into Bone. One would think every body saw Fool and Dupe written in my Face. Miss Williams has Infirmities which would make such a Journey not only dreadful but dangerous and I am myself as the Ballad says—by no means what I was 40 Summers ago: It would be a bad Experiment.

Among other Wonders here is Bath Market and Fruit Shops without a French Bean. I hope you are selling Yours very well. But above all What is become of Newton? Is he Dead or Bankrupt? or what is gone with the Man? Mr. Windle told me *that* Money could not fail; so I depended on it, and gave the Lodging

House Man here and Lucas and Earl their Bills accordingly; and now feel such a Terror on my Spirits: it Actually gives me The Toothach. I! who thought in July to have been free of Debt even without the Sale. But I will add no more than God bless you all——and send us happier on the 23d of May or June than is now Your/ poor H: L: P.—

Text Hyde. *Address* Mr. Alexander Leak/ Streatham Park/ Surrey./ *Postmark* BATH <23 AP 23 1816>; 10 o'Clock Ap 23 1816.

1. JW, the eldest son of Sir John and Ly W, was attempting to make arrangements for his aunt, MW, who was eighteen years younger than HLP.

TO ALEXANDER LEAK

Bath
Thursday 25: April 1816

I feel impatient to tell Leak and his Wife that Mr. Este's zealous Kindness has dictated to *him* that if He attempted Parley with Lord Keith or his Agent——They scarce could refuse *treating.*[1] I have written to beg he would see *You* first——and Mr. Dalgliesh;[2] who knows his Lordship's Motives for Refusal, as well as Yourself. I wonder which Portraits Mr. Watson Taylor pitched upon:[3] and feel surprized that all the People are not in Love with the Saint Cecilia in the Eating Parlour: Was I an Impartial Looker-on, She would be my Choice directly.

Mr. Este will kindly look over the Catalogue and give it a friendly Touch with his charming Pen;[4] I think his Success more likely *there* than with Lord Keith; but there can be no harm in trying,—if he likes it.

What a merciful Escape had poor Bessy Jones Yesterday! passing a Coachmaker's Shop, The Man had Gig Shafts in his Hand high held up; and slipping hold, one of them fell upon her Head.—Poor Soul! and did *not* fracture her Skull as it might have done. I never saw any Creatures so terrified as She and her poor Mistress/ who is—Your true Friend/ H: L: P.

No News of Newton's Money yet:[5] has he paid it in or no?

Text Hyde Collection. *Address* Mr. Alexander Leak/ Streatham Park/ Surrey. *Postmark* 10 o'Clock AP 26 1816; E 26 AP 1816.

1. HLP's "Pocket Book" shows that between 18 April and 1 May she had been corresponding with Charles Este (HLP to SL, 17 November 1787, n. 5). On 26 April she noted that "Mr. Este writes to say Do not sell"; and on 1 May that she "Received a heartbreaking Letter from Mr. Este, *sent* Him mine, and one to Squibb, praying that he will respect Mr. Este's Advice."
2. For Robert Dalgleish, the coal merchant and resident of Streatham, see HLP to JSPS, 24[-26] April 1813, n. 6. For Dalgleish's futile overtures to Lord Keith on HLP's behalf, see HLP to the Leaks, 27 May 1815, and to TSW, 13 August 1815.
3. George Watson-Taylor (ca. 1770–1841), M.P. (1816–32), of 1 Harley Street and Sion Hill, Brent-

ford, Middlesex. He was to buy at the auction the Reynolds portrait of Baretti for £86.2 and of SJ for £378 (*Sale Catalogue*, lots 65 and 68, 10 May). In 1819 HLP was to sell him Murphy's portrait. See her correspondence with JF and Watson-Taylor in March 1819.

According to the *Bath and Cheltenham Gazette* for 13 November 1816: "The wealth of Mr. Watson Taylor . . . is immense . . . he has 95,000£ a year" in addition to income from his estates.

4. An undated letter to HLP (Ry. 555.71) signed C[harles] E[ste] states: "And Pray, Dear Madam, in your great Kindness, Do not let my Humble Endeavours be overrated, as to the *Catalogue*. For, It was not Possible, I should Touch it As The Whole of it, Fair—came to me, so soon after, I had the First Part of it, Foul!"

5. Thomas Newton was the tenant at Crowmarsh, Oxon. See HLP to John Gillon, 18 November 1799, n. 2.

TO ANN LEAK

Bath Thursday
2: May 1816.

My dear Leak

I have no Guess who the Lady is, I do not remember any Lady losing her Wedding Ring at Streatham Park.

Mr. Este—as he says himself is neither Seller nor Buyer;[1] but he was partial to me in former Days and I have every Reason to know he has my Interest at heart; and he has certainly much *Influence* with the *Publick*.

Leak himself went with Mr. Thrale's Will to Sir Vicary Gibbs,[2] and brought back his Opinion that the Pictures Books and China were mine *absolutely*: Lord Keith himself acknowledged it, long after.

All the Furniture is of my own putting-*In* to *Your Knowledge*.

Can I be hindered from Selling my Life Interest in the Place? I should hope not by what Mr. Windle Says; but Selling the *Contents* would I hope pay every Debt: tho' it would *grieve* me to have that House and Expence upon my hands again; when I had so hoped to get rid of it.

And Then the Fear of Dilapidations would come against me too:——Oh I should be very sorry.——Mr. Este thinks I see that 'tis Pity to Sell the Things and the *Place* and so it is; but I have starved long enough: and now——it would be agreeable to me that Mr. Este should know what Obstacles have been thrown in My Way; and I wish You to *inform him of them, and the whole* Story of the Manor &c. &c. rather than it should come from either the Mouth or the Pen of/ H: L: P.

The Post Bell is ringing now; Tell Mr. Este I had not a Moment to write to him in; and shew him this Letter as well as the last.

I have written from haste upon the wrong Side of the Paper: God bless you all and the Dear little Boy.

Text Hyde Collection. *Address* Mrs. Leak/ Streatham Park/ Surrey. *Postmark* BATH 2 MY 2 1816; 3 MY 3 1816; 10 o'Clock < > 1816.

1. Este's name appears once in the *Sale Catalogue* as the purchaser of a multi-volume edition of the *Spectator* (1724) for £2.10. See lot 27 on 8 May.

For Este's former association with HLP, see, e.g., her letters to SL, 17 November 1787 and 23 August 1788; to Sophia Byron, 29 June 1788, 3 August [1789], and 1 September [1789]; to Charles Este, 26 June 1793.

2. See HLP to JSPS, 16–17 April 1811 and n. 12.

TO ALEXANDER LEAK

Bath Sunday
5: May 1816.

Leak's Letter is most generous and kind, but say not that ever *I* passed Censure on Mr. Squibb—or on You—or that I ever expressed Reluctance to the Sale, when all I have said and written *meant* to prove my earnest Desire and steady Resolution to *go on.*

Mr. Squibb has sent the Catalogues, with Two Papers for me to sign; appointing a Person to bid in my Behalf for the Lett or Sale of the House, the Estate &c.——and another for the Furniture.[1]

As Mr. Squibb has so prudently and politely, done all by Advice and Direction of Mr. Windle, I thought it was going hand in hand with *him* to appoint that Gentleman as my Bidder for the Estate, House, &c.—and I have done so; the Letter goes when this goes—by today's Post.

I wish Doctor Burney may bid for his Father's Portrait[2]—but if 'tis a favourite with Mr. Watson Taylor, he will have a poor Chance.

Cannot *you* be the Bidder for the Furniture?[3] and save me more Much ado about nothing—I mean a Bidder to prevent its going too low: My Reserves are so very few—and I feel confident that Mr. Squibb nor you would see my favourite Bottles and old *Vases* given away—I am *sure* you would not.[4]

Murphy's Portrait must not be sold under 100£:[5] but I have no *other* Reserves—unless for the Bed I lay in when last at Streatham Park—and not even *that* if the full Price can be obtained, and which you all think it deserves.

No Letter from Leak today, but a very nice one from Mr. Squibb——and tho' I came *Ill out of Church;* I feel revived by seeing no Epistles to torment the vexed Spirits of your/ poor H: L: P.—

If tis necessary to *appoint a* Person *formally* to act in such Trifling Matters, you must tell me who to *appoint:* but I would rather *Trust upon Leak*—to use our dear Master's Phrase—for as he said Leak shall never deceive you.

Text Hyde Collection. *Address* Mr. Alexander Leak/ Streatham Park/ Surrey. *Postmark* 6 MY 6 1816; 10 o'Clock MY 6 1816.

1. The *Sale Catalogue* shows that a Mr. Matthews bid on furniture, books, pictures, and other household goods for HLP.

He was James Matthews, appraiser and upholder. His firm, Matthews and Taylor of 110 Fenchurch Street, assisted in the auction of Streatham Park.

2. Charles Burney, Jr., bought Reynolds's portrait of CB for £84 (lot 66 on 10 May).

3. The furniture was to be auctioned on the fourth and fifth days of the sale (11 and 13 May), earning approximately £1,282.

4. HLP's "Valuable Oriental China" and miscellaneous vases were sold on the third day (10 May) for approximately £246.10.

5. Matthews bought in the portrait of Arthur Murphy for HLP. The price bid was £102.18.

TO LADY WILLIAMS

Bath Fryday
10: May 1816.

My dear Lady Williams's kind Letters do not deserve *burning*, I am always most happy in reading what gives me such Pleasure, that the good Family are well, and still remember a long-absent Friend.

Were it not for your Ladyship, I should know nothing of my own Country; and the last Letter but one which came from Brynbella brought me the *first* Intelligence of Mrs. Salusbury's *Second* Pregnancy;[1] so you see old News is quite novel to poor me.

I saw Bodylwyddan this Morning at Miss Williams's—in a Superb Frame, and She was trimming up a Rose Tree[2] that She calls dear John——given by her Nephew I conclude. I hope she has done crying about Miss Griffith, for whose Recovery many Tears have indeed been shed, but perhaps the Accounts begin to mend.[3]

Miss Mary Mayhew, who Mr. Williams remembers a pretty Girl here, has lain on a Couch these Three Months, because a Consumption was apprehended; and today Mrs. Lutwyche told me the Bleeding all came from the Throat, and her Doctors advised Air and Exercise. What a waste of Affliction!![4]

General Leighton who I met in the Street this Morning, said his Brother was gone to Brynbella with Mr. Smythe Owen on a Visit,[5] and Some one told me that Mr. Salusbury was Steward of Chester Races.[6] His fair Lady must be better apprized of *My* Affairs than I am of *hers* if She can set any Time for my Journey to North Wales—I can set no Time for *myself*.

Like the dear Myddeltons,[7] *My* House and Property and fag end of Life too— are Upon Sale as your Ladyship sees in the Courier[8]——Not because I have given way to Pomps and Vanities—*at least of late Years:* but because 4700£ hard Money were expended by me on the Fronting, Repairing &c. of Streatham Park——exclusive of Gillow's enormous Bill for Furniture—all which I once vainly hoped might have tempted Mr. Thrale's Daughters either to share the Place with me—amicably,—or take it from me *At any Price they chose*—after my quitting Flintshire. No Application from me however, continued through Two Tedious Years, would prevail;——So now I will trust the Public.

My Dear Lady Williams used to read Books upon Prophesy with serious Attention; and Faber, if I recollect aright, was your Favourite.[9] There is a Mr.

Frere now, who expects the Conversion of the Jews and Destruction of the Infidel Power between March 1822—he says,—and March 1823—and believes that our Blessed Saviour will come in Clouds &c., a *very* few Years after those Events.[10]

Such Thoughts would take one's Breath away—if in the early or middle Part of Life; but Seven Years to *me* is as Seven *Centuries,* I shall be safe under Dymerchion Church.[11]

Meanwhile It is certain that there are Spots in the Sun larger than our whole Earth[12]—to which cause Wise Men attribute the unequalled Coldness of this backward Spring;—I saw a Mazereon Bush today looking as those Shrubs used to look,—in March.

You are a happy Lady in Your Husband and Children; and it was wisely determined in dear Mr. Williams *not* to go abroad this Year—*very* wisely determined.

Paris is in some Respects a Strange Place. A Lady told me today, that She was acquainted with Madam D'Arblaye, who wrote the Wanderer; and lived in France 25 Years. When She returned to England to nurse her Father Old Doctor Burney (who died at Chelsea) in his last Illness:——She asked him one Day what could be the meaning of a New Word She saw, *Trafalgar* House and *Trafalgar* Place &c. I never added She, heard the Word; What does it mean? The Doctor equally astonished, told her it was to commemorate Lord Nelson's Victory. *What* Victory dear Papa? was her Reply, and where was the Battle fought? She told the Lady, who today told it *me;* that no one in Paris had ever heard of the Event any more than herself;[13] who had moved in many Circles, and was married to a Man of Consequence enough,[14] if Consequence would have obtained Information, but What a State must Society have been *in?*

Our Talk at Bath has been as much or more concerning the Separation of Lord and Lady Byron as concerning the Marriage of the Princess.[15] I hope People will find Reason to applaud her Choice instead of finding Fault as we are all apt to do with every body and every thing. Mahometans say (you know) that all Men carry Two Bags: one of their Neighbours Evil Deeds *before* them; The other with their own errors and Crimes—*at their Back.*[16] The Rise of Corn however,[17] and Rise of Stocks will Contribute to put People in better humour,[18]——This last Winter has been a Surly one in every sense of the Word.

Adieu Dearest Madam! make my best Regards to good Sir John, and your incomparable Young ones; and believe me, most faithfully/ Your Ladyship's true and Obedient Servant/ H: L: Piozzi.

I am grieved for the Baby: She seems to be an early Martyr to Medicine, but I hope She *may* recover.[19]

Text Ry. 4 (1812–18). *Address* Lady Williams/ Bodlwyddan/ St. Asaph/ North Wales. *Postmark* BATH 10 MY 10 1816.

1. Angelina Salusbury was to be born 27 July 1816.
2. A rose bush, or "dwarf." See also HLP to HMS, 8 October 1817.

3. For Catherine Griffith, see HLP to Ly W, 21 March 1815, n. 6.

4. Clementina Mary Mayhew was to die at Sidmouth, probably of tuberculosis, on 14 October 1816.

5. For General Baldwin Leighton, see HLP to JSPS, 18 April 1812, n. 4.

His brother was Burgh Leighton (1760–1836), a lieutenant colonel in the 4th Light Dragoons.

6. As steward, JSPS was a manager of a single race at the Chester race course. The position of stewardship had the aura of tradition since it was instituted in 1511 or 1512. See "Extracts from the *Cheshire Observer*," 25 April and 7 May 1925, in the possession of the Chester City Record Office.

7. On 9 May in her "Pocket Book," HLP noted the receipt of "a Letter from Lady Williams . . . says the Myddeltons are quite done up——and will soon sell their effects." But the Gwaynynog estate would be sold only in 1870 to an Oliver Burton of Manchester.

8. Advertisements similar to those in *The Times* and the *Morning Chronicle* also appeared in the *Courier*, 30 April, 6 and 7 May.

9. For George Stanley Faber, see HLP to Q [25 January 1806], n. 22.

10. Discussing the prophecies of Daniel, James Hatley Frere foresaw that the "Period of Infidelity" would conclude in 1822–23 and that the conversion of the "Pagan Nations" and the "Progress of the Kingdom of Christ" would follow. As he continued: in 1867 "the Period of the Perfection of the Kingdom of Christ" would occur wherein "there will be some glorious manifestation of the person of Christ. The Jews will be converted and every one will be delivered 'that shall be found written in the book'" (p. 468).

See HLP to Ly W, 30 April 1815, n. 6, for Frere's *A Combined View of the Prophecies of Daniel, Esdras, and St. John.*

11. HLP was buried there on 16 May 1821.

12. HLP referred to the observation of the Reverend M. Stark, canon and astronomer of Augsburg. He discovered not merely spots on the sun's disk but a cavity, "the apparent diameter of which is three times larger than the real diameter of the earth." See *GM* 86, pt. 2 (1816):551; *The Times*, 26 July 1816.

13. FBA returned to England in August 1812, after living for ten years in France (*Journals and Letters*, vol. 7); for the anecdote about Trafalgar, see Hemlow, p. 332. It was undoubtedly reported to HLP by Marianne or Clement Francis.

14. In 1793 FBA married the *émigré* Alexandre-Jean-Baptiste Piochard d'Arblay. See HLP to PSP, 10 August 1793, n. 17.

15. For the separation of the Byrons, see HLP to JF, 21 February, n. 2.

For the marriage of Princess Charlotte and Prince Leopold on 2 May 1816, see HLP to JF, 16 January, n. 7.

16. A variation on an axiom recorded by George Sandys, *A Relation of a Journey begun An: Dom: 1610. Foure Bookes* (London: Printed for W. Barrett, 1615). In it Sandys states that at the Last Judgment "*Moses, Christ,* and *Mahomet,* shall bring their severall followers to Iudgment, and intercede for them. *Caine* that did the first murder, shall be the ringleader of the damned, who are to passe ouer the bridge of Iustice, laden with their sinnes in satchels. When the greater sinners shall fall on the one side into hell. . . . Those that tumble from the other side of the bridge, are laden with lesse sinnes, and do but fall into Purgatory: from whence they shall shortly be released, and receiued into Paradise" (p. 58).

17. During the agricultural depression of the first quarter of 1816, the price of corn plummeted. Hence, the recent "rapid advance of Grain attracts great interest: Wheat was yesterday fully 6s. higher, making an improvement of 16s. *a* 18s. per quarter . . . within the past three weeks" (*Courier,* 9 May).

18. By the end of May, stock prices had risen significantly. See *GM* 86, pt. 1 (1816):96, 480.

19. "Missey" Salusbury.

TO MRS. ALEXANDER LEAK

Sunday
12 May—1816.

My dear Leak will Write more fully today—though I feel *sure* that when *good* News is coming, I shall see it under her Husband's hand. God Almighty will direct all for the best, and to his Will I shall most contentedly resign myself—— only grieving if I get myself *blamed* on any side.

My Letters have been worded with a very happy Caution, and were written chiefly for fear of offending by Neglect: I *thought* there was something odd in the Correspondence, but could not unravel it.

Mr. Squibb promised to send Catalogues etc. to Brynbella, and I gave him the Direction: and now Mr. Salusbury says he never obtained Intelligence of the Business, till lately through Miss Myddelton. Pray remind Mr. Squibb.

Mr. Este's Letters now breathe nothing but Encomiums on your good Husband; neither you nor I shall ever contradict *Them*. I am just come from Church, and felt struck by the first Psalm in our Morning service, do *do* look in your fine Prayer book and read it as I did; with this Business in my head, and *you* will be struck too.

Oh here comes the Letter from Leak with which I have so much reason to be contented——He has been very good and very diligent, and sincerely do I rejoyce in the hope of Things ending so well: but the Ladies should not have looked *on*, and suffered their Place to go *so*. 'Tis well however we have escaped School Boys pulling that fine Chimney Piece about, it would have been dreadful.

I am ever faithfully yours and your Husband's/ and your Boy's/ H: L: P.

Text Hyde. *Address* Mrs. Leak at Messrs./ Mathews and Taylor's Fenchurch Street/ No. 110/ London. *Postmark* BATH 12 MY 12 1816; 13 MY 13 1816.

TO ALEXANDER LEAK

Bath Sunday
12: May 1816.

Poor Leak! and his little Wife have I fear suffered in the Cause; but *All's well that ends well;* and you do indeed experience what Perkins emphatically called the *Sweets of doing right:*[1] he had another Phrase, saying *how he fought with wild Beasts at Ephesus,* like Saint Paul:[2]——by your account of the mad Volunteer, You have been like him *there* too. I feel sorry for Mr. Squibb.—The Crazy Letters to *me* breathe Encomiums on *Leak* always; but bitter Cries about my Portrait which indeed was worth Twice 78£—even as a *History-Piece.*[3]

Shall you get the *Money* for *Dr. Johnson?*[4] I suppose Burney went to the same

Bidder—but where was Mr. Watson-Taylor? and my Friend Wilson of the European Musæum?

I suppose the Rain kept this last away.[5]

So the Place goes to a Mr. Elliott[6]—and those who will so soon be Owners of it——*let it go*! ! Tis enough to make *any* one go mad: I shall have *Money* however, and no further Debts or Trouble with the Place, and that is a great Matter.

Murphy's Portrait and my dear Santa Cecilia will be agreeable Companions to me here at Bath. The Colossal Magdalene is too large to look well in small Rooms;[7] if Mr. Salusbury behaves to please me, I will send *that* to Brynbella; it will just fit over the Drawing Room Door there—and be seen to Advantage.[8]

When will you be able to come to Bath dear Leak, and accept *My* Congratulations? *They* will be sincere ones.[9]

I hope Mr. Windle has tied my new Tenant hard and fast: he will perhaps take some of the Furniture, and *perhaps* too, the Place will not be degraded by his Residence:[10] He must necessarily admire the Fine Chimney Piece I think,[11] and my Heart feels happy that it will not be exposed to the Touch of School Boys.

Pray what became of my Antique Blue Bottles rimmed with Silver? And the Etruscan Vases?[12] When you have time you must let me hear.

By Mr. Windle's Account when I have deducted Murphy: The Pictures come to 1527£. 8. 0. and I have Three left, Two of them very valuable certainly.—If I have misreckoned you must set me right.

Johnson sold magnificently; I expected more for Garrick, and more for Reynolds—and poor Tasso went a Bargain to somebody: it was a true Titian Head.[13]

God bless you and Yours; I have written to your Wife and hope it will find her not *quite* killed. My Wonder is, how all has been got thro' so well, but Leak conducted it cleverly at last I doubt not./ Ever Yours/ H: L: P.

Oh! If they are all Guineas it does come to 1726.7.—but *are* they all Guineas? Yes Yes I see they are. Adieu the Post waits.

Do as you like about the Coppers—what *you* do, is sure to be well done; and I am sure to think so: You know their Value to a Guinea: They are but just paid for.[14]

Text Hyde Collection. *Address* Mr. Alexander Leak/ Streatham Park/ Surrey. *Postmark* 13 MY 13 1816.

1. For John Perkins, see Elizabeth Montagu to Elizabeth Vesey [25] July 1784, n. 3; John Field to HLP, 28 December 1791, n. 2.
2. 1 Corinthians 15:32.
3. Reynolds' portrait of HLT and Q (lot 58) sold for 78 guineas to Samuel Boddington on 10 May 1816.
4. See HLP to AL, 25 April, n. 3.
5. See HLP to JSPS, 28 April 1813, n. 5. According to the *Sale Catalogue*, John Wilson was not one of the purchasers at the auction.
6. Robert Elliott (d. 1831), a rope, hemp, and flax merchant in Wapping, had lived at Devonshire Place, London, before leasing Streatham Park from June 1816 to ca. 1819. See HLP to MF, 5 March 1818, n. 21; see also the "Streatham Land Tax Assessments," C.R.O., Surrey; for his will signed 11 June 1830 in Farnham and proved 5 November 1831, see P.R.O., Prob. 11/1791/626.

7. The "Study of a Head of a Colossal Female" by Cipriani was bought for HLP.

8. When AL wrote to HLP on 17 May (Ry. 609.14), he asserted that "The Magdalen Head will certainly be better sold, than sent to Brynbella. Mr. Salusbury would refuse to pay the Carriage of it." HLP took this advice to heart. She had it exhibited at Wilson's European Museum. And in 1819 she sold it to Watson-Taylor. See HLP to JF, 11 October 1816; to Watson-Taylor [ca. 19 March 1819] and to Wilson, 2 April 1819.

9. AL and his family were to arrive in Bath on 13 June; see HLP's "Pocket Book" for that date.

10. AL on 17 May informed HLP: "We are proceeding with the Valueation &c. Mr. Eliot say He is ready with the Money whenever We are ready to receive it. I suppose next Week will finish all." The *Sale Catalogue* reveals that Elliott was the largest single purchaser at the auction. He bought books, china, and furniture.

11. The chimney piece designed and carved by Locatelli. See HLP to TSW, 28 March 1811, n. 7.

12. HLP had purchased for fifteen guineas "A Pair of Rare Old Blue and White Bottles, Richly Mounted in Silver, brought overland from India in the 14th century" (lot 49); also "Two Antique Etruscan Vases, found in the ruins of Cicero's villa in Tusculum" for ten guineas.

13. Charles Burney, Jr., bought Reynolds' portrait of Garrick (£183.15); the M.P. Richard Sharp (ca. 1759–1835) purchased Reynolds' self-portrait (£128.2); Mary Anne Kymer acquired Titian's painting of Tasso (£37.16). All were sold on the third day of the sale, 10 May.

For Mary Anne Kymer, see HLP to PSP [8] December 1800, n. 6.

14. On 11 May, the fourth day of the auction, three lots of copper kitchenware were sold to Elliott and another lot of "Nine round copper stewpans" were purchased for HLP.

TO THE REVEREND THOMAS SEDGWICK WHALLEY

Bath Monday
13: May 1816.

My dear Doctor Whalley

when he reads in these Letters how long his poor old Friend has been doing Penance in two Rooms of New King Street with Two Maids only and never a Man: will not wonder, nor I hope feel indignant that I have at last proclaimed an open Sale of Streatham Park: so many Times offered to its Future Possessors,—so constantly refused. The hot boyling Water this Business has kept me in, must likewise account for my long Silence: In vain Bruce Hutchinson and Sir Robert engaged other People's Attention;[1] I poor Soul! could think of no*thing* and no*body* but H:L:P. as vainly Lady Byron dismissed her Husband, and he begged Reconciliation in beautiful Verses[2]—I could see no Letters in the Alphabet but those which composed the Words Streatham Park—of which Place I am at last taking leave for ever. No requests, no Inducements could tempt the Ladies to buy it; so the Public have managed for me, I have sold the Pictures, Bronzes &c. and some Mr. Elliott takes the Naked House and Grounds, standing to all Repairs, Tythes, Taxes, &c., and pays me 260£ o'Year for Life. I shall now discharge the Debts which till this hour have been weighing me down——and which no Oeconomy of mine could reduce, while the Surrey Property drained every Penny from my Purse——and after 4500£ paid for Repairs—brought me in Bills for Hothouses, Greenhouses, &c. to the Tune of 500£ more. Now Dear Sir Wish me joy that I have shaken off this Load of Splendid Misery; that I have by these means set my Income free, and enabled myself to live in a decent Style, such as neither of my Husbands would be shocked to witness.

Dear Salusbury must content himself with what he has, and pray for my Life, as nothing else will so much benefit *him:* And now if you please let me drive away Egotism, and tell you that Mrs. Lambart still lives,[3] and asks for you. Mary Mayhew is in a piteous Case: lying on a Chaise-longue permitted neither to speak or eat—how changed from her who ran Races with Salusbury and Cora at pretty Mendip!![4] Mr. Lutwyche however seems to have gained what *She* has lost, of Health and Strength; and they talk of going abroad when their interesting Invalide is able to bear the Journey and Voyage.

Miss Wroughton looks very grave, and I am told feels sadly deserted; by the loss of a Mother who many Beauties would have thought an Incumbrance, but She has a feeling Heart, and is a most Affectionate Relation.[5]

What else shall I tell you? that I walked thro' the *Snow* to Church Yestermorning, a Strange thing even were we living in Sweden—mais il court des mauvais Bruits du Soleil a ce qu'on dit—and the Spots on his Disk are said to be larger than our Whole Earth—no wonder we are starving—and the Mazereon Bushes out—just like *March.*

Meanwhile Death was never so frequent in England particularly Bath; and *Baby* Sufferers—quite innumerable—Mourning the only Wear; and The long Funerals blacken all the way. You were a wise Man to prefer the Continent, and I hope next Winter will find you in dear *Dear* Italy.[6]

A new Book says the Jews will congregate and go home in 1822: nor would *that* prove Impossible, if this *extraordinary,* if this *Intended* Crusade against Turkey should take Place; and Three great Christian Powers of three distinct Perswasions, should cooperate against the now very feeble Sovereignty of the Ottoman Porte. I think there is an Account somewhere that Harvey who first discovered the Circulation of the Blood—did in the Year 1580 tell in some long forgotten Treatise of his; how an Eastern Prophecy had before *then* assured Mankind, that a *Second* Attack of united Europeans would be decidedly fatal to Constantinople.[7]

Before such Gigantic Events, what Pygmy Triumphs are those of our Valiant Men at Waterloo? how *invisibly* small the Conquests of Whiggism over the Ministry and the Income Tax? yet these Occurrences employ our Mouths—ay and Thoughts too. When I was half Frantic about Streatham Park, I could read nothing but Ducretelle's History of the French Revolution,[8] and the Battle of St. Jean by a Temoin Oculaire[9]—they are written as if on Purpose to withdraw Attention from every thing but the Subjects they discuss, The Adventures they relate.—

I must however return to Self and Streatham. The Portrait of Doctor Johnson sold for 378 Pounds Sterling, and I am told that doctor Burney bought it.[10] That a Scholar of the 19th Century should be able and willing to give such a Sum for a Scholar's Portrait who was the Man most approved by the 18th Century; is pretty and proper: and we must rejoyce it is in such hands. Garrick fetched 175 Guineas Edmund Burke 220;[11] but you will see it all in the Courier.[12] I kept dear Murphy for myself——He was the Playfellow of my first Husband, The true and partial Friend of my second; he loved my *Mother,*—and poor as I am, Murphy remains with *me.* Write to me Dear Sir and you will delight the Heart, if you do not disapprove the Conduct of your ever gratefully and faithfully attached Friend/ H: L: Piozzi.

Mr. Anstey has kindly added to my Letter[13]—and now accept our united Compliments and best Wishes—and Addio!

Text Berg Collection +. *Address* The Revd. Dr. Whalley/ No. 1414/ Rue De La Puterie/ Bruxelles/ Pays Bas. *Postmark* BATH 19 MY 19 1816 109; PAID< > 1816; 208 F 16.

1. In Paris on 13 January, Michael Bruce (1787–1861), John Hely-Hutchinson (1787–1851), a captain in the Grenadiers of the Royal Guard, and Sir Robert Thomas Wilson (1777–1849), a major general, were arrested for having aided the escape of comte Antoine-Marie Chamans de Lavalette (1769–1830), directeur des postes during the *Cent Jours*. A Bonapartist and convicted traitor, Lavalette eluded his prison guards by donning the clothes of his wife, Emelie-Louise, née Beauharnais (1781–1855), niece of Empress Josephine and by walking out of the jail just prior to the scheduled date of his execution on 20 December 1815.
The Frenchman hid out in Paris for three weeks. Wilson and the other two Englishmen fraudulently obtained two British passports, picked up Lavalette on 7 January, and carried him beyond the French frontier to Mons. Wilson was arrested on 13 January, two days after his return to Paris.
The three Englishmen were tried in April, found guilty of aiding Lavalette, but exonerated from the charge of plotting "the subversion of the French government" (*The Times*, 23 April). They were sentenced to three months' imprisonment, the Prince Regent on 10 May expressing through the Duke of York his displeasure with their conduct. See *The Times*, 17 and 18 January, 27 April; *GM* 86, pt. 2 (1816):70; *Journals and Letters*, 9:106 n.–107 n.
2. No sooner had the Byrons separated than he "wrote some verses addressed to his wife, summing up all the sentimental pathos into which his frustrations and regrets now flowed." The first draft of "Fare thee well" is dated 18 March, Byron sending it to his wife a few days later. Her "maddening silence probably provoked [him] to send a copy to Murray," who admired the verses, which soon appeared in newspapers and magazines. In the "Commonplace Book" under the entry *Interesting Verses*, 20 April, HLP includes the poem as "Interesting Verses written by Lord Byron who seems to have been dismissed by his Wife, while so many Ladies are dismissed by their Husbands." See Marchand, *Byron*, 2:594–95; *GM* 86, pt. 1 (1816):351–52.
3. For Elizabeth Lambart, now a Bath resident, see HLT to Q [27 June 1784], n. 10.
4. Cora was William Lutwyche's dog. See HLP to JSPS, 24 July 1819.
5. The elder Susannah Wroughton had died in the early spring of 1816 at Wilcot Manor, Wilts. For her daughter—also Susannah—see HLP to PSW, 21 [November 1792], n. 8; to JSPS, 22 March 1808, n. 2.
6. By autumn 1816, TSW was to be in Modena (Wickham, 2:437).
7. See HLP to John Roberts, 5 March 1816, nn. 2 and 3.
8. Ducretelle is an error for Charles [Jean-Charles-Dominique] de Lacretelle (1766–1855), who between 1801 and 1806 published several works on the changes in the French government from the Revolution to the Directory. See, e.g., *Précis Historique de la Révolution Française. Assemblée Législative* (Paris: chez Onfroy [etc.], 1801).
9. Probably *Campagne de la Belgique . . . sur la Bataille de Waterloo . . . Relation française, par un Témoin Oculaire* (Bruxelles, 1816), as cited in Johann Pohler, *Bibliotheca historico-militaris*, 4 vols. (1887–99; rpt. New York, 1961), 2:132.
10. Watson-Taylor bought the portrait of SJ; see HLP to AL, 25 April 1816, n. 3.
11. Richard Sharp bought the Reynolds' portrait of Burke for £252.
12. The *Courier* for 11 May carried an account of the Streatham Park auction, paying special attention to the sale of the Reynolds portraits (with their buyers and prices).
13. For Robert Anstey, see HLP to Charlotte Lewis, 9 May 1791, n. 2.

TO ALEXANDER LEAK

Sunday 19. May 1816.

It is *I* that am growing stupid—not you indeed: you have shewn great Activity as well as Judgment.[1] What I meant was only to say that I should possess the Portrait so short a Time—It would be like *lending* it to me, for the Bidder would soon have Opportunity to obtain it again.[2] Your delightful Letter must however give me Spirits—or I should be ungrateful to God and Good Friends: and I *will* hope to live and rationally to enjoy so comfortable and desireable an Income.

Making Enemies—especially of young People—is however always imprudent, and tho' I am inclined to be wholly of your Mind about Mr. Salusbury;[3]—— Squibb *ought* to send him the Catalogues and he *promised* to do so.[4] Not a *Priced* one tho'; for I don't want him to see every 20£ I possess, or dispose of: Those days of Confidence are wholly over between *us*.

I think Bob Cotton (I beg his Pardon) would accept the old Cabinet with Pleasure;[5] it belonged to *his* and *my Great* Grandfather: and *his* Name Sake. Old Sir Robert of Combermere, who marrying The Heiress of Lleweney, took *her* Name in addition to his own; and was Sir Robert *Salusbury* Cotton.[6] I saw a Print of him at Streatham Park—*in Mead's Time*, but we never could find him again you know. The Cabinet will crawl as far as Ryegate safe enough.

Magdalene will make her best Figure in the European Musæum, and Mr. Wilson will know how to hang her up high, and shew her off to Advantage, and she will be out of the way.[7]

Stocks rising is a Proof of the Nation's Stability; in no other Sense good to be sure—for me who wish to buy: but there are *so* many Apprehensions when Corn and when Funds are falling—and such melancholy Faces—they fright one.

Mr. Squibb has this Moment written to say the whole is *between* 3 and 4000£ and that what he has already collected is ready for paying in—to Hammersley.

You must get his Account to be sure and bring it hither to me with your own: Is it not provoking to be asked (as I am every day,) Pray Madam who purchased Dr. Johnson's Portrait? And I have only to reply—Indeed I do not know.

A *Priced* Catalogue is what I want first:[8] with Names of the Bidders—no Catalogue came to me, only a civil Letter; to which I may make a civil Answer,— but that is no Account at all: for every part of the whole Business, I rely on *You*; and *that* Mr. Squibb *must* know by this time; but he should give you the full Information, and you must take the Money to Pall Mall.

Be so good as call on Dyde and Scribe for their Bill, when you are at Hammersley's; and bring it with you to Bath: and God speed the Time; for you will be most welcome indeed with the ultimate Intelligence hoped for by your Obliged/H: L: P.

I am making *Estimates* of Hopes and Fears—meaning Debts and Cash to be received, *all Day long:* but I fear we shall at last fall short of our 2800£ per Annum[9] because of that unpaid Money to the Duke of Bedford, and the Taxes incurred by Sir James Fellowes's Visit[10]—and trumpery Debts that operate like Small Shot in an Army, when the Artillery has all been discharged.

The Carriage wants you cruelly I believe;[11] and to tell you the Truth I am weary of burning my Fingers with a Tin Kettle: and long to shew you a pretty *Silver* one that is to be Sold here: but I dare not buy Plate without *you*. I do not understand it.

Text Hyde Collection. *Address* Mr. Alexander Leak/ Streatham Park/ Surrey. *Postmark* BATH 19 MY 19 1816 109; 10 o'Clock MY 20 1816.

1. AL had written to HLP on 17 May (Ry. 609.14): "I do not exactly understand your meaning by Lending the Gentleman Mr. Murphy's Portrait. You never I think, before wrote any thing I could not understand, but this I cannot. I suppose I am grown stupid."
2. Watson-Taylor in 1819 bought the portrait from HLP.
3. AL had also written on 17 May: "I am glad Squibb sent Him no Catalogues or Copy of the Advertisement. He will find Himself of Less *importance* than He thought of."
4. HLP had written to Squibb, who on 21 May replied: "Mr. Squibb had had the honor of Mrs. Piozzi's letter by yesterdays post. . . . [he] is extremely sorry the Catalogue &c. was omitted to be sent to J. S. P. Salusbury Esqr. and will lose no time in attoning for the omission with every apology it is in his power to make" (Ry. 557.200).
5. On the auction's fifth day, 13 May, Matthews bought for HLP "A Very Curious Antique Cabinet, the upper part containing eleven drawers and a cupboard, enclosed by folding doors, finely inlaid, and four drawers under" for £3.11. (lot 26). AL on 17 May had suggested selling the piece because it was "too Old to bear removal any distance."
For Robert Salusbury Cotton, now sixteen, see HLP to AL, 22 October 1815, n. 4.
6. For Sir Robert Cotton of Combermere, see HLP to James Cathrow, 29 November 1813, n. 5.
7. Cipriani's "Head of a Magdalen" is listed in *The Plan and New Descriptive Catalogue of the European Museum* (London: G. Smeeton, 1818), where it is further described as "Being a present from the painter to Mrs. Piozzi" (p. 11, item 108).
8. Squibb in his letter of 21 May wrote that "A priced Catalogue with the Buyers names is making out for Mrs. Piozzi and will be forwarded by Saturdays Mail in the meantime Mr. Squibb subjoins a statement of the prices of the Portraits and the purchasers names."
9. On 17 May AL had predicted: "I should think after having got yourself a House &c. and all that paid, you will have a clear 2800£ per Year."
10. From 1795 to 1800 the Piozzis rented land from the duke of Bedford, paying annually £150 (1795–97) and then £200. Apparently the rent and the interest were never fully paid. See "Streatham Land Tax Assessments," C.R.O., Surrey.
11. In his same letter, AL expressed concern that ". . . something must be done too . . . about your Carriage. I shall see when I arrive."

TO SIR JAMES FELLOWES

Wednesday May 22nd 1816

My dear Sir James Fellowes

has broken the *Mum* at last: and I will now tell him how much at Ease my Heart feels already since the late Transactions. Leak will come with the Bills and Statements in Whitsun Week——and I shall get away on My Journey to Wales towards the longest Day:[1] May not I dip in my own native Sea some of the hottest Mornings of this tardy Summer?——and would it not help to wash away what is left of Care? Your Father had no Notion I had ever been fond of

Bathing, whereas my passing the Season without a few Plunges used to be quite a Punishment.——The last Dip was in the Year 1812 at Prestatyn; and I wrote Verses there which you never saw, I left them in Wales.[2] We are hesitating between a *convenient* House on the Queen's Parade, or dear pretty No. 8 Gay Street—which is particularly *In*convenient for the Servants below Stairs—— Either of them ought to content me well enough; after how I have been liv- ing——a common Expression, but infamous bad English.

Apropos Mrs. Charles Kemble has been here—acting;[3]—and in some part of a Comedy written by Murphy, said "We are like Cymon and Iphigĕnĭa in Dryden's Fables."[4] The Ladies stared, but the Scholars said She was *right*——and I said it were better be wrong than so pedantic: for 'tis always called Iphigēnĭa in common use. Mr. Lutwyche held with the Wise Men, and he you know is a good Prosodist:——*I* quoted Pope's Homer—9th Book—

> Laodice and *Iphigēnia* fair,
> And bright Chrysothemis with Golden Hair.[5]

Oh said Mr. Mangin, Pope is no firm Authority; *he* calls the Wife of Pluto Prōserpine, as in colloquial Chat, when writing his fine Ode on St. Cecilia's Day:[6] but old Milton disdained such Barbarism, *he* calls her Prŏsērpĭna as in the Greek.[7]

We all appealed to Falconer[8]——dear Sir James Fellowes was too far away: I know not the Success of our Appeal yet.

So now do write, and tell about the Bathing and the Verses. Leak will come here in Whitsun Week and I shall know my Affairs exactly. The Pictures will however pay my Debts——The Remainder (not a large one) will buy in 3000£ at least in the 3 per Cents: We have Peace before us, and hope of a rising Stock——which with my 260£ per Annum during Life—all *Repairs, Insurance, Tythes, Taxes,* and so forth paid by the Tenant—will if I live seven Years, make up the Sum I asked for the Place at first. And Then in the Seaman's Phrase, we shall cry—*Steady and all well.* As soon as my Sale was over, the Rain ceased; and now we have a hot Sun and sharp Easterly Winds; I think they affect your Brother Dorset's Health: I hoped he was taking a Cottage here at Freshford,[9] but The all-powerful Ladies attract him to France——There are attractive Ladies *there* too.

Well! here are fine Apple Blossoms, Pink and White as any Lady can make herself, and here is Peace too and I *think Plenty.* When we were all looking at the Fireworks in 1748 from temporary Buildings—fragile enough I sup- pose[10]——Doctor Barton merrily exclaimed Do you call this a good Peace? which brings so many *Heads* to the *Scaffold*?[11]

I take this Letter with me for Lord Gwydir to free. How good he and Lady Willoughby are to pretty Miss Mary Mayhew! and what a pretty Skeleton She is! unable to stand, or speak—so as to be heard——unable to bear Heat or Noise or *anything;* and they all say She will live, and She thinks so herself: Nous verrons:

Adieu Dear Sir, present me with every possible Good Wish to Lady Fellowes, and believe Me ever, Her Ladyship's and Yours/ faithfully/ H: L: P.

Text Yale University Library. *Address* Sir J. Fellowes.

1. HLP is off in her schedule. Whitsun week was to begin 2 June, AL and his family arriving on 13 June.
HLP's "Pocket Book" shows that she was to leave Bath on 4 August to arrive at Brynbella on the evening of 8 August. She returned to Bath on 13 September, writing "Arrived Safe at Bath. God be praised."
2. In 1812 HLP wrote in "Harvard Piozziana," vol. 4: "I went to bathe in the Sea under the Rocks here at wretched Prestatyn . . . the Tides were wonderfully high and proportionately *low*, of course . . . Not a Soul had I to change a word with, and the Nights though long were calm. In distinct Forms of rugged Mountains and shrill Screams from now and then a solitary Sea Gull, were all the Sounds and objects that met my Eyes or Ears. Was it *they* that inspired me at 72 years old whilst wandering on the Beach to break out thus in unpremeditated verses?" The verses, however, do not appear at this point but were inscribed earlier (3:76–79) as some of "my *funny* stuff" for Lady Kirkwall and her mother.
3. The actress-wife of Charles Kemble, Maria Theresa, née De Camp began a six-night engagement at the Theatre Royal on 4 May (*Bath Chronicle*, 2 and 9 May 1816).
For Mrs. Kemble, see HLP to Q, 28 January 1795, n. 6; to DL, 15 February [1795], n. 4.
4. HLP refers to Mrs. Kemble's performance in Arthur Murphy's *The Citizen. A Comedy in Two Acts* (1761). The line appears in act 2.
5. *Iliad*, 9.189–90.
6. *Ode for Musick, on St. Cecilia's Day*, line 85.
7. *Paradise Lost*, 4.269, and 9.396.
8. The physician William Falconer (1744–1824), a recorder of Chester, had an only son, the Reverend Thomas (b. 24 December 1771—buried 25 February 1839), who for a short time was curate of St. James's, Bath. Born in Duke Street, Bath, he lived most of his life at 29 the Circus, where he died. He is buried near his father in the Weston churchyard. See "Weston Burial Record," C.R.O., Somerset.
9. A village in Somerset, near Bath.
10. See HLP to the proprietors of *The Monthly Mirror*, 17 June 1798, n. 11.
11. Philip Barton (ca. 1695–1765) served as canon of Christ Church, Oxford, from 1733 until his death.

TO ALEXANDER LEAK

Wednesday
22: May 1816.

Leak's Letters are really delightful; I think on the Strength of them, I may commission you to buy me that Table Service of Mortlake which we borrowed for Sir James Fellowes—The Shop here in Milsom Street which used to be connected with Mortlake is shut up—so I fear will many be.[1]

Your Wife and Child will be most welcome; and if our Lodgers go *out* next Week, as it is expected they will:—Your Family shall be no further off than *our own* Parlour; if they stay, here are Parlours *close* to us, and Mrs. Sele has disposed of her House &c. for seven Months.[2]

We wait your Decision between a *very* commodious and pretty House on the Queen's Parade; and dear elegant No. 8 Gay Street; which is particularly *in*commodious, and they say actually *Smokes* below Stairs. If you make even temporary Residence at Bath—you can see to *my Affairs* while I run to Wales, and get a Dip in the Sea:

Give my best Love and Wishes to little Dear, his Birthday is about this Time I think.[3]

Mr. Lysons is come,[4] he says *My* Portrait was bought by Mr. Boddington,[5] and that Merrik Hoare bid against him; Is it so? but Mr. Lysons—who knows so many Things—cannot tell who purchased Johnson's Portrait.

Oh! here comes Intelligence from Mr. Squibb: it was Mr. Watson Taylor I find who wished to possess Johnson, Barretti and Murphy[6]—he must wait till my Death produces a Second Sale—Whoever I leave it to, will take *his* Offer without hesitation.

George of the Parade is always good humoured and friendly; and willing to find me a House, and happy to hear he shall soon see Mr. Leak—*I* am happy to hear *that,* and am of your Mind that few Places are cheaper or more comfortable than this.

Somersetshire is beside, the very finest County in England; and here are Farms in Plenty to be had within 10 Miles of the Town; I should think it a most eligible Residence for you: and if anything happened—why Leak would be within Call——*So* far *I* should feel Interested.

Silver does fall in Value,[7] and Tea Kettles are coming into Fashion rather than Urns. I saw nothing at Hamlet's that pleased me as much as many Things that are to be found here in *our* Shops. Apropòs—let me beg you to pay for the Ring at Hamlet's, and take his Receipt:[8] and put a Two Ounce Vial of Cobbe's fine *Tinct. Opii* in your Pocket.[9] There is none so good at Bath: where tho' I pick up my Spirits pretty well in the day—no Sleep visits my poor Eyes in the Night. The *Reaction* Dr. Gibbes talks of, never attacks me till I am a'Bed, and cannot escape. Music will be my best soother; you will find Mr. Stroud, and Miss Sharpe[10] will get me an Instrument. Who bought poor Dear Mr. Piozzi's old Forte Piano?[11]

You see my good Leak that I do purpose enjoying what is left of Life, and Mrs. Gibbes, who prescribes like her Husband, is most earnest for me to take No. 8—it is so near *her* and *him;* and we can perhaps (with your help) find out some Means of making the Kitchen, Servants Hall &c.—*tolerable.*[12]

I have sent a decided Negative to Mr. Watson Taylor's very generous Offer: and I hope Mr. Squibb will shew Him my Letter which contains my Reasons for doing so.

I really wish him to have the Picture after my Death; he is probably a Young Man, and may I am sure *command* it from *any* of the Successors/ of Yours and Your Wife's truly Obliged/ H: L: Piozzi.

Text Hyde Collection. *Address* Mr. Alexander Leak/ Streatham Park/ Surrey. *Postmark* BATH 22 MY 22 1816; 10 o'Clock MY 23 1816.

1. Ellis, Colebrook-Dale, china warehouse, 16 Milsom Street, Bath, had closed between 1812 and 1816 *(Bath Directories).* Many shops were closed by the postwar depression.

2. Samuel Seale (1771–1850) and his wife Mary, née Lockyer (1764–1851) lived at 15 Gay Street. They also owned 6 and 8 Great Pulteney Street, large houses assessed at the value of £70 and £75 a quarter. See the "Walcot Burial Register," C.R.O., Somerset; "Poor Rate Book[s], Bathwick," Guildhall, Bath.

3. Alexander Piozzi Leak, whose first birthday would be on 29 May, see HLP to Ann Leak, 19 [April 1815].

4. SL.

5. Samuel Boddington (d. 1843), a West India merchant, of Boddington, Philips, Sharp, and Company, Mark Lane, London. A man of property both in the West Indies and Great Britain, Boddington was an art collector, whose possessions were so vast that in his will he granted his daughter, Grace Webster, the right to sell anything she "may think not useful to my Grandchildren." See P.R.O., Prob. 11/1980/380, proved 3 June 1843.

6. Squibb informed HLP on 21 May (Ry. 527.200) that Watson-Taylor had "applied to him to obtain Mr. Murphy's Portrait for which he is willing to give 150 Guineas——Mr. W. T. was the purchaser of Mr. Baretti's and Dr. Johnson's portraits and is desirous that Mr. Murphy should complete the triumvirate with his former friends."

7. In May silver was slightly more than 5s. per ounce, "an halfpenny below the mint price." See *GM* 86, pt. 2 (1816):163.

8. For Thomas Hamlet, the goldsmith and jeweler, see HLP to JSPS, 27 October 1811, n. 1.

9. For the chemist William Cobbe, see HLP to AL, 13 December 1814, n. 2. *Tinctura opii* was one of the many authorized preparations of opium, which "in a full dose . . . occasions a pleasant tranquillity of mind, and a drowsiness which . . . always refreshes the patient." See Robert Hooper, *Lexicon Medicum; or, Medical Dictionary* (London: Longman, Rees, Orme, Browne, and Greene, 1831), "Papaver Somniferum," 930.

10. HLP refers to either H. F. Stroud of 3 Lambridge or J. Stroud of Bladud's Bank. For Elizabeth Sharp, see HLP to PSP, 26 April 1801, n. 4.

11. Matthews purchased for £6.10 on 11 May (lot 88), "A Grand Piano-Forte, by Stodart, In a Mahogany Case."

12. Dr. George Smith Gibbes and his first wife Elizabeth, née Sealey (d. 1822). For the doctor, see HLP to Roberts, 20 March 1807, n. 6.

TO ALEXANDER LEAK

Sunday
26: May—1816.

Mr. Windle is a Wise Man and we will mind what He says; *You* are a wise Man and I have always minded what you say, but since I have been poor and in Debt, I have been cowardly, and shall only beg of the Hammersley's to buy me in 1500£ at the most: because I must and will pay every Demand from Greatest to least, and they are really more than you count on: I suppose 930£ will purchase my Stock; which I put there, only because dear Mr. Piozzi put *his* there, and it pleases my Recollection, to do as *he did*.

Is Squibb to have 5 per Cent? or what is he to have? 'Tis a Demand wholly new to me, and I therefore comprehend it not. The Priced Catalogue is arrived, but the Crops, Fixtures &c. have no Place in it——*They* probably belong to *your* Account and Mr. Elliott's Advance Money, and so forth. They did not I suppose go by Auction. I will buy in only 1000£ on Second Thoughts till I see what Money I am worth. Squibb's Total is 3921£—and a handsome Total it is; but who knows how long it will be paying in, and I must (when you come) get me a nice Tea Equipage—you know, with Silver Things; and your Wife knows how

I want Sheets and Table Cloths, and poor Jones knows how I want *Body* Linnen and Pocket Handkerchiefs: you can't Think how sharp we have been Living,——— but for *her* I should certainly have starved.———

And you must see a Man in this Town abut *Wine;* for Lucas has really been very rough with me, and I have no Partiality for *him.*[1]

The People *do* appear very slow to you and me dear Leak—but they are *Sure* I suppose. Your Son will not be among the Tedious souls I think. Give my Love to him and his fretted Mother: I wrote to her only last Night.

Mr. Cotton will be very well pleased with his Cabinet; Pity young Francis got nothing.[2]/ I am very Sincerely/ Your Obliged/ H: L: Piozzi.

Mr. Elliott seems to have purchased a vast Deal of the Furniture; Jones cries after the Bed still: and unless I get *that* House I shall cry too.

Text Hyde Collection. *Address* Mr. Alexander Leak/ Streatham Park/ Surrey. *Postmark* BATH 26 MY 26 1816; 10 o'Clock MY 27 1816.

1. Robert St. John Lucas (d. ca. 1821) began his Bath career as a wine merchant at the York Hotel, as early as 1783. By 1791 he was the proprietor and in 1805 he took as his partner a Mr. Reilly. According to the 1824 directories, Lucas's name had disappeared, the hotel being operated by Reilly alone.

2. The seventh son of Henry Calveley Cotton, Francis Vere (1799–1884) entered the Royal Naval College in 1812 and sailed to North America on the frigate *Pomone* two years later. Returning to England in August 1815, he became a midshipman on the *Albion,* warship. His distinguished naval career included promotion to lieutenant in 1821, captain in 1841, and rear admired in 1874. See *AR,* "Obituary," n.s. 22 (1884):114; O'Byrne, 1:233.

TO SIR JAMES FELLOWES

Bath
30: May 1816.

My dear Sir

Accept a Thousand Thanks for your Letter, it rejoyces my Heart that your Brother and Sister in Law are coming near us;[1] 'Tis the best thing for Them, and the best Thing for No. 13 and all.

Squibb's full Account of all he has sold is close upon 4000£ out of which he will take 400£ of Course; how much more, depends upon his Mercy. Beside all this, there are the Crops and Fixtures which go by Valuation———not open Sale;—and an Annual 260£ for my Life. This you see Comes very hard upon the Sum we first talked about:—if I do not die of this vile Sore Throat and Hoarseness, newly catched; and which will not quit its hold till I get to Rodborough in our Way to Wales I dare say.

Leak has not settled with Mr. Elliott yet,—The Man who takes the House and its Appendages: when he has done there, he will come hither, and I hope fix me in Gay Street against my Return. I will be careful about Seabathing———but if all these Attacks are as I suspect——upon the Nerves, they may perhaps get a little Restoration of Tone by Salt Water, if it is not *quite* too late.

Doctor Gibbes bid me beware of the *Reaction* but what can one do towards keeping such Things at a Distance? Cowper says you know, and *truly* and *sweetly;*

> Fate steals along with Silent Tread,
> Most dangerous when least we dread;
> Frowns in the Storm with angry Brow,
> But in the Sun Shine strikes the Blow.——[2]

Now don't you believe me low Spirited: few People ever had Such uniformly good Spirits. Did I tell you I had saved Murphy from the general Wreck? And that Mr. Watson Taylor wrote after me to beg him for 157£10.—but I am no longer poor, and when I was—There ought surely to be some Difference made between Fidelity—and Unkindness.

When Burneys were treacherous and Baretti boisterous against poor inoffending H:L:P. dear Murphy was faithful found among the faithless, faithful only he.[3]

> He, like His Muse, no mean retreating made,
> But follow'd faithful to the silent Shade.[4]

Equally attached to both my Husbands—he lived with us till he could in a manner live no longer; and his Portrait is now on the Canal with that of Mr. Thrale coming to Bath——my Mother whom both them adored—keeping them Company. Mr. Watson Taylor may make sure of it at my Death;—for Salusbury would sell it instantly, and the Ladies have a very fine Portrait of Mr. Murphy full Length painted by Dance[5]——so they would not say Thank you for it.

Let me however bid you Fare well, and request you to present my best Regards to Lady Fellowes: assuring/ her Ladyship how much I am/ hers and yours/ H: L: P.

Text Princeton University Library. *Address* Sir James Fellowes.

1. Dorset and Julia Fellowes had rented a house at Tivoli in Lyncombe parish, Bath.
2. "A Fable" (1782), lines 36–39, line 37 reading "Found oft'nest in what least we dread."
3. *Paradise Lost*, 5.896–97.
4. Writing in the "Commonplace Book" under *Johnson* about the sale of the Streatham Park portrait, HLP notes: "I have reserved [the painting of Murphy] for myself; nor shall the offered 157£.10—'tho a noble Price, take from my Possession the *only* Man among the Wits I fostered— who did not fly from the Colours unless prevented by Death. . . ." HLP then quotes the same lines (altered to describe Murphy's loyalty) from Pope's "Epistle to Robert Earl of Oxford, and Earl Mortimer" (1721), lines 27–28.
5. Nathaniel Dance Holland (1735–1811), cr. baronet (1800), M.P., portrait painter and foundation member of the Royal Academy, painted a 50″ × 40″ portrait of Arthur Murphy, ca. 1777. Now at the National Portrait Gallery, the painting is of Murphy seated at a table with his hands resting on an opened book and his head turned to the side. The Gallery's file note on the work states that it is a "repetition of the picture formerly at Streatham. This was painted for one of Mr. Thrale's family."

William Ward (1766–1826) engraved the portrait and gave the source as "from an original in the possession of Miss Thrales."

TO ALEXANDER LEAK

Fryday 7: June 1816.

Ah Dear Leak!

and so I *am* ill—and so I was when young Squibb called, but had no Notion of talking to him about my Health—and he of Course thought one old Woman's Ailments were like those of another. My little Skiff has weathered the hard Gale of Wind, but will now I fear sink in the Harbour—not before You arrive *Surely*:— that I may endeavour to express my true Sense of your admirable Management; it is really quite beyond my *Estimates*. With your Letter comes Windle's Lease,[1] and Three Lines under his own hand to bid me send for some Mr. Philip George to witness it.[2] Poor Bessey has been all over the Town to look for him; and says he is an old Superannuated Creature; but She tries to drive him hither, that the Lease may go by the next Coach,—or when will Mr. Leak come? and get us a Man Servant to send of Errands.—Indeed I think of all the Things we are in want of,—*That* is the most pressing.

Poor little Soul! She has her Hands full truly.

My Rash—which was frightful indeed—is dried off and gone: but so violent a Nervous Fit (if nervous) I never did labour under yet, bad as you have seen me; and her Idea is only pampering my Palate with French Beans, Asparagus &c. Today—because She heard Money was within Sight, She has brought me home Green Pease.

Meanwhile here comes Doctor Gibbes, and says my Pulse is much disordered; begs me to take a Table Spoonful of Castor Oyl (like poor dear Piozzi) in Coffee.

I wish this Old Mr. George would come first.

Pay the Bill at Price's, if there *is* a Bill:[3] The Coffee here is exceeding good indeed.

Hamlet is not unreasonable—The wretched Lady very unlikely to enjoy her Ring many Years—or indeed Months.

Good Fortune does not bring Happiness to a Family—any more than it brings health to an Individual; we are in the Habit of Reading and hearing that said perpetually:—but I suppose it will strike *You* more forcibly when exemplified in Your/ poor/H: L: P.

We are quite wild with Impatience to see *you*.

Meanwhile here comes a handsome young Fellow Philip George by Name, who witnesses the Deed:[4] and (for his 1£ Note) has taken the Trouble to tie up the Parcel, and carry it himself to the Coach:—Ay and has witnessed Hammersley's Power of Attorney to receive Dividends, which came by the same

Post——and now God Bless you, I will go take the Castor Oyl. Give my true Love to Wife and Child.——

I sent a Scrap thro' Mr. Davies to Streatham Park last Wednesday.

Text Hyde Collection. *Address* Mr. Alexander Leak at/ Mess: Mathews' and Taylors/ No. 110/Fenchurch Street/ London. *Postmark* BATH 7 JU 7 1816; E 8 JU 8 1816.

1. That is, the lease for Streatham Park signed by Elliott, about which HLP wrote in her "Pocket Book" on this date: "Windle's Lease came, seems a very good one. The Attorney who witnessed it, thought it well drawn and managed. Hammersley sent his Power of Attorney to sign."
2. Philip George Sr. (1748–1822) had practiced law at 7 Belmont Road, Bath, from ca. 1785. He was master extraordinary in chancery and commissioned in the Court of King's Bench. In February 1817, he was to resign as town clerk of Bath, an office which he had held for nearly forty years. See the *Bath Herald,* 15 February 1817; *GM* 92, pt. 1 (1822):190.
3. For Edward Price, a London merchant and shipper, see HLP to AL, 13 December 1814, n. 2.
4. Philip George Jr. (1786–1861) began practicing law with his father and succeeded him as town clerk until ca. 1860. By 1819 he moved from the elder George's office to 14 Seymour Street. There he remained until 1824 when he relocated at 1 Norfolk Crescent. Like his father he was a solicitor and master extraordinary in chancery and was commissioned in the Court of King's Bench, Common Pleas, and Exchequer. See the "Walcot Burial Register," C.R.O., Somerset.

TO MRS. FELLOWES

[ca. 7 June 1816][1]

Dear Madam

I wait till my Steward comes from Streatham Park—and then he shall get me a Servant to send, that I may know how my Neighbours do—and that I may tell kind Enquirers that I have still a little nasty low nervous *Feverette* upon me with a Pain round my Neck, chiefly the Back of it. A good Stroke of the Guillotine would bring me instant Relief.

Meanwhile how is the dear Dr. and Miss Fellowes, *poor* Miss Fellowes!! She has really been a miserable sufferer.

Miss Mary Mayhew too! vit elle encore?

Accept my best Adieux and believe me ever Yours/ H: L: P.

Text Peyraud Collection

1. In her letter to AL of 7 June, HLP indicated that when AL arrived in Bath, she wanted him to find a man servant to send on errands, referred to again here. AL arrived in Bath on 13 June, so the letter must have been written before that date.

TO JOHN SALUSBURY PIOZZI SALUSBURY

Bath
Longest Day
[21 June 1816]

My dearest Salusbury has written me now a very kind and unaffected Letter, and I beg you will accept my kindest and most unaffected Thanks for it.[1] Things seem to do better for me than I hoped in some Respects; and The Sneers and Spiteful Expressions which in my present weak State would destroy me——I hope may be escaped by the Lady's Resolution to leave Wales and England too.[2]

Doctor Cumming's Abergeley Bath is the very Thing for me; we can make it warmer and cooler to my Taste and Powers of Endurance.[3]

At present I could in no wise bear the Motion of a Carriage——tho' by no means (I fear) a *dying* Woman: only a Woman crushed if not wholly broken by Storms of every kind.

Now dearest dear Salusbury, pray for very pity do not go about telling, and hearing, and consulting what *you are to do with me*: but let me alone, and do *nothing* with me.

Think of your own Family, You have—or will have—enough to do with them—if Two Babies are to come every 20 Months.[4]——I do not owe 50£ in the World, and shall very soon have 3000£ in the Consols, besides many Rareties saved out of the Wreck, and a clear Income, and a good House.

When your next Child is born I will send you 100£ for Christening Fee, and Journey Expences if you come to Bath——and when you have talked with Dr. Gibbes you will feel better persuaded of my *Duration.*

Shortening Life and rendering it miserable are by no means the same Thing; neither does Health follow Happiness half as closely at the Heels——as Sickness follows Sorrow.

Besides that the Anxiety and Terror which I suffered concerning Streatham Park whilst it was mine, kept Sleep and Peace at perpetual Distance, nor will I explain the Causes of an Uneasiness which preyed upon my Life——by *Letter* to any Man living.

I am pleased with what you tell me of Mrs. Mostyn: wherever She goes—She will take with her my True Love and good Wishes; While other People's Daughters are disgracing themselves, Mine have all conducted their course of Life completely to the Approbation of the World they live in;——whence I think Some new Name is hissed out every Week. Do you hear or heed these Stories?— better not perhaps: Dear Harriet will however trust you to Bath whilst She is lying in: Our Town will be completely empty at that Time——and virtuous of Course. Miss Wroughton will be gone among the rest; or you would perhaps be sorry to see her broken down by Grief and Disappointment.[5]

Mary Mayhew still exists, a Breathing Corpse—at Sidmouth. Sir Walter James's only Son whom you remember at Oxford, and who married Lady Emily Stuart, is in the last Stage of a Consumption—he has had Two Babies, but both died.[6]

And can you wonder *my* Health suffers? Mrs. Holroyd will be glad to see You; She is no more superannuated than myself, tho' sick enough at Times.

I have been so lame I could scarce go upstairs to Bed without help, but to day I walked 20 Yards in Lady Rivers' Walk,[7] and the Crescent;——Doctor Gibbes was with me, and I had a Chair in waiting: My Hope is to get to Laura next Sunday.

It was a foolish Thing to mention any of this Nonsense *at first*: but I concluded that Miss Williams who weeps for every Cold caught between here and Holy-head——would write word about mine into Wales—and make Discussion concerning what Mr. Salusbury was to *do* with Regard to the Old Quiz his Aunt, at every House in the Neighbourhood.

Dear Love Adieu! and forgive whatever seems like Ill Humour; I feel nothing certainly but Esteem and Tenderness for You and Yours:[8] to whom I will endeavour (as I promised poor Uncle) to do all the little Good I can—and no harm. In this believe your truly Affectionate/ H: L: P.

Dear pretty Harriet will keep quite well till the last Minute; then give a loud Scream or Two, and You will have a Son—Hester Maria must however hold her Post in Papa and Mama's Favour: What a happy Thing it is that She has done being so Ill with her Teeth!!

Longest Day 1816.

The Sun setting at Brynbella behind the Stables.

Text Ry. 589.331. *Address* John Salusbury Piozzi Salusbury Esq./ Brynbella/ near Denbigh/ North Wales. *Postmark* BATH JU 21 1816.

1. On 5 June JSPS had expressed his "fervent hope that nothing will prevent your coming to Brynbella before this month is out." He then added: "I remember perfectly well the longest day was always a favourite period of the year to you" (Ry. 591.8).
2. CMM.
3. For Dr. Cumming as a proponent of hydropathic treatment, see HLP to Ly W, 9 February 1810, n. 11.
4. "Missey" and Angelina were born eleven months apart.
5. Susannah Wroughton was mourning her mother's death.
6. For John James and his wife, Lady Jane, née Stewart, see HLP to JSPS, 20 February 1812, n. 1. They had only one surviving son, Walter Charles (d. 1893), born on 3 June.
7. Lady Rivers' Walk is northeast of the Royal Crescent.
8. On 24 June, JSPS responded to this statement and HLP's letter in general. See below.

TO SIR JAMES FELLOWES

Saturday Night
22–23 June 1816.

My dear Sir James Fellowes will learn from his Sister who is ever partially attached to me, the uneasy Situation I am placed in by the Strange Seizure of poor Leak.[1] He had as I told You settled his Accounts, and given me a Stamped

Receipt in *full of all Demands:* he next went out to see a Farm some six or seven Miles off—This was last Tuesday;—and came home Wet, and neglected to change his Clothes: on Wednesday he dropt down motionless and has lain so ever since. We bleed and blister &c. but the Man seems to have lost all Power except of Speech, and I fear will never recover: tho' Dr. Gibbes and Mr. Norman do all they can to excite Fever and Reaction of *Some* sort,[2] He cannot however bring up the Catarrh which chokes his very Existence——

Ay and *has* choked it: for this Morning Sunday 23d—the wretched Man is no more: and only 41 Years old as he told them.

Your Family ever obliging make me the kindest Offers[3]—but why should I shrink from the Sight or Thought of what so soon must be the Situation/of your faithful/ H: L: P.

Do not fright Sir N. Wraxall with his own fine Clothes, but I am pleased to have something to leave as a Present from Sir James Fellowes.

Leak will be a great Loss to me.

Text Hyde Collection. *Address* Sir James Fellowes.

1. Having arrived in Bath on 13 June, AL was "very Ill in Danger" on 19 June. Two days later, HLP wrote in her "Pocket Book": "Leak not safe at all; a raging Rheumatic Fever expected. Doctor Gibbes called. Terror returned, the Man will sure enough die in the House." She was right; Leak died on 23 June and lay "A Corpse in the House of poor H: L: P." She repeated the events of Leak's death in the "Commonplace Book," noting further that he "declared himself upon his Death-bed 41 Years old only, and without a Disease:—that ever I heard of; & yet so dies his *Body.*"

2. Either James Norman (d. 1827), surgeon at 8 New King Street and founder of the Bath Casualty Hospital, Kingsmead Street, or his son, George (1783–1861), who returned to Bath in 1801 as his father's assistant after studying medicine in London.

The younger Norman was to open his own practice by 1817 at 24 New King Street. See Victor Gustave Plarr, *Lives of the Fellows of the Royal College of Surgeons of England,* rev. by Sir D'Arcy Power . . . with the assistance of W. G. Spencer . . . and . . . G. E. Gask, 2 vols. (Bristol: J. Wright and Sons; London: Simpkin, Marshall, 1930), 2:103–4.

3. See HLP to Mrs. or Miss Fellowes, 23 June 1816, below.

TO MRS. OR MISS FELLOWES

Sunday
23 June 1816.

No I thank you dearest Lady—I have had many kind Offers of the same sort—and yours is particularly soothing to me.—but I am at *Rehearsal* when standing by the Thing I must so soon resemble:

Adieu! and accept my sincerest Thanks and true Love to Mrs. Fellowes from Yours ever/ most faithfully/ H: L: P.

It would suit my Affairs very ill *indeed* to leave my House *so*: and I will not leave it. I have seen many more interesting Deaths than *this*—tho' the Man will be a great Loss to me. Adieu

[In the hand of Sir James Fellowes: Her old Steward Leak died in her House and some of Mrs. Piozzi's Friends sent to offer their accommodations to her at such a distressing moment. Her answer to my Mother is curious—]

Text Princeton University Library AM 14675. *Address* Mrs. or Miss Fellowes/ No. 13 Vineyards

JOHN SALUSBURY PIOZZI SALUSBURY TO HESTER LYNCH PIOZZI

Brynbella
June 24th 1816.

My dearest Aunt

gives a better account of herself and I am rejoiced at it—You have indeed suffered much of the sorrows of this life; it would surely be too much, if sickness, for any length of time, was to follow that sorrow; Let us hope for better things—I make no doubt if once you gain sufficient health to allow you to take your usual exercise you will soon recover. Indeed I *am* glad you are better and trust you still continue to mend—I have heard from Dr. Gibbes and return him many thanks. I would not trouble him with any Letter of enquiries particularly as you are better, therefore I must beg you to acknowledge the receipt of it with my sincere thanks—I shall be glad to hear him give me good reasons for being persuaded of your Duration.

It seems an odd fancy of yours, that whenever I express any anxiety about you, you immediately try to get rid of the subject and appear fearful of my even supposing you to be unwell—indeed I do not see the good sense of that, surely it is better for me to know the truth, than live in a dream—suppose *I* was ill— you would not be at all pleased if I was to keep you ignorant of the circumstance.

Now dearest Aunt let us throw aside this indiscribable nothing that seems to have haunted us since we parted; we used to be very friendly and why not continue so? Why allow that confidence, which we have so long enjoyed in each other, to appear as if lessened when in fact it is not? believe me I have still the same friendship and regard for you as ever and am proud to assure you that I am and ever shall be/ Your affectionate and sincere Nephew/ *J: Salusbury Piozzi Salusbury.*

Harriet keeps pretty well, but begins to complain—she sends her affectionate love and wishes to know what we must call the next Baby. What think you of Angelina—? Adieu.

Text Ry. 591.9 *Address* Mrs. Piozzi/ Bath. *Postmark* DENBIGH < >.

TO ANNA MARIA PEMBERTON

Bath
[ca. 24] June 1816.[1]

If my dear prudent Mrs. Pemberton will consent to read this Letter quietly with her Son Salusbury, and say nothing on the Subject to her amiable Daughter—She shall hear no *un*interesting Story. My last Letters to Brynbella *said* that Leak my Steward, was come from Streatham Park with his Account Books &c.—and some Trifles on which I set Particular Value——The Letters said *True*. It was *true* also that we settled the Balance finally and amicably, and that on The 13: Day of June I paid him up every Penny with and by an *Order* Stamp on Hammersley for 800£——much of it Money lent me for Repairs: in Consideration of which he gave me a Stamped Receipt *in full of All Demands*.

On the Tuesday following, Leak heard of some Farm in the Neighbourhood took a Horse and went to see it—Caught Cold—we believe by neglecting to change his Things, and when he came next Morning to describe the Place to me seemed unwell; walked to the Parlour which his Family occupied because the last Lodger was gone out: said something to *them*, and dropt down Motionless as a Stone. Dr. Gibbes who was in Attendance upon *me*—saw *him* directly; and called Mr. Norman to assist:—

Every thing was done of Course, and every thing was done *in vain*. Leak lived but 50 Hours, and is a Corpse in the house *now*.

He made no Will——and I make few Excuses for troubling you with Stories of my Servants, All sudden Deaths are put in Public Newspapers——and I felt as if I *ought* to prevent Surprizes, Enquiries &c. he died on Saturday *Night*, The shortest Night in the Year. His Widow screams and cries—and I suppose will miscarry. She says however that all he died possessed of, is *hers* and *only hers*; notwithstanding they have a fine Boy a Year old: for that She took Care to have every thing settled on herself before Marriage——a prudent Consideration.—— I have written however to Mr. Windle to know how and to whom my Money must be paid,[2] and shall tell it to Salusbury on the other Side this Letter.

Mrs. Gibbes mean while, and Mrs. Fellowes; and Mrs. Thomas,[3] and Miss Williams—*all* poured in their kind Invitations for me to sleep in any of their Houses rather than my own, with very polite Attention indeed.

I shall not however *quit my Post*——I have many little Valuables which must be watched over, whilst these bustling People are about: and as to starting at the Sight of what I must so soon be myself, that would be foolish *indeed* in/ Dear Madam/ Your Obedient and Affectionate Servant/ H: L: Piozzi.

Best and kindest Regards and tenderest Wishes to the Expectant Lady—A pretty Black-eyed Boy will now be coming very soon to Brynbella.

Text Ry. 594.17.

1. HLP wrote this letter soon after AL's death.
2. Windle wrote on 24 June (Ry. 609.15): "I have had the highest opinion of [Leak]—I am glad

however that you had previously settled with him and took his receipt in full of all demands—his wife I dare say will see that your Draft is paid—at any rate You are not answerable for any further demand, should any be made—as to the Widow's Notion of all his property being hers, she will find herself mistaken in because if he left no will she has her third and the Children the other Two—however this is for More Consideration."

3. For Susanna Isabella Thomas, née Harington, see HLP to SL, 15 November [1788], n. 4.

TO SIR JAMES FELLOWES

Bath
Wednesday 26: June 1816.

It is impossible my Dear Sir for any Thing to be more kind than you and your charming Family. But what should I run away for? or what should I run from? Poor Leak never injured me, nor I him——We sleep quietly enough under the same Roof——The Widow is my Scourge: pressing for prompt,—ay *Immediate* Payment of the Draft her Husband Poor Fellow! never *Indorsed:*—and if he *had* you know, She must prove herself his Heir, and take out proper Letters of Administration before it would be prudent in me to pay the Money.

Hammersley[1] and Windle[2] both applaud the Step I took in *Stopping Matters*——Tho' when She found me resolute, Hysterics and Shrieks,——(deferred till then;) followed; and shock my *Nerves*; but not my *Intentions*. I shall pay nothing to a Person who cannot give me *legal Discharge,* nor Subject my Executors to the Demands of her Son 21 Years hence for 800£ paid to *his Mother*—— and the Interest.

Not I truly. Meanwhile I sincerely believe the Woman will miscarry—and Doctor Fisher thinks so too:[3] Gibbes and Norman dare not come near the House—She says in her Ravings they killed her Husband—I think with 3 Grains of James's Powders——but whether She has Children or no Children, She firmly trusts that all his little Property is *hers*: and says She secured it before Marrying him——A prudent Shropshire Lass! was She not?

Adieu! my poor little Mansion of Misery is like a Fair—Buryers of the Dead, and bringers-forth of the Living.

Poor Leak's Funeral will be the 9th out of this Street since it was Inhabited by/ Dear Sir James Fellowes's,/ Much Obliged and faithful/ H: L: P.

Supply the Compliments and Kind Wishes——my Pen and my Spirits are tired.

[Several lines of faded writing.]

Text Princeton University Library 14675. *Address* Sir James Fellowes.

1. Hugh Hammersley had written on 25 June (Ry. 609.16): "As . . . your accounts had been considerable with [Leak] you must consider yourself fortunate in having settled them, for with his representatives it would have been a troublesome and disagreable business to you.

"You have been quite right in refusing to give the widow the value of the bill which she of course holds: if she be a respectable person administration will be given to her, and she can then endorse the bill and receive the value for it. I conclude Leak had not put his name to it.

"I have seen your Solicitor this morning who will also write to you upon this subject. . . .

"P.S. I have given orders to stop the bill in case the widow should try to get value for it before the necessary forms have been gone through."

2. Windle wrote again on 25 June (Ry. 609.17):

"Pray where is the Draft in question?—if in the hands of the Widow she *cannot* endorse it until *she has administered,* and then on your revoking your orders at Hammersleys the Bill will be paid— I advise you not to Comply with any demand she makes for it is not at present in her Power to give any legal discharge—She had better apply to some respectable Attorney in Bath who will show her the propriety of this Doctrine—I have been at Hammersleys this Morning and they I find have had a Letter from you and will not pay the Bill should it be presented—really this Womans *Interest* surpasses her *Grief* so much that one is led to suspect the latter a little—and particularly after such a friend as You have been to the deceased."

3. For Samuel Fisher, M.D., see HLP to AL, 14 January 1816, n. 9. HLP's "Pocket Book" shows that Fisher attended Ann Leak on 23, 26, and 30 June: HLP paid him £1 for each visit.

TO JOHN SALUSBURY PIOZZI SALUSBURY

Bath
Saturday [28] June 1816.

My dearest Salusbury

The Solemn Stillness that prevails in our little Mansion, from whence a Corpse—somewhat too long kept—has so immediately been driven; gives me a quiet hour to reply to your last agreeable Letter. I hope the new Comer will be a famous Fellow, and do honour to the Names of Owen and of Salusbury[1]— but if another Female should appear, I like the Appellation Angelina vastly:— perhaps 'tis smoother than Angelica upon the whole, and equally preserves dear *dearest* Uncle in our Remembrance. Surely as *his* Representative my Salusbury shall never need to *dun* me for Affection——all that can be felt, I feel for him; and 'tis my Pride to hear that he deserves it.——Yet there are many ways of shewing Regard, without that unlimited Confidence which existed between us when I was the only Connexion that tied you to an Island where Nature had given you none: You have *now* Natural Duties; natural Connexions with Friends of *Your own* making, *Your own* choosing:—Babies of your own begetting, by a Lady You preferred—and justly——(I am well perswaded)—to many Intimate Acquaintance of ours——Dear Love! God preserve your precious Health for them and for yourself: but can you fancy me coming if you *were* a little sick—— to rant and rave and intrude upon a whole Family's Affairs with *my* Afflictions, *my* Remedies et cetera——as I should inevitably have done had it pleased God to send You bad Health when under my immediate Care and Responsibility?—

If you should do The same by Hester Maria after She is married to an Irish Peer, and has caught Cold in a Dublin Ball-Room, as you do now when her Teeth teize her,—I think his Lordship and his Bride 15 Years hence——would be much perplexed and confounded.

Doctor Gibbes will be happy to see You, and I shall be *very* happy *indeed*: my

Spirits would have recovered better but for this last untoward Accident——which really makes one shudder at the very Word Duration when applied to the Term of human Life: My Letter to Mrs. Pemberton contains the Tale I allude to; and till You and She have read that Letter together, The Subject shall not be touched upon. I am certainly alive and mending——and in Correspondence with the great Mr. Wilberforce—[2]The most important Communication I have to *confide.*

My Looks meanwhile, haggard and ferocious; are more altered than even my Temper and my Health.—When Your Wife and Child are safe—come and see:—but if you come soon do not drive up to the House, but send for me to you at the Elephant and Castle just out of Queen Square.[3]

A young Man fresh and full from a distant County has Chance to catch a putrid Fever in *this* unlucky House. Do not risk it dearest; but mind what I say, and take Care of yourself. I shall be glad to shew you my new Habitation, and am only sorry it wants cleaning up after the last Inhabitants—Sir Marcus and Lady Somerville.[4] Besides it is not mine Yet till August, and *these* Apartments (where all my Valuables are deposited:) I am tied to, till next September: your coming will be very convenient to me, and very comfortable, when I know you can come with a clear Conscience; and leave Harriet safe in her Bed: and when we have fumigated the Places all about.

Mrs. Corbet and her Daughter have just sent to ask after me;[5] every body is civil and attentive: They know and feel for my Embarrassment.

Cecilia wrote me a very pleasant Letter, I sent her the least dull Answer in my Power; but my Recovery is much advanced since our Correspondence——She made some Allusion to the Heskeths, but I did not understand her.[6]

God send an easy Labour and happy Delivery to dearest Harriet,——but indeed my Heart does wish for a Black-Eyed Boy. Mrs. Pemberton must accept best Compliments and truest Regards from her affectionate Servant, and My dearest Salusbury's ever/ attached and fond and faithful/ H: L: P.

Is not Haymaking very late? I'm sure you never tell me anything.

Text Ry. 589.333. *Address* John Salusbury Piozzi Salusbury Esq./ Brynbella/ near Denbigh/ North Wales. *Postmark* BATH 28 JU 28 1816.

1. The third child of JSPS and HMS was John Owen Salusbury (1818–1833).
2. For William Wilberforce, see HLP to Sophia Byron, 29 June 1788, n. 10. He had been in Bath to visit his father-in-law Isaac Spooner (b. 1736), who died on 1 June. See *GM* 86, pt. 1 (1816): 571; *Salopian Journal*, 5 June. On 23 June HLP noted in her "Pocket Book" that she had received "a Letter from the great Wilberforce."
   Clement Francis, in a letter of 19 June 1816 (Ry. 584.179), informed HLP that "Mr. Wilberforce desired me to state how sorry he was, that he was absolutely prevented from visiting You. *Twice* he left his own lodgings and was carried home again by the arrival of Relations whom he was obliged to see on so distressing an occasion; when he had nearly arrived at your doors; and afterwards was suddenly summoned to Town by Parliamentary duty."
3. The Elephant and Castle, on Monmouth Street, was owned by Emma Springford (d. ca. 1839) and was one of Bath's leading "family" hotels.
4. Marcus Somerville (ca. 1775–1831), fourth baronet (ca. 1800), M.P. for county Meath, had married in 1801 Mary Anne Gorges Meredyth (fl. 1780–1823).

5. HLP refers to friends of the Pembertons at Longnor; specifically to Anne (fl. 1781–1850), daughter of William Pigott (d. 1811), rector of Chetwynd and Edgmond, Salop (1779–1811). On 19 February 1806, she became the second wife of John Corbet (1751–1817) of Sundorne, M.P. for Shrewsbury (1774–80), high sheriff of Salop (1793). From this marriage, there were four sons and a daughter, Annabella (d. 1864). Mrs. Corbet and Annabella lived at 15 Catherine Place.

6. See HLP to JSPS, 23 December 1813, n. 3.

TO MARY FELLOWES

Bath
5: July 1816.

When my dear Mrs. Fellowes kindly Sent down to ask for a Letter last Night I was very ill indeed—Spasms:—such as Sir James remembers my plaguing him about, Once at Bath and once at Blake's Hotel: They yielded however to Rhubarb and Laudanum, and here I am again—*living*, while Young and healthy People die. Miss Williams has lost her pretty Niece Katherine Griffiths—I am really very sorry, because She feels it so forcibly.[1]

My own Nerves are annoyed and shaken by this Wayward Widow, who will not quit the House without her Money; and who will not entitle herself to receive the Money by administering to her husband's Effects:—because She professes to have a previous Settlement made to her under her Maiden Name which precludes all Necessity of such Expence.[2]

Mr. Windle my Solicitor however bids me not pay her, as She cannot give me Legal Release till She has administered.[3] So we lead wretched Lives—undecided, but not undismayed; for She frighted the poor little Household in such a Manner Two days ago, We thought She must have a Strait Wastecoat.

Meanwhile my dear Friends—happy Creatures! are enjoying themselves in Gloucester Place, and planning new Beauties at Adbury Hall:[4] I am counting the Days for Mrs. Salusbury to be delivered and then her Husband will come and fetch me a nice Frisk into Wales, and I hope bring me back safe to No. 8[5]— all my Difficulties over. But oh, that this Woman would enable herself to be paid! for there lies her Money at Hammersley's useless to every body but *him*;— and the very Name of a Banking House in these Days, keeps me in a fever.[6]

Beg of Sir James Fellowes dear Madam to tell me if what I hear be true; that there has been an Act of Parliament passed lately—making all previous Deeds Settlements &c. meant clearly to avoid the Law—amenable to Punishment by Forfeits.[7] *Is it so*? That Your Son, is my *Oracle* I consider as my best Claim to the very kind Friendship the Doctor and dear Mrs. Fellowes have uniformly shown to Their very much Obliged and truly faithful/ H: L: Piozzi.

Lady Fellowes and Miss Fellowes must accept my finest and tenderest Regards.

How did poor dear Miss Fellowes bear her Journey?——She will write to me I am sure—when She *can*.

Text Hyde Collection. *Address* Mrs. Fellowes/ Gloucester Place.

1. For Catherine Griffith, who died aged twenty, see HLP to Ly W, 21 March 1815, n. 6.
2. According to HLP's "Pocket Book," dated 16 July: "Mrs. Leak departed with her Train of Devourers."
3. Windle on 4 July (Ry. 609.23) wrote: "This Widow of Leaks is I think the most perverse woman ever created—but I am rejoiced to find you adhere to your resolution. . . . You have nothing to do with her, she has your Draft, and has only to Administer and then endorse it, but I would get rid of her . . . if you Cannot get her out of Your House, I would leave it myself and this way at least put an end to her Cries."
4. JF and his bride were temporarily living at Gloucester Place, London; Adbury House was his wife's family home.
5. HLP's "Pocket Book" indicates that she signed the lease for 8 Gay Street on 22 June.
6. Between 1814 and 1817, over eighty banks failed. See also HLP to JSPS, 27 March 1816, n. 3.
7. HLP refers to the recent act of 56 George III. 102: "To amend the Act of the 53rd of his present majesty, intituled 'An Act for the Relief of Insolvent Debtors in England'; and to give further powers to the court appointed by the said act." See *Parliamentary Debates* 34 (1816): 1131–32.

According to *The Times* (17 July), the amended act provided that a person who contracts a debt or enters into an agreement "without any fair prospect or probable means of paying such debts, or fulfilling such engagements" shall not be entitled to his discharge without the creditor's consent.

TO SIR JAMES FELLOWES

Bath
Tuesday 9: July *1816.*

Not yet forgotten by Dear Sir James Fellowes, his old Friend hastens to inform him that She *does* mend; slowly, and heavily; but yet She feels climbing up, rather than sliding down the Hill.

Mrs. Leak seems to have taken Root here—like the Workmen at Adbury— and for the Same Reason doubtless; but Mr. Windle, (you always loved Windle;) says She *must* administer, or forfeit 100£ so we shall get rid of her some day.[1]

Salusbury's Arrival would be very welcome indeed, and when he has put his Lady and Baby to Bed I shall expect him:—he knows who will pay the Expences of his Journey,—*now.*

Your kind Brother Dorset and Mrs. Fellowes will give us a Gay Day at their Tivoli when he comes; but I dare not yet venture on Dinner Parties tho' less distant.

Would not you have been sorry for me when I could not Walk? But blessed be God I have got my Limbs again without ever learning how I lost Them.

So Sheridan is going[2] and Mrs. Jordan gone:[3] *In* Want both of Them, tho' perhaps not actually *of* Want—either of them: Shocking enough! And Mary Mayhew dying, and Miss Katherine Griffith dead. Equo pede pulsat[4] the old *Enemy* Death—[5]

> Le Pauvre en sa Cabane ou le Chaume le couvre
> Et Sujet a ses Loix:
> Et la Garde qui veille—à la Porte du Louvre,
> N'en defend pas nos Rois.[6]

Well! but in the Mean Time Mr. Mangin is married to 26,000£ and a *Young*, if not a conspicuously *fair* Lady:[7] and Horace Twiss is Elected Member of Parliament.[8] So these are on the Gay Side of Life.

Pray, do not Gentlemen Swear to 300£ o'Year Independent as a Qualification?—when I was a Canvasser of Elections I was told so—[9] but Oaths were then thought of very differently from what they are now.

The Misses here are all reading Glenarvon—[10]

"*A monstrous Tale of Things Impossible*"[11]—at least one hopes so. I have finished it, at last—tho' not comprehended it: and can only say with King Lear

"An Ounce of Civet good Apothecary; to Sweeten my Imagination."[12]

My Connection with No. 8 is only for a Year. If it should please God that my fragile Life might last till August 1817—and if I should find the Place *then*, as agreeable as I now fancy it—The Lease will be cheaper and shorter, and more within my Compass: and perhaps as good a Thing to Successors as so much bought into the 3 Per Cents, nor need I much to think on *that* Side my head—if it suits me. Melancholy however are the Accounts of Gentlemen possessing Landed Property; and unless *Horace Twiss* saves the Nation, I *do* think 'tis in no prosperous Case.

Your Dear Father and Mother meanwhile, are happier than the very Poets could dream for them: if Miss Fellowes would but get quite well; I think this World has no more to give them. You dear Sir must present them my truest Regards and make it my Request to Lady Fellowes that She will accept every good Wish from the hand of/ Yours and her Ladyship's ever/ H: L: Piozzi.

I feel sorry the Parliament is broken up; for laugh as one may—in that House does reside the united Wisdom of the Nation—[13] Wisdom says Solomon crieth in the Streets,[14] but no Man heareth:—I think in *London* Streets, the Horn Blowers and the Flowers in Blow, contrive to drown her Voice.[15]

Text Hyde Collection. *Address* Sir James Fellowes.

1. Windle wrote to HLP on 5, 6, and 12 July 1816 (Ry. 609.18, 24, 28) explaining that AL's wife must file an administration, and that "the Act of Parliament expressly attaches a Penalty of £100 as well as ten pounds per Cent on the Duty against her if she touches the Money . . . *before she* administers" (Ry. 609.24). On 12 July Windle enclosed a copy of his correspondence to Ann Leak, in which he stated: "Mrs. Leak, If I understand you correct it is to induce me to advise Mrs. Piozzi to assist in defrauding Government of its Duty. . . ." Informing Ann Leak of the £100 penalty, Windle said of HLP: ". . . now as that Lady settled with your Husband and took his receipt she can have nothing to do with you on this subject.—If he neglected to endorse the Bill that is no fault of hers and you *must* administer to entitle you to do so." AL's administration was filed in Bath on 31 July 1816 (P.R.O., Prob. 6/ 192).

2. R. B. Sheridan had been confined to his home at 17 Savile Row, London, during the spring and was to die there on 7 July. The *Bath and Cheltenham Gazette* for 3 July reported that Sheridan "still lives, but his weakness increases. His shivering fits return daily, and his nights are more restless: he passed a very bad night last night."

3. Mrs. Dorothea Jordan died on 3 July 1816 at St. Cloud, France.

4. Horace, *Odes*, 1.4.13.

5. 1 Corinthians 15:26.

6. "Consolation à M. Du Perier," in *Poésies de Malherbe*, ed. C. H. Lefebvre de Saint-Marc (Paris: Barbou, 1757), 50.

7. At Queen Square Chapel, Bath, on 1 July, EM married as his second wife, Mary (1791–1845), daughter and heir of Lieutenant Colonel Samuel Nangreave (ca. 1756–1815), late of Bond Street, Bath, and the East India Company. See *GM* 86, pt. 2 (1816):80; "Bath Abbey Burial Register," C.R.O., Somerset; *Bath and Cheltenham Gazette*, 1 November 1815. As HLP noted in the "Commonplace Book" under *Marriage:* EM "has . . . made the very best marriage for himself, that his best friends could have wished."

8. During July, Horace Twiss and William Taylor Money (1769–1840) were involved in "the severest parliamentary contest ever remembered" for the borough of Wootton Bassett. After three days of polling, Money was declared the winner, 118 votes to 113 (*Courier*, 10 July 1816). HLP's "Pocket Book" entry of 7 July states that she had learned of Twiss's supposed victory from the Miss Glovers. The Glovers's source may have been the *Bath Chronicle* (4 July 1816), which had reported that "so decided a majority have declared for Mr. Twiss, that Mr. Money has yielded his pretensions and quitted the town. The election will take place on Friday [6 July]." Twiss was to sit in Parliament for Wootton Bassett (1820–30), Newport, Hants. (1830–31), and Bridport (1835–37).

9. HLP refers to her canvassing for HT, who was M.P. for Southwark for several elections from 1765 to 1780.

10. Lady Caroline Lamb, née Ponsonby (1785–1828), *Glenarvon*, 3 vols. (London: Printed for H. Colburn, 1816), a *roman à clef* dealing with the Holland House and Devonshire House circles, featured Byron and the author as its hero and heroine, Glenarvon and Calantha. Published in May, it was to reach a third edition by August.

11. The phrase "of things impossible" and variations may be found in Young's *Night Thoughts*, 1.163–65 and 6.471; in his play *The Brothers*, 4.283; Thomas Southern, or Southerne, *Isabella; or, The Fatal Marriage*, 4.2; in Garrick's version (1757), p. 39.

12. *King Lear*, 4.6.130–31.

13. Parliament had been prorogued from 2 July to 24 August. See *GM* 86, pt. 2 (1816):70.

14. Proverbs 1:20–24.

15. HLP refers to the growing reform movement, which included a meeting of the Hampden Club at the Freemasons' Tavern, Lincoln's Inn Fields, on 15 June. Chaired by Sir Francis Burdett, the meeting was held on the anniversary of the Magna Carta and advertised as: "Reform of Parliament—Liberty and Property being obviously endangered, because of the Commons not being duly represented, of Parliaments having an unconstitutional continuance, of a thousand millions of debt having been incurred since the Revolution, and of the melancholy result, that for paying the interest of such a debt so contracted, the people are oppressed with an intolerable weight of taxes; and likewise because of an immense Standing Army in time of peace . . ." (*The Times*, 14 and 15 June). The featured speaker was Major John Cartwright (1740–1824), who, despite losing his commission in the Nottingham militia in 1792, continued to use his military title. A founder of the Society for Constitutional Information (1780) and longtime political activist, he spoke in favor of annual parliaments and a rate-payer franchise. Meanwhile, hungry colliers from Bilston had marched on London (*The Times*, 6 July 1816).

TO ANN FELLOWES

Bath
18: July 1816

Your Letter Dear Miss Fellowes came to my hand late last Night. I do not this Morning believe this the *last* Day of our foolish and wicked World, but I think it the *worst* Day I ever saw at this Season of the Year.[1] All are uneasy about the Ruin it is causing; and tho' nothing impels English People into Church but a famous Preacher; many feel Alarm at the Effect this extraordinary Weather will have on the Hay and Corn.

Sir James will hear much concerning it when he visits Adbury:—but our

Dividends unmutilated by Income Tax will make us amends, and keep us in Good humour for a short, a *very* short Time.

Meanwhile Your dear Father and Mother are happy; and our Friends here at *pretty* Tivoli would be so, but for the Necessity of Fires in July, and the Oddity of living enveloped with cold Mist, unable to enjoy their beautiful Spot—or see fifty Yards from it.

Death still holds a Court for himself here in New King Street: Whence poor old Colonel Erving will be carried to Walcot in a Day or Two: I shook Hands with him on *Monday* Morning—and passed him in a Chair going out. On *Wednesday* Morning—much *earlier* than that hour, he was a Corpse; without any previous Illness:—except mere old Age. Dr. Fellowes remembers him in America.[2]—

Of Mary Mayhew I hear nothing—but conclude her Veins must be almost empty of Blood by now: That those of her Friends should still beat with Hope;—is—if true, surprising.

You must tell dear Sir James, that Fanny Mostyn Edwards is going to bestow her 2000£ o'Year Estate, on a very worthy Young Man indeed;[3]—a distant Relation of mine; so you see the Marriages and Deaths go on (as we are told they will do,) to the End of the World.

Have you read Glenarvon, and its Key?[4] I hope some newer Foolery has taken up the Londoners' Attention by now. We Bath Folks are content to admire Lady Loudons Moira's beautiful Asiatic;[5] not having Lady Holland's Atheist to stare at,[6]—but *any* thing *will* do. Is Lord Byron really coming home again so soon? He should have <stayed> had it been only in Policy.[7]

But I am detaining you with Questions concerning People and Things by this Time wholly forgotten among *Your* Folks. Distance between Friends produces that certain Vexation; One talks to them on worne-out Subjects always; and that is the grand Cause of Letters being generally insipid——unless they tell of one's *Health:* and I think Yours and Mine Dearest Miss Fellowes, have been long absent from their Owners;——Yours only *Mislaid* I hope,——but *Lost*, and of no Value to those who find it: is the once very strong and active Constitution of/ Your truly faithful Servant and Obliged Friend/ H: L: Piozzi.

If Lady Willoughby and Lord Gwydir recollect me—[8]jettez moi a leurs Pieds, and Farewell!

Make my truest Regards to all the dear Family: I am glad Lady Fellowes is sick *only* in a Morning: 'Tis a Complaint will do her good.[9]

Text Spencer Library, University of Kansas. *Address* Miss Fellowes.

1. In her "Pocket Book" for 18 July, HLP noted "Thunder and Lightning. A *very* cold rough Day, like the end of October." According to the *Bath and Cheltenham Gazette* (24 July), the temperature during the week hovered in the lower sixties Fahrenheit.

2. A retired colonel in the British army, John Erving (ca. 1727–1816) of 48 New King Street died on 17 July.

Born in Boston, Erving during the American Revolution had "sacrificed a splendid fortune and an elevated station to the loyalty which he bore to his lawful sovereign" (*Bath Herald*, 27 July). Dr. Fellowes had served in the same war as a military surgeon to the British army.

3. The marriage was never realized; Frances is identified in her father's will as a spinster. For her father, Thomas Mostyn Edwards, see HLP to AL, 8 February 1813, n. 3.

4. See HLP to JF, 9 July 1816, n. 10; to Ly W, 22 October 1816, n. 8.

5. Flora Mure-Campbell (1780–1840), *suo jure* countess of Loudoun (1786) had married in July 1804 Francis Rawdon-Hastings, second earl of Moira, who had been appointed governor general of Bengal and commander in chief of the forces in India on 18 November 1812.

For Lord Moira, see HLP to PSP, 19 September 1793, n. 10.

6. Elizabeth (Webster), née Vassall (1770–1845), had married in 1797 Henry Richard Fox (1773–1840), third baron Holland (1774). She presided over a literary and political salon at Holland House in Kensington. A Whig and skeptic, she had a so-called "pet atheist," the Scottish John Allen (1771–1843), M.D. and writer, who was engaged to accompany the Hollands on their tour through Spain in 1802. He remained an intimate of the Holland House circle for the rest of his life, acting as family librarian and being treated by Lady Holland—in the words of Macaulay—"no better than a negro slave." See the Earl of Ilchester, *The Home of the Hollands, 1605–1820* (New York: Dutton, 1937), 176–81; Hayward, 2:341n.

7. HLP reports unfounded rumor. Having signed the final deed of separation from Lady Byron on 21 April, Byron left England a few days later, never to return. Far from coming home, he was—according to *The Times* (6 July)—"now one of the great number of English who reside in the vicinity of Geneva."

8. For Baron Gwydir, see HLP to JSPS, 6 January 1815, n. 14; for Lady Willoughby, see HLP to Ly W, 29 March 1815, n. 5.

9. JF's wife was pregnant but lost the child. See HLP to JF, 5 March 1817, n. 2.

TO SIR JAMES FELLOWES

Bath
Monday 22 July—1816.

It was very pretty and very kind in you my Dear Sir to recollect an old Friend so, but you are a charming Family—and Miss Fellowes sent me Word the other Day that H:L:P. was not forgotten.

Here is terrifying Weather indeed—one whole Week have the Meadows over against my Window been completely drenched in Rain to the utter Ruin of the fine Hay which covered them—so there lie the Hopes of the Farmer—and such a Thunderstorm on the 18th as I have seldom seen in England.

Bessy Jones observed the Fire Ball in the *Street*, and Report soon told us the frightful Effects left behind it at poor Windsor's—here in James Street.[1] You must remember to have Copper—not Iron Bell Wires at Adbury; nothing else saved the Lives of those pretty Children: *I* live to the fields You know, and escaped all the Wonders—nor could *quite* believe till Mrs. Windsor shewed me her Floor burned—in Places;—her Wall pushed in—and her Plate Warmer in the Kitchen, perforated very curiously indeed: and all this on a *Cold Rainy Day*.

Worse Storms tear the Atmosphere to Pieces in Italy every Summer Evening, yet I never but once heard of any Life lost or endangered—but then they have no Newspapers—so much may happen without one's hearing of it: It is however worth the while to put up Copper Bellwires.

Miss Williams shewed me a Letter from Lady Trimblestone[2] that Says Mary Mayhew is getting quite well, by taking the Juice of Red Nettles!! I never heard of red Nettles before; and make no doubt but that a few Pebblestones boyled in

Milk would be just as efficacious—but *Hope* is drawn with an *Anchor* always, and Common Sense is never strong enough to weigh it up.

The Mischief is, We seldom drop, or cast it in the proper Harbour;—it would then keep steady, and deserve the name the Romans gave it—*Anchora Sacra*.

Apology;—This is written Sunday Night, tho' meant to be Sent in the Morning.

Meanwhile if Nettles would cure leanness—how fat I should grow! For I have been finely stung of late: Leak's Widow has left me however, and I have left Windle to finish the Battle for me—It is very desirable She should be prevailed on to administer, and by that means render herself capable of granting me *Legal Release:* her Son else, or her Second Husband may give my Successors a World of Trouble, and She has not yet complied—Tho' I trust She cannot help wanting the Money, and tho' There is a forfeiture of 100£ hanging over her in Terrorem; if She flies in the Face of this Act of Parliament.——On the Deed obtained before Marriage, She depends; and if that proves good, I shall be very Sorry.

Our Friend Mr. Hammersley has been playing Boy's Tricks he tells me, and hurt his Knee quite Seriously by jumping: when you call in Pallmall on Your own Affairs—do mention mine, and ask if this perverse Woman has got her 800£ yet. Was not it comfortable for me to receive the whole Dividend—so long sequestered for Debt, and mutilated by Taxation?

I had not a Notion of their paying the whole *clear,* and felt a most agreeable Surprize at Seeing the Old Sum of 777£. 19. 6d. as it used to be 20 or 30 Years ago.

I am glad to hear Lady Fellowes has no Complaints but those She will soon get accustomed to, and which do the Constitution more real Good than harm.—The Event can hardly take Place till the last Weeks of this Year I suppose, or first Weeks of the next—so I shall probably not live to see You in the happy Character of Father: but remember my Words, or rather those of old ArchBishop Leighton;[3] when Speaking of Education—he Said: "Fill you the Bushel with good Wheat yourself;—because then Fools and Foes will have less Room to cram in *Chaff.*" Nothing *better has been ever said* upon the Subject.

Adieu! My Comfort is, this Nonsense costs you nothing;—and you will know how to Get more Such Stuff when You wish it, from Dear Sir Your old and faithful Friend/H:L:Piozzi.

Did you go to Sheridan's Funeral? You will see much concerning him in my Scrap Book.

Make my True love and best Regards to Those you love best, I sent a Packet of Compliments by Miss Fellowes—She appears as its better I think <else> her Letter to me <　　　>.

Text Hyde Collection. *Address* Sir James Fellowes.

1. The *Bath Chronicle* for 25 July 1816 reported that "In the forenoon of Thursday last, during a violent storm, a sudden and tremendous peal of thunder, accompanied by a vivid flash of lightning, burst over the city, when the following awful circumstances occurred at the house of Mr. Windsor, musical professor in James-street." A description much like HLP's follows. The story continues: "Dr. Wilkinson, who examined the house shortly after the occurrence of this phaenomenon," gives a scientific explanation and concludes that "These phaenomenon illustrate the superior conducting

powers of copper to iron; and point out the propriety of having bell-wires made thicker than common, and of copper; it was the contiguity of three copper wires which contributed much to the safety of Mr. Windsor's house." HLP described the "Ball of Fire, which actually rolled down Seymour Street" and "burst in Mrs. Windsor's House" on 21 July 1816 under "Last Day" in her "Commonplace Book." She also mentions the event briefly under "Lightning" a few pages later.

2. Probably Maria Theresa, née Kirwan (d. 1824), wife of John Thomas Barnewall, fifteenth baron Trimlestown.

3. For Robert Leighton, archbishop of Glasgow, see HLP to Clement Francis, [23] July 1816, n. 2.

TO CLEMENT FRANCIS

Bath
[23] July 1816.[1]

My dear Mr. Francis's very kind and Christian-like Consolations are not lost on his much obliged Friend; and the Books are almost exclusively my Favourites. Leighton's little Essay on the four Logical Causes, has really few Equals, and his Life is most interesting and extraordinary.[2]—But Life and Death too, are Strange Things: We have been looking on them, and looking for them pretty near 6000 Years, and can hardly understand them at last.

Poor Leak is a heavy Loss to me, and his Widow is my Scourge. She—and her Friends for her, wish to seduce me to pay her the 800£ without her administering to her Husband's effects; because Administration is expensive, and because She professes to have secured herself by a Marriage Settlement, entitling her to all he should die possessed of, under her Maiden Name Anne Glover.[3] Mr. Windle my Solicitor bids me *not* pay her till She has administered, for that *till then* She can give me no *Legal Release:* and some People here assure me, that Deeds—formed in order to elude the Law incur forfeits—*deservedly* without Doubt; and I shall commit no such Wickedness or Folly as complying with her Demand. Here however She remains, in this Tiney House, its Inhabitants *all too few to wait on her.* Shrieking in Hysterics, when She sees my Resolution unmoved by her Tears.

I am indeed cruelly annoyed and nerve-shaken; desirous above all Things to get the Money paid; which is lying at Hammersley's for her; and listening with Horror to these Stories of Bankruptcies which fright every thinking Person.

Her ostensible Friend Mr. Mathews No. 110 Fenchurch Street seems an excellent Man; You have offered your Services so kindly Dear Sir, you would perhaps be obliging enough to call on him and explain to him the Impropriety of their Request, and the Madness it would be in me to comply with it.

God knows the Sum would never have been what it *is*, had I conjectured what was coming: My Partiality was for Leak always, not for his Wife; and when my Executors see how much Was paid him beyond his strict Demand——They will condemn my Generosity, and find the Expences of Administration already liberally discharged——Tell Mr. Matthews so. And now recollect your own friendly Offers of Service, and pardon my taking the Liberty to employ you. My Solicitor is Mr. Windle No. 1 John Street Bedford Row: You would perhaps go between Mr. Matthews and him, if they should misunderstand each other: I have the most perfect Reliance on the last named Gentleman's Skill in his Profession, and on his unmerited Attachment/ to the True Interests/ of Dear Sir/ Yours most faithfully/ H: L: Piozzi.

Mr. Wilberforce really does do me infinite Honour, I am at least sensible of it: and feel much Obliged to You and Your Sister for bringing me so *near* to A Character I have been so long straining my Eyes to look up to.

Text Berg Collection, m.b. *Address* Clement Francis Esq.

1. On 23 July HLP noted in her "Pocket Book" that she received "Letters from Clement Francis and Susan Thrale [and] answered them."
2. On 19 June (Ry. 584.179) Francis wrote: "You were so kind as to promise that you would accept the writings of my most favorite Religious Author Archbishop Leighton."
Francis refers to Robert Leighton (1611–84), archbishop of Glasgow (1669–74), a new edition of whose *Genuine Works*, 4 vols. had been published by W. Baynes.
3. Hugh Percy Ridpath (1760–1835), an attorney practicing in Bath (1798–1828), wrote to HLP on Mrs. Leak's behalf on 12 July (Ry. 609.27). The auctioneer, James Matthews, wrote on 2, 4, and 13 July (Ry. 609.19, 21, 29). On 2 July, e.g., he asked HLP to "give Mrs. Leak power to receive the £800 which if you will do before she administers it will save her at least £30 or more the administration will be £22 and other expenses will be at least £10 more and I think under all the circumstances it is no more than right to save that expense if possible." See the *Law List[s]* (1798–1828); "Walcot Burial Register," C.R.O., Somerset.

TO THE REVEREND ROBERT GRAY

Brynbella[1]
19th August 1816.

An intelligent gentleman in the neighbourhood has set my mind easy concerning the abolition of tithes notwithstanding.[2] He says the lay impropriations will save the church,[3] just as the rotten boroughs so complained of in the years 93 and 94, when we were trying to imitate the French Revolution.[4] I showed him the ivy twisting among the stones of his old summer house in the park; and asked if he did not remember the people teizing him (and wisely enough *then*) to cut it away. He neglected it, however, and *now* it holds the little building together; if he cut it out, the whole would fall.

Text Hayward, 2:270.

1. Contrary to HLP's expectations, JSPS failed to come to Bath to escort her to Wales. Instead, on 4 August, HLP, accompanied by Bessy and others, left Bath for Rodborough, where they spent the night. From there, they "ran to Bridgenorth—just 60 miles" and "slept at the Crown." Arriving at Chester on 6 August, HLP was treated by Dr. Thackeray for "Spasms, vomiting &c," but was well enough on 7 August to visit Mrs. Thackeray and Sarah Williams, née Hesketh (d. 1824), Sir John's mother. HLP reached Brynbella on the evening of 8 August and recorded finding "a very agreeable Reception." She spent a month in North Wales before returning to Bath on 13 September. See HLP's "Pocket Book" for this period.

2. On 18 June Sir John Nicholl (1759–1838), M.P. for Great Bedwin, presented to the Commons the report of the select committee charged with studying petitions on tithes that had been sent to Parliament from all over Great Britain and Ireland. The report concluded that "the power of leasing tithes, as it at present by law exists, should not be taken away or diminished" (*Parliamentary Debates,* 34 [1816]:1144–45; *AR* 58 [1816]:441–43).

3. In the "Report from the Select Committee on Tithes" (among sixteen resolutions), it was resolved "that it is expedient to enable ecclesiastical proprietors of tithes to grant leases thereof" with the proviso that "such leases should not exceed 14 years," and that "such leases should only be granted to the proprietors of the land." In the same report, it was further resolved "that the lay-owners of impropriate tithes, being tenants for life and for years . . . have the like power of leasing such tithes for any term not exceeding 14 years." See *AR* 58:441–43.

4. See e.g., the "Debate [21 February 1793] on bringing up the Nottingham Petition for Reform." Signed by about 2,500 residents of the city, the petition stated "that as the constitution now stands, with respect to representation in the parliament, the country is amused with the name of a representation of the people, when the reality is gone; that the right of election had passed away from the people almost altogether . . . that [instead] the right of election should be in proportion to the number of adult males in the Kingdom." During the debate Fox, Grey, and Sheridan defended the petition; Pitt and Burke spoke against it. On the vote, twenty-one were for accepting the petition and 109 against (*Parliamentary History,* 30 [1792–94]:460–67).

TO THE REVEREND JOHN ROBERTS

10th September 1816.

Do not *dear* Mr. Roberts write me down from any *Residence* in Flintshire, where You well know that I do not *reside*—Mrs. Piozzi Bath is sufficient.

Accept my best Thanks for Your kind Wishes, and for your Information concerning אוב Ob.——the Analogy between that and the *Obi* of West India is very curious indeed.[1]

Adieu and believe me Dear Sir/ Yours truly/ H: L: P.

Text Victoria & Albert Museum Library. *Address* Rev: John Roberts/ Tremeircheon.

1. In her *Imperial Bible* (1811), HLP had annotated the phrase "a familiar spirit" in 1 Samuel 28:7 as follows: "אוב Ob or Obi, was the name for a familiar Spirit then; It is the Name *now* in West India an *Obi*. She was called Obi at first from her Inflation as the Pythoness &c. & perhaps from that derives our Word Obesity." In the passage in question, Saul, seeking "a familiar spirit," is seeking a medium. (There is no correlation between Obi or Obeah and "obesity"; see *OED*.)

TO SIR JAMES FELLOWES

Bath
Wednesday 18 September 1816.

It was very delightful to me Dear Sir, very delightful *indeed* with an Emphasis,—as we Cambro Britons express it: to have a Letter from You which had performed So long a Journey,—in such starving Weather; and yet caught no

Cold on the Road. Summer Seems to have kept back till my Arrival hither, where so many Matters waited my Arrangement, that I feel well repaid for my Resistance against the Temptations of Pretty Brynbella and its truly amiable Inhabitants.

The Charms of the Country were however completely centered on our own Domestic Circle; for the Changes in the Neighbourhood by Deaths and Desertions were quite melancholy to review.

Yours and Lady Fellowes's Tour have been grand and gay the while; I can fancy Grimsthorpe Castle and Abbey in its ancient Style of Magnificence particularly interesting; and Lady Willoughby will not suffer the Tenants or Farmers in her Environs I dare Say—to *know*, much less to *Suffer* the Sorrows we have been witnessing.

Your dear Brother Henry comes in while I am writing; with him Mrs. Dorset Fellowes to invite us to Tivoli next Fryday, where we Shall dine and have a nice Party: They were going to the Vineyards when they called.

Now for a little about *Self*. I was caught by the Spasms at Ellesmere and putting four Horses to the Carriage drove on to Dr. Thackeray at Chester—he is an old Acquaintance—Well! He *roughed* me very hard with a Calomel Pill, and kept me a Day from Brynbella: whither I went on, when all was over; but felt horribly Shattered. The good Air and Milk however restored me, and Your Father says how well I look; He kissed me in Upham's Library where we first met,—*defying Scandal and the Morning Post*.

My Looks are meantime a little false, because a Spontaneous Diarrhea has harrassed my Inside these last Two Days, but I took *No. 1. Dear* No. 1. you remember; and am mending.

The best Scraps I could pick up you will read over Leaf. They were written in Imitation of the Greek Verses by Metrodorus or Posiedippus (which was it?) *for* Life, and *against* Life—I read them long ago—translated—in the Adventurer; but cannot recollect what Number they are in—besides that I possess not the Book.[1]

For London
Can we thro' London Streets be led
Without rejoycing as we tread?
The City's Wealth our Eye Surveys,
The Court attracts our lighter Gaze;
Whilst Charity her Arm extends
And Sick and Poor find Hosts of Friends.
Wit sparkles round our Rosy Wine
And Beauty boasts her Charms divine:
Musick prolongs our festive Nights,
And Morning calls to fresh Delights;
A London Residence then give,
For here alone I seem to live.

Against London
Can London Streets by Man be trod

Without repenting on the Road?
Where Nobles whelm'd in Shame or Debt,
And Bankrupts swell each Sad Gazette;
All licens'd Death our Frame attacks,
And to his Aid calls Hosts of Quacks;
False Smiles on Beauty's Face appear,
And Wit—evaporates in a Sneer.
Dangers impede our Day's Delights
And Vermin vex our Sleepless Nights:
From London then, lets quickly fly
In rural Shades to live or die.

After a Dose of London—and then Adbury,—I think you will read these Verses *con Amore.*

Make my best Regards as acceptable as you can to Lady Fellowes; I shall be happy to shew You and her my present habitation and the *Trash Rareties* which I saved out of the Streatham Wreck.

Droppers-In leave me not an Instant—and you know it would require a Week to say how I am feeling in my new house, and how sincerely, Every Feeling centers in the Desire of Seeing You at No. 8 how much Your Kindness shewn at No. 17—engaged the Grateful Friendship of Dear Sir Yours ever/H:L:Piozzi.

Text Hyde Collection. *Address* Sir James Fellowes/ Adbury House/ near Newbury/ Berkshire. *Postmark* <BATH >.

1. HLP has also included these verses in her "Commonplace Book" under "London" with a note: "These verses were written in Imitation of Metrodorus & Posidippus's Lines upon *Life. They* are in the Adventurer; I forget what Number. . . . The Parody runs very close, and is well enough adapted to London——but *these* Lines are own'd by H:L:P." In the margin, she has written "In No. 107." In fact, *Adventurer* 107 (13 November 1753) contains English translations of the epigram by Posidippus and that by Metrodorus from the *Greek Anthology* (9.359, 360). A 1794 edition of the *Adventurer* was lot 146 in the first day's sale of the books from Brynbella (17 September 1823). See *Sale Catalogue* (2).

TO RICHARD DUPPA

No. 8: Gay Street Bath
Thursday 26: September 1816.

Mrs. Piozzi presents her best Compliments, and hopes Mr. Duppa has kindly forgiven her *appearance* of Negligence to his Requests so very obligingly urged.[1] But She was that Moment returned to Bath *sick,* and shaken by a Journey of 400 Miles out and home: had her whole Household to remove from New King Street to this Place; and could not it seems remember even what Day of the Month it was.——She does however recollect that Percy Bishop of Dromore was the Man alluded to in the printed Paper:[2] his Lady lived much with us at Brighthelm-stone, and used (foolishly enough perhaps) to shew us her Husband's Letters.[3]—In one of these he Said "I am enjoying the fall of a murmuring Stream (at *such a Place I forget where;*) but to you who reside close to the roaring Ocean, such Scenery would be insipid."

This our Doctor laughed at, as ridiculous Affectation;—and 'tis plain never forgot it. The Anecdote is worth nothing but as it shews how ill those Succeeded who tried to make Dr. Johnson acquiesce in Praise of anything or anybody—— The famous Story of his telling Lady Cotton—Then *Mrs.* Cotton; that her Pease were fit only for a Pig—was wholly *My fault.* I saw them looking Green and Young, and not having taken any on my own Plate, knew now they were half boiled; and in order to force his Admiration, cried out "are not these Charming Pease Sir?"—They might be perhaps—replied he—*for a Pig.*[4]—Mrs. Langton got just such a Reply when shewing off her Grotto. Would it not (said she) in Summer be a pleasing Retreat Dr. Johnson? I believe it would Madam, was the Doctor's Answer—for a *Toad.*[5]

Will this Trash compensate for my past Carelessness? Far as I am advanced in the Way to another Life, I feel a Desire of obtaining in *this* the Good Will of Mr. Duppa; and remain/ Very Sincerely his Obedient Servant:/ H: L: Piozzi.

Text Hyde Collection.

1. For the discovery of SJ's manuscript probably in 1812 and Duppa's edition of *A Diary of a Journey Into North Wales in the Year 1774*, see HLP to Q, 15 May 1813, n. 5; for Richard Duppa, see HLP to LC, 22 May 1799, n. 8.
The Salopian Richard Duppa had graduated LL.B. in 1814 from Oxford, having previously become a student at the Middle Temple in 1810. On 21, 28 August and 11 September 1816 he had written to HLP to request help in elucidating passages and identifying persons in SJ's Welsh journey, which was printed for Robert Jennings by James Moyes in October 1816. Of this edition, HLP wrote in her "Commonplace Book," ". . . I believe nobody read it except H: L: P."
2. The "printed Paper" is missing. For Thomas Percy, bishop of Dromore, see HLP to LC, 5 March 1792, n. 7. SJ had met Percy in 1756 when he was serving as vicar of Easton Maudit, Northants. and visited the vicarage in 1764.
3. Anne Gutteridge, or Goodriche (ca. 1731–1806), had married Percy in 1759. See *GM* 77, pt. 1 (1807):91. The bishop's letter is missing.
4. SJ and the Thrales had visited Robert Salusbury Cotton and his wife, Frances, née Stapleton, at Llewenny from 28 July to 18 August 1774. See Duppa's edition, pp. 85–86; *Boswell's Johnson,* 5:435–46. For the Cottons, see HLP to Q, 17 September 1794, n. 5.
HLT recorded the incident about the peas in *Thraliana,* 1:167; *Anecdotes,* 63.
5. For Mary Langton, see HLP to LC, 30 September 1796, n. 6. For the incident, see Hayward, 1:295.

TO THE REVEREND ROBERT GRAY

No. 8. Gay Street, Bath,
Fryday, 27th Sept. 1816.

Well! now am I returned to the living world again. What do I hear? and what do I see? I hear of dear Doctor Gray's new book from every creature that can hold one;[1] and I see Buonaparte's fine carriage driven up my street by a surly-looking coachman preceded by a showy cuirrassier, in the armour he wore at Waterloo.[2] First of the book however, because *that* captivates all hearts: the other appanage is itself a captive. The chapter treating of Josephus is the general favourite;[3] how much more must it be mine, who have been myself upon the ground trodden by St. Paul and him.[4] Will you laugh at me for fretting that the Old Prediction of Ocyrrhoe the Centauress is omitted? The expressions are *so* strong.

> 'Aspicit infantem, totique salutifer orbi
> Cresce puer, dixit; tibi si mortalia sæpe
> Corpora debebunt animas, tibi reddere ademptas
> Fas erit.'

And again,

> 'Eque Deo Corpus fies exangue Deusque,
> Qui modo corpus eras; et *bis* tua fata novabis.'[5]

Poets do oft prove prophets, as Shakespeare says of jesters.[6] I have, however, passed my last quarter in a region where neither poesy nor prophecy were thought on, except Nixon the Chesshire fool's prediction that

> 'When kings are dismay'd and princes betray'd,
> Our landlords shall stand with their hats in their hand
> And beg of the tenants to take their land.'[7]

My affairs here being all settled, Streatham Park disposed of, and my poor steward, Leak, being dead, I have got a pretty neat house and decent establishment for a widowed lady, and shall exist a true Bath Cat for the short remainder of my life, hearing from Salusbury of his increasing family, and learning from the libraries in this town all the popular topics—Turks, Jews, and Ex-Emperor Buonaparte, remembering still that now my debts are all paid, and my income set free, which was so long sequestered to pay repairs of a house I was not rich enough to inhabit, and could not persuade my daughters to take from me—

> 'Malice domestic, foreign levy,—nothing
> Can touch me further;'

as Macbeth says of Duncan when he is dead.[8] Things will at worst last *my* time I suppose.

Text Hayward, 2:270–272.

1. *The Connection Between The Sacred Writings And The Literature Of Jewish and Heathen Authors, Particularly That Of The Classical Ages, Illustrated, Principally With A View To Evidence In Confirmation Of The Truth Of Revealed Religion* (London: Printed by R. and R. Gilbert, St. John's-Square, Clerkenwell, for the Author, and Sold by F. C. and J. Rivington, 1816).
2. "Open for a Few Days Only in Willis's Auction Room, Milsom Street, Bath, Under the Sanction

of Government, Bonaparte's Costly and Curious Military Carriage, Taken at Waterloo; and sent to the Prince Regent, by Marshal Blücher" (*Bath Herald,* 28 September). Built in Brussels, the dark blue and gilt carriage, with vermilion wheels and bullet-proof panels, was exhibited with Napoleon's "whole personal Camp Equipage, superb Toilette Box, Wardrobe, splendid service of gold and silver Plate, Diamonds, Chronometer, Arms, and complete *Necessaire,* taken at the same time" by the Prussians. The display had earlier attracted 220,000 visitors at the London Museum, Piccadilly (*Courier,* 30 November 1815, 10 and 16 February 1816).

3. What was important to Gray was that Josephus (ca. 37–ca. 95), a "spectator and an historian of events . . . verifies the completion of the divine revelation in every part, and while he thought, possibly, that he was describing only the fulfilment of the Jewish prophecies, he unintentionally substantiated the exact accomplishments of the denunciations of our Lord." See Gray's *Connection,* chap. 31, "Josephus," pp. 267–309, especially p. 308.

4. In chap. 1 of *Retrospection,* "Containing The First Century; from Tiberius to Trajan," HLP discusses the period "when Josephus wrote" (1:25).

5. Ocyrrhoe's prophecy about Aesculapius appears in Ovid's *Metamorphoses,* 2.642–45, 647, 648.

6. *King Lear,* 5.3.71.

7. For Robert Nixon, the "Cheshire Prophet," see HLP to RG, 9 January 1804, n. 2. HLP varies the conclusion of a stanza said to be by Nixon: "Landlords shall stand/ With hats in their hands,/ To desire tenants to hold their lands." See John Oldmixon, *Nixon's Original Cheshire Prophecy, In Doggerel Verse: Published from an Authentic Manuscript* (Gainsborough: Printed by and for Henry Mozley [c 1800]), p. 16.

8. *Macbeth,* 3.2.25–26.

TO SIR JAMES FELLOWES

30: September *1816.*

Why this was kindly done indeed Dear Sir; and requires my earliest as well as truest Thanks.[1] We will talk further about the Lease, but nobody shall turn me out of this house if I can help it; Prince Hoare certainly built it on purpose for H: L: P. who really does not mind the Money-Stuff—a Pin; but one can't go Sell out just now when Stock is so very low.[2] 2500£ o'Year, and my Income is not a farthing less;—with 4000£ besides in the Consols must surely content any Single Woman.—In January 1817 Such will be my Fortune; and who in their Wits *circumstanced as I am* can wish for more? Your dear Mother laughed when I told her I was buying Plate Linen &c. to *begin the World with* like a Boy just come of Age.

But Life is a strange Thing, and has been often compared to a River. Labitur et labetur &c.[3]

> Leave the lofty Glaciere's Side
> Leave the Mountain's solemn Pride;
> Down some gently sloping Hill
> Let's pursue this Silent Rill,
> Noiseless as it seems to flow
> To the distant Lake below.
> Wrapt in some Poetic Dream
> Watch the windings of the Stream.
> In such varied Currents twisting,
> Still escaping, still existing;

Let us find Life's Emblem here:
Haste away!—*The Lake is near.*[4]

Wales inspired these Verses, which of Course Dear Sir James Fellowes never saw—but *he* can make Life valuable as delightful.—God keep the Lake far distant from *him* for A Thousand Sakes. Oh how I shall like to kneel down with and among the dear Cluster at Adbury House! Can it be *hoped* for? I told Mr. Salusbury when he invited me to Brynbella, that (as nobody ever died) I was engaged in Berkshire next May or June—he knows the Place of Course, having resided so long with Shephard of Enborne.[5] Your Parish Scheme appears an excellent one, and England is now *wanting* just such Country Gentlemen as yourself.—Salusbury is very good too; and recollects the Saying I learned of his Uncle, that there are but Three Things worth caring for. L'Anima, la Salute, e la Borsa.[6]—He knows the Value of each, to do him Justice; and will fling none of them away. Doctor Robert Gray who wrote the new book that every one is reading, wrote the Lines round our Sundial at Brynbella—

Umbra tegit lapsas, præsentique imminet Horæ;
Dum lux, dum lucis semita, Virtus agat.[7]

'Ere yet the threat'ning Shade o'erspread the Hour,
Hasten bright Virtue and exert thy Pow'r.

The well-known George Henry Glasse said there was a Fault in the Prosody, and wish'd to correct it,—as thus.

Umbra tegit lapsam, præsentique imminet Horæ;
Hospes, disce ex me vivere, disce mori.

'Ere yet the unreturning Shadows fly,
Go Mortals; learn to live, and learn to die.[8]

Tell me which you prefer; I like the English of the *last* best, myself; but the first—of Course—remains round the little marble Pillar set up by Mr. Piozzi—and very much admired for its Elegance.

Oh what a beautiful House and Place it is!—and how I fret at Sight of *any* Alteration!—however useful and perhaps proper.

Salusbury *did* make me the Compliment of not cutting down a Weeping Willow *we* planted, because I had made Verses on it—and here they are—copied from those close to the Sun Dial.

Mark how the Weeping Willow stands
Near the recording Stone;
It seems to blame our Idle Hands
And mourn the Moments flown.

Thus Conscience holds our Fancy fast
With Fears too oft affected;
Pretending to lament the Past,
The Present—still neglected:

Yet shall this swift-improving Plant
With Spring her Leaves resume;
Nor let th' Example She can grant
Depend on Winter's Gloom.

Loiter no more then near the Tree,
Nor on the Dial gaze:
If but one hour is giv'n to Thee
Act right while yet it stays.[9]

But here comes dear Doctor Fellowes, to whom when I *half* complained of a hurry in my Inside—Bessy Jones wished to make appeal: The Coppers were examined, and the Verdict found *Not guilty* even by your Father himself.

How *well* he is—by the way:—and how kind—as you all are to Your ever Obliged and Grateful/ H: L: P.

Make my best Compliments and Regards acceptable to Lady Fellowes: She is at her *best now:* has done being sick, and not begun being in Pain.

Text Huntington MSS. 6133. *Address* Sir James Fellowes.

1. HLP's letter replies to one by JF, 29 September 1816 (Ry. 555.75). Cf. Shakespeare, *Troilus and Cressida*, 3.1.96.
2. According to the "Walcot Poor Rate Book" (1776), 8 Gay Street had been owned by the portrait painter William Hoare (ca. 1707–1792), who left it to his son, Prince (1755–1834), the playwright and artist (Guildhall, Bath).
3. Horace, *Epistles*, 1.2.43.
4. The poem is HLP's loose imitation of unidentified French verses, dated 1812, in "Harvard Piozziana," vol. 4, and in "Minced Meat for Pyes."
5. JSPS had attended Thomas Shephard's school at Enborne, Berks., between 1806 and 1811.
6. HLP identifies the "Three Things worth caring for" as "an Italian Proverb" in *Thraliana*, 2:1066, n. 2.
7. RG wrote his verses for the Brynbella sundial in the early summer of 1799. See *Thraliana*, 2:999.
8. For George Henry Glasse and his verses, see *Thraliana*, 2:1042, n. 2; "Minced Meat for Pyes"; "Harvard Piozziana," 3:70; Ry. 647.66. For HLP on the Reverend Glasse, see her letters to LC, 2 November 1803, nn. 6, 8, and 25 January 1804, n. 7.
9. On 23 August 1803, HLP wrote the poem (with a few variations) into *Thraliana*, 2:1042, and introduced it with the following: "—when we planted a Weeping Willow over against [our sundial at Brynbella] last Novr these Verses came in my Head."
HLP recalled the verses and anecdotes to comply with JF's request in his last letter to her: "Pray take care of the *loose* scraps and note down every thing—You shall see how I value them."

TO SIR JAMES FELLOWES

Monday 7: October 1816.

When your Dear Mother sent to ask me for something She might Direct to Sir James Fellowes I wrote her word I had nothing to send him but reproaches for Tardiness in our Correspondence.

Upon Recollection however I knew he would be pleased with my boasting Amendment of Health; and attributing it to your Advice and that of Doctor Fellowes—who sent me first to Hetling Court, and now I go regularly.[1]

Whilst drinking there this Day—Lady Keith called here in Gay Street; told my Servant She was only running thro' the Town, and so it proved: for when I sent after her—She was flown.—Provoking enough, that I should be out so mal apropòs: but it can't be helped.[2] Mr. Henry Fellowes slipt away in the same vexatious Manner; Dieu me pardonne but I was certainly no less concerned at losing *him* so perversely.[3]

I have got no New Books to read—Mrs. Whalley recommended me some Verses—a long Poem indeed; but to me very unintelligible. Modern Writers resemble the Cuttle Fish that hides himself from all Pursuers in *his own Ink.* *That* is not Doctor Gray's Case however, I think you will like his Performance exceedingly.

The Weather is as gloomy as November; and the poor Gleaners can get no Corn out of the Stubble, it rots, and grows, and threatens Ruin both to small and great.

Miss Hudson[4] says a Famine will bring us to our Senses, *I* say it will deprive us of the little Wits we have left.[5] The Delirium proceeding from Hunger will have fatal Consequences; because vulgar Minds will feel sure that 'tis somebody's Fault; and Woe to the Mortal they pitch upon.

Send a consoling Word Dear Sir; for my Fancy Sees very bad Visions.——The World always does see most Wonders when most blind—says old Fuller:[6]— perhaps that is now the Case with your/ faithfully and Gratefully/ H: L: P.

Dispose of my Compliments properly and kindly.

Text Hyde Collection. *Address* Sir James Fellowes/ Adbury House/ Berks.

1. The Hot Bath Pump-Room at Hetling Court, near Bath Abbey. See the Bath directories from 1812 to 1824 and advertisements in the *Bath Herald,* especially in 1817.
2. Q is listed in the *Bath Chronicle* for 10 October as a new arrival. In fact between late September and the first week in October, Q had made two passing visits to Bath. See *Journals and Letters,* 9:218, 276, 283.
3. For Henry Fellowes, see HLP to JF, 21 February 1816, n. 8.
4. Catherine Charlotte Hudson (ca. 1767–1825), of 10 Gay Street, was the eldest daughter of Charles Grave Hudson (1730–1813), first baronet (1791), of Wanlip Hall, Leics., a director of the South Sea Company.
5. Behind these statements is an allusion to the looting, rioting, and vandalism of unemployed farmworkers in the eastern counties and of industrial workers in the north and in the midlands. They were protesting economic hardship and dissatisfaction with the government, whom they held responsible for the high cost of bread. See *AR,* "Chronicle," 58 (1816).

6. See Thomas Fuller, *The History of the Worthies of England* [1662], ed. P. Austin Nuthall, 3 vols. (London: Thomas Tegg, 1840), 3:507, which introduces his section on "Wonders."

TO SIR JAMES FELLOWES

Bath: 11: October 1816.

In Adversity—in Prosperity ever dear and kind Sir James Fellowes! My Wraxall is lovely;—opens well as You say, and what Signifies Knowledge *locked up*—either in Man or Book? I think if Lady Keith has a fault—besides her disregard of poor H L P,—that is *hers*. Oh here is a new Book come out, that I know not how She will like, or how the Public will like. Do you remember my telling You that in the Year *1813* when I was in London upon Salusbury's Business, before his Marriage some Months; A Mr. White sent to tell me thro' Doctor Myddelton, that He possessed a Manuscript of Johnson's, and wished me to ascertain that the hand-writing was his own. I invited *both* Gentlemen to Dinner——We were at Blake's Hôtel, and Dr. Gray met them; and I saw that the M: S: was genuine.[1] It was a Diary of the little Journey that Mr. Thrale and *Mr.* Johnson, (such he was then;)[2] and Miss Thrale and myself made into North Wales in the Year 1774.—There was nothing in it of Consequence that *I saw*, except a pretty Parallell between Hawkestone the Country Seat of Sir Richard Hill—and Ilam the Country Seat of Mr. Port in Derbyshire:[3] but the Gentlemen who possessed it seemed shy of letting me read the whole, and did not As it appeared, like being asked how it came into his hands—but repeatedly observed He would print it——only it was not sufficiently bulky for Publication—wished he could swell it out &c.

We parted however, and met no more.——But when I came first into New King Street here—November *1814:*—a poor Widow Woman a Mrs. Parker—offering me Seventeen genuine Letters of Doctor Johnson, which I could by no means think of purchasing for myself—in my then present Circumstances: I recommended her to apply to Mr. White——and She came again in Three Weeks Time better Dressed, and thanked *me* for the 25 Guineas *he* had given her——from which hour I saw her no more, nor ever heard of or from Mr. White again.[4]

——Since you and I parted at Streatham Park however—a Mr. Duppa has written me many Letters chiefly enquiring after my *Family:* what Relationship I bore to Lord Combermere, to Sir Lynch Salusbury Cotton[5] &c. and comically enough asking who my Aunt was; and if She was such a Fool as Doctor Johnson described her.[6]

I replied She was my Aunt only by Marriage; tho' related to my Mother's Brother, who she *did* marry; that She was a Miss Cotton Heiress of Etwall and Belleport in Derby Shire——her youngest Sister was Countess of Ferrers—&c. none of them particularly bright I believe, but as I expressed it—Johnson was a good Despiser.

So now here is Johnson's Diary printed and published with a Fac Simile of his Hand Writing[7]——if Mr. Duppa does not *send me* one,[8] He is as shabby as it seems our Doctor thought me, when I gave but a Crown to the Old Clerk—— see Page 68. The poor Clerk had probably never seen a Crown in his Possession before;[9] Things were very distant A: D: 1774 from what they are *1816*. You must accept the book, and be a truer Friend than Johnson was to Your ever/ Obliged and faithful and/Grateful / H: L: P.

I am sadly afraid of Lady K's being displeased, and fancying *I* promoted this Publication—could I have caught her for a Quarter of a Hour I should have proved my Innocence, and might have shewn her Duppa's Letter but She left neither Note Card nor Message; and when my Servant ran to all the Inns in Chase of her, he learned that She left the White Hart at 12 o'Clock.[10]—Vexatious!—but it can't [be] helped.

I hope the pretty little Girl my People saw with her, will pay [her] more tender Attention.[11]

Your dear Brother looked as grave Yesterday because his and Your own good Father was drawing his Breath too short as if his whole Happiness in both Worlds depended on it:——but You are *such* a Family!

What can Sir James Fellowes do for me in London is next to be considered. I think he must be so good as go to the European Musæum in King Street St. James's, and see what my Old Acquaintance Wilson has done with the Colossal Head of a Magdalen by Cipriani, with which Leak intrusted him.[12] I hope I am not paying for her Ornamenting his high Room where indeed She was likely to shew with great Advantage:—if he has Sold her, The Money should be sent in to Hammersley's.

Text Huntington MSS. 6928.

1. For this incident, see HLP to Q, 15 May 1813, and n. 5; and HLP to Richard Duppa, 26 September 1816.
2. Although SJ received the LL.D. from Trinity College, Dublin, in 1765, he did not allegedly assume the "title of Doctor, till Oxford conferred on him the degree" ten years later (*Boswell's Johnson*, 1:488, n. 3).
3. For SJ's comparison of Hawkestone and Ilam, see *Boswell's Johnson*, 5:434.
4. Perhaps Beatrix Parker, the née Lister (fl. 1756–1815), widow of John Parker (ca. 1755–1797), of Browsholme Hall, West Riding, Yorks., M.P. SJ and the Thrales had seen him at Dovedale on 16 July 1774 (*Boswell's Johnson*, 5:431).
5. For Stapleton Cotton, Baron Combermere, see HLP to Q, 4 January 1801, n. 3 and 22 March 1810. For Sir Lynch Salusbury Cotton, see HLP to Isabella Hamilton, 13 May 1805, n. 2.
6. On 11 September 1816 (Ry. 555.61), Duppa had questioned HLP about her genealogy, particularly with reference to the Cottons. Specifically, he asked, "Who was Sir Lynch Cottons Lady, was she 'weak and ignorant' as Johnson stated in his diary, not that I shall print these offensive words." For the "offensive words," see *Boswell's Johnson*, 5:434.
Elizabeth Abigail, the wife of Sir Lynch, was the daughter of Rowland Cotton of Bellaport, Salop, and Etwall, Derbyshire. For her sister Catherine, who married the sixth earl of Ferrers, see HLP to LC [18] May [1800], n. 5.
7. Facing the title page of Duppa's edition is a "Fac-simile of Dr. Johnson's handwriting from the original Ms.," showing SJ's description of Ilam.
8. Duppa had written to HLP on 11 October (Ry. 555.62): "Enclosed is a copy of the little book which I hope you will do me the honour to accept, and concerning which I have already given you

so much trouble. . . . With the little volume I have sent a duplicate in which I have marked some queries and if in your leisure you will be so good as to answer them in the margin or to add illustrative information it would be acceptable for a 2nd edition which I shall probably at some future time have an opportunity of printing."

9. HLP alludes to the incident of the "old Clerk" at Tremeirchion, who "had great appearance of joy at the sight of his Mistress, and foolishly said that he was now willing to die. He has only a crown given him by my Mistress." See *Boswell's Johnson*, 5:438–40.

10. The White Hart Inn and Tavern, Stall Street, Bath, was kept by Woodhouse, Bishop, and Cooper. See the Bath directories, 1812–19.

11. For Georgiana Augusta Henrietta Elphinstone, now seven, see HLP to Q, 22 March 1810, n. 18.

12. See particularly HLP to AL, 19 May 1816, n. 7. JF was to write on 30 Oct. (Ry. 555.77, 77+) that he saw Wilson, who reported that he would exhibit the "Colossal head" next spring, but that HLP would not get half "the fifty pounds that were offered for it at Streatham."

TO SIR JAMES FELLOWES

Bath 14th October 1816

I have scarce finished Thanking my Dear Friend for one Favour before he does me another.

A Pheasant of *your* Shooting will be to me a Gold and a Silver one; but which of the *Cluster*—The *kind* Cluster—will come and eat it with me? Dr. Fellowes is really not in *Feather:* When I heard He had not been to Hetling Court this Morning—my Feelings, in Unison with those of the Family; sent me Post to the Vineyards.—And I found him better than my Expectations, altho' a few Notes below my Wishes.

Your Brother Dorset has lent me Bubb Dodington's Diary, and I have done Nothing but read in it ever since:[1] Tis a Retrospection of my Young Days, very amusing certainly—but Anecdote is all the Rage, &c. Johnson's Diary is selling rapidly, tho' the Contents are bien maigre I must confess. Apropòs Mr. Duppa *has* sent me the Book, and I perceive has politely suppressed some Sarcastic Expressions about my Family—The Cottons;[2] whom we visited at Combermere and at Lleweney.

I was the last of the Salusburys—so *they* escaped, but I remember his saying once "it would be no Loss if all my Relations were spitted like Larks, and roasted for the Lap-Dog's supper."[3]

It would certainly have been no Loss to *me* as they have behaved themselves, but one hates to see them insulted.

Well! I have been to see Buonaparte's Playthings; They are very fine, and the Workmanship very elaborate: but surely he could never have shot a Pheasant—with an Agate in Place of the Flint—Ah no! The Lyon's heart with the Eagle in Conjunction,—that formed the Star presiding,—or rather the *Constellation* which governed at the Nativity of Louis Quatorze—was far away:—emigrated with the Bourbons to a more Northern Sphere.[4]

This Letter is written in the Dark,—you will hardly be able to read it; but if Words are wanting—supply the Chasm with the kindest: *They* will have best Chance to express the unalterable/ Sentiments of H: L: P,

Your Brother Dorset and I disagree only in our Opinions concerning Buona-parte of whom he thinks much higher than I do: altho' as Balzac says of the Romans,

Le Ciel benissoit toutes leurs Fautes,
Le Ciel couronnoit toutes leurs Folies.[5]

We must however watch the End; for till a Man dies, We can neither pro-nounce him very great or very happy: so said at least one of the Sages of Antiquity.[6]

Adieu!

Text Huntington Library MSS. 6134. *Address* Sir James Fellowes.

1. Henry Penruddocke Wyndham, *The Diary of the late George Bubb Dodington, baron of Melcombe Regis: from March 8, 1748–9, to February 6, 1761. With an appendix, containing some curious and interesting papers, which are either referred to, or alluded to, in the diary. Now first published from his lordship's original manuscripts* (Salisbury: E. Easton, 1784).
2. Duppa (p. 45) printed only SJ's comments that "We left Combermere, where we have been treated with great civility," omitting the subsequent remark that "Sir L. is gross, the Lady weak and ignorant" (*Boswell's Johnson*, 5:434).
3. HLP records the incident in the *Anecdotes* (p. 63): "When I one day lamented the loss of a first cousin killed in America—'Prithee, my dear (said he), have done with canting: how would the world be worse for it, I may ask, if all your relations were at once spitted like larks, and roasted for Presto's supper?'" For Baretti's version, see *Boswell's Johnson*, 4:347.
4. Louis XIV was born early in the morning of 5 September 1638 when superstition decreed that the royal astrologer be in attendance. The governing constellation then consisted of the moon at the end of Sagittarius and the beginning of Capricorn in trine aspect with Regulus.
    In late 1789, however, the constellation that had appeared so fortuitous for Louis and the house of Bourbon "was far away"—decidedly not in the ascendant. Rather, about then there was a conjunc-tion of Regulus (and Leonis)—the heart of the lion; and Jupiter—the eagle. And at that time, coincidentally, the mobs put an end to Bourbon rule.
5. Jean-Louis Guez de Balzac, *Pensées de Balzac* (Paris: Potey, 1808), 139–40. "De l'incertitude de nos jugemens": ". . . Il y a eu des hommes dont la vie a été pleine de miracles, quoiqu'ils ne fussent pas saints, et qu'ils n'eussent pas dessein de l'être: le ciel bénissait leurs fautes; le ciel couronnait toutes leur folies."
6. Ovid, *Metamorphoses*, 3.135–37. Addison's translation of the lines is the motto for *Adventurer* 120. Cf. *Rambler* 21.

TO LADY WILLIAMS

Bath Tuesday
22: October 1816

I think my Dear Lady Williams will be soon ready to feel pleased at the Sight of an old Friend's Hand Writing, and I have now to congratulate my Country Folks on the Arrival of fine Weather—the more prized as it has been absent so long. The People round Bath are making diligent Use of it, and I flatter myself it will be still more useful and valuable at a Distance. The Rage for leaving England is cooling; but Mrs. Mostyn is gone I believe; and possibly the Death of a Mr. Strong,[1] which we read in the Newspapers, will give her Son a Dismissal—with Permission to follow and protect her.—I should certainly feel happier was he with her. Meanwhile Miss Williams and I have to lament poor Mrs. Lutwyche's Loss of pretty Mary Mayhew,[2] and of an old sickly Foreign Nobleman that used to share their House and Friendship——Le Chevalier de Boisgelin a Knight of Malta;[3] Mr. Williams remembers him well. These Privations will send *them* abroad, and one can in no Wise blame them for going.

Will Sir John like to hear that we are going to War again? It is conjectured that the Turks will not submit to take Lessons of Good Behaviour from England.[4] Well! Buonaparte's Spoyls, his Carriage, Muskets, Trinkets &c. have attracted much Notice, and 'tis to be hoped that Folks will Soon have done admiring their late Possessor; who if he did not rise like a *Rocket,* is sure enough fallen at last like a *Stick* in the Island of St. Helena.[5]

Mr. Salusbury sends me Word that he was to accompany Some Young Ladies—Shropshire ones of Course—to Bodylwyddan a few Days ago—how happy the Music there will make him!—Upon my Word I think the Notion of making home the Scene of Contentment is a capital good Notion: The professed Pleasure-hunters are never contented—Parties are too empty—or too crouded:—Theatres repeat the Same Thing too often; or the Same Actors tire their greatest Admirers in the Course of one Season.

Are you all tired yet of Miss Myddelton and Mr. Yorke?[6] or will her return to the Country bring up the Subject again? Is Mrs. Hemans writing?[7] or does every body and every Thing feel the Influence of this universal *Damp* which will take so many of these short tho' bright Days to dry?

Miss Williams has been looking ill, lately, but seemed in good Spirits this Morning, and we are to meet next Wednesday at Mrs. Whalley's. No matter where we meet if we do but talk of Wales; and of dear Sir John; and how well Your Ladyship looks—and how beautiful the Children grow—no longer Children, as I tell her; but very lovely Girls.—

The Criticism you make on Glenarvon is excellent; I have really heard none so good.

The Key that was shewn *me,*[8] barely said that Lord Avonside represented Mr. L[ambe] and Lady Calantha—his Wife. That Lord B[yron] was Hero of the Piece, and that the Princess of Madagascar stood for Lady O[xford]; whilst People made themselves believe that the Duchess of D[evonshire] was meant by Lady Margaret.——I suppose they make the Bells play what Tune they please; and as none of these characters are familiar to me, 'tis Impossible for me to judge of the Resemblance real or fictitious.—As a Novel 'tis very Entertaining, but the Author of *Discipline* would not approve it I should think:[9] Oh I have read *those* three Volumes a Second Time, and really do find them incomparable. But here comes Miss Williams—heart-broken at Thought of the Lutwyches leaving Bath—and *they* go on Tuesday for Paris, to meet Lady Baynton and pass the Winter together. Mr. Robert Hesketh's Marriage should console her,[10] Old People *must depart* in *some* Sense of the Word; Young ones must go on, and be merry while they may.

I hear Mrs. Salusbury of Brynbella grows fat; how perfect the Resemblance will soon be, between her and her Mama! Are Miss Leycesters beautiful?[11] and is dear Mr. Williams in Love with Them? Present him my truest Compliments and Good Wishes: and Dear Madam, let me beg your Ladyship to divide with Sir John the most perfect and positive Regard of *your own*/ H: L: P.

Text Ry. 4 (1812–18). *Address* Lady Williams/ Bodylwyddan/ near St. Asaph/ Flintshire.

1. An error for Mrs. Strong: i.e., Catherine, née Maxwell (b. 1784), the wife of William Strong (1788–1866), of Stanground, Hunts. For their marriage on 27 August 1811, see the "Fletton Marriage Register" and "Stanground Burials," C.R.O., Cambridgeshire. Her death is reported in the *Bath Chronicle*, 17 October; the *Bath Journal*, 14 October; *GM* 86, pt. 2 (1816):381.

HLP implies a possible association between CMM and the new widower, who was to marry twice more.

For the late Catherine Strong's parents-in-law, whom both HLP and Ly W knew, see the former's letter to Ly W, 26 February 1816, n. 8.

2. For Clementina Mary Mayhew, niece of William Lutwyche, see HLP to Ly W, 30 January 1802, n. 7. Suffering from a "long and debilitating illness," she died at Sidmouth on 14 October 1816.

3. Pierre-Marie-Louis de Boisgelin de Kerdu had died on 10 September at Pleubian.

4. Turkey was threatened not only by persistent Russian ambitions but by her refusal to placate Napoleonic exiles. Thus, Lallemand and Savary, who had sought refuge in Constantinople, were driven out, the Grand Seignior having refused to allow any of the adherents of Napoleon "to abide in his territories."

Internally Turkey was rocked by insurrection: e.g., the Janissaries at Adrianople revolted and killed several of the governing officers there.

Trebisond, moreover, was occupied by four thousand rebels, whose soldiers "committed all kinds of excesses against the peaceable inhabitants. The French Consul, M. Dupré, was obliged to barricade his house, and defend himself against the factions." See *GM* 86, pt. 2 (1816):361.

5. Napoleon had arrived at St. Helena on 15 October.

6. The eldest daughter of the late Robert Myddelton of Gwaynynog was Caroline May, now twenty, marriageable, and hence the subject of gossip. Only on 4 October 1823 did she marry the Reverend William Carr Fenton (1783–1855) of Grinton Lodge, Yorks. Ordained in 1820, he served as rector of Cowthorpe near Witherby (1824–35); vicar of Mattersey near Bawtry (1835–55).

7. The poet Felicia Dorothea Hemans, née Browne (1793–1835), grew up at Gwrych, near Abergele and from 1809 to 1825 lived with her brother, Sir Thomas Henry (1787–1855) at Bronwylfa, near St. Asaph. That HLP knew the poet is suggested by a letter written by L. Gardner, 23 September 1816 (Ry. 892.66), wherein the latter offers HLP "our best thanks upon your obliging Introduction to Mrs. Brown and Mrs. Hemans—we called upon them in our Road from Abergele." See also HLP to PSP, 10 February 1821.

8. One such "Ms. Key to the Characters in Lady Caroline Lambe's 'Glenarvon'" may be found in the Huntington Library as Mss. 132900. This "Key" identifies the characters as follows: Glenarvon-Byron; Miss Monmouth-Lady Byron; Calantha-Lady Caroline Lambe; Princess of Madagascar-Lady Holland; Lady Margaret-Duchess of Devonshire, etc.

9. For Mary Brunton's *Discipline*, see HLP to Ly W, 15 June 1815, n. 2.

10. HLP responds to unfounded rumor. A relative-in-law of Ly W, Robert Hesketh (1764–1824) of Rossall and North Meols had married in 1790 Maria Rawlinson (d. 1824). Their second son was Robert Fleetwood (1798–1817).

11. The Miss Leicesters were the daughters of Charles Leicester (see HLP to Ly W, 15 June 1815, n. 5), by his first wife, Mary, née Egerton (d. 1797). They were Louisa (d. 1840), Emily Elizabeth (d. 1863), and Lavinia Sophia (d. 1847).

TO SIR JAMES FELLOWES

Fryday 1: November 1816.

When my Heart first made Election of Sir James Fellowes, not only as a *present* but as a *future* Friend; I *felt* rather than *knew* that he would never forget or forsake me—Everything I see and hear, confirms my saucy Prejudice.

Your dear Father and Mother with whom I dined Yesterday are as well as ever I saw them—and the Doctor gave me Lozenges for a Cough, that I really think is the Effect of a nerve-shaken Frame, no Cold at all:—but *Sunday Evening,*— *such* a Sunday Evening! passed in Marlborough Buildings where I used to meet Friends so beloved, Companions so chearful:—sent me home to Bessy Jones with a half-breaking heart, and in every Vein Johnson's well-founded Horror of the *Last.*[1] The Family left Bath next Day, for Paris, where they have taken a House for a Year.! Poor Boisgelin is dead you know: one could not care in Earnest for Boigelin; but at my Age, 'tis like losing the Milestones in the last Stage of a long Journey——

When I knocked at my Door that same Sunday Night, my servant told me how Doctor Parry was at the Point of Death. Oh Dear! but those who can't cry, *must* cough I think:——Miss Williams weeps loud and long;——

> She foams out all the Passion at her Lips,
> And so the Poyson kills not.

We shall however—*both* of us,—have a cruel Loss in the Lutwyches. How happy, how elegant is Your Epitaph on poor Mary.—Beautiful! and not too shewy; just as it should be: I am afraid to trust myself with translating—or even praising it——The *Hand* is visible enough, ever light and easy; The Heart soft as Velvet, the Mind bright and strong as Adamant.

Pray let the Ruin have an Inscription (when Time comes,) as well as the Frontispiece.[2]

The Colossal Magdalene by Cipriani was put up at 15£: 15: 0—and to avoid the Disgrace of *reducing;*—Mathew, (Partner to Squibb)—who lives in Fenchurch Street bought it in for me.

But I have had other *Small* Shot fired from Streatham Park. You remember my Saying that the Ladies complained they had lost their Deeds and that Lord Keith begged to look over my Papers etc.——It was—as Leak said—to prevent my getting a *Sum* of *Money* for the Place which was what I wanted, for purpose of paying my Debts; and Mr. Windle by letting the Place to the best Bidder, managed for me—*Second-best.*—They have found the Deeds now; and Lord Keith has applied to Windle for Payment of Arrears to the Duke of Bedford, of a Quit Rent—12£ per Annum—setting *his* Steward at me:—Likewise our Friend Mr. Hill demands 35£ Tythe Money, which with the other comes close to 200£ but that will not now *distress,* however it may vex me.

I cannot indeed fulfill my Intention of purchasing a *fourth* Thousand into the

3 Per Cent Consols *this* Year, but Mr. Salusbury must pray for my Life, that I *may* do it in Course of Anno Domini 1817.

Meanwhile my Money goes for my own conveniencies; and no Comforts of Life do I now deny myself. You will see when you come.

How your Brother Dorset did make our Blood run cold telling of your Exploit in pulling the Tree almost on your head! Oh for a hundred Sakes, have Care of your own Life and Health, and do not dine so late and then eat so hastily—'tis dreadful: Mr. Thrale owed his Death to the Practice; and Doctor Parry whose person was not unlike his, turns *his* Life out at the same Door.

Mr. Dorset Fellowes says he obtained a Promise from You of dining at 5 o'Clock,—keep it I intreat you; for the Workmen neglected today will come again tomorrow—*as surely*—as the Stomach Complaint neglected one Day will return the next. But I will release you from this Schooling, lest you should say to your Self—as Pierre to Jaffier

> What feminine Tale hast thou been listning to?
> Of unair'd Shirts, Catarrhs and Tooth-achs caught
> ——by wearing thin-soal'd Shoes! !³

Oh! but here's a Rumour in the Town that Buonaparte has been shot—trying to make his Escape—Should you like these Lines for *his* Epitaph? They are not of Course mine—but could have suited no one so well—says the *Compiler.*

> Adsta Viator: Quo properas!
>   Hic videbis
> Reliquias N
> Magnus Ingenio—et Fortunâ mirabilis:
> Tormentum seculi sui, quam Ornamentum.
> Galliam subegit, Italiam spoliavit;
> Afflixit Hispaniam, turbavit Angliam,
>   Lusit Europam.
> Ofluxa Mortalibus, quam tenue Momentum
>   Inter Omnia et Nihil.
> Hoc te volui Viator, hic te metire—et abi.

Your Father calling in so kindly, hurried me; and I dare say there are Twenty Faults; if so, Correct them, for the Bell is ringing, and I shall stop the Man to say—Remember Five! for your future Dinner hour; as I see plainly Doctor Fellowes thinks it very wrong to wait longer—and your Health is growing every Day and every hour more Important.

I wish my Pen was as Perswasive and as Impressive as the Voice of Dear Siddons when She Says in Belvidera's Part *Remember Twelve.*⁴

Farewell! would you believe that your good Father fancies *he* can discern a Taste for the Science he has professed so many Years, in/ his and Your Obliged/ H: L: P.?

Once more Adieu! and present me with affectionate Respect to Lady Fellowes.

Text Huntington MSS. 6135. *Address* Sir James Fellowes/ Adbury House/ near Newbury/ Berks. *Postmark* BATH NO 1 1816.

1. Samuel Johnson's most famous discussion of the "last" appears in his final *Idler* essay (103): "There are few things not purely evil, of which we can say, without some emotion of uneasiness, 'this is the last.'"
2. In a note addressed to Sir James Fellowes at the Vineyards, the home of his parents, and dated "Monday 30," HLP writes: "We lamented your situation last night——tho' it was not a bad one; between a beautiful Frontispiece the N:M., and an interesting Ruin—The poor H:L:P." The thirtieth was on a Monday in January 1815, September and December 1816, and June 1817. References in the note to HLP's book of travels and to Floretta suggest an early date when the two were becoming acquainted after a first meeting on 1 January 1815. On 11 July 1996 this note was donated to the Huntington Library by Thomas V. Lange in honor of Edward and Lillian Bloom.
3. Thomas Otway, *Venice Preserved*, 3.2.242–44.
4. *Venice Preserved*, 3.2.227.

TO LADY WILLIAMS

Bath
5: November 1816.

My dearest Lady Williams will easily believe my truly unfeigned Concern when opening the first Letter I ever received from my Godson, I read of his Brother's Accident.[1]

The Story was told indeed in such a Manner, I guess not *where,* or *how much* my amiable young Friend has been hurt: Let me hear the particulars I earnestly beg, either from Your Ladyship or from his own dear hand.

The Account of the Rioters would interest me deeply,[2] if a nearer Interest did not intervene; and it pleases *me* as much as it does *him,* to be told that my Godson is going soon to Harrow:[3] It will be a famous Change for him, will open new Scenes of Life, and produce Improvement in his Person and Mind, beyond what his Family can be aware of.—

These are Times when every body's best Wits are wanted—and I understand that much Pains are taken to excite Commotions in the Very heart of the Metropolis. *My* old Residence the Borough of Southwark is certainly run raving Mad, by what the Papers exhibit of their outrageous Resolutions;[4] and *Britons to Arms* are printed on Hand-bills, and thrust under Doors whose Owners would be quiet if they could.

I fancy the bad Weather and bad Harvest has put them all out of humour; but cutting each other's Throats will mend the matter only by thinning the Population.

Bath is quiet, and will remain so: a Town dedicated either to Sickness or Amusement will not be disturbed by Political Transactions; and our Folks are only thinking on the Election of a Master of the Ceremonies[5]——Miss Williams is to be excepted: She thinks *chiefly*—I might say *only* on dear Bodylwyddan, and how She will be affected by to day's News from thence, I dread to see and hear.—Meanwhile our great Physician Doctor Parry lies senseless and at

Death's Door under a Stroke of Apoplexy, or Palsy; Poor Fellow![6] People here
are much interested about *him:* and these numerous Chapels or Meeting-houses,
or Whatever we must call them Seem to have awakened our Members of Parliament—Rector &c.—and they are coming to live among us——as 'tis Pity but
they had done long ago.

Adieu Dear Madam! I can write no *Good* News, but am desirous to be told that
no *Ill* is approaching Bodylwyddan; which has no truer,/ or more respectfully
Affectionate/ Wellwisher than/ H: L: Piozzi.

Text Ry. 4 (1812–18). *Address* Lady Williams/ Bodylwyddan near St. Asaph/
Flintshire/ N: Wales. *Postmark* NO 6 1816.

1. On 5 November HLP recorded in her "Pocket Book" receiving a "bad Letter from Hughey
Williams—saying his eldest Brother had been hurt while Shooting. Miss Williams is in Despair.
Evening at Mangin's. He thinks Williams's Accident is in the Paper,—we could not find it."
2. England's unrest was evident in the "alarming conspiracies of the frame-breakers" in Nottinghamshire, "serious riots" among ironworkers in Glamorganshire and Monmouthshire, protests
among workers for better wages in Birmingham, and a "very large meeting" of thirty thousand
persons in Manchester demanding parliamentary reform (*The Times*, 21, 22, 23, 28 October; 1,
2 November).
3. For Hugh Williams at Rugby (rather than Harrow), see HLP to Ly W, 26 February 1816, n. 12.
4. Prompted by "the distressed state of the country," householders and electors of Southwark
met on 17 October at the borough town-hall and pointed to the "stagnation in commerce and
agriculture," "degradation of public morals," and "lack of confidence . . . in Parliament" as "signs
of the calamitous complexion of the times." The meeting passed seven resolutions, including calls
for parliamentary reform, reassessment of pensions and sinecures, and a petition to the Regent (*The
Times*, 18 October). "Britons to Arms" was printed on five thousand bills, posted throughout London, to publicize the first meeting at Spa Fields, which was to be held on 15 November. See *Cobbett's
Weekly Political Register*, 32 (1817): 313.
5. The sudden death on 16 October of James King (1740–1816), master of the ceremonies of the
Upper Assembly Rooms in Bath since 1805, necessitated an election in November to choose a
successor. Captain George Wyke (fl. 1780–1835) defeated James Heaviside and Lewis P. Madden;
he held the post until his resignation on 1 February 1818. See *Bath Herald*, 19 October, 27 December
1817; Mainwaring, *Annals of Bath*, 169–70.
6. See HLP to PSW, 1 September [1789], n. 7. In October 1816, Caleb Hillier Parry suffered a
paralytic stroke that deprived him of the use of his right side and impaired his speech. His mental
faculties remained alert, however, and he was to spend the remaining six years of his life reading,
dictating, and superintending his farm and gardens.

TO JOHN SALUSBURY PIOZZI SALUSBURY

9–10 November 1816.

My dearest Salusbury's Letter but echoes the Conversation of every Day. The
Times are indeed very bad—I told you long ago that bad Times were coming—
tho' I knew not the Form they would appear in: That which is presented to us
is formidable enough; for tho' the Corn in some of these Counties is got in,
much remains out to perplex the Farmer and rob Gentlemen of their Rents.——
Few of them even pretend to pay Taylors, Shoemakers, &c. So they shut their
Shops, and increase the List of Bankrupts.

Poor Duke of Rutland the while! and how beautifully he has behaved![1] Lord Stanhope and the Marquis Wellesley are no more;[2]—and Dr. Parry lies a *breathing*,—not a *Speaking* Corpse in the house where his Wife and Children eat only by his exertions.[3] Our heroic Friend Gibbes with Two more of the Profession offered to take, and keep his Practice safe for *him* that the Insurance Money might not be forfeited: but Life is a Cutfinger Club,[4] and as Dr. Charles Parry says, What did he come here for, but to succeed to his Father's Business?[5]

To understand this——which you cannot care about;——I must tell you that the old Doctor long ago agreed to pay so many Hundred Pounds per Annum— out of his Gains as would secure The Wife and unmarried Children 30000£ among them at his Death.[6] But here he lies getting nothing and if the Money is not paid up to the very hour—*All is forfeited!*

The Gentlemen Who offered to hold his Practice for him were therefore generous to the Widow and Orphans. While I am writing comes in My Correspondent Mr. Duppa, who going thro' the Town resolved to come and see one of its Antiquities—Your Old Aunt H: L: P.——He is the Man with whom The Reviewers have connected me, with Regard to Dr. Johnson's Diary.[7]——He came for Five Minutes he said, and staid Three hours; and will soon make me a longer Visit, by putting himself in a Post Chaise; and taking A Lodging in Edgar House[8]—wait on me every Day.

You would not like such Adventures——but I *do:* They serve to amuse and flatter me; he is Intimate with Colonel Barry,[9] Laureate Southey;[10] all the People I like to talk and hear about. He looked with a very warm Interest at the little Drawing of Brynbella; said he knew Arch Deacon Corbet so well, and Mrs. Katherine Plimley,[11] and that they had often conversed with him in Praise of the fair Owner, and Paintress of the Mansion.[12]

Now don't you be frighted as You were about Miss Somebody whose Name I have forgotten. Depend on it, You never need hear of *him* more.[13]

Young Williams's Accident was in the News papers before any Letter informed either his Aunt or Me of it,——so you see there are no Tales told out of School; it ended very happily indeed, but I suppose the Family must have felt uneasy at the Time.

This is Saturday 9: November Lord Mayor's Day and a lovely Bustle our Metropolis will exhibit.[14] The Rain this Morning at Two o'Clock was as if—in the Scripture Phrase—the very Windows of heaven had been opened.[15] Apropos to Scripture Phrases, I will write to Mr. Moore.[16]

Sir Henry Rivers—Son to the Lady who owns half this Town, is very wisely come hither to make Residence: he is a Clergyman, a Young Man and a handsome Man—completely of the Old School, and I *hope* his Fortune will give him Consideration among the Inhabitants.[17] It were *too* much to hope from Heaven that he had Talents to make himself respected; but his Conduct I hear is examplary, his Wife I see is pretty; and all *that* will go further than Scholarship.[18] He will do whatever is in his Power to check the cantagious Infatuation of following any Thing rather than the Established Church, any Person rather than a plain Man who reads his Sermon.—Lady John Thynne confest herself convinced by my Arguments that He would be a pernicious Counsellor who should perswade my Lord to go abroad[19]——and the General Election so near.[20]

Indeed the MDs, the MCs and the MPs, have each—sufficient for them to look to, and The Town is MT—all the while.

Do you trouble your head about the Eclipse?[21] Or shall you rise early enough to see it? There will be none so compleat again till the Year 1820,——and the last of 1793 was less perfect.

A curious Thing has chanced among the Lawyers; Mr. Duppa told it me. A rich Man well known to Fame by Name of Memory Middleton, died many Years ago—as 'twas supposed—Intestate. By the breaking up a Banking House last Week his Will has been found——and the Legatees &c. &c. are all half-distracted——still more so those by whom the Land has been sold, the Money squandered &c. It will make fine Work.[22]

Meanwhile, The Papers tell me poor Peggy Owen is gone;[23] She has *the Start of me.*

So Adieu Dear Creatures and God bless; and do not wonder that I write you Things wholly uninteresting——because it can't be otherwise. But you need only read how sincerely I remain Yours and Your Family's/ ever H: L: P.

Sunday Morning 10 November 1816
The Eclipse 19: November.

Text Ry. 589.343. *Address* John Salusbury Piozzi Salusbury Esq./ Brynbella/ near Denbigh/ North Wales. *Postmark* BATH 10 NO 109.

1. On 26 October Belvoir Castle, Grantham, seat of John Henry Manners (1778–1857), fifth duke of Rutland (1787), was ravaged by fire. Among the many losses were several valuable paintings, including Reynolds's *Nativity.* Although the castle was insured for £40,000, damages exceeded three times that sum (*Bath Herald,* 2 and 9 November); Farington, 14:4916.

2. Charles Stanhope (1753–1816), third earl Stanhope (1786), M.P., died of a liver complaint and dropsy on 15 December at Chevening (*The Times,* 17 December 1816).

Hyacinthe Gabrielle, née Roland, the estranged wife of the Marquess Wellesley, died on 7 November, aged fifty-six. For Richard Colley Wellesley, marquess Wellesley, see HLP to JSPS, 15 May 1812, n. 5.

3. Caleb Hillier Parry and his estranged wife Sarah had six living children in 1822: Charles Henry (1779–1860), Sarah Matilda (d. 1852), Mrs. Gertrude Trevor, William Edward (1790–1855), Caroline Bridget, and Mrs. Mary Garnier (P.R.O., Prob. 11/1657/ 275, proved, in London, 23 May 1822). See also *GM,* n.s. 37 (1852): 428.

For Dr. Parry and his wife, see HLP to PSW, 1 September [1789], n. 7.

4. Under "Poltroon" in the "Commonplace Book," HLP writes: "The word in old French means Cut Thumb: a Fellow so cowardly, that he cuts off his Thumb to avoid being killed in the Service of his Country." (HLP perpetuates a specious etymology of *poltron.*)

5. Parry's eldest son, Charles Henry, studied medicine at Göttingen, traveled with Coleridge in the Harz, and received an M.D. from Edinburgh (1804). A licentiate of the Royal College of Physicians in 1806, he became F.R.S. six years later. He practiced at 27 the Circus, Bath, and from 1818 to 1822 would serve as physician to the Bath General Hospital. Retiring early, he was to settle at 5 Belgrave Place, Brighton.

6. Dr. Parry left bequests to all his children, but the bulk of his wealth went to his unmarried daughters, Sarah and Caroline Bridget. His wife inherited the house at 7 Sion Place.

7. In the final paragraph of the "Preface" to the *Diary* (p. xi), Duppa "acknowledges his obligation to Mrs. Piozzi, for her kind assistance in explaining many facts in this Diary, which could not otherwise have been understood." The *Monthly Review* (81 [1816]: 220) speculated that "were [SJ]

alive, he would shake both his sides with laughter at seeing the detail of all his calls at Lichfield, and the amount of his washing-bill at Chester, illustrated with notes by Mrs. Piozzi and Mr. Duppa."

8. A boardinghouse maintained by John Wooderspoon, or Woodderspoon (1773–1837), and his wife, Frances (1772–1849) at 1 Edgar Buildings. See the "Walcot Burial Register" and the "Bath Abbey Burial Register," C.R.O., Somerset; "Walcot Poor Rate Book[s]," Guildhall, Bath.

9. For Henry Barry, see HLP to PSW, 11 June 1789, n. 2.

10. Robert Southey had been appointed poet laureate in 1813.

11. The Oxonian Joseph Corbett (ca. 1759–1830), archdeacon of Salop, assumed the surname Corbett in lieu of his patronymic Plymley in 1804, upon inheriting the Longnor Estates from his uncle, Robert Corbett (d. 1804). The archdeacon and his sister, Katherine Plymley (1758–1829), also of Longnor, were friends and neighbors of the Pembertons.

12. HMS painted a watercolor of Brynbella. See HLP to HMP, [ca. 8] June 1814.

13. HLP alludes to John Bather (1781–1839), whose family at Dinthill, Salop, were friends of the Plymleys/Corbetts and neighbors of the Pembertons. John had courted HMP during 1813–1814 and had competed with JSPS for her hand. Educated at Trinity College, Oxford, and Lincoln's Inn, Bather became a barrister-at-law, and, was according to Katherine Plymley, "more than commonly ill used" by HMP and her mother, who had taken "every pain . . . to convince him he was beloved" until they learned "he was not so rich as they had expected." Katherine further notes that Bather was "kept away" from HMP whenever JSPS called, but that he "immediately supplied [JSPS's] place" at his departure. "Greatly hurt" when HMP accepted JSPS's proposal, Bather married on 20 December 1814 Elizabeth, née Gipps (d. 1880). See "Katherine Plymley's Diary," C.R.O., Salop.

14. "Saturday [9 November] being the day on which the Lord Mayor [of London] usually takes upon himself the insignia of office was as usual celebrated by a grand civic feast." The lord mayor, Matthew Wood (1768–1843), and city officers proceeded not by water, as was the custom, but rode in state from Palace Yard through Parliament Street, the Strand, etc. to Guildhall (*Bath Herald,* 16 November).

15. Genesis 7:11.

16. John Moore, the surgeon of Vale Street, Denbigh.

17. Henry Rivers (ca. 1780–1851), ninth baronet (1805) of Chafford, Kent, had attended St. John's College, Cambridge, receiving his B.A. in 1801 and M.A. in 1805. A priest since 1804, he had in March 1816 been "preferred to the rectory of Walcot, on the presentation of his mother," Martha, Lady Rivers, née Coxe (ca. 1749–1835). She, as lord of the manor of Walcot, held the advowson. Her late husband Peter Rivers (ca. 1721–90), sixth baronet (1743), had acquired the Walcot estates in 1767, leasing such land for development as the Royal Crescent, Catharine Place, Rivers Street, Russel Street, the western part of Bennett Street, and the area north of the Royal Crescent to St. James's Square. See Walter Ison, *The Georgian Buildings of Bath from 1700 to 1830,* rev. ed. (Bath: Kingsmead Press, 1980), 173, 231–32, 233.

Sir Henry was to serve as rector of Walcot until June 1817 (*Bath and Cheltenham Gazette,* 11 June 1817).

18. The Reverend Sir Henry Rivers had married in 1812 Charlotte Eales (d. 1870).

19. M.P. for Bath, John Thynne (1772–1849), later third baron Carteret (1838) had in 1801 married Mary Anne, née Master (ca. 1777–1863).

20. A general election was not called until May 1818. In June of that year, John Thynne, the youngest son of the first marquess of Bath, would be returned as M.P. for Bath. See *The Times,* 12 May and 17 June 1818.

21. "The Eclipse of the Sun, on Tuesday morning, the 19th inst. will be the greatest which has happened in this country in 52 years" (*Bath Herald,* 16 November). For the eclipse of 1793, see *The Times,* 5 September 1793, and for that of 1820, see *GM* 90, pt. 2:254; HLP to DL, 12 August 1820.

22. Nathaniel Middleton (d. 1807), an employee of the East India Company from 1770 to 1788, had earned the sobriquet "Memory Middleton" because of his constant "prevarication, evasions, and famous lapses of memory" that characterized his testimony (April–June 1788) in the prolonged trial (February 1788–April 1795) of Warren Hastings (1732–1818). See Peter J. Marshall, *The Impeachment of Warren Hastings* (London: Oxford University Press, 1965), 52. According to the *Courier* (5 November), the recent cessation of a Pall-Mall banking business, in which Middleton had been a partner, produced a hitherto unknown will. Because it had been assumed that Middelton died intestate, his eldest son, "as heir at law, took possession . . . of his landed property" near Southampton, which he had since sold and which had been resold in lots, and the house, worth £20,000 that stood on the property, razed: "This affair . . . made no little stir in that place." But on 8 November, the *Courier* reported that the recently discovered will had been superseded by another will, duly proved, which left the estate in question to the eldest son; hence, "all the titles . . . are . . . secure."

23. Margaret Owen had died in late October at her home in the Claremont Buildings, Shrewsbury. See HLP to Q, 17 August [1784], n. 9.

TO LADY WILLIAMS

Bath Sunday
10: November 1816.

You are very good indeed dearest Lady Williams to write so soon upon my saucy Requisition—but it was quite cruel to leave us looking to the Newspapers for Intelligence we considered as so deeply Interesting. My Godson's Letter having alarmed me—a Gentleman present said he saw the Story in the public Prints—how then should it escape poor Miss Williams, whose Family Fondness circulates thro' every Vein of her Heart.

Your Account of the Weather, the Corn &c. is truly dismal: I never saw such a storm of Hail and Rain as we had Yesterday Morning before Daybreak: My house lies, or rather *stands* on an Inclined Plane; so the Torrent rushed by *us*, and roared down the Hill most frightfully. Our little River Avon swells apace, and looks extremely angry, I think those who Inhabit my last Year's wretched Habitation will have heavy Floods to encounter.

Nothing goes well, but dear Williams's Bag of Game;—let us never have done rejoycing that his precious Life was saved for a hundred Sakes. Meanwhile your Ladyship's Intelligence from the noble Cities of Dysert and Prestatyn make my very Hair stand on End. 600£ o'Year!!![1] while so many Gentlemen and Clergy of first Rate Abilities in *these* Parts of the World are starving. 600£ o'Year! why Mr. Williams can assure Your Ladyship that such an Allowance at Oxford or Cambridge would entitle a Man to keep the best Company in the University.

Well! I have a Letter from Mrs. Hoare to say her youngest Sister is gone to Geneva—and that *She,* Sophia, is very glad of it, because when in London She was lowspirited. A charming Place Geneva to be sure for lowspirited Ladies that want Society and Amusement!—why Paris is the only Place for *that.* The Switzers are the most hum-drum Companions one can find; see always the same faces, tell always the same stories; live the quietest Lives possible—sit still amidst the stormy Mountains, and fret when their favourite Fish are disturbed, by such and such Winds; resolving not to eat the other Fish, which Heaven sends them in Plenty. In a hot Summer Geneva is enchanting—The Glaciers so cool and so majestic. The Views of Nature so sublime after being wearied with the works of Art in Italy. But what should drive an Inhabitant of North Wales to pass their Christmas in that wild Country, they must be clever who can tell.

Buonaparte 'tis said keeps up his regal State and acts the Emperor very prettily—I wonder whether his Work is done, or whether more is reserved for him to do.[2]

I think your Ladyship will miss poor dear old Lloyd of Wygfair, next Tuesday sennight when the Eclipse will create Conversation—for if his House did stink of mangey Dogs, and sour Paste; he could always tell one Something it was pleasant to learn, and this Eclipse—the best we have many Years, would have amused *him*, and given him some-thing to talk about, and amuse *droppers-in*.[3] I think there is a fashion in Fears as in every thing else. I remember my Father somewhat ill-looked-on, because he would not be afraid of an Eclipse which He was peeping at thro' Telescopes and smoked Glasses some time about 1747 or 48. We were at my Uncle Robert's house in Albemarle Street London; and there was a bit of a Garden and an Alcove and I had permission to entertain Baby Visitants with Baby Teadishes &c. which interested me more than the Eclipse, of which I recollect no trace except some Catholic Lady reproaching my father for not being frighted, and saying These Wicked Heretics fear neither God nor Devil—while my heart told me and the other Children—one of whom was Sir George Osborne—dead long since, and one—Peggy Owen of Penrhôs dead last Week——that there was nothing to be afraid of.—We observed no Darkness whatever.[4]

I suppose there is no one now, Catholic or Protestant; that thinks about such Matters, except as Matters of mere Curiosity.

The Lady who was to have married the Father of those pretty Miss Leicesters, met Miss Williams and me in the Street together one Day about a Week ago:[5] and your Sister in Law with officious Kindness cried—*This* is Mrs. Piozzi; when with the true Salopian Terror having her Dignity intruded on, Miss Russel hastily retired: tho' in no Danger whatever/ from Dearest Madam/ Your Ladyship's ever Obedient/ and Obliged and faithful/ H: L: P.

Present me most respectfully and affectionately to Dear Sir John—and his and Your Ladyship's Darlings.

H: L: P. sends her true Love to Dear Mr. Williams and begs him to be careful in future——Miss Price had beautiful bright black Eyes a Dozen Years ago: how happy they are not yet *shorn of their Beams*.[6] Adieu! I wish you would write to Me.

Text Ry. 4 (1812–18). *Address* Lady Williams/ Bodylwyddan/ St. Asaph/ Flintshire/ North Wales. *Postmark* BATH <10> NO 1816.

1. Because HLP is responding to a remark in Ly W's now missing letter, we can only speculate as to the original statement, which had to do with the worth of livings in the diocese of St. Asaph.

According to the Ecclesiastical Revenues Commission's report of 1835, there were some eight or nine livings in the St. Asaph diocese with gross incomes of £600 per annum. Dyserth does not seem to be appropriate, since its income in 1835 was valued at £113 annually, unless HLP's exclamation refers to the income from the tithes of the parish of Dyserth, which belonged to the archdeacon of St. Asaph, an office habitually held *in commendam* by the bishop of the said diocese.

There is yet another interpretation. The date of HLP's letter accords with an event that occurred on 16 October, viz., the institution of the bishop's eldest son, Charles Scott Luxmoore, to a prebendary in the Cathedral of St. Asaph. Having graduated from St. John's, Cambridge, in 1815, he was already in possession of two rectories and a prebendary in his father's former diocese of Hereford. It may be that HLP associates £600 per annum with a young and inexperienced Luxmoore.

2. At St. Helena, Napoleon had instituted elaborate rituals: guests, for example, were welcomed by liveried servants "'in the name of the Emperor'"; his luxurious meals, served with exquisite linen, silver, and china, were announced, "'Your Majesty's dinner is served.'" Gilbert Martineau says that "this elaborate procedure was laid down and organized by Napoleon himself, with the evident . . . intention of giving the British the impression that he was a sovereign living incognito

rather than a prisoner of State." See *Napoleon's St. Helena,* trans. Francis Partridge (London: John Murray, 1968), 43, 47, 48–49.

3. John Lloyd had been a particularly welcome presence during the time of an eclipse. He had several astronomical instruments, including a "15-feet acromatic telescope by Dolland." See the *Bath and Cheltenham Gazette,* 28 February 1816.

4. On 20 April 1788, HLP had reminisced in *Thraliana* (1:284) about the "fine House in Albemarle Street" belonging to her maternal uncle, Robert Salusbury Cotton. It was there that she saw "the famous Eclipse of the Sun in 1748 [14 July]. the present Sir George Osborne & his Brother came over . . . & we played together all Day, & saw the Eclipse thro' smok'd Glasses."

George Osborne, or Osborn, or Osburne (1742–1818), fourth baronet (1753) of Chicksands Priory, Beds., was an army general.

5. See HLP to Ly W, 22 October 1816, n. 11 for the "pretty Miss Leicesters."

Between the death of his first wife, Mary, in 1797 and his wedding in 1798, Charles Leicester may have courted a cousin, the daughter of the Reverend William Russell (b. 1733) of Cardington, Salop, and his wife, Elizabeth, née Byrne (d. 1805).

For Charles Leicester, see HLP to Ly W, 15 June 1815, n. 5.

6. *Paradise Lost,* 1.596.

TO SIR JAMES FELLOWES

Bath
Monday 18 November *1816*

The Punishment is all my own, *Cruel que vous êtes;*—but you are coming to Town at last—and Sir James and Lady Fellowes will do Mrs. Piozzi the Honour to dine with her on Wednesday 27th of this Month to meet the Dear Family from the Vineyards &c.—at five o'Clock.

Our Cluster has been withering for a Week or two, from blighting Apprehensions of Ill Health at Adbury;—but I say

> Peace Friends! and be not over exquisite
> To cast the Fashion of uncertain Evils;
> For grant they prove such, while they rest unknown
> What need a Man forestall his Date of Grief
> Running to meet what he would most avoid?
> And if they be *like these* mere false Alarms,
> How bitter were such Self Delusion!——[1]

Oh 'tis delightful News that you are coming, and Joy comes well in Such a needful Time. What a disgraceful Account do the Papers give of the State of our *Enlightened* Metropolis![2]—Will the Moment never arrive when even Careless Lookers-on will be alarmed, and torpid Sensualists awaked to Reflection; when the Man who fears not for his Soul, shall at least tremble for his Possessions; and discover that decent Morality and Subordination to constituted Authorities can alone protect the Rich from Robbery and the Poor from Oppression. I am not apt to be *ambitiously sententious* and have wholly forgotten the Character of my last Letter—not recollecting if I had then been told how Two Clergymen of respectable Situations had thrown off their Gowns because the Church of England would not Throw off the Ten Commandments.—They go about now I hear from Meeting House to Meeting House preaching against the Decalogue.[3]

Such Times would put *any Puddle* into a Storm. Well! but all this is Talking, in order to keep immediate Feeling away: Yet I do think you are not very bad when *Such Stuff* cures you. I never recommended solid or *heavy* Food even at Noon day. Strong Chicken *Soup*—but without Ham in it—and such elegant Sweet Jellies as Your Cook knows how to make, would be a Luncheon at once light and nutritive, and I am sure you *keep moving* till Dinner Time, which at this Season of the Year closes the Day *naturellement*. The Pain about the Pylorus is monitory, will keep you from eating too fast for fear of crouding the *doorway;*[4] and will send you to Hetling Court where a Snuffy-nosed old Woman has replaced a very ordinary Young one. Such is the Choice which human Life affords.

Did not you once tell me what a pretty Genius I had for the Study of Medicine?——Oh you were more ill then, than you are now. Bessy Jones and I have both had Coughs; and I persuaded myself that my broken out Nose was a Cancer—and her tightness of Breathing an incipient Phtisis:[5] till dear Doctor Fellowes came and laughed at us,——protesting that her Pulse was good, and assuring *himself* (without telling me So,)—That my Head was addle.

So now We are looking forward to Two Gay Days—27th of January and February the 14th. We will have a Harp for the little Welshwoman's Birthday, and devise Sports for that of your good Father when we meet and are merry next Wednesday Sennight—Is it not from the French that we even learn to *call* it *dressing* a Dinner?—*dresser* les Apprêts d'un Banquet they say; and *deshabiller* un Lapin is cutting one up pour le *Fracasser:* all this I learned from poor Boisgelin—from whom I shall learn no more.[6]

Doctor Parry still breathes—poor Dr. Parry! but he was *so* unsuccessful in his Care of Mr. Piozzi, I never felt my heart attracted to his house.

Adieu! This Letter has been written all by Scraps and Snatches: People coming in without ceasing, and stealing the Wits from my head The Pen from my Fingers every Moment. Let it at least do its Duty in presenting my best Regards and Compliments to Lady Fellowes's Acceptance

> Paper therefore fly with Speed
> Let thy Friend make haste to read
> To be read—is all thy Meed
> Hark! the Bell is ringing!

Can such Stuff come from any Creature but *your* much honoured/ H: L: P.?

Text Huntington MSS. 6136. *Address* Sir James Fellowes/ Adbury House/ near Newbury/ Berkshire. *Postmark* < > NO 18 <1816>.

1. Milton's *A Mask* ["Comus"], lines 358–64.
2. There were many riots in London, but HLP refers to one provoked by Henry Hunt (1773–1835), a reformer who gained attention in 1812 when he stood unsuccessfully for Bristol's parliamentary seat.

On 15 November he addressed over five thousand people gathered at Spa Fields, London. There he urged support for distressed mechanics and manufacturers who petitioned the Prince Regent for tax relief. At nightfall, with the meeting adjourned until 2 December, two mobs formed: one pillaged food shops and broke windows while the other attacked the home of Viscount Castlereagh and attempted to tear up the iron railings at Leicester Square. By 9 p.m. the Bow Street officers quelled the disturbances (*The Times*, 16 and 18 November).

3. HLP relates a rumor. Accepting its authenticity, she wrote it up in the "Commonplace Book" under *Methodists*:

"Methodists are now perswading our Clergy to throw off their Gowns, because the Church of England will not throw away the Decalogue—If we once *do* discard the Ten Commandments what will become of us? Cant in our Mouths, Crime in our Hearts and Hands; Terror—The *Reign* of Terror will be begun, and Military Despotism must be called in, to save us from Anarchy and Madness:——putting the Power of murdering their Neighbours into Professors' Hands, that we may escape Torture administered by Dilletanti.—!!!"

4. A bit of HLP's medical humor. The pylorus—at the juncture of the stomach and intestine—is literally from the Greek word for "gatekeeper."

5. Phtisis: a progressive wasting disease; specifically pulmonary consumption *(OED)*.

6. He died 10 September 1816. See HLP to Ly W, 22 October 1816, n. 3.

TO SIR JAMES FELLOWES

Bath
29: November 1816
Fryday

Another Letter You shall have Dear Sir—and that directly; to thank you for fixing to come *in Earnest* next Fryday and dine once more with Your old Acquaintance Murphy and Thrale; and Santa Cecilia——tanta Cara:[1] and my lovely Mother, who looks *so* well among them all.[2]

I am glad the Thousand Trees are arrived *un*spoiled this Weather as they surely are: because You closed your Letter in Good humour, and a Failure would have full surely vexed You. Such Conduct as Yours however will always keep the Mind in a *Disposition* to give and receive Pleasure:——Would to God you had *Treble* your Income! but it will encrease, not diminish by Such Management:—and bad as the People are encouraged to grow, they will not cease to love and reverence such a Landlord, Master, &c. as my Friend Sir James Fellowes, of whom I am daily more and more proud.

Cobbett had been Galvanizing the Multitude finely I am told in his last Paper——Be *scum* no longer, says he;—be no longer called *Scum* I say.[3]

Did I ever tell you a Story of which this reminds me, concerning the blind Lord North's Father, old Guildford;[4] who delighted in affecting coarse Expressions; and used to say to his Friends when he met them—"Oh Such a one, how does the Pot boyl?" Some Democrate who probably disliked the rough Address;——when Wilkes and Liberty set London madding:[5] called to Lord Guildford across a Circle of Ladies round the Tea Table—and cried exultingly— "Well my good Lord, how does the Pot boyl *now?*" "Troth Sir, replied the Peer without Hesitation, just as you Gentlemen would wish it to do—Scum uppermost." I am so afraid this Tale is not new to You any more than baptizing the Bells. We have Two in England you know that were Christened *Thomas*.[6]

The Oxford one I forget all Account of;[7] but When the Devil was set up to look over Lincoln Cathedral, The *wise* Folk found baptizing the Bell was an efficacious Method of Sending him off:—some of their Conclave however being Incredulous—Let us said They baptize the Bell by Name of the *doubting* Apostle—*and that will do.* So he is *Tom* o'Lincoln.[8]

I fancy the Phænomenon you allude to at Valencia—where they are I trust not much Improved in Philosophy, was a real Meteor:[9] The Atmosphere is loaded with Vapour certainly, in a Way not wholly natural: and has been all the Summer—if Summer it may be called——Mrs. Mostyn is at Geneva—starving of Cold in a larger and more Icy Valley than the Vale of Llwydd, and surrounded with higher and more snowy Mountains. I am half uneasy about her, She is subject to Pleurisy[10]—and the East Winds in Switzerland are dreadful; but she says She is amused, and lives cheap.

Be careful of your own health Dear Sir, and come to Bath *unaltered:* and let us see out this Tedious Year 1816. On Fryday when you dine here, there will be but 21 Days of it left.

Doctor Fellowes has the Gout, Your Sister blythe and bonny; and fit to encounter Switzerland after her last Journey through the Snow.—Mrs. Dorset sent here last Night for a little Book——I was a'Bed; but jumped up and sent it her: General Garstyn leaves Bath[11]—like Betty *Bolèyne* without saying a Word to me[12]——Oh false and fickle Mortals! but here is a Young Captain Montague who makes Verses on me, so that must go for Compensation.[13]

My Spirits are not bad, but like your good Father I am teized with Cough and Choke; and *Face*-ach, which he has not.

Mrs. Fellowes has best Health of any of us. My Eyes are good however, or I could not see the Lines of this Paper but tomorrow is Saturday and if this Nonsense does not go directly, You will not know till Sunday, how *hasty* I was to thank You and Lady Fellowes for all your undeserved/ Kindnesses to Your poor/ H: L: P.

I was at Grosvenor Place when your Dear Letter came,[14] and the House has been full of Droppers *In* ever since.

I hope there are a great many Larches among the New Comers. They are so Good natured—they are at home everywhere.

Text Huntington MSS. 6137. *Address* Sir James Fellowes/ Adbury House/ near/ Newbury/ Berks. *Postmark* BATH 29 NO 29 1816.

1. JF would have been acquainted with these paintings from having spent his honeymoon at Streatham Park in spring 1816. Apart from Cipriani's "Head of a Colossal Female," on loan to the European Museum, HLP had saved only these painting from the sale of the contents of Streatham Park.

2. For the Zoffany portrait of Hester Maria Salusbury, see HLP to AL, 8 February 1813, n. 8, and to JF, 21 February 1816.

3. Addressing the "Journeymen and Labourers of England, Wales, Scotland, and Ireland," William Cobbett remarks that several of the London dailies represent those groups as "the *Scum* of Society, They say, that you have *no business at public meetings. . . . that your voice is nothing. . . .* I trust they will change their tone, and that the day of change is *at no great distance!*" See his *Weekly Political Register* 31 (2 November 1816):561–62.

4. For Frederick North, first lord of the treasury, who had become blind in 1787, see HLP to PSP [ca. 31 December 1792], n. 5. He was the son of Francis North (1704–90), first earl of Guilford (1752) from whom he inherited his title.

5. "Wilkes and Liberty" was the slogan used between spring 1763 and autumn 1774 by the London supporters of John Wilkes in his various parliamentary elections. See HLP to PSP, 15 October 1820.

6. In *Retrospection*, 1:141, HLP writes of bells being "baptized formally, and blest" in Italian churches, and she observes: "I have half a notion, that since the Reformation, bells have been solemnly and seriously christened here in England. Two yet remain at Lincoln and at Oxford: their names are *Thomas*; I know not their age."

7. Great Tom, "the loudest thing in Oxford," was moved from Osney Abbey's tower to Christ Church when the monasteries were dissolved. See James Morris, *Oxford* (New York: Harcourt, Brace, and World, 1965), 131.

8. Great Tom, the bell of more than five tons in the central tower of Lincoln Cathedral.

9. On 19 October at 7:15 p.m. "an extraordinary phenomenon was witnessed" at Valencia, Spain: "A sun and seven stars appeared in the atmosphere, and their light illuminated the whole City. The stars then united themselves with the sun, and the whole disappeared" (*Courier*, 23 November).

10. CMT had symptoms of pleurisy in the autumn of 1792.

11. For John Garstin, see HLP to JF [19 October 1815], n. 3.

12. HLP records the anecdote about Betty Boleyne in the "Commonplace Book" under *General Garstin*:

"General Garstin . . . told me such *funny* Stories, about some Female, Betty Boleyne by Name, and her Engagements with Lord Keith, who trapt her when in a tender Humour out of a Bond for 1500£ that I laughed myself dead almost. . . . The Lady's miserly Habits sleeping at an Almshouse near Rochester erected for the Benefit of *poor* Travellers, when She was worth 30,000£: and a Number of other unaccountable Tricks making the Connection very comical indeed—with his Escape as they were just going to Church, by Her saying—Well my Dear, as every thing is now settled, give me the Bond. He did so, and She threw it into the Fire—— running away at another Door, and never suffering herself to be seen again, or solicited to perform her Engagements."

13. George Wroughton Montagu (d. 1871), a captain in the 82nd Regiment of Foot (1815–18), was the eldest son of Susannah Wroughton's younger sister, Charlotte (d. 1839), and her husband, George Montagu (1750–1829), G.C.B. (1815), an admiral. The younger Montagu was to rise to the rank of colonel. He disappears from the *Army Lists* in 1825, the year that his aunt Susannah died, and he succeeded to the Wroughton family property, Wilcot Manor, Wilts.

14. HLP visited the Reverend and Mrs. Josiah Thomas, who lived at 12 Grosvenor Place, Bath.

TO JOHN SALUSBURY PIOZZI SALUSBURY

Bath
6: December 1816

I thank You dearest Salusbury for your Letter, and am Sorry to see that it confirms all we are told about the unwholesome Corn &c. Would it not provoke one to hear of Two Thousand Sacks of fine Wheat Flour burned last Week at Chippenham Twelve Miles from this Town—at such A Moment!—Madness; is it not?[1] Sir James Fellowes however, says they are tolerably quiet about *him*—in Your old favourite County—Berkshire:——where the Critics whooted me for Italicking my Words in Letters to you. I think no Emphasis Strong enough now to express the general Uneasiness, or particular Absurdity of the Londoners.[2] Had Government not been provided with Guards for the Bank, Property would scarce have had a Name in England—and my poor Daughters—(Self I care not for;)—must have been totally ruined. They attempted to take Arms from the

Tower too: but there Government was beforehand with them, else half the Lives in London would have been lost by now: Do not think I exaggerate,——every Newspaper tells the Same Tale; and 'tis only because you do not read them, that I make my Letters into an Abridgement of public and daily Prints.

The Old Wheat you mention is indeed a Blessing——To make it go further——some People bake it in *Biscuit*—Sea Biscuit as 'tis called: and beat it into Powder for Babies. This Calamity has been long been Threatening us, but no one will expect Misfortune till they feel it—and those who tell them that 'tis coming, make themselves less welcome by doing so.

I had a Small Party last Night—mere Tea and Talk—and Dr. Gibbes said the Epidemic Diseases consequent on bad Food would sweep many of us away.—— A Gentleman in Company replied, fame had always told, and History had constantly related, that such Things *were*—but he trusted—They were far from *us*.

They are no further off now than France and Germany however.[3]

> So from Plague Pestilence and Famine
> Good Lord deliver us.[4]

I do not walk either to or from the Parties at this Time of Year indeed; Books and Chairhire constitute much of my Expences, but the first amuse me when at home, and the last take me out to be amused.

Meantime my old Enemy Toothach or Pain in the face worries me just as it has always done every Winter, whether in Surrey Somersetshire or Wales.

Mrs. Mostyn has written, She seems to like Geneva very much: The Society is all English, they live but little if any with the *Natives* who She observes are very Moral meaning I suppose very dull; but praising the Scenery She compares it to the Vale of Llwydd, on a large Scale; with a great immense Blue Lake in the middle. Doctor Whalley is safe in Modena; *He* proposes to return next June.[5] I am sorry dear Williams's rich Match is off[6]—for Joy comes well in such a needful Time, and he deserves every thing for staying quietly in his own Country among peaceable Folks—there are no Mobs in Wales I believe, and no Morality at Modena,——so *those* Friends will do well enough. Mr. Hunt, The Man who set London o'raving, ran thro' our Town to Bristol yesterday:[7] and altho' the Poor say they have not a Penny to purchase Food——The very Beggars subscribe a Penny each, to pay the Fine of—— ——who robbed the Stock-Exchange, and was punished by being made to forfeit so much Money.[8] He is said to be worth 300000£ but if his Friends pull down the Bank, he will be no richer than They. All Beggars, and no one to beg from; So that will be Liberty and Equality:——They *do* hoist the French Rebel Colours.[9]

Adieu and God bless; and pardon for disturbing your more rational Tranquillity, the agitated Fingers of your/ H: L: P.

We are very much to be envied, we Bath Inhabitants,—Invalides are respected by all Ranks——and Residents in this Town are ranked—I know not why—as Sick People. My chief Symptom of Bodily Distress is my Drinking Asses Milk in a Morning by Doctor Gibbes's Prescription; It is very good for that Catarrh which teizes all old Subjects in cold Weather——and as to Teeth, they come and go with equal pain I believe: Hester Maria scarce suffers more than her Godmother and your Affectionate Aunt is enduring at this very Moment, but tis Idle to think about Self—and that Self an old Woman;—while such Distress and Danger hang over all. It was Captain Montagu suggested to me the Notion of saving Wheat Flour by baking it into *Sea Biscuit* instead of Loaves; The Trick may perhaps be worth trying,—*in Country Places.*

Once more Farewell and when you want a Letter write to/ your faithfully attached/ H: L: P.

Make my Affectionate Love acceptable to your *Three Darlings.*

Compliments to enquiring Friends—Doctor Cumming, Mr. Moore &c. Sir Watkin Williams is again reported to be at the Brink of Matrimony, Is it true?[10]

Text Ry. 589.345. *Address* John Salusbury Piozzi Salusbury Esq./ Brynbella/ near Denbigh/ North Wales. *Postmark* BATH 7 DE 7 1816.

1. Having received "an incendiary letter" threatening arson "unless the price of flour was lowered," Messrs. Dowling and Gaby, proprietors of a corn and flour mill at Chippenham, sustained losses in excess of £10,000, when their mill burned down at 3 a.m. on 2 December. "The immediate consequence of this is, that on our next market wheat will . . . rise considerably." See *AR*, "Chronicle," 58 (1816): 190; *Bath Chronicle,* 5 December.

2. Crowds had gathered at the second Spa Fields meeting on 2 December to hear Henry Hunt, John Cartwright (HLP to JF, 9 July 1816, n. 15), James Watson, Sr. (1766–1838), James Watson, Jr. (ca. 1797–1836), and Arthur Thistlewood (1770–1820) call for reform. Thistlewood harangued the mob, with the younger Watson waving a French tricolor and exhorting the crowd to follow him. Plotting to attack the Bank and Tower, dubbed "the old Lady and the old Gentlemen," the rioters reached the Royal Exchange, where they were met and repelled by the lord mayor and the police. (See also HLP to JSPS, 17 December 1816, n. 2.) While this was occurring, Hunt was addressing those who had remained at Spa Fields on the subject of the Regent's refusal to receive petitions for annual parliaments and male suffrage. All was quiet in London by nightfall, and as the *AR* remarks, "The tumult, daring and alarming as it might seem, was wholly inadequate to endanger the safety of the capital." See *AR* 58 (1816):190–91; *GM* 86, pt. 2 (1816):556–57; *Bath and Cheltenham Gazette,* 4 December; and the *Bath Chronicle,* 5 December.

3. HLP refers to articles in the *Bath Chronicle* (5 and 12 December) that reported near-famine conditions on the Continent: Paris was "in a very perturbed state, owing chiefly to the distresses of the lower orders," and Germany was suffering a "melancholy" harvest, the result of "whole fields of young corn [being] destroyed by snails."

4. See, e.g., Leviticus 26:25; Numbers 14:12; Deuteronomy 28:21; Jeremiah 14:12; Ezekiel 5:12, 6:11, 7:15.

5. TSW had written to his wife, Frances, from Modena in the autumn of 1816. See Wickham, 2:437–40.

6. JW was not to marry until 1842.

7. By profession a gentleman-farmer from Wiltshire, Hunt was currently traveling around the provinces seeking support for another Spa Fields meeting to be held after Parliament opened on 28 January 1817. (See HLP to JF, 23 January 1817, n. 6.) On 27 December he was to address a peaceful gathering of two thousand persons at Brandon Hill, Bristol, on the issues of annual parliaments and election reform (*Bath Herald,* 28 December). See also HLP to JSPS, 17 December 1816, n. 1.

8. Sentenced to a year's imprisonment allegedly for seeking to defraud the stock exchange, Thomas Cochrane upon his release threw himself into political reform and opposition to government. When he participated in a reform meeting at the London Tavern in August 1816, he was arrested on charges of having escaped from the King's Bench Prison seventeen months earlier. His jail term deferred, he was fined £100 in November, primarily as retribution for his political activism. He refused to pay the fine and was again imprisoned. But on 7 December, he was released after having served sixteen days; his fine had been paid by a *"penny* subscription." See the *Bath Chronicle,*

5 and 12 December. Cobbett was to write that "the *Penny Subscription* set on foot to pay his fine . . . excited an enthusiasm that never was surpassed, and in which all ranks, except tax-eaters, participated." See his *Weekly Political Register*, 32 (13 September 1817):743; also the *Courier*, 6 December 1816.

9. The "lower classes" at the Spa Fields meeting wore "green, white and red cockades" and carried a tricolor flag bearing the inscription, "'Truth and Justice, that is all we want'" (*Bath Chronicle*, 5 December).

10. For Sir Watkin Williams-Wynn and rumors of his marriage, see, e.g., HLP to JSPS, 21 February 1815.

TO MARY MANGIN

11: December [1816]

How is dear Mrs. Mangin today?[1] I hoped to have come and satisfied myself concerning the State of her Health;—but Fear of being sent back to Prison by Doctor Gibbes, keeps me another day within:—though the Pain in my Face now plagues me but little.[2]

Collins has filled my Book-Shelves—and I have read with Delight the Introductory Pages to Pamela.[3]——It would not surprize me if I should be Seduced to go on through the whole Work of our darling Richardson./ Ever Yours/ H: L: P.

Text Princeton University Library. *Address* No. 11/ Queen's Parade/ [Bath].

1. For Mary Mangin, see HLP to JF, 9 July, n. 7.
2. But by 12 December, HLP was to write in her "Pocket Book": "Toothach and Pain in the Face to Distraction."
3. Edwin Collings, the Bath bookseller, had—according to HLP in her "Pocket Book"—"brought me home *Ben:* Jonson's Works by Gifford and Mr. Mangin's nice new Edition of Richardson's Works." The latter was *The Works of Samuel Richardson. With a Sketch of his Life and Writings*, 19 vols. (London: W. Miller, 1811).

TO THOMAS WINDLE

Bath
12: December 1816.

My dear Sir

I have (tho' tormented with Toothache) looked over the *Only Lease* in my Possession, most carefully; It is to Reynold Davies:—and no one else, not a Word about Parsons. The Date is April 1804—The Expiration of course 1830— he binds himself to Gabriel Piozzi and *his* Wife, John Mostyn and *his* Wife— and Three Miss Thrales——to keep Gates and Platts and Hedges and Ditches &c.—or forfeit his Lease:——paying 27£ per Annum. He has paid it regularly and shall not be disturbed by *me*. Let my Successors do *their own* Way,—Mine is to be quiet, and leave my old Friends so. I shall buy in a Thousand Pounds next January if I live so long,—My Balance at Hammersley's is 400£ now which with Newton's 200£ payable on the 23d Instant—as the Bankers tell me, will purchase as much Stock 3 Per Cent Consols as will make my present Three Thousand Pounds into four Thousand: borrowing 50£ or so from my January Dividends, and leaving me enough to pay my *few*, my *very* few Debts: and go on till Spring and Summer supply more Money to/ Dear Sir/ Yours faith[fully]/ H: L: Piozzi.

You see as I told you My Adversity—so I confide in you to rejoice in my Prosperity—You have been always a true Friend, and my Heart is not an ungrateful one.
My Love to the Dear Ladies.
Rev: Reynold Davies's Lease is for what was then called Town's End Field.[1]— I believe he built a House upon it—but all that has nothing to do with Ray the Bricklayer, who used to pay Rent to Mr. Thrale and afterwards to Mr. Piozzi for Some Land or House or Place of which I know nothing, and can give no Description;——When he died—meaning Ray the Bricklayer—his Successors paid;[2] and Parsons is the Name which stands in the Banker's Book[3]—Leak said there was no such Person now, it was a Mr. L'Estrange who married Parsons's Daughter.[4] I have had no Money from them since December 1814—so I suppose they owe me 40£.——
You once worried Parsons out of 18£ I remember, when Property Tax took off Two; and Leak could not get the Money without your Help.——

Text MS Eng. 71 Boston Public Library. *Address* Thomas Windle Esq./ No. 1/ John Street/ Bedford Row/ London. *Postmark* BATH DE 12 < >; E 13 DE 13 1816.

1. For RD and the Streatham land that he rented from the Piozzis, see HLP to JSPS, 15 December 1810, n. 12.
2. Richard Ray rented Streatham land from HT as early as 1780. After Ray's death in 1795, the land was rented by his widow, Sarah, until 1811. See "Streatham Land Tax Assessments," in C.R.O., Surrey.
3. See HLP to RD, 7 November 1813, n. 1.
4. Perhaps Thomas L'Estrange (ca. 1792–1822), who, residing at Euston Place, St. Pancras, was buried from St. Leonard's Church. See the church's "Register of Burials," at the Greater London Record Office.

TO JOHN SALUSBURY PIOZZI SALUSBURY

Tuesday
17: December 1816

Your Letter Dear Salusbury is really a very kind one: but The Time is yet far distant I hope, when poor Aunt shall stand in need of an Asylum.
The blundering Rebellion is completely stifled[1]—smothered like a Man bit by a Mad Dog in Ireland, between Two Featherbeds. Our Bristol Folks—who are

proverbially said to sleep with one Eye open;—are too well aware of Mr. Hunt's and Mr. Cobbet's conduct and Intentions——and since their Friends Attack upon the Bank and Tower, No Man worth 50£ will venture himself among them. It was fortunate the Trick was tried; Every Tradesman in London instantly shut his Shop and began providing for the Defence of their Property.

Mr. Platt's being shot too, was to the *Publick* a lucky Circumstance;[2] Young Watson will be taken I dare say——750£ is *such* a Reward you know:[3]—and hanging that one Man will be better than the Guards killing Rioters in the Street.

All is quiet: The foolish Creatures fancied they should have support from every Country Town; but Common Sense carried the Day, and saved the Nation from such Distresses as poor France experienced, and cannot yet recover from.

I enclose you the Song so admired that 3000£ of them have been printed to give about. It is written by one of *us* chattering Old Women, (Hannah More they say:)[4]

> whose *Tongues*
> *of Aspen Leaves been made.*[5]

So if we annoy our Neighbours *one Way,* we assist them in *another.*

Newton has sent a Bill in to Hammersley's for 200£ payable the 23d of this Month—tardy you'll say,—but steady: It will enable me—with what I have saved, and what I shall borrow from January Dividends, to *keep my Word;* and make my Self Possessor of *four* Thousand Pounds Stock in the 3 per Cents—by this Day next Month.

The five per Cents will be made four immediately on meeting of Parliament which must instigate us all to drive Money in *now* if possible.

And here is a great Saving to be made in Wine the Gentlemen of my Acquaintance tell *me.*

Port Wine you know is so called from O*port*o in Por*tug*al: but Wise Men have found the way to plant *their* Grapes in *our* Colony at the Cape of Good Hope: whence The Produce made—being our own, comes cheaper to the Mother Country—old England;—*as* cheap however as home-made Stuff consisting of Sugar and Brandy.[6] 'Tis a new Contrivance, and will lower the Price of Sugar too in Time, and make a monstrous saving. So you see I learn something useful by living in the *World*—which my long Habits make necessary to my Existence;—it would be Shortened by playing the Recluse and not knowing what past *even close to me. You* who are blest with the Companion of Your Choice may live delighted and see no one else: but I, poor Solitary Cast-off, could not breathe without Light and Noise and Acquaintance:—Droppers-*In* as I call them, and justly:—for they do drop-*in* by ones and twos and Threes all Morning, and after dinner I spend the hours in Study or in Prayer, or both till Bed-Time——scarce ever going to a Party now, it is so cruel cold: Lady Willoughby asked me this Evening—and I refused. But Spring will make me more active, I shall come out with the Butterflies.

What Thunder and Lightning we had on the early Morning of the 15th December worthy a hot August——but the Weather is very surprizing. Sir James

Fellowes came cum multis aliis—to see if it had frighted me. He goes to Town today, and takes my Banker's Book to settle. He and his Lady have been to Bath on a Visit to their adored Father and Mother: When I wish my Dear Salusbury to be the happiest Man upon Earth, I can *but* wish him the Fate of old Doctor Fellowes: who has spent 56 Years with the chosen Wife of his Heart—and who at fourscore Years old lives—and will die surrounded by Children and Grand Children—all striving who shall shew themselves most Affectionate to *him* and *her*:—disinterestedly so without a doubt—for they are all well provided for; and what the Parents leave among them cannot be felt in their Fingers. If Happiness may be found on Earth, I think 'tis at No. 13 in the Vineyards Bath: and When a Letter comes from Brynbella telling of the health of its Dear Inhabitants, no Small Felicity is brought to their/ truly faithful and Attached H: L: P. at No. 8 Gay Street.

Text Ry. 589.347. *Address* John Salusbury Piozzi Salusbury Esq./ Brynbella/ near Denbigh/ North Wales.

1. Although the violence that followed the Spa Fields meeting on 2 December was suppressed, the reform movement continued to strengthen, with another meeting planned for 28 January 1817. Meanwhile Sheffield experienced "alarming symptoms of riot" when the cavalry on 10 December dispersed a mob carrying a "loaf of bread (dipped in blood) stuck upon a long pole" and breaking windows along its route. See the *Bath and Cheltenham Gazette*, 4 December; the *Bath Chronicle*, 12 December.

2. Meeting first at Spa Fields, James Watson Jr. and his followers sought arms at Snow Hill. Entering Mr. Beckwith's gunshop, Watson was "told to go about his business by a Mr. [Richard] Platt, who was casually present." Watson allegedly "drew a pocket-pistol, and discharged its contents into Mr. Platt's body." Platt sustained a minor wound. See *Bath and Cheltenham Gazette*, 11 December; *AR* 58:190–91; *GM* 86, pt. 2 (1816):556–58; HLP to JSPS, 6 December, n. 2.

3. On 7 December the City of London offered a £500 reward for the "apprehension of *James Watson* the younger, late of Hyde-street, Bloomsbury, surgeon" (*Bath and Cheltenham Gazette*, 11 December). After the Platt incident, Watson had escaped to the United States. In the meanwhile, however, the £200 was added to the original reward. See *The Times*, 12, 14, 16 December.

4. Hannah More had written a number of "songs" derogatory of the Spa Fields orators and contributed them to the eight numbers (15 February–5 April 1817) of the *Anti-Cobbett*. HLP had seen one of the "songs" prior to its publication and made a copy for JSPS. See *Journals and Letters*, 9:431 and n. 25. The "songs" are not in the collected works of 1818–19 or 1830, nor have they been identified.

5. As Tilley observes (p. 745), the comparison of a woman's tongue to an aspen leaf has long been proverbial.

6. The *Bath Herald* (29 June and 21 December) advertised the medicinal benefits of "Cape Wines," including "Madeira, Hock and Port" imported from the Cape of Good Hope.

TO JOHN WILLIAMS

Bath
25 December 1816.

My dear Mr. Williams
While Salusbury reposes in the noiseless Tranquillity of Brynbella—and while you sit reading old History at Bodylwyddan; and believing as Dr. Johnson did,

that when *Consternation* was described by the Writers in pompous Terms,—nobody was *consternated:*[1]—*I have to assure you that War in the Streets* of London and *Famine* in the Fields;[2] are very serious, not to say dreadful Things.

He however, who guided the Gun from Your Eye, and your Artery,[3]—will if such be his good Pleasure, still the Raging of the Winds, and the Madness of the People. In him we must confide.

Methodism sapps the Church, assisting Sedition which batters the State: They will go together, when they do go.[4]

Mr. Hunt is here, pressing for a Place to convene Listeners; he has tried Bristol and failed. The Rioters shewing a Disposition to Seize the Bank,—frighted our Moneyed Men—who wisely reflecting that half a Loaf is better than no Bread, will I doubt not quietly submit to see their 5 Per Cents become 4;—rather than witness a sudden Destruction of *all* Property by *Le Peuple Souverain.*

When all is concluded—no Country in Europe is more prosperous than our own. A very Intelligent Young Friend—Mr. Harrington who came home but Three Days ago,[5]—says He saw Corn *Standing* in Picardie—and that neither France nor Germany have produced a Bunch of Grapes that would make even Vinegar.—Hearing he had seen Rome, I enquired how my old friends in Lombardy went on? for said I, If they get no Wheat They can eat Chesnut Bread.—But The Chesnuts have *failed* was the Reply—*every*thing has failed; and such are the enormous Falls of Snow from the Mountains, many of the Lombard Peasants are destroyed; particularly the Inhabitants of Piedmont.

These are Facts.
&c.

Now if Dear Mr. Williams possesses the happy Alchemy of deducing Consolation from Them, saying we are at worst better off than our Neighbours &c. France especially, who has Foreign Troops quartered on her starving Provinces:—why then I shall pronounce an uncontrovertible Truism,—that 'tis better be a young Man than an Old Woman—who sees nothing but Sorrow in the Probability of wanting Food when there will be no People to sell us any.

Mrs. Mostyn has written to me, She seems to like her Situation—but I do not much like it for her. Such a Climate in such a Season! Poor Thing, I am so afraid of her getting a Pleurisy.[6]

Dear Miss Williams apprehends no *public* Calamities—She is wholly wrapped up in the Events of Bodylwyddan; and Strange Things in*deed* must befall, before She can withdraw one Thought from the Principality.

We had settled it that Your Honour was soon to be married to 60,000£ and I said it was a good Thing—Lord Byron protests his Wife was—a Fortune without Money,—a Belle without Beauty; and a Bas-bleu without either Wit or Learning[7]—I am for some one positive Possession.

Sir Watkin will obtain Rank Riches, and Interest in his County Your Aunt says;—and those are *Three* good Things, after waiting ½ a Century, and spending away all the while.[8]

Old Roberts however makes—in proportion—a better Match still. A pretty

Wench with Money, at his Time o'Day, must surely have been unhoped for;— but every thing shews how much may be gained by Delay.[9]—

I have gained a Frank, directed to Brynbella which carries Loves Compliments &c. a Million from/ Your H: L: P.

What ails Miss Ellen's pretty White Hand? no great harm I hope. But *Aunty* is restless about it: She is indeed full of the tenderest Affection for her Brothers and their Children.

Corn is coming in every day, so we shall escape Epidemic Diseases, but Money must be found to pay for it.

Mr. Hunt is gone away without saying a Word.

Text Ry. 6 (1813–1821). *Address* John Williams Esq./ Bodylwyddan/ St. Asaph. *Postmark* < >.

1. See HLP to EM, 25 July 1819, n. 18.
2. HLP refers not only to the Spa Fields riots but to the answers emanating from the circular letter put out by the board of agriculture. No one could deny "the present deplorable state of the National Agriculture.—Bankruptcies, seizures, executions, imprisonments, and farmers become parish paupers . . . with great arrears of rent, and in many cases, tithes and poor-rates unpaid; improvements of every kind generally discontinued; live-stock greatly lessened; tradesmen's bills unpaid; and an alarming gangs of poachers and other predators." All these symptoms denote "extreme distress, and absolute ruin in a variety of instances." Moreover, among farm workers there was a "want of employment . . . amounting to great misery and wretchedness." See *AR* 58 (1816):461–69.
3. For JW's shooting accident, see HLP to Ly W, 5 November 1816, n. 1.
4. For HLP's recent attack on Methodism, see her letter to JF, 18 November, n. 3. For her earlier suspicion of the aims of Methodism or any religious reform organization, see her letter to RG, 11 January 1799, n. 1.
5. A grandson of Dr. Henry Harington, Edward Musgrave Harington (1789–1842), was serving in the Royal Navy, becoming in time a commander. In 1826 he married his cousin, Jane Ann Thomas (1798–1893).
6. CMM was in Switzerland. HLP's fears that CMM was susceptible to pleurisy went back to 1792. See HLP to PSW: 9, 15, 29 September; 1 October 1792.
7. Byron had been a consistent subject of Bath gossip. His separation from Anne Isabella, née Milbanke, was still less than a year old. Moreover, the poet himself was much in the news. His continental travels were reported in the press (*The Times,* 22 and 31 October; *Morning Post,* 31 October). *The Prisoner of Chillon* and the third canto of *Childe Harold* were advertised for publication on 23 November (*Courier,* 19 November). Extracts from the latter poem on Waterloo appeared in the *Courier* on 19 and 21 November.
8. For Sir Watkin's engagement and marriage on 4 February 1817 to Lady Henrietta Antonia Clive, see HLP to JSPS, 21 February 1815, n. 16.
9. Probably the ironmonger and tax assessor in Flintshire. See HLP to John Lloyd, 11 November 1809, n. 2.

Index

The Piozzi Letters